Land Records
of
Somerset
County
Maryland

by

Ruth T. Dryden

HERITAGE BOOKS
2020

HERITAGE BOOKS

AN IMPRINT OF HERITAGE BOOKS, INC.

Books, CDs, and more—Worldwide

For our listing of thousands of titles see our website
at
www.HeritageBooks.com

Published 2020 by
HERITAGE BOOKS, INC.
Publishing Division
5810 Ruatan Street
Berwyn Heights, Md. 20740

Originally published 1985

International Standard Book Numbers
Paperbound: 978-0-7884-3291-0
Clothbound: 978-0-7884-8597-8

Dedicated to

James H. Farish who helped

immeasurably with this book

and its index.

NOTES ON USING THIS BOOK

All land records are in Capital letters and in alphabetical order. Where "no name" or "unnamed" is used there could be a question as to the verification of this deed. These are my determination as to which lands were exchanged so beware of these entries.

Widows were entitled to one third of their husbands estates. This was called Dower Rights and are indicated when she relinquished her claim on land sold. She is usually referred to as the relic of her husband.

Variations in the spelling of a name are due to the original deed or patent, i.e. Benson could be Benston, McReady could be McCready, McGrath is also Magraugh.

When the land is sold for 5 shillings, it is usually to a relative, daughter, brother, nephew, since this is a token payment. The term, no acreage, means that the land was described in the deed but the exact number of acres sold was not included. One moity is one half of the land.

The index omits titles such as Jr., Sr., Esq. Rev. & Col.since these titles vary and the same person could have any or all of these.

The land sometimes passed from one generation to another and there is no deed or will to indicate this. It descends by law to the eldest son. If there are no sons, to a brother or nephew, or occasionally to daughters and their husbands or dower rights to the widow's second husband.

Note that the names of lands when patented can be a clue to the origin of the patentee such as BELFAST, also in Ireland. The name can be also an indication of the owners personality, MISORY, HARD FORTUNE, LUCK, MISTAKE, or a description of the land itself such as FLATLAND and MEADOW.

LIST OF ABBREVIATIONS

exec= Executor of the will
adm.=administrator of the estate
Dorc.Co.= Dorcester County Maryland
Acco.Co.Va.= Accomack County Virginia
Worc.Co.= Worcester County Maryland
etc= and so forth
d/o= daughter of   w/o= wife of   s/o= son of
Del.=state of Delaware
mtg.= mortgage
aka= also known as or alias.

SOURCES

Deed books of Somerset County Maryland thru 1810
Will books of Somerset County Md. abstracted by Dryden
Marylander Calendar of Wills by Baldwin
Old Somerset on the Eastern Shore of Md. by Torrence
1783 tax lists abstracted by Dryden
1666-1723 Rent Rolls abstracted by Dryden
Federal Census Records.
Marylander & Herald newspaper, Princess Anne Md.
Maps - Harry L. Benson, tract maps of Somerset County.
    MDHR G.1727-437 Maryland hall of Records.Comission, Department of
    General services, Annapolis,Maryland.
Card Index, patent files, Hall of Records, Annapolis, Maryland.

ABBINGTON

Patented 10 May 1683 for Thomas Hobbs, 300 acres. in the Mt.Vernon
Wicomico 100. Election district 5. map#1 south east.
10 Dec.1691 will of Thomas Hobbs- to son Joy Hobbs
1666-1723 Rent Rolls, possessed by Joy Hobbs
1735 will of Joy Hobbs, to sons Thomas Hobbs, Joy Hobbs and Matthias
Hobbs.
16 May 1758 Stephen Hobbs (son of Thomas Hobbs) and his wife Margaret
Hobbs sold his rights to Henry Waggaman.
18 August 1762 Joy Hobbs and wife Mary Hobbs, Noble Hobbs and wife
Priscilla Hobbs of Dorcester County, sold to Matthias Hobbs of Somerset
County 100 acres.
1759 will of Henry Waggaman, to son John Waggaman.
1762 resurveyed to GOOD LUCK, 275 acres by Matthias Hobbs.
1771 AUSTINS ADVENTURE surveyed by Robert Austin within the lines of
ABBINGTON.
17 Oct.1781 Joseph Austin sold 6 3/4 acres to Mary Covington of AUSTINS
ADVENTURE.
1 Aug.1780 Joseph Austin sold to George Austin and John Wright AUSTINS 86
1/2 acres.(c/b other lands)
1783 tax- Mary Covington 16 3/4 acres ADVENTURE
28 Jan.1783 Margaret Hobbs for 5 shillings paid by Josiah Hobbs son of
Stephen Hobbs, deceased, husband of Margaret, releases her dower rights
to CARNEYS CHANCE & ABBINGTON (conveyed by Stephen Hobbs to Henry
Waggaman) Margaret Hobbs age 50 said that her son Josiah Hobbs was 7 or 8
years old at the time of her husbands death.
29 April 1792 Henry Waggaman son of Henry & Mary Waggaman, with wife
Sarah Waggaman of Dorcester Co.,attorney, sold to George Waggaman of
Somerset County 200 acres with CARNEYS CHANCE,CUMBERLAND,DAVIDS CHANCE,
ADVENTURE, etc.
5 Feb.1799 Nehemiah Covington,wife Nancy Covington sold to Benjamin Hobbs
16 3/4 acres AUSTINS ADVENTURE.

ACCIDENT

Patented in 1752 for James Tull, 37 acres, in Annamessex. Lawsons,
Election district 8,map #18.
1753 possessed by Elijah Tull
1783 tax list, Elijah Coulbourn 37 acres.(mar. Sarah Tull)
11 Jan 1790 Elijah Coulbourn Sr.and wife Rachel Coulbourn and John Tull
son of James Tull sold to Benjamin Conner with SCOTLAND,POOR SWAMP,
PUZZLE, COME BY CHANCE, BUCK RIDGE- no acres mentioned.
11 Jan 1790 Benjamin Conner (son-in-law of Elijah Coulbourn) returned
same as above.

ACKMANS CHANCE

Patented in 1792 for George Aikman in St.Peters,Election district 2,
map#6
23 Dec.1806 Ann Aikman admx. of George Aikman dec'd.

ACQUINTICA

Two adjacent patents in 1665 by the same name, one for 300 acres and one

for 200 acres, by George Wale, located in the Lower Dublin, Dividing
Creek 100, Election district 4, map #13.
17 Oct 1671 George Wale and Sarah Wale his wife sold 300a. to Edward
Wale.
8 Dec.1678 Edward Wale sold to Thomas Newbold 400 acres.
1666-1723 Rent Rolls 400 acres Thomas Newbold
1712 the will of Thomas Newbold of Pocomoke, gave to son Thomas Newbold.
20 Aug.1766 William Hayward of Talbot County released his claim
(mortgage?) of 400 acres to Purnell Newbold .
3 Feb 1767 Purnell Newbold sold to Samuel Wilson 400 acres.
12 Nov 1767 Samuel Wilson sold 12 acres to John Perkins.
1783 tax list- 338 acres possessed by Samuel Wilson in Dividing Creek
100.
1790 will of Samuel Wilson, to son Samuel Wilson lands on the north side
of the Pocomoke River (Unnamed).
28 Feb 1786 Samuel Wilson sold 2 1/2 acres to John Perkins.
15 Oct.1795 Samuel Wilson, wife Leah Wilson, of Samuel sold to Eli
Gibbons 29 acres with NEWTOWN.
19 Nov.1795 Major Samuel Wilson, wife Leah Wilson sold to Littleton
Dennis 815 acres of ACQUINTICA,FRIENDSHIP,CONTENT, NEWTOWN, NELGLECT,
POWELLS CHANCE, MIDDLE,EXCHANGE, etc.
25 May 1805 Eli Gibbons, wife Amelia Gibbons sold to Henry Cluff 29
acres.
6 June 1806 Jesse Taylor, wife Delitta Taylor, sold to Littleton Dennis
ACQUINTICA, NEWTOWN and saw mill and grist mill and mill pond.
6 April 1809 Henry Cluff sold to Elizabeth Morris Hayward 29 acres.
17 May 1810 Elizabeth Morris Hayward of Worc.Co. sold to Levin Pollitt of
Somerset Co. 29 acres, with NEWTOWN.
1 June 1830 Chancery Court Sale-Thomas Gibbons vs. Esther Broughton admx.
of Josiah Broughton part purchased of Thomas Jones.

ADAMS CHANCE

Patented in 1764 by John Adams, 49 acres in West Princess
Anne, Election district 1, map#2.
14 May 1782 John Adams sold 49 acres to son John Adams.
25 Oct 1792 William Adams, wife Louisa Adams, son of John Adams,sold to
William Brereton, all, no acres given.

ADAMS CHANCE

Resurveyed from PLANNERS ADVENTURE & LITTLEWORTH by Thomas Adams in 1762
for 148 acres. In Brinkleys, southwest, Election district 3, map#17.
1769 Thomas Adams, wife Adria Adams, sold to Col.Sampson Wheatley 17
acres.
1773 will of Sampson Wheatley (wife Mary Wheatley), to daughter Betty
Wheatley, bought of Thomas Adams.(Betty Wheatley married Benjamin
Schoolfield.)
18 Jan 1781, will of Thomas Adams Jr, to grandson Thomas Adams son of
David Adams after the decease of my wife Adria Adams, lands (unnamed).
1783 tax lists- Wheatley Adams 128 acres
1783 tax lists- Mary Wheatley 17 acres
1798 will Benjamin Schoolfield, 30 acres to daughters, Betsy Schoolfield,
Polly Schoolfield, Amelia Schoolfield and Ann Schoolfield that bounds
William Adams plantation (unnamed)

24 June 1786 Caleb Jones and wife Betty Jones daughter of Sampson Wheatley, sold to Kellum Lankford, Elijah Coulbourn and Thomas Jones (of Annamessex) 17 acres, with IRISH GROVE, MERCHANTS TREASURE, PRIVILEDGE, WHEATLYS SECOND ADDN.,etc.

24 April 1805 Benjamin Conner, wife Grace Conner, Noah Lankford, wife Ann Lankford, Benjamin Bedsworth, John Broughton, wife Mary Broughton, Richard Hall, wife Sarah Purnell Hall, and Mary Bedsworth sold to Mordicai Jones of St.Marys County devised by Sampson Wheatley to daughter Betty Jones and conveyed by Caleb Jones and wife Betty Jones to Kellam Lankford, Elijah Coulbourn and Thomas Jones, now deceased.

ADAMS CONCLUSION

Patented in 1749 for William Adams, Brinkleys northeast. Election district 3, map #15, 535 acres.

1742 will of William Adams, to sons William Adams and Dennis Adams.

1756 will of William Adams, parts to sons William Adams and Phillip Adams.

26 Jul.1780 Micajah Adams sold to Fountain Beauchamp

3 Nov 1780 William Adams son of Dennis Adams, and Micajah Adams sold to John Beauchamp son of John (that William Adams willed), dividing between sons Dennis Adams and Phillip Adams, no acres.

18 Oct.1781 William Adams son of Dennis Adams,sold to William Adams son of William, 25 acres.

1782 will Fountain Beauchamp, lands (unnamed) to son Isaac Beauchamp if no issue to son Phillip Adams Beauchamp.(wife of Fountain Beauchamp was Rhoda Adams.)

1783 tax list- William Adams 250 acres

1783 tax list- Mary Adams 140 acres

1783 tax list- Joshua Beauchamp 59 acres

21 Feb.1787 John Beauchamp and Mary Beauchamp sold to Samuel Smith 52 acres purchased of Micajah Adams with pt. LEDBOURN, HOG YARD and ENLARGEMENT.

12 May 1788 William Adams son of Dennis Adams sold to William Adams son of William 25 acres,to correct error in past conveyance.

1789 will of William Adams, 1/2 each to sons Dennis Adams and Asa Adams.

5 Feb 1789 Beauchamp Davis, Planner Beauchamp, wife Martha Beauchamp, William Adams of William, Levin Beauchamp and Thomas Beauchamp sold to Samuel Smith 7 3/4 acres with ADAMS VENTURE,BEAUCHAMP VENTURE, LEDBOURN.

20 Jan 1789 Mary Adams leased to Fountain Beauchamp 25 acres of MITCHELLS CONCLUSION and part of ADAMS CONCLUSION.

5 Feb 1789 Samuel Smith sold to Pierce Chapman for 5 shillings 2 1/2 acres.

6 Aug 1792 Planner Beauchamp, wife Martha Beauchamp,and Pierce Chapman, wife Rebecca Chapman sold to Samuel Smith 4 acres with BEAUCHAMPS VENTURE.

13 Oct.1797 Dennis Adams mortgaged 100 acres to James Adams

24 Nov.1801 Margaret Adams alias Peggy Adams daughter of William Adams and Sarah Adams and Sarah Adams widow of William Adams sold all rights to real esated that was the property of brother Asa Adams, deceased 60 acres, no name.

2 Nov.1801 Dennis Adams sold to William Adams RICHARDS ADVENTURE or VENTURE & ADAMS CONCLUSION 200 acres.

7 Nov.1801 James Adams of William Adams and William Adams, wife Polly Adams sold to Samuel Smith 133 acres conveyed from Dennis Adams 133

acres, no name.

14 Jan 1802 Joshua Ross and Nancy Adams sold to Samuel Smith 40 acres land adj. ADAMS CONCLUSION no name.

14 Jan 1802 Samuel Smith,wife Esther Smith and Nancy Adams sold to Joshua Ross 121 acres, description, no name.

2 Sep.1803 Joshua Ross and wife Mary Ross sold to Thomas Davis 32 1/4 acres.

13 Sep. 1804 Thomas Davis and wife Sally Davis sold to William Broughton 32 1/4 acres.

10 May 1805 Elisha Beauchamp sold to William Smith of Samuel 2 acres where he and mother Leah Beauchamp live.

23 April 1806 Samuel Smith sold 200 acres to Isaac Gibbons of WHITBY, ADAMS CONCLUSION, ADAMS SCHEME.

ADAMS DELIGHT

Date of patent unknown. 16 1/2 acres out of ADAMS PURCHASE, in Dublin district, map#12, Election District 4.

23 May 1804 Samuel Adams sold to Burton Cannon and Isaac Mitchell Adams, no acreage given.

2 July 1805 Phillip A. Adams sold to Collins Adams 200 acres of NORFOLK, ADDN. TO NORFOLK, ADAMS DELIGHT.

ADAMS DISCOVERY

Patented in 1760 by John Adams, 667 acres in West Pr. Anne district 1 map#2. Repatented in 1762 by William Adams.

16 Dec.1766 William Adams and wife Leah Adams sold to Isaiah Banks 32 acres

1776 will Isaiah Banks, 32 acres to brother Henry Banks on south side of the Wicomico River.

1783 tax lists-John Adams Sr. 188 1/2 acres. Wicomico 100

1783 tax lists-Priscilla Banks 32 1/2 acres.

1783 tax lists-John Adams Jr. 40a.

22 Apr. 1784 Henry Banks sold to William McBryde with HALLS ADVENTURE & KINGS NEGLECT.

17 Dec.1804 Thomas Hamilton and Charles Nutter, wife Louisa Nutter (late Louisa Adams agree to divide the RE of William Adams Jr. YOUNG TINSON, TONYS VINEYARD, JOHNS DESIRE & ADAMS DISCOVERY.

28 Aug.1807 Charles Nutter and wife Louisa Nutter sold 70 acres to Elias Bailey.

17 March 1809 Charles Nutter, wife Louisa Nutter sold to Elias Bailey 70 acres.

10 Oct.1809 James Ritchie, trustee on behalf of the heirs of William McBryde sold to James Bennett 32 1/2 acres.

18 Dec.1810 Dr. Charles Nutter sold to Daniel Whitney, shipright, 558 acres of YOUNG TINSON, TONYS VINEYARD, JOHNS DESIRE & ADAMS DISCOVERY.

ADAMS FIRST CHOICE

Resurveyed in 1746 by Isaac Adams from KINGS LOTT for 208 acres, in Brinkleys, north east. Election district 3, map #15.

1777 Isaac Adams, dec'd, Jacob Adams his heir.

1795 will William Wood, wife Nancy Wood, to son Joshua Wood (under 21)

9 Feb.1786 Ephraim Adams sold 120 acres to William Wood.

18 March 1789 Ephraim Adams sold to William Wood 57 1/2 acres.

ADAMS FOLLY

Patented in 1739 by Samuel Adams from HUDSONS FOLLY & HUDSONS FORTUNE, 345 acres. In Brinkleys southeast, Election district 3, Map #16.
23 Nov.1745 Jacob Adams sold to Teague Matthews 44 acres, once called Hudsons Folly, now called Matthews Folly (not patented by this new name.)
1783 tax lists- Samuel Adams 301 acres (s/o Samuel Adams)
6 Aug.1792 David Matthews sold to Samuel Taylor with EDENS & MEADOW GROUND.
6 Aug.1792 Samuel Taylor sold to David Matthews same as above-probably division of lines.

ADAMS FOLLY

Patented in 1815 by Daniel Whitney for 9 1/4 acres, in West Princess Anne, upper part. Election district 1 map #2.

ADAMS GARDEN

Patented 18 May 1670 by Phillip Adams. In the Brinkleys Election district 3, map#17, 100 acres. There were two patents by this name.
1696 Phillip Adams, gave 100 acres to son Thomas Adams.
1735 Thomas Adams (wife Ann Adams), per will, gave to son David Adams part, and part to son Thomas Adams.
Rent Rolls 1666-1723 shows 100 acres possessed by Thomas Adams.
1753 Phillip Adams the younger, son of Abraham Adams deceased sold to Isaac Adams 36 acres part of KINGS LOTT and ADAMS GARDEN, 22 acres.
11 Nov. 1753 Phillip Adams sold to Isaac Adams KINGS LOTT and ADAMS GARDEN, no acreage mentioned.
1761-64 tax lists, possessed by William Adams.
24 Mar.1774 Ephraim Adams sold 75 acres to Stephen Coulbourn with KINGS LOTT, total 200 acres.
1783 tax lists-Sarah Adams (of Morumsco) held 106 1/4 acres with HAPHAZARD and KINGS LOTT.(Poc.100)
1783 tax lists-Stephen Coulbourn 75 acres.(Pocomoke 100)
1783 tax lists-Ephraim Adams 50 acres, (Pocomoke 100)

ADAMS GARDEN

Patented in 1676 by Phillip Adams for 100 acres, in Brinkleys, northwest, map#14 Election district 3.
6 July 1677 Phillip Adams and Ann Adams his wife, sold to George Trehearn, 100 acres.
22 April 1680 George Trehearn and Ann Trehearn his wife sold to John Rowell. John Rowell and wife Margaret Rowell sold to William Adkins.
1692 William Adkins granted by deed to Thomas Williams. Thomas Williams and wife Frances Williams deeded to William Horn. William Horn and wife Elizabeth Horn sold to Coventry Parish.
1719 Coventry Parish traded the 100 acres to Randall Mitchell for 150 acres of MITCHELLS LOTT.
25 Jan 1750 John Mitchell sold to Thomas Williams (As Randall Mitchell died with only one daughter Mary Mitchell. She married Thomas White by whom she had one child that died before the mother who is since dead, and

5

no other issue. Thomas Mitchell is now possessed as tennant. John
Mitchell being the eldest uncle of Mary Mitchell, is entitled.
1766 Thomas White gave to cousin Abraham Outten(who married Betty White)
3 April 1760 Thomas Williams gave 100 acres to grandson Thomas White
Williams.
11 Feb 1772 Thomas Williams sold 100 acres to Kellam Lankford.
1783 tax lists- Kellum Lankford (Gr.Annamessex 100)
1796 Kellum Lankford gave to son Noah Lankford.
5 April 1803 Noah Lankford son of Kellum Lankford sold to William
Williams, merchant, lands in Morumsco, no name.
11 Nov 1803 William Williams, wife Mary Williams sold to Thomas Robertson
Jr. lands where Noah Lankford lived in Morumsco, no name.
1 Sep.1806 William How Adams sold to Dr.Thomas Robertson Jr. 15 12 acres.
13 Sep.1808 Thomas Robertson, wife Harriett Robertson sold to William How
Lankford 188 acres.
1838 Richard Hall, per will, gave to son Henry Hall.

ADAMS GREEN

Patented 24 June 1679 by William Stevens who assigned to Phillip Adams by
purchase. In Brinkleys, southwest, Election district 3, map#17.for 50
acres.
Rent Rolls 1666-1723 possessed by Thomas Adams (s/o Phillip)
1735 Thomas Adams, per will left lands to son Thomas.
1783 tax lists- Ephraim Adams, 50 acres.

ADAMS LUCK

Patented in 1775 by George Adams in Brinkleys, northeast, Election
district 3, map #15.
12 Jan 1788 George Adams, wife Sarah Adams sold to William Broughton 26
acres.
11 July 1792 George Adams, wife Sarah Adams and Hope Adams, wife Martha
sold to William Broughton 7 acres.

ADAMS PRIVILEDGE

Patented 1774 by Phillip Adams for 20 acres in Westover, Election
district 13, map#11.
1789 Tax lists- Phillip Adams
1812 Phillip Adams willed to son John Adams.

ADAMS PURCHASE

Patented in 1758 by Samuel Adams, a resurvey of tract NORFOLK for 539 1/2
acres. Dublin, map#12, Election district 4.
13 Aug.1782 Phillip Collins Adams deeded to brother Samuel Adams, part,
29 acres with NORFOLK
1783 tax lists- Samuel Adams, 327 1/4 acres. Dividing Ck.100
1783 tax lists- Phillip C. Adams 200 acres. Div.Ck.100
24 May 1785 Phillip Collins Adams and wife Priscilla Adams sold to Joshua
Boston part with NORFOLK 101 acres.
4 April 1786 Joshua Boston purchased of Phillip Collins Adams, part.
19 Feb. 1787 Phillip Collins Adams, wife Priscilla Adams sold to Samuel
Adams 48 acres for 5 shillings of BECKLES & ADAMS PURCHASE.

26 May 1792 Joshua Boston and Nancy Boston sold part to Samuel Adams.
26 May 1792 Joshua Boston, wife Nancy Boston, Zorobable King and William
Turpin sold to Samuel Adams NORFOLK & ADAMS PURCHASE 30 acres.
29 Nov.1794 Phillip Collins Adams sold to George Miles of Samuel Miles
250 acres NORFOLK,ADAMS PURCHASE, mtg.
13 April 1799 George Miles released mtg. to Phillip Collins Adams 250
acres of NORFOLK, ADAMS PURCHASE.
4 April 1786 Phillip Collins Adams sold to Joshua Boston 102 1/2 acres
including BECKLES.
13 March 1803 Joshua Boston, John Morrison and Levin King sold to James
Boston of Joshua Boston 100 acres of NORFOLK & ADAMS PURCHASE.
13 March 1804 Joshua Boston sold to son Levin Boston.
15 Aug.1803 Phillip Adams wife Priscilla Adams sold part to Jonathan
Mills with NORFOLK.
14 Mar 1804 Joshua Boston conveyed to his son Levin Boston except parts
conveyed to son James Boston and Samuel Adams.
23 May 1804 Samuel Adams sold to Burton Cannon and Isaac Mitchell, no
acreage given.
13 Feb 1804 Burton Cannon, wife Sally Cannon sold to Matthias Coston
Taylor 16 acres.
11 Feb 1806 James Boston sold to Isaac Mitchell Adams 10 1/4 acres of
NORFOLK & ADAMS PURCHase.
11 Feb 1806 Jonathan Mills, wife Leah Mills & William Williams and
Alexander McAllen sold to James Boston 30 acres of NORFOLK & ADAMS
PURCHASE.
26 April 1809 Joshua Boston and son Levin Boston mortgaged to Jesse King
and his brother William King 202 1/2 acres of BECKLES and ADAMS
PURCHASE..
1815 Burton Cannon willed to son Winder Cannon, tract bought of Joshua
Boston.
23 Dec 1820 James Boston sold to Nathan Milbourn 10 acres.
13 Feb 1821 James Boston purchased from Nathan Milbourn 10 acres.
1822 will Matthias Coston Taylor, to Matthias C.T. Beauchamp, bought of
Burton Cannon.
23 Mar.1825 James Boston purchased at sheriff's sale, 408 acres.
including NORFOLK & ADAMS PURCHASE.
1836 Levin Pollitt willed to William Bowland son of John.

ADAMS PURCHASE

Patented 23 July 1679 for 100 acres by Phillip Adams. In Brinkleys, south
west, map #17, Election district 3.
Rent Rolls 1666-1723 possessed by Thomas Adams son and heir to Phillip
Adams.
1735 Thomas Adams willed to son David Adams 50 acres and to son Thomas 50
acres of marsh. This land not named in will.
12 Nov 1755 Phillip Adams, the younger, son of Abraham Adams who was the
eldest son of Thomas Adams, sold to Samuel Collins Adams.
1761-1764 tax lists- William Adams son of Thomas Adams.
26 Feb 1778 Jacob Adams sold to Gertrude Adams, with HOUSTONS
CHOICE,ADVENTURE,SNOW HILL.   50 acres.
1783 tax lists- Gertrude Adams 50 acres.
1783 tax lists- Kellum Lankford, 100 acres
1817 will of Andrew Adams, to nephew Andrew son of John Adams.
26 July 1831 Sheriff's sale-suit of George Dashiell against Isaac M.

Adams.
1833 Matthias Coston Taylor willed to Matthias C.T. Beauchamp son of John Beauchamp.

ADAMS SCHEME

Patented 1788 a resurvey of HICKORY RIDGE, by William Adams for 248 3/4acres in Brinkleys, northeast, map#14, Election district 3.
11 May 1805 William Adams mortgaged to Littleton Dennis
11 May 1805 William Adams, wife Sarah Adams sold to James Adams, all.
21 March 1806 William Adams, wife Sarah Adams sold to John Chapman 58 1/8 acres
21 March 1806 James Adams, wife Elizabeth Adams sold to John Schoolfield 101 acres
21 March 1806 Willliam Adams and son James Adams, wife Elizabeth Adams mortgaged to Littleton Dennis ADAMS SCHEME & WHITBY RECTIFIED 142 acres.
21 March 1806 Littleton Dennis sold the mortgage to John Schoolfield and John Chapman.
21 March 1806 William Adams, wife Sarah Adams sold 101 acres to John Schoolfield.
21 March 1806 James Adams, wife Elizabeth Adams sold to John Chapman 59 acres.
23 April 1806 Samuel Smith sold to Isaac Gibbons 200 acres of WHITBY, ADAMS CONCLUSION, ADAMS SCHEME.
20 jan 1808 John Schoolfield, wife Mary Schoolfield, sold 6 acres to Isaac Gibbons.

ADAMS TROUBLE

A resurvey from PARTNERS AGREEMENT in 1770 for 182 acres by David Adams, possessed by Thomas Adams, in Brinkleys, southwest, map#17, on Planners Creek, Election district 3.

ADAMS VENTURE

Patented in 1750 by Phillip Adams, for 21 acres, in Brinkleys northeast, map #15, Election district 3.
5 Feb 1789 Beauchamp Davis,Planner Beauchamp, wife Martha Beauchamp, William Adams of William, Levin Beauchamp and Thomas Beauchamp sold to Samuel Smith 11 acres with BEAUCHAMPS VENTURE, LEDBOURN, ADAMS CONCLUSION.

ADDITION

Patented on 6 April 1680 by Owen Magraugh in West Princess Anne, map#3.Election district 1. 100 acres.
11 May 1687 Owen Magraugh and wife Mary Magraugh sold 100 acres to William Laws.
1703 Will of William Laws, to son James Laws.
1757 James Laws willed to son James, dwelling plantation.
29 Oct 1765 William Laws sold to Levin Ballard, 100 acres.
23 March 1769 Levin Ballard sold to William Noble 3 1/4 acres.
23 March 1769 Levin Ballard sold to Henry Newman, 6 acres.

19 Sep.1776 Levin Ballard sold to Levin Woolford and John McGrath with
HAYWARDS PURCHASE,DORMANS FOLLY, WOLFS DEN,etc. 100 acres of this land.
13 March 1779 Levin Woolford and John McGrath sold to Samuel Wilkins that
Levin Ballard purchased of William Laws.
100 acres, with HAYWARDS PURCHASE,TURKEY RIDGE,etc.
27 Feb.1793 John Wilkins, wife Sally Wilkins, sold to James Ewing 100
acres purchased by Levin Ballard in 1765, with HAYWARDS PURCHASE,TURKEY
RIDGE, DORMANS FOLLY & 17 acres of marsh.
29 March 1799 Thomas Noble sold to Arnold Elzey purchased in 1769 by
William Noble.
1794 James Ewing willed real estate, unnamed, to brother Isaac Ewing.
Deed of Bargain, 13 May 1808 Dr. Arnold Elzey of Washinton D. C. sold to
William Done.

ADDITION

Patented in 1724 for 74 acres by William Smith in East Pr. Anne, Election
district 15, map #5.
1775 Resurveyed to LAWS PURCHASE.

ADDITION

Patented in 1727 by William Smith for 82 acres. in East Princess Anne,
Election district 15,map #5.
1783 tax- William Strawbridge, 82 acres.
17 Oct.1794 Sarah Porter and William Porter sold to William Davis Allen
for 5 sh. WIDOWS CHANGE,CONVIENCY,ADDN.LITTLE LESS & LEAST. They became
possessed at death of Jane Strawbridge d/o Dr. William Strawbridge in
right of her grandmother Mary Williams half sister to Dr. William
Strawbridge.
15 April 1796 John Williams of Worc.Co. sold to William Davis Allen, John
Williams eldest male heir of Jane Strawbridge daughter of Dr. William
Strawbridge deceased, 1128 acres of WIDOWS CHANGE,CONVIENCY, ADDITION.

ADDITION

Patented in 1728 for 100 acres in Fairmount, Election District 6, map #9
by John Tull
1787 resurveyed to TULLS ADDITION 95 acres.

ADDITION

A resurvey of Hackland in 1730 for 1630 acres. West Princess Anne. map#2,
Election district 1.
1783 tax- Levin Gale Jr. 50 acres
1783 tax -Levin Gale Sr. 1130 acres
27 March 1786 Levin Gale the younger, wife Ann Gale sold to Levin Gale
the Elder 250 acres.
1786 resurvey to STONEY POINT 1963 ACRES.
2 June 1803 Levin Gale sold to George Gale all lands devised by Uncle
George Gale, ADDITION.
6 Aug.1807 George Gale son of Levin Gale, sold to George Gale of Cecil
Co. Md. 250 acres.

ADDITION

Patented in 1730 by George Waggaman for 11 3/4 acres in East Pr. Anne, Election district 15, map #5.
19 Nov.1795 George Waggaman sold to Major William Jones WAGGAMANS LOTT & ADDITION
14 Feb 1797 George Waggaman sold to Elizabeth Jackson 33 1/4 acres of WAGGAMANS LOTT, ROWLEY RIDGE & ADDITION.
20 Aug.1803 Henry Waggaman wife Sarah Waggaman, of Dorc.Co. sold to Levin Jones.
8 July 1806 Levin Dashiell Jones sold to Matthias Hobbs 47 1/2 acres of ADDITION, CUMBERLAND, WAGGAMAMS CONCLUSION, GOOD LUCK, CONVENIENCE.

ADDITION

Patented 1732 for 52 acres. West Princess Anne, Election district 1, map#2.
1757 resurveyed to WHITE CHAPPELL.

ADDITION

Patented in 1738 by Elijah Conner, for 31 acres in Brinkleys, Election district 3, map #17.
26 May 1806 John Conner, wife Jane Conner sold to Mordicai Jones of St. Marys. Co. WARE POINT, CONNERS ADDN. & OUTTENS VENTURE.
6 April 1810 John Conner sold to Henry James Carroll 800 acres of WARE POINT, OUTTENS ADDITION, CHEESEMANS CHANCE, etc.
23 July 1810 Mordicai Jones of St. Marys Co. sold to Thomas Jones 400 acres of OUTTENS ADDITION, WAREPOINT & CONNERS ADDITION.

ADDITION

Patented in 1743 by Thomas Rencher for 66 acres. Mt.Vernon district, map #1, Election district #5.
8 Apr.1776 Robert Dashiell and wife Sarah Dashiell of Talbot County sold to Samuel Ingersol of Somerset, 263a. of VENTURE, ADDITION, and FATHERS CARE.
1783 tax- Samuel Ingersol 30 acres
17 March 1790 James Roberts and Rachel Roberts his wife sold to William James of Worc. Co.property of Samuel Ingersol either in Somerset or Worc.Co.'s.
24 April 1790 Mary Ingersol sold to William James, lands held by her father Samuel Ingersol.
23 June 1795 Richard Ingersol sold to William Roberts 30 acres on the south side of his plantation, unnamed (could be COVINGTONS MEADOW)
1 Oct.1800 Richard Ingersol son of Samuel Ingersol, with Elizabeth Ingersol sold to David Walston, with FATHERS CARE & VENTURE.
1806 will of Thomas Rencher, to son John Rencher lands on Wicomico River where Richard Ingersol now lives in Sassafras Neck.

ADDITION

Patented in 1746 by Thomas Hayward for 45 acres, Dublin, map #12, Election district 4.
1765 Thomas Hayward sold to Thomas Hayward Jr. 740 acres of

PROFFIT,ADDITION and other tracts.
1769 resurveyed to IRELAND 353 acres.

ADDITION

Patented in 1746 by John Broughton for 40 acres,in Dublin map #13
Election district 4.
3 May 1775 John Broughton and wife Mary Broughton sold to Robert Jenkins
King, part, with BROUGHTONS PURCHASE, 5 1/2 acres.
1783 tax -John Broughton, 36 acres.
1788 Robert Jenkins King, will, to son Levin King part of land bought of
John Broughton (not named).

ADDITION

Patented 1749 by William Jones for 52 acres in St.Peters, Election
district 2, map #6
6 Mar.1790 John Jones Sr. sold to William Jones 52 acres with
WOOLFORD,JONES ENLARGMENT, BOZMANS ADVENTURE,ROBERTSONS ADDITION.

ADDITION

Patented in 1755 for 6 acres in Lawsons, Election district 8, map #18.
17 March 1810 Benjamin Lankford sold to William Williams 4 1/2 acres.
10 April 1810 Matthias Dashiell, sheriff sold to William Williams 4 1/2
acres per judgement against Benjamin Lankford.

ADDITION

Patented in 1758 by Southy Whittington, in Lawsons, Election district 8
map #18. 100 acres.
1770/3 will Southy Whittington, to son Isaac Whittington.
1783 tax- Isaac Whittington 100 acres. Little Annamessex.
1818 resurveyed to WHITTINGTONS CONCLUSION 163 3/4 acres

ADDITION

Patented in 1758 by Thomas Dixon for 6 acres, in Brinkleys northwest,
Election district 3, map#14.
1794 Thomas Dixon gave most of his land to Sarah Dixon Furniss wife of
Thomas Furniss.

ADDITION

Patented in 1760 for 7 acres. In Dublin, map #12, Election district 4,
adjacent MILES LOT.
21 Feb 1787 Samuel Smith, wife Esther Smith, Samuel Miles and William
Waters Sr. sold 102 acres to Nehemiah King, BAD LUCK, MILES LOTT, MILES
ADDITION, BACHELORS HOLE, and 7 acres of ADDITION.
21 March 1787 Nehemiah King sold to Levin King son of Robert Jenkins
King, the 5 parcels afsd.

ADDITION

Patented in 1761 by Thomas Cottingham for 4 1/2 acres in Brinkleys southwest, Election district 3, map #17.

ADDITION

Patented in 1762 by Isaac Hayman for 17 1/2 acres. in East Princess Anne, map#4, Election district 15.
1770. will of Isaac Hayman, to son Joshua Hayman with WOLFSPITT RIDGE, the east end.
1783 tax - Isaac Hayman, Wicomico 100.

ADDITION

Patented in 1763 by Charles Hayman for 13 1/2 acres, in East Princess Anne, Election district 15, map#4.
1774 will of Charles Hayman, to son Revel (with CHARLES CHANCE) and to wife Betty Hayman.
1783 tax- Revel Hayman 13 1/2 acres(NEW ADDITION) Wicomico 100.
1796 will of Revel Hayman, lands (unnamed) to wife Sarah Hayman and then to son William Brown Hayman.
4 March 1797 Sarah Hayman, devisee of Revel Hayman sold to John Hayman Jr. of Worc. Co. 13 1/2 acres.
8 March 1806 John Hayman, wife Esther Hayman of Worc.Co. sold to Joshua Morris 13 1/2 acres.
1819 Joshua Morris willed to daughter Priscilla Morris 12 acres.

ADDITION

Patented in 1764 for 5 acres in East Pr.Anne, Election district 15, map#5, out of GRAYS ADVENTURE.
1853 resurveyed to ANNIE'S DELIGHT-SEDGEWICK

ADDITION

Patented in 1765 by Thomas Williams Jr. for 24 acres in Brinkleys, Election district 3 map#14.
1767 resurveyed by William Green 644 2/4 acres.

ADDITION

Patented in 1770 by John Puzey for 251 acres in East Pr.Anne, Election district 15, map#5.
1783 tax - John Puzey, Div.Ck.100, 251 acres.

ADDITION

Patented in 1771 for 23 acres, Westover, Election district 13, map #10, adjacent AMITEE & ARRACOCO on Kings Branch.

ADDITION

Patented in 1773 by Stephen Ward for 10 acres in Lawsons Election district 8, map # 19.
1783 tax - Stephen Ward, 10 acres. Little Annamessex
1783 will of Stephen Ward, to wife Mary Ward.
7 Jan.1800 John Ward son of Stephen Ward, now of Kentucky, sold to John

Cullen.
15 Feb.1802 John Cullen sold to Hance Croswell.
23 April 1808 Hance Croswell sold to William Ward.

ADDITION

Patented in 1774 for 15 1/2 acres by George Waggaman, East Princess Anne, Election district 15, map #4.
19 Nov.1795 George Waggaman sold to Major William Jones WAGGAMANS LOTT & ADDITION, no acres given.

ADDITION

Patented in 1774, for 174 acres by William Miles Jr. in East Pr.Anne, Election district 15, map# 4. (adj. BEAR RIDGE,BROWNS CHANCE)

ADDITION

Not patented, per Bensons maps and probably surveyed as IMPROVEMENT & SMALL ADDITION, in 1775 by Thomas Whitney for 50 acres, in West Princess Anne, Election district 1, map#3.
1796 will of Thomas Whitney, to son William Whitney, plantaton where I live, after death to grandson William son of William Whitney.
1800 will of William Whitney, to son William (under 21) plantation (unamed).
1 Nov.1807 William Whitney sold to William McNider land devised by grandfather Thomas Whitney to his father William Whitney, no name. He took a mortgage for this.

ADDITION

Patented in 1790 for 11 1/4 acres in East Pr. Anne, Election district 15, map#5, adjacent BRIDGERS LOTT & BECKFORD.

ADDITION

Patented in 1794 for 13 1/2 acres in Mt.Vernon, Election district 5, map#1 adjacent CUMBERLAND & HOBBS CONCLUSION.

ADDITION

Patented in 1807 by Thomas Cottingham for 6 1/2 acres in Brinkleys southwest, Election district #3, map #17.

ADDITION TO GEORGES ADVENTURE

Patented in 1791 by Ballard Reed for 46 acres in St.Peters, Election district 2, map#6.

ADVENTURE

Patented in 1724 for 70 acres by John Ellis, in Brinkleys southeast, Election district 3, map#16.
24 Oct. 1765 John Ellis sold 70 acres to Robert Pitts.
21 Nov. 1770 Robert Pitts and wife Milcah Pitts, sold to Thomas Robertson

626 acres with ENTRANCE,GLENDORE,MORRIS HOPE,etc.
1784 Dr. Thomas Robertson and wife Martha Robertson sold to William Waddy
626 acres with ENTRANCE, GLENDORE, ETC.
3 Sep. 1785 William Waddy and wife Mary Sewell Waddy and Thomas Handy
Jr. and wife Mary Handy sold to William Miles 212 3/4 acres, 70 acres of
ADVENTURE,with ENTRANCE, MORRIS HOPE.
29 Oct.1796 William Miles, wife Nancy Miles, sold to Thomas Williams 70
acres with ENTRANCE,MORRIS LOTT.
8 July 1809 Thomas Williams Wilkins sold to Lodowick Milbourn land of
Thomas Williams of David Williams, purchased of William Miles, no name.

ADVENTURE

Patented on 9 Dec.1688 by John Rensher for 100 acres in Dames Quarter,
Election district 9, map #7.
Rent Rolls 1666-1723 possessed by John Rensher.
1709 John Renshaw and Frances Renshaw his wife sold 200 acres to John
Bozman.
11 July 1720 William Bozman Sr. and Sarah Bozman his wife, son of John
Bozman and Sarah Bozman, sold to William Stoughton Esq. 200 acres.
1728 ADVENTURES AMENDMENT, resurvey to add 37 acres by William Stoughton.
25 July 1734 William Bozman and William Stoughton sold 37 acres to James
Robertson near the mouth of the Manokin River, patented for 200 acres
7 Jan 1745 James Robertson and wife Mary Robertson sold to Henry Waggaman
100 acres of ADVENTURE and 37 acres of AMENDMENT.
1783 tax- William Waggaman, 200 acres.
29 Apr.1792 Henry Waggaman s/o Henry and Mary Waggaman, with wife Sarah
Waggaman of Dorcester County sold to George Waggaman of Som.Co. with
CARNEYS CHANCE, OWENS DELIGHT,LONG MEADOW, ADVENTURE & ADVENTURES
AMENDMENT, etc.
1 Nov.1794 George Waggaman sold to John Bedsworth 21 3/4 acres with LONG
MEADOW.
1 Nov.1794 William Waggaman sold to George Waggaman LONG MEADOW,
ADVENTURE, ADVENTURES AMENDMENT. Mortgage.

ADVENTURE

Patented on 8 Nov.1695 by James Curtis in Fairmount, Election district 6,
map#9, for 200 acres.
1666-1723 rent rolls-possessed by James Curtis
1720 will of James Curtis, to daughters Catherine Curtis and Rachel
Curtis, CURTIS ADVENTURE.
11 Oct.1734 Charles Curtis and Mary Curtis his wife sold to Solomon Long
tracts ADVENTURE & HORSE HAMMOCK, 200 acres, granted to James Curtis
late father of Charles Curtis and willed by James Curtis in 1720.
21 October 1746 Solomon Long and wife Margaret Long, sold to James Polk
with HORSE HAMMOCK, 100 acres.
1756 Solomon Long gave 100 acres to son David Long.
26 Apr. 1768 Solomon Long sold 50 acres for 5 shillings to David Long.
2 Jan 1807 Solomon Long, wife Nelly Long sold to William Parks, part.

ADVENTURE

Patented 10 Feb.1665 for 400 acres by Jeffrey Minshull,from MINSHULLS
ADVENTURE,in Brinkleys, Election district 3, map #15..

1668 Jeffrey Minshull deeded 200 acres to William Green.
20 Sep.1679 Jeffrey Minshull son of Jeffrey and widow Frances Minshull of
Jeffrey sold to William Stevens of Pocomoke. It was resurveyed in 1679 by
Col. William Stevens for 450 acres.
Rent Rolls 1666-1723 possessed by Samuel Layfield
1709 will of Samuel Layfield does not mention this land.
1765 William Adams willed to son Phillip Adams.
1768 will of Hope Adams, to son Hope (MITCHELLS ADVENTURE)
26 Feb.1778 Jacob Adams sold to Gertrude Adams 119 acres with HOUSTONS
CHOICE,SNOW HILL,ADVENTURE,ADAMS PURCHASE.
1783 tax lists- Hope Adams 105 acres.
1783 tax lists- Gertrude Adams 70 acres
1783 tax lists- Fountain Beauchamp 5 acres
1783 tax lists- Rhoda Beauchamp 60 acres
1783 tax lists- Duncan Livingston 94 acres
1783 tax lists- Sabrah Adams (with LONG RIDGE 125 acres)
2 March 1789 Levi Beauchamp sold to Hope Adams son of Hope 10 acres of
ADVENTURE & GOOD HOPE, called THE TAN YARD.
9 April 1792 George Adams sold to Isaac Beauchamp 3 3/8 acres.
6 Aug.1792 Fountain Beauchamp and Beauchamp Davis sold to Dr. Thomas
Robertson- division of lines, to settle dispute.
9 June 1792 I George Adams sell to Joshua Davis 1 3/4 acres.
11 July 1792 George Adams, wife Sarah Adams, sold to Thomas Robertson 120
acres except part already sold,with ADAMS LUCK.
26 May 1795 Isaac Beauchamp sold to Thomas Robertson 3 3/8 acres conveyed
by George Adams.
13 Dec.1797 James Adams,wife Elizabeth Adams sold to Thomas White, 11
acres.
5 Aug.1797 Samuel Adams sold to Thomas Williams all lands devised by Hope
Adams, no name or acreaage.
3 Jan 1799 Thomas Williams Jr. sold to William Adams Schoolfield 200
acres bought of Samuel Adams, no name.
2 Nov.1801 Dennis Adams sold to William Williams 200 acres of ADVENTURE &
ADAMS CONCLUSION.
7 Dec.1801 James Adams of William Adams and William Adams, wife Polly
Adams sold 133 acres to Samuel Smith, conveyed from Dennis Adams.
7 Feb.1803 William A. Schoolfield and wife Mary Schoolfield sold 6 acres
to Elijah Broughton of tracts ADVENTURE & GOOD HOPE.
26 Dec.1805 Mary Beauchamp daughter of Fountain Beauchamp sold her part
to Thomas Catlin.
27 Feb.1806 Thomas Catlin, and Mary Beauchamp sold to William Williams,
property of Fountain Beauchamp deceased, 40 acres.
15 June 1807 Benjamin Lankford Sr. sold to William Williams.
11 Apr. 1810 Daniel Ballard, sheriff, sold to Isaac Miles 105 acres, per
judgement against William A. Schoolfield.

ADVICE

Patented 1793 by John Jones for 10 acres. East Princess Anne Election
district 15, map #4.
1803 Thomas Jones willed to sons John Jones & Tubman Jones
11 June 1808 Thomas Curtis, trustee to sell the RE of Thomas Jones sold
to Matthias Miles 10 acres.

AGREEMENT

Patented on 6 Jun 1683 by John Hill and James Price, in Asbury, Election
district 12 map #21. for 100 acres
Rent Rolls 1666-1723 Possessed 100 acres by Mary Price widow of James
Price.
18 Nov.1736 Cornelius Ward son of Cornelius, and Alice Ward his wife sold
to Jacob Ward son of Thomas Ward their 1/2 interest in two tracts PRICES
VINEYARD & AGREEMENT that James Price willed to daughters Margaret Price
and Ann Price. Ann Price married Cornelius Ward and Margaret Price
married Thomas Ward.
21 December 1736 I James Ward son of Thomas Ward am bound to Jacob
Ward(division of lands). Thomas Ward and Margaret Ward his wife
possessed 1/2 of tracts PRICES VINEYARD & AGREEMENT 300 acres. Thomas
and Margaret with sons James Ward and Jacob Ward, afsd.
1783 tax- Stephen Ward 50 acres
1783 tax- Thomas Ward 52 acres.
7 Jan 1800 John Ward son of Stephen Ward, now of Kentucky, sold to John
Cullen.

ALLENS CONTENT

Patented on 4 Sep. 1666 by Richard Allen for 100 acres. Also known as
ALLENS CONTEST, in Brinkleys northeast.map#15 Election district 3.
Rent Rolls 1666,1723 possessed by Robert Wood.
1 May 1727 I Thomas Wood of Coventry Parish, give to grand son William
Wood, his mother to use during widowhood.
1751 resurveyed to WOODS CONTENT-161 acres.

ALLENS VALE

1797 resurvey of WIDOWS CHANGE & ILLCHESTER,by William Davis Allen for
1297 acres, in East Princess Anne, Election district 15, map #5.
9 April 1799 William Davis Allen sold to William Stewart and John Cottman
Stewart 115 acres.
1802 William Polk willed to son John Polk.
18 Oct.1830 Sheriff's sale-suit of Levin Miller against Henry J. Riggin,
179 acres of PANTHERS DEN,ALLENS VALE,COME BY CHANCE.

ALMODINGTON

Patented on 10 Nov. 1663 by John Elzey for 1000 acres in St. Peters,
Election district 2, map #6. Resurveyed in 1672 for 1200 acres.
1667 John Elzey willed to son Arnold Elzey.
Rent Rolls 1666-1723 Possessed by Capt. Arnold Elzey for 1000 acres.
17 June 1681 Arnold Elzey sold to Sarah Ballard 300 acres.
6 Feb.1705 Arnold Elzey deeded for use of Somerset Parish, 1 acre.
1729/33 will of Arnold Elzey, to son John Elzey all lands and to
daughters Sarah Elzey and Elizabeth Elzey land on Manokin River (not
named).
(Sarah Elzey died single person,1747, no land in will.
Elizabeth died s.p. 1777/81. John Elzey died 1777, no land mentioned in
will. Plantation to wife Ann Elzey and son Robert Elzey.)

3 Oct 1734 John Elzey sold to Jarvis Ballard for 5 shillings, 300 acres
now called EXCHANGE.
3 Oct. 1734 Jarvis Ballard sold to John Elzey 300 acres that Arnold Elzey
deeded on 17 Jun 1681 to his mother Sarah Ballard. After her decease, to
Jarvis Ballard called RECOVERY 300 acres on Goose Ck. being part of 1000
acres patented John Elzey.
1783 tax lists- Sarah Ballard 250 acres.
1783 tax lists- James Ballard 50 acres
1783 tax lists- Arnold Elzey (with SUPPORT) 1242 acres.
1786 resurvey by William Elzey.
23 Feb 1791 William Jones and wife Sarah Jones sold to Rev. Jacob Ker
23 Feb 1791 Rev.Jacob Ker sold to Sarah Jones wife of William Jones. no
acres given.
23 Sep.1807 Thomas Jones gave to his brother Arnold Elzey Jones, from
mother Sarah Jones, where father Col. William Jones now lives. no
acreage.
5 Jan 1980. forclosure-Mortgage from George H. Ritter to Elizabeth
Chandler 203.20 acres, 43 acres of marsh and timber and 160 acres
cultivated. 15 room Colonial Home, 9 room caretakers home and out
buildings. House built by Arnold Elzey c1700.= Marylander and Herld
newspaper.
Also the site of "Homewood" National Register House on Oriole Road the
house John Elzey built for a daughter who married a Waters.

AMBROSIA

Patented in 1692 by Teague Riggin and wife Mary Riggin (Mary London) and
deeded to son Ambrose Riggin. Also known as GOLDEN LYON. In Brinkleys
southeast, Election district 3 map #16.
1721 Teague Riggin willed to son Solomon Riggin 200 acres.

AMITY

Patented 13 Oct.1673 by Alexander Draper who assigned to William Furniss
for 900 acres.
Resurveyed in 1677 by William Furniss. in Westover, Election district 13,
map #10.
4 March 1684 William Furniss and wife Honour Furniss gave to John
Bennett and wife Sarah Bennett (daughter of Wm.Furniss) 100 acres called
WILLS LOTT in Manokin.
1703 John and Sarah Bennett sold 100 acres to William Turpin, called
WILLS LOTT.
Rent Rolls 1666-1723 possessed by William Turpin 200 acres and James
Furniss 700 acres.
13 March 1725 William Furniss and wife Ann Furniss sold to James
Furniss(gr.father Wm.Furniss of afsd William s/o James, gave to his son
James) now known as BROTHERS AGREEMENT. 200 acres.
18 Nov. 1726 William Furniss s/o James Furniss of William, and Ann
Furniss sold to Stephen O'Dear.
19 Nov. 1729 William Furniss heir of James dec'd lately who was the son
of William the Elder sold to Solomon Long 150 acres. (William Furniss the
Elder died intestate and his son James Furniss died intestate.)
10 Feb.1734/5 John O'Dear and Isabelle O'Dear his wife and Stephen O'Dear
his brother sold to Moses Tilghman that James Furniss and Judith Furniss
his wife sold to Stephen O'Dear and Elizabeth O'Dear his wife now called

BEARS HALL. 100 acres.
17 Jun. 1734/5 Stephen O'Dear and Mary O'Dear his wife sold 186 acres to Joseph Tilghman (also see BEARS HALL)
13 Jan.1737/8 William Turpin and Sarah Turpin his wife sold for 5 shillings to Woncy McClemmy two parcels on Manokin taken up by Alexander Draper, and purchased from John Bennett. 200 acres (daughter Elizabeth Turpin married Woncy McClemmy)
1741 I Isaac Mitchell am bound to William Conner of Annamessex-condition William Mitchell son of Isaac Mitchell will in six months be age 21 and he will make over to Conner tr SUCESS(Good Sucess) 100 acres. If he dies not Isaac shall alienated to Conner tract AMITY 200 acres where Isaac now lives on Kings Mill Branch 17 Nov. 1743.
5 Nov 1747 William Furniss son of William sold 5 acres to James Furniss.
18 Nov.1747 William Furniss sold to Solomon Long 88 acres.
20 July 1762 William Furniss eldest son of William who was the son of William who was the son of James Furniss who was the son of William, and Elizabeth McClemmy and Mary McClemmy daughters of Woncy McClemmy, deceased (only children) sold to Isaac Mitchell for 5 shillings 200 acres.
19 Jul. 1764 Isaac Mitchell gave to son William Mitchell 200 acres.
1763 Joseph Tilghman gave to son Isaiah Tilghman 186 acres.
1765 Solomon Long gave to son Solomon Long 260 acres.
16 Mar.1768 William Mitchell sold 200 acres to William Miles of Manokin.
4 Aug 1772 William Furniss sold to Josiah Long 2 3/4acres.
31 Mar.1772 David Long heir of Solomon Long sold to Solomon Long, land Solomon Sr. purchase from Wm. Furniss on 20 Nov 1766 (no name) 10 acres.
19 March 1773 William Miles sold to William Mitchell 200 acres (redemption of Mtg.)
1783 tax- James Elzey 97 1/2 acres
1783 tax- Solomon Long 247 acres
1783 tax- heirs of David Long 2 3/4 acres
1783 tax- Bridget Mitchell 66 1/2 acres
1783 tax- William Mitchell 133 1/2 acres
1783 tax- Isaiah Tilghman 196 acres
23 March 1787 William Mitchell sold to James Bowland 200 acres.
24 March 1787 James Bowland sold to William Mitchell 200 acres.
15 May 1787 William Mitchell and Rebecca Mitchell his mother sold to Solomon Long 30 acres.
1790 Isaiah Tilghman willed to son William Tilghman land conveyed by deed from Stephen O'Dear to Joseph Tilghman, and to son William part purchased of Solomon Long.196 acres.
7 Sep.1790 Eli Furniss, wife Matilda Furniss, sold to Jesse King all from his father William Furniss. no acres given.
24 Feb 1795 Solomon Long sold to William Done 299 acres of AMITY & BEVERLY adjacent.
27 May 1795 William Done sold to Jesse King 30 acres
12 March 1797 Solomon Long son of Solomon sold to Isaiah Tilghman 8 3/4 acres.
11 Dec 1798 Jesse King sold to James Wilson
2 Jan 1798 William Done,wife Margaret Done sold to Jesse King 299 acres of AMITY & BEVERLY.
11 Dec 1798 Josiah Furniss sold to Jesse King AMITY 200 acres called BROTHERS AGREEMENT and 5 acres.
2 Dec 1800 Jesse King mortgaged to John Woolford, part AMITY & BEVERLY, desc. no acreage given.

14 April 1801 Josiah Long son of Josiah Long, of Northampton Co. Va. sold
to William King of Jesse of Som.Co. all his part.
6 June 1801 William Mitchell son of William sold to Jesse King 18 acres.
6 Aug.1805 Jesse King mortaged to Arthur Woolford his interest.
6 Aug.1805 John Woolford released older mortgage to Jesse King.
27 June 1807 Peggy Mitchell sold to Jesse King and Zadock Long for 5
shillings her dower rights from husband William Mitchell.
9 Feb 1808 Arthur Woolford released mortgage to Jesse King.

AMITY

18 Nov. 1685 patented by Richard Peakes of Gr. Money at Mt.Vernon
Election district 5, map #1 for 50 acres.
Rent Rolls 1666-1723, possessed by Phillip Covington.
1732/3 will of Phillip Covington, to wife and then to son John Covington.
1733/8 possessed by John Covington.
1750 became part of SWEETWOOD, in a resurvey.

ANDERSONS ADVENTURE

1748 part resurveyed from BECKFORD for 254 acres in West Princess Anne,
Election district 1 map #3. by John Anderson.
1742 John Anderson gave part to wife Rachel Anderson, guardian to son
James Anderson and sold 140 acres to John White of Princess Anne.
20 Dec.1752 John Cannon and wife Rachel Cannon, formerly widow of John
Anderson, exec. sold to John White of Princess Anne Town 140
acres,(confirmation of sale)
1795 resurveyed back to BECKFORD.

ANDREWS DISAPPOINTMENT

Patented in 1769 by John Adams, from WALLERS CHANCE, for 91 3/4 acres. in
West Pr.Anne, Election district 1, map #2.
1783 tax- John Adams Sr. in Wicomico 100, 91 3/4 acres.
25 March 1807 Thomas Hamilton mortgaged to Benjamin F. A. C. Dashiell.

ANGOLA

Patented on 29 Aug.1677 by William Green for 50 acres.
Rent Rolls 1666-1723- Wm. Green assigned to John Johnson,a negro on the
south side of the Wicomico River. No heir appears so land escheats to his
lordship. Not found on Benson's maps.

ANGSLEY

Patented on 8 Dec. 1701 by Thomas Davis for 100 acres. Also known as
ANGLESE, in Brinkleys southeast., Election district 3, map #16.
Rent Rolls 1666-1723 possessed by Thomas Davis.
10 Nov.1726 I Sarah Davis for love, give to daughter Mary Cox wife of
William Cox tract WATERFORD 450 acres and 100 acres
formerly belonging to Sampson Allen(unnamed).
1762 John Davis son of Thomas Davis, willed to the eldest son of John Cox
of William Cox(Mary Davis daughter of Thomas Davis married Wm.Cox.)
1783 tax lists- William Cox 100 acres.

19

ANNAMESSICKS

Patented 1665 by Benjamin Summers for 300 acres. See EMESSEX.

ANNAMESSEX (Marsh)

Patented on 31 Dec 1701 by James Gray in Lawsons District, Election district 8, map #19.
Rent Rolls 1666-1723 possessed by James Gray
1701, Thomas Jones willed to son Thomas

ANNIES DELIGHT SEDGEWICK

Patented in 1853 for 319 acres out of GRAYS ADVENTURE, MANLOVES DISCOVERY, COME BY CHANCE, THE KEY AND ADDITION.

APES HOLE

1679 patented by Edward Furlong for 200 acres in Asbury, Election district 12, map 21. 8 October 1689 Thomas Jones resurveyed a piece of escheat land.
Rent Rolls 1666-1723 possessed by William Jenkins by the appointment of Robert Catherwood, guardian to Jones' orphans.
1701 Thomas Jones willed to son John Jones.
10 Apr. 1734 John Jones of Dorcester County Md. sold to John Sterling.
1741 John Sterling willed part to son Henry Sterling and part sold to James Ward.
18 May 1769 James Ward the elder, gave to son Thomas Ward, 8 acres.
1783 tax lists- Henry Sterling 160 acres
1783 tax lists- Thomas Ward 8 acres
1784 Henry Sterling willed to wife Deborah Sterling and to son Ephraim Sterling.
1796 will of Thomas Ward, 1/2 of plantation to wife Hannah Ward and 1/2 to son James Ward(unnamed land)

ARABIA

Patented in 1758 by Isaiah Tilghman in Westover, Election district 13, map# 10 for 83 acres.   Resurveyed in 1784 by Isaiah Tilghman for 113 acres.
1783 tax lists- Isaiah Tilghman 71 acres
1790 Isaiah Tilghman willed parts to sons William Tilghman and James Tilghman.
13 March 1810 William Tilghman son of Isaiah Tilghman sold to Isaac Gibbons of Thomas Gibbons, 2 3/4 & 16 3/4 acres.

ARCADIA

Patented in 1787 by Denwood Wilson in West Pr. Anne, Election district 1, map #3, for 182 1/2 acres. Was part of WILSONS CONCLUSION.
1798 will of Denwood Wilson, to sons William Witherspoon Wilson and George Wilson.
22 Apr.1794 Denwood Wilson sold to Arnold Elzey 3/4 acre to correct division lines.
26 April 1807 William Wilson of Northampton Co. Va. sold to Littleton

Dennis Teackle 80 3/8 acres.
29 Oct.1807 Littleton Dennis Teackle sold to John Teackle of Georgetown
D.C.
May 1981 Sale by auction, described in 1864 as part of ARCADIA (alias
Bellmont) on road from Princess Anne to Monie Church. (20 acres belongs
to Thomas Dixon from Samuel Jones.) 10 acres, conveyed to Hiram Bacon
from H.Filmore Lankford,assigned by deed dated 27 Aug 1927, total of
13.39 acres. Marylander and Hearld newspaper.

ARMSTRONGS LOTT

This land included ARMSTRONGS PURCHASE both out of SKIPPERS PLANTATION
patented 1666 by Matthew Armstrong 600 acres and 200 acres, in Westover,
Election district 3 map #11.
Rent Rolls 166-1723 possessed by James Curtis 250 acres and by Samuel
Handy 500 acres.
1670 Matthew Armstrong sold to Stephen Bond. He and wife Jane Bond
willed to a neice who married a Handy 300 acres SKIPPERS PLANTATION.
1671 Hannah Armstrong of Boston Mass.widow of Matthew Armstrong sold to
Daniel Curtis 250 acres and also part of ARMSTRONGS LOTT.
1681 Daniel Curtis died and gave plantation to son James.
1720 James Curtis son of Daniel Curtis died and left to son Charles
Curtis.
1741 Charles Curtis gave to son James Curtis 250 acres of ARMSTRONGS
LOTT.
1734 Samuel Handy per will gave to son Thomas Handy ARMSTRONGS PURCHASE
250 acres.
1737 Thomas H. Handy son of Samuel Handy died, lands descended to his son
Sewell Handy.
1766 James Curtis resurveyed ARMSTRONGS LOTT 311 acres.
17 Nov. 1771 Sewell Handy and James Curtis divided the 200 acres.
ARMSTRONGS PURCHASE and 300 acres of ARMSTRONGS LOTT.
1777 Sewell Handy died and land(dwelling plantation went to his son
Thomas Handy.
1800 Sewell Handy petitioned to divide the Real Estate of Thomas Handy
(his father) who died intestate and was possessed of 348 acres ARMSTRONGS
and other lands.
1 May 1802 Sewell Handy son of Thomas Handy and wife Harriett Handy of
Queen Anne Co. sold to Thomas Beauchamp 1/6th part.

ARMSTRONGS LOTT

Resurvey in 1766 of ARMSTRONGS PURCHASE by James Curtis for 311 acres in
Westover, Election district 13, Map #10.
1783 tax list- James Curtis (resurvey) 311 acres.
6 Dec 1786 James Curtis sold to Thomas Handy Jr. 311 acres.
6 Dec 1786 Thomas Handy Jr. to James Curtis 311 acres.
1816 William J. Curtis died in possession of ARMSTRONGS LOTT ENLARGED,172
acres.

ARRACOCO

Patented on 19 Nov. 1679 by Randal Revell and Alexander Draper, the
surplus land adjacent to DOUBLE PURCHASE included in a resurvey of 2800
acres made by Revell called DOUBLE PURCHASE. Westover, Election district
13, map #10.

20 May   1678 Randal Revell and wife Katherine Revell sold to George Downes 200 acres called KIQUITAN CHOICE.
13 May 1685 Randal Revell and wife Katherine gave to Stephen Horsey and his wife Hannah Horsey 500 acres called HANNAHS DELIGHT out of DOUBLE PURCHASE in ARRACOCO.
13 May 1685 Randall Revell and wife Katherine Revell gave to John Webb and wife Katherine Webb 160 acres called GREAT HOPES.
18 Aug.1692 Randal Revell sold to William Bannister part 340 acres. Thomas Bannister son of William called it FATHERS PURCHASE(unpatented) also called WILLIAMS PURCHASE.
1709 Randall Revell son and heir of Randall Revell, deeded to his son Charles Revell a part 333 1/3 acres, includes part of DOUBLE PURCHASE.
1728 Thomas Bannister sold to Thomas Mitchell 60 acres being part of DOUBLE PURCHASE & ARRACOCO.
1768 part resurveyed to GREAT HOPE 774 1/2 acres.

ASCUES CHOICE

Patented 7 Nov.1679 by Edward Dickenson and assigned to Phillip Ascue for 150 acres in West Pr.Anne, Election district 1, map #2.
Rent Rolls 1666-1723 possessed by Phillip Ascue.
2 Jan. 1688 Phillip Ascue and Lydia Ascue his wife sold to James Ingram and Mary Ingram his wife(daughter of Phillip Ascue and Lydia Ascue) 150 acres for 6 shillings.
1 Jan.1725 George Clifton, carpenter and Mary Clifton his wife sold to John Disheroon 150 acres.
13 Jul 1761 John Disheroon, planter, of Worcester County for 5 shilings sold to son Obediah Disheroon, part devised to John by his father John Disheroon deceased of Worc.Co.(divided between John and his brother Michael Disheroon) 92 acres.
1756/62, will of Michael Disheroon, to wife Mary Disheroon 58 acres part and to son Constant Disheroon, dwelling plantation and aforesaid after wifes death.
1783 tax- Mary Disheroon 58 acres(w/o Michael Disheroon))
1783 tax- Stephen Disheroon (s/o John Disheroon)
1795 Constant Disheroon willed to daughter Milla Stanford (wife of Thomas Stanford) 50 acres where I live.

AUSTINS CHANCE

Patented in 1787 by George Austin for 48 1/2 acres in St Peters, Election district 2, map #2.
29 March 1791 George Austin sold to Levin Dashiell- deed of mortgage.
29 May 1792 George Austin sold to John Dashiell 48 1/4 acres.
26 Jan 1809 Mary Austin widow of George Austin, William Austin, Lewis Phoebus and wife Mary Phoebus, Sarah Austin, Milla Austin, Nancy Austin and Nelly Austin children of George Austin deceased, sold to John Dashiell Sr. 48 1/4 acres.
1817 John Dashiell willed to be sold.

AUSTINS ADVENTURE

see ABBINGTON

AYR

A resurvey in 1794 from RIGGINS AMENDMENT & HILLIARDS DISCOVERY and part
of HILLARDS ADVENTURE, by Teague Riggin for 357 3/4 acres, in Brinkleys
southeast,Election district 3, map #6.
23 May 1795 Teague Riggin sold to George Riggin 356 3/4 acres of RIGGINS
AMENDMENT.

BACHELERS HOLE

Patented in 1754 by Edward Waters for 302 acres in Dublin, Election
district 4, map #13 and map #12.. Resurveyed in 1775 for 501 1/2 acres by
William Waters that includes WATERS ADDITION TO TIMBER TRACT, part of
WATERS FOLLY, and upper part of HOG YARD, total of 1110 3/4 acres.
1784 will of Edward Waters, to waiting man Adam use of BATCHELORS HOLE &
LONG RIDGE (he freed him)
1787 Part of Addition resurveyed to DEER PARK.
21 Feb.1787 Samuel Smith, wife Esther Smith, Samuel Miles and William
Waters Sr. sold to Nehemiah King, 40 acres with MILES LOTT, BAD LUCK,
ADDITION. MILES ADDITION.
20 Feb 1798 Samuel Smith, wife Esther Smith, Samuel Miles and William
Waters Sr. sold to Nehemiah King 7 acres of BACHELERS HOLE & BAD LUCK.
21 March 1787 Nehemiah King sold to Levin King son of Robert Jenkins
King, same as above.
12 Nov.1799 Francis Hutchins Waters sold to William Waters of John Waters
interest in real estate of uncle Edward Waters, no name or acreage given.
1808 will of William Waters, to son William Gillis Waters my Pocomoke
Lands 1100 acres(unnamed)
28 Nov.1808 Levin King sold for 5 shillings to Mary A King, BAD LUCK,
BACHELORS HOLE, MILES LOTT & ADDITION TO MILES LOTT.

BAD EXCHANGE

Patented in 1768 by Josiah Polk for 190 acres, in Dublin, Election
district 4, map #13.
21 Feb 1775 Josiah Polk quitclaimed to John Broughton and Jonathan Cluff
his rights. no acres mentioned.

BAD LUCK

Patented on 7 July 1756 by Samuel Miles, in Dublin, Election district 4,
map #12.
22 Nov 1758 Samuel Miles,carpenter, and wife Rebecca Miles sold to
William Smith, weaver, part of two tracts 45 acres of MILES LOT and 40
acres of BAD LUCK.
1783 tax- Samuel Smith, 10 acres, Dividing Creek 100
1783 tax- Samuel Miles 122 acres, Dividing Creek 100
1760 this land was resurveyed to MILES ADDITION.
21 Feb 1787 Samuel Smith,wife Esther Smith, Samuel Miles and William
Waters Sr. sold to Nehemiah King, 40 acres with MILES LOTT, ADDITION,
MILES ADDITION, BACHELORS HOLE.
21 March 1787 Nehemiah King sold to Levin King s/o Robert Jenkins King 40
acres, and afsd. lands.
21 Feb 1787 Samuel Smith, wife Esther Smith, Samuel Miles and William
Waters Sr. sold to Nehemiah King 102 acres.7 acres of BACHELORS HOLE,
with BAD LUCK,MILES LOTT,ADDITION,MILES ADDITION.

23

21 March 1787 Nehemiah King sold to Levin King son of Robert Jenkins King for 5 shillings, same as above.
14 Feb 1805 George Miles of Worc.Co. mortgaged to Littleton Robins.
28 Nov.1808 Levin King sold for 5 shillings to Mary A. King BAD LUCK, BACHELORS HOLE, MILES LOTT, ADDITION TO MILES LOTT.
16 June 1808 George Miles son of Samuel Miles of Worc.Co. sold to Littleton Robins with MILES LOTT.

BAINES ADDITION (BANES ADDITION)

Patented in 1762 for 36 acres by Duncan Banes(Baine) in East Pr.Anne, Election district 15, map #4. In 1769 Duncan Banes added ADDITION 210 ACRES. and in 1794 Stephen Banes (son of Duncan Banes) patented THIRD ADDITION 212 1/4 acres.
28 Oct.1765 Duncan Banes sold to Jonathan Pollitt 4 1/2 acres.
22 March 1775 Duncan Banes and wife Sarah Banes sold to Mills Bailey.
1783 tax- Mills Bailey 52 acres, Wicomico 100
1783 tax- Jonathan Pollitt Jr. 4 1/2 acres.
1788 will of Mills Bailey, lands (unnamed) to wife Rebecca Bailey, after her death to son James Bailey. If he has no issue to sons Asa Bailey and Hambleton Bailey.
18 March 1790 Stephen Baine sold to Isaac Hayman 9 1/2 acres
19 May 1795 Stephen Baine,wife Anne Baine sold to Isaac Hayman, BAINES ADDITION with vacancy now called BAINES THIRD ADDITION 57 acres.
19 May 1795 Stephen Baine,wife Anne Baine, sold to Jonathan Pollitt Jr. 3 acres BAINES THIRD ADDITION.
15 Jan.1798 Stephen Baine,wife Anne Baine sold to Jacob Morris 155 acres.
21 Aug.1805 James Bailey sold to negro Jesse Purnell 28 acres of WHAT YOU PLEASE, BAINES ADDITION & HENRYS ENDEAVOUR(now in Wicomico Co.)
15 April 1807 Jonathan Pollitt, wife Nicy Pollitt sold to John Morris Jr. BAINES THIRD ADDITION 2 3/4 acres and BAINES ADDITION 4 3/4 acres with CACKMORE.

BALD RIDGE

On 19 March 1680 William Stevens assigned to John Roach 200 acres in Brinkleys northwest, Election district 13, map#14.
1708 John Roach willed to son Nathaniel Roach 200 acres.
Rent Rolls 1666-1723 Possessed by John Roach.
1746/47 Henry Smith willed to son William Smith part of land deeded of 8 Dec.1742 to son Henry Smith.
8 Dec.1742 I Henry Smith give to son William Smith of Coventry Parish, BALD RIDGE.
1 Sep.1747 William Smith traded 9 acres for 10 acres of DIXONS CHOICE ENLARGED, with Thomas Dixon.
1756 Thomas Dixon sold to Isaac Dixon 9 acres with 20 acres out of DIXONS BULL.
2 Sep.1779 Henry Smith and wife Mary Smith sold to Samuel Bedsworth 96 3/4acres.
1783 tax- Samuel Bedsworth 106 acres.
21 March 1787 Samuel Bedsworth sold to Thomas Jones, 80 acres with BEDSWORTHS CHOICE, COLEPIT, BRADDOCKS DEFEAT, PROVIDENCE.
1788 will of Isaac Dixon, plantation(unnamed) to son Isaac.
14 Nov.1793 Samuel Bedsworth sold to Benjamin Lankford rights in tracts that William Smith willed 1/3rd part to Sarah Archiblad Smith

grandaughter of grantor 33 1/3 acres (could be other lands.)
17 Apr.1800 Lambert Hyland trustee, sold to Thomas Jones, as Thomas Jones
in Dec.1797 obtained a decree against Samuel Bedsworth.
22 Apr.1800 Thomas Jones, wife Mary Jones, sold to William Williams.

BALLARDS AND KINGS LOTT

Patented in 1771 by Jarvis Ballard for 97 acres, includes part of
HAMILTONS FORTUNE. Resurveyed in 1782 for William Ballard in East
Pr.Anne, Election district 15, map#5.
1773 John King willed to son Whittington King, land taken up by Jarvis
Ballard.
1783 tax-William Ballard 48 acres.
12 March 1799 William Ballard of Jarvis Ballard sold to Levin Ballard 77
acres.
29 March 1800 William Ballard of Jarvis Ballard sold to Lambert Hyland 97
acres.
30 March 1803 Priscilla Walston sold to Lambert Hyland, land of Jarvis
Ballard, her first husband, dower rights.

BALLYHACK

Patented on 8 Nov.1700 by Robert Polk in Dames Quarter, Election district
9, map #7.for 200 acres
Rent Rolls 1666-1723 possessed by Robert Pollock.
1718 Robert Pollock died intestate.
16 Aug.1748 Joseph Pollock of Dorcester County Md. sold to John Shores
and William Shores 200 acres with FORLORN HOPE,CLOMMELL & FORLORN HOPE
ADDITION, total 440 acres.
1783 tax- George Austin 200 acres.

BALLYS PURCHASE(BAILYS PURCHASE)

Patented in 1748 by Benjamin Bailey for 50 acres in East Pr.Anne,
Election district 15, map #4.
20 Aug. 1762 George Bailey gave to son Mills Bailey
1783 tax- Mills Bailey 50 acres. Wicomico 100.
1788 will of Mills Bailey, land (unnamed) to wife Rebecca Bailey and then
to son James Bailey.
4 May 1804 James Bailey sold to Jacob Morris 38 acres.

BALTIMORE

Patented in 1770 by Neil Ritchie for 482 acres in Dublin, Election
district 4, map #12.
19 Nov.1772 John Tull sold 105 1/4 acres to Joseph Cottman.
19 Nov.1772 John Tull sold 20 acres to Benjamin Cottman.
1 Jun 1773 John Tull sold 25 acres to Levin Maddux.
17 Mar 1773 John Tull sold 68 1/4 acre to Zorobable King.
1780 will of John Tull, to daughter Rhoda Hall and to daughter Sarah
Tull.
1783 tax-Zorobable King 68 1/2 acres
1783 tax-Sarah Coston 32 acres
1783 tax-Rhoda Hall 50 acres
1783 tax-Neil Ritchie 90 acres

1783 tax-Levin Maddux 26 acres
14 Sep.1791 Joseph Cottman sold to Benjamin Cottman and Levin Maddux, and
Henry Coston heir of Isaac Coston, Zorobable King, Rhoda Hall and Neil
Ritchie and wife Sarah Ritchie,division of lands that John Tull had
called Indian Ridge 42 1/3 acres and added 439 3/4 acres of vacant land
not called BALTIMORE 482 acres. John Tull willed to daughters Sarah Tull
and Rhoda Hall.
21 Oct 1791 Neil Ritchie and wife Sarah Ritchie sold 105 1/4 acres to
Zorobable King.
21 Oct 1791 Neil Ritchie and wife Sarah Ritchie sold to Joseph Cottman
105 1/4 acres.
21 Oct 1791 Neil Ritchie and wife Sarah Ritchie sold to Nehemiah King
remaining part 42 1/4 acres, with BEAR POINT & HARRISONS ADVENTURE.
21 Oct 1791 Neil Ritchie and wife Sarah Ritchie,sold to Levin Maddux 25
acres.
21 Oct 1791 Neil Ritchie and wife Sarah Ritchie sold to Henry Coston 82
1/2 acres.
1791 repatented by John Tull
1794 Zorobabel King willed to son Levin King, lands(unnamed)
3 Feb 1793 Nehemiah King sold to Henry King land conveyed in 1791 from
Neil Ritchie, several tracts 343 1/2 acres, unnamed.
5 Feb 1793 Nehemiah King sold to Neil Ritchie 23 3/4 acres of BEAR POINT
& BALTIMORE.
6 April 1796 Neil Ritchie, wife Sarah Ritchie sold to William Cottman 21
acres.
16 Oct.1798 Levin Maddux,wife Polly Maddux, sold to William Coston 14 1/2
acres.
27 Aug. 1799 Levin Maddux, wife Mary Maddux sold to William Cottman 21
1/4 acres of ADDITION TO BEECH RIDGE & BALTIMORE.
15 April 1807 Levin Farrington, William Cottman, Lazarus Cottman sold to
Andrew Adams, all lands of Wiliam Cottman, deceased, no name.

BARBADOS

Patented 21 Nov.1722 Robert King for 300 acres by Robert King on Devils
Island(Deals Island) in Dames Quarter, Election district 14, map #8.
1783 tax- Nehemiah King, 300 acres.
14 Feb.1795 Nehemiah King sold to David Wallace 300 acres

BARE HOLE

Patented 1700 Peter Benton for 50 acres, in Dublin, Election district 4,
map #12.
1718 possessed by Matthias Coston 50 acres.
1728 Peter Benton willed to Benton Coston BEARSHOLE. (Peter Benton
married Comfort Coston w/o Stephen Coston)
17 Jun 1767 Mathias Coston and wife Abigail Coston sold to Samuel Miles
50 acres.

BARES CHANCE

Patented in 1745 by Thomas Bannister for 15 acres in East Pr.Anne,
Election district 15, map#5.
1751 will of Thomas Bannister, to son William Bannister(planation) and to
son Ezekiel Bannister BARES CHANCE & LOW GROUND.

25 Oct.1759 Mitchell Bannister and wife Abigail Bannister and William
Bannister his brother, sold to James Furniss Jr. son of James with WOLFS
HARBOUR & INDIAN BONES, that father Thomas willed to his sons. 15 acres.
17 Mar.1772 James Furniss sold to Isaac Handy, attorney, 15 acres with
WOLFS HARBOUR & INDIAN BONES.
8 Jan 1805 Richard Henry Handy, wife Elizabeth Handy, as heir of Isaac
Handy sold to Littleton Dennis Teackle.
19 Oct.1807 Littleton Dennis Teackle sold to John Teackle of Georgetown
D.C.
12 May 1810 John Teackle of DC sold to John Pershouse of Philadelphia Pa.

BARNABYS LOTT

Patented 12 Mar.1663 by James Barnaby for 200 acres in Fairmount,
Election district 6, map #9.
1667 James Barnaby willed to son James.
1667 Mary Barnaby widow married Edward Jones.
Rent Rolls 1666-1723 Possessed by John Henderson who married Elizabeth
Barnaby, 146 acres and James Willis who married Rebecca Barnaby,54 acres.
13 Nov.1688 John Henderson and wife Elizabeth sold to Lazarus Maddux 6
acres that James Barnaby willed to John Henderson and wife Elizabeth
Henderson and James Willis and wife Rebecca Willis.
1711 John and Elizabeth Henderson deeded her share of her fathers land to
her son William Henderson.
1720 William Henderson gave 96 acres to brother Joseph Henderson.
26 Aug. 1727 Barnaby Willis and Collebrah Willis his wife sold to William
Turpin 32 acres taken out of BARNABYS LOTT and WILLISES CHOICE.
14 Sep.1736 John Henderson Sr and wife Elizabeth Henderson gave to
Barnaby Willis 200 acres.
1 Apr.1738 Nathaniel Roach and Hannah Roach his wife sold to David
Wilson, now called ADDITION. Hannah Roach being the daughter and sole
heir of Joseph Henderson.
5 Jan 1747 David Wilson sold to Thomas Seon, part now called ADDITION.
8 Dec.1747 Nathaniel Roach and Hannah Roach his wife sold to David
Wilson, all her one half part.
1755 William Turpin willed to son Whitty Turpin land bought of Barnaby
Willis, unnamed.
4 Jan.1760 James Henderson (s/o John Henderson and Elizabeth Henderson
(both deceased) sold to Nathaniel Whitaker 100 acres.
13 Aug.1761 Nathaniel Whitaker sold to Thomas Seon his interest in two
parcels SALISBURY & BARNABYS LOTT.
7 Jan.1772 Jabez Willis (eldest son of William Willis) sold to James
Willis with tract ENVY, no acres mentioned.
6 Mar.1772 James Willis sold to Thomas Seon, 8 acres with part of ENVY.
total 10 acres.
1783 tax-Thomas S. Sudler 11 1/4 acre
1783 tax-Whitty Turpin 10 acres
1783 tax-James Willis 30 1/2 acre.
1782 Thomas Seon Sudler inherited and changed the name by resurvey in
1789 to SUDLERS CONCLUSION 419 3/4 acres.
1784 Whitty Turpin willed lands to wife Elizabeth, then to daughter Sarah
Fountain and then to grandson Whitty Fountain.
23 Dec 1789 John Wilson and wife Peggy Wilson sold to Thomas Seon Sudler
30 acres.

BARNETT

Patented 20 Dec.1701 by Richard Barnes for 35 acres in Asbury, Election district 12, map # 21.
1718 John Sterling with Richard Barnes purchased of James Ward and Mary Ward his wife, Morris Dugan and Sarah Dugan, sisters of John Sterling who inherited from their father.
31 Aug 1762 Aaron Sterling sold(lease trust) to Southy Whittington and after the death of Aaron, then on behalf of son Littleton Sterling.
1783 tax-Aaron Sterling 30 acres.
1795 will of Aaron Sterling, to son Aaron Jr.

BARRETTS CONCLUSION

Patented in 1786 by Joseph Barrett for 114 acres a resurvey of LANKFORDS CONTENT & TREHEARNS TROUBLE, in Brinkleys, Election district 3, map #14.
31 Jan 1806 Joseph Barrett gave to son James Barrett
31 Jan 1806 James Barrett sold to William Williams.

BAY BUSH HALL

Patented by William Stevens who assigned on 14 March 1680 to John Hill 100 acres, in Asbury, Election district 12, map #21.
8 March 1681 John Hill and wife Alice Hill sold to Amos Cook.
Rent Rolls 1666-1723 Amos Cook died without heirs and land escheats.
1739 a resurvey by William Williams 100 acres.
1747/51 William Williams gave to wife Elizabeth Williams.
18 Oct.1775 Job Williams and John Williams of Dorchester County sold to Isaac Moore of Somerset County.50 acres between Arthur Williams and Job Williams.
1783 tax- Isaac Moore 60 acres.
16 Sep.1790 William Williams sold to Hance Lawson, formerly the property of father Arthur Williams. no acres given.
1819 Job Moore willed to son Stephen Moore.
1857 James Lawson gave to daughters Sally R. Moore, Susanna Nelson and Grace L. Sterling.

BEACH AND PINE

Patented on 3 Nov.1685 by John Dorman,in Westover, Election district 13, map 11, for 100 acres.
Rent Rolls 1666-1723 possessed by Richard Tull Jr.
1710 will of Richard Tull, to son Solomon Tull.
10 Aug 1734 Solomon Tull and Elizabeth Tull his wife sold 50 acres to William Wharton.
7 May 1739 Isaac Barnes of Lewis Town Delaware sold to Solomon Tull land where he now lives, 100 acres.
14 April 1742 William Wharton and wife Mary Wharton sold to Edward Rook, 50 acres.
15 Dec.1746 Edward Rook and wife Sarah Rook, mariner, sold to John Howard, blacksmith, 50 acres with 20 acres of WILSONS LOTT.
25 Feb.1752 John Howard and wife Christian Howard sold 50 acres to William Waters, with Wilsons Lott.
1783 tax- Joshua Tull 50 acres.
1783 tax- William Waters Jr. 50 acres.

31 Dec.1798 Solomon Tull sold to William Waters of William for 5
shillings all interest in with WATERTOWN,WILSONS LOT
2 Nov.1830 Sheriff's sale, Elisha Whitlock against Edward M. Waters.

BEARD NECK

Surveyed on 19 Sep.1676 for William Stevens who assigned to Robert Dukes,
350 acres in Lawsons, Election district 8, map #18.
Rent Rolls 1666-1723 Held by Robert Dukes son of Robert.
1704/5 John Dukes son of Robert and Frances Dukes, and wife Ann Dukes
sold to David Lindzey.50 acres.
1708 Robert Dukes, wife Frances Dukes sold to James Dickenson, 50 acres.
19 Nov.1719 David Lindzey and wife Esther Lindzey sold to Mary Prior
widow, and Mary Prior her daughter. (John White married the afsd widow
Mary.) 50 acres.
10 Nov.1719 James Dickinson and wife Elizabeth Dickinson sold 50 acres to
Robert Scott.
21 Aug 1740 John White and Mary White his wife and Joshua Merrill and
Mary Merrill his wife sold 52 acres to John Scott.
6 Nov.1770 John Scott and Sinor Scott, his wife sold 190 acres to Smith
Horsey.
1783 tax- Smith Horsey's heirs 100 acres
1783 tax- Samuel Long 100 acres
1781 will of Smith Horsey, to son Smith.
16 April 1806 Smith Horsey sold to John Wilkins 190 acres
16 April 1806 John Wilkins sold to Smith Horsey 190 acres
16 April 1806 Smith Horsey sold to John Horsey of Smith Horsey 190 acres
with MEADOW GROUND 5 or 6 acres and tract purchased of Thomas Robertson
executor of Robert B. Holland.
9 Feb.1809 William Coulbourn of Robert Coulbourn sold to Thomas Merrill
Tull 50 1/2 acres.
1819 resurveyed to GREAT ANNAMESSEX 832 acres by Samuel Horsey.

BEARE POINT (BEAR POINT)

William Stevens assigned on 10 July 1679 to Stephen Coston 500 acres in
Dublin, Election district 4, map #12.
1697 Stephen Coston willed to sons and daughters, 150 acres to Eliza
Coston (she married William Townsend) 150 acres to Esther Coston (she
married John Tull) and 200 acres to Isaac Coston.
Rent Rolls 1666-1723 350 acres possessed by Peter Benton in his wife's
part (he married Comfort Coston widow of Stephen)
1725 Southy Whittington,surveyor, laid out for John Harris, tract HARRIS
ADVENTURE, being taken out of a tract of Stephen Coston Jr., BARE POINT,
150 acres which part Stephen Coston left to his daughter Elizabeth
Coston, which part was sold by the heirs to said John Harris; signed
Elizabeth Townsend, John Tull and Isaac Coston.
1728 Peter Benton gave Matthias Coston 50 acres.
1729 John Tull, wife Esther Tull gave lands (unnamed) to son John Tull.
19 Nov.1729 John Harris and Rebecca Harris his wife, sold to John Tull
150 acres now called HARRIS ADVENTURE.
1743 Isaac Coston willed to wife Rose Coston and son Oliver Coston.
20 Aug.1754 Ahab Coston and wife Abigail Coston, sold to Isaac Coston for
5 shillings devised by deceased Isaac Coston to son Oliver Coston which
descended to Ahab as brother and heir at law 150 acres and FLATTLANDS.

9 Jul. 1764 John Tull and Esther Tull traded 200 acres with Isaac Coston for 175 acres.
9 Apr.1767 Esther Tull and John Tull sold 175 acres to William Hayward.
1772 Isaac Coston willed to son Henry Coston priviledge to ditch thru any part of BEAR POINT, and to son Isaac Coston remainder of lands, if he dies to son Eli Coston- this tract not named.
10 Nov.1775 William Hayward of Talbot County sold to John Tull of Somerset Co. for 10 shillings, his interest.
1780 John Tull, wife Esther Tull, gave lands(unnamed) to son John.
1783 tax- Sarah Coston 100 acres
1783 tax- Rhoda Hall 120 acres
1783 tax- John Riggin 125 acres
2 Jan.1788 Alexander Draper and Rachel Draper his wife of Sussex Co. Del. sold to John Riggin of Som.Co. 125 acres (from Elizabeth Coston who married William Townsend and had issue Stephen Townsend, and Stephen had issue William Townsend and William had issue of afsd Rachel Townsend now wife of Alexander Draper. Deed also signed by Matthias Coston.)
21 Oct 1791 Neil Ritchie and wife Sarah Ritchie sold to Nehemiah King, Mary Gray and Rhoda Hall, that was possessed by John Tull and devised to Esther Tull,mother of said John Tull by her father Stephen Coston in his will,150 acres with HARRISONS ADVENTURE & BALTIMORE.
29 Jan.1793 Eli Townsend of Worc Co sold to John Riggin, all rights, no acreage given.
3 Feb.1793 Nehemiah King sold to Henry Coston land conveyed in 1791 by Neil Ritchie and wife Sarah Ritchie several tracts 343 1/2 acres, unnamed.
5 Feb.1793 Nehemiah King sold to Neil Ritchie 23 3/4 acres of BEAR POINT & BALIMORE.
19 Jan 1793 Rachel Draper of Slaughter Neck in Cedar Creek 100 in Sussex Co. Del. sold to Neil Ritchie of Som.Co. for 5 shillings 7 acres formerly conveyed from John Harris and Rebecca Harris to John Tull.
26 April 1796 Neil Ritchie, wife Sarah Ritchie, sold 7 acres to Henry Coston.
26 April 1796 Neil Ritchie, wife Sarah Ritchie, sold 2 3/4 acres to Isaac Coston.
18 April 1810 Robert Riggin, wife Peggy Riggin sold to Littleton Harris 340 acres of HARRISONS ADVENTURE & BEAR POINT.
1807 Henry Coston willed to son Henry K. Coston, no name

BEAR RIDGE

Patented in 1731 by Daniel Long for 49 acres, in Dublin, Election district 4, map # 12.
20 March 1755 Daniel Long and wife Sarah Long, and James Ward son of Joseph Ward sold to William Waters. (Joseph Ward married Elizabeth Long daughter of Solomon Long.)49 acres.
1761 Resurveyed to WATERS ENLARGEMENT 165 acres, by William Waters.
1780 will of William Waters, to son George Waters, BEAR RIDGE part of WATERS ENLARGEMENT.

BEAR RIDGE

Patented on 23 March 1687 by Thomas Manlove for 200 acres in East Pr.Anne, Election district 15, map 4.
Rent Rolls 1666-1723 possessed by Samuel Handy.

1776 Saywell Handy gave to son Saywell 218 acres
4 Dec. 1781 Thomas Handy (son of Saywell deceased) sold to Matthias Miles
200 acres.
1783 tax- Matthias Miles 172 acres.
1792 resurveyed to FOUR-IN-ONE 739 1/8 acre.

BEARS DEN

Patented on 23 Jan.1687 to William Goldsmith for 100 acres. in East
Pr.Anne, Election district 15, map #5.
Rent Rolls 1666-1723 William Goldsmith dead in Pennsylvania and no one
possesses.
12 May 1807 Thomas Reynolds and wife Sarah Reynolds, of Broadkill 100 in
Sussex Co.Del. sold to Josiah H. Hanbury of same. William Goldsmith died
in Sussex Co. Del. leaving issue, Neomi Goldsmith, Patience Goldsmith,
Comfort Goldsmith & Jamima Goldsmith. Sarah Reynolds only surviving
daughter and heir of Neomi Goldsmith. 100 acres.

BEARS HALL

This 100 acres was not patented but is part of AMITY in Westover,
Election district 13, map 10.
10 Feb.1734/5 John O'Dear and Isabelle O'Dear his wife and Stephen O'Dear
his brother sold to Moses Tilghman 100 acres part of AMITY.
31 May 1735 Moses Tilghman sold to Joseph Tilghman 100 acres.
1763 will of Joseph Tilghman, to son Isaiah.
1783 tax- Isaiah Tilghman 100 acres.
1790 Isaiah Tilghman willed to son William Tilghman 100 acres.

BEARS QUARTER

Patented 25 May 1689 by John Parsons in West Princess Anne, Election
district 1, map #2, for 100 acres.
Rent Rolls 1666-1723 possessed by John Parsons.
15 Oct. 1749 Ahab Coston and wife Abigail Coston(d/o John Parsons) sold
to Thomas Gillis, SECOND CHOICE and 20 acres of BEARS QUARTER.
15 Oct.1749 Thomas Gillis sold to Ahab Coston part of SECOND CHOICE,
(this was a trade of lands)
15 Feb.1760 Thomas Gillis sold to Levin Gillis part purchased of Ahab
Coston, with other lands for 5 pounds.
31 March 1763 Matthias Coston and Abigail Coston his wife(d/o John
Parsons and widow of Ahab Coston)sold to Jessey Lister and Coulbourn
Long, SECOND CHOICE & BEARS QUARTER (except part conveyed by said Abigail
and Ahab Coston her then husband to Thomas Gillis, total of 250 acres.
18 Aug.1763 Coulbourn Long sold to Abigail Coston wife of Matthias Coston
for 5 shillings 250 acres of SECOND CHOICE & BEARS QUARTER.
10 April 1764 Matthias Coston and wife Abigail Coston leased for seven
years 300 acres to John Davis of SECOND CHOICE,BEAR QUARTER & GOOD LUCK.
24 April 1771 Oliver Coston (son of Ahab Coston)and wife Sophia Coston
sold to Rev. Samuel Sloan and Eden School visitors, SECOND CHOICE & BEARS
QUARTER, except part conveyed by Ahab Coston and wife Abigail Coston to
Capt. Thomas Gillis-no acreage mentioned.
13 April 1771 Oliver Coston sold 40 acres to Ahab Coston with 110 acres
of SECOND CHOICE.
22 Nov.1771 Oliver Coston sold to Samuel Sloan, etc. of Eden School 169

acres of SECOND CHOICE,BEAR QUARTER, GOOD LUCK, conveyed by Thomas Gillis
to Ahab Coston father of Oliver Cosston and to Abigail Coston his wife.
18 July 1773 Ahab Coston and wife Betty Mary Coston, sold to Gillis Polk,
SECOND CHOICE, & BEAR QUARTER, per deed from Oliver Coston to Ahab, no
acreage mentioned.
7 Sep.1779 Oliver Coston sold to Andrew Adams part of three tracts,
SECOND CHOICE, GOOD LUCK, BEARS QUARTER in all 50 acres.
13 Oct.1788 Oliver Coston son of Abigail Coston, daughter of John Parsons
the younger, sold to Andrew Adams 100 acres with SECOND CHOICE.

BEAUCHAMPS CHANCE

Patented in 1752 by Robert Beauchamp for 206 acres in Westover, Election
district 13, map #11.
7 March 1762 Robert Beauchamp and wife Esther Beauchamp sold to Stacey
Miles 206 acres.
1770/85 will of Stacey Miles, to son Thomas Miles
1783 tax lists- Thomas Miles (calls it Beauchamps Conclusion.)
1786 resurveyed to MILES ADDITION, 230 1/4 acres

BEAUCHAMPS PRIVILEDGE

Resurveyed from part of TILLMANS PURCHASE in 1752 by Marcy Beauchamp for
79 acres in Westover, Election district 13, map#11.
12 Sep.1763 Stephen Garland mortgaged to John Logan of the City of
London, merchant 90 acres BEAUCHAMPS PRIVILEDGE and interest in THREE
BROTHERS,DAVIDGES PURCHASE & SALISBURY.
2 Jan 1766 Stephen Garland bonded to Thomas Dashiell,sheriff, as attorney
on behalf of a prisoner in jail (for bail) with other lands.
10 March 1767 Thomas Dashiell, sheriff sold 79 acres to John White.
10 March 1767 John White sold 79 acres to Stephen Garland.
1762 Resurveyed to DAVIDGES PURCHASE 335 acres.

BEAUCHAMPS VENTURE

Patented in 1746 by Thomas Beauchamp for 145 acres in Brinkleys,
northwest, Election district 3, map #14.
1757 resurvyed ADVENTURE by Thomas Beauchamp inlcuding part of LEDBOURN,
for a total of 608 1/2 acres.
1759 Thomas Beauchamp willed to brother William Beauchamp.
1759 Thomas Beauchamp willed to Beauchamp Davis lands (unamed)
1 April 1769 Fountain Beauchamp and wife Rhoda Beauchamp sold to Phillip
Adams son of Hope Adams 161 acres of LEDBOURN which includes 44 acres of
BEAUCHAMPS VENTURE willed to Fountain by his father Edward Beauchamp in
1750.
15 Dec.1769 Handy Beauchamp sold to William Boston Jr. 13 1/2 acres with
LEDBOURN.
24 Nov.1769 Beauchamp Davis Sr. sold to Beauchamp Davis Jr. for 5
shillings 21 acres (that Thomas Beauchamp willed to Beauchamp Davis Sr.)
18 Jun 1771 William Beauchamp gave to son John Beauchamp 36 acres.
4 Aug.1780 Levin Beauchamp sold to James Hall 5 4/5 acres.
17 Dec.1781 Richard Boston and wife Mary Boston sold to brother Levin
Boston 13 1/2 acres and part of LEDBOURN that William Boston purchased of
Handy Beauchamp. William died intestate and Richard was the eldest

brother.
1783 tax- Levin Boston 25 acres
1783 tax- Phillip Adams of Hope Adams, 44 acres.
1783 tax- Thomas Beauchamp 173 1/2acres
1783 tax- Beauchamp Davis 21 acres and ADDITION 126 acres.
1783 tax- Joshua Beauchamp, with ADAMS CONCLUSION 59acres
1783 tax- Levin Beauchamp 241 1/3 acres
1783 tax- James Hall, with CHANCE 20 acres.
1794 Pierce Chapman (wife Rebecca Chapman)willed estate to son John
Chapman if he lives to adulthhood.
24 Sep 1787 Elijah Beauchamp, wife Martha Beauchamp, sold to Pierce
Chapman BEAUCHAMPS VENTURE & ENLARGEMENT 32 3/4 acres
12 Jan 1788 Pierce Chapman sold to Thomas Beauchamp 32 3/4 acres of
BEAUCHAMPS VENTURE & ENLARGEMENT.
12 Jan 1788 James Hall, wife Mary Hall sold to Henry Schoolfield 5 1/5
acres with pt. CHANCE.
12 Jan 1788 Thomas Beauchamp, wife Sarah Beauchamp, sold to Pierce
Chapman 52 3/8 acres
12 Jan 1788 Levin Beauchamp, wife Mary Beauchamp sold to Pierce Chapman 8
1/4 acres.
12 Jan 1788 Planner Beauchamp sold to Pierce Chapman 8 1/4 acres.
12 Jan 1788 Planner Beauchamp sold to Samuel Smith 3 3/4 acres.
8 Jan 1790 Thomas Beauchamp, wife Sarah sold to Pierce Chapman 30 acres.
6 Aug.1792 Planner Beauchamp, wife Martha Beauchamp, Pierce Chapman, wife
Rebecca Chapman sold to Samuel Smith, 79 acres with ADAMS CONCLUSION.
5 Feb.1792 Planner Beauchamp sold to Thomas Jones 80 acres.
15 March 1796 Levin Beauchamp sold to Thomas Jones, merchant 104 acres.
20 Sep.1796 Thomas Beauchamp Sr.,wife Sarah Beauchamp sold to William
Williams 166 3/4 acres of LEDBOURN,HOGYARD,ENLARGEMENT,SMALL HOPES,
BEAUCHAMPS VENTURE.
17 April 1797 Joshua Beauchamp, wife Mary Beauchamp sold to Samuel Smith
BEAUCHAMPS VENTURE & LEDBOURN, formerly belonging to Handy Beauchamp 60
acres and 1/3rd part held by Joshua in right of his wife Mary Beauchamp.
1798 tax- Levin Boston 25 acres
18 March 1797 Levin Beauchamp,wife Mary Beauchamp sold to Rebecca Chapman
87 3/4 acres & 25 3/4 acres.
18 March 1797 Thomas Jones,merchant sold to Levin Beauchamp 104 acres.
11 Jan 1798 William Williams,wife Polly Williams sold to Thomas Adams
with ENLARGEMENT,LEDBOURN,HOG YARD,SMALL HOPE
11 Jan 1798 William Williams,wife Polly Williams sold to David Potter 78
1/4 acres SMALL HOPES,BEAUCHAMPS VENTURE.
11 Jan 1798 William Williams sold to Samuel Smith 33 1/2 acres of
LEDBOURN,HOG YARD,ENLARGEMENT & afsd.
11 Jan 1798 David Potter sold to Phillip Adams 78 1/4 acres of BEAUCHAMPS
VENTURE & SMALL HOPES.
7 Nov.1798 Whittington Polk,wife Rebecca Polk, (was widow of Pierce
Chapman) sold to William Boggs 113 1/2 acres.
17 Feb. 1808 Levin Boston sold part to William Adams.
1813 Samuel Smith willed to sons James Smith & Samuel.
29 Jan 1820 Elijah Boston sold part to Thomas Adams (of Phillip Adams)
with LONG RIDGE, LEDBOURN,BOSTONS LOTT & MILBOURNS PURCHASE.
1831 Thomas Adams willed to four children, Morris Henry Adams, Mary Pitt,
Leah Jane Adams and Emeline Rounds land purchased of Elijah Boston-
unnamed.
28 Oct.1786 Rhoda Beauchamp and Levi Beauchamp sold to Isaac Beauchamp 42

acres, his rights to BEAUCHAMPS VENTURE & GOOD HOPE.

26 Aug.1794 Planner Beauchamp,wife Martha Beauchamp and Thomas Jones sold to Samuel Smith 80 acres.

1 July 1799 Samuel Smith, wife Esther Smith sold 169 acres to William Boggs.

1 July 1799 William Boggs,wife Betsy Boggs sold to Samuel Smith, 113 1/2 acres that on 18 March 1797 Rebecca Chapman bought of Levin Beauchamp and part to William Boggs land from Rebecca Polk and her husband Whittington Polk.

14 Sep.1804 David Potter, wife Mary Potter sold to Phillip Adams 78 1/4 acres of BEAUCHAMPS VENTURE & SMALL HOPES.

17 Feb.1810 Levin Boston sold to William Williams 40 acres of LONG RIDGE.

1813 Samuel Smith willed to daughter Rosanna Smith land bought of Pierce Chapman & William Boggs 92 1/2 acres, unnamed.

BEAVER DAM BRANCH

Patented in 1769 by Isaiah Tilghman for 65 acres in Westover, Election district 13, map #10.

1783 tax- Isaiah Tilghman possessed.

1790 will of Isaiah Tilghman, to son William Tilghman 65 acres.

BECKFORD

24 Nov.1679 William Stevens assigned to Edmund Howard 500 acres in East Princess Ann, Election district 15, map #5.

Rent Rolls 1666-1723 Possessed by Peter Dent. (Edmund Howard married Margaret Dent)

1 March 1697 Edmund Howard sold to Peter Dent, except 93 acres.

1710/11 will of Peter Dent, lands not mentioned by name but he willed land except 93 acres to daughter Rebecca Dent. (Rebecca married David Brown)

13 March 1732/33 The Maryland General assembly laid out for lots in a new town PRINCESS ANNE, and Rebecca Brown and David Brown were given first choice, lots two and three. These were sold before his death by David Brown. Rebecca Dent then married James Anderson. 25 acres.

5 Nov.1736 James Anderson and Rebecca Anderson his wife sold to John Tunstall 500 acres excepting all such part within the bounds of Princess Anne town.

2 March 1747 James Anderson now of Chester County Pennsylvania sold 500 acres to Patrick Allison of Somerset County Md. containing the town of Princess Anne formerly the inheritance of Peter Dent that descended to the widow Rebecca, widow of David Brown and lately wife of said James Anderson, and James had issue in life of said Rebecca Anderson now living, and several lots in Princess Anne town,he to pay rents for eleven years. Signed, Patrick Stewart, attorney, and James Anderson.

1752 John Anderson gave per will to wife Rachel Anderson, guardian (he had sons James Anderson and John Anderson) He was the son of James and Rebecca Anderson.

1771 John Anderson sold the remaining part of the BECKFORD estate, excluding the Princess Anne Lots, to Mr. Henry Jackson, excepting one acre conveyed to Denwood Wilson.

31 Jan 1770 Lawrence Gothree, late of Nova Scotia but now of Somerset

County purchased from John Anderson, part, 1/4 acres adjacent Princess
Anne Town,
8 Oct. 1771 John Anderson and wife Elizabeth Anderson sold 1 acre to
Denwood Wilson.
17 Oct. 1771 John Anderson and wife Elizabeth sold to Henry Jackson part,
(no acreage mentioned)
10 Oct. 1771 John Anderson sold 1/4th acre to Matthias Miles.
1 May 1778 Denwood Wilson sold to Henry Jackson, 1 acre.
1783 tax- Henry Jackson 470 3/4 acre.
14 May 1788 John Wilkins sold to William Lowber for 50 years, lot
belonging to the Presbyterian Meeting House, called the TAN YARD- lease.
1793 will of William Brittingham, to son William.
1795 resurveyed to 549 acres including CROUCHES CHOICE.
1794/5 will of Henry Jackson, to son George Wilson Jackson.
16 Oct.1798 Matthias Miles sold to Isaac Ewing 1/4 acre
17 Sep.1799 Levin Ballard and Nehemiah King sold to Rebecca Mitchell aka
Rebecca Hammond(as Henry Jackson willed to John Done 3 1/2 acres, whereas
by writ of the court on 28 May 1795 on behalf of Ann Thorpe admx. of
William Thorpe
deceased against John Done)
1800 Rebecca Mitchell (Rebecca Hammond) willed to sons John Hammond,
Solomon Hammond, Benjamin Hammond land in Pr. Anne town devised to John
Done,late, by Henry Jackson deceased and after wards by deed of 17
Sep.1799 conveyed me by Levin Ballard and Nehemiah King.
28 June 1800 William Lowber of Philadelphia and wife Elizabeth Lowber
sold to Samuel Lippincott of Acco.Co.Va.lot and tan yard near Pr.Anne
Town 2 acres purchased of John Wilkins- no name.
1800 will of John Dennis, to son Littleton James Dennis
19 May 1802 George Wilson Jackson of Pr.Anne town, merchant sold to John
Dennis Esq. attorney at law, lot 6 acres 1 rod, 3 perches.
19 May 1802 George Wilson Jackson sold to Littleton Dennis Teackle 9
acres.
12 Apr.1803 George Wilson Jackson sold to William McNider, part,
description no acres mentioned.
25 Oct 1803 George Wilson Jackson sold to Matthias Jones lot contiguous
with Pr.Anne Town, 3 1/2 acres.
23 Apr.1804 Samuel Lippincott of Acco.Co.Va. sold to Littleton Dennis
Teackle lot in BECKFORD.
17 Dec.1804 Littleton Dennis Teackle sold to John Dennis piece of
BECKFORD 2 miles from Pr.Anne called THE RIDGE.
11 Dec 1804 John Dennis, Esq.attorney at law, wife Eleanor Dennis sold to
Littleton Dennis Teackle, merchant, part west of the Prot.Episcopal
Church.
26 June 1805 George Wilson Jackson sold 66 acres to George Handy,
adjacent Pr. Anne Town.
1805 Benjamin Hammond sold to John Hammond lot lately belonging to
Rebecca Hammond where John Done lived.
11 Mach 1806 George Wilson Jackson sold 4 acres to William Gillis Waters.
1 April 1806 Samuel Hammond sold to Samuel Mullen 1/4th part of lot in
BECKFORD where John Done lives purchased by Rebecca Mitchell, alias
Rebecca Hammond.
14 Oct.1806 Robert Leatherbury, sheriff sold to John Custis Wilson, per
judgement against Isaac Ewing, tract with houses, contiguous to Pr. Anne
Town 1/2 acre.

16 Dec.1806 Josiah Wilson Heath, wife Mary Heath and Samuel Heath with
Peggy Heath sold to Jesse Wainright lots adjacent Pr. Anne Town 1/2 acre.
29 Oct 1807 Littleton Dennis Teackle sold to John Teackle of Georgetown
DC. lands purchased of John Dennis.
13 April 1809 John Teackle of Georgetown DC and Littleton Dennis Teackle
sold to Charles N. Bancker of Philadelphia part of BECKFORD & houses in
Princess Anne Town.
20 Feb 1810 John Hammond sold to Elizabeth Bond Mitchell part formerly of
Rebecca Hammond.
1828 will of Henrietta Dennis, to brother Littleton Dennis house at
BECKFORD.
1841 Isaac Newman gave to sons Samuel Newman, Littleton Newman and Dennis
Newman, BECKFORD mansion in Princess Anne purchased of Littleton Teackle,
Aaron B.Quimby and wife Elizabeth Quimby.
(note; many of these entries for BECKFORD are actually within the bounds
of PRINCESS TOWN.)

PRINCESS ANNE TOWN

Established on 13 March 1732 for 25 acres out of BECKFORD

LOT-1

1742 Possessed by John Tunstall
1746 John Tunstall willed to grandson Tunstall Hack and Peter Spence
Hack.
10 March 1752 John White purchased.
3 Oct.1766 John White of Pr.Anne sold to William Smith a lot, as per
mortgage from David McGrath to John White on 14 Feb.1764.
19 July 1770 James Dick of Ann Arundel Co. surviving partner in trade
with Thomas Richardson deceased sold to William Pollitt 3/4 acre where
John White lived in Pr.Anne, no number of lot given.
1783 Frederick Digner had 3 lots in town, this is one.
21 Dec.1784 Frederick Digner sold to William Waddy.
5 June 1798 Levin Ballard, sheriff, sold to George Waggaman, per
judgement against Lambert Hyland against Frederick Digner, 1 lot 11/15th
acre. No lot number given.
2 Apr.1799 George Waggaman sold to Henry Jones.
20 May 1801 Henry Jones, wife Elizabeth Jones sold to Thomas Jones son of
John Jones.
8 Feb.1803 Thomas Jones of John Jones,wife Margaret Jones sold to Thomas
Jones.
17 Nov.1803 John Wilkins, sheriff, sold to Josias Cox, merchant, lot of
Henry Jones and Thomas Jones per judgement against them.
29 May 1804 Henry Waggaman of Dorc.Co. sold to Littleton Dennis Teackle
8030 sq.ft.
29 May 1804 Littleton Dennis Teackle sold to Josias Cox.
5 May 1806 Josias Cox with wife Mary Cox sold to Polly Digner.
16 July 1810 John Teackle of DC sold to John H. Bell.

LOT-2

29 April 1738 David Brown and wife Rebecca Brown sold to James
Strawbridge, David Polk and James Polk 1/3rd part each.
29 April 1739 Sale confirmed by James Anderson and wife Rebecca Anderson
(Rebecca Brown)
1788 David Polk willed 1/3rd part to son William Polk.
15 April 1788 James Polk sold to Frederick Digner- no lot number given.
15 April 1796 John Williams sold to William Davis Allen 1/3rd part.

22 Sep.1796 Frederick Digner sold to Solomon Long.
11 April 1797 Frederick Digner sold part to Solomon Long.
17 May 1798 Solomon Long sold to Levin King and William Ballard and William Pollitt.
1 April 1800 Josiah Furniss sold to Parker Selby 1/3rd part.
27 May 1800 Parker Selby sold 1/3rd part to William McNider.
24 June 1800 William Polk sold to William McNider 1/3rd part.
12 March 1805 William McNider sold to James Mullen.

LOT-3

14 Sep.1737 David Brown and wife Rebecca Brown sold to Col. Robert King and Capt.David Wilson.
14 Sep.1737 James Anderson and wife Rebecca Anderson (Rebecca Brown) confirms sale.
11 Oct.1791 John Woolford sold to Parker Selby bought of John Jones.
11 Aug.1795 Dr. John Woolford sold to Arnold Elzey.
11 May 1801 Parker Selby sold to Levin Woolford.
14 May 1801 Arnold Elzey of Washington City sold to Levin Woolford.
15 May 1805 Dr. Arnold Elzey, wife Henrieta Elzey of Washington DC sold to John Stevens of Worc.Co.
15 Oct.1805 Parker Selby sold to William McNider
29 July 1806 John Woolford, Arthur Woolford, Whittington King, wife Nancy King, representatives of Levin Woolford sold to Parker Selby. They also gave a mortgage to Arnold Elzey.
26 Sep.1809 William McNider sold to Parker Selby
1811 William McNider willed to Parker Selby and Levina Selby, house and lot in Pr.Anne now occupied by Thomas Smith, watchmaker. To nieces Eleanor Adams and Mary Dryden house and not now occupied by Samuel Talbot and house occupied by Milly Benson, no numbers given. He also owned lot #25.

LOT-4

1748 Heber Whittingham ,wife Mary Whittingham, willed to be sold to pay debts.
13 Feb.1749 Heber Whittingham mortgaged to John Done.
22 Feb.1764 Mary Whittingham sold to William Geddes, mortgage.
17 Feb.1767 William Geddes released the mortgage.
18 May 1774 John Graham and wife Mary Elizabeth Graham and John Gordon and wife Ann Gordon of Northumberland Co. Va. sold to Peter Waters lot where Heber Whittingham lived with lot #5. Mary Elizabeth Graham and Ann Gordon daughters of John Tunstall, legal heirs.
1783 tax- Heber Whittingham.
8 Oct.1806 Heber Whittingham sold to William B. Jones.
29 Aug.1818 William B. Jones sold to William R. Warwick.

LOT-5

18 March 1774 John Graham and wife Mary Elizabeth Graham and John Gordon and wife Ann Gordon (daughters of John Tunstall) sold to Peter Waters, where Isaac Handy built a house as a study.
1805 Isaac Handy inherited and held by son Richard Henry Handy.
8 Jan.1805 Richard Henry Handy sold to Littleton Dennis Teackle.
29 Oct.1807 Littleton Dennis Teackle sold to John Teackle of Georgetown DC purchased of Robert Henry Handy.
16 July 1810 John Teackle of D.C. sold to John H. Bell.

LOT-6

3 Oct.1769 William Geddes of Kent Co. Md. sold to Isaac Handy 3/4 acre. no lot number.
25 Nov.1782 Nehemiah King sold to Charles Jones

37

25 Nov.1782 Charles Jones sold to Nehemiah King.
1805 Henry Handy willed to son Richard Henry Handy.
8 Jan.1805 Richard Henry Handy sold to Littleton Dennis Teackle.
29 Oct.1807 Littleton Dennis Teackle sold to John Teackle of Georgetown
DC, purchased of Robert Henry Handy.

LOT-7

1755 Heber Whittingham sold to heirs of William Geddes.
10 Nov.1755 Samuel Whittingham sold to William Geddes.
8 Jan 1805 Richard H. Handy,wife Elizabeth Handy sold to Littleton Dennis
Teackle.
20 June 1807 Littleton Dennis Teackle, wife Elizabeth Teackle sold to
John Gale.

LOT-8

1763 James Anderson sold to Thomas Gillis
22 Sep.1767 Thomas Gillis sold to William Geddes.
8 Jan 1805 Richard H. Handy, wife Elizabeth Handy sold to Littleton
Dennis Teackle.
20 June 1807 Littleton Dennis Teackle,wife Elizabeth Teackle sold to John
Gale.

LOT-9

2 Oct.1751 John Anderson purchased.
18 Mach 1763 John Anderson sold part to Thomas Gillis
Aug.1764 Thomas Gillis sold to William Geddes.
22 June 1769 John Anderson sold to Collier Fountain.
19 Oct.1787 Nicholas Tull of Baltimore Co. sold to George Robertson.
22 Oct.1787 Ann Hall sold to George Robertson
1 Aug.1780 Collier Fountain sold to Elijah Tull of Baltimore Co.

LOT-10

16 Nov.1745 John Anderson sold to Patrick Allison, innkeeper back 2 lots
and 10 acres- no number.
1748 Patrick Allison willed to daughter Grace Allison who married David
Caldwell of Pennsylvania.
1752 John Anderson willed to son James Anderson, lot formerly belonging
to Patrick Allison where the Public House stood.
17 April 1761 David Caldwell sold to Samuel Wilkins.
11 May1762 Samuel Wilkins sold to Thomas Bond 1 lot and 1/2 lot of Levin
Gale.-no numbers.
22 Sep.1789 John Bond sold to James Ewing 1 moity.no lot number.
29 March 1798 Archibald Moncrieff of Baltimore survivor of Charles
Crookshank deceased sold to John Erskin, as Archibald Patison willed to
Archibald Moncrieff and Charles Crookshank, lot occupied by James Ewing,
no number.
25 May 1790 James Ewing sold to Nehemiah King 1 moity of lot purchased by
Thomas Bond of Samuel Wilkins, no number.
24 May 1804 Evans Willing sold to Littleton Dennis Teackle (Evans Willing
was appointed trustee to dispose of the RE of John Purss)
21 Nov.1804 Littleton Dennis Teackle sold to George Robertson, Peter
Waters and John Hamilton Bell.
21 Feb.1805 Josias Cox sold to George Robertson, Peter Waters and John H.
Bell.
5 Apr.1807 Littleton Dennis Teackle, wife Elizabeth Teackle sold part to
William McNider.

LOT-11

1748 Patrick Allison willed to only child Grace Allison-no number.
2 Oct.1751 Robert Allison, executor of Patrick Allison.

17 April 1761 David Caldwell and wife Grace Caldwell daughter of Patrick Allison sold to Samuel Wilkins.
11 May 1762 Samuel Wilkins sold 1/2 to Levin Gale- no number.
11 May 1762 Samuel Wilkins sold part to Thomas Bond.
2 March 1788 John Purss, wife Mary Purss sold to John Denwood
6 May 1788 John Denwood sold to John Jones.
6 May 1788 John Jones,wife Elinor Jones sold to John Denwood.
24 Jan.1794 John Lathberry sheriff, sold to James McCulloch property of John Denwood, conveyed for Lambert Hyland.
10 March 1795 Lambert Hyland sold to James McCulloch.
1 June 1798 Edward Parnell of Baltimore, exec. of James McCulloch sold to William Curtis and John Curtis and Thomas Curtis lots 11 & 15.
5 May 1798 John McCulloch of Philadelphia exec. of James McCulloch sold to William Curtis, John Curtis, and Thomas Curtis.
21 May 1803 William Curtis,wife Elizabeth Curtis, John W. Curtis, wife Margaret Curtis, Thomas Curtis, wife Sarah Curtis, sold to Josias Cox.

                                LOT-12
2 Oct 1751 James Anderson sold to Benjamin Fransway
21 March 1754 Benjamin Fransway sold to Edmond Hough of Worc.Co.
25 March 1761 Benjamin Fransway sold to John Cox lots 12 & 13, one and 1/2 acres.
4 Feb.1767 John Cox sold to William Dashiell
3 Sep.1766 William Heath sold to John Cox
6 Apr.1764 John Anderson and John Cox sold to William Heath
1765 John Cox gave to grandaughter Elizabeth Jacobs lots 12 & 13.
26 Oct.1787 Neil Ritchie and wife Sarah Ritchie and Rhoda Hall and Mary Gray sold to John Denwood.
17 Oct.1791 William Dashiell sold to John Denwood.
4 July 1797 Thomas Denwood Woolford sold to John Howard Adams.
4 July 1797 John Lathberry, sheriff, per suit against John Denwood sold to Thomas Denwood Woolford.
23 July 1799 John Howard Adams sold to George Wilson Jackson.
27 March 1804 George Wilson Jackson sold to John Howard Adams, lot in Pr. Anne Town, no number.
27 March 1804 John Howard Adams sold to George W. Jackson and John H. Anderson 1 acre, 6 perches.

                                LOT-13
1764 James Anderson sold to William Heath
2 Oct.1751 James Anderson sold to Benjamin Fransway.
21 March 1754 Benjamin Fransway sold to Edmond Hough of Worc.Co.
25 March 1761 Benjamin Fransway sold to John Cox lots 12 and 13, one 1/2 acres.
4 Feb 1767 John Cox sold to Benjamin Dashiell
13 Sep.1766 William Heath sold to John Cox.
6 Apr.1764 John Anderson, John Cox sold to William Heath
1765 John Cox gave to grandaughter Elizabeth Jacobs
26 Oct.1787 Neil Ritchie and wife Sarah Ritchie, Rhoda Hall and Mary Gray sold to John Denwood.
17 Oct.1791 William Dashiell sold to John Denwood.
9 July 1797 Thomas Denwood Woolford sold to John Howard Adams.
4 July 1797 John Lathbury, sheriff, suit against John Denwood sold to Thomas Denwood Woolford.
23 July 1799 John Howard Adams sold to George Wilson Jackson.

                                LOT-14
12 Feb.1750 Levin Gale willed to children, George Gale and Leah Gale.

26 July 1752 George Gale and Leah Gale sold to Nehemiah Dorman
6 July 1757 Nehemiah Dorman sold to Henry Waggaman.
1759 Henry Waggaman willed to son George Waggaman 1/2 lot purchased of
Nehemiah Dorman
26 Nov.1776 William Elliott Waggaman and Henry Waggaman sold to George
Waggaman.
1783 tax- George Waggaman
19 Nov.1789 George Waggaman sold to Francis Manning
8 Apr.1789 George Waggaman sold to Adam Anderson
8 Apr.1789 George Waggaman sold to Samuel McClemmy.
14 Sep.1790 John Denwood sold to Francis Manning, a lease.
26 May 1791 Adam Anderson sold to Robert Leatherbury
22 July 1794 George Waggaman sold to Francis Manning, no number.
1796 Francis Manning willed to son James Manning one lot, no number
given.
4 July 1797 Thomas Denwood Woolford sold part to Whitty Sasser.
21 May 1799 Whitty Sasser sold to Nehemiah King.
2 Marcy 1802 Henry Waggaman of Dorc.Co. sold to Littleton Dennis Teackle,
part.
2 March 1802 Henry Waggaman of Dorc.Co. sold part to Zadock Long
9 March 1802 Littleton Dennis Teackle sold to Isaac Whitney 25 sq.
perches.
13 May 1805 Robert Leatherbury sold to Zadock Long.
29 July 1806 Joseph Whitney,(that was conveyed to Isaac Whitney brother
of Joseph) sold to Littleton Dennis Teackle.
21 July 1807 Isaac Whitney, wife Elizabeth Whitney sold to Littleton
Dennis Teackle.

LOT-15
2 Oct.1751 John Bell purchased.
17 March 1752 John Bell, wife Joyce Bell sold to Henry Waggaman
1755 Henry Waggaman sold to John Done.
1 Feb.1780 David Wilson and wife Sarah Wilson and Robert Done (her
trustee) sold to John Done lot, that Sarah Done is seized by right of
dower, with DONES NEST EGG.no number given of lot.
18 Nov.1788 John Done sold to Sarah Done widow of John Done deceased.
9 Aug.1797 David Wilson, wife Sarah Wilson of Worc.Co. sold to John Done.
7 June 1797 John Done sold to Zadock Long.
1 June 1798 Edward Parnell of Baltimore, exec. of James McCullock
deceased sold to William Curtis, John Curtis,Thomas Curtis lots 11 & 15.

LOT-16
2 Oct.1751 John Bell purchased.
2 Dec.1751 John Bell and wife Joyce Bell sold to Charles Franks and wife
Isabelle Franks, daughter of John Bell.
26 Apr.1763 John Anderson sold to Robert Hopkins.
20 Jan 1764 Robert Hopkins sold to William Robertson and Lane Robertson.
25 April 1766 Robert Hopkins sold to William Robertson and Lane
Robertson.
30 Apr.1766 William Robertson, wife Rachel Robertson and Walter Lane
Robertson and wife Mary Robertson sold to Levin Gale.
1783 tax- Levin Gale- 13 lots.
28 June 1803 Leah Gale sold to John Dennis, lots, no numbers.
28 June 1803 George Wilson Jackson sold to John Dennis, lot with
BECKFORD, of Levin Gale.
1820 site of the New Court House.

LOT-17

1 751 Henry Lowes purchased from John Anderson
11 May 1762 John Anderson sold to Elijah Tull
17 May 1762 Elijah Tull of North Carolina sold to Thomas Ballard, lease.
1761 Henry Lowes willed to son Tubman Lowes, if he returns. house and not, no number.
21 Apr.1769 William Geddes of Kent Co. Md. sold to William Smith, innholder, lot on New Market St. where Elijah Tull lived., no number.
1783 tax- Heber Whittingham for Elijah Tull
1783 tax- Heirs of Robert Moncur, 3 lots.
14 Aug.1792 William Moncur and Revel Horsey sold to Esme Bayley 1/2.
1799 Esme Bayley willed to son Josiah Bayley, 2 lots in Pr. Anne, no number.
22 March 1803 Thomas Bayley sold to Robert Jenkins King.

LOT-18

1752 held by John Anderson.
31 Oct.1765 John Anderson sold to Thomas Bond
12 May 1767 Thomas Bond,wife Elizabeth Bond sold to Robert Geddes.
22 March 1803 Thomas Bayley sold to Robert Jenkins King.

LOT-19

1765 James Anderson sold to Robert Geddes.
20 Nov.1767 Robert Geddes willed part to son Robert Geddes.
26 May 1767 Robert Geddes sold part to Levin Ballard.
March 1771 William Geddes of Kent Co. Md.inherited part and sold to William Miles.
1781 William Miles willed to grandson George Miles house and lot purchased of John Hopkins and to grandaughter Peggy Pollitt of Thomas Pollitt house and lot purchased of William Geddes.
2 May 1797 Peggy Pollitt sold to Levin Woolford, lots 19 & 20 from the will of her grandfather William Miles.
7 March 1797 Elizabeth Ballard wife of Levin Ballard, and Thomas W. Ballard sold to John Bloodsworth her 1/3rds.
13 June 1801 Revel Horsey sold to Littleton Dennis Teackle with lot #21.

LOT-20

3 July 1750 William Heath and William Gray sold to Henry Lowes.
18 Aug.1773 Henry Lowes sold to Peter Waters.
10 May 1777 Peter Waters sold to John Denwood.
2 May 1797 Peggy Pollitt sold to John Woolford, 18 & 20 willed her by her grandfather William Miles.
21 March 1782 Peter Waters sold to Thomas Maddux lot conveyed by Henry Lowes, no number.
1765 James Anderson sold to Robert Geddes
26 May 1767 Robert Geddes sold to Levin Ballard.
20 Nov.1767 Robert Geddes probate, part to son William Geddes.
13 June 1801 Revel Horsey sold to Littleton Dennis Teackle.
2 Oct.1807 Littleton Dennis Teackle sold to John Teackle of Georgetown DC land purchased of Revel Horsey, unnamed.

LOT-22

3 Nov.1751 William Stoughton conveyed to daughter Mary Sloss wife of Thomas Sloss and balance to daughters Mary Stoughton and Ann Stoughton.
26 March 1793 Thomas Sloss and wife Mary SLoss sold to Edward Gantt and wife Ann Gantt (Ann Stoughton) and Levin Winder and wife Mary Winder (Mary Stoughton.)
11 Oct.1796 Levin Winder and wife Mary Winder sold to James McCulloch for 5 shillings.

41

11 Oct.1796 Edward Gantt and wife Ann Gantt of Berkley Co.Va. and Levin Winder of Somerset Co. sold to James McCulloch for 5 shillings.
25 May 1798 John McCulloch of Philadelphia sold to William Curtis, John Curtis and Thomas Curtis, no number.
25 Nov.1791 Edward Gantt and wife Ann Gantt of Montgomery Co. sold to James McCulloch.
1 June 1798 Edward Gantt and Ann Gantt sold to William Done, release of mortgage.
15 Dec.1798 William Bell of Philadelphia, attorney, of John McCulloch sold to John Done.
27 Jan 1807 William Done, wife Margaret Done sold to Benjamin F.A.C.Dashiell.

LOT-23

2 Oct.1751 Benjamin Hobbs sold to William Geddes.
31 March 1761 John Anderson sold to Robert Geddes.
14 Dec.1762 Robert Geddes sold 30 ft. to son William Geddes.
1769 Robert Geddes sold to Levin Ballard, part (store on this lot.)
8 Nov.1769 William Geddes and wife Mary Geddes mortgaged to Alexander Spiers, John Bowman, William French, John Crawford, George Crawford merchants of Glasgow Scotland and Ebenezer Mackie in Maryland his store lot.
27 April 1771 William Geddes of Kent Co. Md. sold to Levin Ballard 3/4 acres

LOT-24

21 Nov.1754 Robert Geddes sold to George North of Philadelphia Pa.
2 June 1762 George North sold to John Done.
11 May 1762 Robert Geddes, John Anderson, William Gray and William Miles released interest to John Done.
1 Feb.1780 John Done sold to John Bloodsworth
1783 tax- John Bloodsworth 2 lots.
11 Sep.1776 Levin Ballard sold 2 lots, lot 24, to Robert Moncur
2 Dec.1777 Levin Ballard sold to John Bloodsworth where Robert Geddes lived, no number.
5 Sep.1809 John Bloodsworth sold to Col. William Jones.

LOT-25

22 June 1758 Benjamin Hobbs sold to Francis Cheney lot where he lives.
24 June 1760 John Anderson sold to Andrew Francis Cheney
1783 tax- Dr. Andrew Francis Cheney, 2 lots.
12 July 1790 Andrew Francis Cheney gave to son Francis Tubman Cheney and wife Elizabeth Cheney.
12 May 1803 Littleton Dennis Teackle sold to Richard Waters of William Waters.
12 March 1805 Richard Waters of William Waters, wife Polly Waters sold to William McNider.

LOT-26

17 March 1762 John Anderson sold to John Hopkins
28 Nov.1768 John Anderson sold to William Miles.
1781 Wiliam Miles willed to grandson George Miles lot purchased of John Hopkins.
24 July 1795 George Miles, wife Bridget Miles, sold to William Done, lot from grandfather of George Miles.
27 Jan.1807 William Done, wife Margaret Done, sold to Benjamin F.A.C. Dashiell.

LOT-27

1765 John Anderson sold to Robert Geddes

17 Feb.1767 Robert Geddes sold to the Vestry of Somerset Parish.
LOT-28
1765 James Anderson sold to Robert Geddes
17 Feb.1767 Robert Geddes sold to the Vestry of Somerset Parish.
LOT-29
10 Apr.1759 John Anderson sold to Samuel Ingram
28 Aug.1770 Samuel Ingram mortgaged to William Miles
1781 William Miles willed to grandson William Miles of Samuel Miles,
mortgage of Samuel Ingram
21 Feb.1786 Matthias Miles son of William Miles sold to Robert Ingram son
of Samuel Ingram, mortgage.
LOT-30
1 June 1755 Thomas Jones sold to Andrew Francis Cheney.
1 Nov.1785 Andrew Francis Cheney sold to Lambert Hyland
1 Nov.1785 Lambert Hyland, wife Elizabeth Hyland sold to Arnold Elzey.
1 Dec.1795 Arnold Elzey sold to William Done.
6 May 1800 William Done, wife Margaret Done sold to Thomas Curtis.
9 June 1802 Thomas Curtis sold to Thomas Winder Handy, 2 lots.

Unidentified deeds
17 Aug.1758 Ephraim Wilson sold to Samuel Wilson two lots in Pr.Anne Town
bounds East Broad St, south by long alley, west by Manokin River being
the two lower most lots by the river.

19 Oct.1779 Thomas Gullott sold to Frederick Digner 3/4 acres.

1794 Henry Jackson willed to daughter Leah Gale, store lot in Princess
Anne.

19 Nov.1794 Isaac Betts sold to Josiah Wilson Heath and Samuel Heath 1/8
acres adj. Dr. Winders land.

23 Sep. 1796 George Gale of Cecil Co., Levin Gale and Samuel Wilson and
Leah Littleton Wilson sold to Leah Gale wife of Levin Gale and Jane Gale
widow of Robert Gale for 5 shillings, one lot.

1800 Rebecca Mitchell (Rebecca Hammond) willed to sons John Hammond,
Solomon Hammond, Benjamin Hammond land in Pr.Anne town devised to John
Done late, by Henry Jackson deceased, and afterwards by deed of 17 Sep.
1799 conveyed me by Levin Ballard and Nehemiah King.

18 May 1802 John Campbell, merchant of Pr.Anne, sold to Littleton Dennis
Teackle lot purchased of Parker Selby, no number.

26 Jan 1802 Richard Waters of William Waters,sold to Littleton Dennis
Teackle, lot Francis Cheney died possessed.

28 June 1803 Leah Gale sold to John Dennis BECKFORD and inherited lots in
Pr. Anne, of Levin Gale, no numbers.

28 June 1803 George Wilson Jackson sold to John Dennis lots of Levin Gale
in Pr.Anne, with BECKFORD.

28 June 1803 John Dennis,wife Eleanor Dennis sold to George Wilson
Jackson same as above.

27 Sep.1803 John Wilkins,sheriff, sold to John Hammond, to settle debts
of Saul Hammond 1/4 part house and lot devised by Rebecca Hammond to Saul
Hammond, no number.

21 Feb.1804 William McNider sold to Samuel Mullin lot adj. Pr.Anne Town
for 99 year lease.

1805 will of Revel Horsey, to Media Whittingham part of lot in Pr.Anne
formerly property of Heber Whittingham purchased at sheriff's sale.
26 June 1805 Parker Selby, constable, sold to Revel Horsey 1/5th part of
house and lot in Pr.Anne town, per suit of John Wilkins against Samuel
Adams and suit of Leah Adams. admx. of John H. Adams, deceased. Land of
Samuel Adams, that Heber Whittingham once. had.

1816 John Stewart willed to son James Stewart house and lot purchased of
John H. Bell.

1837 William Jones willed to wife Nelly Jones and daughter Margaret Jones
house and lot purchased of John Done.

1834 Stephen Shepherd willed to daughter Fedda Ann Selby lot bought of
Littleton D. Teackle.

1842 Thomas Langsdale willed to John N. Bowland property in Pr. Anne.

1846 George S. Clayton of Acco.Co.Va. gave to daughter Elizabeth Clayton
house and lot.

1849 Henrietta B. Haynie willed to grandniece Henrietta H. Jones land
bought of Samuel W. Jones Esq.

1855 William Handy had an office and lot in Pr.Anne.

1858 George C. Dixon willed to sons Thomas Dixon, George Dixon and John
Dixon house in Pr.Anne.

                              BECKLES

Patented 1 Jun 1679 by William Harper for 200 acres in Dublin, Election
district 4, map #12.
1702 will of William Harper (wife Elizabeth Harper) this land not
mentioned.
Rent Rolls 1666-1723 possessed 100 acres by George Tull and 100 acres by
Edward Harper (son of William Harper.)
18 April 1732 I George Tull for affection give to son Noble Tull part of
two tracts, BECKLES & COLEMANS ADVENTURE.
3 Apr.1751 Noble Tull and wife Katherine Tull, sold 7 acres to Samuel
Adams.
3 July 1759 Jonathan Tull and wife Mary Tull sold to Samuel Adams 28
acres with COLEMANS ADVENTURE & CHANCE.
3 Jul 1759 Jonathan Tull and wife Mary sold to Thomas Hayward the elder(
that George Tull father of Jonathan conveyed to him) 23 acres.

18 Aug.1763 John Pollitt appointed guardian of George Tull son of George, in possession of COLEMANS ADVENTURE & BECKLES.
21 Jun 1764 George Tull sold to John Pollitt part, his rights that father George Tull willed to him.
2 June 1767 Jonathan Tull sold 4 acres to Thomas Hayward for 5 shillings.
20 Aug.1767 Jonathan Tull sold to Samuel Adams 3 acres.
1763 Samuel Adams willed to son Samuel land bought of Jonathan Tull (unnamed.)
4 March 1771 William Tull and Catherine Tull his mother sold to Samuel Adams, part with COLEMANS ADVENTURE (no acreage.)
13 Aug 1782 Samuel Adams deeded all of BECKLES to Phillip Adams.
13 August 1782 Phillip Adams deeded to brother Samuel Adams.
1783 Samuel Adams, wife Nanney Adams sold for 5 shillings 3 3/4 acres to Phillip Collins Adams.
1783 tax- Phillip C. Adams 10 acres
1783 tax- Samuel Adams 95 acres
1783 tax- John Pollitt 40 acres
4 April 1786 Phillip Adams conveyed part to Joshua Boston 102 1/2 acres with ADAMS PURCHASE.
19 Feb 1787 Phillip Adams, wife Priscilla Adams sold to Samuel Adams for 5 shillings 48 acres of BECKLES & ADAMS CHOICE.
3 Oct.1787 John Pollitt sold to Levin Pollitt son of John, of Worc.Co. part BECKLES & COLEMANS ADVENTURE that was conveyed to John by George Tull in 1765.
1790 part resurveyed to POLLITTS ADVENTURE 246 acres. part.
1793 Thomas Hayward willed to son Thomas, part.
15 Nov.1795 Joshua Boston bought part from Phillip Collins Adams.
14 Mar.1804 Joshua Boston conveyed his part to son Levin Boston.
26 April 1809 Joshua Boston and son Levin Boston mortgaged to Jesse King and William King 202 1/2 acres of ADAMS PURCHASE & BECKLES..
12 Jan 1812 James Boston bought 44 acres from Levin Pollitt
1836 Levin Pollitt gave to Levin P. Bowland son of John Bowland and to William Bowland son of John and to William T. Hargis son of Thomas Hargis.

BEDLAM GREEN

Certificate issued to James Johnson and was assigned to Robert Crouch on 5 October 1683 for 150 acres in Princess Anne, Election district 1, map #2.
Rent Rolls 1666-1723 possessed by Robert Crouch Sr.150 acres
1711 will of Robert Crouch Sr.,(this land not mentioned)
17 June 1727 John Crouch sold 51 acres to Thomas Gillis.
24 Jan.1734 John Crouch sold to James Gillis 100 acres.
1757 resurveyed to WHITE CHAPPELL 502 acres.

BELLS AND HORSEYS CONCLUSION

See WATKINSES POINT.

BELLS PURCHASE

Patented on 10 Sept.1723 by Anthony Bell in Lawsons, Election district 8, map #18 for 100 acres.
Anthony Bell willed to son Thomas Bell.

4 Apr.1745 Thomas Bell, wife Elizabeth Bell sold to Josephus Bell.
12 Nov.1762 Daniel Bell of Dorcester County Md. son of Thomas Bell sold
to Josephus Bell of Somerset County part devised by Anthony Bell to
Thomas Bell.
1765 resurveyed to EXPENSE 340 1/4 acres by Josephus Bell.

BETTERSWORTH (BEDSWORTH) CHOICE

Patented in 1751 by John Bedsworth(Bettsworth) in Brinkleys, Election
district 3, map #14 for 62 1/2 acres.
1783 tax- Samuel Bedsworth (s/o John Bedsworth) 62 1/2 acres.
21 March 1787 Samuel Bedsworth sold to Thomas Jones 62 1/2 acres with
PROVIDENCE,COLEPIT,BALD RIDGE,BRADDOCKS DEFEAT, total 410 1/2 acres.
17 Apr.1800 Lambert Hyland trustee sold to Thomas Jones by decree of
court against Samuel Bedsworth.
22 Apr.1800 Thomas Jones,wife Mary Jones,sold to William Williams.

BEECH RIDGE

Patented by Matthias Coston in 1755 for 27 acres in Dublin, Election
district 4, Map #12. He also patented ADDITION to BEECH RIDGE in 1760
for a total of 357 acres.
20 June 1746 Matthias Coston sold to Benjamin Cottman 39 acres of
ADDITION TO BEECH RIDGE.
20 Jun 1746 Matthias Coston sold to Joseph Cottman 100 acres of ADDITION.
2 Nov 1764 Matthias Coston and wife Abigail Coston sold to Isaac Coston
73 acres of ADDITION.
1772 will of Isaac Coston, to son Henry Coston, if he dies to son Eli
Coston.
20 Nov.1782 Benjamin Cottman sold to Levin Maddox for 5 shillings part
conveyed by Matthias Coston 20 3/4 acres.
22 Sep.1783 Matthias Coston sold to Joseph Cottman 8 1/2 acres of
ADDITION (trade for part of COSTONS VENTURE)
1783 tax- Sarah Coston (Addition) 73 acres
1783 tax- Matthias Coston(Addition) 135 acres
1783 tax- Joseph Cottman (Addition)
1783 tax- Benjamin Cottman 38 1/4 acre
1783 tax- Levin Maddux 20 3/4 acre
1788 will of Sarah Coston (wid/o Isaac Coston) to youngest son Eli
Coston, tract formerly disposed of by my husband to his son Isaac which
being confiscated and purchased by me, but if son Eli never returns to
son Henry Coston(unnamed so this could be other lands.)
3 March 1795 John Spencer and wife Frances Spencer and Thomas Barnes and
Sophia Barnes his wife of Worcester Co. sold to Levin Maddux land
belonging to Benjamin Cottman by any name 67 1/3 acres- no names of land
mentioned.
16 Oct.1798 Levin Maddux,wife Polly sold to William Cottman ADDITION 10
acres.
27 Aug.1799 Levin Maddux and wife Mary Maddux sold to William Cottman 21
1/4 acres of ADDN. TO BEECH RIDGE & BALTIMORE.
17 Dec.1805 Matthias Coston Taylor sold to Margaret Coston, ADDITION TO
BEECH RIDGE.
15 April 1807 Levin Farrington, William Cottman and Lazarus Cottman sold
to Andrew Adams all the land of William Cottman, deceased, no name or
acreage.

BELLFAST

Patented in 1753 by Thomas Sloss for 75 1/2 acres in St. Peters, Election district 2, map #6.
1 Nov 1763 Thomas Sloss and George Irving sold to William Smith 75 acres with GEORGES ADVENTURE & CHANCE.
1783 tax- James Campbell 25 acres
1783 tax- Mary Smith(with CHANCE 87 1/2 acres)
5 Feb.1789 Samuel Smith, wife Esther Smith, sold to Henry Walston Miles 64 1/4 acres with CHANCE,ST.PETER'S NECK,GEORGES ADVENTURE.

BENGAL

A resurvey on HARRINGTON & PRIVILDEGE in 1793 by Thomas Holbrook for 988 acres in Mt.Vernon, Election district 5, map#1.
1795 Thomas Holbrook per will, to sons Thomas and Samuel Holbrook.
26 Oct.1802 Thomas Holbrook son of Thomas mortgaged to John Teackle, Littleton Dennis and Littleton Dennis Teackle.
4 Oct.1803 Thomas Holbrook sold to Samuel Holbrook, all.
21 Aug.1804 Thomas Holbrook, wife Peggy Holbrook and Littleton Dennis Sr. and Littleton Dennis Teackle sold to Levin Jones 140 acres of POWERFIELD, BENGAL & LAST VACANCY.
14 Nov.1804 Littleton Dennis, Littleton Dennis Teackle and Thomas Holbrook sold to Tubman Lowes, HOBBS CONCUSION now included in a resurvey to BEGAL 252 acres, conveyed by Matthias Hobbs and Thomas Holbrook father of Thomas afsd.
11 Nov.1808 Littleton Dennis, Littleton Dennis Teackle sold 300 acres to Samuel Holbrook.
1 Nov.1808 Littleton Dennis and Littleton Dennis Teackle sold to George Robertson 200 acres.
2 Nov.1808 Thomas Holbrook, wife Peggy Holbrook sold to Samuel Holbrook 300 acres.
13 April 1809 John Teackle of Georgetown DC sold to George Robertson of Somerset County.
13 April 1809 John Teackle of DC sold to Samuel Holbrook, part.
18 Oct. 1809 Samuel Smith, wife Esther Smith sold 252 acres to John Cottman, was HOBBS CONCLUSION, now BENGAL
25 March 1809 George Robertson sold to John Cottman 200 acres.
14 Sep.1830 Sheriff's sale, suit against Thomas Holbrook 40 acres.

BENJAMINS ADVICE

Patented on 28 Sep.1721 by John King for 50 acres in Dublin, Election district 4, map #12.
Rent Rolls 1666-1723, possessed by John King
2 Mar.1743 Whittington King(son of John) and wife Eleanor King sold to Daniel Long, 50 acres.
24 Mar.1749 Daniel Long sold to George Gale surviving trustee of Samuel Chase, grandson of Thomas Walker deceased, 50 acres. (mortgage)
22 Feb 1758 Daniel Long quitclaimed his right to Solomon Long with CONEY WARREN (heretofore mortgaged to Col.George Gale.)
He appoints attorneys Littleton Dennis and William Allen to convey.   50 acres.
4 April 1758 Solomon Long and wife (unnamed) sold to John Porter 50 acres.

1763 resurveyed to PORTERS PURCHASE 319 acres.

BENJAMINS DISCOVERY

Patented in 1813 by Benjamin Lankford for 52 3/4 acres in Lawsons east,
Election district 8, map #18.

BENSTONS LOTT

This land is not on the maps but is in Lawsons district, map #19 and was
surveyed in 1775 by Stephen Ward for 30 acres, adj.MIDDLE OF NECK,WHITE
OAK SWAMP,WARDS FOLLY.
1783 Stephen Ward willed to wife Mary Ward with BOTTOM OF THE SPOUT.
7 Jan 1800 John Ward son of Stephen Ward, now of Kentucky sold to John
Cullen 500 acres with ADDITION TO BENSTONS LOTT.
6 Nov.1801 John Cullen, wife Betsy Cullen sold to Jacob Miles(free negro)
20 acres of MIDDLE OF THE NECK, & BENSTONS LOTT.
15 Feb 1802 John Cullen sold to Hance Croswell 23 acres of BOTTOM OF THE
SPOUT, MIDDLE OF THE NECK & BENSTONS LOTT.
23 April Hance Croswell sold to William Ward 23 acres of BOTTOM OF THE
SPOUT, MIDDLE OF THE NECK & BENSTONS LOTT.

BERETONS MISTAKE

Patented in 1802 a resurvey of part of WHITE CHAPPELL for 177 3/4 acres
by Levin Pollitt in West Princess Anne, Election district 1, map #2.
13 Dec 1806 Levin G. Pollitt and wife Nelly Pollitt sold to Samuel Polk.

BERRERS LOTT

Patented on 13 Mar.1663 by Phillip Berrer for 600 acres in Westover,
Election district 13, map #11
Rent Rolls 1666-1723 possessed by William Davis.
1696 will of Richard Davis, to sons Richard Davis, William Davis and John
Davis 250 acres between Fishing and Broad Creeks (not named)
1703 Richard Davis willed to sister Rose Davis and brother John Davis
(from father Richard Davis.)
1713 John Davis willed to cousin David Wilson 400 acres.
7 Sep. 1727 Ephraim Wilson gave to son David Wilson (Rose
Davis married Robert Murray (page torn) who conveyed to Ephraim Wilson)
part, no acres given.
11 Nov.1732 William Davis and Bridget Davis his wife sold 1/2 to Edmund
Beauchamp. (that Richard Davis bequeathed to son William Davis father of
afsd. William and John Davis.)the part which was not sold to William
Bannister late by William Davis his father. (could be other lands since
this deed did not name the land.)
1734 resurveyed to WILSONS LOTT 800 acres.

BETTS PURCHASE

Patented on 1 June 1666 by George Betts for 100 acres in St. Peters,
Election district 2, map#6.
Rent Rolls 1666-1723 possessed by George Betts
1688 resurveyed to GEORGES ADVENTURE 364 acres.

BEVERLY

8 Oct.1678 Randal Revell, wife Katherine Revell sold to Christopher Rousby of Calvert County 500 acres of DOUBLE PURCHASE & ARRACOCO, called BEVERLY.
See DOUBLE PURCHASE, surveyed by Randall Revell.
5 Nov.1751 Tripart- Peter Spencer Hack and wife Sarah Ann Hack sold to James Knight and Nehemiah King 500 acres BEVERLY part of tract DOUBLE PURCHASE in Native Arracoco Neck. James Knight tenent in freehold-agreement.
24 Feb 1795 Solomon Long sold to William Done 299 acres of AMITY & BEVERLY adjacent.
2 Jan 1798 William Done,wife Margaret sold to Jesse King 299 acres of AMITY & BEVERLY.
2 Dec.1800 Jesse King mortgaged to John Woolford.
6 Aug.1805 John Woolford released mortgage to Jesse King.
6 Aug.1805 Jesse King mortgaged to Arthur Woolford.

BILLINDICT

1679 this is part of SMITHS RECOVERY, in West Pr. Anne, Election district 1, map #3.
11 Jun 1752 William Raisen of Kent Co. Maryland sold to Ephraim Wilson, part of SMITHS RECOVERY 150 acres.
18 Mar.1762 Ephraim Wilson sold to Thomas Jones (as David Wilson deceased purchased of Tunstall Hack and willed to David Wilson. A certain Thomas Stott of Kent Co. conveyed to Ephraim Wilson.
1764 resurveyed to WILSONS PURCHASE.

BLACK RIDGE

Patented 5 Sep.1667 by Ambrose London for 16 acres in Fairmount, Election district 6, map#9.
11 March 1678 Ambrose London and wife Mary London sold to Joseph Mason 16 acres.
Rent Rolls 1666-1723 possessed by Samuel Handy.
1734 Samuel Handy willed lands to sons Samuel and John Handy.
24 Sep.1751 John Handy of Dorcester Co. Md. and wife Elizabeth Handy deeded to Samuel Handy.
2 Oct 1747 George Tucker of the Isle of Barbadoes and wife Mary Tucker (Mary Handy d/o Thomas Handy) sold 16 acres of BLACK RIDGE, and parts of LONDONS ADVENTURE,JERICHO,HANDYS CHOICE, etc. total of 514 acres.
2 Sep.1767 Thomas Seon sold to Whitty Turpin with HANDYS MEADOW, JERICHO, STEPHENS MEADOW, etc.
1 Aug.1796 Thomas Holbrook and wife Peggy Holbrook(daughter of Whitty Turpin) sold to Henry Coston and Whittington King land deeded Whitty Turpin by Thomas Seon in 1767, no names or acreage given.
22 May 1804 Whittington King and wife Nancy King and Henry Coston and wife Ann Coston sold to William King land conveyed by Thomas Holbrook, unnamed.

BLAKES HOPE

Patented on 9 Mar.1663 by Joel Blake for 700 acres in Dublin, Election district 4, map #13.

49

17 March 1663 Joel Blake assigned to William Smith
10 Dec.1667 William Smith willed to wife Mary Smith, at decease to Hannah Smith.
26 Feb 1671 Vincent Atchison and wife Hannah Atchison (Hannah Smith) sold to William Coulboun
10 Sep.1672 William Coulbourn and wife Margaret Coulbourn sold to Henry Smith
9 June 1679 Henry Smith and wife Ann Smith gave to Edward Stevens.
1684 Edward Stevens gave 1/3rd to wife Ruth Stevens, per will.
Rent Rolls 1666-1723 Possessed by -
233 1/3 acres Edward Stevens
233 1/3 acres William Stevens
233 1/3 acres John Stevens and his mother.
1695 Edward Stevens gave to John Broughton 100 acres.
1716 Edward Stevens gave to daughter Tabitha Stevens or unborn son.
12 Jan 1727 William Stevens and Isabel Stevens his wife, Samuel Stevens and Jane Stevens his wife and Eleanor Stevens widow of William, deceased, sold to Thomas Hayward 200 acres. (that Edward Stevens had willed to the three sons of Florence Tucker commonly known by the name of Edward Stevens, William Stevens and John Stevens. They sold to John Broughton 100 acres. William Stevens Sr. bequested to his youngest sons William and Samuel Stevens and wife Eleanor Stevens.
8 Nov.1730 John Stevens sold to Edward Cluff 1/3rd of 600 acres, 200 acres.
17 Feb 1734/5 John Broughton traded 25 acres of WILLIAMS HOPE for 21 acres of BLAKES HOPE, with Thomas Hayward.
6 Feb 1734 Edward Stevens, William Stevens and John Stevens were seized of this land and by deed became the property of Thomas Hayward, Edward Cluff and William Stevens (this is a division of the land)
1734 Resurvey 200 acres to HAYWARDS LOTT.
26 Jan 1737 William Stevens son of Edward Stevens sold to Thomas Hayward, 1 acre and 9 perches.
1758/9 William Stevens left to son John.
10 July 1765 Thomas Hayward gave to son Thomas Jr. 1 acre and 9 perches.
22 Jun 1768 Charles Broughton sold to Thomas Hayward 100 acres where Bruff Broughton father of Charles lived, originally BLAKES HOPE, alias LITTLE ACTON.
6 Sep 1768 Thomas Hayward sold 100 acres to Michael Cluff and William Broughton.
1783 tax- John Broughton Jr. 53 1/3 acres
1783 tax- Michael Cluff 233 acres
1783 tax- Thomas Hayward 100 acres
1783 tax- Mary Stevens 66 acres
1783 tax- William Stevens 134 acres
1783 tax- Hannah Tilghman widow of Aaron Tilghman (Hannah Broughton) 33 1/3 acres.
1792 William Stevens patented part of BLAKES HOPE 5 3/4 acres.
1792 will of Thomas Hayward, to son John Hayward, lot at Stevens Ferry, BLAKES HOPE.
13 Oct.1795 William Stevens sold to Jesse King part devised to William Stevens father of William by the will of Edward Stevens.
13 Oct.1795 Jesse King sold to William Stevens s/o William.
1802 will John Hayward, to son John Elzey Hayward, lot at Stevens Ferry.
28 Feb.1803 John Broughton gave to son Isaac Broughton 185 acres of BLAKES HOPE & WILLIAMS HOPE.

11 Nov 1806 Pierce Riggin, constable, sold to Kellum Broughton 36 acres
of WILLIAMS HOPE & BLAKES HOPE per judgement against Isaac Broughton,
Esq.
7 May 1813 John Wilkins, sheriff, per judgement against John Broughton
sold to Kellum Broughton the highest bidder,134 acres of WILLIAMS HOPE &
BLAKES HOPE.
1842 will of Thomas Langsdale, to mother-in-law Mary D. Stevens.(no
acreage mentioned)
1857 Mary Stevens (widow of Thomas Stevens) gave to Sidney C. Dougherty
son of Maria Dougherty. (no acreage)
1883 ADDITION TO BLAKES HOPE, patented for 175 1/4 acres by James W.
Dougherty.

BLOOMSBURY

Patented in 1787 by Thomas Sloss for 820 1/4 acres. a resurvey of
RAINSBURY, PENNY WISE, BLOYCES HOPE, THE SUCESS. In St.Peters, Election
district 2, map #6.
1 June 1798 deed of release,partition and conveyance, Levin Winder and
Mary Stoughton Winder his wife to Rev. Edward Gantt and Ann Stoughton
Gantt, as Mary Stoughton daughter and sole heiress of William Stoughton
had tracts, she married Thomas Sloss and obtained a resurvey.(Mary Winder
and Ann Gantt only daughters of Thomas Sloss.)
26 Feb. 1808 Edward Gantt, wife Ann Stoughton Gantt in Fairfax Co. Va.
agreed to execute a deed to Levin Winder of Somerset County Md.
16 April 1808 Rev. Edward Gantt, wife Ann Stoughton Gantt sold to Levin
Winder 820 1/4 acres.

BLOYCES HOPE

Patented on 1 Nov.1666 by Thomas Bloyd(Bloyce) in St. Peters, Election
district 2, map #6, for 150 acres..
Rent Rolls 1666-1723, possessed by Bloyce Wright.
Rent Rolls second entry, possessed by Thomas Shaw.
2 Dec.1681 Thomas Bloyce of Little Money sold to Thomas Walker 150 acres.
18 Jun 1729 William Stoughton on behalf of William Robinson sold to
Thomas Wright 50 acres out of BLOYCES HOPE, CHANCE & RAINSBURY.(1716 will
of Thomas Shaw names William Robinson as grandson.)
26 Feb 1782 John Wright sold to Gowan Wright tract (unamed) that William
Robinson and wife Sarah Robinson deeded in 1727 to Thomas Wright
grandfather of John at Little Creek for 101 acres.
1783 tax- Thomas Sloss (resurvey) 100 acres
1783 tax- Gowan Wright 30 acres
1787 resurveyed to BLOOMSBURY, 820 1/4 acres.

BLUFF HAMMOCKS

Patented on 26 Feb.1723 by James Strawbridge for 100 acres on Smiths
Island, Election district 10, map 22.
7 Mar.1774 John Graham and wife Mary Elizabeth Graham and John Gordan
and Ann Gordan his wife of Northumberland Virginia, sold to Henry
Lowes.(pat. James Strawbridge who sold to John Tunstall, Ann Gordon and
Mary Graham legal heirs.)

BOARD TREE

Patented in 1753 by Samuel Owens and Michael Owens for 100 acres in East Princess Anne, Election district 15, map #4, also known as BOARD TREE RIDGE.
18 Aug 1757 John Owens Sr, Michael Owens and Samuel Owens with wife Elizabeth Owens, sold to John Done (no acreage mentioned)
1758 resurveyed to DONES NEST EGG 565 acres, by John Done.

BOARD TREE HOLLOCK

Patented in 1761 by Spencer Harris for 25 acres in Dublin, Election district 4, map #12.
1794 will of Spencer Harris, lands to wife Sinah Harris (unnamed) and after death to sons Littleton Harris and Isaac Harris.
1813 Littleton Harris willed all property to wife Amelia Harris, unnamed land.

BOSTON

Patented on 16 Sep. 1676 by William Stevens and assigned to to Thomas Cottingham for 300 acres in Brinkleys southwest, Election district 3, map #17.
Rent Rolls 1666-1723 possessed by Charles Cottingham son of Thomas Cottingham.
19 June 1735 Charles Cottingham and Ann Cottingham his wife, sold to Thomas Lindzey 15 acres, with CHEESMANS CHOICE (as Thomas Cottingham died intestate and it descended to eldest son Charles.)
4 Sep. 1742 Charles Cottingham gave to son Thomas, BOSTON and balance of land not sold to Jonathan Cottingham VULCANS VINEYARD.
4 Sep.1742 Charles Cottingham and wife Ann Cottingham sold to Thomas Tull, part of this and GOSHEN, total of 189 acres, called THE EXCHANGE.
28 March 1747 Charles Cottingham sold to Charles Cottingham Jr. part 16 acres called CHANCE being part of BOSTON.
1753 will of Charles Cottingham, to wife Ann Cottingham and son John Cottingham.
27 Feb.1756 Thomas Lindzey sold to Charles Cottingham 50 acres part of BOSTON & MUMFORD.
1750 will of John Jarman,(wife Sarah Jarman) gave to son William Jarman, BOSTON in Annamessex.
12 May 1761 Thomas Lindzey sold to Nehemiah Turpin 140 acres, GLAZIERS HALL, BOSTON & MUMFORD (mortgage)
23 Oct. 1764 Nehemiah Turpin sold to Thomas Lindzey,(release of above mortgage.)
23 Oct.1764 Thomas Lindzey sold to Nehemiah Turpin part of CHEESMANS CHANCE,MUMFORD,BOSTON, lately resurveyed and called EDEN 95 acres.
29 Dec.1768 Thomas Williams to Benjamin Lankford(agreement of partition) 5 acres.
29 Dec.1768 Benjamin Lankford sold to Thomas Williams for 5 shillings 5 acres of BOSTON,with DISCOVERY & DISCOVERY ENLARGED.
26 Mar.1772 John Cottingham heir of Charles Cottingham sold to Thomas Tull (confirmation that Charles Cottingham the elder deceased did deed land to Thomas Tull deceased father of Thomas) 23 acres.
1783 tax- John Cottingham 132 acres
1783 tax- Benjamin Lankford 181 acres
1783 tax- David Lindzey 8 acres

1783 tax- Thomas Tull 23 acres
1783 tax- Nehemiah Turpin 220 acres.
1798 tax- William Cottingham(with MUMFORD & REVENGE)
2 Jan 1787 William Turpin son of Nehemiah Turpin sold to John Turpin son
of Nehemiah Turpin 95 acres, parts of MUMFORD,BOSTON, EDEN.
1798 tax- Ephraim Cottingham (son of John Cottingham)
27 March 1829 Josiah Cottingham son of William Cottingham sold right to
the trustees of the Methodist Episcopal Church.
23 June 1834 Josiah Cottingham sold balance to Levin Conner (no acreage
mentioned)
24 Jun 1795 John Turpin, wife Sarah Turpin, of Worc.Co. sold to Thomas
Whittington 91 1/4 acres, parts of CHEESEMANS CHANCE,MUMFORD & BOSTON.
10 March 1796 Thomas Whittington sold to Isaac Whittington 95 acres of
BOSTON, EDEN, MUMFORD.
10 March 1796 David Lindzey sold to Thomas Whittington 95 acres of
BOSTON,EDEN,& MUMFORD.
28 Dec.1801 Levi Holland and wife Sally Holland sold to Samuel Tull
BOSTON & TURKEY SWAMP all land Ephraim Cottingham died possessed.
13 Sep.1801 Samuel Cottingham sold to William Williams BOSTON, VULCANS
VINEYARD & TURKEY PINE devised Samuel by his father David Cottingham, no
acres given.
27 Jan.1806 Thomas Tull Sr. sold to Thomas Merrill Tull 170 acres of
BOSTON, CHANCE & TROUBLE.
24 April 1805 Benjamin Conner, Noah Lankford, Benjamin Bedsworth, John
Broughton and wife Mary Broughton, Richard Hall and Mary Bedsworth sold
to Mordicai Jones of St. Marys Co.devised by Sampson Wheatley.
9 Feb.1809 Thomas Merrill Tull, wife Polly Tull sold to Joshua Tull 203
1/2 acres of BOSTON, GOSHEN, TROUBLESOME, WILLIAMS LOTT.

BOSTONS ADDITION

Patented on 19 July 1748 by John Houston for 6 acres in Brinkleys
northwest, Election district 3, map #14.
3 March 1767 John Houston of Worcester County and wife Mary Houston sold
to Thomas Williams. 6 acres
1783 tax- Thomas Cottingham with CHANCE 137 3/4acres in Gr.Annamessex.
1783/91 Thomas Cottingham willed to son Randall Cottingham dwelling
plantation and lands to son David Cottingham, unnamed land.

BOSTONS ADVENTURE

Patented 1 February 1664 by Henry Boston for 400 acres in Brinkleys north
west, Election district 3, map #14.
4 October 1669 Henry Boston, wife Ann Boston, sold to Samuel Long, who
deeded to sons John Long, Daniel Long,Jeffrey Long and David Long.
1671 Ann Sasser now wife of Henry Boston sold to Samuel Long.
Rent Rolls 1666-1723- possessed by John Long 250 acres and Helena
Minshull relic of Jeffrey Minshull.
13 Sep.1716 agreement as to division of LONGS PURCHASE, BOSTONS ADVENTURE
& LONGS PREVENTION 442 acres, by John Long, Jeffrey Long, David Long and
Daniel Long.
21 Feb 1720 Eleanor Dikes relic of Jeffrey Minshull and John Minshull son
of Jeffrey deceased sold to Daniel Long, now known as MOTHERS & SONS
ENJOYMENT and 10 acres of land out of two tracts granted Samuel Long
called LONGS PREVENTION & LONGS PURCHASE.

1718 John Long per will bequeathed land to son Samuel Long.

29 Mar.1739 John Minshull of Bath County North Carolina sold to Daniel Long 150 acres of tract MOTHER AND SONS ENJOYMENT, part of BOSTONS ADVENTURE.

30 June 1739 William Hutchison and Ann Hutchison his wife sold to Solomon Long MOTHER AND SONS ENJOYMENT and 10 acres taken out of LONGS PURCHASE & LONGS PREVENTION.

19 April 1740 Daniel Long and Samuel Long sold 150 acres to Solomon Long of MOTHER & SONS ENJOYMENT, part of BOSTONS ADVENTURE.

3 Dec.1743 Solomon Long and Margaret Long his wife sold 150 acres to Jeffrey Long MOTHER & SONS ENJOYMENT. (mentioned grandfather Samuel Long.)

28 Oct.1747 David Long and wife Abigail Long sold to Jeffrey Long 110 acres of BOSTONS ADVENTURE, LONGS PURCHASE, & LONGS PREVENTION.

22 Aug.1748 William Long and wife Neomi Long of Worcester county sold to Coulbourn Long of Somerset Co. his moity of three tracts LONGS PREVENTION, LONGS PURCHASE & BOSTONS ADVENTURE (53 acres) (divided from lands of Uncle Daniel Long deceased uncle of Samuel)100 acres that Samuel Long willed in 1740 to William Long 1/2 part and other 1/2 part to Coulbourn Long.

4 Sep.1750 John Long, Jeffrey Long, David Long, David Long the younger, shipwright, sold to Coulbourn Long tailor, 110 acres of BOSTONS ADVENTURE, LONGS PURCHASE & LONGS PREVENTION (division of lands.)

15 Sep. 1753 David Long Jr, shipwright, sold to Jeffrey Long, parts 110 acres of BOSTONS ADVENTURE, LONGS PURCHASE, LONGS PREVENTION.

1753 resurveyed to LONGS CHANCE 1130 acres.

26 July 1756 Isaac Boston sold to Thomas Marshall 181 acres with BOSTONS GREEN and 47 vacant acres.

15 Oct 1767 Littleton Long sold to Nehemiah Turpin (from father David Long) 110 1/2 acres with LONGS PURCHASE, LONGS PREVENTION.

2 Jan 1787 Orpha Turpin gave to son William Turpin her rights that she is entitled to with CONVENIENCY as heir of Jeffrey Long.

3 Oct.1808 William Williams, Thomas Williams, John Williams and Thomas Furniss comissioners sold to Sewell Turpin. As William Turpin of Nehemiah Turpin had LONGS CHANCE, BOSTONS ADVENTURE and he died intestate and it descended to Sewell Turpin, John Turpin, Anne Turpin, William Turpin, Anna Maria Turpin and Mary T. Whittington.

BOSTONS CHANCE

Resurveyed in 1754, part from SEWARDS PURCHASE 260 1/2 acres by Isaac Boston in Brinkleys northeast, Election district 3, map #15.

20 April 1774 Thomas Marshall gave to Isaac Marshall 240 1/2 acres with BOSTONS GREEN, SHOEMAKERS MEADOW, BOSTONS PURCHASE, etc, with 523 2/3 acres.

1783 tax list- Isaac Marshall 240 1/2 acre.

21 Dec.1808 Thomas Marshal of Isaac Marshall sold 100 acres to Asia Dicks.

29 Nov.1808 William Marshall of Isaac, wife Sarah Marshall sold to brother Thomas Marshall 100 acres.

BOSTONS CHANCE

Patented in 1782 by Levin Boston, probably a resurvey of FIRST CHOICE, in Westover, Election district 13, map #11, for 102 acres.

1783 tax lists - Levin Boston 102 acres.
12 Feb.1785 Levin Boston, wife Gertrude Boston traded with Thomas King
for equal tracts of CONCLUSION & LONG LOTT on Morumsco Creek.

BOSTON GREEN

Patented on 10 June 1695 by Isaac Boston for 25 acres in Brinkleys
northeast, Election district 3, map #15.
Rent Rolls 1666-1723 possessed by Adrain Marshall.(Adrain Marshall
married the widow Elizabeth Boston widow of Isaac.)
6 July 1756 Isaac Boston Jr. sold 25 acres to Thomas Marshall.
7 July 1757 Rachel Boston widow, sold to Thomas Marshall 1/3rd part of
BOSTONS GREEN, & SAYWARDS PURCHASE, that her late husband Isaac died
possessed.
20 April 1774 Thomas Marshall gave to son Isaac Marshall 5 tracts,
including 25 acres of BOSTONS GREEN.
1783 tax- Isaac Marshall 25 acres.

BOSTONS LOTT

Patented 18 May 1746 by William Boston for 86 acres in Westover, Election
district 13, map #11.
1777 will of Wiliam Boston, parts to son Richard Boston and to son Levin
Boston and 20 acres to daughter Martha Boston.
1783 tax- Richard Boston 43 acres
1783 tax- Levin Boston 37 1/2 acres
19 Jan.1787 Levin Boston sold to John Milbourn, 7 acres inherited from
his father of unspecified land. John Milbourn to convey to Levin's son
Elijah Boston.
9 Sep 1788 John Milbourn sold to Joshua Turpin 5 3/4 acres with MILBOURNS
PURCHASE, CONCLUSION, 93 1/4 acres.
1798 tax- Levin Boston.
20 Feb.1808 Levin Boston mortgaged to Michael Cluff, willed Levin by his
father William Boston.
12 April 1811 Levin Boston sold 38 acres to son Elijah Boston.
29 Jan.1820 Elijah Boston sold to Thomas Adams of Phillip Adams, with
LONG RIDGE,BEAUCHAMPS VENTURE,LEDBOURN & MILBOURNS PURCHASE.
1831 Thomas Adams willed to four children, Morris Henry Adams, Mary
Pitts, Leah Jane Adams, Emeline Rounds, land purchased of Elijah Boston,
unnamed.

BOSTONS PURCHASE

Patented 12 Jun 1688 by Isaac Boston and brother Esau Boston bought of
Cornelius Morris and wife Ann Morris formerly SEWARDS PURCHASE, 200 acres
in Brinkleys southwest, Election district 3, map #15.
21 April 1720 Esau Boston and wife Ellis Boston deeded to his sister
Betty Boston. 200 acres.
29 Oct.1750 Obed Taylor nephew of Esau Boston, relinquished his claim to
BOSTONS PURCHASE, as heir at law to his deceased mother Betty Taylor, 100
acres to Esau Boston.
8 Dec.1750 Isaac Boston and Esau Boston, arbitrated SAYWARDS PURCHASE,
NEW BOSTONS PURCHASE,19 acres to Esau and 201 acres to Isaac.
13 Jan 1756 Isaac Boston sold to Samuel Adams 19 2/3rds acres.(from his
father Isaac Boston)

6 March 1758 Samuel Boston sold to Thomas Marshall 19 2/3rds acre with SHOEMAKERS MEADOW.
20 Apr.1761 Thomas Marshall sold to Esau Boston 200 acres (mortgage agreement)
25 April 1761 Esau Boston sold part to Thomas Marshall, 200 acres.
4 Jan 1768 Naboth Boston sold to Kellum Lankford (that Isaac Boston father of Naboth devised 1/2 to son Naboth. 78 acres.
20 April 1774 Thomas Marshall gave to son Isaac Marshall 200 acres.
1783 tax- Isaac Marshall 200 acres.

BOSTONS PURCHASE

1745 an escheat of HASFORTS PURCHASE in Brinkleys southwest, Election district 3, map #17, of 182 acres from Richard Brittain to Isaac Boston and 173 acres of vacant land for a total of 355 acres.
15 April 1765 Isaac Boston deeded to Kellum Lankford 355 acres patented by his father Isaac. Isaac Sr. gave to sons David Boston and Samuel Boston. Both died intestate without issue and it became the right of brother Isaac Boston the younger.
1783 tax- Kellum Lankford 355 acres
1795 will of Kellum Lankford, to son Noah Lankford.
5 Apr.1803 Noah Lankford son of Kellum Lankford sold to William Williams, merchant, lands in Morumsco, no name.
11 Nov.1803 William Williams and wife Mary Williams sold to Thomas Robertson Jr. land of Noah Lankford. no name.
8 May 1804 Dr. Thomas Robertson, wife Sarah Robertson sold to Richard Hall 10 acres.
8 May 1804 Dr. Thomas Robertson,wife Sarah Robertson sold to William Coulbourn of Stephen Coulbourn, tracts where William Gibbons lives except part of BOSTONS PURCHASE that was conveyed to Richard Hall, no names of land.
11 Sep.1804 William Coulbourn of Stephen Coulbourn, sold to Benjamin Lankford Jr. son of Lazarus Lankford 69 1/2 acres called LANKFORDS SECOND PURCHASE.
11 Sep.1804 William Coulbourn sold to Nathan Cahoon 39 3/4 acres.
11 Sep.1804 William Coulbourn sold to Dr.Thomas Robertson Jr., tracts where William Gibbons lives except parts of BOSTONS PURCHASE, no name or acreage given.
3 Oct.1805 Richard Hall and Benjamin Lankford sold to George Wilson 2 3/4 acres.
5 April 1806 Dr. Thomas Robertson sold to Richard Hall 10 acres.
9 Jan 1807 Benjamin Lankford, wife Archibald Lankford, sold to Nathaniel Bell 69 1/2 acres BOSTONS PURCHASE now called LANKFORDS SECOND PURCHASE.
22 Feb.1809 Richard Hall, wife Sally Hall, Nathan Cohoon, sold to Noah Lankford Hall 30 1/4 acres of TURKEY PINE, COHOONS FOLLY, BOSTONS PURCHASE & WILSONS CONCLUSION.

BOSTON TOWN

Patented on 20 August 1663 by Henry Boston for 350 acres in Brinkleys northwest, Election district 3, map #14.
15 Nov.1677 Henry Boston Jr. sold to Capt. Thomas Walker, 350 acres
1 March 1678 Thomas Walker and wife Jane Walker sold to William Planner, all.
2 Oct.1682 John Bird of Ann Arundel Co. and now wife Elizabeth Bird late

wife of Henry Boston sold her dower rights to William Planner.
1682 resurveyed for 500 acres by William Planner.
1733 William Planner son and heir of William, per will left to Benjamin Lankford and heirs.
1733 Benjamin Lankford gave 61 acres to Lucy Ballance.
20 Aug. 1747 Thomas Dixon Sr. and Benjamin Lankford sold to Thomas Dixon Jr. part of BOSTONTOWN & DIXONS CHOICE, 60 acres and part of DIXONS ADDITION 31 acres.
1 Sep.1747 Thomas Dixon traded 10 acres with William Smith DIXONS CHOICE ENLARGED for 9 acres of BALD RIDGE.
21 Jan.1767 John Purnell of Worc. Co. and wife Sarah Purnell sold to Thomas Williams 296 acres and 10 acres. (as William Planner deceased had devised by will to Benjamin Lankford part and part to Lucy Ballance and after decease to Sarah Ballance and to Margaret McClemmy 10 acres and after her death to Sarah Ballance who married John Purnell.)
1783 tax- Thomas Dixon 30 acres
1783 tax- Thomas Williams 285 acres
1795 will Thomas Dixon, to Sarah Dixon Furniss daughter of Thomas Furniss, 30 acres.

BOTTOM OF THE SPOUT

Patented in 1760 by Thomas Montgomery for 4 1/2 acres in Lawsons, Election district 8, map #19.
13 April 1776 Dennis Montgomery sold to Stephen Ward.
1783 tax- Stephen Ward 4 1/2 acres
1783 will of Stephen Ward, to wife Mary Ward.
7 Jan.1780 John Ward son of Stephen Ward, now of Kentucky, sold to John Cullen.
15 Feb.1802 John Cullen sold to Hance Croswell 23 acres of BENSTONS LOTT, BOTTOM OF THE SPOUT, MIDDLE OF THE NECK & ADDITION.
23 April 1808 Hance Croswell sold to William Ward 23 acres of above lands.

BOYERS SECURITY

Patented 10 Nov. 1737 by William Boyer for 34 acres in Brinkleys southeast, Election district 3, map #16.
15 March 1753 Henry Rich and wife Dorcas Rich otherwise called Negro Harry formerly slave of Robert Boyer deceased, and freed by him, sell to Hannah Clifton, widow of John Clifton, land devised him by Robert Boyer 34 acres.

BOYCES BRANCH

Patented on 9 April 1664 by William Boyce for 300 acres in Westover, Election district 13, map #11.
27 Dec.1681 Thomas Sewell and wife Jane Sewell sold to Robert Catlin 30 acres of BOYCES BRANCH & HOLWELL, called CONTENTION.
Rent Rolls 1666-1723, Possessed by Edward Stockdell in right of his wife Joan Stockdell the daughter of William Boyce.
Edward and Joan Stockdell had children Edward and Joan Stockdell. Edward Stockdell(Stogell) died intestate and left two daughters Jean Stockdell and Suffiah Stockdell. Suffiah married Benjamin Cottman.
18 June 1755 Benjamin Cottman and wife Suffiah Cottman sold 67 acres to William Turpin.

23 July 1757 Stacey Miles quitclaim to William Turpin all interest in
tract where Benjamin Cottman lived and William Catlin lately mortgaged to
Stacey Miles in Gr. Annamessex.(same date. William Turpin released to
Stacey Miles, part. (division of lands)
1767 will of William Turpin, to son John Turpin land, where I live(not
named) bought of Benjamin Cottman.
1783 tax- Stacey Miles 80 acres
1783 tax- John Turpin 80 acres.
1785 will of Stacey Miles, 100 acres to son Levin Miles.
1795 will Jane Miles (w/o Stacey) to grand-daughter Peggy Perkins
daughter of John Beauchamp.
25 Oct.1798 William Perkins,wife Peggy Perkins sold to Julyann Lister and
Martha Lister heirs of Thomas Lister 80 acres.

BOSEMANS ADDITION (BOZMANS)

1 March 1694 John Bozman patented for 250 acres in West Pr. Anne,
Election district 1, map #3.
Rent Rolls 1666-1723 possessed by John Bozman.
20 June 1744 John Bozman sold 52 acres to Rev. James Robertson.
23 Nov.1744 Triparte Bonds, John Bozman, wife Eleanor Bozman, to John
Tunstall, and Samuel Wilson (200 acres that John Bozman father of John
from grandfather John Bozman on 21 March 1711)
3 May 1746 James Robertson purchased of to Samuel Wilson and wife Martha
Wilson. 52 acres
23 Aug. 1759 Martha Wilson and Levin Wilson sold to Thomas Wilson(as
Samuel Wilson died intestate and Levin heir at law, gave to Thomas part
of BOZMANS ADDITON & WOOLFORD adjacent.)
6 Nov.1770 Thomas Robertson and wife Martha Robertson son of Rev. James
Robertson sold to Rev. Hamilton Bell 52 acres.
1 Jan 1773 Martha Wilson widow of Samuel Wilson and Levin Wilson gave to
George Wilson all the land deeded to Thomas Wilson deceased on the north
side of the Manokin River (unnamed)
16 June 1779 Ballard Bozman sold to Levin Wilson his rights to land,
unnamed , between William Bell and Levin Woolford.
12 Aug.1783 Hamilton Bell sold for 5 shillings to brother William Bell
all land purchased of Dr. Thomas Robertson on the Manokin River(unnamed)
1785 William Bell and wife Eleanor Bell sold to Levin Wilson 32 3/4 acres
of BOZMANS ADDITION & MORE AND CASE IT.
1783 tax- Levin Wilson 148 acres
1783 tax- William Bell 52 acres
1791 Levin Wilson willed to nephew George Wilson Jackson lands on Manokin
River between William Bell and Levin Woolford, unnamed.
4 April 1808 Elizabeth Jackson and George W. Jackson sold to William
Jones 30 acres.

BAWSMANS ADVENTURE(BOZMANS)

Patented in 1734 by Daniel Bawsman and Philomon Bawsman for 268 acres a
resurvey of WOOLFORDS CHANCE, in St.Peters, Election district 2, map #6.
1750 will of Levin Bozman, to brothers Levin and Philomon Bozman.
2 March 1754 triparte, Philomon Bozman to Jarvis Ballard and John
Robertson 133 acres.
11 April 1760 George Robertson son of John Robertson deceased, sold to
Nehemiah Bozman 42 1/2 acres and part of ROBERTSONS ADDITION.

18 April 1760 George Robertson and wife Eleanor Robertson sold 84 1/2 acres to Arnold Elzey.
15 Nov.1779 Arnold Elzey once of Somerset County, now of Baltimore Town, Baltimore County sold to Henry Jackson and John Jones of Goose Creek 217 1/4 acres, with ROBERTSONS ADDITION.
1783 tax- John Jones of Goose Creek (with ROBERTSONS ADDN. 110 1/2 acres)
1783 tax- Henry Jackson (with ROBERTSONS ADDN. 110 1/2 acres.
28 Feb.1792 John Jones of Goose Creek quitclaimed to Henry Jackson with ROBERTSONS ADDN. This was a division of lines.
6 March 1790 John Jones Sr, sold to William Jones Sr. 1/2 of with WOOLFORD,JONES ENLARGEMENT, ROBERTSONS ADDITION.
1794 Henry Jackson willed to son George Wilson Jackson land bought of Arnold Elzey.
8 Sep.1807 William B. Jones sold to Littleton Dennis Teackle.
29 Oct.1807 Littleton Dennis Teackle sold to John Teackle of Georgetown DC land sold to him by William B. Jones, unnamed.
4 April 1808 Elizabeth Jackson and George W. Jackson sold to William Jones 45 acres and 110 acres of BOZMANS ADVENTURE & ROBERTSONS ADDITION.

BOZMANS CHOICE

Surveyed on 2 March 1663 for William Bozman in West Pr. Anne, Election district 1, map #3 for 300 acres.
1663 will of William Bozman, to sons John Bozman, George Bozman.
Rent Rolls 1666-1723 possessed by Lazarus Maddux by the name of MOTHERS CARE (William Bozman married Eleanor Maddux widow of Alexander Maddux and mother of Lazarus Maddux)

BOZMANS MARSH

Patented 1723, a resurvey to include JAMES MEADOW, for 460 acres in Dames Quarter, Election district 11, map #7 by Massey Bozman (?)

BRADDOCKS DEFEAT

Surveyed for Henry Smith in 1770 but not patented or found on maps. This is in Brinkleys northwest, Election district 3, map #14.
21 March 1787 Samuel Bedsworth sold to Thomas Jones 2 1/2 acres of COLEPIT, BALDRIDGE,BEDSWORTH CHOICE, PROVIDENCE, a total of 410 1/2 acres in Annamessex.

BRANCH

Patented in 1786 by Thomas Pollitt for 2 1/4 acres in West Princess Anne, Election district 1, map #2.

BRANFIELD

Patented on 19 Oct.1685 by Robert Catlin for 100 acres in Westover Election district 13, map #11.
1699 will of Robert Caltin, estate to son William Catlin (unamed)
11 March 1767 William Catlin sold to Joshua Catlin for 5 shillings, 7 acres with 42 acres of HARTFORD BROAD OAK.
21 March 1768 William Catlin gave to his son William Catlin Jr. lands in Annamessex (unnamed)
14 Oct. 1772 Joshua Catlin sold to William Catlin part of HARDFORD BROAD

OAK and BRANFIELD, that William Catlin father of Joshua Catlin deeded to
him 49 3/4 acres.
1783 tax- William Catlin 16 acres.

BRERETONS CHANCE

Patented on 10 Nov. 1675 by William Brereton for 300 acres in West
Princess Anne, Election district 1, map #2.
1690 will of William Brereton, to wife Sarah Brereton and then to son
John Brereton.
Rent Rolls 1666-1723 possessed by William Brereton son of William.
26 Oct.1728 William Brereton conveyed part SMITHS ADVENTURE, BRERETONS
CHANCE & MILES END to Alexander Adams except the 100a Brereton in 1718
conveyed to John Waltham, total 150 acres.
1783 tax- John Adams Sr. 10 acres
1783 tax- William Brereton 150 acres.
23 Nov.1790 William Brereton gave to Salathiel Griffith all real
estate-(for keeping him during his lifetime) no name or acres.
1799 Joseph Brereton gave to brother Scott Brereton.
11 March 1802 Scott Brereton sold to William Brereton 27 1/4 acres of
BRERETONS CHANCE, & SMITHS ADVENTURE.
11 May 1802 William Brereton, wife Ann sold to Scott Brereton 60 1/4
acres of same.
23 May 1802 William Brereton sold to Scott Brereton, balance.

BRICKLE HOE

Patented on 23 August 1679 by John White and assigned to John Carter, in
Lawsons, Election district 8, map #18. 300 acres.
Rent Rolls 1666-1723 Possessed by John Carter Jr. 300 acres.
1 Nov.1722 John Carter and Elizabeth Carter of Dorcester County gave 200
acres of BRICKLE HOE and part of LONG RIDGE to Sarah Davis.
18 June 1727 I Sarah Davis for love give to son John Davis land bought of
John Carter.
1736/7 John Carter per will gave his plantation to son Charles Carter
(unanmed)
25 Feb.1765 Samuel Cox sold to Solomon Bird 100 acres, as John Davis had
parcels in Annamessex that he willed in 1762 to Samuel Cox, unnamed land.
10 Aug.1767 Samuel Cox sold to Revel Horsey 95 1/2 acres devised to
Samuel Cox by John Davis.
8 Nov.1769 Samuel Cox sold to Solomon Bird 15 1/2 acres(that John Davis
willed to Samuel) with UPPER ANDUE.
Jan 1772 Samuel Cox sold to John Horsey 70 acres.
1781 Revel Horsey willed to daughter Zipporah Horsey lands purchased of
Samuel Cox (unnamed) and if no issue to son Edward Horsey.
1783 tax lists- Sarah Horsey 250 acres.
26 Dec.1796 Zipporah Bruff of Worc.Co. sold to Aaron Sterling of John
Sterling, 80 acres.

BRIDGERS LOTT

Patented in 1663 by Joshua Bridges (includes ROWLEY RIDGE) for 1000 acres
in West Princess Anne, Election district 15, map #5.
Resurveyed in 1673 for Joseph Bridges for 1100 acres and sold to Thomas
Jones.

Rent Rolls 1666-1723 possessed by Robert Catherwood in right of Thomas
Jones' orphans.(Robert married Martha Jones the widow.)
1700 will of Thomas Jones, to son William Jones and daughter Sarah Jones.
21 March 1742 Samuel Wilson and Martha Wilson his wife one of the heirs
of Sarah Woolford daughter of Thomas Jones deceased, Henry Waggaman and
wife Mary Waggaman another daughter and co-heir of Sarah Woolford sold to
Ephraim Waggaman of Worcester County for 5 shillings now called WAGGAMANS
LOTT, 600 acres.
1748 resurvey by Thomas Jones, 370 acres.
26 April 1750 Henry Waggaman and wife Mary Waggaman sold 600 acres for 5
shillings to George Gale now called WAGGAMANS LOTT.
1783 tax- William Jones (of Manokin) 370 acres.
4 Jun 1788 George Waggaman sold to John Laws and wife Nelly Laws, and
William Handy, wife Margaret Handy and Mary Smith, 9 acres.
23 Sep.1807 William Jones, wife Eleanor Jones gave to son Thomas Jones
370 acres.
1855 will of William W. Handy, to son William Collins Handy (Cherry Grove
Farm) called BRIDGERS LOTT.

BRIDGETS LOTT

Patented 9 Dec.1719 for 100 acres by Bridget Kirk widow of John Kirk, in
Lawsons, Election district 8, map #18.
Rent Rolls 1666-1723 possessed by Bridget Kirk.
3 May 1746 Littleton Townsend and wife Sarah Townsend(Sarah Kirk) sold to
Southy Whittington, RECOVERY,PUZZLE & BRIDGETS LOTT.
1752 resurveyed to RECOVERY.

BROTHERS AGREEMENT

See AMITY
BROTHERS AGREEMENT

Patented in 1749 by John Phoebus for 79 acres in St. Peters, Election
district 2, map #6.
1783 tax- John Phoebus 79 acres.
23 Jan 1795 John Phoebus Sr. sold to John Phoebus Jr. for 5 shillings
200 acres of NICHOLSONS ADVENTURE,BROTHERS AGREEMENT, LITTLEWORTH.
2 Sep.1795 John Phoebus sold to Lewis Phoebus for 5 sh. 16 3/4 acres of
BROTHERS AGREEMENT & NICHOLSONS ADVENTURE.
22 Feb 1808 Evans Willin sold to John Wilkins.
12 Dec.1810 Thomas Rutter, marshall, sold to Joshua Dorsey of Baltimore
County, per judgement against Evans Willin, 50 acres.

BROTHERS CONTRIVANCE & BROTHERS GOOD WILL

See Double Purchase.

BROTHERS LOVE

This land was not patented but was surveyed in 1671 for Edward Smale and
John Smale, and in 1685 was possessed by William Traile on the north side
of the Pocomoke River, who had 133 1/3 acre.
1691 Mrs. Eleanor Traile sold to Archibald White 90 1/3 acres.
1750 Isaac White patented ADDITION TO BROTHERS LOVE for 415 acres in

Brinkleys southeast, Election district 3, map #16, presumably this same
land.
9 Jan 1762 John Matthews gave to son Elijah Matthews 100 acres of
BROTHERS LOVE, now called SONS CHOICE
22 Feb 1765 John Walton of Sussex Co. Del. sold to James Nairn of Som.Co.
15 acres, part of PIMMORE & BROTHERS LOVE.
21 March 1770 Isaac White,heir of Henry White, sold to Elijah Matthews
part,(with CORK and and now called SONS CHOICE
1771 resurveyed to ISAACS FORTUNE 449 acres.
1783 tax- Elijah Matthews 100 acres of SONS CHOICE.

BROTHERS LOVE

see SONNES CHOICE

BROTHERS UNITED

This is part of DOUBLE PURCHASE pat. by Randall Revell.

BROUGHTONS PURCHASE

Patented in 1763 by John Broughton for 274 acres in Dublin, Election
district 4, map #13.
14 Feb. 1769 John Broughton and wife Mary Broughton sold 45 acres to
Gideon Tilghman.
14 Feb.1769 Gideon Tilghman and wife Tabitha Tilghman sold to Robert
Jenkins King 31 1/2 acres.
3 May 1775 John Broughton and wife Mary sold 28 1/2 acres to Robert
Jenkins King with part of ADDITION.
22 Dec.1778 John Broughton sold 16 acres to John Perkins.
1783 tax- John Broughton 144 acres
1783 tax- Robert Jenkins King
1788 will of Robert Jenkins King, to son Levin, part bought of John
Broughton Sr.
5 Nov.1798 George Broughton son of John Broughton, wife Alce Broughton
sold to Elzey Maddux 43 acres.
8 Nov.1803 Dr. Robert Jenkins King sold to Eli Gibbons 399 3/4 acres that
includes TILGHMANS CARE, TILGHMANS SECURITY, GIDEONS LUCK & WILLIAMS
HOPE.
3 Jan 1809 Levin King of Robert J. King, sold to Lazarus Cottman with
ADDTION 446 1/4 acres.
6 Nov.1827 Sheriff's sale of William Coston vs. Elisha Whitlock, part of
BROUGHTONS PURCHASE, lands of Josiah Broughton- Village Herald.

BROWNS CHANCE

Patented in 1754 by George Brown for 113 acres in East Princess Anne,
Election district 15, map #4.
1783 tax- David Brown 113 acres.
1795 ADDITION TO BROWNS CHANCE, patented by David Brown 245 acres.
8 Jan 1803 David Brown Sr. and William Brown of Worc. Co. sold to Thomas
Brown 113 acres patented George Brown father of David Brown and
grandfather of William Brown.
1829 David Brown willed real estate to son Thomas Brown, no name.

BROWNS LOTT

Patented in 1738 a partial resurvey of BETHERTON, in West Princess Anne,

Election district 1, map #3 for 182 acres.
2 May 1749 Margaret Brown sold to William Skirven (with
MEADOW,HACKALLA,OWENS CHOICE,THOMAS ADDITION.) 180 acres.
12 July 1750 John Woolford and wife Mary Woolford sold to William Skirven
his rights to, with OWENS CHOICE
1783 tax- Mary Skirven 168 1/2 acres.
7 Dec 1786 Denwood Wilson and wife Margaret Wilson sold to James Wilson
all tracts near the Manokin River which descended to Margaet Skirven as
the only child of William Skirven. no name or acres.

BROWNS VENTURE

Patented in 1811 by Thomas Brown for 22 acres in East Princess Anne,
Election district 15, map #4

BROWNSTONE

Patented on 6 March 1666 by John Westlock for 300 acres. in West Princess
Anne, Election district 1, map #3.
1 May 1669 John Westlock, wife Magdalene Westlock, sold to Richard
Ackworth 300 acres.
7 Nov. 1685 Richard Ackworth and wife Sarah Ackworth sold to Levin
Denwood.
Rent Rolls 1666-1723 possessed by Arthur Denwood
16 Sep.1740 Thomas Denwood and George Denwood divide the and of
grandfather Levin Denwood.
16 Sep.1741 George Denwood sold to David Wilson a total of 420 1/2 acres
with WEATHERLYS CHANCE, FIRST CHOICE,NUTTERS DELIGHT, DENWOODS INCLUSION.
1746 Patented Thomas Denwood for 410 acres.
1750 will David Wilson, to son James Wilson plantation purchased of
Thomas Denwood.
20 Aug.1772 James Wilson and Josiah Polk sold to George Hayward, that
David Wilson deceased devised to James, part with WILSONS CONCLUSION.
1783 tax- James Wilson 300 acres.
1856 will of George Handy, son-in-law John W. Crisfield to dispose of
farm BROWNSTONE.

BUCK LODGE

Patented on 6 May 1683 by William Stevens for 150 acres, who assigned to
Edward Dikes in Brinkleys northeast, Election district 3, map #15.
Rent Rolls 1666-1723 possessed by Edward Dikes.
1783 tax- James Dikes 150 acres.
12 Feb 1799 Stephen Dakes son of James sold to David Dakes 82 3/4 acres
of BUCK LODGE & HIGNOTTS CHOICE.

BUCK RIDGE

Patented in 1729 by Edward Beauchamp for 100 acres in Lawsons, Election
district 8 Map #18.
1750 Edward Beauchamp sold to George Adams, per will.
15 Oct.1765 John Juett sold to William Juett 108 acres his rights to BUCK
RIDGE,POOR SWAMP,SCOTLAND, in Annamessex, parts willed by John White to
his daughter Alice Juett wife of John Juett.
1783 tax- George Howard 24 1/2 acres

1783 tax- Daniel Cullen 40 acres.
18 March 1788 George Disharoon and wife Alice Disharoon of Worcester Co.
sold for 5 shillings to William Juett (her son by John Juett) left Alice
by her father John White. no name or acreage.
13 Dec 1789 William Juett, wife Alice one daughter of John White sold to
William Kellum, lands John White gave to daughter -no name or acres.
11 Jan 1790 Elijah Coulbourn Sr. and wife Rachel Coulbourn and John Tull
son of James Tull sold BUCK RIDGE that was devised by John White and
Rachel White to his daughter now wife of Elijah Coulbourn, with
ACCIDENT,COME BY CHANCE,SCOTLAND, etc.
to Benjamin Conner (his son-in-law)
11 Jan 1790 Benjamin Conner sold to Elijah Coulbouurn,same.

BUCK RIDGE

Patented in 1755 by John Benson for 31 1/2 acres in East Princess Anne,
Election district 15, map #5.
1783 tax- Rebecca Benson 31 1/2 acres
13 July 1788 Rebecca Benson sold to Richard Bounds, with WOOLVER, no
acres given.

BUNKER HILL

Patented in 1793 by Denwood Wilson for 18 1/4 acres in West Princess
Anne, Election district 1, map #3.
1798 will of Denwood Wilson, to son George Wilson.
9 Dec.1794 Denwood Wilson gave to Samuel Wilson 18 1/4 acres

CABIN RIDGE

See tract CRAMBURNE

CABIN SWAMP

Patented 19 March 1680 to William Stevens who assigned it to John Roach,
150 acres in Lawsons, Election district 8, map #19.
Rent Rolls 1666-1723 possessed by John Roach, 150 acres
1708 John Roach willed to son Samuel Roach, 105 acres.
1736 Samuel Roach willed to cousin Michael Roach
1758 William Wheatley and wife Alice Wheatley sold to Aaron Sterling 99
1/2 acres of EXCHANGE & CABIN SWAMP.
22 Jan 1763 William Wheatley Sr. and wife Alice Wheatley, cabinetmaker,
sold to Aaron Sterling 10 acres with EXCHANGE.
22 Jan 1763 William Wheatley and wife Alice sold to Daniel Cullen 53
acres with WHEATLEYS PLEASURE.
13 Oct.1767 William Wheatley sold part 11 acres to William Roach with
EXCHANGE.
8 June 1771 Daniel Cullen sold to Outerbridge Horsey 53 acres of
WHEATLEYS PLEASURE & EXCHANGE.
31 Oct.1772 William Wheatley sold to John Johnson two tracts formerly
belonging to Henry Cullen and Michael Roach now deceased,50 acres of
EXCHANGE & CABIN SWAMP.
17 Aug.1774 Outerbridge Horsey sold to Daniel Cullen 53 acres with
WHEATLEYS PLEASURE, EXCHANGE. (probably a release of mortgage.)

25 Jun.1775 Daniel Cullen sold to Isaac Coulbourn, 53 acres with WHEATLEYS PLEASURE & EXCHANGE.
14 Dec.1781 William Wheatley sold 10 acres to John Riggin (son of Jonathan Riggin.)
13 March 1782 William Wheatley Sr. sold to Isaac Johnson CABIN SWAMP & EXCHANGE, formerly belonging to Nathaniel Roach in Annamessex.
1783 tax- Isaac Johnson (with EXCHANGE 60 acres)
1783 tax- William Roach 14 acres
1783 tax- Aaron Sterling 10 acres
1783 tax- William Wheatley 75 acres
1783 tax- John Roach 100 acres.
5 March 1784 John Johnson sold to Isaac Johnson part of EXCHANGE & CABIN SWAMP, 50 acres.
11 June 1785 William Wheatley sold to Michael Wheatley 25 acres of CABIN SWAMP & ROACH'S FOLLY.
23 Aug.1786 Michael Wheatley, wife Martha Wheatley, sold to Jesse Cullen 25 acres.
10 Oct. 1787 Daniel Cullen sold to William Wheatley and Michael Wheatley, 7 acres of ROACHS FOLLY & CABIN SWAMP.
21 May 1788 William Wheatley sold to John Riggin 14 1/2 acres of CABIN SWAMP & ROACHS FOLLY.
25 July 1788 William Wheatley Sr, sold to Dickerson Dougherty 10 acres of CABIN SWAMP & ROACHS FOLLY.
10 Sep.1789 Samuel Cullin sold to Littleton Johnson 39 3/4 acres.
16 Oct 1789 James Haynie sold to Dickerson Dougherty 14 1/2 acres of CABIN SWAMP & ROACHS FOLLY.
3 Feb.1792 Daniel Cullen sold to John Handy 133 3/4 acres of CABBIN SWAMP, EXCHANGE,WHEATLEYS PLEASURE.
1795 Aaron Sterling willed to son Aaron tracts bought of William Wheatley.
31 Oct 1797 William Williams,wife Polly Williams sold to John Handy, released their mortgage claim on lands of Daniel Cullen.
8 Jan 1803 John Handy,wife Sarah Handy sold to John Lawson 130 3/4 acres of EXCHANGE & WHEATLEYS PLEASURE, CABBIN SWAMP
2 Feb 1808 John Riggin sold to Littleton Johnson 25 acres of CABIN SWAMP & ROACHS FOLLY.
27 Feb.1808 John Riggin Sr., wife Betsy Riggin sold to Isaac Johnson 12 acres.
11 June 1808 John Lawson sold to Benjamin Lankford 2 acres.

CACKMORE

Patented 30 May 1681 by Richard Chambers for 200 acres in East Princess Anne, Election district 15, map #4. AKA COCKMORE
1726/8 Richard Chambers willed to grandson Richard Brereton 100 acres (other 100 acres not mentioned.)
17 June 1735 Richard Chambers sold to David Vance 100 acres that Richard Chambers late, willed to son Richard afsd.
1738 David Vance sold 40 acres to Alexander Vance (for 14 years)
1743 Richard Brereton willed to brother Henry Brereton land left by uncle Richard Chambers, 100 acres.
6 Oct.1761 Asa Hall of Cecil Co. Md. sold to Jonathan Pollitt of Somerset County, 100 acres.
8 March 1762 James Vance of North Carolina sold 20 acres to Jonathan Pollitt (adjacent land that Pollitt bought of Asa Hall.)

14 Feb. 1764 James Vance sold 20 acres to Jonathan Pollitt.
4 Sep.1772 Judith Lagoe of Baltimore Co. Md. widow, and daughter of
Thomas Bratan sold 100 acres to Jonathan Pollitt, part formerly belonging
to Richard Brereton (with HIGH MEADOW.)
21 July 1773 William Douglas of Queen Anne Co. Md. sold to Jonathan
Pollitt, rights to HIGHMEADOW and CACKMORE. No acreage mentioned.
10 Oct.1774 I Judith Legoe witnessed that her sister Winifred Brereton
married John Leaton and left no children except Wealthy Leaton and Mary
Thrift wife of James Thrift; sworn before Aquila Hath of Hartford County,
Md.
10 Sep.1774 James Thrift and wife Mary Thrift of Hartford County sold to
Jonathan Pollitt, all rights to HIGH MEADOW formerly belonging to Thomas
Brereton and rights to COCKMORE, adjacent.
10 Oct.1774 Weathly Leaton of Hartford Co. sold to Jonathan Pollitt her
rights to HIGH MEADOW,CACKMORE.
13 Oct.1774 Judith(Judah) Legoe of Hartford Co. sold her rights to
Jonathan Pollitt.
1783 tax- Jonathan Pollitt Jr. 140 acres.
16 March 1785 James Vance of Sussex Co. Del. sold to James Houston 50 1/4
acres.
7 March 1786 Chambers Hall of Newcastle Co.Del. sold to Jonathan Pollitt
Jr. 1/4th part of 100 acres willed by Richard Brereton.
24 March 1786 Jonathan Pollitt Sr. gave to son Jonathan Pollitt Jr. (no
acres given)
15 April 1807 Jonathan Pollitt, wife Nicy Pollitt sold to John Morris Jr.
152 acres.

CAHOONS FOLLY

A resurvey partly from CHEESEMANS CHANCE, in 1783 by Nathan Cahoon for
202 1/2 acres in Brinkleys, southwest, Election District 3, Map #17.
9 June 1794 Nathan Cahoon sold to Isaac Outten 32 3/4 acres
1796 will of Kellum Lankford, 150 acres to son Noah Lankford, bought of
Isaac Outten.
25 May 1795 Isaac Outten sold to Kellum Lankford 15 acres.
25 May 1795 Nathan Cahoon sold to Kellum Lankford 20 1/2 acres, to use of
Elizabeth Hall daughter of Kellum Lankford
5 April 1803 Noah Lankford sold to William Williams all lands in
Morumsco, unnamed.
11 Nov.1803 William Williams, wife Mary Williams sold to Thomas Robertson
Jr. lands in Morumsco Noah Lankford had from his father Kellum Lankford,
no name or acreage.
22 Feb.1809 Richard Hall and wife Sally Hall & Nathan Cahoon sold to Noah
Lankford Hall, part.

CAIPS MOUTH

Patented in 1745 by John Williams for 12 1/2 acres in Westover, Election
district 13, map #11.
1783 tax- John Williams 12 1/2 acres
12 July 1791 John Williams sold to Levin Ballard 12 1/2 acres with
WILLIAMS LOTT,NORTH BORDER,FIRST CHOICE, CONCLUSION.
12 July 1791 Levin Ballard sold to John Williams 12 1/2 acres, same as
above.
20 Nov.1812 John W. Curtis sold to William Williams.

1815 William Curtis purchased of William Williams 12 1/2 acres.

CALDICUTT

Patented 30 June 1667 by William Stevens for 500 acres in Brinkleys
northeast, Election district 3, map #15.
1687 William Stevens willed 500 acres of land(unnamed) to cousin William
White and heirs.
Rent Rolls 166-1723 possessed 500 acres by Stevens White.
17 June 1760 Stevens White and wife Elizabeth White, sold to Littleton
Dennis part of two tracts REHOBETH & CALDICOTT, except 100 acres.
1761 Stevens White willed to brother Elias White.
7 Sep. 1776 Thomas Bruff and Betty Bruff his wife, silversmith, sold to
William Stevens White(as Stevens White father of William Stevens White
had two tracts. Betty White the relic married Thomas Bruff) Sold her
dower rights.
16 March 1774 William Allen sold 62 acres to Littleton Dennis.
1783 tax- Thomas Bruff, 150 acres
1783 tax- William S. White 100 acres
1783 tax- Susannah Dennis (w/o Littleton Dennis)
8 April 1790 Brittian Powell and Littleton Dryden sold to Littleton
Dennis of Worcester County with WOODHALL (This deed to determine
boundaries of property)
8 April 1790 Brittian Powell sold part to William Stevens White. Also
settlement of boundaries.
8 April 1790 Brittian Powell to Thomas Bruff with WOODHALL
8 April 1790 Thomas Bruff, William Stevens White and Littleton Dennis to
Brittian Powell. same as above.
8 April 1790 Littleton Dennis of Worc. Co. sold to Littleton Dryden for 5
shillings, same as above.
11 May 1791 William Stevens White sold to Littleton Dennis of Worcester
County, 16 1/4 acres of REHOBETH & CALDICUTT.
6 Aug.1792 Samuel Smith, wife Esther Smith and William Stevens White
traded Pierce Chapman 3 1/4 acres for 2 3/4 acres of same.
21 Feb 1794 William Stevens White sold to Littleton Dennis all his rights
to REHOBETH & CALDICOTT.
3 March 1797 Thomas Miles sold to Rebecca Chapman 50 3/4 acres.
3 March 1797 Thomas Miles sold to Elizabeth Bruff for life, 1/3 part.
3 March 1797 Thomas Miles sold to John Bruff, part. no acres mentioned.
3 March 1797 John Bruff sold to Littleton Dennis 9 1/2 acres
3 March 1797 John Bruff sold to Rebecca Chapman 50 acres
3 March 1797 John Bruff sold to William Stevens White of Accomac Co. Va.
88 acres- mtg.
13 April 1796 Elizabeth Bruff and son John Bruff and daughters Ann Bruff
and Susanna Bruff sold to Thomas Miles 250 acres.
27 July 1797 William Stevens White of Acco.Co.Va. released mortgage to
John Bruff, held by Major Thomas Bruff deceased
27 July 1797 John Bruff and mother Betty Bruff sold to Rebecca Chapman 90
1/2 acres.
27 July 1797 John Bruff and mother Betty Bruff widow of Thomas
Bruff(releases her dower right) to Rebecca Chapman her 1/3rds 62 acres.
27 July 1797 Capt. John Bruff and mother Betty Bruff sold to Rebecca
Chapman- she to pay Joseph Bruff, Richard Bruff,Benjamin Bruff and James
Bruff sons of Thomas Bruff.
18 Nov.1797 John Bruff mortgaged to John Cochran of New Castle Co.Del.his

interest.

17 Sep.1798 John Bruff sold to Ann Bruff and Susanna Bruff 100 acres.
7 Nov.1798 Whittington Polk and wife Rebecca Polk sold to Thomas King 50 acres and 90 1/2 acres conveyed to Rebecca Polk from Thomas Miles and John Bruff.(same sale 15 May 1799)
7 Nov.1798 Thomas King sold to Whittington Polk 140 1/2 acres.(same sale 15 May 1799)
8 Nov.1800 John Cochran of New Castle Co.Del. sold to Elizabeth Bruff, William Bruff, Susanna Bruff of Maryland 100 acres, release of mortgage.
8 Nov.1800 Elizabeth Bruff, Ann Bruff and Susanna Bruff sold to Whittington Polk 100 acres.
8 March 1804 Whittington Polk, wife Rebecca Polk, sold to Littleton Dennis 100 acres.

CALF PASTURE

Patented 1775 for 27 acres by Samuel Wilson in Lower Dublin, Election district 4, map #13
1783 tax- Samuel Wilson 27 acres
1790 Samuel Wilson willed to nephew Samuel Ker, a small piece of land between Col. Corbin and Nehemiah King (unnamed).
8 Jan 1795 Samuel Ker, wife Betsy Ker sold to John Custis Wilson devised by will of Samuel Wilson, 5 acres-no name.

CALF PASTURE

Resurveyed from COX'S BILL and patented in 1742 by Thomas Hayward for 247 acres in Brinkleys southeast, Election district 3, map #16.
16 August 1755 Thomas Hayward sold 212 acres to Obed Riggin.
(less that 35 acres that Thomas Hayward sold to William Cox.)
2 Oct. 1766 Obed Riggin and wife Rebecca Riggin sold to Thomas King 212 acres.
17 Aug.1779 Thomas King sold 212 acres to Zadock Wheeler of Worc.Co.Md.
23 Aug.1784 Zadock Wheeler and wife Rebecca Wheeler of Worc. Co.,shipwright, sold 212 acres to Jesse Ward.
17 March 1787 Jesse Ward sold to William Cox, all.

CAMELS LOTT

Patented in 1761 by Isaac Dickerson for 11 acres in Brinkleys southeast, Election district 3, map #16.
1771 Isaac Dickerson willed to wife Catherine Dickerson plantation and after death to son James Dickerson(unnamed land)
1783 tax- Catherine Dickerson 11 acres.

CANNAAN

This land was not patented but is part of SCOTTS FOLLY AND SCOTLAND in Lawsons, Election district 8, map #18.
6 Jun 1737 articles of agreement- Joshua Atkinson sold to Southy Whittington (as William Scott deceased father of Elizabeth Scott now wife of Joshua Atkinson was seized of tract SCOTLAND and also 50 acres of SCOTTS FOLLY, now called CANAAN 200 acres)
22 June 1763 Southy Whittington Sr. gave 140 acres to Southy Whittington Jr.

CANEDY ISLAND

Patented on 5 June 1683 by John King for 50 acres in Fairmount, Election
district 6, map #9 (aka CANADA, CANDEE ISLAND)
1696 John King willed to son Benjamin King, 50 acres
Rent rolls 166-1723 possessed by Benjamin King, 50 acres.
1733 Benjamin King willed the land to be sold.
15 Nov.1737 Capt. Capell King sold to Benjamin Sharp 50 acres formerly
occupied by Benjamin King brother of Capell, that Benjamin willed to be
sold.
15 Apr.1760 Benjamin Sharp sold to Whittington King 50 acres.
1762 resurvey by Isaiah Tilghman 219 1/2 acres, includes part of FURNISS
ADVENTURE & WINTER HARBOUR.
1783 tax- Isaiah Tilghman 275 1/2 acres.
1790 Isaiah Tilghman willed to son William Tilghman.
23 Oct.1804 William Tilghman son of Isaiah Tilghman, wife Sarah Tilghman
sold to Samuel Ford 5 acres.

CANES CHOICE

Patented on 18 March 1683 by James Caine, in Fairmount, Election district
6, map 9 for 300 acres.
14 Aug.1675 Eleanor Caine relic of James Caine sold to Thomas Avery part
and 100 acres now called TROUBLESOME, to Henry Miles.
1695 will of Henry Miles, to daughter Alice Miles, TROUBLESOME.
9 Jun.1746 Samuel Miles sold to Stacey Miles, 100 acres.
7 June 1755 Stacey Miles. wife Jane Miles, sold to Thomas Seon,
TROUBLESOME 100 acres and also 50 acres of TROUBLE.

CANTERBURY

Patented 20 July 1677 by John Parsons who assigned to Alexander Mitchell,
50 acres in West Princess Ann, Election district 1, map #2.
16 Dec.1734 John Mitchell sold to Peter Surman Sr. all the moiety given
John by his father being 1/2 of that John left to sons Richard Mitchell
and John Mitchell, CANTERBURY & HORSEYS CHANCE, 100 acres.
2 Oct.1734 Richard Mitchell and Mary Mitchell his wife, sold to Alexander
Adams, rector of Stepney Parish 100 acres, 84 acres out of HORSEYS CHANCE
and 16 acres of CANTERBURY.
15 Oct.1748 Peter Surman and wife Mary Surman sold to Thomas Gillis 13
acres with parts of TROUBLE,CRAMBURNE,HORSEYS CHANCE.
1779 will of Thomas Gillis, to dau-in-law Sarah Gillis widow of Levin
Gillis (with CRAMBURN)
1783 tax- Thomas Fountain, 17 acres.
28 Sep.1790 Joseph Gillis son of Thomas Gillis with wife Elizabeth Gillis
sold to Thomas Fountain, 13 acres of CANTERBURY since resurveyed on 15
Jan 1735 by the name of HORSEYS CHANCE, with CRAMBURN & TROUBLE.

CARLISLE

Patented on 24 Nov.1686 by Thomas Horseman for 100 acres in West Princess
Anne, Election district 1, map #2.
Rent Rolls 1666-1723 possessed by Adrain Gordon.
22 Jun 1743 James Chadwick and wife Ann Chadwick of Kent Co. Del. sold to

Abraham Heath two tracts, CARLISLE 100 acres & CHADWICKS ADVENTURE 50 acres.
15 July 1757 I Abraham Heath and wife Priscilla Heath deed to Walter Taylor 100 acres of CARLISLE & CHADWICKS ADVENTURE.
17 Aug.1779 Walter Taylor sold to David Prior 42 acres.
1783 tax- Stephen Taylor 48 1/2 acres.
1 Sep.1790 Walter Taylor of Kent Co. Del. sold to Henry Banks of Som. Co. 46 3/4 acres with PRIVILEDGE & GOOD LUCK.

CARYS ADVENTURE

Patented 20 Nov.1666 by Thomas Carey for 300 acres in Mt. Vernon, Election district 5, map #1.
Rent Rolls 1666-1723 possessed by Thomas Carey, 300 acres.
1681 Thomas Carey willed to wife Jane Carey.
26 Jan 1709 Richard Carey and wife Mary Carey gave to Thomas Carey.
26 March 1722 Thomas Carey son of Richard and Mary Carey sold to Betty Gale, 300 acres.
4 Nov.1732 Betty Gale alienated to Thomas Carey (Alias Thomas Crouch 300 acres.
7 Oct 1740 Thomas Carey (otherwise called Thomas Crouch) sold to Edward Chambers 355 acres except small part of Eleanor Covington widow of Phillip Covington,and also one moiety of WASHFORD.
3 Nov.1741 Edward Chambers, Collector of Customs of the port of Pocomoke, sold to Henry Waggaman for 5 shillings 400 acres at Money Creek, CAREYS PURCHASE, purchased of Thomas Carey.
4 Sep.1750 Eleanor Covington widow of Phillip, Nehemiah Covington and Phillip Covington son of Phillip sold to Henry Waggaman(per deed from Richard Carey and wife Mary Carey to Thomas Carey.)
1742 resurveyed to WAGGAMANS PURCHASE, 947 1/2 acres

CARYS CHANCE

Patented 12 March 1687 for 164 acres in West Princess Anne, Election district 1, map #3, taken out of MOTHERS CARE, by Richard Carey.
Rent Rolls 1666-1723 possessed by Richard Carey.

CARNYS CHANCE

Patented on 14 Feb.1666 by Thomas Carny Jr.in Mt. Vernon, Election district 5, map 1, for 300 acres.(Thomas Carny went to Bristol England by Oct.1667 and gave power of Attorney to James Dashiell.)
12 Jun.1667 James Dashiell deeded to William Layton.
13 May 1678 William Layton, wife Ursulla Layton sold to Thomas Hobbs, all.
Rent Rolls 1666-1723 Possessed by Joy Hobbs
1735 Joy Hobbs willed to sons Thomas Hobbs, Joy Hobbs, Matthias Hobbs and Noble Hobbs.
19 March 1754 Noble Hobbs of Dorchester Co.Md. sold 50 acres to Robert Hopkins of Somerset Co.(the part possessed by Marcellas Hobbs.)
16 May 1758 Stephen Hobbs and wife Margaret Hobbs sold to Henry Waggaman, his rights to CARNYS CHANCE and ABBINGTON.
1759 Henry Waggaman willed to son John.
24 Sep.1765 Marcellas Hobbs and wife Agnes Hobbs sold 46 1/2 acres to

Matthias Hobbs.
27 Feb.1768 Robert Austin and wife Rachel Austin sold to Mary Covington 50 acres.
14 Jan 1768 Marcellas Hobbs and wife Agnes Hobbs sold to Mary Waggaman 100 acres, the lower part, with CUMBERLAND & GOOD LUCK.
1780 Mary Waggaman, with son Henry Waggaman land bought of Matthias Hobbs (unnamed)
28 Jan.1783 Margaret Hobbs for 5 shillings paid by Josiah Hobbs son of Stephen Hobbs her deceased husband released her dower rights to CARNYS CHANCE & ABBINGTON (conveyed by Stephen to Henry Waggaman.)
1783 tax- Levin Gale 164 acres
1783 tax- Matthias Hobbs 46 3/4 acres
1783 tax- Mary Covington 46 3/4 acres
1783 tax- Henry Waggaman 103 acres and 100 acres.
1798 Matthias Hobbs gave to wife Mary and to dau Mary Hobbs.
29 April 1792 Henry Waggaman son of Henry and Mary Waggaman, with wife Sarah Waggaman of Dorc.Co. sold to George Waggaman of Som.Co. 100 acres with CUMBERLAND, DAVIDS CHANCE, REFUGE, WAGGAMANS PURCHASE, etc.
12 Nov.1793 George Waggaman sold to Elias Bayley 27 acres of CARNYS CHANCE & GOOD LUCK.
3 Aug.1803 Henry Waggaman sold to Nehemiah Covington 4 acres
20 Aug.1803 Henry Waggaman and wife Sarah Waggaman of Dorc.Co. sold to Elias Bayley 64 1/4 acres of CARNEYS CHANCE & GOOD LUCK.
20 Aug.1803 Henry Waggaman and wife Sarah Waggaman of Dorc.Co. sold to Littleton Dennis Teackle 906 1/4 acres of WAGGAMANS PURCHASE,OWENS DELIGHT,OWENS IMPROVEMENT, etc.
20 Aug.1803 Henry Waggaman and wife Sarah Waggaman of Dorc.Co. sold to Levin Jones 483 acres of WAGGAMANS PURCHASE, CARNEYS CHANCE,GOOD LUCK, CUMBERLAND,etc.
20 Aug.1803 Henry Waggaman sold to Jesse Covington 68 1/3 acres of CARNEYS CHANCE & GOOD LUCK that Jesse Covington gave him a mortgage for.
2 Jan 1810 Levin F. Jones sold to Matthias Hobbs 47 1/2 acres of George Waggaman land, no name.
1841 Matthias Hobbs willed to son Samuel Hobbs, land purchased of Solomon Harris, and to son Matthias Hobbs, formerly land of brother Benjamin Hobbs.

CARNYS ORDER

Patented on 6 Jun 1667 for 100 acres near Mt. Vernon. This land was cut off by other surveys, and not found on the maps.

CASEYS VENTURE

Patented in 1769 by Samuel Casey for 114 1/4 acres in Brinkleys southeast, Election district 3, map #16.
4 Nov. 1787 Peter Carsley, wife Catherine Carsley, sold to Levi Adams of Accomack Co.Va. 114 1/4 acres, CARSLEYS VENTURE (shown on maps as CASEYS VENTURE.)

CATHERINES CONTENT

This is part of DOUBLE PURCHASE, 3000 acres patented by Randall Revell in Westover, Election district 13, map #10

CATLINS LOTT (CATTLYNS LOTT)

Patented 9 April 1664 by Robert Catlin for 300 acres in Westover,
Election district 13, map 11.
This was later resurveyed in 1666 to HARTFORD BROAD OAK, 400 acres.

CATLINS LOTT

Patented in 1749 by William Catlin for 21 acres in Westover, Election
district 3, map #11.
21 Nov.1766 William Catlin Sr. sold to Jesse Lister 100 1/2 acres taken
out of CATLINS LOTT, CATLINS VENTURE & HARTFORD BROAD OAK.
1776 Jesse Lister willed all lands to son William Lister (unanmed)

CATLINS VENTURE

Patented in 1727 by William Catlin for 50 acres in Westover, Election
disrict 13, map #11.
21 Aug.1766 William Catlin Jr. sold to Isaac Beauchamp, part HARTFORD
BROAD OAK & CATLINS VENTURE, 41 1/5 acres.
21 Nov.1766 William Catlin Sr. sold to Jesse Lister 100 1/2 acres out of
three tracts, CATLINS LOT, CATLINS VENTURE, HARTFORD BROAD OAK.
16 Mar.1768 William Catlin Jr. sold 40 acres to John Turpin part of
CATLINS VENTURE, HARTFORD BROAD OAK.
31 March 1768 William Catlin willed to son William lands in Annamessex
(unnamed)
6 Apr.1768 William Catlin Jr.(mtg.) to John Williams part of CATLINS
VENTURE, HARTFORD BROAD OAK, BRANFIELD (this mortgage was released on 20
Aug.1771.)
1776 Jesse Lister willed to son William Lister, land (unnamed)
1783 tax- William Lister, 100 acres
1783 tax- John Turpin 14 acres
1783 tax- Jean Beauchamp 41 acres.
2 Oct.1807 William Turpin son of John Turpin sold to Tubman Mitchell 10
acres father purchased of William Catlin.
6 April 1808 William Turpin son of John Turpin, and wife Elizabeth Turpin
sold to Isaac Miles.

CEDAR HAMMOCK

Patented in 1768 by Traves Sterling for 40 acres in Asbury, Election
district 12, map #21.
1783 tax- Traves Sterling 20 acres and 40 acres unknown.

CEDAR HILL

Patented in 1786, a resurvey of FAIR SPRING, by Samuel Wilson for 541 1/2
acres, in Westover, Election district 13, map #11.
18 Aug.1795 Milcah Gale Chaille sold to Levin Miles 39 acres of CEDAR
HILL & CHANCE.
18 Aug.1795 Milcah Gale Chaille sold to William Tilghman Sr. 129 acres of
POOLS HOPE, FAIR SPRING & CEDAR HILL.
18 Nov 1794 Milcah Gale Chaille sold to William Tilghman Sr. 33 1/2
acres.
6 July 1802 Matthias Jones, & Milcah Gale Chaille sold to George W.

Jackson 200 acres.
6 July 1802 George W. Jackson sold to Milcah Gale Chaille and Matthias
Jones 200 acres.
1806 William Tilghman willed to daughter Nancy Tilghman land bought of
Milcah Gale Chaille, no name.
23 June 1806 Nancy Tilghman daughter of William Turpin conveyed to
Stephen Tilghman land father William bought of Milcah Gale Chaille, he to
support his sister Sally Tilghman diring life, no name. 169 3/4 acres.
1817 Stephen Tilghman willed to brother William Tilghman 169 3/4 acres,
no name.

CEDAR LANDING

Patented in 1819, probably was part of POMFRET, in Lawsons, Election
district 8, map #18, for 235 1/4 acres by William Williams.

CHADWICKS ADVENTURE

Patented on 15 July 1720 by James Chadwick for 50 acres in West Princess
Anne, Election district 1, map #2.
Rent Rolls 1666-1723 possessed by James Chadwick.
22 June 1743 James Chadwick and wife Ann Chadwick of Kent Co. Del. sold
50 acres to Abraham Heath with CARLISLE.
15 July 1757 I Abraham Heath,wife Priscilla Heath deed to Walter Taylor
50 acres with CARLISLE.
17 Aug 1778 I Walter Taylor sell to David Prior 3 1/2 acre, with CARLISLE
& BIRCH SWAMP.

CHANCE

Patented 17 June 1667 to Roger Woolford for 300 acres in Dublin District,
Election district 4, map#12.
Rent Rolls 166-1723 possessed by Roger Woolford
1701/2 Roger Woolford willed plantation to son Roger and to son James
Woolford land at Dividing Creek (both unnamed lands)
1730 Roger Woolford of Dorcester County Md, willed 300 acres to son John
Woolford except 30 acres sold to John Jones (note; Sarah Woolford married
John Jones).
3 Nov.1740 John Fleming sold to Robert Harris (a quitclaim, trade for
MINSHALLS ADVENTURE,adjacent, 300 acres.
26 Feb.1741 John Woolford and wife Mary Woolford sold to Robert Harris
and wife Mary Harris, that Roger Woolford son of Roger bequeathed to son
John Woolford.
31 Aug.1742 Thomas Woolford of Dorcester Co. Md. eldest son of Roger of
Dorcester Co. and grandson of Roger Woolford of Somerset County, and wife
Sarah Woolford sold 300 acres to Robert Harris.
1745 resurvey by Robert Harris to 316 acres
1755/6 Robert Harris willed to son John Harris, 316 acres
4 Oct. 1790 Littleton Dennis and wife Elizabeth Dennis of Worc.Co. sold
to John Mitchell 136 1/2 acres near Dividing Creek.
1788/93 John Harris willed to son John, 316 acres.
1809 Resurveyed to HEATHS EXPERIMENT 739 3/4 acres.

CHANCE

Patented on 16 Feb 1673 by Henry Smith for 90 acres in East Princess

Anne, Election district 15, map #5.

11 Oct.1681 Henry Smith, wife Ann Smith sold to Andrew Whittington 90 acres.

Rent Rolls 1666-1723 Know not the right of possession of this land unless it is John King who married Ursula Whittington.

1715 John Smith of Sussex Co. Del. grandson of Henry Smith sold all lands in Somerset County Maryland.

10 Feb.1734/5 Whittington King son of John and Ursula Whittington King (daughter of Andrew Whittington) gave to his brother John King.

29 March 1738 Jane Olandman sold to Robert King 58 1/3 acres, three tracts, CHANCE conveyed from John and Eleanor King, with DUBLIN & PIMINE, that descended to daughters of Dennis Olandman,(Jane as youngest daughter, age 21 last February)

20 June 1745 Whittington King, principal vestryman conveyed to the rest of his brethern of Somerset Parish 2 acres, whereon the chapel of Somerset stands known by the name of KINGS MILL CHAPEL (abandon in 1767)

24 May 1760 Whittington King sold to William Dawson for 21 years.

4 Oct 1760 William Dawson sold to Benjamin Hobbs 5 acres for 20 years bought of Whittington King.

27 Oct.1760 William Dawson sold to Benjamin Hobbs part to be paid for in seven years. no acreage given.

20 Aug.1762 Jesse King sold to John Furlong, part that William Dawson leased from Whittington King, and later leased to Benjamin Hobbs who released to Jesse King.

25 Aug 1765 John Bozier and Priscilla Bozier sold to John King 1/3rds, the right of dower of Priscilla King who was the widow of Whittington King.

27 May 1766 Christian Hobbs widow of Benjamin Hobbs leased to John Furlong, part leased by Benjamin Hobbs of William Boston 5 acres, for 14 years.

12 May 1767 Vestry of Somerset parish sold 2 acres to William Miles.

21 March 1772 Rev. Hamilton Bell traded John King for 8 1/4 acres of HAMILTONS FORTUNE, for 2 1/4 acres of CHANCE.

9 Jun 1772 William Layfield and wife Agnes sold to William Miles 80 acres of CHANCE at Trading Branch.

25 July 1775 William Miles sold to Levin Dorman 80 acres.

CHANCE

Patented in 1683 for 50 acres in St. Peters, Election district 2, map #6 by Peter Elzey.

1715 Peter Elzey per will gave to friend William Wallace.

18 Jan.1721 William Wallace conveyed to William Stoughton with GEORGES ADVENTURE, BELFAST, etc.

1 Nov.1763 Thomas Sloss and George Irving sold to William Smith.

23 Mar.1775 Thomas Sloss and wife Mary sold to William Smith 50 acres. (as Peter Elzey willed to William Wallace and he convyed to William Stoughton who died with one daughter now wife of Thomas Sloss.

11 Sep 1779 John Elzey of Sussex Co. Del. sold to Samuel Smith 50 acres.

5 Feb.1789 Samuel Smith, wife Esther Smith, sold to Henry Walston Miles 44 acres with GEORGES ADVENTURE, BELFAST, being part of tract devised to William Wallace by Peter Elzey.

CHANCE

Patented 19 March 1694/5 by Thomas Walter for 150 acres in St. Peters,

Election disrict 2, map #6.
Rent Rolls 1666-1723 possessed by Thomas Shaw.
1716 Thomas Shaw (wife Mary Shaw) willed estate to Thomas Hudson,
preacher and lands to grandson William Robinson (no name of land
mentioned)
18 Jun 1729 William Stoughton on behalf of William Robinson sold to
Thomas Wright 50 acres out of BLOYCES HOPE & CHANCE, and RAINSBURY..
1754 resurveyed to CONCLUSION 226 acres.

CHANCE

Patented 2 May 1705 for 23 acres by Alexander Brown, in East Princess
Anne, Election district 15, map #5.
20 Oct 1707 Alexander Brown willed to son Thomas Brown.
1 March 1738 Thomas Brown eldest son of Alexander Brown, and Mary Brown
and Margaret Brown , two daughters of Alexander, gave 23 acres to brother
David Brown.(Elizabeth Brown wife of Alexander also lately deceased.)
5 Dec.1739 David Brown sold 23 acres to William Miles.
1769 resurveyed to MEADOW LAND 120 acres.

CHANCE

Patented on 20 June 1715 for 15 acres to Charles Wharton in Dublin,
Election district 4, map #13.
18 Nov.1735 William Wharton and Mary Wharton his wife, sold to John
Dennis Jr, that Charles Wharton willed to his son William.
20 Aug. 1755 John Dennis gave 15 acres to son Littleton.
9 Sep.1773 Littleton Dennis of Worcester Co. sold to Samuel Sloan.
1783 tax- Samuel Sloan, 15 acres.
15 April 1806 Samuel Sloan sold to Levin Pollitt 10 acres.
1807 Samuel Sloan willed part to wife Elizabeth Sloan.

CHANCE

Patented on 28 April 1721 by John Kellam for 50 acres in Lawsons,
Election district 8, map #18.
1783 tax- John Kellam Jr, 50 acres.
19 Oct.1793 John Kellam son of John sold to Jessee Lankford.
15 Jan 1794 John Kellam Sr., wife Elizabeth Kellam sold to Jesee Maddux
Lankford 50 acres.
Also see KELLUMS ADDITION

CHANCE

Patented by George Tull in 1722 for 50 acres in Dublin, Election district
4, map 12.
10 Nov.1736 I George Tull give to son Jonathan Tull CHANCE & JOES OLD
FIELD.
3 July 1759 Jonathan Tull and wife Mary Tull sold to Samuel Adams 50
acres and part of COLEMANS ADVENTURE & BECKLES.
1763 Samuel Adams gave to son Samuel lands bought of Jonathan
Tull.(unnamed)
1783 tax- Samuel Adams, 50 acres.

CHANCE

Patented in 1725 for 100 acres in Dublin, Election district 4 map #13.
1740 resurveyed part 29 acres to CHANCE
1747 resurveyed part 15 acres to CYPRESS SWAMP.
1775 Balance resurveyed to LITTLE DERRY.

CHANCE

A resurvey of CHANCE of 1725 for 29 acres, in Dublin, Election district
4, map #13, by Robert Geddes.
17 Aug. 1749 Robert Geddes and wife Susannah Geddes, inholder sold to
John Hamilton 29 acres, with CYPRESS SWAMP.
1775 resurveyed to ADDITION TO LITTLE DERRY 343 1/2 acres.

CHANCE

Patented in 1734 by Daniel Long for 25 acres, in Brinkleys northwest,
Election district 3, map #14.
Daniel Long bequeathed to son David.
25 Feb 1752 David Long and wife Abigail Long sold 99 acres to John Howard
that David Long resurveyed and added 74 acres and now called DAVIDS
ADVENTURE at Morumsco Creek.
1757 Resurveyed to DAVIDS ADVENTURE 99 acres.

CHANCE

Patented in 1741 for 50 acres in Brinkleys northeast, Election district
3, map #15.

CHANCE

Patented in 1741 to Southy Whittington for 50 acres in Lawsons, Election
district 8, map #18, part from tract INCREASE.
25 March 1757 Southy Whittington and wife Mary Whittington sold to
Lazarus Lankford 4 acres, adjacent MIDDLE RIDGE.
14 Apr. 1763 Southy Whittington gave to son William Whittington 79 acres
with PUZZLE & RECOVERY.
22 Jun 1763 Southy Whittington Sr.gave 13 acres to son Southy Jr.
1773 Southy Whittington willed to son Isaac Whittington not given to sons
William Whittington or Southy.
1783 tax- Isaac Whittington
15 June 1807 Benjamin Lankford sold to William Williams 4 acres unnamed
that Lazarus Lankford purchased of Southy Whittington.
17 March 1810 Benjamin Lankford Sr. sold 8 acres to William Williams.
10 Apr.1810 Matthias Dashiell, sheriff, sold to William Williams, per
jugement agains Benjamin Lankford, 8 acres.
1813 resurveyed a part to WHITTINGTONS CONCLUSION 13 acres.

CHANCE

Patented in 1741 by Kirk Gunby for 50 acres in Lawsons, Election district
8, map #18.
10 Nov.1752 Kirk Gunby sold to Southy Whittington to settle dispute of
boundaries.

1775 will Kirk Gunby, to son John Gunby.
1783 tax- John Gunby
1783 tax- Sarah Gunby
1791 will John Gunby to son Kirk Gunby.
10 Nov.1804 Elisha Gunby sold to Benjamin Lankford 8 1/2 acres of CHANCE
& MIDDLE RIDGE.

CHANCE

Patented in 1741 for 50 acres in Brinkleys northeast, Election district
3, map #15.

CHANCE

Patented in 1746 by John Peden Sr. for 20 acres in Dublin, Election
district 4, map #13.
1769 John Peden willed all lands to son John.
1783 tax- John Peden, 20 acres
1795 John Peden willed lands(unanamed) to son John Peden.

CHANCE

Patented in 1748 by Stephen Tull for 111 acres in Dublin, map #12,
Election district 14.
1750 resurveyed to KNIGHTS PURCHASE and then in 1760 became part of TULLS
ADDITION.

CHANCE

Patented in 1749 for 36 acres in Brinkleys northwest, Election district
3, map #14.
1783 Thomas Cottingham wih BOSTONS ADDITION 137 3/4 acres.

CHANCE

Patented in 1751 for 80 acres, in East Princess Anne, Election district
15, map #5.
1783 Levin Dorman, 80 acres.
19 March 1793 Levin Dorman sold to William Adams 80 acres with DORMANS
PURCHASE.
12 Aug.1810 Levin Dorman Sr. gave to Levin Dorman Jr. 200 acres DORMANS
CONCLUSION & CHANCE.

CHANCE

Patented in 1751 for 63 acres to Charles Cottingham in Brinkleys
southwest, Election district 3, map #17.
1760 William Cottingham son of Charles, resurveyed the land belonging to
Charles Cottingham.
1783 tax- William Cottingham, 63 acres
23 Feb.1805 Josiah Cottingham son of William sold part to Thomas
Cottingham.
23 June 1834 Josiah Cottingham sold the balance to Levin Conner.
23 March 1833 Josiah Cottingham sold to William Henry Lankford, 2 acres.

CHANCE

Patented in 1753 by Hope Adams for 68 acres in Brinkleys northeast, Election district 3, map #15.
1783 tax- Sarah Adams 60 acres (widow of Hope)
17 Jan 1787 Hope Adams sold to William Broughton part 27 1/4 acres.
1 Aug 1791 Hope Adams son of Jesse and wife Martha Adams sold to William Broughton 23 acres.
11 July 1792 William Broughton,wife Martha Broughton, Hope Adams, wife Martha Adams sold to Thomas Robertson Sr. 10 1/2 acres.
11 July 1792 George Adams, wife Sarah Adams, Hope Adams, wife Martha Adams sold to William Broughton 7 1/2 acres with ADAMS LUCK.

CHANCE

Patented in 1753 to William Miles for 35 acres, in Lawsons, Election district 8, map #19.
24 Oct.1765 William Miles mortgaged to Matthias Gale of London, merchant, HEARTS EASE,DIXONS LOTT,HOG PEN SWAMP, FORTUNE & 35 acres of CHANCE.
1773 resurveyed to HEARTS CONTENT 257 1/4 acres.

CHANCE

Patented in 1753 for 22 acres in Tangier, Election district 9, map #7.
1792 became part of CHANCE surveyed for John Jones for 227 1/4 acres.

CHANCE

Patented in 1757 for 50 acres by William Taylor in Brinkleys northeast, Election district 3, map #15.
1760 ADDITION TO CHANCE patented for 30 acres by Henry Schoolfield.
William Taylor sold to James Hall 13 1/4 acres
1777 will Henry Schoolfield, to son Henry, ADDITION TO CHANCE.
1783 tax- Henry Schoolfield 30 acre (ADDITION)
1783 tax- James Hall, with BEAUCHAMPS VENTURE 20 acres.
12 Jan.1788 James Hall, wife Mary Hall, sold to Henry Schoolfield 13 1/4 acres with BEAUCHAMPS VENTURE.
12 Jan.1788 Henry Schoolfield, with Elizabeth Schoolfield sold to Pierce Chapman 69 1/4 acres of SCHOOLFIELDS CHANCE,ADDITION TO SCHOOLFIELDS CHANCE, BEAUCHAMPS VENTURE AND CHANCE.

CHANCE

Patented in 1760 by Kellum Lankford for 36 acres in Brinkleys northwest, Election district 3, map #14.
1783 tax- Kellum Lankford 36 acres.
1796 will of Kellum Lankford, to grandson Benjamin Lankford son of Noah Lankford (under 21)

CHANCE

Patented in 1760 by Matthew Puckam for 50 acres in East Princess Anne, Election district 15, map #4.
17 Jan.1764 Matthew Puckam sold to Charles Redding for 5 shillings, 50 acres.

21 Feb.1743 Charles Redding sold to Joseph Dashiell 50 acres with 30 acres of CONTENT, that Matthew Puckam and Richard Puckam sold to him.
2 Apr.1771 Charles Redding and wife Esther Redding sold to John Johnson, 50 acres, with CONTENT.
8 Aug.1807 John Johnson sold to Elzey Maddux 50 acres.

CHANCE

Patented in 1762 by John Nairn for 4 acres in Brinkleys southeast, Election district 3, map #16.

CHANCE

Patented in 1766 to Thomas Tull for 129 1/2 acres in Brinkleys southwest, Election district 3, map #17
27 Jan 1806 Thomas Tull sold to Thomas Merrill Tull 170 acres of BOSTON, CHANCE & TROUBLESOME.
9 Feb.1809 Thomas Merrill Tull, wife Polly sold to Joshua Tull 203 1/2 acres of BOSTON, CHANCE, TROUBLESOME & WILLIAMS LOTT.

CHANCE

Patented in 1774 by William Miles, for 4 acres in Westover, Election district #13, map #11.
28 Feb 1786 William Miles son of Samuel Miles sold to Samuel Wilson 8 3/4 acres on south side of Back Creek adj.TILGHMANS ADVENTURE.
18 Aug.1795 Milcah Gale Chaille sold to Levin Miles, all with CEDAR HILL & FORTUNE.

CHANCE

This land was not patented. It is part of MITCHELLS LOTT,in Brinkleys northwest, Election district 3, map #4 and contains 75 acres, possessed by Thomas Marshall.
20 April 1774 Thomas Marshall gave to son Stephen Marshall MITCHELLS LOTT, now called CHANCE, with PRIVILEDGE, etc. 481 1/4 acres.
1740 probably resurveyed to MARSHALLS INHERITANCE 438 acres.

CHANCE

Patented in 1784 for 12 acres by Henry Walston on Deal Island, Election district 14, map #8.
9 Sep. 1803 Isaac Noble,wife Peggy Noble sold to Thomas Jones, as Henry Walston willed 1/3rd part to daughter Peggy Noble on Deal Island.
22 Sep.1804 Henry Evans sold to Thomas Jones his 1/4th part of the 1/3rd part that Henry Walston willed to son David Walston and grandson Henry Evans.

CHANCE

Patented in 1792 by John Jones for 227 1/4 acres in Tangier, Election district 9, map #7, a resurvey of LUMS AMENDMENT & CHANCE(1752)
1846 John Jones of Robert Jones, willed to son Robert CHANCE bought of John Jones of John, and to son Rufus Jones 50 acres.

CHANCE

Patented in 1792 by Thomas Waters for 559 1/4 acres in Mt.Vernon,
Election district 5, map #1.and was part of LAST PURCHASE.

CHANCE

Patented in 1801 by Matthias Miles for 114 acres in East Princess Anne,
Election district 15, map #15.
1801 ADDITION TO CHANCE, patented for 74 acres by Matthias Miles
1848 resurveyed to ADDITION TO PASTURAGE 261 acres.

CHANCE

Patented in 1817 for 11 acres in East Princess Anne, Election district
15, map #5.

CHARLES CHANCE

Patented in 1744 by Charles Hayman for 20 acres in East Princess Anne,
Election district 15, map #4
1763 ADDITION TO CHANCE, 13 1/2 acres
1774 will of Charles Hayman, to son Revel Hayman
1783 tax- Revel Hayman, CHANCE & ADDITION 33 1/2 acres
1796 will of Revel Hayman, lands(unnamed) to wife Sarah Hayman and then
to son William Brown Hayman.
7 Feb.1797 Sarah Hayman sold to John Hitch 20 acres that Revel Hayman
willed to wife Sarah to be sold to pay debts. She releases all her claim
on the lands.

CHARLES HIS ADVENTURE

Patented on 28 March 1705 by Charles Williams in Dames Quarter and
Tangier (on lines) Election districts 9 and 11, map #7, for 140 acres.
Also known as WILLIAMS ADVENTURE.
1734 will of Charles Williams, to son John Williams, WILLIAMS ADVENTURE
1783 tax- Charles Williams, 140 acres.
1829 will of Zorobable Williams, to brother Elijah Williams.

CHEAP PRICE

Patented 4 Sep.1663 by Thomas Price for 500 acres in Brinkleys northwest,
Election district 3, map#14.
11 Jan.1695 Thomas Price died in Sussex Co. Del. and he sold to William
Planner 300 acres.
20 Sep.1685 Thomas Price, wife Katherine Price sold to William Planner
200 acres now called PLANNERS PURCHASE.
3 Aug.1695 resurveyed by William Planner for 725 acres
Rent Rolls 1666-1723 William Planner 725 acres.
1783 tax- Planner Williams (with PLANNERS BLOSSOM 1232 acres)
1788 Planner Williams gave 230 acres to daughter Amelia Gale.

CHEESEMANS CHANCE

Patented 28 June 1676 by William Cheeseman for 100 acres in Brinkleys southwest, Election district 3, map #17.
Rent Rolls 1666-1723 possessed 40 acres by George Hey and 60 acres by Joseph Evans.
8 March 1682 William Cheeseman, wife Jane Cheeseman sold 60 acres to Henry Potter.
16 May 1682 William Cheeseman and wife Jane Cheeseman sold to William Stevens, 40 acres now called GLAZIERS HALL. William Stevens left to wife Elizabeth Stevens who married George Layfield. George and Elizabeth Layfield sold to Langdon Goddard who sold to George Hey.
George Hey died and it descended to Ann Taylor wife of Dennis Taylor, daughter of George Hey. Dennis Taylor and wife Ann sold the 40 acres to Charles Cottingham.
5 Jan 1687 Henry Potter, wife Alee Potter sold to John Coulbourn and Joseph Evans 60 acres called GLAZIERS HALL.
19 Jun 1735 Charles Cottingham and Ann Cottingham his wife sold 40 acres to Thomas Lindzey(with 15 acres of BOSTON)
24 Feb.1735/6 Joseph Evans, schoolmaster, gave to friend John Cahoon- no acreage given.
1749 John Cahoon willed to wife Mary Cahoon and after her death to son Henry Cahoon, plantation (unnamed).
1750 part resurveyed to EDEN 89 3/4 acres
12 May 1762 Thomas Lindzey sold to Nehemiah Turpin, 140 acres GLAZIERS HALL, BOSTON, MUMFORD. (Mortgage)
23 Oct 1764 Nehemiah Turpin sold to Thomas Lindzey the same as above.
23 Oct.1764 Thomas Lindzey sold to Nehemiah Turpin 95 acres called CHEESEMANS CHANCE, MUMFORD, and BOSTON lately resurveyed and called EDEN.
8 Oct.1765 Henry Cahoon sold to Abraham Outten 60 acres.
1775 Henry Cahoon willed to son Nathan Cahoon, all lands(unanamed)
7 Sep.1776 Isaac Outten sold to Nathan Cahoon, with SECURITY, no acres given.
1783 tax- Nathan Cahoon 60 acres
1783 tax- Isaac Outten 60 acres
1793 resurveyed to CAHOONS FOLLY 202 1/2 acres.
9 June 1794 Nathan Cahoon to David Lindzey, to settle bounds.
17 Jan 1799 Isaac Outten, wife Margaret Outten of Acco.Co.Va. sold to John Conner 569 acres, several tracts.
6 April 1810 John Conner sold to Henry James Carroll, total 800 acres.

CHERRY GARDEN

Patented on 15 Aug.1695 for 86 acres to William Noble in Dublin Election District 4, map #13.
1721 Jonathan Noble willed to sons William Noble and Jonathan Noble.
22 Nov.1734 John Lewis and Rebecca Lewis, Elizabeth Noble of Sussex Co.Del. conveyed 1/3rd of a share to John Paden.
28 May 1736 John Lewis and Rebecca Lewis his wife and Elizabeth Noble all of Sussex Co.Del. sold to David Dryden Jr. As William Noble made over to son James who died intestate and so it descended to son James Noble Jr. James Jr. conveyed to Jonathan Noble.(William and Jonathan Noble of William Noble died in minority so land descended to three daughters Rebecca Noble, Hannah Noble and Elizabeth Noble.
18 Aug.1786 Hannah Dryden devised her maiden dower to son Ephraim Dryden

and grandson James Dryden.
1792 part resurveyed to PADENS PUZZLE 56 3/4 acres, unpatented.
9 Aug.1804 John Peden sold to Stephen Beauchamp son of Stephen, 86 acres.
23 Aug.1805 Stephen Beauchamp sold to Isaac Dryden, all rights.
21 Oct.1806 Robert H. Dryden son of James Dryden sold to Teague Donoho of
Worc. Co. 102 1/4 acres of HACKLEY, TIMBER GROVE & CHERRY GARDEN.
9 March 1805 Robert H. Dryden mortgaged to Michael Cluff part of CHERRY
GARDEN & HACKLEY.
10 June 1806 Teague Donoho sold to Michael Cluff his rights to HACKLEY &
CHERRY GARDEN.

CHERRY HINTON

Patented on 14 March 1680 by William Stevens who assigned it to Francis
Martin, for 150 acres in Asbury, Election district 12, map #21.
1699 Francis Martin gave 150 acres to son John Martin.
Rent Rolls 1666-1723 Possessed by William Brittingham by marriage to the
widow Martin.
1741 John Sterling gave 150 acres to son Joseph Sterling.
22 March 1744 Aaron Sterling bought from brother Joseph.

CHESTNUT RIDGE

Patented 4 July 1677 by William Stevens and assigned to Cornelius Ward
for 100 acres in Lawsons, Election district 8, map #19.
Rent Rolls 1666-1723 possessed by Cornelius Ward.
7 July 1725 Samuel Ward, son of Cornelius, and Mary Ward his wife sold
100 acres to Francis Lord, with WHITE OAK SWAMP & part of CORKE all now
called PUZZLE.
1739 Francis Lord willed to sons Randall Lord and Henry Lord part now
called TROUBLESOME, part of PUZZLE.
28 March 1747 Randall Lord for 5 shillings sold to Henry Lord 75 acres
with WHITE OAK SWAMP & CORK.
15 March 1774 Henry Lord sold 44 acres to John Ward.
1783 tax- Thomas Lord Jr. 75 acres.
27 Aug.1795 John Lord, wife Jemima Lord, Anne Lord and Nathaniel
Dougherty and wife Betty Dougherty sold to Joshua Dougherty 30 1/2 acres,
their rights.
13 June 1796 Stephen Ward of John, wife Leah Ward, sold to Littleton
Johnson of Lame 29 1/4 acres of CORK,CHESTNUT RIDGE,WHITE OAK SWAMP.
17 Feb.1797 Ezekiel Ward sold to Littleton Johnson 27 1/4 acres of CORK,
CHESTNUT RIDGE, LITTLEWORTH, WHITE OAK.
9 Jan 1800 Mary Lord sold rights to Isaac Dougherty
1832 Village Herald newspaper- Easter Dougherty administratrix of Joshua
Dougherty sold to William Ward of Elijah Ward, to pay debts.
14 June 1804 George Davey sold to David Follen 25 acres of LITTLEWORTH &
CHESTNUT RIDGE.
12 May 1804 John Ward Jr. leased to William Johnson son of Littleton
Johnson part during life of John Ward.
21 April 1807 Robert Leatherbury Esq. sheriff, sold to Robert Cluff the
highest bidder, per judgement against William Perkins and Samuel Long 83
acres of NEWTOWN, LITTLE WORTH, CHESTNUT RIDGE & NEGLECT.
31 Dec.1807 John Ward of John, sold to John Taws of William Taws, all
rights.

CHESTNUT RIDGE

Patented in 1737 for 102 acres in Dublin, Election Disrict 4, Map #13.
1759 resurveyed to LITTLE PROFIT.

CHOICE

Patented in 1744 to Aaron Sterling for 20 acres in Asbury, Election
district 12, map #21.
(this land is within the bounds of COMICLE JOKE)

CHOICE

Patented in 1754 by George Pollitt for 42 acres in East Princess Anne,
Election district 15, map #4
9 April 1805 George Furniss sold to James Pollitt, James to support the
wife of George Furniss, mother of James Pollitt during her life. All
rights. Lands of George Pollitt deceased he claims by marrying the widow
of said George Pollitt.

CLONMELL

Patented on 20 Sep.1700 by Ephraim Polk for 100 acres in Dames Quarter,
Election district 11, map #7.
Rent Rolls 1666-1723 possessed by Ephraim Polk
16 Oct 1739 Charles Pollock sold to Joseph Pollock 100 acres (Charles as
lawful heir of Ephraim Pollock.)
16 Aug.1748 Joseph Pollock of Dorcester Co. sold to John Shores and
William Shores 100 acres, with FORLORN HOPE,BALLYHACK, FORLORN HOPE
ADDITION.
(note Clonmell is a city in Ireland)

CLONWELL

Patented on 1 Oct.1696 by Pierce Bray for 40 acres in Brinkleys
southeast, Election district 3, map #14.
Rent Rolls 1666-1723 possessed by Pierce Bray.
17 Nov. 1740 Michael Vestry and Mary Vestry his wife sold to John White
of Pocomoke, 40 acres. (as Edward Bray deceased had two tracts CORK &
CLONWELL, that he willed in 1716 to his sister Mary Bray now wife of
Michael Vestry.
1782 Isaac White willed to daughters Abigail White and Nancy White.
28 May 1798 Josiah Lankford and wife Abigail Lankford sold to Isaac
Riggin 20 acres.
1834 will of Isaac Riggin, to son Stephen Riggin land purchased from
Josiah Lankford and wife, unnamed.

CLOSURE(The)

This 50 acres is part of FIRST CHOICE in Westover.

CLOVERFIELDS

A resurvey from FRIENDS CHOICE & WOODLAND and patented on 2 Oct. 1749 for
1250 acres by David Wilson in East Princess Anne, Election district 15,
map #5.

1750 David Wilson gave part to Zorobable King and the balance to son
David.
7 Nov.1760 David Wilson and wife Nancy Wilson sold 113 acres to Hamilton
Bell.
23 Nov.1765 Zorobable King sold 106 1/2 acres to Dorman Turpin of
CLOVERFIELD,INDIAN BONES & KINGS GLADE.
22 Jun.1768 William Turpin Jr. sold to Zorobable King and Denwood Turpin
1/3rd part of his right of dower of his now wife Betty Turpin (unnamed
land)
22 Nov.1771 Denwood Turpin sold to William Miles 106 acres of land bought
of Zorobable King, no name.
7 Jan 1772 William Miles sold to Isaac Handy land that Denwood Turpin
conveyed to William Miles that he purchased of Samuel Prior and Zorobable
King 106 1/2 acres (unnamed)
16 Dec.1779 David Wilson sold to Sarah Done and Robert Done of
Worc.Co.(this was difficult to read. It was included with a gift of
personal estate)
1783 tax- Rev. Hamilton Bell Sr. 113 3/4 acres
1783 tax- David Wilson 808 1/2 acres
1783 tax- Zorobable King 92 acres
1783 Hamilton Bell willed to son Rev. Hamilton Bell, lands where I live
and plantation on Manokin River (unnamed)
7 May 1786 David Wilson and wife Sarah Wilson of Worc.Co. sold to John
Wilson, all not previously sold with FRIENDS CHOICE & GULLETTS
ADVISEMENT.
20 Dec 1791 Nehemiah King sold to John Wilson DOUBLE PURCHASE, etc. for
John Wilson to convey to Nehemiah King CLOVERFIELD purchased of David
Wilson, which he and wife Peggy Wilson did on same date.
24 Jan.1793 David Wilson of Worc.Co. sold to Richard Henry tract per
conveyance to Isaac Handy deceased by Planner Williams and Samuel Wilson.
1794 Zorobable King willed lands to son Levin King (unnamed)
3 Dec.1795 David Wilson of Worc.Co. sold to Richard Henry Handy, per
agreement of Isaac Handy who died. Lands of William Wilson. no acreage
given.
8 Jan 1805 Richard Henry Handy, wife Elizabeth Handy sold to Littleton
Dennis Teackle.
29 Oct.1807 Littleton Dennis Teackle sold to John Teackle of Georgetown
DC. lands purchased of Richard Henry Handy.
12 May 1810 John Teackle of Georgetown DC sold to John Pershouse of Phil.
Pa. 750 acres of CLOVERFIELDS, CONEY WARREN, WOOLFS HARBOR, BARES CHANCE
& INDIAN BONES.
1810 part possessed by George Wilson Jackson

CLOVERGROUND

Patented in 1763 by Matthias Hobbs for 111 1/2 acres in Mt. Vernon,
Election district 5, map #1
1788 resurveyed to HOBBS CONCLUSION 463 1/4 acres

COAL PIT

Patented in 1748 by John Bedsworth for 50 acres in Brinkleys northwest,
Election district 3, map #4.
1753 resurveyed to PROVIDENCE 215 1/2 acres.
21 March 1787 Samuel Bedsworth sold to Thomas Jones 50 acres with

BEDSWORTHS CHOICE,PROVIDENCE,BALD RIDGE, BRADDOCKS DEFEAT.
17 Apr.1800 Lambert Hyland trustee of the court, by decress sold to
Thomas Jones lands of Samuel Bedsworth.
22 Apr.1800 Thomas Jones,wife Mary Jones sold to William Williams.

COLD RAIN

Patented in 1726 by Thomas Goldsmith for 50 acres in East Princess Anne,
Election district 15, map #5
1783 tax- Matthias Miles 50 acres
25 Nov.1783 William McDorman and wife Mary McDorman sold to Matthias
Miles 50 acres (as Hannah Goldsmith devised to William McDorman.)

COLEBROOK

Patented on 20 Oct.1662 by William Cole for 550 acres in St. Peters,
Election district 2, map #6
Rent Rolls 1666-1723 Possessed by William Turpin in right of George
Jones' orphan who married Richard Whitty, heir, to whom it belongs.
1698 Richard Whitty willed to daughter Sarah Whitty.
1702 George Jones (married Sarah Whitty) willed to son George.
5 Dec.1737 William Turpin and Sarah Turpin (daughter of Richard Whitty)
sold to William McClemmy 550 acres.
1750 William McClemmy willed to son Whitty McClemmy dwelling plantation,
if no heir to son William McClemmy.
27 Aug.1771 William McClemmy sold to George Dashiell son of George, and
Josiah Polk 550 acres. Triparte agreement.
19 Aug.1772 Whitty McClemmy and George Hayward of Worc.Co. sold to Josiah
Polk that William McClemmy willed to Whitty, part of dwelling plantation
35 acres.
21 July 1772 Josiah Polk sold to Ezekiel Gillis his rights. no acreage
mentioned.
1783 tax- Ezekiel Gillis 200 acres
1783 tax- Whitty McClemmy 350 acres.
6 May 1794 William Waller sold to Ezekiel Gillis, with WALLERS ADVENTURE,
Mt.PLEASANT, agrees to boundaries.
17 Feb.1798 George Jones conveyed to Ezekiel McClemmy Gillis devised by
Whitty McClemmy to Ezekiel.
17 Feb.1798 Ezekiel McClemmy Gillis conveyed to George Jones
1827 William Jones Sr. willed to wife Eleanor Jones and then to son
William C.E. Jones.

COLEBURN

Patented on 18 August 1663 by Stephen Horsey for 650 acres in Brinkleys,
northwest, Election district 3, map #14.
Rent Rolls 1666-1723 possessed- 250 acres by Nathaniel Horsey, 150 acres
by Samuel Horsey, 250 acres by Isaac Horsey.
4 Feb.1725 Nathaniel Horsey and wife Sarah Horsey gave 1/3rd part to son
Nathaniel Horsey Jr.
4 Feb.1726 Revel Horsey son of Nathaniel and grandson of Stephen Horsey,
sold to Nathaniel Horsey son of Nathaniel his 1/3rd interest(that Stephen
Horsey willed to his three sons Samuel Horsey,Isaac Horsey and Nathaniel
Horsey father of Revel Horsey.
31 Dec.1731 Isaac Horsey, gave to grand daughter Sarah Outerbridge and

her husband John Outerbridge his interest on the south side of Great
Annemessex where I dwell. 250 acres.
23 Jan.1734 Stephen Horsey son of Stephen deceased for 10 shillings gave
200 acres to Isaac Horsey.
23 Jan.1734 Stephen Horsey son of Stephen gave to John Outerbridge part
for 10 shillings, no acreage mentioned.
15 Sep.1736 Stephen Horsey sold to Michael Holland COULBOURNS BUTTED. 50
acres.
4 Nov.1743 Nathaniel Horsey gave to his only son Outerbridge Horsey 216
acres.
15 April 1745 Stephen Horsey, the elder brother and heir of John Horsey
deceased who was heir at law to his grandfather Stephen Horsey conveyed
426 acres to Nathaniel Horsey the elder.
6 Jan.1745 Outerbridge Horsey sold to John Tunstall 1/3rd (patented
Stephen Horsey great grandfather of Outerbridge being the 1/3rd part that
was deeded by Nathaniel Horsey father of Outerbridge (to be used only
during the lifetime of Outerbridge Horsey)
23 Jan 1744/5 Stephen Horsey sold his 1/3rd for 5 shillings to Samuel
Horsey.
3 May 1746, John Tunstall returned to Outerbridge Horsey the 1/3rd part.
28 Jan.1747/8 Smith Horsey quitclaims all rights to Nathaniel and
Outerbridge Horsey.
1752 Isaac Horsey gave to daughter Sarah Bozman 216 acres.
17 Oct 1748 division of lands between Outerbridge Horsey and Isaac
Horsey.
17 Oct 1748 Isaac Horsey and Jacob Aires and wife Sarah Aires quitclaim
to Outerbridge Horsey.
16 Nov.1748 Jacob Aires, cabinet maker, and wife Sarah Aires (formerly
Sarah Outerbridge the wife of John Outerbridge) sold to Outerbridge
Horsey. 195 acres.
22 Jan 1748, Ann Prior wife of Thomas Prior, Samuel Prior eldest son of
Thomas Prior and John Scott sold to Outerbridge Horsey 24 acres of
COLEBURN, and 100 acres DIXONS KINDNESS, as Samuel Prior laid out
adjacent land 24 acres not patented with PRIORS ADVENTURE, and claim to
BEARS NECK 300 acres patented Robert Dukes (within the tr. COLBURN)
27 Jan. 1749 Outerbridge Horsey sold to Ann Prior, Samuel Prior and John
Scott, BEAR NECK (this was a trade of lands.)24 acres.
6 Nov.1750 Capt. Stephen Horsey Sr, sold 216 acres to Smith Horsey,
merchant, for 5 shillings.
21 Nov.1753 Stephen Horsey sold for 5 shillings to Outerbridge Horsey, no
acres given, description only.
21 Nov.1754 William Outerbridge son of John Outerbridge deceased sold to
Jacob Aires, 195 acres.
26 Jan 1756 William Outerbridge sold to George Bozman 4 acres.
26 Aug.1758 Stephen Horsey son of Samuel Horsey sold for 5 shillings 542
acres of COLEBURN, & HORSEYS CONCLUSION to Outerbridge Horsey.
27 Feb.1764 Michael Holland the elder gave to son Michael part of
PRIVILDEGE,POMFRET, COLEBURN.
18 Mar.1767 Stephen Horsey of Worc.Co. sold to Smith Horsey of Somerset
Co. 108 acres.
7 April 1767 Michael Holland sold to Smith Horsey, 23 acres of COLEBURN &
POMFRET.
1783 tax- George Bozman 22 1/4 acres
1783 tax- Outerbridge Horsey 216 acres
1785 Outerbridge Horsey willed to son William Horsey.

6 Sep.1794 George Bozman sold to Rizdon Bozman 220 acres
1 March 1797 Outerbridge Horsey son of William Horsey and grandson of
Outerbridge sold to William Hitch (William Horsey died before his father
Outberbridge Horsey)
12 March 1797 William Hitch sold to Outerbridge Horsey.
1 Dec.1808 Rizdon Bozman sold 200 acres to Thomas Robertson Jr.
1823 Elizabeth B. Ward purchased from Major William A. Schoolfield 28
acres where Charles Hall lived.
1838 Elizabeth Ward sold the 28 acres to Littleton U. Dennis.

COLEMANS ADVENTURE

Surveyed on 25 Jan.1666 for John Coleman for 500 acres in Dublin,
Election district 4, map #12 and patented in 1679 to Richard Tull.
1688 possessed by Richard Tull
Rent Rolls 1666-1723 possessed 200 acres by George Tull and 300 acres by
Richard Tull.
1710/11 Richard Tull willed 300 acres to son Richard.
1 May 1720 Richard Tull son of Richard, and Naomi Tull his wife gave 300
acres to George Tull.
18 April 1732 George Tull gave to son Noble Tull, part of BECKLES &
COLEMANS ADVENTURE.
21 Dec.1758 Noble Tull and wife Catherine Tull sold 130 acres to Jonathan
Tull.
3 July 1759 Jonathan Tull and wife Mary Tull sold to Isaac Mitchell 13
acres
3 July 1759 Jonathan Tull and wife Mary Tull sold to Samuel Adams 19
acres, with BECKLES & CHANCE.
18 Aug.1763 John Pollitt was appointed guardian of George Tull son of
George. who possessed pt. of COLEMANS ADVENTURE & BECKLES.
21 June 1746 George Tull sold to John Pollitt part of BECKLES & COLEMANS
ADVENTURE, that George Tull willed to son George (no acres given)
5 Feb.1765 George Tull s/o George deceased sold to John Pollitt his
interest in BECKLES & COLEMANS ADVENTURE.
1763 Samuel Adams willed to son Samuel, lands bought of Jonathan Tull 4
March 1771 William Tull and Catherine Tull his mother sold to Samuel
Adams, part BECKLES, COLEMANS ADVENTURE, no acres given.
1783 tax- Jonathan Tull Sr. 133 acres.
3 Oct.1787 John Pollitt sold to Levin Pollitt son of John, of Worc.Co.
his rights to BECKLES & COLEMANS ADVENTURE that George Tull conveyed to
John Pollitt.
15 Nov.1802 Jonathan Tull, wife Sarah Tull sold to Major Levin Pollitt of
Worc.Co. 31 acres.
25 Nov.1806 Joshua Mitchell, wife Nancy Mitchell sold to Joseph Richards
of Worc.Co. 239 1/3 acres of MIDDLESEX & COLEMANS ADVENTURE
29 Jan. 1807 Joseph Richards mortgaged to Joshua Mitchell same as above.
7 Jan.1815 James Boston bought from William Melvin, part.
18 July 1817 James Boston sold to Samuel Taylor.
1836 Levin Pollitt willed to Levin P. Bowland son of John Bowland.

COLLINS ADDITION

A resurvey from KINGS NECK in 1700 by Samuel Collins and patented for 233
acres in Brinkleys southeast, Election district 3, map #14.
1707 Samuel Collins willed to wife Eliza Collins, then to son John

Collins.
Rent Rolls 1666-1723 Samuel Collins.

COLLINS ADVENTURE

Patented in 1748 by Collins Adams for 199 acres in Brinkleys southeast,
Election district 3, map #14.
1755 Collins Adams willed to son Phillip Adams.
27 May 1777 Phillip Adams son of Collins Adams am bound to Jacob Adams
for 500 pounds, that Collins gave to son Phillip Adams,part HOUSTONS
CHOICE, SNOW HILL & COLLINS ADVENTURE.
1783 tax- Samuel Collins 139 acres
1796 patented AMENDMENT 84 acres by Esme Merrill and wife.
1813 Jacob Milbourn willed to son Lodowick Milbourn (home plantation?
1854 Lodowick J. Milbourn willed part to son James Milbourn.

COLLINS LOTT

Patented in 1742 by Samuel Collins for 5 1/4 acres in Brinkleys
southeast, Election district 3, map #16.

COLRANE

Patented on 2 Feb. 1682 in Dublin, Election district 4, map #12 for 200
acres and assigned to James Conner.
Rent Rolls 1666-1723 James Conner knows not this land nor rent paid. He
pretends the right not in him. James Conner and Dorothy Conner his wife
left son Nixon Conner who died at age 16, and son Richard Conner age 22
on 17 June 1742 is about to sell 200 acres and 50 acres of STOOPING PINE
to Benton Harris.
1777 Will of Capt. Benton Harris, land bought of Richard Conner to be
sold.
28 Aug.1779 Frederick Conner of Worc.Co. sold to Matthias Miles of
Somerset Co. 200 acres with STOOPING PINE.
6 Aug.1796 Frederick Conner of Worc.Co. sold to Matthias Miles all of
COLRAIN & pt. STOOPING PINE.
27 Dec.1796 Matthias Miles sold to George Miles 200 acres.
8 Feb.1797 Thomas Hall, Joshua Bowen, Levin Hall, George Hall, James M.
Hall of Worc.Co. sold to Isaac Harris as devised by Benton Harris to
Esther Hall wife of Richard Hall and mother to all afsd.
9 Oct.1798 Robert Hudson of Worc.Co. sold to Isaac Harris of John Harris,
all claim.
1821 Matthias Miles gave to daughter Molly Miles and 41 acres to grand
sons Tubman Jones and John Jones.
31 March 1795 Matthias Miles sold to George Miles 200 acres
1847 William Mills per will gave to wife Sally Mills.

COME AT LAST

Patented in 1741 by William Shores for 10 acres in St. Peters, Election
district 12, map #6.
19 March 1756 William Shores sold to John Shores and Henry Spear 10 acres
with WHITTYS LOTT.

COME BY CHANCE

Patented 14 June 1682 by Christopher Nutter in East Princess Anne, Election district 15, map #5 for 150 acres.
Rent Rolls 1666-1723 Possessed by the widow Margaret Nutter.
1853 Resurveyed to ANNIES DELIGHT, SEDGEWICK, 319 acres.

COME BY CHANCE

Patented on 4 April 1706 by Samuel Davis for 100 acres in Dublin, Election district 4, map #12.
Rent Rolls 1666-1723 possessed by Samuel Davis.
20 March 1720 Samuel Davis son and heir of Samuel Davis, deceased sold to Joseph Ward, planter.
17 Nov.1760 Joseph Ward,gave to son Joseph Ward Jr. 5 acres with PAXEN HILL, 100 acres
1775 Joseph Ward willed to son Joseph 5 or 6 acres
11 March 1775 Rebecca Benston sold to Saul Ward 10 acres on Dividing Creek.
1783 tax- Jesse Ward 80 acres -Dividing Creek 100.
17 Apr 1787 Joseph Ward, wife Elizabeth Ward and Elizabeth Ward sold to John Perkins 121 acres of PAXON HILL, WARWICKS DISCOVERY, COME BY CHANCE, etc.
28 March 1789 John Perkins, wife Rachel Perkins sold to Mary Broughton 216 acres of PAXON HILL,WARDS VENTURE,CROOKED RIDGE,WORTH LITTLE,etc.
17 Apr 1790 Joseph Ward sold 6 acres to Jesse Ward.
7 Feb.1792 Jesse Ward, wife Esther Ward of Worc. Co. sold to John Layfield 86 acres.(Jesse Ward s/o Cornelius and neighbor of Joseph Ward of Joseph) with WARDS VENTURE & LITTLEWORTH.
1799 John Layfield willed to son John Layfield tract bought of Jesse Ward, unnamed.
20 Oct.1807 Mary Broughton gave to son Edward Broughton.
28 March 1808 Thomas Layfield, wife Henny Layfield sold to Isaac Mitchell Adams.
29 March 1808 Isaac Mitchell Adams sold to Josiah W. Heath.

COME BY CHANCE

A resurvey in 1714 by William Polk for 20 acres that was part of FATHERS CARE, in East Princess Anne, Election district 15,map #4.
27 Aug.1739 William Polk gave to son David Polk 10 acres.
5 March 1776 David Polk gave to son Gillis Polk, ROXBERRY,TAMAROONS RIDGE & COME BY CHANCE, no acres given.

COME BY CHANCE

Patented in 1724 by Randal Long for 103 acres in Lawsons, Election district 8, map 18
17 Nov.1762 Randal Long sold to Elijah Coulbourn 6 acres surveyed for Randal Long the elder now deceased in Annamessex.
12 Nov.1767 Randal Long sold to Samuel Kellum 3 acres.
1767 will Randal Long, to mother Sarah Long.
11 Nov.1768 Samuel Kellum sold to Elijah Coulbourn 3 acres with SCOTLAND.
1783 tax- Sarah Long 100 acres.
11 Jan 1790 Elijah Coulbourn Sr, and wife Rachel Coulbourn and John Tull son of James Tull sold to Benjamin Conner (son in law of Elijah

Coulbourn) COMEBY CHANCE with SCOTLAND,POOR SWAMP,ACCIDENT,PUZZLE,BUCK
RIDGE. no acres given
11 Jan 1790 Benjamin Conner sold to Elijah Coulbourn, same.
9 Feb.1810 William Coulbourn of Robert Coulbourn sold to Thomas Merrill
Tull 37 1/4 acres with HOG HAMMOCK & BEARD NECK.

COME BY CHANCE

Patented in 1740 for 150 acres in East Princess Anne, Election district
15, map #4 for 150 acres and was part of GOLDEN QUARTER & LABOUR IN VAIN.
1750 became part of LABOUR IN VAIN 170 acres.

COME BY CHANCE

Patented in 1744 by Robert King for 40 acres on Deal Island, Election
district 14, map #8.
22 Nov.1750 Robert King and wife Ann King sold to James Windsor 40 acres.
1780 will James Windsor, estate to sons James Windsor, Isaac Windsor,
Henry Windsor. Wife Elizabeth Windsor. He mentions COME BY CHANCE and
SMALL ADDITION on Devils Island.

COME BY CHANCE

Patented in 1762 for 19 3/4 acres in East Pr. Anne, Election district 15,
map #4.
13 Oct.1795 Mary Broughton sold to John Layfield, part.

COME BY CHANCE

Patented in 1769 by Matthias Miles for 45 acres in East Princess Anne,
Election district 15, map #5.
1783 tax- Matthias Miles 45 acres in Manokin 100.
1818 will Matthias Miles, to grandsons Tubman Jones and John Jones 26
acres.

COME OUT

Patented in 1816 for 95 acres by Francis White of Francis, on the line
between Tangier and Dames Quarter, elections districts 9 and 11, map #7.

COMFORTS ADVENTURE

Patented in 1707 for 100 acres in Mt.Vernon, Election district 5, map #1
and resurveyed in 1729 for 190 acres by Phillip Covington, of COVINGTONS
ADVENTURE & COVINGTONS COMFORT..
11 Feb 1756 Daniel Jones, wife Elizabeth Jones and Nehemiah Covington,
with wife Betty Covington sold to John Dorman Jr. 42 acres part of
COVINGTONS MEADOW and COMFORTS ADVENTURE that Phillip Covington willed to
son Nehemiah.
6 July 1757 Phillip Covington, Daniel Jones, Nehemiah Covington of
Dorc.Co. sold to Thomas Jones part of three tracts. COVINGTONS
MEADOW,COMFORTS ADVENTURE, SASSAFRAS NECK for a total of 341 acres.
21 Oct.1769 William Rencher Sr, and wife Martha Rencher, sold to Thomas
Roberts 205 acres of COVINGTONS MEADOW, & COMFORTS ADVENTURE.
1783 tax- John Jones for Thomas Jones heirs 28 acres.
1783 tax- Arnold Ballard of Monie 140 acres.

22 Oct 1792 George Jones son of Thomas Jones sold to Thomas Rencher COVINGTONS MEADOW, SASSAFRAS NECK, COMFORTS ADVENTURE, no acreage given.
27 April 1804 William Roberts, wife Sarah Roberts sold to Richard Ingersol 279 acres of COVINGTONS MEADOW, MIDDLE, FATHERS CARE, AND COMFORTS ADVENTURE.
3 Sep.1806 Robert Leatherbury, sheriff sold for debts of Robert Ingersol to John Kirwin 30 acrs of COVINGTONS MEADOW & COMFORTS ADVENTURE.
10 Nov.1807 Richard Ingersol, wife Elizabeth Ingersol, sold to John Kirwin 30 acres afsd land.
11 Feb 1808 Richard Ingersol, wife Elizabeth sold to Jacob Kirwin 147 1/2 acres of COVINGTONS MEADOW & COMFORTS ADVENTURE.
12 Nov.1834 John Kirwin Jr. sold to William A.D. Bounds, that was conveyed from John Kirwin Sr. to John Jr. 33 acres of COMFORTS ADVENTURE and COVINGTONS MEADOW AND COMFORT.

COMICLE JOKE

Patented in 1753 by Joseph Sterling for 26 acres in Asbury,Election district 12, map #21.
1783 tax- Aaron Sterling 26 acres.
1795 will Aaron Sterling, to son Aaron.

COMPLYANCE

see WATKINS POINT

CONCLUSION

Patented in 1717 for 20 acres in Westover, Election district 13, map #11.
1760 John Williams willed to son John 20 acres, if no issue to son Josiah Williams.
1759 resurveyed for John Williams
12 July 1791 John Williams sold to Levin Ballard 20 acres, with WILLIAMS LOTT, NORTH BORDER, FIRST CHOICE, CAIPS MOUTH.
12 July 1791 Levin Ballard sold to John Williams, same as above.

CONCLUSION

Patented on 20 April 1720 by John Caldwell and assigned to Robert Wilson for 138 acres in East Princess Anne, Election district 14, map #4.
1735 Robert Wilson willed to wife Mary Wilson and to brother George Wilson 150 acres and then to son-in-law William Scott.
11 Jan.1752 George Wilson and wife Jane Wilson sold to Thomas Sloss 138 acres.
8 Jun 1753 Thomas Sloss mortgaged to Alexander Hamilton of Philadelphia 138 acres.
22 Dec.1758 Alexander Hamilton of Philadelphia released the mortgage to Thomas Sloss.
1763 Resurveyed by Thomas Sloss.
17 Aug.1775 Thomas Sloss sold to Samuel Miles 138 acres.
1783 tax- Elizabeth Miles 138 acres.
29 May 1782 Samuel Miles, wife Mary Miles sold to Matthias Miles with FRIENDS ADVICE, SAMUELS LOTT.- 138 acres.
1776 resurveyed to GREAT HOPES, 787 acres.

CONCLUSION

A resurvey in 1726 of STREIGHTS, JOHNSTONE, EVERDONS LOTT, etc. by Robert King II for 1500 acres in Westover, Election district 13, map #11.

25 Nov.1741 Thomas Williams quitclaimed to Robert King STREIGHTS and since a resurvey of that land and others called CONCLUSION.

1753 Robert King willed 1566 acres to grandson Thomas King son of Robert King Jr.

21 Feb 1775 Thomas King sold 73 acres to Thomas Robertson.

1783 tax- Thomas King 1500 acres.

1783 tax- John Williams 73 acres.

1783 tax- Levin Boston

12 Feb 1785 Thomas King traded Levin Boston 102 acres of CONCLUSION & LONG LOTT for same of BOSTONS CHANCE.

19 Jan 1787 Levin Boston sold to Thomas King 8 1/8 acres.

19 Jan 1787 Levin Boston sold 8 1/4 acres to John Milbourn.

19 Dec.1791 Levin Boston exchanged 14 acres with Thomas King for 10 acres of LONG LOTT.

16 Dec.1802 Henry James Carroll,wife Elizabeth Barnes Carroll sold to Robert Jenkins King land inherited by Elizabeth Barnes Carroll by her father Thomas King, unnamed at head of Gr. Annamessex River.

16 Dec.1802 Dr. Robert Jenkins King sold to Henry James Carroll Sr. lands of Thomas King 800 acres

16 Dec 1802 Dr. Robert Jenkins King sold to Henry James Carroll Sr., on road from Rehobeth to Pr.Anne town 800 acres, unnamed (could be other lands)

2 Aug 1804 Levin Boston sold to William Williams 102 acres bought from Thomas King.

29 Aug.1806 Levin Boston sold to William Williams 102 acres CONCLUSION & LONGS LOTT.

This was the sight of KINGSTON HALL. 19 Sep 1837 the Court of Somerset sold for debts to John W. Dennis.

29 Aug.1806 Levin Boston sold to William Williams 102 acres of CONCLUSION & LONGS LOTT.

CONCLUSION

Patented in 1734 for William Polk for 85 acres in East Princess Anne Election district 15, map #5.

1783 tax- James Polk 85 acres.

1795 resurveyed by William Polk that included SMITHS RESOLVE for a total of 380 acres.

1802 William Polk gave to son Samuel Polk (no acreage mentioned)

CONCLUSION

Patented in 1751 by Ann Prior for 47 acres in Brinkleys. southwest, Election district 3, map #17.

1772 will of Ann (Long) Prior (widow of Thomas Prior) to son Randal Prior.

1783 tax- William Cottingham for heirs of Randal Prior.

20 Feb 1787 Thomas Prior sold to Kellum Lankford 16 acres.

CONCLUSION

Patented in 1751 for Thomas Holbrook 459 acres in Mt. Vernon, Election district 5, map #1, a resurvey from HARRINGTON.
13 Aug.1808 Daniel Ballard, sheriff sold to Zadock Long 81 1/2 acres of CONCLUSION, LAST VACANCY, FLOWERFIELDS per judgement against Thomas Holbrook.

CONCLUSION

Resurveyed from CHANCE in 1754 for 226 acres in St. Peters, Election district 2 map #6.

CONCLUSION

Patented in 1769 for 19 3/4 acres by William Miles in East Princess Anne Election district 15, map #5.

CONCLUSION

Patented in 1789 by Henry Walston for 5 acres. This land has not been located on Benstons maps.
1796 Henry Walston willed, lands in Muddy Hole to son David Walston (unnamed)

CONCLUSION

This land was surveyed but not patented in 1793 by William Waller from part of WALLERS ADVENTURE & FRIENDS ADVICE for 6 3/4 acres in St. Peters, Election district 2, map #6.

CONCLUSION

A resurvey in 1797 from INTENT & LOTT & WRIGHTS FOLLY by Gowan Wright for 307 1/4 acres in St. Peters, Election district 2, map #6.
1805 Gowan Wright willed to daughters Mary Wright, Sarah Wright and Ann Wright, land unnamed.
10 June 1806 Thomas White, wife Nancy White, Sarah Wright and Molly Wright agree to divide the lands of Gowan Wright deceased, CONCLUSION, SUCESS, 62 acres, 88 acres and 30 acres of marsh.

CONDOQUE

Surveyed on 4 Nov.1668 by William Stevens for 100 acres and assigned to Phillip Conner in Brinkleys, southwest, Election district 3, map #17.
Rent Rolls 1666-1723 possessed 50 acres by the widow of Phillip Conner and 50 acres by John Outten.
1703 Phillip Conner died and left a wife Mary Conner.
1735/6 John Outten Jr, willed to son Purnell Outten 50 acres which his father had alienated from Phillip Conner.
1769 Phillip Adams willed to grandson Phillip Adams son of Thomas Adams, 25 acres CONDOQUE MARSH and to daughter Grace Marshall 25 acres of same.
19 Nov.1741 William Conner and wife Mary Conner sold to John Conner, that Phillip Conner gave to his son William, 50 acres.
1783 tax- Purnell Outten
1783 tax- Isabelle Conway 50 acres.
1795 Purnell Outten willed lands to son Purnell(unnamed)
6 April 1810 John Conner sold to Henry James Carroll.

1831 Thomas Adams gave to son Samuel Adams 1/2 of land purchased of John
Conner and balance to daughter Eleanor Gillis Smith (Eleanor Adams mar.
James Smith) CONDOCKAWAY excepting the Isle called THE PLANTING ISLAND.

CONEY WARREN

Patented on 29 Oct. 1674 by John King for 125 acres in East Princess
Anne, Election district 15, map #5.
1696 John King willed to son John.
Rent Rolls 1666-1723 John King 125 acres.
2 Mar.1743 Whittington King and wife Eleanor King sold to Daniel Long,
patented John King father of Whittington.
24 Mar 1749 Daniel Long sold to George Gale surviving trustee of Samuel
Chase grandson of Thomas Walker deceased, who by appointment of said
Thomas Walker by will devised to Samuel Chase certain lands to Jacob
Sarly with the payment thereof to go to Chase, with BENJAMINS ADVICE. -
mortgage.
22 Feb 1758 Daniel Long quitclaimed his right to Solomon Long 125 acres
(heretofore mortgaged to Col. George Gale)
4 Apr. 1758 Solomon Long mortgaged 125 acres to Thomas Prior.
5 Jan 1768 John King and wife Ann King sold to Isaac Handy 125 acres.
17 Nov.1768 Thomas Prior and wife Esther Prior sold the mortgage to Isaac
Handy, 125 acres.
8 Jan.1805 Richard Henry Handy, wife Elizabeth sold to Littleton Dennis
Teackle, as heir to Isaac Handy Esq.
29 Oct.1807 Littleton Dennis Teackle sold to John Teackle of Georgetown
DC land purchased from Richard Henry Handy, unnamed.

CONSOLIDATION

Patented in 1791 by Hannah Polk, as resurvey of ROXBOROUGH & MATTHIAS
CHOICE, for 820 3/4 acres in East Princess Anne, Election district 15,
map #4.

CONTENT

Patented in 1714 by Thomas Newbold for 77 acres in Dublin, Election
district 4, map #13.
3 Feb. 1767 Purnell Newbold sold to Samuel Wilson 77 acres with
ACQUANTICO & FRIENDSHIP.
1775 resurveyed to COW PASTURE 112 acres.
19 Nov.1795 Major Samuel Wilson,wife Leah Wilson sold to Littleton Dennis
815 acres with ACQUINTICA, COW PASTURE,HOGYARD,GREEN MEADOW,NEWTOWN, etc.

CONTENT

Patented in 1762 by Matthew Puckam for 30 acres in East Pr. Anne,
Election district 5, map #4
21 Feb 1743 Charles Redding sold to Joseph Dashiell 50 acres CHANCE and
30 acres of CONTENT sold to Charles Redding by Matthew Puckam and Richard
Puckam.
2 Apr.1771 Matthew Puckam sold to Charles Redding 30 acres.
2 Apr. 1771 Charles Redding and wife Esther Redding sold to John Johnson
30 acres with CHANCE.
1783 tax- Jonathan Stanford 30 acres.
8 Aug.1807 John Johnson sold to Elzey Maddux 30 acres with CHANCE.

CONTENTION

Patented on 1 Feb 1666 by Edward Dickerson a resurvey from DICKSTON for 300 acres in Westover, Election district 13, map #11.

Rent Rolls 1666-1723 Possessed by Somerset Dickerson the heir and Thomas Beauchamp.

12 Jun 1668 Edward Dickerson and wife Elizabeth Dickerson sold to Edmund Beauchamp 300 acres.

2 Oct 1669 Edmund Beauchamp gave to wife Sarah Beauchamp, alias Sarah Dixon daughter of Ambrose Dixon and Mary Dixon.

1716/7 Thomas Beauchamp son of Edward Beauchamp willed to sons Isaac Beauchamp and John Beauchamp. no acreage mentioned.

1733 Edmund Beauchamp son of Edmund Beauchamp willed to wife Sarah Beauchamp - no acreage mentioned.

18 June 1734 William Beauchamp gave to brother John Beauchamp all rights to fathers dwelling house and plantation at head of Annamessex River.(unnamed)

1 Oct.1744 William Beauchamp and wife Comfort Beauchamp sold to Robert King 1 acre with 5 acres of JOHNSTON.

13 Oct.1744 William Beauchamp and wife Comfort Beauchamp sold 92 acres to Isaac Beauchamp for 10 shillings.

20 Aug. 1746 John Williams quitclaimed all right to Isaac Beauchamp for HARTFORD BROAD OAK.

1783 tax- Sarah Beauchamp 168 acres

1783 tax- Jean Beauchamp 45 acres.

12 July 1784 Isaac Beauchamp sold 18 acres to Thomas Jones and wife Mary Jones and then to the heirs of said Mary Jones.

CONTENTION

Patented on 9 Feb 1672 by John Renshaw for 100 acres in St.Peters, Election district 2, map #6

1695 Interest granted to Henry Wright by John Renshaw.

5 Jan 1743 David Pollock of Dorc. Co. sold 7 acres to Thomas Wright of Som. Co. part CONTENTION on east side of Little Creek.

8 Nov.1747 David Pollock of Dorc. Co. sold to Henry Wright 100 acres except 7 acres POLKS FOLLY sold to Thomas Wright.

1748 Thomas Wright willed to son Henry Wright all right to land that was bought of David Polk 100 acres and to son Gowan Wright and 100 acres to son Thomas Wright.

18 Jun.1754 Henry Wright and wife Mary Wright sold to brother Thomas Wright, 50 acres.

17 Dec.1762 Thomas Wright once of Somerset County but now of Ann Arundel Co. sold to Thomas Akeman, part of CONTENTION & INTENT, no acres given.

2 May 1775 John Wright son of Henry Wright deceased, sold to Gowan Wright 242 acres that Thomas Wright willed in 1750 to son Henry to make over to Gowan his right to land bought of David Polk and Henry Wright died before conveying.

1783 tax- Gowan Wright 50 acres.

1783 tax- Thomas Akeman 26 1/2 acres with DISCOVERY.

1783 tax- Robert Cavanaugh 95 acres with INTENT.

24 April 1800 Whittington White, wife Tabby White sold to Thomas White of Francis White 36 acres.

2 Sep.1800 John Webb,wife Hetty Webb sold to Thomas Noble with WELL MENT,

DISCOVERY, INTENT.
1805 Gowan Wright willed lands to daughters Mary Wright, Sarah Wright and
Ann Wright- no name.

CONTENTION

Patented on 5 Feb 1674 by John Bozman and assigned to Lazarus Maddux in
Fairmount, Election district 6, map #9, 100 acres.
Rent Rolls 1666-1723 possessed by Lazarus Maddux. 100 acres
1679 resurveyed to MADDUX ADVENTURE 150 acres.

CONTENTION
see HOLLOWELL & BOYCES BRANCH, 30 acres.

CONTENTION

Patented in 1737 by Matthew Wallace for 50 acres in West Pr. Anne,
Election district 1, map #2.
11 Jun.1771 Thomas Gillis willed 50 acres to son Joseph Gillis, with
GILLIS DOUBLE PURCHASE,WHITE CHAPEL,END OF STRIFE.

CONTENTION

Patented in 1791 by Thomas Sudler for 4 acres in Westover, Election
district 13, map #11.

CONVENIENCE

Patented in 1739 by Jeffrey Long for 25 acres in Brinkleys southwest,
Election district 3, map #17
1762 Jeffrey Long willed to daughter Orpha Brittingham land below
COULBOURNS LONGS (not named)
1783 tax- Nehemiah Turpin 25 acres.
2 Jan 1787 Orpha Turpin gave to son William Turpin all rights she is
entitled to CONVIENCY as heir of Jeffrey Long.

CONVENIENCE

Patented in 1794 by George Waggaman for 1 3/4 acres in Mt.Vernon,
Election district 5, map #1.
20 Aug.1803 Henry Waggaman and wife Sarah Waggaman of Dorc.Co. sold to
Levin Jones, joiner.
8 July 1806 Levin Dashiell Jones sold to Matthias Hobbs 47 1/2 acres of
CUMBERLAND, ADDITION,WAGGAMANS CONCLUSION, GOOD LUCK & CONVENIENCE.

CONVENIENCY

Patented on 13 Dec.1701 by Richard Waters for 80 acres in Fairmount,
Election district 6, map #9.
Rent Rolls 1666-1723- Richard Waters.
1720 Richard Waters willed land to sons William Waters Richard Waters and
Littleton Waters.(this land not named)
1732 William Waters names son Richard Waters, brother Littleton Waters
and daughters Sarah Waters and Eliza Waters.
1783 tax- Richard Waters 80 acres.

8 Nov 1786 Richard Waters Sr. sold to William Waters Sr., divised Richard
Waters by his father William Waters (this is a division of lands.)

CONVENIENCY

Patented in 1721 by James Strawbridge, a resurvey from ILLCHESTER, for
100 acres in East Princess Anne, Election district 15, map #5.
Rent Rolls 166-1723 James Strawbridge 100 acres.
1766 William Strawbridge gave to daughter Jane Strawbridge who died
intestate by 1796 and the lands were sold.
1783 tax- William Strawbridge 100 acres.
17 Oct 1794 Sarah Porter and William Porter sold to William Davis Allen
for 5 shillings land they became possessed at the death of Jane
Strawbridge d/o Dr. William Strawbidge and in right of her grandmother
Mary Williams half sister to Dr. William Strawbridge. WIDOWS CHANGE,
CONVIENCY, ADDITION, LITTLE LESS & LEAST.
15 Apr.1796 John Williams of Worc.Co. Co. and William Davis Allen sold to
William Davis Allen.

CONVENIENCY

Patented in 1722 or 60 acres in Brinkleys southwest, Election district 3,
map #17.
15 April 1791 Merrill Maddux mortgaged to Nathan Cahoon 206 1/2 acres
with RUSCOMMON & MITCHELLS CHOICE.

CONVENIENCY

A resurvey on 26 May 1755 from WINDERS PURCHASE, for 344 acres in
Westover, Election district 13, map #11 by Ephraim Wilson.
14 June 1735 Nicholas Fountain and wife Tabitha Fountain sold 5 acres to
William Turpin son of William
14 March 1755 Marcy Fountain sold to Ephraim Wilson.
19 Feb.1757 Ephraim Wilson and wife Mary Wilson sold to William Fountain
45 acres.
1777 Ephraim Wilson willed to daughter Henrietta Wilson land bought of
Marcy Fountain, with COW QUARTER.
1783 tax- Robert J. Henry 134 1/2 acres
3 June 1800 Dr. Arnold Elzey, wife Henrietta Elzey (daughter of Ephraim
Wilson) sold to Josiah Furniss.
11 Dec 1798 Josiah Furniss sold to James Wilson 344 1/2 acres.
1853 Josiah Furniss gave to sons Thomas J. Furniss and Edward F. Furniss.

CORBY

see LAST CHOICE-Day Scott 1747 to Edward Corby.

CORK

Patented on 12 Sep.1678 by William Stevens for 500 acres and assigned to
Cornelius Ward in Lawsons, Election district 8, map #19.
7 July 1725 Samuel Ward son of Cornelius Ward and Mary Ward his wife sold
to Francis Lord 150 acres with CHESTNUT RIDGE & WHITE OAK SWAMP, and a
part of CORK all now called PUZZLE.
9 Oct.1743 William Ward sold to John Ward 100 acres. that Cornelius Ward

willed on 27 Dec.1722 to son Stephen Ward 100 acres and if no issue to William Ward son of Samuel Ward. Stephen Ward died and William possessed 100 acres excepting 1/3rd part held by the widow of Stephen during her lifetime.

28 Mar.1747 Randall Lord gave to Henry Lord his brother 75 (sons of Francis Lord) part of CHESTNUT RIDGE & WHITE OAK SWAMP, CORK called PUZZLE, this part now called TROUBLESOME.

13 Nov.1751 John Ward sold 25 acres to Joseph Ward.

15 Oct.1768 Cornelius Ward Sr. and Cornelius Ward Jr. sold 25 acres to James Ward son of Cornelius Sr. with PRICES CONCLUSION,WHITE OAK SWAMP.

20 May 1772 John Ward purchased from Henry Lord 31 acres of CORK & CHESTNUT RIDGE.

5 Jun 1784 John Ward and Ann Ward sold to John King and Sarah King his wife. 15 acres for 10 shillings.

14 Jun 1784 Cornelius Ward Sr. sold to John Ward and Ann Ward 25 acres with 8 acres of FOLLY.

5 Jun.1784 William Ward sold to Cornelius Ward Sr. 25 acres with 8 acres of FOLLY.

19 Dec 1784 Matthias Ward sold 25 acres to Stephen Ward.

18 July 1788 Stephen Ward sold to Levi Miles his rights to CORK & LITTLEWORTH.

5 Mar 1790 Jonathan Riggin sold to Elisha Riggin for his maintenance, his interest in CORK, no acreage mentioned.

5 Mar.1790 John Ward Sr. sold for 5 shilings to Joseph Ward, with FOLLY, no acreage given.

1791 William Ward, willed to son William land bought of brother William Ward 100 acres, unnamed.

1783 tax- James Ward 25 acres
1783 tax- William Ward 50 acres
1783 tax- Samuel Ward 50 acres
1783 tax- William Ward 25 acres
1783 tax- John Ward 100 acres
1783 tax- Cornelius Ward 25 acres
1783 tax- John King 8 acres
1783 tax- Jonathan Riggin 25 acres
1783 tax- Samuel Lawson 50 acres
1783 tax- John Taws 15 acres

3 Nov.1794 Joshua Ward, wife Lydia Ward sold to Joseph Ward 25 acres.

27 Aug.1795 John Lord,wife Jemima Lord, Anne Lord and Nathaniel Dougherty and wife Betty Dougherty sold to Joshua Dougherty 30 1/2 acres CHESTNUT RIDGE,CORK,WHITE OAK SWAMP.

13 June 1796 Stephen Ward of John Ward, and wife Leah Ward sold to Littleton Johnson of Lame Johnson 29 1/4 acres of CORK,CHESTNUT RIDGE & WHITE OAK SWAMP.

17 Feb. 1797 Ezekiel Ward sold to Littleton Johnson 27 1/4 acres CORK,CHESTNUT RIDGE,LITTLEWORTH,WHITE OAK SWAMP.

17 Feb 1797 Hance Croswell sold to Ezekiel Ward 5 acres of FOLLY, WHITE OAK & CORK.

18 Apr. 1797 Levi Miles sold to James Turner 1 acre.

18 Apr. 1797 Joseph Ward sold to Hance Croswell CORK & FOLLY 30 acres.

18 Apr.1797 Levi Miles sold to George Davey 1 acre

18 Apr.1797 John Knipe sold to George Davey 15 acres.

18 Apr.1797 George Davey sold to John Knisse and wife Sarah Knisse during their lives.

1798 will William Ward, son John executor, to wife Martha Ward my fathers

manor plantation (unnamed).
8 March 1799 Stephen Ward of Matthias Ward and Ezekiel Ward sold to George Davey 25 acres.
9 Jan 1800 Mary Lord sold to Isaac Dougherty all rights in CORK,CHESTNUT RIDGE,WHITE OAK SWAMP,& CORK.
2 Aug. 1804 Elisha Riggin sold to Capt. Aaron Sterling 25 acres.
12 May 1804 John Ward Jr. leased to William Johnson son of Littleton Johnson, part.
22 Sep 1804 Samuel Ward sold 20 acres to Joseph Ward Jr.
10 May 1805 Joseph Ward son of Joseph, wife Martha Ward, sold 4 acres to Isaac Riggin.
29 June 1805 Joseph Ward (of Anne Ward) wife Martha Ward sold to Isaac Riggin 4 acres.
11 May 1805 Levi Miles sold to George Davey 10 acres.
9 Nov.1805 Joseph Ward (of Anne Ward) wife Martha Ward, sold to Isaac Riggin 4 acres.
25 Aug.1806 John Miles, constable of Little Annamessex sold to William Roach 15 acres lands of Joseph Ward.
25 Aug.1806 Samuel Ward sold to John Lord 40 or 50 acres of CORK, BAKERS LOTT & WHITE OAK.
31 Dec.1807 Ezekiel Taws sold to John Ward of William Ward, 9 acres.
6 Dec.1807 Levi Miles sold 6 acres to Stephen Ward.
10 Jn 1807 Joseph Ward (of Anne Ward) sold to Mary Ward and Nancy Ward for 30 years part where he lives.
10 Jan 1807 Mary Ward and Nancy Ward sold to John ward of William Ward.
10 Jan 1807 William Roach sold to Joseph Ward of Joseph Ward 30 acres.
11 June 1808 Traves Sterling Jr. wife Leah Sterling (Leah Ward) sold to William Roach, claim to lands of Stephen Ward in Little Annamessex, no name.
4 June 1808 John Miles, constable, sold to William Roach, per judgement against Levi Miles, with LITTLEWORTH.
13 Aug.1808 John Miles, constable, sold to William Ward 100 acres, lands of Ezekiel Ward, DUBLIN, CORK, WHITE OAK SWAMP.
18 March 1809 James Turner, wife Mary Turner sold to Thomas Smallwood Cottingham, purchased of Levi Miles.
17 May 1809 George Davey sold 10 acres to James Montgomery.
9 June 1810 William Roach sold all rights to James Montgomery.
5 July 1810 Isaac Denson, wife Rhoda Denson, sold to John Huston of Worc.Co. 53 1/4 acres.
Dec 1832 Village Herald Newspaper Ad. Esther Doughtery admx. of Joshua Dougherty tract CORK taken from William Ward of Elijah Ward, to settle debts; to be sold.

CORK

Patented on 2 Apr.1707 by Pierce Bray for 200 acres in Brinkleys southeast, Election district 3, map #16.
Rent Rolls 1666-1723 Pierce Bray.
1713 Pierce Bray willed to son John White and Archibald White orphan of Archibald White 62 acres part of CORK.(Archibald White married Mary Bray)
17 Nov.1740 Michael Vestry and Mary Bray Vestry his wife sold to John White of Pocomoke two tracts patented Edward Bray who willed 5 May 1716 to sister Mary Bray 100 acres CORK and CLOMELL.

1750 Resurveyed to ADDITION TO BROTHERS LOVE 415 acres according to Benson's Maps.
21 March 1770 Isaac White son of Henry White sold to Elijah Matthews 100 acres part now called SONS CHOICE, once BROTHERS LOVE.
1772 Isaac White willed 40 acres to daughter Abigail White and to daughter Nancy White.
1789 William White willed to son Robert White(no acreage given)
13 Aug.1790 Elijah Matthews sold to Stephen Collins 100 acres of BROTHER LOVE & CORK with MEADOW & ADVENTURE.
1 Feb 1797 Josiah Lankford and wife Abigail Lankford sold to Stephen Collins 40 acres given Abigail by her father Isaac White.

CORNER

Surveyed in 1795 by Revel Hayman for 4 acres. Cannot locate on maps but believed to be in East Princess Anne District.
7 Feb.1797 Sarah Hayman sold to John Hitch, that Revel Hayman willed in 1796 to wife Sarah Hayman to be sold to pay debts. She sold 2 acres of CORNER and all her claim to CHARLES CHANCE,LAST CHOICE.

CORPORALLS RIDGE

Patented 3 Aug.1687 by Charles Jones and Assigned to Henry Smith for 50 acres in East Princess Anne, Election district 15, map #5.
Rent Rolls 1666-1723 William Smith son of Thomas Smith 50 acres,
1697 Thomas Smith willed to son John.
8 Feb.1743 Thomas Smith son of Robert Smith deceased sell 50 acres to William Walton with part of HARTHBERRY.
1750 resurveyed to WALTONS IMPROVEMENT 294 acres.

CORRECTION

Patented in 1792 for 9 acres by Samuel Smith in Brinkleys, Election district 3, map #15.
1813 Samuel Smith willed lands to sons James Smith, Samuel Smith and to daughter Rosanna Smith.

COSTONS BAY SIDE

Patented in 1759 by Matthias Coston and resurveyed in 1768 for 81 acres in Brinkleys southeast, Election district 3, map #14.
1783 tax- Levi Riggin 59 1/2 acre.

COSTINS CARE

A resurvey of COSTONS TROUBLE by Matthias Coston in 1794 and patented for 553 acres in Dublin, Election district 4, map #12.
19 Nov.1799 Matthias Coston sold to Isaac Coston 11 acres.
1803 Matthias Coston willed to son William Coston.

COSTONS TROUBLE

Patented on 11 Jun 1679 and assigned Henry Coston for 450 acres in Dublin, Election district 4, map #12.

1696 Stephen Coston willed to sons Isaac 100 acres and to son Stephen Coston 300 acres.

Rent Rolls 1666-1723 300 acres by Peter Benton and 150 acres by John Tull.

1715 Matthias Coston of Dorcester County willed to daughter Rebecca Coston 50 acres.(she married Thomas Perkins.)

1729 John Tull and wife Esther Tull(was Esther Coston daughter of Stephen Coston) gave lands (unnamed) to sons Richard Tull, Stephen Tull, Joshua Tull and John Tull.

1728 Peter Benton who married Comfort Coston widow of Stephen Coston who willed COSTONS TROUBLE to sons Isaac Coston and daughters Elizabeth Coston and Esther Coston.

14 Apr.1740 Thomas Perkins and Rebecca Perkins his wife sold to Stephen Coston of Stephen, 50 acres.

1743 Isaac Coston son of Stephen Coston willed 100 acres to son Isaac Coston.

21 Feb.1748 Stephen Coston sold 200 acres to Matthias Coston.

23 Nov.1749/50 Stephen Coston, wife Rodiah Coston sold to Matthias Coston, joyner 350 acres.

16 March 1757 Isaac Coston and wife Sarah Coston sold to Benjamin Cottman 47 acres with COSTONS VINEYARD.

20 Jun 1764 Benjamin Cottman and wife Sophia Cottman sold 25 acres to Matthias Coston.

22 March 1769 Benjamin Cottman and wife Sophia Cottman sold 19 1/2 acres to Levin Maddux, part with COSTONS VINEYARD.

12 Dec.1769 Matthias Coston sold to Isaac Coston(agreement to partition) as Stephen Coston grandfather of Matthias Coston and Isaac Coston and and he willed in 1697 to son Isaac father of Isaac Coston 100 acres and to his son Stephen Coston 300 acres of same and said Isaac Coston father of Isaac willed in 1743 to son Isaac Coston 100 acres and Stephen Coston father of afsd. Matthias Coston died intestate and his part fell to his son Stephen Coston brother of Matthias. Stephen Coston conveyed to brother Matthias Coston.

22 Mar 1770 Oliver Coston, grandson of Isaac Coston deceased sold to Matthias Coston nephew of Isaac 25 acres that Isaac Coston willed in 1743 to son Isaac but not to his heirs, and his son Isaac conveyed part to Benjamin Cottman who conveyed to Matthias Coston. Isaac Coston deceased and by law descends to the heirs of his brother Ahab Coston and Oliver afsd. being present heir of Ahab Coston, knowing it was his grandfather Isaac Coston's intent to leave part of tract to Isaac Coston.

22 Mar.1770 Oliver Coston sold to Isaac Coston for 5 shillings 53 acres(division of lands.)

20 Nov.1782 Levin Maddux and Oliver Coston sold for 5 shillings rights to Matthias Coston, no acreage given.

1783 tax- Sarah Coston 35 acres

1783 tax- Matthias Coston 397 acres

1794 resurveyed to COSTONS CARE 553 acres.

2 March 1795 John Spencer and wife Frances Spencer and Thomas Barns and wife Sophira Barns of Worc.Co. sold to Levin Maddux lands belonging to Benjamin Cottman by any name 67 1/3 acres.

1803 Matthias Coston willed to son William Coston both tracts COSTONS TROUBLE & COSTONS CARE.

19 May 1804 Isaac Mitchell Adams and Burton Cannon and wife Sally Cannon sold to Matthias Coston, part.

24 June 1808 John Williams of Worc.Co., sold to Sarah Cannon wife of

Burton Cannon (formerly Sarah Adams) that John Williams in 1796 gave bond to Sally Adams, for lands willed to Isaac Costen by father Isaac coston, and lands willed by Henry Coston to Sarah Coston, in Dividing Creek, no name or acreage.

COSTONS VENTURE

Patented in 1751 by Benton Coston for 78 acres in Dublin, Election district 4, map #12.
5 Apr.1753 Benton Coston and wife Elizabeth Coston sold 78 acres to Joseph Cottman, also called WINTER QUARTER.
22 Sep 1783 Joseph Cottman sold to Matthias Coston part 1 1/4 acres (trade for ADDITION TO BEACH RIDGE)
1783 tax- Joseph Cottman
1788 resurveyed for 140 1/2 acres
15 Mar.1787 Joseph Cottman, wife Margaret Cottman sold to Samuel Miles 4 acres with GLADE SWAMP.
11 Sep.1810 George Miles of Samuel Miles, of Worc.Co. sold to Isaac M. Adams.

COSTONS VINEYARD

Patented in 1732 by Isaac Coston for 100 acres in Dublin, Election district 4, map #12.
1756 Ahab Coston sold to Benjamin Cottman.
16 March 1757 Isaac Coston, wife Sarah Coston sold to Benjamin Cottman 91a. with COSTONS TROUBLE.
22 March 1769 Benjamin Cottman and wife Sophia Cottman sold 36 3/4 acres to Levin Maddux with COSTONS TROUBLE.
1783 tax- Sarah Coston 29 acres
1783 tax- Levin Maddux
1783 tax- Benjamin Cottman 52 acres.
3 March 1795 John Spencer and wife Frances Spencer and Thomas Barns, wife Sophira Barns of Worc.Co. sold to Levin Maddux lands belonging to Benjamin Cottman by any name 67 1/3 acres.
16 Oct.1798 Levin Maddux, wife Polly Maddux, sold to William Cottman 21 acres.
17 Aug.1799 William Cottman,wife Ann Cottman sold to Levin Maddux 13 1/4 acres.

COTTINGHAMS CHANCE

Patented in 1748 by Thomas Cottingham for 40 acres in Brinkleys southwest, Election district 3, map #17.

COTTINGHAMS LOTT

Patented in 1771 by David Cottingham for 6 acres. Not found on Benson's maps.

COTTMANS FREEHOLD

Patented in 1751 by Benjamin Cottman for 86 acres in Mt. Vernon, Election district 5, map #1.
26 April 1768 Benjamin Cottman and wife Jane Cottman sold to Joseph Cottman.
1783 tax- Joseph Cottman 74 acres
1783 tax- Benjamin Cottman 12 acres

COTTMANS POINT

Patented on 29 April 1680 by William Stevens and assigned to Benjamin Cottman, in Mt.Vernon, Election district 5, map #1.
Rent Rolls 1666-1723 Possessed by Benjamin Nesham who married the widow Cottman. 50 acres.
31 Oct 1734 Benjamin Cottman gave to Benjamin Cottman Jr, now of Pennsylvania, 50 acres
7 Feb.1743 Benjamin Cottman the younger, of Philadelphia County Pa. sold to Joseph Cottman of Somerset Co. 236 acres.
50 acres of COTTMANS POINT and TANTON DEANE.
1783 tax- Joseph Cottman 50 acres
1819 resurveyed to Mt.PLEASANT 763 1/2 acres.

COTTMANS PURCHASE

Patented in 1769 by Benjamin Cottman for 31 acres in Mt.Vernon, Election district 5, map #1.
1703 tax- Benjamin Cottman 31 acres.

COTTMANS VENTURE

Patented in 1760 by Benjamin Cottman for 69 acres in Mt. Vernon, Election district 5, map #1.
1783 tax- Benjamin Cottman 69 acres.

COULBOURNS RIDGE

Patented in 1746 by Edward Scandell in Lawsons district, Election district 8, map #18.
21 Nov.1752 Edward Scandell sold to Thomas Ward 100 acres.
3 Nov.1766 Thomas Ward and William Ward sold 65 acres to Smith Horsey.
1804 resurveyed to GREAT ANNAMESSEX 832 acres by Samuel Horsey.

COVINTONS ADVENTURE

Patented in 1755 by Nehemiah Covington and Phillip Covington for 60 acres in Mt.Vernon, Election district 5, map #1.
20 June 1759 Nehemiah Covington and wife Betty Covington of Dorcester County and Daniel Jones, wife Elizabeth Jones of Somerset Co. sold to Phillip Covington all interest in land in Som.Co. at Money Creek, 60 acres with SWEETWOOD.
9 July 1766 Mary Covington admx. of Phillip Covington deceased sold 60 acres to Levin Gale, the highest bidder with COVINGTONS CONCLUSION & SWEETWOOD.
1783 tax- Levin Gale 60 acres.
25 Oct 1800 Littleton Gale of Cecil Co. Md. sold to Levin Jones, and John Leatherbury of Somerset Co. 650 acres of COVINGTONS CONCLUSION, COVINGTONS ADVENTURE & SWEETWOOD
18 May 1801 Samuel Wilson and wife Leah Wilson (late Leah Gale) sold to Levin Jones and John Leatherbury her claim.

COVINTONS ADVENTURE

Patented on 10 Nov. 1707 by Phillip Covington in Mt.Vernon, for 100

acres, Election district 5, map #1.
1729 resurveyed to COMFORTS ADVENTURE.190 acres.
1783 tax- Thomas Roberts with Covingtons Meadow 205 acres.

COVINGTONS COMFORT

Patented on 6 May 1706 by Nehemiah Covington for 180 acres in
Mt.Vernon,Election district 5, map #1.
Rent Rolls 1666-1723 Phillip Covington.
1710 Nehemiah Covington willed to wife Rebecca Covington and then to son
Levin Covington and daughters Sarah Lloyd, Elizabeth Wailes and Eliza
Covington.
10 Oct.1727 Margery Covington of Pr. George Co. Md. executrix of Levin
Covington deceased, sold to Phillip Covington of Somerset Co. 3 tracts
COVINGTONS VINEYARD,COVINGTONS COMFORT, WHITE MARSH adjacent.
1729 resurveyed to COMFORTS ADVENTURE. 190 acres.

COVINGTONS CONCLUSION

Patented in 1751 a resurvey from LOWER WOOD, by Levin Covington, Nehemiah
Covington and Phillip Covington in Mt Vernon,Election district 5, map #1.
9 July 1766 Mary Covington admx. of Phillip Covington deceased sold 348
acres to Levin Gale.
25 Oct.1800 Littleton Gale of Cecil Co. Md. sold to Levin Jones and John
Leatherbury of Somerset Co. 650 acres of COVINGTONS CONCLUSION,
COVINGTONS ADVENTURE, NEGLECT & SWEETWOOD.
18 May 1801 Samuel Wilson and wife Leah Wilson (late Leah Gale) sold
their rights to Levin Jones and John Leatherbury.
8 Jan 1802 John Leatherbury, wife Sally sold to Levin Jones Sr. 220 7/8
acres of COVINGTONS CONCLUSION, SWEETWOOD, MANNINGS RESOLUTION
8 Jan 1802 Levin Jones sold to John Leatherbury of Robert Leatherbury 400
acre of same as above.
3 Aug.1807 John Leatherbury of Robert Leatherbury, wife Sally Leatherbury
soldto Lucretia Jones 306 1/4 acres of COVINGTONS CONCLUSION, NEGLECT AND
SWEETWOOD.

COVINGTONS FOLLY

Patented on 6 May 1705 by Samuel Covington for 70 acres in Mt. Vernon,
Election district 5, map #1.
Rent Rolls 1666-1723 possessed by Samuel Covington
1703/4 will of Samuel Covington, this land not mentioned.
1 Dec 1736 Thomas Covington son of Samuel Covington sold to John
Leatherbury 70 acres.
1756 John Leatherbury gave to son Robert Leatherbury land bought of
Thomas Covington.
1783 tax- Robert Leatherbury 70 acres
1785 Robert Leatherbury willed to son John Leatherbury.
2 Oct.1800 John Leatherbury,wife Sarah Leatherbury sold to Richard
Ingersol.
24 Dec 1801 Richard Ingersol sold to Robert Leatherbury, with SECURITY &
MY OWN BEFORE, description no acres given.
7 April 1804 Richard Ingersol sold 350 acres to William Roberts of
COVINGTONS FOLLY, SECURITY & THE LOTT.
1832 William Roberts willed 25 acres to nephew Thomas Ingerson.

1837 Sarah Jones willed to grandson Henry Vitry-no acres given.

COVINGTONS HARD BARGAIN

Patented in 1800 by Nehemiah Covington for 6 1/2 acres in West Princess Anne, Election district 1, map #2.

COVINGTONS MEADOW

Patented on 1 Dec.1699 by Phillip Covington for 460 acres in Mt.Vernon, Election district 5, map #1.
Rent Rolls 1666-1723 Phillip Covington
9 July 1715 Phillip Covington and wife Eleanor Covington conveyed to William Jones and Daniel Jones 295 acres.
18 Feb 1756 Daniel Jones and Nehemiah Covington conveyed to John Dorman 42 acres that was willed to Nehemiah by his father Phillip Covington. Elizabeth Jones wife of Daniel Jones was Betty Covington widow of Nehemiah Covington. This deed included part of COMFORTS ADVENTURE.
6 July 1757 Phillip Covington,Daniel Jones and Nehemiah Covington of Dorc. Co. sold to Thomas Jones 341 acres of COVINGTONS MEADOW,COMFORTS ADVENTURE, SASSAFRAS NECK.
25 April 1765 William Jones and wife Priscilla Jones sold to Daniel Jones all rights. William Jones is heir at law to William Jones and Daniel Jones is heir of Daniel.
14 Aug. 1765 Nehemiah Covington of Dorc.Co. sold to Thomas Holbrook of Somerset Co. his rights, for 5 shillings.
22 Oct 1765 Daniel Jones sold 100 acres to Charles Ballard
22 Oct 1765 Daniel Jones sold 50 acres to Thomas Rencher
22 Oct 1765 Daniel Jones sold 145 acres to Thomas Holbrook
8 April 1767 John Dorman and wife Mary Dorman sold 42 acres to Thomas Jones.
1769 ADDITION patented for 33 3/4 acres by Thomas Holbrook.
21 Oct. 1769 William Rencher Sr. and wife Martha Rencher sold to Thomas Roberts 205 acres of COVINGTONS MEADOW, COMFORTS ADVENTURE.
17 Feb.1779 Thomas Holbrook sold to Samuel Ingersol pt. two tracts 11 acres COVINGTONS MEADOW, MIDDLE.
9 Mar.1779 Thomas Holbrook sold to Thomas Rencher 178 3/4 acres.
1783 tax- Samuel Ingersol, 11 acres of MIDDLE.
1783 tax- Thomas Rencher 105 acres
1783 tax- John Jones(for Thomas Jones' heirs.)
1783 tax- Thomas Roberts, 202 acres with COVINGTONS ADVENTURE
1783 tax- George Ballard 100 acres
1783 tax- Arnold Ballard 3 acres.
31 Mar.1785 Charles Ballard sold for 5 shillings to George Ballard son of Charles, 100 acres.
17 Nov.1791 Henry Jones sold to Josiah Hobbs for 5 shillings land devised him by father Thomas Jones in 1774- no name or acreage so could be other lands.
18 May 1792 Arnold Ballard and wife Elizabeth Ballard sold to Josiah Hobbs as Thomas Jones of Monie willed in 1774 to son Henry ADDITION TO(not finished on deed) Elizabeth Jones the widow became wife of Arnold Ballard, sold her dower rights.
22 Oct 1792 George Jones sold to Thomas Rencher COVINGTONS MEADOW, conveyed in 1757 to Thomas Jones father of George Jones, with SASSAFRAS NECK, COMFORTS ADVENTURE. no acreage given.

27 April 1804 William Roberts, wife Sarah Roberts sold to Richard
Ingersol.
1806 Thomas Rencher Sr, willed to son John Rencher lands on Wic.River
extending to Monie Creek now called SASSAFRAS NECK, where Richard
Ingersol now lives and land at Foskeys Gut- unnamed.
3 Sep.1806 Robert Leatherbury sheriff, sold to John Kirwin 30 acres of
COVINGTONS MEADOW & COMFORTS ADVENTURE for debts of Robert Ingersol.
10 Nov.1807 Richard Ingersol, wife Elizabeth Ingersol sold to John Kirwin
30 acres of COVINGTONS ADVENTURE, COVINGTONS MEADOW.
21 March 1808 Eleanor Ballard, Ann Muir Ballard, Samuel Rencher and wife
Elizabeth Rencher, Thomas Rencher and wife Priscilla Rencher, John Gray
and wife Margueritte Gray, Robert Venables, wife Sarah Venables, Joshua
W. Langsdale and wife Matilda Langsdale sold 100 acres to Smith Sims.
11 Feb 1808 Richard Ingersol, wife Elizabeth Ingersol sold to Jacob
Kirwin 147 1/2 acres fo COMFORTS ADVENTURE & COVINGTONS MEADOW.
12 Nov 1834 John Kirwin Jr. sold to William A.D. Bounds, that conveyed
him by his father John Kirwin Sr. COVINGTONS MEADOW & COMFORTS ADVENTURE
33 acres. Part of COVINGTONS MEADOW & COMFORT 65 acres, and LOTT &
COVINGTONS MEADOW 30 acres.
1849 will John Jones, 10 acres to son George Jones.

COVINGTONS PURCHASE
see MANNINGS RESOLUTION

COVINGTONS VINEYARD

Patented on 1 March 1663 by Nehemiah Covington for 300 acres in
Mt.Vernon,Election district 5, map #1.
Rent Rolls 1666-1723 Nehemiah Covington
20 Jan 1679/80 Nehemiah Covington and wife Ann Covington deeded to sons
John Covington and Nehemiah Covington Jr.
1710/13 Nehemiah Covington gave to wife Rebecca Covington. At her decease
to son Levin Covington and daughters Sarah Lloyd (wife of Edward Lloyd)
Elizabeth Wailes (wife of Benjamin Wailes) and Eliza Covington.
10 Oct.1727 Margery Covington of Pr.Georges Co.Md. executrix of the will
of Levin Covington dec'd., sold to Phillip Covington, three
tracts,COVINGTONS VINEYARD, COVINGTONS COMFORT & WHITE MARSH, no acreage
given.
7 Oct.1725 Margery Covington and Phillip Covington sold to John
Leatherbury two parcels on south side Money Creek, unnamed.
1783 tax- Sally Leatherbury 300 acres
1794 repatented 564 acres by Robert Leatherbury.
27 April 1830 Sheriff's sale-at suit of Zadock Long against Robert
Leatherbury, Levin K. Leatherbury and Adam Rencher, 250 acres of
COVINGTONS VINEYARD.

COW MARSH

Patented in 1718 by Somerset Dickerson for 50 acres in Brinkleys
southeast, Election district 3, map #14
15 May 1724 Somerset Dickerson and wife Hannah Dickerson sold 50 acres to
Mary Hampton.
1744 Mary Hampton willed to son Robert Jenkins Henry.
1764 will Robert Jenkins Henry, to son Robert Jenkins Henry all land at
the mouth of Morumsco Creek.-unnamed.
1783 tax- Robert Jenkins Henry 50 acres.

106

COW PASTURE

Patented in 1775, a resurvey of CONTENT, by Samuel Wilson for 112 acres, in Dublin, Election district 4, map #13.
1783 tax- Samuel Wilson 112 acres
20 Aug.1787 Thomas Benston, division of lands with Samuel Wilson of MIDDLE, COWPASTURE, GREEN MEADOW,HOG YARD.
19 Nov. 1795 Major Samuel Wilson son of Samuel, wife Leah Wilson sold to Littleton Dennis 815 acres 112 1/2 acres of COW PASTURE, CONTENT, NEWTON, NEGLECT, EXCHANGE, FRIENDSHIP,etc.

COW PASTURE

Patented on 16 Aug 1688 by William Robinson for 50 acres in Mt. Vernon, Election district 5, map #1.
Rent Rolls 1666-1723 Benjamin Cottman.
15 Aug.1766 William Robertson and Walter Lane Robertson sold to Thomas Holbrook, ROBERTSONS LOTT & COW PASTURE.
17 May 1766 Thomas Holbrook and wife Sarah Holbrook sold to James Polk, all rights to ROBERTSONS LOTT & COW PASTURE.
13 June 1767 John Robinson sold to William Polk, with ROBERTSONS LOTT, no acreage given.
21 Feb.1769 John Robinson and wife Priscilla Robinson sold to William Polk his rights.
25 Sep.1770 James Polk sold to William Polk, all rights, no acreage given.
1783 tax- William Polk

COW QUARTER

Patented on 13 July 1677 by Stephen Horsey for 150 acres in Lawson, Election district 8, map #18.
Rent Rolls 1666-1723 50 acres, assigned to John Horsey, possessed by Stephen Horsey.
10 Jun 1702 Stephen Horsey sold to Thomas Davis 45 acres.
2 Apr.1720 Thomas Davis sold to John Davis 45 acres.
1754 Stephen Horsey willed to grandson Isaac Horsey except 45 acres that father Stephen Horsey sold to Thomas Davis.

COW QUARTER

Surveyed on 5 Jun 1683 by William Stevens and assigned to John King, for 50 acres in Fairmount, Election district 6, map #9.
Rent Rolls 1666-1723 possessed by James Curtis
1720 James Curtis of Annamessex, willed to daughter Esther Curtis.
20 Aug.1740 Charles Curtis and wife Mary Curtis sold to Solomon Long 50 acres, with SAMPIER that was received by Charles from the will of his father James Curtis.
1756 Solomon Long gave to son David Long 50 acres with SAMPIER.
2 Jan 1807 Solomon Long,wife Nelly sold to William Parks, part.
1836 William Parks willed unnamed land to grandson Hezekiah Mead Parks son of Isaac Parks.

COW QUARTER

Patented on 6 Dec.1688 by George Phoebus for 60 acres in St.Peters,
Election district 2, map #6.
22 Feb.1808 Evans Willin sold to John Wilkins.

COW QUARTER

Patented on 10 Dec.1701 by James English for 100 acres in St.Peters,
Election district 2, map #1, and possessed by John Irving.
1783 tax- Thomas Irving 100 acres
1784 Thomas Irving willed 100 acres to son George Irving.
25 May 1785 George Irving, executor of Thomas Irving sold 100 acres to
John Irving.
17 Jan 1786 John Irving sold to William Jones 50 1/2 acres.
9 June 1795 John Irving sold 25 acres to Evans Willin.
9 June 1795 John Irving sold 25 acres to Isaac Willin.
1787 William Jones willed to son William Bozman Jones 50 acres.

COW QUARTER

Patented on 6 Jun 1721 by Thomas Maddux for 160 acres in Brinkleys,
southwest, Election district 13, map 17.
19 Nov.1741 Bell Maddux and wife Rachel Maddux, sold 10 acres to Henry
Potter with 50 acres of DANIELS DEN, surveyed for Thomas Maddux.
20 Nov.1751 Bell Maddux sold to David Matthews 100 acres.
14 Jun 1760 Bell Maddux, wife Margaret Maddux, sold 47 acres to Levin
Powell.
1760/4 Levin Powell willed to wife Rachel Powell and then to son Levin
Powell.
20 March 1783 Zorobable Maddux, wife Esther Maddux, and Margaret Maddux
sold to Merrill Maddux of Worc.Co., 150 acres, their rights to RUSCOMMON,
DANIELS DEN & COW QUARTER.
28 Oct.1786 David Matthews Sr, sold his rights to Nathan Cahoon 100 acres
with GOLDEN LYON 100 acres.
24 Mar.1788 Nathan Cahoon,wife Elizabeth Cahoon, sold to George Howard
200 acres of GOLDEN LYON & COW QUARTER except 20 acres conveyed to John
Riggin.
1805 Thomas Wood Potter willed to son Thomas Potter.
23 Apr.1810 Thomas Potter, wife Jamima Potter and Merrill Maddux, &
Nathan Cahoon sold to Henry Cahoon 60 acres of DANIELS DEN & COW QUARTER.

COW QUARTER

Patented in 1757, a resurvey from HANDYS CHOICE,LONDONS ADVISEMENT,
JERICHO, PROMISE LAND,STEVENS MEADOW by Thomas Seon for 678 acres in
Fairmount,Election district 6, map #9.
23 Mar 1758 Thomas Seon sold 350 acres to Ephraim Wilson.
22 Nov 1769 Thomas Seon sold 80 acres to Ephraim Wilson for 5 shillings.
1783 tax- John Wilson of Samuel 287 acres.
1783 tax- Thomas Seon Sudler 40 1/4 acres.
19 July 1796 Dr. Arnold Elzey and wife Henrietta Elzey (daughter of
Ephraim Wilson) sold to Jesse King 350 nd 80 acres of COW QUARTER.
17 Jan 1809 Solomon Evans sold to Jesse King.
10 Jan 1809 Jesse King sold to Solomon Evans Jr.

Patented in 1769 by Thomas Ward for 3 1/2 acres in Asbury, Election
district 12,map #21.
1796 Thomas Ward willed lands to wife Hannah and son James Ward, unnamed.

COX'S BILL

Patented in 1732 by Edmund Ruck for 167 acres in Brinkleys, southeast,
Election district 3,map #16. There was a second patent on this land in
1732 for 145 acres called RUCK PREVENTED.
10 April 1742 Edmund Ruck and wife Sarah Ruck sold to Thomas Hayward 167
acres.
25 Oct 1746 Thomas Hayward and wife Sarah Hayward sold to William Cox 35
acres of CALF PASTURE but originally called COX'S BILL. 25 Nov.1768 Elias
White of Som.Co. sold to Littleton Dennis of Worc.Co. 50 acres adjacent
MORRIS HOPE that Robert Boyer purchased of Edmund Ruck and sold to
Michael Clifton, COXES BITT.
3 July 1770 Littleton Dennis of Worc.Co. sold to David Williams 50 acres
with PERSIMON POINT & MORRIS HOPE.
22 Nov.1773 Elias White, wife Sarah White, sold to David Williams 50
acres with WHITES GIFT,MORRIS HOPE,PERSIMON POINT being land Robert Boyer
devised to Negro Harry.
1742 RESURVEYED TO CALF PASTURE 247 acres.

COXES CHOICE

Patented on 20 March 1673 by Thomas Cox for 150 acres in Mt.Vernon,
Election district 5, map #1.
Thomas Cox conveyed 70 acres to John Hust.
Thomas Cox died without disposing of the balance and it descended to his
son Thomas Cox and then to Hill Cox.
22 Feb.1752 Hill Cox sold 80 acres to Thomas Holbrook.
18 July 1753 Lydia Wright sold to Daniel Jones 150 acres.
11 March 1762 Daniel Jones sold to Thomas Holbrook pt. PRIVILEDGE taken
out of COX'S CHOICE, with LAST VACANCY & FLOWERFIELDS.

COXES LOTT

Patented 6 Oct.1677 by John White and assigned to Thomas Cox for 100
acres in Mt.Vernon, Election district 5, map #1.
Rent Rolls 1666-1723 Patrick Conner who purchased of Thomas Cox 100
acres.
4 May 1686 Thomas Cox, wife Rebecca Cox sold to James Bradshaw.
28 Feb 1733 Robert Austin son of Joseph Austin sold to Matthias Gale 100
acres.
23 Nov.1787 Levin Gale sold to James Elzey Jr, 100 acres with WHITE HAVEN
TOWN, PRIVILEDGE.
1783 tax- Levin Gale 100 acres.
18 Aug.1794 Nehemiah King and William Jones of Thomas of Manokin sold to
James Elzey for 5 shillings, SECOND PURCHASE,COXES LOTT,ELLIS
CHANCE,WHITE HAVEN & PRIVILEDGE.
19 Aug.1794 James Elzey,wife Sarah Elzey sold to William Jones of Thomas,
same as above.
1794 resurveyed to WORKINGTON 502 acres.

25 March 1794 James Elzey sold to Nehemiah King and William Jones of
Thomas of Manokin for 5 shillings SECOND PURCHASE, COXES LOTT,ELLIS
CHANCE,WHITE HAVEN & PRIVILEDGE.
27 Aug.1800 William Jones sold to Ann Elzey 70 acres.

COXES MISTAKE

Patented on 27 Aug.1677 by William Green and assigned to Cornelius
Johnson for 200 acres in Mt.Vernon,Election district 5, map #1.
Rent Rolls 1666-1723 William Jones 200 acres.
1685 Cornelius Johnson gave to Margaret Jones daughter of William Jones
and to Daniel Jones (land ncot mentioned by name) and to William Jones
Jr.
1734 Resurveyed to JENKINS MISTAKE 163 acres
1795 resurveyed to MISTAKE RECTIFIED 479 1/4 acres.

CRAMBURN

Patented on 2 April 1680 by William Stevens for 350 acres and assigned to
George Goddard, in West Princess Anne, Election district 1, map #2.
Rent Rolls 1666-1723 250 acres George Goddard, 100 acres Peter Surman
1705 George Goddard conveyed 220 acres to Alexander Carlysle
1709 Alexander Carlysle conveyed back to George Goddard 220 acres
18 Sep 1722 George Goddard gave 60 acres to Rev. Alexander Adams.
15 Oct 1748 Peter Surman son of Peter, and wife Mary Surman sold 50 acres
to Thomas Gillis of CABBIN RIDGE conveyed by George Goddard to Peter
Surman father of Peter, being part of CRAMBURN and also another 50 acres
of CRAMBURN, with TROUBLE, HORSEYS CHANCE & CANTERBURY.
1779/80 will Thomas Gillis, to son Joseph Gillis part of 3 tracts
CANTERBURY, CRAMBOURN, HORSEYS CHANCE, 200 acres.
1783 tax- Thomas Fountain.
29 Sep.1790 Joseph Gillis,son of Thomas Gillis Sr. and wife Elizabeth
Gillis sold to Thomas Fountain 50 acres, with TROUBLE,HORSEYS CHANCE &
CANTERBURY.
1802 resurveyed to EDINBURGH.
25 March 1807 Thomas Hamilton mortgaged to Benjamin F.A.C. Dashiell.
3 April 1810 Robert J. King sold to Levin King Jr. 192 acres of CRAMBURN,
WALLEYS CHANCE OR HORSEYS CHANCE, EDINBURGH.

CRIPPLE

Patented in 1766 by John Harris for 14 1/2 acres in Dublin, Election
district 4, map #12.
1788/93 John Harris willed to son John.
1809 resurveyed to HEATHS EXPERIMENT 739 2/3 acres.

CROLLERS FOLLY

Patented in 1683 by John Croller for 100 acres in East Princess Anne,
Election district 15, map #4
Rent Rolls 1666-1723 Escheatable and entered by Robert Wilson for whom it
is reserved. 100 acres
1735/6 Will of Robert Wilson, this land not mentioned.
1748 resurveyed to POLLITTS VICTORY 198 acres.

CROOKED ISLAND

see DALES ADVENTURE 3 1/4 acres.

CROOKED RIDGE

Patented in 1745 by Joseph Ward for 25 acres in East Pr. Anne, Election district 15, map #5
4 Feb 1771 Joseph Ward sold to Saul Ward 25 acres
12 Feb.1785 Saul Ward sold to Joseph Ward 25 acres with PAXON HILL & WORTH LITTLE.
21 Feb.1786 Joseph Ward sold to Matthias Miles 25 acres with PAXON HILL, WORTHLITTLE, PHILLIPS CONCULSION
22 Mar.1786 Joseph Ward, wife Elizabeth Ward sold to John Layfield 100 acres of CROOKED RIDGE,PAXON HILL,PHILLIPS CONCULSION, WORTH LITTLE.
17 Apr.1787 Joseph Ward, wife Elizabeth Ward, and Elizabeth Ward sold to John Perkins 121 acres PAXON HILL,WARWICKS DISCOVERY,CROOKED RIDGE, WORTHLITTLE, etc.
28 Mar.1789 John Perkins, wife Rachel Perkins sold to Mary Broughton 216 acres of WARDS VENTURE,WORTH LITTLE,WARDS CONCLUSION,WINDSOR SWAMP, etc.
13 Oct.1795 Mary Broughton sold to John Layfield 8 acres of CROOKED RIDGE,COME BY CHANCE,PHILLIPS CONCLUSION,PAXON HILL, WARWICKS DISCOVERY
20 Oct. 1807 Mary Broughton gave to son Edward Broughton.
15 Feb.1808 Edward Broughton sold to William Fleming 28 3/4 acres
20 March 1808 Thomas Layfield, wife Henny Layfield sold to Isaac Mitchell Adams.
29 March 1808 Isaac Mitchell Adams sold to Josiah W. Heath.

CROSS

Patented on 29 Aug.1677 by William Green for 36 acres and assigned to Thomas Rowe on Deals Island, Election district 14, map #8.
1702 Thomas Rowe willed to son Nicholas Rowe.
Rent Rolls 1666-1723 Possessed by Francis Gradon in right of the orphan of Thomas Rowe.
8 Mar.1725 Nicholas Rowe and wife Elizabeth Rowe sold 36 acres to Robert King.
1783 tax- Nehemiah King 36 acres.

CROUCHS CHOICE

Patented on 20 Jan 1664 by Ambrose Crouch for 500 acres in East Pr. Anne, Election district 15, map 5. Ambrose Crouch left no heirs and it escheated.
1679 resurveyed to BECKFORD and assigned to Edmund Howard who resurveyed to BECKFORD. The town of Princess Anne is on this property, laid out in 1733.

CULLENS LOTT

Patented in 1765 by Jacob Cullen, a partial resurvey of JOHNSONS LOTT, 149 1/2 acres in Asbury, Election district 12,map 21.
1783 tax- Jacob Cullen

CUMBERLAND

Surveyed on 12 Oct.1705 by John Waters for 150 acres. This land is part
of WATERS RIVER in Annamessex 100a.

CUMBERLAND

Patented in 1747 by Marcellas Hobbs for 50 acres in Mt.Vernon, Election
district 5, map #1
14 Jan 1768 Marcellas Hobbs and wife Agnes Hobbs sold to Mary Waggaman
widow of Henry Waggaman 40 acres with part of GOOD LUCK & CARNEYS CHANCE.
1780 Mary Waggaman, willed to son Henry Waggaman lands purchased of
Marcellas Hobbs.
29 April 1792 Henry Waggaman, wife Sarah Waggaman of Dorc.Co. sold to
George Waggaman of Somerset Co. 40 acres with CARNEYS CHANCE, WAGGAMANS
PURCHASE, DAVIDS CHANCE, etc.
20 Aug.1803 Henry Waggaman and wife Sarah Waggaman of Dorc.Co. sold to
Levin Jones.
8 July 1806 Levin Dashiell Jones sold to Matthias Hobbs 47 1/2 acres of
ADDITION, CUMBERLAND, WAGGAMANS CONCLUSION, GOOD LUCK & CONVIENCE.
1841 Matthias Hobbs willed to son Matthias.

CURSLEYS JOKE

Patented in 1744 by William Carsley for 60 acres in Brinkleys northwest,
Election district 3, map #14. Sometimes called CARSLEYS YOAK.
1745/1764 debt books, Robert Kersley.
29 Jun 1765 William Carsley Jr, Mary Carsley widow of Robert Carsley sold
60 acres to William Smith.
1783 tax- Mary Smith of William Smith 60 acres.
8 Jan 1803 Benjamin Lankford sold to Robert Lankford 60 1/2 acres.
15 April 1806 Robert Lankford, wife Sarah sold to Jesse Jackson 60 1/2
acres.
15 April 1806 Jesse Jackson sold to Dr. Thomas Robertson Jr.
1816 Dr. Thomas Robertson willed lands in Annamessex to son Thomas,
unnamed.

CURTIS LOT

Patented on 3 April 1762 by Samuel Curtis for 100 acres in Westover,
Election district 13,map #11.
1783 tax- Samuel Curtis 100 acres.
15 Feb 1798 Samuel Curtis sold to son Henry H.Curtis for 5 shillings,100
acres with THREE BROTHERS

CURTIS LOT

Patented on 15 May 1704 by James Curtis for 75 acres in Westover,
Election district 13, map #10.
Rent Rolls 1666-1723 James Curtis 75 acres.
1720 James Curtis willed to daughter Rachel Curtis
1741 Charles Curtis son of James, gave to son Charles Curtis.
12 May 1760 Samuel Curtis sold 75 acres to William Long.
1783 tax- William Long 75 acres.
6 Aug.1792 John Turpin of Nehemiah Turpin, and wife Sarah Turpin sold to
Thomas Lister 60 1/4 acres of HOLLWELL,CURTIS LOTT & WILSONS LOTT
adjacent, property of William Long deceased. One fourth part became

right of Sarah Turpin wife of John Turpin.
17 Jan 1805 Samuel Long wife Elizabeth Long, sold to Isaac Beauchamp,
George Beauchamp 57 3/4 acres of lands of father William Long, unnamed.

CYPRESS SWAMP

Patented in 1746 from CHANCE, by Robert Geddes for 15 acres in Dublin,
Election district 4, map #13.
17 Aug.1749 Robert Geddes and wife Susannah Geddes, inholder, sold 15
acres to John Hamilton, with CHANCE & CYPRESS SWAMP.
1783 tax- Rev. Hamilton Bell
1797 Jonathan Cluff willed to son Robert Cluff with TIMBER GROVE.

CUT CLOSE

Patented in 1803 by Thomas Mitchell in East Pr. Anne, Election district
15, map #5.
12 May 1805 Thomas Mitchell, wife Mary Mitchell of Worc.Co. sold to
William Mitchell.
18 May 1805 William Mitchell, wife Sally Mitchell sold to Kirk Gunby.
1806 ADDITION TO CUT CLOSE patented for 209 acres to Kirk Gunby.
23 Dec.1828 Villiage Hearld= Sale by decree of Somerset County Court of
the Real Estate of Kirk Gunby, CUT CLOSE,ADDITION TO CUT CLOSE and other
tracts.

DAINTRY

Patented on 19 July 1677 by John Parsons for 150 acres in West Princess
Anne, Election district 1, map #2 and map #4 in East Pr. Anne.
Rent Rolls 1666-1723 150 acres possessed by John Parsons but lately held
by William Alexander Jr.who repatented in 1728 for 300 acres..
1734 William Alexander willed to son James Alexander.
1737/8 Liston Alexander son of William Alexander gave to William son of
Moses Alexander and to sister Agnes Alexander.
24 June 1736 Moses Alexander, clocksmith, son of William Alexander sold
to Liston Alexander for 5 shillings all interest in the lands of William
Alexander, HUNGARY NECK 380 acres being part of TROUBLE and part of
DAINTRY.
2 Nov.1738 Moses Alexander sold to Agnes Alexander 150 acres with part of
TROUBLE.
1743 Thomas Pollitt willed to son Thomas Pollitt, TROUBLE & DAINTRY.
24 May 1749 John Laws and wife Agnes Laws, sold to Thomas Pollitt 170
acres part of DAINTRY & TROUBLE, that Moses Alexander deeded to Agnes
Alexander now wife of John Laws.
9 April 1745 Moses Alexander and his eldest son John Alexander,blacksmith
of Wicomico 100 sold to Alexander Adams rector of Stepney Parish 230
acres of DAINTRY & TROUBLE.
(As William Alexander was married to Catherine Wallace and has several
children and all his sons died childless except his second son Moses
afsd.)
20 Sep.1763 Matthias Coston and wife Abigail Coston sold to Thomas
Pollitt (dispute of lands, SECOND CHOICE included in original tract
DAINTRY)

25 Sep.1781 Oliver Coston son of Abigail Coston who was the daughter of
John Parsons the younger, sold to Thomas Pollitt for 5 shillings 150
acres with GOOD LUCK.
1783 tax- Thomas Pollitt 150 acres.
1788 Thomas Pollitt, willed to son Thomas part granted to William
Alexander and pt. granted to John Parsons.
13 Nov.1798 Dr. Charles Nutter, wife Louisa Nutter sold to Capt. Thomas
Jones 28 acres.
17 Jan 1810 Thomas Curtis sold to Matthias Miles 125 1/4 acres, as
trustee to sell the realestate of Thomas Jones, with SECOND ADDITION TO
HOG QUARTER.

DALES ADVENTURE

Patented on 9 July 1679 by David Dale for 400 acres in Brinkleys,
southeast, Election district 3, map #16.
20 Nov.1681 Henry Dale son of David Dale, and Elizabeth Dale sold to
Gideon Tilghman 200 acres called TILGHMANS REST.
26 Sep.1689 Henry Dale son of David Dale and wife Elizabeth Dale sold 200
acres to Samuel Handy, called HANDYS HALL.
Rent Rolls 1666-1723 Possessed 200 acres by Samuel Collins and 200 acres
Gideon Tilghman.
1720 will Gideon Tilghman, to son Moses Tilghman 200 acres.
28 Sep.1724 Gideon Tilghman and wife Esther Tilghman, sold to Ralph
Milbourn 200 acres called GIDEONS REST.
3 Sep.1753 Samuel Collins sold 3 1/4 acres to John Evans.
3 Sep.1753 John Evans sold to Jabez Pitts HANDYS HALL taken out of DALES
ADVENTURE whereon John Evans now lives called CROOKED ISLAND 3 1/4 acres.
1757 Ralph Milbourn gave to son Lodowick Milbourn.
1774 possessed by Lodowick Milbourn.
28 Feb.1760 John Evans, wife Elizabeth Evans sold to Nathaniel Evans,
part of HANDYS HALL being part of DALES ADVENTURE 61 acres.
22 Dec.1764 Jabez Pitts gave to son Robert Pitts land purchased of John
Evans with all lands he has an interest in.
13 Apr.1762 John Evans sold to Zorobable Merchant of Worc.Co. 1/2 acre.
12 Oct 1765 John Evans sold to Lodowick Milbourn, HANDYS HALL taken out
of DALES ADVENTURE 1 acre.
23 Oct.1766 Robert Pitts sold to Lodowick Milbourn part of CROOKED ISLAND
that Jabez Pitts purchased of John Evans, with part of MILBOURNS MISTAKE,
no acres given.
23 Oct.1766 John Evans and wife Elizabeth Evans sold to Lodowick Milbourn
1 acre of HANDYS HALL.
20 March 1767 Nathaniel Evans sold to Zorobable Merchant HANDYS HALL 61
acres.
1783 tax- Lodowick Milbourn 100 acres.
1783 tax- Tabitha Merchant 60 acres HANDYS HALL.
27 Aug.1787 Jonathan Bunting, wife Ann Bunting and Rose Evans one of the
coheirs of Ephraim Evans sold to Jonathan Milbourn 18 acres of HANDYS
HALL near Oystershell town.
27 Aug.1787 Jonathan Bunting and Rose Evans sold to Jonathan Milbourn 1/2
acre, land sold by Ephraim Evans to Zorobable Merchant deceased. unnamed.
in Oystershell town.
19 March 1792 Abigail Collins sold to Jonathan Bunting and wife Ann
Bunting, Thomas Bunting and wife Rose Bunting for 5 shillings 151 1/2
acres of HANDYS HALL, OWEN GLENDORE, OYSTER SHELL and HANDYS MEADOW,that

Ephraim Evans mortgaged to John Collins.
19 March 1792 Thomas Bunting, wife Rose Bunting, sold to Jonathan Bunting
for 5 shillings HANDYS HALL, OYSTER SHELL BANKS, HANDYS MEADOW.
1 Feb 1797 John Merchant, son of Zorobable Merchant sold 61 acres to
Tabitha Ward HANDYS HALL.
31 March 1797 Ralph Milbourn sold all his interest to James Milbourn of
OWEN GLENDORE,HANDYS HALL,OYSTER SHELL BANKS
12 March 1799 Ralph Milbourn sold to Stephen Collins 116 acres at
Oystershell Town.
19 March 1800 James Milbourn, and Ralph Milbourn mortgaged to William
Waters Sr.HANDYS HALL,CROOKED ISLAND, HANDYS MEADOW,OWEN GLENDORE,
OYSTERSHELL BANKS.
18 Nov.1798 Ralph Milbourn sold to Stephen Collins 10 acres.
18 Nov.1798 Ralph Milbourn sold to Tabitha Ward 16 acres
20 Dec.1803 James Polk, wife Polly Polk, George Parker, wife Rebecca
Parker, sold to Stephen Collins 77 3/4 acres had by Tabitha Ward,
deceased, HANDYS HALL & DALES ADVENTURE.

                              DAMSWAMP

This land not patented and not on Benson's maps. It is in Brinkleys
southwest ,Election district 3, map #17 and surveyed in 1758 by Sampson
Wheatley.
1773 Sampson Wheatley willed to daughter Betty Wheatley after wifes
death.
1783 tax- Mary Wheatley 26 1/2 acres
24 Jun 1786 Caleb Jones and wife Betty Jones, daughter of Sampson
Wheatley sold to Kellum Lankford, Elijah Coulbourn, and Thomas Jones
DAMSWAMP with ADAMS CHANCE,WHEATLEYS DIFFICULT PURCHASE,IRISH GROVE,
MERCHANTS TREASURE,PRIVILEDGE, WHEATLEYS SECOND ADDN.,LITTLEWORTH, NEW
BOSTON.
24 April 1805 Benjamin Conner, Noah Lankford, Benjamin Bedsworth, John
Broughton and wife Mary Broughton, Richard Hall and Mary Bedsworth sold
to Mordicai Jones of St. Marys County, divised by Sampson Wheatley.
17 Feb 1807 Caleb Jones of Parish of St. Marys Co. York province of New
Brunswick and wife Betty Jones sold to Mordicai Jones of St. Marys
Co.USA.
23 May 1807 Mordicai Jones, wife Mary Jones of St. Marys Co. sold to
Robert Bell of Somerset County.

                             DAM QUARTER

Patented on 22 Feb 1666 by William Stevens who assigned to Thomas Ball,
for 150 acres in Dames Quarter, Election district 11, map #7.
11 Oct 1673 Major Thomas Brereton of Northumberland Co. Va. sold to John
White of same. 150 acres.
Rent Rolls 1666-1723 possessed by John White.
1718 John White gave to daughter Grace Wallace 40 acres and to son John
White, plantation.
14 June 1736 John White son of John sold to Richard Wallace part where
Grace Wallace lived 40 acres.
8 March 1774 John White Sr, gave to son John, with OXFORD, FRIENDS
CONTENT, 333 acres.
8 Sep.1774 John White, wife Rebecca White, sold to Joseph Wallace 84
acres with 22 acres of FRIENDS CONTENT.

13 July 1779 David Wallace gave to Richard Wallace with FRIENDS
ACCEPTANCE, FRIENDS CONTENTMENT,MEADOW, etc. no acres given.
1783 tax- Margaret Wallace & Mary Wallace 40 acres.
8 Jun 1788 John White sold to John Thomas of Dorcester Co. DAMES QUARTER,
FRIENDS CONTENTMENT 116 acres.
29 July 1788 Richard Wallace, wife Rebecca Wallace sold to William
Roberts all his rights to FRIENDS ACCEPTANCE,MEADOW, DAM QUARTER,etc.
1794 William Roberts gave to neice Nancy Lemon wife of Robert Lemon, no
acres mentioned.
25 Sep.1792 John Thomas of Dorc.Co. sold to Thomas White 94 acres of
DAMES QUARTER & FRIENDS CONTENTMENT.
16 July 1793 John White sold to Francis White 303 acres of DAM QUARTER,
OXFORD, FRIENDS CONTENTMENT.
14 Jan 1794 John White sold to Francis White Jr.5 1/2 acres.
9 Feb.1805 Whittington White, wife Tabitha White sold to Matthias Wingate
6 acres, for 5 shillings.
9 Feb.1805 Whittington White, wife Tabitha White, sold to Henry White 43
acres of DAMES QUARTER & FRIENDS CONTENT.
2 Dec.1806 Whittington White, wife Tabitha sold to Peter White 9 1/2
acres of DAMES QUARTER & FRIENDS CONTENT.

DAM QUARTER

Patented on 23 May 1683 by William Stevens who assigned to Thomas Dixon,
for 100 acres in Brinkleys northwest, Election district 3, map #14.
Rent Rolls 1666-1723 Thomas Dixon
1718 Thomas Dixon willed 100 acres to son William Dixon.
10 Jan 1736 Thomas Dixon and wife Sarah Dixon sold to Joseph Lankford 100
acres.
1736 debt books- Joseph Lankford 36 acres
21 April 1755 Joseph Lankford deeded to Puzey Lankford 36 acres.
1755 debt books- Puzey Lankford 36 acres.
9 Sep.1756 Isaac Dixon and wife Sarah Dixon sold to Outerbridge Horsey 20
1/2 acres (from Thomas Dixon grandfather of Isaac Dixon.)
9 Sep.1756 Isaac Dixon sold to Robert Carsley.
1764 debt books- Robert Carsley
29 Jun 1765 William Carsley Jr. and Mary Carsley widow of Robert Carsley
sold 19 1/4 acres to William Smith.
1783 tax- Puzey Lankford 36 acres
1785 Outerbridge Horsey willed land from Isaac Dixon to son Isaac Horsey,
after his death to son Lazarus Horsey.
9 Apr.1792 Thomas Dixon of Worc.Co. sold to Benjamin Lankford of Lazarus
Lankford, 3 acres.
9 June 1792 Thomas Dixon of Worc.Co. sold to Joseph Lankford of Puzey
Lankford 44 1/4 acres.
8 Jan 1803 Benjamin Lankford sold to Robert Lankford 19 acres that Robert
Carsley purchased of Isaac Dixon.
15 Arpi 1806 Robert Lankford sold to Jesse Jackson land purchased of
Benjamin Lankford in 1803.
15 April 1806 Jesse Jackson sold to Dr. Thomas Robertson.

DANIELS DEN

Patented on 3 March 1674 by Daniel Donoho for 100 acres in Brinkleys,
Election district 3, map #17.

Rent Rolls 1666-1723 Alexander Maddux 100 acres.
19 Nov 1741 Bell Maddux and wife Rachel Maddux sold 50 acres to Henry
Potter with 10 acres of COW QUARTER.
20 March 1783 Zorobable Maddux,wife Esther Maddux and Margaret Maddux of
Worc.Co. sold rights 150 acres to Merrill Maddux with RUSCOMMAN,COW
QUARTER.(Zorobable as son of Thomas Maddux and Margaret Maddux)
1783 tax- Henry Potter 40 acres
1783 tax- Merrill Maddux 150 acres with RUSCOMMON.
30 Oct.1784 Merrill Maddux sold 49 acres to Jesse Powell.
1805/8 Thomas Wood Potter willed to son Thomas Potter.
23 April 1810 Thomas Potter, wife Jamima Potter, & Merill Maddux, &
Nathan Cahoon sold to Henry Cahoon 60 acres COW QUARTER & DANIELS DEN.

DAUGHERTYS ADVENTURE

Patented in 1818 by Dickerson Daugherty for 8 acres in Lawsons, Election
District 8, map #19.

DAUGHERTYS PURCHASE

Patented in 1818 by Dickerson Daugherty for 58 7/8 acres in Lawsons,
Election district 8, map #19.

DAUGHTERS RECOVERY
see GREENFIELD,MIDDLE & EXCHANGE-Dublin Distict

DAUGHTERS DOWER

This is part of DOUBLE PURCHASE- Randall Revell.

DAVIDGES PURCHASE

Patented in 1762 by Stephen Garland, a resurvey of BEAUCHAMP
PRIVILEDGE for 395 acres in Westover, Election district 13, map #11.
1783 tax- Stephen Garland 335 1/2 acres.
12 Sep.1763 Stephen Garland, mortgaged to John Logan of the city of
London, merchant his interst in THREE BROTHERS, DAVIDGES PURCHASE,
SALISBURY, BEAUCHAMPS PRIVILEDGE.
2 Jan 1766 Stephen Garland gave a bond for release of a prisoner in jail
to Thomas Dashiell, sheriff for DAVIDGES PURCHASE,THREE BROTHERS,
SOMERSET, SALISBURY LOTT, etc.
335 1/2 acres.
10 March 1767 Thomas Dashiell, sheriff sold to John White
10 March 1767 John White sold to Stephen Garland 335 1/2 acres.

DAVIDS ADVENTURE

Patented in 1757 by David Long for 99 acres, a resurvey including CHANCE,
in Brinkleys, northwest, Election district 3, map #14.
1752 David Long and wife Abigail Long sold 99 acres to John Howard.
9 March 1755 John Howard and wife Christian Howard, sold to George Miles
99 acres (a resurvey of Chance that Daniel Long willed to son David Long)
1783 tax- Levi Johnson (mulatto) 99 acres.
18 Feb.1798 Evans Willin and wife Ruth Willin sold to Nathaniel Bell 99
acres.

117

DAVIDS CHANCE

Patented in 1754 by David McGrath for 205 1/2 acres in West Princess
Anne, Election district 1, map #3.
14 Feb 1764 David McGrath mortgaged to John White, 186 acres.
3 Oct.1766 John White, sold to William Smith (the mortgage) 186 acres
with OWENS IMPROVEMENT,OWENS DELIGHT, MIDDLE, REFUGE,etc.
29 March 1769 Isaac Coulbourn, sheriff, sold to Mary Waggaman widow (as
Edward Lloyd of Talbot Co. had a judgement against John White, David
McGrath and William Smith.sold to settle against David McGrath 271 acres
of OWENS IMPROVEMENT,MIDDLE,OWENS DELIGHT, DAVIDS CHANCE, etc.
1783 tax- John McGrath 38 acres
1783 tax- William Waggaman
1788 John McGrath willed to son David Gahergan McGrath.
29 April 1792 Henry Waggaman son of Henry and Mary Waggaman, with wife
Sarah Waggaman of Dorc.Co. sold to George Waggaman of Som.Co. with OWENS
IMPROVEMENT,LONG MEADOW, ABINGTON, REFUGE, etc.
20 Aug.1803 Henry Waggaman and wife Sarah Waggaman of Dorc.Co. sold to
Littleton Dennis Teackle
11 Dec 1804 John Dennis sold to Elias Bailey 3/4 acre of OWENS IMPROVMENT
& DAVIDS CHANCE.
13 April 1809 Sarah McGrath, widow of John McGrath and David G. McGrath
her son sold to Robert J. King 50 acres, no name.

DAVIDS DESTINY

Patented on 21 May 1668 for 350 acres by David Williamson in Dames
Quarter, Election district 11, map #11.
Rent Rolls 1666-1723 Possessed by the widow Ann Roberts that David
Williamson alienated to Thomas Kendal.
18 Dec.1673 Francis Roberts sold to Alexander Draper 350 acres.
18 April 1676 Alexander Draper sold to Francis Roberts 350 acres.
16 Nov.1683 Francis Roberts sold to Christopher Little 100 acres with
OUTLETT.
26 Nov.1754 Edward Roberts sold 250 acres to William Roberts at Dames
Quarter
14 Nov.1762 Edward Roberts sold to William Roberts all except part
conveyed by Francis Roberts to John White.
21 March 1780 William Roberts sold to Noah Nelms 49 acres.
1783 tax- William Roberts 150 acres.
2 Aug.1796 Francis White gave to son William White DAVIDS DESTINY now
called JAMES DELIGHT, ELLIOTTS CHOICE, OUTLETT.
13 Jan 1798 Noah Nelms of Baltimore sold to Thomas White Sr. 49 acres.
15 Jan 1799 George Jones, wife Leah Jones sold to William White of
Francis White, 38 3/4 acres.
15 Jan 1799 William White of Francis White, wife Nancy White sold to
Thomas White Sr. 12 1/2 acres.
20 Jan 1801 Charles Jones, wife Hetty Jones sold to Thomas White 25
acres.
30 Jan 1801 Thomas White, wife Nancy White sold to Charles Jones 16
acres.

DAVIS'S CHOICE

Patented on 14 March 1663 by James Davis for 600 acres in East Princess

Anne, Election district 15, map #5.
30 March 1669 James Davis, planter, and Margaret Davis his wife sold to
John Smith and Henry Smith son of Henry of Accoc. Co.Va. 600 acres.
6 Nov.1681 Henry Smith sold to George Phillips 330 acres now called
GEORGES DELIGHT
30 Oct.1682 Henry Smith sold to Jacob Warring 130 acres now called .
TURNERS CHOICE
12 Jan 1685 Jacob Warring sold to Thomas Wilson 130 acres.
Rent Rolls 1666-1723 possesed by -
 150 acres belongs to Mary Smith
 330 acres John Fisher
 120 acres Ephraim Wilson and Peter Dent.
1709/10 John Fisher and wife Jane Fisher willed to son Barkley Fisher 300
acres.
9 March 1721 Thomas Davis son of Thomas Davis, of Nasamond Co.Va. sold to
Ephraim Wilson 25 acres now called KINGS PURCHASE out of DAVIS CHOICE.
15 Apr.1737 Ephraim Wilson and Frances Wilson his wife sold to James
Lindow and Margaret Lindow his wife for 5 shillings 1/2 of TURNERS
PURCHASE being part of DAVIS CHOICE.
28 May 1742 Margaret Lindow widow of James Lindow sold to the Vestrymen
of Somerset Parish 130 acres purchased by Thomas Wilson deceased, who
puchased of Jacob Warring, where Margaret Lindow now lives, TURNERS
CHOICE being part taken out of DAVIS'S CHOICE.
6 Dec.1747 David Wilson and wife Abigail Wilson, son of Ephraim Wilson
deceased,sold to the Vestrymen of Somerset Parish, William Turpin,
Mitchell Jones, Panter Laws, William Jones of Goose Creek, Marcy
Fountain, Henry Ballard, TURNERS CHOICE taken out of DAVIS CHOICE 103
acres that Thomas Wilson grandfather of David Wilson purchased from Jacob
Warring.
5 Jan 1747/8 Samuel Wilson, executor of the will of Margaret Lindow
deceased gave to David Wilson TURNERS PURCHASE.
26 March 1752 Randall Mitchell and wife Sarah Mitchell sold to Hamilton
Bell 146 acres now called GEORGES DELIGHT.
17 Feb.1756 John Parker, wife Elizabeth Parker, sold to Rev. Hamilton
Bell 4 acres.
25 March 1772 Randall Mitchell and Stephen Mitchell his son sold 12 acres
to Hamilton Bell.
1783 tax- John Parker 179 acres.
1783 tax- Rev. Hamilton Bell 12 acres.
26 Dec.1799 Vestry of Somerset Parish sold to John Byrd.
12 March 1800 John Parker and George Parker sold to John Bird for 5
shillings, description, no acres given.
12 March 1800 John Parker sold to George Parker with PARKERS FORTUNE
12 March 1800 George Parker sold to John Parker with PARKERS FORTUNE
12 Mar. 1800 John Byrd sold to John Parker and George Parker.
25 Aug.1802 Levin Irving sold to John Byrd part.
25 Aug.1802 Levin Irving sold to Margaret Byrd wife of John Byrd and Mary
Smith, part.
14 Sep. 1804 John Byrd, wife Margaret Byrd, and Mary Smith sold to Zadock
Long DAVIS CHOICE, with WALTONS IMPROVEMENT & LAWS PURCHASE.
1 Feb.1831 Constables sale-suit of Isaac P.Smith against Lorenzo D.
Parker,Clement J.B. Parker 45 acres of DAVIS CHOICE devised by John
Parker.
1837 George Parker, willed to wife Esther Parker.

DAVIS CHOICE

Patented on 20 March 1663 by Thomas Davis for 450 acres in Westover, Election District 13, map #11
4 Aug.1685 Thomas Davis of James River Virginia sold to Lewis Knight 160 acres..
11 June 1688 Thomas Davis sold to Edward Jones 100 acres now called LONG SINCE EXPECTED.
11 June 1688 Thomas Davis sold to William Turpin 175 acres now called LONG LOOKED FOR.
1750 resurveyed to MOTHERS CARE 795 acres.

DAVIS CHANCE

Patented on 25 Aug.1679 by John White and assigned to Richard Davis for 100 acres in Westover, Election district 13, map #11.
1702 Richard Davis willed to brother William Davis 300 acres of DAVIS LOTT and CHANCE.
Rent Rolls 1666-1723 Poss. by Ephraim Wilson 100 acres
1750 resurveyed to MOTHERS CARE 795 acres.

DAVISES CHANGE

This was surveyed in 1666 by James Davis for 140 acres,and not patented but was part of POOLS HOPE, in Westover, Election district 13, map #11.
13 March 1669 Thomas Pool, wife Elizabeth Pool sold to James Davis 200 acres called DAVIS'S CHANGE.
13 May 1678 James Davis, wife Margaret Davis sold to Gideon Tilghman 100 acres DAVIS CHANGE out of POOLS HOPE.
30 March 1669 James Davis, wife Margaret Davis sold to William Thompson of Virginia 100 acres of DAVIS CHANGE out of POOLS HOPE, called THOMPSONS ADVENTURE.
9 Jan.1671 William Thompson of Virginia sold to Henry Smith 100 acres.
5 Aug.1677 William Thompson sold to Henry Smith 100 acres who assigned 100 acres to Gideon Tilghman.
1709 Edward Davis son of James Davis willed to son Edward.
1740 Edward Davis willed to son Edward Davis. no acres mentioned.

DAVIS'S CONQUEST

Patented on 14 March 1663 by William Davis for 300 acres in Westover, Election district 13, map #11.
8 Sep.1674 William Davis and Anne Davis his wife sold to Richard Davis 50 acres now called ADDITION TO DAVIS LOTT.
17 April 1751 David Wilson and wife Betty Wilson sold to Samuel Wilson.
(as William Davis died intestate and land descended to Elizabeth Davis and Martha Davis daughters of William. Elizabeth married Ephraim Wilson now deceased and had sons David Wilson and Samuel Wilson alive at her death. Martha deeded on 12 Aug 1702 (then Martha Jones w/o Thomas) to Ephraim Wilson.
1750 Resurveyed to MOTHERS CARE 795 acres.

DAVIS GOOD WILL

Patented in 1767 by Thomas Handy for 777 acres in Lawsons Election

district 8, map #18.A resurvey of UNDUE & UPPER UNDUE.
1783 tax- Thomas Handy Sr. 663 acres.
1793 Thomas Handy willed to sons Thomas and John Handy.
13 Mar.1796 Thomas Handy s/o Thomas sold to Henry Handy the balance of
DAVIS GOOD WILL.
10 March 1796 Thomas Handy son of Thomas sold 102 acres to John Handy.
2 Aug. 1796 Thomas Handy son of Thomas sold to William Williams 500
acres.
19 Aug.1797 Henry Handy sold to John Handy 42 1/4 acres
29 May 1797 William Williams, wife Polly Williams sold to Henry Handy 580
acres.
27 Aug.1796 Thomas Handy sold to Henry Handy given me by father except
100 acres sold to brother John Handy.

DAVIS INLET

Patented on 12 Jun 1689 by Thomas Davis for 50 acres in Asbury, Election
district 12,map #21
24 Feb 1765 Samuel Cox sold to Solomon Bird 100 acres as John Davis had
parcels in Annamessex and devised to Samuel Cox, sold part of afsd.
lands.
1762 John Davis, son of Thomas Davis sold to nephew Samuel Cox (Mary
Davis married William Cox) 50 acres.

DAVIS LOT

Patented on 5 March 1663 by Richard Davis for 300 acres in Westover,
Election district 13, map #11.
6 Oct 1674 Richard Davis sold to William Furniss, part now called LONG
TIME AGREED UPON
1703 will of Richard Davis, to brother William Davis 300 acres.
Rent Rolls 1666-1723 possessed by Ephraim Wilson
1783 tax- John Gunby Sr. 100 acres
7 Nov 1785 Thomas Furniss sold to Samuel Wilson (mortgage) 337 acres of
FAIR SPRING,DAVIS LOTT,GREAT HOPES.

DEAR PURCHASE

See WATERS RIVER

DEAR QUARTER

Patented 11 Sep.1701 by John Duer for 160 acres in East Princess Anne,
Election district 15, map #5.
Rent Rolls 1666-1723 Possessed by Archibald Smith but denies rent so John
Duer must pay who has the right.
21 March 1721 Archibald Smith of Sussex Co.Del. sold to Archibald Stitt.
1774 Archibald Stitt willed to William Knox son of Robert Knox of North
Carolina, 160 acres.
17 Apr.1775 William Owens of Worc.Co. sold to John Pollitt land patented
by John Duer, DEAR QUARTER, no acres given.
14 Oct.1783 Josiah Knox of Pitt Co. North Carolina sold to John Pollitt
of Somerset County 160 acres.
1783 tax- John Pollitt 160 acres.

DEEP

Patented on 8 March 1663 by John Shipway for 300 acres in East Princess
Anne, Election district 15,map #4
1687 John Shipway willed to John Heath.
Rent Rolls 1666-1723 possessed by, 150 acres by Henry Dorman and 150
acres by John Lokey.
1727/8 John Lokey willed dwelling plantation and estate to Dorman Heath.
2 March 1731/2 Henry Dorman gave to son Henry two tracts 300 acres of
DEEP & 250 acres of SHIPWAYS CHOICE.
17 June 1732 Henry Dorman Jr. and wife Catherine Dorman sold to John
Finch, part two tracts DEEP & SHIPWAYS CHOICE that is not included in
part belonging to Abraham Heath, 150 acres and another parcel sold by
John Shipway to Thomas Pollitt.
24 Aug.1733 John Pollitt of Dorcester Co. sold to John Finch 100 acres
above the WADING place, part of DEEP & SHIPWAYS CHOICE, called POLLITTS
CHOICE, conveyed to Thomas Pollitt of Som.Co. by the late Henry Dorman.
1 July 1737 John Finch sold 150 acres to John Tunstall, merchant DEEP &
SHIPWAYS CHOICE sold by John Shipway to Thomas Pollitt now called FRIENDS
ASSISTANCE and also a tract POLLITTS CHOICE being part of DEEP 100 acres
and now called PROPERTY RESTORED.
7 June 1740 Dorman Heath gave to wife Perthenia Heath and daughters
Rachel Heath and Sarah Heath 100 acres of DEEP and SPITTLE, and 50 acres
patented by John Shipway.
13 May 1749 I Spencer Hack release to Heber Whittingham 1/2 part of DEEP
& SHIPWAYS CHOICE, devised Spencer Hack by grandfather John Tunstall.
7 March 1769 I Heber Whittingham devisee of Heber Whittingham deceased,
assign rights to John Jones son of William Jones.
1740 36 acres resurveyed to SHIPWAYS CHOICE.
1749 this part resurveyed to MOORS BARROW 323 acres.

DEEP STILL

Patented in 1763 for 94 acres out of DEEP by Wilson Heath in East
Princess Anne, Election district 15, map #4.
4 Dec.1783 Wilson Heath and Jesse Heath sold to Josiah Hobbs of Sussex
Co.Del.92 acres originally called DEEP and since resurveyed by Wilson
Heath and wife Rachel Heath and now called DEEP STILL, with tract
SPITTLE.
7 April 1795 Josiah Hobbs, wife Rebecca Hobbs sold 92 acres to Ezekiel
Haynie that was resurveyed by Wilson Heath and wife Rachel Heath.

DEER PARK

A resurvey in 1787 by William Waters of WATERS ADDITION TO TIMBER TRACT,
part of WHARTONS FOLLY, ADDITION TO BATCHELORS HOLE and the upper part of
HOG YARD. 1110 3/4 acres in Dublin, Election district 4, maps #12 & #13.
1834 will of George Miles, to daughter Eliza Dickerson,(wife of Parker
Dickerson) DEER PARK, part bought at sheriffs sale being part of the
property of James Boston.

DENNIS ADDITION TO GOOD SUCESS

Patented in 1774 by Samuel Sloan for 170 1/2 acres in Dublin Election
district 4, map 13.

1836 Levin Pollitt willed to neice Mary Dennis Stevens
DENNIS LOT

see DOUBLE PURCHASE

DENWOODS INCLUSION

Patented on 6 March 1685 by Levin Denwood for 21 acres in West Princess
Anne, Election district 1, map #3.
Rent Rolls 1666-1723 poss. by Arthur Denwood.
16 Sep.1740 Thomas Denwood sold to George Denwood the lands of
grandfather Levin Denwood.
16 Sep 1741 George Denwood sold to David Wilson 21 acres.
1783 tax- James Wilson 20 acres.

DERRY

Patented on 2 Feb 1721 by John Gray for 77 acres in East Princess Anne,
Election district 15, map #5
Rent Rolls 1666-1723 John Gray
1731 John Gray willed to son William Gray.
1743 William Gray willed 77 acres to son William Gray.
26 Nov.1754 James Gray and William Gray sold to Jarvis Ballard 77 acres
with SMITHSFIELD,SMITHS RESOLVES, GOLDSMITHS DELIGHT.
6 Apr 1756 William Gray son of ALlen Gray sold to William Polk and
Benjamin Polk 77 acres, with KILLMAYAN.
1783 tax- William Ballard 77 acres.
12 March 1799 William Ballard of Jarvis Ballard sold to Levin Ballard, 77
acres
29 March 1800 William Ballard of Jarvis Ballard sold 77 acres to Lambert
Hyland.

DESERT

Patented in April 1675 by David Brown for 100 acres in East Princess
Anne, Election district 15, map #4.
Rent Rolls 1666-1723 Alexander Brown, 100 acres.
1697 David Brown willed lands to Alexander Brown, unnamed.
1 March 1738 Thomas Brown eldest son of Alexander Brown deceased and Mary
Brown and Margaret Brown the two daughters of Alexander Brown gave to
brother David Brown, 100 acres.
5 Dec.1739 David Brown sold to William Miles 100 acres.
8 Apr.1749 David Wilson eldest son of Ephraim Wilson, deceased, and John
Woolford and wife Mary Woolford and Margaret Brown (heir of Alexander
Brown and Margaret Brown his wife) sold to William Miles.
(note; the land of David Brown became vested in David Wilson son of
Ephraim Wilson and Margaret Wilson daughter of Thomas Wilson. She died
intestate. Was married to James Lindow, as heir of Thomas Wilson, and
Mary Woolford and Margaret Brown heirs of Margaret Erskin their mother.
Thomas Brown brother died intestate also.)
1783 tax- Matthias Miles 100 acres.

(The)DESART

Patented on 10 March 1665 to Stephen Horsey for 400 acres in Fairmount,

123

Election district 6,, map #9.
Rent Rolls 1666-1723 possessed 246 acres by Thomas Walston and 154 acres by John Tull.
1702 resurveyed to 525 acres, by Thomas Walston.
1726 Thomas Walston (wife Mary Walston) willed real estate to sons William Walston and Thomas Walston.
1729 John Tull willed to son Joshua Tull, part.
1754 Stephen Horsey willed to sons Revel Horsey, Stephen Horsey and grandson John Horsey.
4 May 1754 Benjamin Sharp and wife Mary Sharp, William Walston and Thomas Walston sold 175 acres to Zorobable Hall(that Thomas Walston willed to wife Mary Walston)
4 May 1754 Boaz Walston as eldest son of Thomas Walston sold his interest to Zorobable Hall except part conveyed to John Tull and Hugh McNeale.
1785 Zorobable Hall willed that wife Ann Hall give the tract to any of my sons the tract formerly belonging to William Walston and Thomas Walston (unnamed land). Sons George Hall and James Hall.
1783 tax- Zorobable Hall 175 acres.
1783 tax- Thomas Tull 154 acres.
20 Oct 1794 Joshua Tull Sr, s/o of John Tull gave to son Thomas Tull 150 acres with MEADOW,WINTER RANGE, etc.
2 Sep.1808 George Hall, wife Polly Hall of Baltimore Co. Md. sold to Edward Hall of Somerset County, the balance.

DICKERSONS HOPE

Patented on 28 July 1679 by William Stevens and assigned to Edward Dickenson for 300 acres in Brinkleys, Election district 3, map #16.
1703 Somerset Dickerson sold to brother Peter Dickerson part of this tract called PETER DICKERSON PASTURE.
Rent Rolls 1666-1723 40 acres Peter Dickerson and 260 acres Somerset Dickerson.
15 May 1724 Somerset Dickerson and wife Hannah Dickerson sold part to Mary Hampton (part now sold before to Peter Dickerson and Rev. John Henry, now deceased.)
1733 Peter Dickerson gave unnamed plantation to son Charles Dickerson.
1744 Mary Hampton gave to son Robert Jenkins Henry (Mary King wife of John Hampton)
1783 tax- Robert Jenkins King 125 1/2 acres.
1783 tax- Levi Riggin 40 acres.

DICKERSONS CHOICE

see DIXONS CHOICE

DICKERSONS FOLLY

Surveyed on 21 April 1680 by William Stevens for 200 acres in Lawsons, Election district 8, map #18.
Rent Rolls 1666-1723 Assigned to John Kirk.
1718/20 John Kirk willed estate to wife Bridget Kirk and after death to daughter Sarah Kirk (she married Littleton Townsend.)
19 Aug.1736 Littleton Townsend and wife Sarah Townsend sold to Joseph McClester 200 acres.
1783 tax- John Kellam Jr. 100 acres.

1793 John Kellum Sr, sold to Jesse Maddux Lankford.
15 Jan 1794 John Kellum Sr. & wife Elizabeth Kellum sold to Jesse Maddux
Lankford 92 acres.

DISCOVERY

Patented on 2 May 1688 by William Cheesman for 150 acres in Westover,
Election District 13, map #11.
Rent Rolls 1666-1723 Assigned to George Johnson and belongs to his heirs
in England, guardian Capt. Thomas Dixon.
1681 George Johnson willed to wife Frances Johnson,lands to be sold.
20 Feb.1695 George Johnson's attorney sold to William Planner.
5 Mar.1771 William Planner son and heir of William sold to Joshua
Kennerly.
7 Nov.1727 Joshua Kennerly of Dorcester Co. sold to Edmund Beauchamp.
18 June 1734 William Beauchamp gave to brother Robert Beauchamp all
rights.
1 Apr.1745 Robert Beauchamp and wife Esther Beauchamp sold for 5
shillings to William Beauchamp.
1 Apr.1745 William Beauchamp and wife Comfort Beauchamp sold to William
Jones 90 acres of the lower part of DISCOVERY and pt. of CONTENTION now
called PUZZLE.
1 Apr.1745 Robert King and William Beauchamp quitclaimed 100 acres to
Robert Beauchamp.
17 Mar.1762 Robert Beauchamp, wife Esther Beauchamp, sold to Thomas Tull
100 acres.
22 Mar.1769 Thomas Tull and wife Esther Tull sold to Thomas Davis 100
acres, with MIDDLE SWAMP, the tract that lies on the dividing line
between John Beauchamp and brother Robert Beauchamp.
19 Aug.1806 Thomas Davis sold all his lands to Beauchamp Davis, unnamed.
18 May 1807 Thomas M. Jones, wife Margaret Jones sold to Thomas Beauchamp
1/3rd Part divised by Thomas Davis to sons Robert and Thomas who died
intestate leaving James Davis, brother and Hetty Furniss and Margaret
Jones, sisters.
18 May 1807 James Davis and wife Mary Davis sold to Thomas Beauchamp
1/3rd part DISCOVERY & MIDDLE STRAND.
9 June 1807 James Furniss and wife Hetty Furniss sold to Thomas Beauchamp
1/3rd part.

DISCOVERY

Patented on 28 May 1684 in Brinkleys southwest, Election district 3, map
#17 by John Outten for 225 acres.
1708/9 John Outten willed to son John land in Condoqua Neck.
1745 debt Book, possessed by William Kersey
1755 debt Book, possessed by Samuel Kersey.
21 Jun 1769 William Kersey gave to Isaac Adams and wife Mary Adams
daughter of William Kersey SHOEMAKERS MEADOW,KERSLEYS INDUSTRY and
DISCOVERY. 12 1/2 acres.
1783 tax- Purnell Outten 50 acres
1783 tax- Isaac Outten 175 1/4 acres
1783 tax- Gertrude Adams 22 acres
1783 tax- Peter Kersey
1783 tax- William White Sr. 11 acres
17 Jan 1799 Isaac Outten, wife Margaret Outten of Acco.Co.Va. sold to

John Conner, several tracts 569 acres, no names.
11 Nov.1805 James Conner sold to William Coulbourn and William Lankford
lands purchased of Isaac Outten, unnamed.

DISCOVERY

Patented in 1734 by Benjamin Lankford for 50 acres in Brinkleys
northwest, Election district 3, map #14.
1749 DISCOVERY ENLARGED patented for 64 acres by Benjamin Lankford.
29 Dec.1769 Benjamin Lankford sold part to Thomas Williams of BOSTONS
DISCOVERY AND DISCOVERY ENLARGED 5 acres.
1783 tax- Benjamin Lankford Sr. 63 acres of ENLARGED.

DISCOVERY

Patented in 1745 for 3 acres in Lawsons, Election district 8, map #18 by
Kirk Gunby.
1767 resurveyed to GUNBYS CONCLUSION 3 1/4 acres by James Gunby.

DISCOVERY

Patented on 10 Aug.1753 by Thomas Wright for 45 acres in St.Peters,
Election district 2, map #6.
3 May 1759 Thomas Wright late of Somerset Co. but now of Ann Arundel Co.
sold to Thomas Aikman and John Webb of Somerset County.
25 May 1761 Thomas Aikman and John Webb agree to partition DISCOVERY,
CONTENTION & INTENT.
1783 tax- Thomas Aikman 45 acres with CONTENTION.
2 Sep.1800 John Webb, wife Hetty Webb sold to Thomas Noble

DISCOVERY

AKA- RECOVERY,1757 West Princess Anne.

DISCOVERY

Patented in 1757 by William Coulbourn for 92 acres in Lawsons, Election
district 8, map #18.
19 Dec. 1760 William Coulbourn, wife Elizabeth Coulbourn sold 30 acres
to brother Isaac Coulbourn.
1775 Isaac Coulbourn willed to nephew William Coulbourn of William, land
conveyed me by brother William Coulbourn, unnamed.
1783 Tax - William Coulbourn Jr. 60 acres.
1788 William Coulbourn willed real estate to son William, unnamed.

DISCOVERY

Patented in 1794 by Nathan Cahoon for 14 1/4 acres in Brinkleys
southwest, Election district 3, map #17.
7 Jan 1802 Nathan Cahoon sold to William Adams 4 5/8 acres.

DISPENCE

Patented on 8 Dec.1663 by David Spence for 1000 acres in Mt.Vernon,
Election district 5, map #5

Rent Rolls 1666-1723 James Spence son of David Spence 250 acres
John Spence son of David Spence 250 acres
Thomas Walker 242 acres by the name of WOODBRIDGE.
The remainder cut off by an older survey after sold to Thomas Holbrook.
30 Jun.1668 David Spence deeded to James Dashiell
8 Nov.1670 James Dashiell and Ann Dashiell made over 500 acres to Thomas Rowe.
4 June 1672 Thomas Rowe and wife Ann Rowe sold to Thomas Holbrook and John Holland 258 acres.
5 June 1675 Thomas Rowe and wife Ann Rowe sold to Thomas Walker 242 acres now called WOODBRIDGE.
1 Sep.1675 John Holland sold to Thomas Holbrook 258 1/4 acres called HOLD HOLLAND.
1678 will David Spence, to sons John Spence and James Spence at the age of 18 years, 500 acres.
4 Dec. 1710 James Spence and John Spence sold to George Dale the elder, one half.
22 June 1750 George Gale brother and executor to the will of Levin Gale deceased and Leah Gale only child and heir of Levin Gale sold to Henry Lowes 500 acres.
1761 Henry Lowes willed to son Tubman Lowes dwelling plantation purchased from the heirs of Levin Gale (unnamed)
9 Mar.1773 Henry Lowes sold to James Dickenson and William Hayward of Talbot County 500 acres with FATHERS CARE,HEREAFTER,RALPHS PREVENTION, ROBERTSONS LOTT.(mortgaged to pay debts.)
1783 tax- Henry Lowes 50 acres.
1786 Matilda Bounds, Jane Dashiell, Margaret Waters sold to Thomas Waters, Thomas Waters Stone and Daniel White.

DIVIDEND

See AMITY

DIVISION

Patented in 1770 by John Hayman for 30 acres in East Princess Anne, Election district 15, map #4.
1824 will of John Hayman, to daughters Leah Hayman and Molly Hayman.

DIXONS ADDITION

Patented in 1745 by Thomas Dixon for 167 acres in Brinkleys, northwest, Election district 3, map #14.
20 Aug.1747 Thomas Dixon Sr, and Benjamin Lankford sold to Thomas Dixon Jr. 31 axres of DIXONS ADDITION & part BOSTONTOWN, & DIXONS CHOICE.
9 Sep 1756 Isaac Dixon sold part to Thomas Dixon
16 Feb.1775 Isaac Dixon sold to Outerbridge Horsey 15 acres for 5 shillings, part that Thomas Dixon willed to Isaac.
1783 tax- Thomas Dixon 45 acres.
1785 Outerbridge Horsey willed to son Isaac Horsey land from Isaac Dixon (unnamed)
15 April 1807 Lazarus Horsey sold his interest to Thomas Robertson.

DIXONS BULL

Patented in 1738 by Thomas Dixon for 40 acres in Brinkleys northwest, Election district 3, map #14.

1756 Thomas Dixon sold to Isaac Dixon 20 acres with 9 acres of BALD
RIDGE.
9 Jan 1759 Isaac Dixon sold to Outerbridge Horsey his interest HORSEYS
PREVENTION,DIXONS CHOICE, PT. DIXONS BULL.
This was actually a settlement of bounds and division of lands.
15 April 1807 Lazarus Horsey sold his interest to Thomas Robertson.
7 Aug.1807 Isaac Dixon, wife Patty Dixon sold to Thomas Robertson 18 1/2
acres.

DIXONS CHOICE

Patented on 19 Aug.1663 by Ambrose Dixon for 500 acres in Brinkleys
northwest, Election district 3, map #14.
Rent Rolls 1666-1723 possessed by Capt. Thomas Dixon.
1740 ENLARGED pat. 425 acres by Thomas Dixon.
20 Aug.1747 Thomas Dixon Sr. and Benjamin Lankford sold to Thomas Dixon
Jr. 60 acres with BOSTON TOWN & DIXONS ADDN.
1 Sep 1747 Thomas Dixon traded William Smith 10 acres of DIXONS CHOICE
ENLARGED for 9 acres of BALD RIDGE.
9 Jan.1759 settlement of boundaries between Isaac Dixon and Outerbridge
Horsey.
10 Feb.1759 Triparte agreement, Thomas Dixon, Isaac Dixon for 214 1/2
acrew with Planner Williams.
1783 tax- Thomas Dixon (Enlarged) 216 acres.
1783 tax- Isaac Dixon 249 acres with DIXONS BULL.
1783 tax- Outerbridge Horsey 4 1/2 acres of enlarged.
1794 Thomas Dixon gave to daughter Sarah Dixon Furniss DIXONS CHOICE
ENLARGED.
15 April 1807 Lazarus Horsey sold his interest to Thomas Robertson

DIXONS KINDNESS

Patented on 16 Nov.1694 by George Hughs for 100 acres in Brinkleys
northwest, Election district 3, map #14.
Rent Rolls 1666-1723 Thomas Prior
12 June 1700 George Hughs deeded to Thomas Prior who willed to wife Ann
Prior and son Samuel Prior.
27 Jan 1748 Ann Prior widow of Thomas Prior, and Samuel Prior eldest son
of Thomas Prior, and John Scott quitclaimed to Outerbridge Horsey 100
acres, with PRIORS ADVENTURE & BEARS NECK with tract COULBOURN.
17 Jan 1756 Ann Prior relic of Thomas Prior and Samuel Prior heir at law,
sold 100 acres to Outerbridge Horsey. Confirmation of previous deed.
1783 tax- Outerbridge Horsey 20 1/2 acres
1785 Outerbridge Horsey willed to grandson William Horsey.
11 March 1797 Outerbridge Horsey son of William Horsey and grandson of
Outerbridge Horsey sold to William Hitch.
12 March 1797 William Hitch returned same to Outerbridge Horsey.
15 April 1807 Lazarus Horsey sold his interest to Thomas Robertson.

DIXONS LOTT

Patented in 1663 by Ambrose Dixon for 300 acres in Brinkleys southwest,
Election district 3, map #17.
May 1667 Ambrose Dixon, wife Mary Dixon, sold to George Wilson Sr.of
Nansemond Co.Va. 300 acres.
17 Feb.1672 George Wilson and wife Elizabeth Wilson sold to Robert Dukes

150 acres
14 July 1685 Robert Dukes and Elizabeth Dukes (Elizabeth Wilson) sold to
George Wilson 150 acres out of 300 acres of DIXONS LOTT in Morumsco
called DUKES PLACE.
1709 George Wilson III devised his land to sons George Wilson and William
Wilson.
Rent Rolls 1666-1723. 150 acres George Wilson, 150 acres William Wilson.
21 Nov.1721 George Wilson and Susannah Wilson his wife sold 100 acres to
James Trehearn.
1783 tax- Stephen Marshall 50 acres
1783 tax- Isaac Marshall 50 acres.

DIXONS LOTT

Patented on 14 Nov.1694 by Thomas Dixon in Crisfield, Election district
7, map #20, for 1200 acres..
Rent Rolls 1666-1723 Thomas Dixon.
4 March 1720 Division of lands by sons of Thomas Dixon, William Dixon and
Thomas Dixon.
20 May 1734 William Dixon wife Elizabeth Dixon, and Thomas Dixon, wife
Sarah Dixon, of Coventry Parish sold 150 acres to Thomas Williams Jr. now
called WINTER REFUGE.
21 Jan 1737 Thomas Dixon and William Dixon sold 150 acres to Thomas
Williams.
27 Aug.1739 William Dixon gave to daughter Mary Horsey wife of
Outerbridge Horsey 100 acres.
15 Aug.1748 Thomas Dixon sold 75 acres to Henry Miles called DIXONS
HAMMOCK.
15 Aug.1748 Thomas Dixon sold to Patrick McKemmy 75 acres.
15 Aug.1748 Thomas Dixon sold 50 acres to Isaac Williams
Nov.1756 Henry Miles willed to son William 75 acres of HOG PEN SWAMP adj.
DIXONS HAMMOCK.
2 Apr.1751 Isaac Williams and wife Ann Williams, traded 50 acres with
Thomas Williams with WILLIAMSTOWN,WILLIAMS CONQUEST and VACANCY.
1768 Thomas Williams willed to grandson Levin Williams 100 acres of marsh
at Jeans Island, unnamed and to grandson Thomas 1/2 of marsh at Jeans
Island DIXONS LOTT.
28 Nov.1771 Levin Williams sold to Planner Williams and Thomas Williams
for 5 shillings land Thomas Williams deceased grandfather of Levin willed
to him -no name.
11 Dec.1756 Ambrose Dixon, wife Martha Dixon, sold to Kirk Gunby 150
acres devised him by will of his father William.
24 Oct.1765 William Miles sold to Matthias Gale of London, merchant, 75
acres DIXONS LOTT,HOGPEN SWAMP,FORTUNE PLEASURE,CHANCE & HEARTS EASE.
2 Dec.1765 Thomas Williams gave to grandson Thomas Williams Jr. 25 acres
of DIXONS LOTT with other lands.
2 Dec.1767 Thomas Williams gave to Planner Williams his grandson 1000
acres in Annamessex where Isaac Williams brother of Thomas lived adjacent
lands given to Thomas Williams Jr.
1768 will of Thomas Williams, to grandson Thomas Williams land at Jeans
Island.
1770 Stacey Miles willed to Henry Miles son of William Miles 1/3rd part.
7 Aug.1774 Thomas Williams sold to Isaac Marshall and Stephen Marshall
100 acres, out of a deed from Thomas Dixon and William Dixon to Capt
Thomas Williams the elder, formerly called DIXONS LOTT but now called

WINTERHARBOR, and also by the will of Thomas Williams.
19 Jan 1775 Kirk Gunby willed to son John Gunby 100 acres bought of
Ambrose Dixon and to son Levin Gunby 50 acres bought of Ambrose Dixon on
Janes Island marsh.
29 Apr.1777 Isaac Coulbourn sold to William Coulbourn son of William for
10 shillings 50 acres purchased of Isaac Dixon
21 Apr.1777 Isaac Dixon sold to Isaac Coulbourn for 10 shillings 100
acres.
1783 tax- Thomas Dixon Jr. 110 acres
1783 tax- William Dixon Sr. 25 acres
1783 tax- Ambrose Dixon 25 acres
1783 tax- Thomas Dixon 30 acres
1783 tax- Samuel Trehearn 55 acres
1783 Ambrose Dixon willed lands to son William Dixon and after death to
grandson William Dashiell Dixon, unnamed
1797 Thomas Dixon willed land to son William Dixon, unnamed..
1802 Thomas Williams willed to grandson Thomas W. Williams land that
descended to me at the death of Thomas Williams, unnamed.
1881 resurveyed to 1181 1/3rd acres by Thomas I.Dixon.

DOE PARK

Patented in 1747 by John Johnson for 50 acres in Lawsons, Election
district 8, map #18.
1783 tax- John Johnson Jr. 50 acres
1792 John Johnson Sr. willed to son John and after death to grandson John
Henry Johnson.
1802 resurveyed to NEGLECT 110 1/2 acres.

DOGWOOD RIDGE
Also see PITCHCROFT on Deals Island

DOGWOOD RIDGE

Patented on 11 Aug.1753 by James Laws for 100 acres in West Princess
Anne, Election district 1, map #3.
1757/8 James Laws willed 100 acres to son James Laws.
31 May 1763 James Laws, wife Jane Ann Laws traded to William Hayward 8
1/2 acres for same of NUTTERS PURCHASE.
20 March 1764 James Laws and wife Jane Laws sold to William Hayward Esq.
with part of NUTTERS PURCHASE 8 acres.
19 March 1764 William Hayward and wife Margaret Hayward sold to Andrew
Francis Cheney 100 acres.
1765 resurveyed to FRIENDSHIP 172 acres.

DONES NEST EGG

Patented in 1761 by John Done,a resurvey of LABOUR IN VANE & BOARD TREE
RIDGE for 565 acres in East Pr.Anne, Election district 15, map #4.
25 May 1784 John Done sold part to William Heath, description but no
acreage mentioned.
1 Oct.1785 John Done, eldest son of Dr.John Done sold to John Denwood 270
acres.

1 Feb 1789 David Wilson, wife Sarah Wilson (Sarah was the widow of
John Done and was seized of dower rights) and Robert A. Done sold to John
Done, with lot in Princess Anne Town.
31 March 1795 Abraham Heath,wife Martha Heath sold to Josiah Hobbs, as
William Heath willed in 1783 to son Abraham, HATHS CHANCE, HATHS SECOND
ADDN.TO HATHS CHANCE,DONES NEST EGG, HAPHAZARD,WILSONS FIRST, HATHS GIFT,
HOG RIDGE.
31 March 1795 Abraham Heath, wife Martha Heath, sold to Josiah Hobbs with
HATHS CHANCE,HOG YARD,WILSONS FIRST,etc.
24 Feb.1800 John Wilkins sold to William Done LABOUR IN VAIN & BOARD TREE
RIDGE bought at public sale now in DONES NEST EGG 220 3/4 acres.
29 March 1803 John Done sold to William Done 29 3/4 acres
29 March 1803 William Done and wife Margaret Done sold to John Done, no
acres mentioned.
13 Aug 1804 Comissioners to sell real estate of William Heath sold 22
acres to Rebecca Hobbs daughter of William Heath. Division of lands to
children, Abraham Heath, John Heath, Nelly Morris, Leah Beauchamp, Polly
Anderson, Betsy Pollitt, Priscilla Morris, Esther Fooks, and Rebecca
Hobbs.
26 March 1805 William Done sold to John Done 29 3/4 acres.

DORMANS ADDITION

Patented in 1749 to Nehemiah Dorman for 104 acres in West Pr. Anne,
Election district 1, map #2.
25 Nov.1756 Nehemiah Dorman sold to Levin Ballard with DORMANS PURCHASE &
NELSONS CHOICE. mortgage 104 acres.
21 July 1756 Levin Ballard released back to Nehemiah Dorman.
20 Nov.1767 William Hayward of Talbot Co. sold to Levin Ballard of
Som.Co.(that was mortgaged to William Hayward)except part conveyed to
Andrew Francis Cheney, with TURKEY RIDGE,HAYWARDS PURCHASE, NELSONS
CHOICE.
4 Feb.1768 Sheldon Dorman quitclaimed 104 acres to Levin Ballard.
15 Oct.1768 Levin Ballard sold to William Geddes 84 1/2 acres with
NELSONS CHOICE,HAYWARDS PURCHASE.
7 Oct.1769 William Geddes and wife Mary Geddes sold to William Winder 84
1/2 acres with NELSONS CHOICE,HAYWARDS PURCHASE, DORMANS ADDITION.
13 March 1779 Levin Woolford and John McGrath sold 104 acres to Samuel
Wilkins.
1783 tax- Dr. John Winder 69 acres
1783 tax- Samuel Wilkins 97 1/2 acres
1792 William Winder willed to son John Winder lands bought of William
Geddes (unnamed)
27 Feb.1793 John Wilkins, wife Sally Wilkins sold to James Ewing 104
acres with HAYWARDS PURCHASE,TURKEY RIDGE, DORMANS ADDITION.
18 April 1807 Hans Creevey of Baltimore trustee,of Isaac Ewing heir of
James Ewing, sold to William Winder 20 5/8 acres.
1808 William Winder willed to son William Henry Winder part purchased of
the trustee of James Ewing.

DORMANS CONCLUSION

Patented in 1768 to Michael Dorman for 276 acres in West Princess Anne,
Election district 1, map #2.
1769 Michael Dorman willed to son John Dorman part of tract on the road

from Wicomico Creek to Princess Anne town and balance to son Chase Dorman.

11 Aug.1772 Chase Dorman sold 54 acres to Levin Ballard.

19 Sep.1776 Levin Ballard sold to Levin Woolford and John McGrath 104 acres.

21 Jan.1778 Levin Ballard of Calvert Co. and wife Elizabeth Ballard sold to Samuel Wilkins(Elizabeth Ballard was entitled by dower to lands conveyed by Levin Woolford and John McGrath to Samuel Wilkins. Henry Ballard deceased father of Levin was willed by Charles Ballard 17 acres of marsh on Monie Creek.)

13 March 1779 Levin Woolford and John McGrath sold 54 acres to Samuel Wilkins with HAYWARDS PURCHASE & DORMANS ADDITION, etc.

1783 tax- Samuel Wilkins 54 acres

1783 tax- Chase Dorman 92 acres

1783 tax- Isaiah Dorman 17 acres

1783 tax- John Dorman 139 acres

13 May 1792 John Wilkins, wife Sarah Wilkins sold to Nehemiah King 54 acres.(part conveyed by Chase Dorman to Levin Ballard.)with HAYWARDS PURCHASE.

1793 Chase Dorman willed 50 acres to son Thomas Chase Dorman

9 July 1796 Levin Pollitt,wife Eleanor Pollitt sold to Stephen Right 12 acres with JOHNS HILL.

9 Aug.1796 Nehemiah King sold to Samuel Wilson 54 acres with HAYWARDS PURCHASE.

1797 Chase Dorman willed dwelling plantation to son Hezekiah Dorman, unnamed.

26 Feb 1799 George Handy,sheriff sold to highest bidder Benjamin Dashiell- for debts of Isaiah Dorman devised from Michael Dorman, DORMANS DISCOVERY & DORMANS CONCLUSION.

13 April 1802 Hezekiah Dorman son of Chase Dorman and wife Amelia Dorman sold to Zadock Long

25 Jan 1806 Thomas Purnell Dorman sold to Solomon Dorman 12 3/4 acres.

20 Dec.1808 Thomas Purnell Dorman sold to Solomon Dorman 8 acres.

13 Feb.1810 Thomas Purnell Dorman sold to Randal Hayman 59 1/4 acres of ODRMANS CONCLUSION & ADDN. TO HOG QUARTER.

DORMANS CONCLUSION

Patented in 1794 to Levin Dorman for 411 acres in East Pr. Anne, Election district 15, map #5.

12 April 1810 Levin Dorman Sr. gave to Levin Dorman Jr. 200 acres with CHANCE.

DORMANS DISCOVERY

Patented in 1749 by Michael Dorman for 171 acres in West Pr. Anne, Election district 1 map #2.

1771 Michael Dorman willed to sons Isaiah Dorman and Chase Dorman.

1783 tax- Chase Dorman 40 acres

1783 tax- Elizabeth Dorman with GOLDEN QUARTER 31 1/2 acres

1783 tax- Isaiah Dorman 131 acres

1793 Chase Dorman willed 60 acres to son Jesse Dorman and plantation to son Hezekiah Dorman.

9 Oct 1794 Isaiah Dorman s/o Michael sold to George Dorman all land willed by father Michael Dorman, no name 150 acres.

26 Feb.1799 George Handy,sheriff sold to highest bidder Benjamin Dashiell

for debts of Isaiah Dorman.
19 April 1803 Hezekiah Dorman, wife Amelia, sold to Littleton Dennis
Teackle 60 acres, description, from brother Jesse Dorman, no name.
19 April 1803 Ezekiel Dugan and wife Eleanor Dugan sold to Littleton
Dennis Teackle 60 acres, received by Eleanor Dugan from deceased brother
Jesse Dorman, no name.
19 April 1803 Levin Pollitt, wife Margaret Pollitt sold to Littleton
Dennis Teackle, land from the brother of Margaret Pollitt, Jesse Dorman.
19 April 1803 Hezekiah Dorman son of Chase Dorman, wife Amelia Dorman
sold to Zadock Long, DORMANS DISCOVERY, DORMANS CONCLUSION, GOLDEN
QUARTER, NELSONS CHOICE, devised to Chase Dorman by his father Michael
Dorman except 60 acres Chase devised to son Jesse Dorman and 50 acres
DORMANS CONCLUSION Chase Dorman devised to son Thomas.
9 Jan 1807 I Nelly Benson widow of Matthias Benson, daughter of Samuel
Dorman and Catherine Dorman deceased; Catherine my mother was Catherine
Stevens of Bath Co. Va. appointed Charles Bannister Robins my sisters
grandson, of the town of Lewisburg, Green Briar Co. Va. attorney to take
land in Somerset County owned by Zadock Dorman, my undivided part to
sell. May father was Samuel Dorman who married Catherine Stevens. Their
children were Catherine Dorman, Elizabeth Dorman, Samuel Dorman, Sarah
Dormanlly Dorman, John Dorman, Tabitha Dorman or Levinia Dorman.
Know I Rachel Dorman widow of John Dorman eldest son of Samuel Dorman,
and daughter of Nehemiah Tilghman and wife Catherine Tilghman. Catherine
Tilghman was the daughter of Samuel Dorman. I have children John Dorman,
Nehemiah Dorman, Samuel Dorman, Stephen Dorman of Lewisburg, Greenbriar
Va. and I appoint the same attorey, Charles Bannister Robins son of Levi
Robins who was son of Joseph Robins and his wife Catherine Robins which
said Catherine married Nehemiah Tilghman of Lewisburg Va.
28 March 1807 Charles Bannister Robins of Greenbriar Co. Va. attorney for
Nelly Benson, Rachel Dorman, Nehemiah Dorman, Samuel Dorman and Stephen
Dorman John Dorman sold to Henry King 128 acres, held by Zadock Dorman
who died intestate leaving one daughter Lovey Dorman who died intestate.

DORMANS DISCOVERY

Patented in 1760, a resurvey of TOSSITER for 128 1/2 acres in Dublin
District, Election district 4, map #13.
1783 tax- Zadock Dorman 89 acres (div. Ck.100)
1783 tax- Katherine Dorman 43 acres.
1792 patented to Zadock Dorman.
16 Nov.1793 Zadock Dorman sold to Sarah Cluff 1 acre.
1801 Zadock Dorman died intestate. His daughter Lovey Dorman died so it
was sold by Charles Collins of Virginia to Henry King.
19 Feb.1796 Zadock Dorman leased to Henry King 2 acres for 20 years.
12 May 1800 Zadock Dorman leased 5 acres to Henry King for 15 years.

DORMANS FOLLY

Patented in 1768 by Andrew Adams for 103 3/4 acres in West Pr. Anne,
Election district 1, map #2.
19 Oct.1773 Andrew Adams sold for 5 shillings all to Levin Ballard.
1773 Levin Ballard sold 103 3/4 acres to Levin Woolford and John McGrath.
13 March 1779 Levin Woolford and John McGrath sold to Samuel Wilkins 103
3/4 acres with HAYWARDS PURCHASE, TURKEY RIDGE, etc.
1783 tax- Samuel Wilkins 103 3/4 acres.

13 Mar.1792 John Wilkins sold to Solomon Dorman 30 acres.
27 Feb.1793 John Wilkins, wife Sally Wilkins sold to James Ewing 103 3/4
acres with TURKEY RIDGE,HAYWARDS PURCHASE and 17 marsh on Monie Crek.

DORMANS PRIVILEDGE

Patented in 1729 by Matthew Dorman 30 acres in West Pr. Anne. Election
district 1, map #2.
9 July 1758 Nehemiah Dorman sold to William Allen

DORMANS PRIVILEDGE

Patented in 1729 by Matthew Dorman for 30 acres in West Pr.Anne,Election
district 1, map #2.
Triparte agreement 9 July 1758 Nehemiah Dorman sold to William Allen and
William Hayward with NELSONS CHOICE 75 acres.
21 June 1758 Levin Ballard sold to Nehemiah Dorman 30 acres with DORMANS
PURCHASE, DORMANS ADDN. & NELSONS CHOICE.
2 Nov 1758 William Hayman and Nehemiah Dorman sold to Henry Newman 30
acres.
1759 resurveyed to NEWMANS ADDITION 192 1/4 acres.

DORMANS PURCHASE

Patented in 1771 by Levin Dorman for 206 acres in East Pr. Anne, Election
district 15, map #5.
1783 tax- Levin Dorman 206 acres.
19 March 1793 Levin Dorman sold to William Adams 206 acres with 80 acres
of CHANCE.

DORMANS PURCHASE

Patented on 29 Nov.1682 by Phillip Carter and assigned to Matthew Dorman
for 150 acres in West Pr. Anne, Election district 1, map #2.
1692 Matthew Dorman willed to son Matthew.
Rent Rolls, 1666-1723- Matthew Dorman
25 Nov.1756 Nehemiah Dorman sold to Levin Ballard (conveyed by Matthew
Dorman to Nehemiah Dorman) 30 acres.
17 June 1758 Levin Ballard released mortgage of 150 acres to Nehemiah
Dorman.
16 June 1762 Matthew Dorman son of Matthew sold to Levin Ballard 55 acres
of parcel which Matthew Dorman grandfather of Matthew willed to son
William Dorman near head of Manokin River. (unnamed- probably DORMANS
PURCHASE & NELSONS CHOICE) 9 Oct 1794 Isaiah Dorman son of Michael sold
to George Dorman

DOUBLE PURCHASE

Patented on 19 Nov.1679 by Randall Revell & Ann Toft for 3000 acres in
Westover (Revells Neck) Election district 13, map #10.
25 Feb.1681 Randall Revell and wife Catherine Revell sold to William
Shurman 255 acres called MIDDLE PLANTATION
19 March 1682 Randall Revell and wife Catherine Revell sold to Robert
King 300 acres called KINGSLAND.
13 Oct.1682 Randall Revell and wife Catherine sold to George Downs 200

acres called DOWNS LOTT
13 April 1683 Randall Revell and wife Catherine Revell gave for affection
to children, William Coulbourn and wife Ann Coulbourn 300 acres.
13 May 1685 Randall Revell gave to wife Catherine Revell 500 acres, to
son Randall Revell 500 acres and to daughters Ann Revell, Katherine
Revell and Sarah Revell 500 acres each.
1667 Ann Toft of Accomac Co.Va. gave to Katherine Revell and Hannah
Revell 300 acres.
5 Feb.1681 Randall Revell sold to Thomas Pool 245 acres called WELCOME
POOL.
1701 Jeffrey Mitchell gave to son Thomas Mitchell 250 acres at Condoway
Point.
Rent rolls 1666-1723- possessed by-
 Randall Revell 1160 acres
 Thomas Mitchell 250 acres
 Ann Coulbourn 250 acres (Ann Revell married William Coulbourn Jr.)
 Stephen Horsey 500 acres and 240 acres (he married Hannah Revell)
 Nathaniel Horsey 500 acres (he married Sarah Revell)
 Mary King 300 acres (widow of Capt. John King.)
 Capt. John West 1570 acres. (he married Katherine Revell)
 William Foxon 200 acres
 Andrew Thompson 125 acres
 Abel Wright 75 acres and 45 acres
 William Bannister 340 acres
 James Furniss 245 acres
note; 1st town SOMERSET TOWN or Summertown built on this property.
1703 John Lane gave to son Ephraim Lane 100 acres.
1715/6 John West willed to wife Katherine West 1/2 of CATHERINES
CONTENT,GREAT HOPES & BROTHERS UNITED.
12 July 1720 Katherine West widow and Randall West one of the sons of
John West and Katherine West, sold 214 acres to Robert King.
1730/1 Randall West son of John West, gave to daughter Ann West 1570
acres, dwelling plantation had from mother.
1720 William Bannister died single person, estate to brothers Thomas
Bannister and Charles Bannister and sisters Rachel Bannister and Mary
Bannister.
10 Oct 1722 Charles Revell son of Randall of Randall Revell sold to Boaz
Walston part of ARRACOCO & DOUBLE PURCHASE 333 1/3 acres, 100 acres being
part called GOSHAN.
15 Dec 1722 Sarah Horsey gave to son John Horsey 200 acres of part called
SARAHS JOY.
7 March 1726 Randall West and wife Hannah West, William West and Rachel
West his wife, Anthony West and Mary West his wife sold to Robert King 79
acres that Katherine Revell West willed to aforesaid on 1 Jan. 1722
called ADDITION.
31 July 1726 Sarah Horsey, relic of Nathaniel Horsey gave to son William
Horsey 100 acres that Randall Revell gave to daughter Sarah Revell tract
now called SARAHS JOY being part of DOUBLE PURCHASE.
27 Nov.1728 Thomas Bannister son of William Bannister sold to Thomas
Mitchell 60 acres being part of DOUBLE PURCHASE & ARRACOCO now called
FATHERS PURCHASE being part of afsd purchase called WILLIAMS PURCHASE.
13 Nov.1729 Hannah Horsey and John Horsey son of Hannah gave to her
daughter and his sister Elizabeth Outerbridge wife of Burr Outerbridge
late of the island of Bermuda, part of two tracts HANNAHS DELIGHT &
EXCHANGE 200 acres hence forward to be called MOTHERS CARE & BROTHERS

GOOD WILL.

4 Feb.1729 William West and Rachel West his wife sold to Randall West 150 acres of BROTHERS CONTRIVANCE called CATHERINES CONTENT, part of DOUBLE PURCHASE.

27 Aug.1730 Randall West sold to Ephraim Wilson 165 acres adj. CATHERINES CONTENT, patented Randall Revell that he conveyed part called GREAT HOPES to John West father of Randall West (this was actually part of ARRACOCO.)

1735 William Thompson son of Andrew Thompson, willed to son William Thompson 125 acres left by father. Is no issue to brother Andrew Thompson.

12 June 1741 I Ann Mitchell wife of Thomas Mitchell give to sons Randall Mitchell and Stephen Mitchell, dwelling plantation on Manokin River, all lands(unnamed.)

8 May 1742 Andrew Thompson sold 95 acres to David Wilson

7 Apr 1750 Nathaniel Horsey sold to Abraham Covington for 5 shillings 100 acres of land devised to Nathaniel Horsey by the will of his grandmother Sarah Horsey.

21 Jan 1750 Charles Cottingham and wife Margaret Cottingham sold to John Dennis land bequeathed to Margaret by Charles Revell (no name)

5 Oct.1752 Stephen Horsey Sr, sold to Sarah Bannister widow, tract purchased by Stephen Horsey of Randall Revell 43 acres, unnamed.

20 Nov.1750 Randall Revell sold 106 acres to John Dennis.

25 Sep.1752 Hannah Horsey for 5 shillings sold to Robert King all interest in KINGSLAND coveyed by Randall Revell and wife Hannah Revell to the father of Robert King containing 300 acres and all DENNIS LOTT 200 acres conveyed to Robert King by William Foxon and wife Judith Foxon, 214 acres called DOUBLE PURCHASE conveyed to Robert King by Katherine and Randall West and 79 acres of ADDITION conveyed to Robert King by Randall West, William West, and Anthony West and their wives and all Robert King is possessed of between Back Creek and Manokin River in Revells Neck.

1754 Stephen Horsey willed to son Stephen Horsey lands between William Outterbridge and HANNAHS DELIGHT.

31 Dec 1754 William Bannister son of Thomas Bannister sold to Thomas Hayward 137 acres in Revells neck(no name)

20 June 1758 Ephraim Wilson deeded to brother Samuel Wilson (from David Wilson father of Ephraim) no acres given.

12 Feb 1760 John Covington son of Abraham Covington, and wife Teresay Covington, sold to George Irving 100 acres.

19 Aug.1761 John Dennis sold to Ballard Bozman 107 acres

8 Oct 1765 Thomas Hayward Jr. sold to James Elzey tracts in Revells Neck bought of William Bannister (no name or acres)

13 Nov.1767 Michael Robins and wife Agnes Robins of Accoc.Co.Va. eldest son of John Robins who was the eldest brother and heir of Sarah Bannister deceased, sold to Mitchell Bannister of Somerset County.

13 Nov.1767 Michael Robins of Acco.Co.Va. sold to Levin King one of the children of Nehemiah King(per contract with Nehemiah) who willed to son Levin King. 43 acres.

1777 Miitchell Bannister willed to son Charles Bannister lands on south side of Middle Gut and to son William Bannister, same (unnamed)

1783 tax- Ballard Bozman 500 acres & 107 1/4 acres
1783 tax- Heirs of Charles Bannister 160 acres
1783 tax- Phillip Barnabus 25 acres
1782 tax- Heirs of Mitchell Bannister 80 acres
1783 tax- James Elzey 200 acres
1783 tax- Grace Furniss 81 3/4 acres

1783 tax- George Corbin 401 acres
1783 tax- William Furniss 165 1/4 acres
1783 tax- Revel Horsey 300 acres
1783 tax- Levin King of Nehemiah 293 acres & 50 acres and ADDITION 30 acres.
1783 tax- John Irving 200 acres
1783 tax- Nehemiah King 200 acres with FREE PURCHASE
1783 tax- Samuel Muir 100 acres
1783 tax- Benjamin Polk 50 acres
1783 tax- James Polk 113 acres
1783 tax- Randall Revell Jr. 100 acres
1783 tax- Randall Revell Sr. 333 1/2 acres
24 May 1786 Nehemiah King sold 300 acres to Thomas Hayward for 5 shillings, KINGSLAND taken out of DOUBLE PURCHASE.
21 Jun 1786 Thomas Hayward sold to Nehemiah King same as above.
25 May 1786 William Bowen of Worc.Co. and Ann Bowen who was the daughter of Mitchell Bannister and sister of Charles Bannister deceased, sold to Rev.Jacob Ker, part of a tract in Revells neck (no name) 8 acres.
20 March 1787 Littleton Walston sold to Thomas Evans 100 acres that John Walston had. Betsy Walston wife of Littleton Walston lived there until age 21 and then conveyed 1/4th part which Mitchell Bannister willed to son William Bannister, now deceased (no name or acreage)
27 Fe.1790 Thomas Evans, wife Sally Evans sold to Littleton Walston 1/4 pt. devised by Mitchell Bannister to son William Bannister (no name or acres)
17 Mar 1790 Littleton Walston,wife Betty Walston sold to Thomas Fitchett 100 acres that Charles Revell conveyed to Boaz Walston
19 Mar.1790 Jesse Walston sold to Thomas Fitchett lands of mortgage that Littlton Walston being indebted to Jesse
Walston that Joy Walston died seized in Revells Neck (no name) 100 acres.
26 Feb 1791 Littleton Walston sold to Thomas Fitchett 1/4th pt.(no name).
1 Jun 1791 James Elzey and wife Nelly Elzey daughter of Ballard Bozman dec'd, gave to son Robert Elzey land devised Nelly by her father.(Nelly now pregnant and to live with daughters peaceably on land) and if son Robert Elzey has no issue and if a son is born, then to him(no name or acres.)
8 May 1792 Littleton Walston,wife Betsy Walston' sold to Thomas Fitchett 1/4 pt. land (Littleton married Betsy Bannister).
11 March 1794 John Wilson gave to kinsman Samuel Ker 60 acres purchased of Nehemiah King.
11 May 1793 Thomas Fitchett, wife Susanna Fitchett, sold to Smith Horsey land bought of Littleton Walston.
24 Feb,1795 Solomon Long sold to William Done 299 acres of BEVERLY(pt. DOUBLE PURCHASE) and AMITY adjacent.
8 Jan 1795 John Custis Wilson and Samuel Ker,wife Betsy Ker sold to John Irving 109 acres of ESKRIDGES & ROBINS adj.
8 Jan 1795 John Custis Wilson, wife Peggy Wilson sold to Samuel Ker, ESKRIDGES & ROBINS 106 acres.
12 May 1807 John Revell and Randal Revell sold to William Fleming 252 1/2 acres.
       Part of DOUBLE PURCHASE Called BROTHERS UNITED
1715/6 John West willed to wife Katherine West 1/2 of CATHERINES CONTENT, GREAT HOPES & BROTHERS UNITED.
1722 Katherine West willed to son Anthony West 150 acres and to son Thomas West 100 acres (unnamed)

1736 Anthony West sold to Joseph McClester,(mortgage to David Wilson)165
acres of BROTHERS UNITED & GREAT HOPES part of DOUBLE PURCHASE.
20 May 1746 Samuel Feddeman of Acco.Co.Va. and wife Ann Feddeman only
surviving daughter of Randall West of Som.Co. who was one of the sons of
John West by Katherine West his wife , sold all to David Wilson of
CATHERINES CONTENT, GREAT HOPES & BROTHERS UNITED.
10 Nov.1771 Elijah West son of Anthony West,late, of Kent Co.Del. sold to
Isaac Coulbourn of Som.Co. with Samuel Wilson 1/5th pt. for life,
BROTHERS UNITED 405 acres and GREAT HOPES both part DOUBLE PURCHASE
4 Nov.1784 Anne Feddeman,heir of Randall West sold to Samuel Wilson all
her rights to CATHERINES CONTENT,GREAT HOPES & BROTHERS UNITED.

Part of DOUBLE PURCHASE called CATHERINES CONTENT
2 March 1684 Randall Revell and wife Katherine Revell gave to youngest
daughter Katherine Revell 500 acres called CATHERINES CONTENT.
1720 Katherine West, widow of John West sold to Robert King 214 acres,
part that was called BROTHERS CONVIENCE.
4 Feb.1729 William West and Rachel West his wife sold to Randall West
150 acres of BROTHERS CONVIENCE called CATHERINES CONTENT.
16 Jan 1734 Anthony West and wife Mary West son of John West and
Catherine West, sold to Robert King 30 acres, now called NEW ADDITION.

10 Feb 1734 Anthony West and wife Mary West sold to Daniel Wilson 100
acres now called WILSONS LOTT being part of CATHERINES CONTENT.
1734 Stephen Horsey, John Stevens and wife Ann Stevens quitclaimed 100
acres to David Wilson, WILSONS LOTT being part of CATHERINES CONTENT.
12 Mar.1737 Anthony West and wife Mary West sold to David Wilson
CATHERINES CONTENT now called TRIBLE PURCHASE.
20 May 1746 Samuel Feddeman of Acco.Co.Va. and wife Ann Feddeman only
surviving daughter of Randall West of Som.Co. who was one of the sons of
John West by Katherine West his wife sold all to David Wilson, with
BROTHERS UNITED & GREAT HOPES.

Part of DOUBLE PURCHASE called DAUGHTERS DOWER
Thomas Mitchell resurveyed FATHERS GIFT by Southy Whittington on request
of William Eskridge, part of 500 acres dividing from the land of Thomas
Mitchell, laid out for 217 acres on 29 June 1722.
20 March 1755 Stephen Mitchell sold to Randall Mitchell 250 acres being
1/2 part of FATHERS GIFT, original tract DOUBLE PURCHASE.
8 Dec.1767 Randall Mitchell sold to Mitchell Bannister 38 1/2 of
DAUGHTERS DOWER.
8 Dec.1767 Mitchell Bannister sold to Randall Mitchell 62 1/2 acres that
Randall Revell sold to William Bannister called DAUGHTERS DOWER, part
WILLIAMS PURCHASE, all part of DOUBLE PURCHASE.
13 Oct.1772 Randall Mitchell sold to Samuel Wilson 174 acres land William
Coulbourn and Ann Coulbourn deeded to Thomas Mitchell.
Samuel Wilson sold to Jacob Ker 273 acres purchased of Randall Mitchell,
no name.
1783 tax- Rev. Jacob Ker 225 acres of DAUGHTERS DOWER & BANNISTERS LAND

Part of DOUBLE PURCHASE called FATHERS PURCHASE
6 Feb.1749 Thomas Mitchell and Thomas Bannister sold 60 acres to Nehemiah
King out of DOUBLE PURCHASE
20 Dec.1791 Nehemiah King sold 60 acres to John Wilson with ADDITION,
DEAR PURCHASE,CLOVERFIELD,COME BY CHANCE.

20 Dec.1791 John Wilson and wife Peggy Wilson sold to Nehemiah King same tract as above, trade of lands.

Part of DOUBLE PURCHASE called GOSHEN
1722 Randall Revell sold to Boaz Walston 100 acres.
10 Jan 1785 Samuel Mure and wife Elizabeth Mure sold to Jesse Walston her right of dower to 1/3 of GOSHEN where Joy Walston lived in Revels Neck.
18 July 1786 Jesse Walston sold to Littleton Walston all rights of discovery 1/3rds where Joy Walston lived.
8 July 1786 Littleton Walston traded 100 acres with Jesse Walston.
27 Feb.1790 Thomas Evans,wife Sally Evans sold to Littleton Walston and wife Betsy Walston- agreement- that Mitchell Bannister had that descended to four sisters 100 acres.
23 Mar.1790 Thomas Fitchett, wife Susannah Fitchett sold to George Corbin of Acco.Co.Va. 100 acres of part sold to Boaz Walston.
28 June 1799 Smith Horsey and wife Mary Horsey of Acco.Co.Va. and William SLocomb and wife Ann Slocomb of Worc.Co. sold to Revel Horsey 100 acres, devised by Mitchell Bannister to son William Bannister (unnamed land)

Part of DOUBLE PURCHASE called HANNAHS DELIGHT & EXCHANGE
15 Mar.1684 Randall Revell and wife Katherine Revell gave to Stephen Horsey and wife Hannah Horsey 500 acres out of DOUBLE PURCHASE, called HANNAHS DELIGHT.
13 Nov.1729 Hannah Horsey and John Horsey son of Hannah gave to Burr Outerbridge late of the Island of Bermuda and Eliza Outerbridge his wife for love of her daughter part of HANNAHS DELIGHT & EXCHANGE, hence forward to be called MOTHERS CARE & BROTHERS GOODWILL. 200 acres
20 June 1750 Stephen Horsey Sr, and wife Elizabeth Horsey and son Stephen Horsey sold to Thomas Bannister part called HANNAHS DELIGHT & EXCHANGE.
1783 tax- Samuel Kellum 200 acres.
7 Aug.1795 Edward Horsey sold to John Shepherd Ker of Acco.Co.Va. 200 acres of HANNAHS DELIGHT & EXCHANGE

Part of DOUBLE PURCHASE called SARAHS JOY
2 March 1684 Randall Revell, wife Katherine Revell gave to daughter Sarah Revell 500 acres called SARAHS JOY.
16 Jan 1759 Isaac Horsey son of Revel Horsey and devisee of John Horsey, deceased, sold to Thomas Hayward Jr.,as John Horsey willed in 1744 part to son William Horsey,if no issue to daughter Betty Horsey,if no issue to son Isaac Horsey afsd.(they died as minors) his interest.
4 Aug.1755 Rachel Rowe, sold to Nehemiah King, that John Henry former husband of Rachel Rowe willed to William Henry eldest son of John Henry when of age, 200 acres and her dower rights.
2 June 1759 Isaac Horsey, tailor, and wife Mary Horsey sold to brother Revel Horsey 200 acres.
24 Feb.1760 Revel Horsey sold 200 acres to Thomas Hayward the younger.
21 May 1765 George Irving sold 200 acres to John Irving.
13 Jan 1778 Thomas Hayward sold to Revell Horsey part purchased of Isaac Horsey.
1783 tax- John Irving

Part of DOUBLE PURCHASE and ARRACOCO called WELCOME
POOL(FREE PURCHASE)
5 Feb.1681 Randall Revell wife Katherine Revell sold part 245 acres to Thomas Pool called WELCOME POOL.

139

20 March 1685 Thomas Pool sold to Hannah Carpenter wife of Nicholas
Carpenter, part called FREE PURCHASE 100 acres.
2 July 1691 Eliza Pool relic of Thomas Pool and John Pool with wife
Martha Pool sold to Hannah Carpenter, ADDN. TO FREE PURCHASE. (John Pool
died intestate with no issue,Thomas Pool his brother being the last son
of Thomas Pool on 20 Jan 1708 sold to Thomas Thompson LAST ADDN. FREE
PURCHASE being all remaining part of WELCOME POOL and said Thomas
Thompson willed to son Andrew Thompson. 95 acres.
8 Aug.1742 Andrew Thompson sold 95 acres to David Wilson.
3 July 1761 William Thompson, wife Mary Thompson & Sarah McDonald widow
of William McDonald sold to Nehemiah King 100 acres of FREE PURCHASE and
50 acres of WELCOME POOL.
1766/67 Nehemiah King willed to son Robert King land bought of William
Thompson
1783 tax- Nehemiah King 50 acres.

DOUBLE PURCHASE

Patented 10 March 1679 by William Stevens for 150 acres in Brinkleys,
northwest, Election district 3, map #14.
Rent Rolls 1666-1723 assigned to William Planner and possessed by William
Planner son and heir.
1767 resurveyed to WILLIAMS GREEN 644 3/4 acres

DOUBLE PURCHASE

Patented in 1744 for 163 acres in East Pr.Anne, Election district 15, map
#5.
1802 William Polk willed to sons John Polk and Samuel Polk

DOUBLE PURCHASE

Patented in 1757 by Stephen Adams, a resurvey from JERSEY and GUERNSEY
for 288 3/4 acres in West Pr.Anne, Election district 1, map #2.
1770 ADDITION TO DOUBLE PURCHASE pat. by Stephen Adams for 415 1/4 acres.
17 Jun.1766 Stephen Adams sold 3 1/2 acres to Walter Taylor
27 Mar.1792 Stephen Adams mortgaged to Levin Gale, Henry Jackson and John
Stewart 288 3/4 acres
19 Jan.1793 Stephen Adams, wife Jemimah Adams, sold to James Adams
GUERNSEY & DOUBLE PURCHASE, description, no acreage given.
1805 Alexander Stewart executor of John Stewart who was the surviving
partner of GALE, JACKSON & STEWART, sold to John Whittingham Adams- a
release of mortgage.
17 July 1806 John Whittingham Adams sold to Thomas Prior 49 acres.
6 April 1809 John W. Adams sold to Lewis Smith,except part belonging to
Henrietta Adams daughter of James Adams deceased, and 49 acres already
sold.
1811 Thomas Taylor willed to son Purnell Taylor 50 acres.

DOUBLE PURCHASE

Patented in 1791 for 4 acres by Michael Cluff in Dublin District,
Election district 4, map #13.

DOVE DALE

Patented in 1813 by William Crockett for 2 1/4 acres in West Pr. Anne, Election district 1, map #3.

(The) DOWNS

Patented on 5 Sep.1675 by Francis Roberts in Tangier Quarter, Election district 9, map #7 for 100 acres.
Rent Rolls 1666-1723, poss. by the widow Ann Roberts 100 acres.
26 April 1684 Francis Roberts sold to Henry Leaton 100 acres.
1696/7 Henry Leaton willed to son Henry Leaton, no acreage.
1744 Lewis Jones willed to son Lewis Jones 100 acres.
19 Nov.1750 Thomas Roberts and Sarah Roberts sold 100 acres to John Roberts, conveyed to John Roberts (alias Grandee) by Francis Roberts on 1 Sep.1697 at Dogwood Ridge (unnamed).
1756 John Jones willed to son James Jones 100 acres(DOWNS CHOICE adjacent JONES CHANCE.)
1783 tax- Lewis Jones 100 acres.

DOWNS LOTT

see DOUBLE PURCHASE

DREDDENS DESTINY

Patented in 1759 by David Dryden, resurvey from DAVIDS DESTINY, for 258 1/2 acres in Dublin, Election district 4, map #13.
8 Nov.1762 Thomas Benston sold 100 acres to William Dryden
1775 will David Dryden, to son Littleton Dryden 109 acres.
10 Nov.1772 William Dryden and Thomas Benston, wife Sarah Benston sold to David Dryden 109 acres for 5 shillings.
1783 tax- Littleton Dryden 100 acres.
1788 resurveyed to DREDDENS CONCLUSION 353 acres.
1 March 1790 Thomas Benston sold to Littleton Dryden 30 acres of DREDDENS DESTINY, DREDDENS CONCLUSION.
31 March 1810 Thomas Benston and James Barrett, wife Catherine Barrett sold to Littleton Dennis devised by grandfather Thomas Benston.
17 April 1810 Thomas Dashiell, sheriff sold to Thomas Mitchell Jones, per judgement against Thomas Benston.
10 Sep.1810 Thomas M. Jones, wife Margaret Jones sold to Littleton Dennis.

DREDDENS CONCLUSION

Patented in 1788 from DREDDENS DESTINY by Thomas Benston for 353 acres in Dublin, Election district 4, map #13.
Thomas Benston son of Thomas married Sarah Dryden. He died in 1802 and gave lands to grandson Jesse Boston.
1 March 1790 Thomas Benston sold to Littleton Dryden 30 acres of DREDDENS DESTINY, DREDDENS CONCLUSION.
1803 Littleton Dryden willed to son John Dryden 100 acres, unnamed.
23 March 1810 John Dryden son of Littleton Dryden sold to William Williams 100 acres, unamed.

DROWN COVE

See POMFRET

DUBLIN

Patented on 5 Nov.1665 for 100 acres by John Mackitt in Brinkleys,
northeast, Election district 3, map #15.
2 March 1696 John Mackitt sold to son-in-law Robert Hall 100 acres who
sold to Joseph Bowle.
1691 Joseph Bowle sold to Hope Taylor 100 acres.
1696 Hope Taylor willed to son Robert Taylor
Rent Rolls 1666-1723 possessed by the widow Taylor 100 acres.
Resurveyed 1725 by Robert Taylor 186 acres.
1742 Robert Taylor son of Hope Taylor and Elias Taylor son of Hope Taylor
divided this land.
2 Aug.1748 Robert Taylor and wife Elizabeth Taylor, Elias Taylor and wife
Susannah Taylor(son of Dennis Taylor deceased) and John Hall of Kent Co.
Del.(son of Robert Hall and his wife Elizabeth Hall, daughter of John
Mackitt) sold to William Wood tract at Morumsco. no acreage given.
2 Aug.1748 John Hall of Kent Co.Del.,son of Robert Hall sold 75 acres to
Elias Taylor
1770 Elias Taylor died with 100 acres.
1773 Levi Wood willed to sister Leah Wood, if no issue to Levi Wood son
of Elijah.
1783 tax- Sarah Taylor 70 acres
1783 tax- William Wood 92 acres
1795/7 William Wood gave to son Joshua Wood.

DUBLIN

Patented 4 June 1693 by Denum Olandman for 125 acres in Dublin, Election
district 4, map #12.
Rent Rolls 1666-1723 Dennum Olandman 125 acres.
1710 Dennum Olannum gave to son William Olandman 25 acres.
17 March 1730 Ann Olandman sold 125 acres to William Bowland.
1734 will of William Bowland, to son William,realestate unnamed.
4 Dec.1733 Duncan King and Eleanor King his wife sold to William Bowland
1/3 part of 175 acres being part of DUBLIN,KINGS CHANCE & PREMINE, that
Dennum Olandman left to son William Olandman who died without issue and
falls to daughters of Duncan Olandman Jr, Ann Olandman, & Eleanor
Olandman now wife of Duncan King.
13 Jan 1734 Alexander Chain and Ann Chain(Ann Olandman) his wife sold to
Robert King 33 1/3 a. being 1/2 of 175 acres of Dennum Olandman Sr.
29 Mar.1738 Jane Olandman sold to Robert King, part of three tracts,
CHANCE,DUBLIN, PEMINE that descended to her as youngest daughter of
Dennis Olandman Jr. Now age 21 last February.
4 Apr.1745 William Bowland son of William and Eleanor Bowland his mother
sold 40 acres to Robert King of PEMMINE,KINGS CHANCE & DUBLIN.
15 Aug.1755 William Bowland eldest son of William, and Eleanor Bowland
widow of Wiliam deceased sold to Nehemiah King, pt. DUBLIN,KINGS CHANCE,
PEMMINE (confirmation 143 acres.)
19 Dec.1766 Nehemiah King,wife Frances King, gave to son Nehemiah King
(under 21) lands on Kings branch-unnamed.

DUBLIN(DOUBLIN)

Patented in 1742 by Thomas MacGummery for 75 acres in Lawsons, Election
district 8, map #19.
17 Aug.1769 Dennis Montgomery sold to John Ward 75 acres.
1783 tax- Ezekiel Ward 50 acres.
1791 John Ward willed to son Ezekiel Ward,land bought of Dennis
Montgommery (unnamed).
12 May 1804 Ezekiel Ward transferred to John Miles, constable of Little
Annamessex, to pay debts.
1 Feb.1806 John Miles sold to Ezekiel Ward 150 acres.
1 Feb.1806 Ezekiel Ward sold 150 acres of WHITE OAK SWAMP, FOLLY, DUBLIN
to Thomas Ward.
25 July 1808 Ezekiel Ward sold to Henry Ward, Whitty Ward, Ezekiel Ward
Jr., Betsy Ward, Lovey Ward and John Ward.
13 Aug.1808 John Miles Constable, sold to William Ward lands of Ezekiel
Ward, 100 acres of DUBLIN, CORK & WHITE OAK SWAMP.
10 June 1809 William Ward of Ezekiel Ward, sold to Traves Sterling Jr.,
part.
15 July 1809 William Ward sold 26 1/4 acres to Henry Ward.
13 Feb. 1810 Traves Stering Jr. sold 22 acres to John Sterling.

                              DUBLIN

Patented in 1762 by John Peden for 157 acres in Dublin, Election district
4, map #13.
1795 John Peden willed lands to son John Peden.

                              DUBLIN

Patented in 1763 by Elijah Tlghman out of CEDAR HILL for 120 acres in
Westover, Election district 13, map #11.
25 May 1773 Elijah Tilghman of Dorc.Co. Md. sold to Samuel Wilson 120
acres, with TILGHMANS CHANCE.
Aug.1786 Samuel Wilson sold to William Gibbons 38 1/4 acres with
TILGHMANS CHANCE.
6 Mar.1787 William Gibbons mortgaged to Samuel Wilson with all his other
lands, HOPEWELL,GOOD LUCK,TILGHMANS LUCK, TILGHMANS CHANCE, etc.
13 July1788 William Gibbons mortgaged to Samuel Wilson and Levin Miles,
all his lands, same as above.
13 Aug.1792 William Gibbons, wife Mary Gibbons, sold to Levin Miles 200
acres with POOLS HOPE,TILGHMANS ADVENTURE, GOOD LUCK, HOPEWELL, etc.
6 Apr.1804 Edward Stogdol Miles and Levin Miles, sold to George
Robertson, Peter Waters and John Bell merchants lands from father Levin
Miles, all, no names.

                              DUDLEY

Patented on 28 Sep.1681 by Elizabeth Smith and assigned to Abraham Heath
for 50 acres in East Pr.Anne, Election district 15, map #5.
1691 Abraham Heath died, land not in will- sons were Thomas Heath, Jacob
Heath, William Heath and Abraham Heath.
Rent Rolls 1666-1723, Abraham Heath heir denies any such land.
10 Jun 1723 Anthony Moore who moved to Carolina sold 50 acres to James
Strawbridge with ROWLEY HILL. that Abraham Heath willed to daughter Mary
Heath wife of Henry Dorman and Henry Dorman and Mary Dorman made over to
Anthony Moore.
1735 James Strawbridge, wife Jean Strawbridge, sold to John Phillips 50
acres with ROWLEY HILL.

31 Jan 1775 I John Phillips am bound to William Miles 50 acres of
DUDLEY,with PHILLIPS CONCLUSION,ROWLEY HILL,etc.
1783 tax- John Phillips 50 acres.
22 March 1786 Jonathan Stanford and wife Grace Stanford sold for 5
shillings to John McDaniel and wife Elizabeth McDaniel 50 acres of ROWLEY
HILL & DUDLEY with PRIVILEDGE.
5 Jan 1796 Elizabeth McDaniel coheir of John Phillips sold to David
McDaniel 67 1/2 acres of ROWLEY HILL & DUDLEY.
5 Jan 1796 Elizabeth McDaniel sold to Caleb Bevans McDaniel 2 1/2 acres
with PRIVILEDGE.
22 May 1805 John Stewart, Samuel Smith, Henry Coston and Jesse King sold
to Jesse Dukes of Sussex Co. Del.170 acres in right of his wife Sarah
Dukes. He to pay the other representatives of the deceased the value of
their share- as John Phillps died and these are the comissioners to
divide lands GRAYS PURCHASE, ROWLEY HILL, PRIVILEDGE & DUDLEY.
22 May 1805 Jesse Dukes, wife Sarah Dukes of Sussex Co.Del. sold all
rights to Pierce Riggin of Somerset County.

DUKES PLACE

1685 This is part of DIXONS LOTT, Robert Dukes sold to George Wilson,
originally owned by Ambrose Dixon who gave to daughter Elizabeth Dixon
who married Robert Dukes.150 acres.

DUMFRIES

Patented in 1792 by Levin Denwood for 4 acres in West Pr.Anne, Election
district 1, map #3.
1798 Denwood Wilson willed to son George Wilson.
9 Dec.1794 Denwood Wilson gave to son Samuel Wilson 4 acres

EASTERN BOUNDS

Patented in 1741 by Thomas Williams for 100 acres in Brinkleys,
northwest, Election district 3, map #4.
1768 Resurveyed to PLANNERS BLOSSOM 577 acres.

EDEN

Patented in 1750 by Thomas Lindzey for 89 3/4 acres in Brinkleys,
southwest, Election district 3, map #17.
23 Oct.1764 Thomas Lindzey sold to Nehemiah Turpin 95 acres, part
CHEESEMANS CHANCE & MUMFORD, BOSTON lately called EDEN.
30 July 1765 Thomas Lindsey sold to Nehemiah Turpin 8 acres.
2 Jan 1787 William Turpin son of Nehemiah Turpin sold to John Turpin son
of Nehemiah Turpin, pt. MUMFORD,BOSTON, EDEN, 95 acres.
24 June 1795 John Turpin, wife Sarah Turpin, of Worc.Co. sold to Thomas
Whittington 91 1/4 acres of CHEESEMANS CHANCE or EDEN, MUMFORD & BOSTON.
10 March 1796 Thomas Whittington gave to Isaac Whittington 95 acres of
BOSTON, EDEN, MUMFORD.
10 March 1796 David Lindzey sold to Thomas Whittington 95 acres of
BOSTON, EDEN & MUMFORD.
24 Feb 1810 James R. Mills sold to Henry Lankford 89 3/4 acres.

EDGE HILL

Patented in 1849 by John W. Crisfield, as resurvey of FRIENDS ASSISTANCE, ADDITION, OWENS CHOICE, for 520 acres in West Pr. Anne, Election district 1, map #3.

EDINBURGH

Patented in 1793 by Thomas Robertson for 158 acres in Brinkleys, northeast, Election district 3, map #15.
1816 Thomas Robertson willed to daughter Louisa Robertson land in Morumsco.

EDINBURGH

Patented in 1802 by Thomas Hamilton for 1235 1/8 acres, a resurvey of GLASCOW SWAMP, ADAMS DISCOVERY, YOUNG TINSON & WILSONS FOLLY & CRAMBURN, in West Pr.Anne Election district 1, map #2.
17 Dec.1804 Charles Nutter, wife Louise Nutter, late Louise Adams, agree with Thomas Hamilton to divide the lands of William Adams Jr.except ANDREWS DISAPPOINTMENT & ADAMS DISCOVERY 1087 3/4 acres of several tracts, unnamed.
24 June 1806 Thomas Hamilton sold to Elias Bailey 10 1/4 acres
25 March 1807 Thomas Hamilton mortgaged to Benjamin F.A.C. Dashiell, divised by William Adams Jr.
3 Nov.1807 William Cottman and John Stewart trustees of Thomas Hamilton to sell RE to Thomas Byrd 572 3/4 acres.
13 Sep.1808 William Cottman and John Stewart executors of Thomas Hamilton sold to John Gould 652 1/4 acres.
9 Nov.1808 Thomas G. Fountain sold to Robert J. King 165 1/4 acres of CRAMBURN, WALLEYS CHANCE, HORSEYS CHANCE & EDINBURGH.
3 April 1810 Robert J. King sold to Levin King Jr.

EDWARDS CHANCE

Surveyed for Edward Roberts in 1743 for 100 acres and resurveyed in 1751 for 168 acres by same, in Dames Quarter, Election district 11, map #7. This was part of BOZMANS MARSH and BALLY HACK.
1783 tax- William Roberts 100 acres.

EDWARDS LOTT

Patented on 29 March 1705 for 200 acres by Ann Roberts in Dames Quarter, Election district 11, map #7, originally surveyed for Francis Roberts.
It was resurveyed in 1720 for 220 acres and patented to Edward Roberts.
1783 tax- Bartlett Roberts 50 acres
1783 tax- William Roberts 113 acres
1783 tax- John Roberts 50 acres
1783 tax- John Windsor for Frank Roberts heirs (with JESEMINE 30 acres)
24 Nov.1797 Samuel Phillips and wife Betsy Phillips of Dorc.Co. Md. sold to Whittington White- as Joseph Wallace conveyed to John Roberts by mortgage. He died and left unpaid and left only daughter Betsy Roberts wife of Samuel Phillips and encumbered with mortgage and dower 1/3rds now held by Job Parks and wife Mary Parks, 200 acres between Manokin and Wicomico River, not named.

5 March 1805 Samuel Roberts sold to Whittington White land mortgaged to John Roberts in Dames Quarter, no name.
1820 Resurveyed to NEGLECT- unpatented for 406 acres.

EDWIN

Patented on 3 Jun 1664 by William Edwin and Marguerite Edwin of St. Mary's County Md. in Brinkleys Southeast, Election district 3, map #16. 350 acres.
Rent Rolls 1666-1723 William Matthews 350 acres.
1718 William Matthews willed to son Teague Matthews 350 acres.
1726 Teague Matthews willed part to son William Matthews and part to son John Matthews, land from William Matthews.
3 June 1760 John Matthews sold to Joshua Dickerson, blacksmith, 100 acres given him by his deceased father William Matthews.
27 July 1768 Joshua Dickerson and wife Eleanor Dickerson sold to John Collins 100 acres with SMITHS CHANCE.
1768 John Collins willed to son Stephen Collins land purchased of Joshua Dickerson (unnamed)
1777/84 Samuel Matthews willed to son Boaz Matthews dwelling plantation (unnamed)
1783 tax- Samuel Matthews Jr. 40 acres
1783 tax- David Matthews Sr. 100 acres
1783 tax- Samuel Matthews Sr. 100 acres
16 May 1788 Henry Matthews son of Boaz Matthews sold to Samuel Bedsworth and Thomas Jones, merchant of Kingston 150 acres (no name)
13 Aug.1790 Samuel Bedsworth and Thomas Jones sold to Elijah Matthews land on north side Morumsco Creek that descended from Samuel Matthews to his son Boaz Matthews.
22 Aug.1789 Samuel Bedsworth sold to Thomas Jones purchased to Henry Matthews (no name or acreage.)
21 July 1800 Isaac Matthews sold 1 moity to Elijah Matthews of EDWIN & MEADOW GROUND 119 acres.
21 July 1800 Zachariah Matthews, Thomas Evans and wife Sophia Evans, Molly Matthews, Ruth Matthews,& Eleanor Matthews sold to Isaac Matthews 119 acres of EDWIN & MEADOW GROUND
16 Feb 1802 Elijah Matthews sold to Zachariah Matthews 119 acres of EDWIN & MEADOW.
10 June 1806 Zachariah Matthews sold to George Carsley 45 acres of EDWIN & MEADOW.
1844 David Walston gave 40 acres to wife Betsy M. Walston.

ELGATE

Patented on 3 June 1664 by William Elgate for 150 acres in Brinkleys southeast, Election district 3, map #16.
17 Feb.1672 William Elgate and wife Hannah Elgate sold to Thomas Owen 150 acres.
26 Oct.1675 Thomas Owen and wife Mary Owen sold 150 acres to George Hasfort.
20 Oct.1678 George Hasfort sold to John Ellis.
Rent Rolls 1666-1723 John Ellis
1709 Samuel Adams gave part to son Samuel.
19 March 1739 Jacob Adams gave to son Samuel Adams after death of wife Catherine Adams.

1745 tax list- Samuel Adams 100 acres.
1783 tax list- Samuel Adams 150 acres.

ELLIOTTS CHOICE

Patented on 20 May 1668 by Stephen Elliott for 200 acres in Dames
Quarter, Election district 1, map #7.
28 Nov 1669 Stephen Elliott sold to Richard Poak.
5 Aug 1674 Richard Poak sold to Alexander Draper.
18 April 1676 Alexander Draper sold to Francis Roberts 200 acres.
17 Nov.1683 Francis Roberts sold to Samuel Jones.
Rent Rolls 1666-1723 Widow Ann Roberts 200 acres.
100 acres AKA ROWLANDS RIDGE.
20 Aug.1754 Samuel Jones sold to Francis Roberts ROWLANDS RIDGE conveyed
by Francis Roberts to grandfather of afsd. Francis Roberts and to Samuel
Jones, grandfather of afsd Samuel Jones.
1783 tax- William Roberts 100 acres
1783 tax- William Winder for Frank Roberts heirs 100 acres.
1794 William Roberts willed to wife Mary Roberts.
2 Aug.1796 Francis White gave to son William White, OUTLETT,DAVIDS
DESTINY, ELLIOTTS CHOICE,JAMES DELIGHT

ELLIOTTS IMPROVEMENT

Patented on 9 May 1673 by Thomas Manlove who made it over to Matthew
Dorman, for 200 acres in West Pr.Anne Election district 1, map #2.
1 Oct.1679 Thomas Manlove,wife Jane Manlove, sold to Matthew Dorman 200
acres.
1691 Matthew Dorman willed to son Henry Dorman
Rent Rolls 1666-1723 Matthew Dorman 200 acres.
Henry Dorman and wife Mary Dorman deeded to John Hales Sr. John Hales Sr.
sold part to John Brown, Since the death of John Hales the Elder and
John Brown Sr, William Brown son and heir of John Brown, and Matthew
Dorman possessed to confirm fathers agreement.
6 July 1727 John Hales and Margaret Hales his wife sold their part to
Matthew Dorman.

ELLIS CHANCE

Patented in 1739 by Alice Ellis for 100 acres in Mt Vernon, Election
district 5, map #1.
1739 Alice Ellis willed to nephew John Elzey 100 acres.
1783 tax- Ann Elzey.
25 March 1794 James Elzey sold to Nehemiah King and William Jones of
Thomas Jones of Manokin for 5sh. SECOND PURCHASE,COXES LOTT,ELLIS CHANCE,
WHITE HAVEN & PRIVILEDGE.
18 Aug.1794 Nehemiah King and William Jones of Manokin sold to James
Elzey for 5 shillings same as above.
19 Aug.1794 James Elzey,wife Sarah Elzey sold to William Jones of Thomas
Jones, same as above.
12 April 1808 George Jones of Robert Jones, wife Leah Jones, sold to John
Adams 6 3/4 acres.

ELLIS HIS LOTT

Patented on 3 Dec.1676 by William Stevens and assigned to John Ellis for
50 acres in Brinkleys southeast, Election district 3, map #16.
Rent Rolls 1666-1723 John Ellis 50 acres.
1726 William Matthews gave part to sons William Matthews and Samuel
Matthews.
1729 William Matthews sold to Samuel Matthews 50 acres.
1783 tax- Samuel Matthews Jr. 50 acres.

EMMESSEX

Patented on 10 Feb 1663 for 300 acres by Benjamin Summers in Crisfield,
Election district 7, map #20. Resurveyed in 1676 and found to be only 250
acres.
Rent Rolls 1666-1723 Benjamin Summers
1709 Benjamin Summers willed to sons William Summers, Thomas Summers,
John Summers.
4 May 1723 William Summers, sailor, and wife Martha Summers appointed
William Coulbourn, attorney, to make over to Southy Whittington tract
EMMESSEX according to our grandfather Benjamin Summers.
29 June 1725 Joseph Summers only surviving son of William Summers
deceased, who was one of the sons of Benjamin Summers sold to Southy
Whittington 1/3rd part of 250 acres, 84 acres. William Summers at death
left to sons Benjamin Summers, William and Joseph Summers. Benjamin
Summers and William Summers died intestate without issue so 1/3rd fell to
Joseph Summers with LITTLEWORTH.
27 Aug.1732 I Thomas Summers give to sons Jonathan Summers and George
Summers and in Annamessex.
20 Aug.1734 Southy Whittington and Mary Whittington his wife sold 84
acres to William Juett.
24 Jan 1782 Jonathan Summers and Thomas Summers sold 35 acres to Dukes
Riggin.
1783 tax- Dukes Riggin 50 acres
1783 tax- Jonathan Summers 60 1/2 acres
1783 tax- Thomas Summers 60 1/2 acres
1783 tax- David Summers 90 acres
1783 tax- Richard Summers 90 acres
1783 tax- Nathaniel Juett 100 acres
16 Mar.1784 Jonathan Summers sold 17 acres to Dukes Riggin
16 Feb.1785 Jonathan Summers sold to Thomas Summers son of Jonathan
Summers and Jonathan Summers and Thomas Summers son of Thomas, his
rights.
13 Nov.1790 Elisha Riggin, William Turner husband of Nancy Riggin, Sophia
Riggin, Martha Riggin, Betty Riggin, Grace Riggin,Jeremiah Riggin,
Horatio Riggin, Noah Riggin am bound to John Riggin- bond- to make over
land belonging to George Summers deceased, to John Riggin from will of
Dukes Riggin their father.
26 Nov.1798 Thomas Summers Sr. sold to son Jonathan Summers EMMESSEX and
SUMMERS ADDITION to EMMESSEX 54 acres.
27 Feb.1802 Thomas Summers sold 100 acres to William Roach
13 June 1803 Nathaniel Juett sold to Thomas Nelson 3 acres.
4 Feb 1804 Thomas Summers sold to William Roacch 100 acres.
31 Oct.1804 William Roach sold to Hance Croswell.
1805 Nathaniel Juett willed to son Whittington Juett, land purchased of

Joseph Summers.
8 March 1806 John Riggin sold to John Newman 4 acres.
14 March 1806 Richard Summers, wife Edlealiah Summers sold to David
Follen 90 acres.
14 March 1806 David Follen sold to Michael Summers 90 acres.
14 March 1806 Richard Summers sold to Elijah Summers 90 acres
19 Feb.1807 Elijah Summers sold to John Summers part sold him by Richard
Summers.
2 Jan 1808 Whittington Juett son of Nathaniel Juett sold all his
interest to Nathan Bradshaw.
2 Jan 1808 Nathan Bradshaw sold to Whittington Juett, same.
12 Dec.1807 George Davey and wife Betsy Davey sold to Elijah Summers 25
acres.
12 Dec.1807 John Summers sold to Elijah Summers 90 acres.
1872 this is the site of the town of CRISFIELD incorporated as SOMERS
COVE and renamed in 1886 named for John Woodland Crisfield.

END OF STRIFE

Patented in 1757, a resurvey of LAZARUS LOTT, by Lazarus Maddux for 609
acres in Fairmount,Election district 6, map #9.
20 Nov.1766 Lazarus Maddux, wife Sarah Maddux sold to Samuel Tull 89
acres.
19 March 1773 Lazarus Maddux, wife Sarah Maddux for 10 shillings sold to
Elzey Maddux son of Lazarus 150 acres (division of lines of Stoughton
Maddux, Daniel Maddux, and Thomas Maddux deceased.)
10 March 1773 Lazarus Maddux gave to son Stoughton Maddux 363 acres.
19 Feb.1799 Elzey Maddux sold 150 acres to Littleton D. Maddux.
9 Oct.1810 Levin Tull, wife Peggy Tull sold to Littleton Dorsey 89 acres.

END OF STRIFE

Patented in 1721 by Thomas Gillis for 510 acres in West Pr.Anne, Election
district 1, map #2. A resurvey of part of SAMUELS ADVENTURE.
15 Feb 1760 Thomas Gillis sold to Levin Gillis 400 acres except part
conveyed to Ahab Coston, with SUPPORT, SECOND CHOICE & BEAR QUARTER.
11 June 1771 Thomas Gillis gave to son Joseph Gillis 80 acres with GILLIS
DOUBLE PURCHASE,WHITE CHAPPEL, CONTENTION, END OF STRIFE.
1772 Levin Gillis willed lands to sons Thomas Gillis and Levin Gillis at
Wading place, unnamed.
1783 tax- Thomas Gillis 285 acres
1783 tax- Levin Gillis 125 acres
1783 Thomas Gillis willed lands to son Joseph Gillis, if no issue to
grandson Levin Gillis, no name.

END OF STRIFE

Patented in 1751 by Abraham Heath in East Pr.Anne, Election district 15,
map #4, for 37 acres.
22 March 1770 Stephen Heath son of Abraham Heath sold to Matthias Miles
34 1/2 acres.
1783 tax- George Bailey 2 acres.

ENLARGEMENT

Patented in 1785 by John Beauchamp for 109 acres in Brinkleys northeast, Election district 3, map #15.

21 Feb 1787 John Beauchamp and Mary Beauchamp sold to Samuel Smith 160 acres of LEDBOURN, HOG QUARTER, ENLARGEMENT.

13 Feb 1787 Elijah Beauchamp and John Beauchamp settled division of lands.

8 Jan 1790 John Beauchamp, wife Ann Beauchamp sold to Thomas Beauchamp 38 acres of LEDBOURN, HOGYARD, ENLARGEMENT.

24 Jan.1790 Thomas Beauchamp, wife Martha Beauchamp sold to Thomas Adams 203 1/4 acres of LEDBOURN, HOGYARD, ENLARGEMENT, THREE BROTHERS.

8 Jan 1790 Ann Beauchamp and Thomas Beauchamp sold to Thomas Adams, part of THREE BROTHERS, HOGYARD, LEDBOURN, ENLARGEMENT.

20 Sep.1796 Thomas Beauchamp, wife Sarah Beauchamp sold to William Williams 166 3/4 acres of LEDBOURN, HOGYARD, ENLARGEMENT, BEAUCHAMP VENTURE, SMALL HOPES.

11 Jan 1798 William Williams, wife Polly Williams sold to Thomas Adams, part.

11 Jan 1798 William Williams, wife Polly Williams, sold part to Samuel Smith

1800 will of Jesse Jones, to son Handy Jones, part.

ENTRANCE

Patented on 25 April 1683 by Edward Howard for 850 acres in Brinkleys, southeast, Election district 3, map 16.

1687 William Stevens willed 400 acres to Edward Howard and to his son William Stevens Howard 400 acres.

11 Aug.1684 Edward Howard and wife Margaret Howard sold to William Stevens for 5 shillings.

Rent Rolls 1666-1723 William White 400 acres and 450 acres to Thomas Williams in right of Edward Howard.

1706 William White willed to son John White.

13 April 1720 William Stevens Howard of Charles County Md. assigned friend Thomas Peale of Somerset Co. to make over to Thomas Bollin, part.

19 Aug.1720 Thomas Bollin and wife Katherine Bollin sold to William Holland 95 acres.

4 Sep.1733 Thomas Bollin, mariner, and wife Katherine sold a small parcel taken out of the tract to William Holland.

4 March 1735/6 Thomas Bollin and wife Katherine Bollin sold to James Nairn part not contained in last deed now called NAIRNS CHANCE.

20 Feb 1744 William Howard of Charles Co. Md. son of William Stevens Howard deceased, sold for 5 shillings to William Holland. no acreage given.

19 Feb.1744 James Nairn sold to William Holland NAIRNS CHANCE being part of THE ENTRANCE.

26 Feb 1744 William Howard of Charles Co. Md. heir at law of William Stevens Howard sold to Stevens White of Somerset County son of William White deceased who was the son of Stevens White Esq. conveyed land already sold by grandfather to Stevens White.

31 Aug.1748 William Holland and wife Margaret Holland sold to Jabez Pitts of Acco. Co. Va. 400 acres.

13 Feb.1752 Stevens White eldest son of William White gave all to Elias White, son of William of Stevens White.

22 Dec 1764 Jabez Pitts gave to son Robert Pitts.
24 Aug.1765 Elias White sold 110 acres to Robert Pitts and another part
of same 30 acres.
29 Oct 1765 Elias White sold 200 acres to John Collins.
20 Nov.1766 Elias White sold to John Nairn 325 acres of GLEANEATH & SIPE
resurveyed and called THE ENTRANCE (mortgage)
21 Nov.1770 Robert Pitts, wife Milcah Pitts, sold to Thomas Robertson 400
acres with GLENDORE,WHITES GIFT, ADVENTURE, MORRIS HOPE.
1783 tax-William Waddy 500 acres.
1784 Thomas Robertson and wife Martha Robertson sold to William Waddy 400
acres.
3 Sep.1785 William Waddy and wife Mary Sewell Waddy and Thomas Handy and
wife Mary Handy sold 145 3/4 acres to William Miles.
29 Oct 1796 William Miles,wife Nancy Miles sold to Thomas Williams 142
3/4 acres with ADVENTURE & MORRIS LOT.
8 July 1809 Thomas Williams Wilkins sold to Lodowick Milbourn, land
Thomas Williams of David Williams purchased of William Miles, descended
to Uncle Thomas Williams who devised to grandson Thomas Williams Wilkins,
no name or acres.

ENVY

Patented in 1752 by John Waters for 478 acres in Fairmount, Election
district 6, map #9.
1775 ADDITION TO ENVY pat. by Littleton Waters for 417 3/4 acres.
25 May 1763 Richard Waters exchanged with John Waters for tract
PARTNERSHIP in Annamessex 70 acres, conveyed to Richard Waters by John
Waters.
21 Jan.1778 John Waters sold to Littleton Waters 417 3/4 acres.
23 Dec 1789 Richard Waters, wife Eleanor Waters sold to Joshua Tull the
younger 70 acres, with MILES CHOICE.
3 April 1797 Joshua Tull the younger sold to Elisha Walston 70 acres,
with MILES CHOICE.
16 July 1802 Littleton Waters of Baltimore sold to Samuel Ford 175 acres
of ADDITION TO ENVY.
3 Oct.1805 Littleton Waters of Baltimore Md.sold to George Davey of
Somerset 242 3/4 acres.

ERLINDY

Patented on 20 May 1663 by John Elzey for 350 acres in Mt.Vernon,
Election district 5, map #1.(name means Clean Air)
1693 John Elzey gave to wife Sarah Elzey.
1704 Sarah Elzey sold to Charles Ballard and Eleanor Ballard.
1706 Charles Ballard and Eleanor Ballard sold to Joseph Austin.
1711 Charles Austin and Ann Austin sold to John Renshaw.
Rent Rolls 1666-1723 John Renshaw
1711 John Renshaw left to son Samuel Renshaw and to sons Thomas Renshaw
and Underwood Renshaw 250 acres.
7 Nov.1722 Samuel Renshaw of Albarmarle Co. of Pasetank appointed Richard
Chambers attorney sell 50 acres.
1743 resurvey by Thomas Renshaw and Underwood Renshaw for 381 acres.
1753 Thomas Renshaw and Alice Renshaw deeded 23 acres to William Renshaw.
19 Sep.1769 William Renshaw and wife Martha Renshaw sold to Levin Gale
230 acres.
1772 Ann Waller sold 100 acres of William Renshaw, his share to John

Crockett who sold to Levin Gale.
1783 tax- Thomas Renshaw 149 acres
1783 tax- William Waller 252 acres
17 Feb 1785 Levin Gale sold to Ann Huggins for 5 shillings, part, no
acres given.
1813 became Town of MT VERNON
1813 Moses Horner purchased 100 acres
1877 Moses Horner possessed (Maryland & Herld newspaper)

EVERDENS LOTT

Patented on 16 July 1689 by Thomas Everton for 500 acres in Westover,
Election district 13, map #11.
Rent Rolls 1666-1723 Thomas Everton in Dorcester Co.
1710 will Thomas Everton of Dorcester County, to grandson William
Kennerly 500 acres.
19 Aug.1724 William Kennerly cf Dorcester County sold 500 acres to Robert
King of Somerset Co.
1726 resurvey to CONCLUSION 1500 acres, Robert King.

EXCHANGE

SEE BOSTON & GOSHEN-1701 John Cottingham
1742 Charles Cottingham sold to Thomas Tull 189 acres out of BOSTON &
GOSHEN called THE EXCHANGE.
24 Mar.1760 Thomas Tull Jr. sold to William Tull 189 acres.
29 Jun 1765 William Tull of Annamessex sold to Thomas Tull 189 acres.

EXCHANGE

Patented in 1762 by Samuel Handy for 80 acres in Dublin, Election
district 4, map #12.
1783 tax- Susannah Dennis 30 acres
18 Oct.1778 Samuel Handy of Worcester Co. sold 80 acres to Littleton
Dennis of same.
2 Aug.1790 Littleton Dennis, wife Elizabeth Dennis, sold to Lazarus
Cottman, all.

EXCHANGE

Patented in 1769 by Samuel Smith for 9 1/4 acres in Westover, Election
district 13, map #10
21 Feb 1787 Samuel Smith and wife Esther Smith, sold to Joseph Tilghman 9
1/4 acres.
5 Nov.1798 Joseph Tilghman,wife Mary Tilghman sold to George Broughton.
24 Feb 1801 George Broughton and wife Alee Broughton sold to William
Beauchamp 57 1/4 acres of HUNTSMANS FOLLY, SMYTHS LOTT & EXCHANGE.
24 Feb.1801 William Beauchamp sold to George Broughton lands he holds by
deed from Joseph Tilghman and George Broughton 8 1 1/2 acres.
24 Feb.1801 George Broughton, wife Alee Broughton sold to John Miles 81
1/4 acres of HUNTSMANS FOLLY, JOSEPHS FOLLY, SMYTHS LOTT & EXCHANGE.
24 Feb 1801 John Miles sold to George Broughton 126 acres of same as
above.

EXCHANGE

Patented on 2 July 1667 by Robert Jones for 100 acres in Dublin, Election

district 4, map #13.
14 July 1668 Robert Jones and wife Martha Jones of Northumberland Co. Va. sold to Thomas Walker.
8 Nov. 1670 Thomas Walker sold to Walter Powell
10 Sep. 1679 Walter Powell sold to Elizabeth Hudson and Violetta Hudson daughters of Nicholas Hudson 200 acres of GREENFIELD, MIDDLE, & EXCHANGE, not called DAUGHTERS RECOVERY
6 Feb.1686 Richard Warren and wife Violetta Warren and John Snow, wife Elizabeth Snow and Elizabeth Hafford, mother of Violetta and Elizabeth, widow of John Hafford sold to John Lowder of Boston, New England, 200 acres of EXCHANGE & MIDDLE.
12 March 1687 John Lowder of Boston, sold to John Starrett of Maryland 200 acres of MIDDLE & EXCHANGE.
1695 Walter Powell devised to son William Powell
1715 William Powell gave to son John Powell 200 acres and balance to son William Powell.
20 May 1740 William Powell and wife Ellen Powell of Pr.William Co.Va. sold to Thomas Benston GREENFIELD & EXCHANGE.
21 Feb.1757 William Benston eldest son of Thomas Benston deceased,wife Martha Benston sold to his brother Thomas Benston 100 acres.
10 March 1767 William Benston and wife Martha Benston sold to Samuel Wilson 110 acres of EXCHANGE & MIDDLE.
25 March 1780 Samuel Wilson sold to William Benston son of Thomas Benston 14 1/2 acres of MIDDLE & EXCHANGE.
1783 tax- Thomas Benston 31 acres
1783 tax- Samuel Wilson 96 acres
1 Mar.1790 Thomas Benston sold to Samuel Wilson MIDDLE & EXCHANGE, no acres given.
1790 Samuel Wilson willed to son Samuel Wilson lands on northside of Pocomoke River(unnamed)
8 Apr.1790 Samuel Wilson sold to Stephen Collins and Littleton Dryden 35 acres(contract that Samuel Wilson gave back to Thomas Benston, and Thomas Wiliamson Benston for use of Rebecca Benston during life and after death for use of Thomas Benston)
19 Nov.1795 Major Samuel Wilson,wife Leah Wilson sold to Littleton Dennis.
31 March 1810 Thomas Benston and James Barrett, wife Catherine Barrett sold to Littleton Dennis, devised by grandfather Thomas Benston.
17 April 1810 Thomas Dashiell, sheriff, sold to Thomas Mitchell Jones 133 1/4 acres of EXCHANGE, DREDDENS DESTINY & part of GREENFIELD.
10 Sep.1810 Thomas Mitchell Jones, wife Margaret Jones sold to Littleton Dennis same as above.

EXCHANGE

Patented on 24 July 1679 by John Roach for 200 acres in Lawsons, Election district 8, map #19.
Rent Rolls 1666-1723 200 acres, John Roach.
1709 John Roach Sr, willed 50 acres to son John Roach and son Michael Roach 150 acres.
1726 John Roach willed to son Charles Roach 50 acres.
20 June 1744 Michael Roach son of Michael Roach deceased, sold to Henry Cullen 10 acres.
22 Jun 1754 William Roach sold to Thomas Cullen (division of lands)
28 March 1757 Thomas Cullen sold to William Miles 150 acres.

11 Nov.1758 William Wheatley and wife Alice Wheatley sold to Aaron
Sterling 99 1/2 acres of EXCHANGE & CABIN SWAMP.
16 Jun 1761 William Miles and Thomas Cullen sold to Daniel Cullen 150
acres(devised by the will of John Roach)
22 Jan 1763 William Wheatley Sr. and wife Alice Wheatley sold 72 1/2
acres to Aaron Sterling.
22 Jan 1763 Daniel Cullen, wife Wineford Cullen sold 87 acres to William
Wheatley.
13 Oct.1767 William Wheatley sold 3 acres to William Roach
8 Jun 1771 Daniel Cullen sold 150 acres to Outerbridge Horsey.(mortgage)
31 Oct 1772 William Wheatley sold to John Johnson 50 acres of EXCHANGE &
CABIN SWAMP.
17 Aug.1774 Outerbridge Horsey sold to Daniel Cullen(release of mortgage)
25 Jan.1775 Daniel Cullen,ship carpenter, sold to Isaac Coulbourn 153
acres of WHEATLEYS PLEASURE & CABIN SWAMP & EXCHANGE.
13 Mar.1782 William Wheatley Sr. sold 13 acres to Isaac Johnson.
1783 tax- Isaac Johnson
1783 tax- William Roach 34 acres
1783 tax- Rachel Roach 16 acres
1783 tax- Aaron Sterling 72 1/2 acres
5 March 1784 John Johnson Jr. sold to Isaac Johnson 50 acres of EXCHANGE
& CABIN SWAMP.
1785 William Roach willed to son Billy Roach, lands in Annamessex
(unnamed)
3 Feb.1792 Daniel Cullen sold to John Handy 133 3/4 acres of EXCHANGE,
CABIN SWAMP, WHEATLEYS PLEASURE.
1795 Aaron Sterling willed to son Aaron tracts bought of William Whitney.
31 Oct.1797 William Williams,wife Polly Williams released theirr claim on
lands of Daniel Cullen, to John Handy.
21 June 1799 Isaac Johnson sold to William Wilson Jr. 1 acre
21 June 1799 William Wheatley sold 1 acre to James Morrison
8 Jan 1803 John Handy, wife Sarah Handy sold to John Lawson 130 3/4 acres
of CABIN SWAMP, WHEATLEYS PLEASURE & EXCHANGE
12 Nov.1803 Stephen Wheatley sold to John Riggin son of Jonathan Riggin,
carpenter 5 acres.
23 Jan 1808 Stephen Wheatley sold to William Wilson 4 or 5 acres.

EXCHANGE

see LONGS LOTT 1680 & CONCLUSION 1726

EXPENSE

Patented in 1765 by Josephus Bell, a resurvey of BELLS PURCHASE, etc. for
240 1/2 acres in Lawsons, Election district 8, map #18.
1783 tax- Josephus Bell 340 acres.

FAIR BRIDGE

see FERRY BRIDGE

FAIR MEADOW

Patented in 1728 by James Hayman, a resurvey out of GREAT HOPES, for 24
acres in East Princess Anne, Election district 15, Map #4.
22 Oct 1765 James Hayman sold to Charles Hayman for 5 shillings 24 acres.

1774 Charles Hayman willed to daughter Catherine Hayman.
23 May 1780 Isaac Hayman and wife Catherine Hayman sold to Matthias Miles
(devised by Charles Hayman to Catherine) 24 acres.
1783 tax- Matthias Miles 24 acres.

FAIR MEADOW

Patented in 1748 by William Miles for 109 acres in East Princess Anne,
Election district 15, map #4.
1763 resurveyed for 296 acres by William Miles.
1783 tax- Matthias Miles 196 acres.
1792 resurveyed to FOUR IN ONE 739 1/8 acres.

FAIR MEADOW

Patented in 1766 by Robert Geddes for 17 acres in East Princess Anne,
Election district 15, map #4.
19 Nov.1768 William Geddes son of Robert Geddes and wife Mary Geddes sold
to William Pollitt 17 acres with ADDITION, HAYMANS PURCHASE.
20 Nov.1772 Thomas Pollitt sold to William Pollitt 17 acres with GEDDES
OUTLETT, ADDITION, HAYMANS PURCHASE, LAST CHOICE.
1783 tax- William Pollitt 17 acres.

FAIR SPRING

Patented on 4 Feb.1679 by William Stevens and assigned to William Furniss
for 300 acres in Westover, Election district 13, map #11.
Rent Rolls 1666-1723 James Furniss son of William Furniss 300 acres.
1765 James Furniss willed dwelling plantation to son William.
1775 William Furniss gave to son Thomas Furniss
1783 tax- Grace Furniss 100 acres
1783 tax- Thomas Furniss 200 acres
22 Apr 1783 Thomas Furniss sold 75 acres to Samuel Wilson
12 Sep.1785 Thomas Furniss, wife Sarah Furniss sold to Samuel Wilson FAIR
SPRING & pt. GREAT HOPES.
7 Nov.1785 Thomas Furniss sold to Samuel Wilson 337 acres of DAVIS LOTT,
GREAT HOPES, FAIR SPRING.
1786 resurveyed to CEDAR HILL 541 1/2 acres by Samuel Wilson
18 Aug.1795 Milcah Gale Chaille sold to William Tilghman Sr. 129 acres of
POOLS HOPE & FAIR SPRING,CEDAR HILL.
1806 William Tilghman willed to daughter Nancy Tilghman land bought of
Milcah Gale Chaille.
3 June 1806 Nancy Tilghman daughter of William gave to Stephen Tilghman,
he to support his sister Sally Tilghman during life, land conveyed
William Tilghman by Milcah Gale Chaille 169 3/4 acres, no name.
1817 Stephen Tilghman willed to brother William 169 3/4 acres, no name.

FANCY

Surveyed but unpatented in 1787 by George Miles for 7 3/4 acres in St.
Peters, Election district 2, map #6.
22 Feb.1808 Evans Willin sold to John Wilkins.

FATHER AND SONS DESIRE

Patented on 18 Nov.1699 by John White and Richard Wallace for 85 acres in
Dames Quarter, Election district 11, map #7.
Rent Rolls 1666-1723 possessed by same.
1718 John White willed to daughter Grace Wallace 40 acres in Dames
Quarter (son-in-law Richard Wallace) unnamed land.
14 Jun 1736 Richard Wallace sold to John White 168 acres being two tracts
FATHER & SONS DESIRE & FRIENDS CONTENTMENT.
13 July 1779 David Wallace gave to Richard Wallace
1783 tax- John White Jr. 39 acres
1783 tax- Mary Wallace & Margaret Wallace 121 1/2 acres
1783 tax- Thomas White 92 acres with FRIENDS CONTENT
29 July 1788 Richard Wallace, wife Rebecca Wallace sold to William
Roberts all his rights.
14 April 1804 Whittington White and wife Tabitha White, sold to Thomas
White of Thomas, 15 acres of FATHER & SONS DESIRE & FRIENDS CONTENT.
2 Dec.1806 Whittington White, wife Tabitha White, sold to Thomas White of
Thomas 40 acres of FATHER AND SONS DESIRE & FRIENDS CONTENT.

FATHER AND MOTHERS GIFT

This is part of GOLDEN LYON

FATHERS CARE

Patented on 1 March 1705 by John Conner for 50 acres in Fairmount,
Election district 6, map #9.
Rent Rolls 1666-1723 John Conner
1 Dec 1750 resurvey by Ephraim Wilson to 200 acres
23 July 1751 Ephraim Wilson sold to William Turpin 40 acres
20 March 1752 Ephraim Wilson sold to William Turpin 90 acres
20 Sep.1767 Ephraim Wilson and wife Mary Wilson, sold to Henry Miles for
5 shillings 103 acres of FATHERS CARE, HOPEWELL.
27 Feb.1801 John Conner sold 50 acres to Merrill Maddux

FATHERS CARE

Patented on 18 March 1705 by John Conner for 50 acres in Brinkleys
southwest, Election district 3, map #17.
Rent Rolls 1666-1723 possessed by the widow Conner in her son's right.
18 Mar.1769 Elijah Conner sold to Sarah Potter widow of Thomas Potter 50
acres.
1778/84 Samuel Matthews willed to wife Sarah Matthews (Sarah Potter) with
RUSCOMMON and then after death to son Boaz Matthews.
7 March 1791 Henry Potter of Pittsilvania Co.Va. sold to Nathan Cahoon 73
acres of RUSCOMMON & FATHERS CARE.

FATHERS CARE

Patented in 1753 for 283 1/2 acres in East Pr.Anne, Election district 15,
map #4 by David Polk.
1783 tax- Gillis Polk 283 1/2 acres
1791 resurveyed to CONSOLATION 820 2/4 acres.

156

FATHERS CARE

Patented in 1714 for 250 acres in Mt.Vernon, Election district 5, map #1.
9 March 1773 Henry Lowes sold to James Dickinson and William Hayward of
Talbot County Md.(mortgaged for Mr. Ogle's debt) 250 acres with DISPENCE
& HEREAFTER, etc.

FATHERS CARE

Patented in 11 Oct 1737 by Thomas Dashiell, a resurvey from part of LOTTS
WIFE, originally THE LOTT 85 acres and added 81 acres of vacant land for
a total of 166 acres, in Mt. Vernon, Election district 5, map #1.
4 Jan 1741 Thomas Dashiell gave to son Charles Dashiell 166 acres with
VENTURE.
12 Feb 1770 Levin Dashiell and wife Frances Dashiell sold to Robert
Dashiell 363 acres of FATHERS CARE, ADDITION & VENTURE.
8 April 1776 Robert Dashiell, wife Sarah Dashiell of Talbot Co. sold to
Samuel Ingersol of Somerset County 263 acres of FATHERS CARE, VENTURE
ADDITION.
1783 tax- Samuel C.Ingersol 166 acres.
17 March 1790 John Roberts and wife Rachel Roberts sold to William James
of Worc.Co. property in Somerset Co. & Worc.Co. of Samuel Ingersol, no
name or acres.
24 Apr.1790 Mary Ingersol sold to William James, lands held by her father
Samuel Ingersol.
16 May 1797 Richard Ingersol sold to William Roberts 54 1/4 acres of
MIDDLE & FATHERS CARE.
13 May 1800 John Ingersol of Worc.Co. sold to Richard Ingersol of
Somerset Co. lands, as heir of Samuel Ingersol- unnamed.
1 Oct 1801 Richard Ingersol son of Samuel Ingersol, and wife Elizabeth
Ingersol sold his rights to David Walston, with ADDITION & ADVENTURE.
27 April 1804 William Roberts and wife Sarah Roberts sold to Richard
Ingersol, part.
19 Dec.1804 Richard Ingersol, wife Elizabeth Ingersol sold to Fairfax
Smith 50 acres of MIDDLE & FATHERS CARE.
10 Nov.1807 Fairfax Smith, wife Rebecca Smith sold to Thomas Rencher 7
1/4 acres of FATHERS CARE & MIDDLE.
20 Jan 1808 Fairfax Smith sold to John Kirwin 44 acres of MIDDLE &
FATHERS CARE.
13 March 1808 Richarrd Ingersol sold 4 12 acres to Jacob Kirwin of MIDDLE
& FATHERS CARE.

FATHERS GIFT

This is part of DOUBLE PURCHASE. 29 June 1722 Southy Whittington
surveyor on request of William Eskridge laid out for him part of 500
acres called FATHERS GIFT with consent of Thomas Mitchell, possessor.
13 Oct.1714 Ann Coulbourn, William Coulbourn and Jean Coulbourn his wife
conveyed to Abigail Coulbourn now wife of William Eskridge 1/2 of FATHERS
GIFT conveyed to Thomas Mitchell and wife Ann Mitchell now in possession
of said Ann Mitchell. On the south side of the Manokin river dividing
from the land laid out for Thomas Mitchell called DAUGHTERS DOWER.
9 Dec 1735 William Eskridge and wife Abigail Eskridge sold to Nehemiah
King 1/2 of FATHER GIFT now called COME BY CHANCE 250 acres.
8 April 1748 I Ann Mitchell sell to Richard Mitchell and Stephen Mitchell

and William Wheatley(has a judgement against lands DAUGHTERS DOWER 250
acres being 1/2 of FATHERS GIFT containing 500 acres, all being part of
DOUBLE PURCHASE, patented by Randall Revell.

FATHERS GIFT SECURED

See MITCHELL LOTT

FATHERS INTENT

See POMFRET.- 18 Aug.1750 Samuel Handy and wife Elizabeth Handy sold to
William Coulbourn FATHERS INTENT, part of a tract surveyed for William
Coulbourn called POMFRET 55 acres, 15 rods.
1765 William Coulbourn willed to wife Elizabeth Coulbourn POMFRET,
FATHERS INTENT, after death to son John Coulbourn.

FATHERS PURCHASE

See DOUBLE PURCHASE

FERRY BRIDGE

Patented on 10 May 1685 by William Coulbourn for 200 acres in Lawsons,
Election district 8, map #18.
Rent Rolls 1666-1723 Ann Coulbourn relic of William Coulbourn 200 acres.
1744/8 Solomon Coulbourn son of William Coulbourn Jr, gave to sons
Solomon Coulbourn, William Coulbourn, Isaac Coulbourn, Benjamin Coulbourn
taken up by grandfather William Coulbourn.
18 May 1750 William Coulbourn Sr, and William Coulbourn Jr. sold to
Michael Holland 200 acres (formerly given by William Coulbourn to his
daughter Penelope Coulbourn who married Michael Holland.)
2 March 1753 Michael Holland gave to son Robert Holland 100 acres
21 Nov.1754 William Coulbourn, Isaac Coulbourn, Benjamin Coulbourn (sons
of Solomon Coulbourn deceased)sold to Robert Holland 200 acres.
15 Oct.1765 Robert Holland sold 100 acres to Michael Holland.
2 Feb 1769 Michael Holland the elder gave to son Michael Holland all not
before conveyed.
15 March 1773 Michael Holland Jr. sold 100 acres to Robert Holland for 5
shillings, with HOLLANDS CHANCE.
1759 part resurveyed to HOLLANDS CHANCE 220 1/4 acres
1783 tax- Robert Holland 100 acres.
10 Nov.1792 Michael Holland sold 21 1/2 acres of FERRY BRIDGE & POMFRET
to John Horsey.
1795 Robert Holland willed to nephew Daniel Holland son of Edward, land
no name.
4 April 1797 Jesse Holland son of Michael Holland sold to William
Williams, his rights.
28 Sep.1801 Mary Holland widow of Robert Holland released her dower
rights to Daniel Holland,no name or acres.
12 March 1810 Daniel Holland sold to Nathaniel Bell land devised to him
by Robert Holland, no name.
12 March 1810 Nathaniel Bell sold to Daniel Walston, lands in Little
Annamessex willed him by Robert Holland, no name.

FERRY HILL

Patented in 1763 by Thomas Holbrook in Mt.Vernon, Election district 5, map #1, for 17 1/4 acres
1783 tax- William Dockery 17 1/4 acres
1791 Thomas Holbrook, willed to son Samuel Holbrook.

FIRST CHOICE

Patented on 23 Sep.1663 by Richard Acworth for 210 acres in West Pr.Anne, Election district 1, map #3.
17 Nov.1685 Richard Acworth and wife Sarah Acworth sold to Levin Denwood 210 acres..
Rent Rolls 1666-1723 possessed by Arthur Denwood who purchased of Acworths heirs.
16 Sep.1740 Thomas Denwood conveyed 210 acres to George Denwood lands of grandfather Levin Denwood.
16 Sep.1741 George Denwood sold to David Wilson 420 1/2 acres of FIRST CHOICE,NUTTERS DELIGHT,DENWOODS INCLUSION, WEATHERLYS CHANCE, BROWNSTONE.

FIRST CHOICE

Patented on 4 March 1677 by Thomas Dixon for 200 acres in Brinkleys, northwest, Election district 3, map #14.
Rent Rolls 1666-1723 Thomas Dixon 200 acres
1744 resurvey to SECOND CHOICE 215 acres.
1747 William Dixon willed to son Thomas Dixon
1751 William Dixon gave to son Thomas 212 acres.

FIRST CHOICE

Patented on 17 June 1679 by Robert Catlin for 250 acres in Westover, Election district 13, map #11 resurvey of JOHNSONS FIRST CHOICE.
16 March 1686 Robert Catlin, wife Hannah Catlin sold 75 acres
1666-1723 Rent rolls, possessed by William Catlin son of Robert Catlin.
21 Nov.1722 John Taylor and Mary Taylor sold to Edmund Beauchamp, patented Robert Catlin and sold by William Catlin and wife Jane Catlin to John Taylor.
27 July 1729 William Catlin only son of Robert Catlin sold 50 acres to Robert King now called THE CLOSURE.
18 March 1729 William Beauchamp gave to son Edmund Beauchamp, FIRST CHOICE, HOG YARD, LOSS & GAIN.
24 Sep 1745 William Catlin sold to Edmund Beauchamp 75 acres including all the part called FORKED NECK for 10 shillings.
8 Sep.1745 William Beauchamp of Kent Co. Del. sold to his brother Edmund Beauchamp of Somerset Co.,planter, 75 acres with 100 acres of LOSS & GAIN with FORKED NECK.
20 Aug.1745 Edmund Beauchamp and wife Elizabeth Beauchamp sold 40 acres to William Jones, carpenter.
5 Aug.1750 Edmund Beauchamp, wife Elizabeth Beauchamp sold to John Williams 21 acres.
14 Aug.1752 Edmund Beauchamp sold to William Walston LOSS & GAIN, FIRST CHOICE. description, no acres given.
2 Dec 1752 William Walston, wife Ann Walston sold to Nathaniel Dougherty 39 3/4 acres.

159

19 June 1754 Nathaniel Dougherty sold to William Turpin 39 3/4 acres, with LOSS & GAIN.
7 June 1761 William Walston sold to Nathaniel Dougherty 8 acres with LOSS & GAIN.
12 Feb 1763 Nathaniel Dougherty, wife Rebecca Dougherty sold to William Turpin 39 3/4 acres with 8 acres conveyed by William Walston and LOSS & GAIN.
1767 William Turpin willed to son Joshua Turpin tract bought of Nathaniel Dougherty 100 acres, unnamed.
12 July 1791 John Williams sold to Levin Ballard 21 acres.
12 July 1791 Levin Ballard sold to John Williams 21 acres.

FIRST CHOICE

Patented in 1727 by Alexander McCready for 100 acres in Brinkleys, southeast, Election district 3, map #16
1742 Alexander McCready willed 100 acres to son Solomon McCready.
1782 Solomon McCready willed to son Alexander McCready
1783 tax- Isaac McCready 100 acres.
1810 Isaac McCready willed to grandson Samuel McCready son of Solomon McCready 1/2, 100 acres and to grandson Stephen McCready son of Isaac McCready.

FIRST CHOICE

Patented in 1754 by Isaac Denston for 66 acres in East Princess Anne, Election district 15, map #4.
1771 Isaac Denston willed to son William Denston 66 acres.
22 Apr.1794 Ephraim Denston sold to Samuel Banks 66 acres with MISFORTUNE.
4 July 1798 Ephraim Adams Denston sold to Samuel Banks 66 acres.
14 Nov.1804 Ephraim Adams Denston and Samuel Banks of Worc.Co. sold to Thomas Brown 67 acres.

FIRST CONCLUSION

Patented in 1768 by Matthias Miles for 92 acres in West Pr.Anne, Election district 1, map 2.
1783 tax- Matthias Miles 92 acres.
25 May 1803 Matthias Miles sold to Thomas Jones of John Jones 92 acres.
25 May 1803 Thomas Jones of John Jones, and wife Betsy Jones sold to Littleton Dennis Teackle 92 acres.

FISHING ISLAND

Patented in 1681 for 20 acres by George Lane, in Fairmount, Election district 6, map #9.
Rent Rolls 1666-1723 Possessed by Dennis Lane widow of George Lane, 20 acres.
30 May 1703 George Lane gave to son George.
20 Oct.1720 George Lane son of George Lane, and wife Temperance Lane sold 20 acres to Marcy Fountain.
1726/7 Marcy Fountain willed to son Samuel Fountain
25 April 1755 Marcy Fountain mortgaged to Henry Lowes
1761 Henry Lowes willed to son Tubman Lowes land mortgaged by Marcy

Fountain.
18 Aug.1767 Henry Lowes sold to William Fountain for 10 shillings land
conveyed by Marcy Fountain to Henry's father.
14 May 1771 Thomas Pollitt and wife Betty Pollitt sold to William
Fountain 20 acres with NEWFOUNDLAND, MARSHGROUND.
13 Aug.1786 William Fountain, wife Sarah Furniss Fountain sold to John
Williams 1/2 tr. MARSH GROUND and 1 moity of NEWFOUNDLAND & FISHING
ISLAND.
14 Feb.1789 William Fountain, wife Sarah Fountain, sold to John Williams
1 moity of same as above.
4 May 1807 John Curtis, wife Margaret Curtis and William Fountain sold to
John C. Wilson 314 1/4 acres of FISHING ISLAND, NEWFOUNDLAND & MARSH
GROUND.
1850 Whitty Fountain willed to daughter Margaret Hall 1/2 of and to son
William Fountain, part.

FLATT CAPP

Patented on 18 April 1689 by Thomas Jones for 50 acres in Lawsons,
Election district 8, map #19.
Rent Rolls 1666-1723 Possessed by Robert Catherwood in right of Thomas
Jones orphans (Robert Catherwood married the widow of Thomas Jones.)
14 Oct.1749 Thomas Jones, merchant, sold to John Williams 50 acres for 5
shillings, with MISTAKE.
11 Nov.1768 John Williams sold to Kirk Gunby, 400 acres of FLATT CAPP &
MISTAKE.
29 Dec.1768 John Williams sold to Josephus Bell 1/4th part of FLATTCAPP &
MISTAKE.
1775 Kirk Gunby willed to son John Gunby
1783 tax- John Gunby Sr. 25 acres.
1783 tax- Sarah Gunby, her 1/3rds.
1783 tax- Josephus Bell
1788 John Gunby willed to son Kirk Gunby.

FLATLAND

Patented in 1764 by Isaac Coston for 277 acres in Dublin, Election
district 4, map #12.
20 Aug 1754 Ahab Coston and wife Abigail Coston sold to Isaac Coston 100
acres for 5 shillings, and part of BEAR POINT.
1758 10 1/2 acres resurveyed to TURKEY RIDGE.
1772 Isaac Coston willed 177 acres to son Henry Coston.
1783 tax- Sarah Coston 277 acres.

FLATTLAND ·

Patented on 1 June 1696 by Thomas Everton for 850 acres in Fairmount,
Election district 6, map #9.
1710 Thomas Evernton willed to Richard Waters and wife Elizabeth Waters
and heirs 850 acres.
Rent Rolls 1666-1723- Richard Waters.
1720 Richard Waters willed to sons William Waters, Richard Waters,
Littleton Waters and to son John Waters 70 acres.
1752 Elizabeth Waters gave to son Richard Waters part left me by Thomas
Everton.

1775 15 1/2 acres added called ADDITION but not patented by Isaiah Tilghman.
1783 tax- Richard Waters 840 acres.
8 Nov.1786 Richard Waters Sr. sold to William Waters Sr. devised by his father William(division of lands) with LONDONS GIFT,FRIENDS KINDNESS, WATERS RIVER,CONVIENCE.
15 Nov.1787 Richard Waters Sr, wife Eleanor Waters sold to James Waters, part, no acres given, description.
20 Feb.1788 Richard Waters, wife Eleanor Waters, sold to Isaiah Tilghman 149 1/2 acres of FLATLAND,FRIENDS KINDNESS & LONDONS GIFT.
20 Dec.1788 Richard Waters, wife Eleanor Waters, sold to the heirs of William Long 149 1/2 acres.
20 Dec.1788 Richard Waters,wife Eleanor Waters, sold to Thomas Lister 149 1/2 acres with FRIENDS KINDNESS.
20 Dec.1788 Richard Waters sold to Joshua Boston 149 1/2 acres.
17 March 1790 John Beauchamp sold to Thomas Beauchamp 50 acres that is part of FLATLAND,FRIENDS KINDNESS.
17 March 1790 John Beauchamp sold 99 1/2 acres to Samuel Curtis of FLATLAND, and FRIENDS KINDNESS.
1790 Isaiah Tilghman willed to daughter Amelia Tilghman and to son William Tilghman and to grand-daughter Leah Beauchamp conveyed to brother William and me from Richard Waters Sr, with ADDITION.
1790 John Beauchamp sold part to Samuel Curtis.
19 April 1790 Richard Waters sold 99 1/2 acres to Samuel Curtis of FLATLAND,FRIENDS KINDNESS.
10 April 1790 Richard Waters sold 50 acres to Thomas Beauchamp of FLATLANDS,FRIENDS KINDNESS.
25 Feb.1790 Joshua Boston, wife Nancy Boston sold 149 acres to Isaiah Tilghman and William Tilghman.
1790 Isaiah Tilghman willed part to son William Tilghman and part to daughter Amelia Tilghman and son James Tilghman and grandaughter Leah Beauchamp.
6 Aug.1792 John Turpin of Nehemiah Turpin, and wife Sarah Turpin, sold to Thomas Jones,merchant 37 1/2 acres. Purchased by William Long and conveyed to the heirs of William Long 1/4th part which became the property of John Turpin in right of his wife Sarah who was the daughter of William Long.
18 June 1799 Samuel Long and William Long sold to Isaiah Tilghman purchased by William Long, 149 1/2 acres.
1802 Daniel Ballard and wife Dolly Ballard sold 130 acres to William Curtis.
12 July 1802 Daniel Ballard, wife Dolly Ballard sold 130 acres to William Curtis.
12 July 1802 James Waters sold to William Curtis 130 acres.
12 July 1802 Thomas Seon Sudler, wife Nelly Sudler sold 130 acres to William Curtis.
1802 Thomas Sudler and wife Nelly Sudler sold part to William Curtis.
1804 Joshua Boston conveyed part to son Levin Boston.
31 Oct.1804 Samuel Smith executor,sold to Isaac Beauchamp that Thomas Jones purchased of John Turpin, and willed to be sold 37 1/2 acres.
1808 Jesse Lister willed to niece Martha Lister.
1815 William Curtis sold 130 acres to William Thomas.

FLEMINGS BEGINNING

Patented in 1753 by William Fleming for 16 acres in Dublin, Election
district 13, map #12.

FLEMINGS CONCLUSION

Patented in 1756 by William Fleming for 275 acres, a resurvey of
HARRISONS ADVENTURE, in Dublin, Election district 4, map #2.
21 June 1769 William Fleming sold to Teague Riggin Sr. of Perryhawkin 9
1/2 acres.
20 June 1769 William Fleming sold to James Harris, an infant son of James
Harris,deceased. 17 acres.
1783 tax- William Fleming.
6 April 1796 John Harris sold 17 acres to William Fleming.
6 April 1796 Ephraim Collins,wife Sarah Collins, James Collins and wife
Mary Collins sold to Andrew Brown of Worc.Co. tracts willed to Caleb
Harris by his father. All interest in FLEMINGS CONCLUSION, FLEMINGS LOSS,
except the graveyard.
12 April 1806 William Wilson, wife Leah Wilson sold to John Riggin all
interest in lands of Teague Riggin 65 acres, unnamed.
1809 resurvyed to FLEMINGS SECURITY 852 1/4 acres.

FLEMINGS LOSS

Patented in 1744 by Caleb Harris for 60 acres in Dublin, Election
district 4, map #12.
1751 Caleb Harris willed 60 acres to son Abraham Harris.
17 June 1752 James Harris sold to Abraham Harris 115 acres of MIDDLETON,
FLEMINGS LOSS,HARRISONS VENTURE and on the same date Abraham Harris sold
120 acres of MIDDLETON & FLEMINGS LOSS to James Harris- to settle
boundaries.
16 Dec.1776 Abraham Harris,wife Director Harris sold 16 acres to William
Fleming.
1783 tax- William Fleming.
27 Aug.1788 John Sheldon Alexander and wife Leah Alexander of Worc. Co.
sold 60 acres to John Harris with MIDDLETOWN,HARRISONS ADVENTURE.
6 April 1796 John Harris sold 60 acres to William Fleming.
6 April 1796 Ephraim Collins,wife Sarah Collins, James Collins and wife
Mary Collins, sold to Andrew Brown of Worc.Co. tracts willed to Caleb
Harris by his father and all interest in FLEMINGS CONCLUSION & FLEMINGS
LOSS.

FLEMINGS SECURITY

Patented in 1809 by William Fleming, a resurvey of FLEMINGS CONCLUSION &
MINSHALLS ADVENTURE, in Dublin, Election district 4, map #12, for 852 1/4
acres.
6 Nov.1827 Sheriffs sale- Charles Jones vs William Fleming 800 acres.
1831 ADDTION TO FLEMINGS SECURITY patented by Jehu Parsons for 4 acres.
1859 Jehu Parsons willed to son William Sydney Parsons with the small
ADDITION.

FLINT

Patented on 29 July 1679 by Edward Jones for 50 acres in Fairmount,
Election district 6, map #9.
Rent Rolls 1666-1723 Possessed by Miles Gray.
1717 Miles Gray willed to son-in-law William Turpin and his son John

Turpin.
1736 John Turpin willed to son William Turpin the right in GRAYS
IMPROVEMENT out of the original patented (FLINT not mentioned.)
2 April 1754 William Turpin sold to Whittington King and Whitty Turpin 50
acres.

FLOWERFIELD

Patented in 1761 by Thomas Holbrook, a resurvey of part of SWEETWOOD, for
115 1/2 acres in Mt.Vernon,Election district 5, map #1.
11 March 1762 Daniel Jones sold to Thomas Holbrook, PRIVILEDGE, LAST
VACANCY & FLOWERFIELDS. no acreage given.
1783 tax- Thomas Holbrook 115 1/2 acres
2 Feb.1788 Thomas Holbrook deeded to son Henry Holbrook 207 1/2 acres of
LAST VACANCY,FLOWERFIELD.
1789 Henry Holbrook gave to son Thomas Holbrook.
7 Jan.1794 John Holbrook sold to Thomas Holbrook Jr. as Henry Holbrook
willed to son John Holbrook 207 acres to be sold to pay debts. Priscilla
Holbrook released her dower rights. No name mentioned.
24 May 1804 John Teackle of Acco. Co. Va. sold to Littleton Dennis
Teackle of Som.Co. the lands of Thomas Holbrook.
21 Aug.1804 Thomas Holbrook, wife Peggy Holbrook, Littelton Dennis and
Littleton Dennis Teackle sold to Levin Jones 140 acres of FLOWERFIELD,
BENGAL & LAST VACANCY.
29 Oct.1807 Littleton Dennis Teackle sold to John Teackle of Georgetown
DC lands of Thomas Holbrook.
13 Aug.1808 Daniel Ballard, sheriff, sold to Zadock Long Sr. 81 1/2 acres
of CONCLUSION,LAST VACANCY & FLOWERFIELDS per judgement against Thomas
Holbrook.
17 Oct.1808 Levin Jones, wife Elizabeth Jones sold to Joseph Whitney 80
acres of RECTIFIED MISTAKE & FLOWERFIELDS.

FLOWERFIELDS

Patented in 1814 by Nathan Cahoon for 116 acres in Brinkleys,southwest
Election district 3, map 17.

FOLLY

Patented in 1752 by Cornelius Ward for 19 acres in Lawsons, Election
District 8,map #19.
15 Oct.1768 Cornelius Ward Sr, and Cornelius Ward Jr. sold to James Ward
son of Cornelius Ward Sr 8 1/2 acres with CORK,PRICES CONCLUSION,WHITE
OAK SWAMP.
1783 tax- Cornelius Ward 9 1/2 acres.
5 Mar.1790 John Ward Sr. sold to Joseph Ward for 5 shillings, FOLLY &
CORK.
17 Feb.1797 Hance Croswell sold to Ezekiel Ward for 5 shillings FOLLY,
CORK, WHITE OAK.
18 Apr.1797 Joseph Ward sold to Hance Croswell 30 acres of CORK & FOLLY.
9 April 1803 Ezekiel Ward sold 5 acres to George Davey.
12 May 1804 Ezekiel Ward transfered to John Miles, constable of Little
Annamessex, to pay debts 150 acres with WHITE OAK SWAMP & DUBLIN.

1 Feb.1806 John Miles sold to Ezekiel Ward 150 acres of FOLLY, DUBLIN &
WHITE OAK SWAMP.
25 July 1808 Ezekiel Ward sold to Henry Ward, Whitty Ward, Ezekiel Ward
Jr., Betsy Ward, Lovey Ward and John Ward FOLLY & DUBLIN.

FORCE PUTT

Patented in 1745 by Charles Roach for 168 acres in Lawsons, Election
district 8, map #19.
1783 tax- William Roach 92 acres
1783 tax- Rachel Roach 46 acres
7 Jan 1800 John Ward son of Stephen Ward, now in Kentucky sold to John
Cullen.
25 Feb.1806 William Roach sold to John Lawson 37 2/3 acres.
1874 ADDITION TO FORCEPUTT patented by Thomas K.Walton.

FORKED NECK

See FIRST CHOICE in Annamessex.

FORLORN HOPE

Patented in 1683 for Augustine Stanford for 100 acres in Dames Quarter,
Election district 11, map #7.
Rent Rolls 1666-1723 possessed by the widow of Robert Pollock by the name
of POLLOCKS LOTT.
1702 Robert Polk willed to sons David Polk and Robert Polk.
1712 ADDITION TO FORLORN HOPE 90 acres.
1726 William Polk of Dorc.Co. gave to daughter Ann Polk, at head of Dames
Quarter, 50 acres.
1727 Robert Polk of Dorcester Co. sold to brother Joseph Polk.
5 Jan 1743 David Pollock, James Pollock and John Pollock of Dorc.Co. sold
200 acres to Edward Roberts POLKS MEADOW at FORLORN HOPE in Dame Quarter.
16 Aug.1748 Joseph Pollock of Dorc.Co. sold to John Shores and William
Shores of Somerset County 100 acres of POLKS FOLLY, and 50 acres FORLORN
HOPE, patented Augustine Stanford and Robert Polk.
16 Aug.1749 Joseph Pollock of Dorc.Co. sold to John Shores and William
Shores 50 acres of FORLORN HOPE and 90 acres of ADDITION.
1783 tax- George Austin 100 acres and ADDITION.
1794 William Roberts willed to niece Nancy Lemon wife of Robert Lemon,
POLKS MEADOW.
9 Jan 1802 George Austin leased to Mary Miles 3 acres during lifetime.
13 March 1810 Lewis Phoebus, wife Polly Phoebus sold to William Austin
son of George Austin 87 1/4 acres and ADDITION 6 acres.
1847 Edward Shores willed to son Thomas Shores 12 1/2 acres.

FORTUNE

Patented in 1762 by William Miles for 36 1/2 acres in Lawsons, Election
district 8, map #18.
14 Oct 1765 William Miles mortgaged to Matthias Gale of London, merchant,
HEARTS EASE,PLEASURE,FORTUNE etc- 36 1/2 acres
18 Aug.1795 Milcah Gale Chaille sold to Levin Miles all CHANCE & FORTUNE.

FOSCOTT

Patented on 2 Jan.1688 by Henry Miles for 50 acres in Fairmount,Election district 6, map #9.
1695 Henry Miles willed to sons Samuel Miles and Henry Miles.
Rent Rolls 1666-1723 Samuel Miles heir of Henry Miles.
1782 will of Samuel Miles, to brother Matthias Miles old plantation 50 acres, unnamed.

FOUL MEADOW

Surveyed in 1784 by Isaiah Tilghman from TILGHMANS ENLARGEMENT, for 183 3/4 acres in Dublin, Election district 4, map #12.
1790 Isaiah Tilghman willed to daughter Amelia Tilghman 183 acres and part to son James Tilghman. (Amelia married Edward Gibbons in 1799.)

FOUNTAINS ADDITION

see MARISH GROUND

FOUNTAINS LOTT

Patented on 12 March 1663 by Nicholas Fountain for 300 acres in Westover, Election district 13, map #11.
1708 Nicholas Fountain willed to sons Nicholas Fountain and Stephen Fountain.
Rent Rolls 1666-1723 Nicholas Fountain 300 acres.
29 July 1727 Stephen Fountain son of Nicholas Fountain sold to Nicholas Fountain son of Marcy Fountain 175 acres with NORMANDY.
7 June 1732 Nicholas Fountain Sr gave to Nicholas Fountain Jr. 1 moity of OLD RIGHTS 126 1/2 acres adjacent NORMANDY, unnamed land.
14 June 1735 Nicholas Fountain and wife Tabitha Fountain sold to William Turpin son of William, the west moity of FOUNTAINS LOTT & NORMANDY and 10 acres of CONVENIENCY.
1743 Nicholas Fountain willed lands purchased from Stephen Fountain to son Marcy Fountain (unnamed)
1758 resurvyed to NORMANDY 261 acres
1783 tax- Denwood Turpin 115 acres.
7 July 1800 Whitty Turpin Fountain and William Turpin agreed to division of lines.

FOUR IN ONE

Patented in 1792, a resurvey of FAIR MEADOW,BEARE RIDGE,DESERT, for 739 1/8 acres in East Pr.Anne,Election district 5, map #4, by Matthias Miles.

FOXES HALL

Patented in 1774 by Thomas Pollitt for 46 acres in East Princess Anne, Election district 15, map #4.
1783 tax- Thomas Pollitt, 46 acres
1788 Thomas Pollitt willed to son Thomas Pollitt.

FRANCIS'S ADVENTURE

Surveyed in 1761 for Francis Roberts for 15 acres in Dames Quarter,

Election district 11, map #7.

FREE CHOICE

see SUFFOLK

FREE PURCHASE & ADDITION TO FREE PURCHASE

See DOUBLE PURCHASE, patented Randall Revell, part called WELCOME POOL.

FRIENDS ACCEPTANCE

Patented on 13 Aug.1701 by Richard Wallace for 95 acres in Dames Quarter,
Election district 11 map #7.
Rent Rolls 1666-1723 possessed by Richard Wallace.
13 July 1779 David Wallace gave to Richard Wallace 95 acres with MEADOW,
DAM QUARTER, FATHER & SONS DESIRE,etc.
1783 tax- Mary Wallace & Margaret Wallace 25 acres.
29 July 1788 Richard Wallace, wife Rebecca Wallace sold to William
Roberts all his rights.

FRIENDS ADVICE

Patented on 1 April 1699 to William Waller for 45 acres in St.Peters,
Election district 2, map #6.
Rent Rolls 1666-1723 William Waller
1700 resurveyed, 45 acres
1841 Isaac Newman willed to son Thomas William Newman land purchase of
William Waller and also to son Isaac Newman.

FRIENDS ADVICE

Patented in 1742 to Thomas Wright for 40 acres in St.Peters, Election
district 2, map #6.
1703 tax- John Wright 40 acres
1785 resurveyed to RIGHTS CONCLUSION 264 1/4 acres.

FRIENDS ADVICE

Patented on 15 July 1750 to Benjamin Fransway for 356 acres in East
Pr.Anne,Election district 15, map #5.
11 Feb 1751 Benjamin Fransway sold to Thomas Jones 356 acres and this
sale was confirmed on 25 Feb.1758.
1783 tax- William Jones 356 acres.
13 Sep.1806 William Jones, wife Eleanor Jones sold to William Gillis
Waters 135 acres.

FRIENDS ADVICE

Patented in 1771 by William Miles for 123 acres in East PR. Anne,Election
district 15, map #4.
19 March 1777 William Miles sold to Samuel Miles for 5 shillings 123
acres.
29 Nov.1782 Samuel Miles, wife Mary Miles sold to Matthias Miles 123
acres with CONCLUSION & SAMUELS LOTT.
1783 tax- Matthias Miles 123 acres.

167

1776 resurveyed to GREAT HOPES.

FRIENDS AGREEMENT

Patented in 1742 by Thomas Wright for 28 acres in St. Peters,Election
district 2, map #6.
26 Feb.1782 John Wright sold to Gowan Wright 28 acres.
1783 tax- Gowan Wright 28 acres.

FRIENDS ASSISTANCE

Patented in 1771 by John Phillips for 185 acres in East Pr.Anne,Election
district 1, map #3.
17 July 1787 John McDaniel and wife Elizabeh McDaniel and Phillip Riggin
sold to Matthias Miles 185 acres with PHILLIPS CONCLUSION.
17 March 1801 Matthias Miles sold to John Layfield 10 acres.
1818/21 Matthias Miles gave to son Levin C. Miles 97 acres where Stephen
Heath lives and to nephew William Miles.
1833 resurveyed to FRIENDS GOOD WILL 175 acres.

FRIENDS ASSISTANCE

Patented on 29 June 1685 by Charles Ballard for 200 acres in West
Pr.Anne, Election district 1 map #3.
9 Oct 1756 Robert Ballard sold to William Hayward 200 acres with NUTTERS
PURCHASE,TURKEY RIDGE.
1758 resurveyed to HAYWARDS PURCHASE 549 1/2 acres.

FRIENDS CHOICE

Patented on 14 Oct.1673 by Thomas Jones for 300 acres in East Pr.Anne,
Election district 15, map #5.
1675 Capt. Thomas Jones sold to William Stevens.
1 Oct.1679 William Stevens sold to Henry Smith
17 Jan 1687 Henry Smith and wife Ann Smith sold to Edward Wheeler and
wife Margaret Wheeler and Thomas Everton and wife Jean Everton. They all
sold on 4 Aug.1694 to William Porter.
6 Dec.1695 William Porter willed his wife Elizabeth Porter to sell.
18 June 1718 Elizabeth Porter and her son Joseph Porter and his wife
Eliner Porter sold to Esther Murray.
25 Feb.1746 Esther Murray, widow sold to David Wilson 300 acres.
1749 resurveyed to CLOVERFIELDS 1250 acres.
4 May 1786 David Wilson,wife Sarah Wilson of Worc.Co. sold to John Wilson
of Somerset CO. with CLOVERFIELDS, GULLETTS ADVISEMENT, all not
previously sold.

FRIENDS CONTENT

Patented on 24 Feb.1666 to Percival Reed for 300 acres and assigned to
Thomas Jerrett, in Dames Quarter, Election district 11 map #7.
AKA-FRIENDS CONTENTMENT
Rent Rolls 1666-1723 It hath been escheated for John White and Richard
Wallace. Thomas Jerrett is deceased.
1701 resurveyed by John White and Richard Wallace for 270 acres.

1718 John White gave 40 acres in Dames Quarter to son-in-law Richard Wallace- land not named.
14 Jun 1736 Richard Wallace sold to John White 168 acres of FRIENDS CONTENTMENT & FATHER & SONS DESIRE.
1766 John White willed to sons William White and John White FRIENDS CONTENTMENT.
8 March 1774 John White Sr. gave to son John White 333 acres DAME QUARTER,FRIENDS CONTENT,OXFORD.
8 Sep.1774 John White, wife Rebecca White sold to Joseph Wallace 22 acres.
13 July 1779 David Wallace gave to Richard Wallace with FRIENDS ACCEPTANCE,DAMES QUARTER, etc. no acreage given.
May 1782 William White son of William sold 108 acres to Thomas White.
1783 tax- John White Jr. 27 acres
1783 tax- Thomas White 92 acres with FATHER & SONS DESIRE
8 June 1788 John White sold to John Thomas of Dorc.Co. 116 acres of DAMES QUARTER & FRIENDS CONTENTMENT
29 July 1788 Richard Wallace,wife Rebecca Wallace, sold to William Roberts all his rights.
18 Jun 1788 John White sold 6 3/4 acres to Thomas White.
19 Jan 1793 John White leased to Francis White 303 acres of OXFORD,DAME QUARTER,FRIENDS CONTENTMENT,during life of John White.
1799 Thomas White gave to son William White.
28 Sep.1803 Whittington White sold 12 acres to David Wallace
14 April 1804 Whittington White,wife Tabitha White sold to Thomas White of Thomas 15 acres of FATHER & SONS DESIRE AND FRIENDS CONTENT.
9 Feb 1805 Whittington White, wife Tabitha White sold to Henry White 43 acres of DAMES QUARTER & FRIENDS CONTENT.
27 May 1805 David Wallace Jr. sold to Peter White 13 3/4 acres.
27 May 1805 David Wallace Jr. sold to Peter White, part conveyed by Whittington White.
2 Dec 1806 Whittington White, wife Tabitha White sold to Thomas White of Thomas FATHER & SONS DESIRE, FRIENDS CONTENT except dower of Mary Parks.
2 Dec.1806 Peter White sold 8 acres to Thomas White.
2 Dec.1806 Nelly Roberts sold to Whittington White her rights, mortgaged by Joseph Wallace to John Roberts.
2 Dec.1806 Whittington White, wife Tabitha White sold 34 acres to Henry White.
7 Dec.1807 Peter White sold to Henry White 6 acres purchased of David Wallace, no name.

FRIENDS CHOICE

see HARRISONS ADVENTURE-1715

FRIENDS CHOICE

Patented in 1734 by John Harris for 18 acres in Dublin,Election District 4, map #12
1783 tax- John Riggin 18 acres.

FRIENDS GOOD WILL

Patented in 1833 by Levin Miller for 175 acres a resurvey of FRIENDS ASSISTANCE in East Princess Anne,Election district 15, map #5.

FRIENDS KINDNESS

Patented on 14 March 1723 by Richard Chambers for 100 acres in East Pr.Anne,Election district 15, map #5.
1743 Richard Chambers willed to cousin Richard Brereton and cousin Samuel Collins.
c6 Oct 1746 Henry Brereton of Baltimore Co. Md. and Thomas Brereton of same sold to Woncy McClemmy of Somerset CO. all rights to VULCANS FORGE,MANLOVES VENTURE,FRIENDS KINDNESS, that brother Richard Brereton willed to them.
7 April 1748 Samuel Collins and wife Elizabeth Collins of Worc.Co. sold to Woncy McClemmy their rights.
7 Nov.1749 Creditors join to sell the land of Woncy McClemmy (George Gale,Nehemiah King, Ephraim Wilson, James Polk,Thomas Jones,Joseph Gillis, Marcy Fountain)MANLOVES VENTURE,VULCAN FORGE,FRIENDS KINDNESS. Solomon Long adm. of Woncy McClemmy and Elenor McClemmy widow of Woncy (had two infant daughters) sold to Hamilton Bell 100 acres.

FRIENDS KINDNESS

Patented in 1754 by Ezekiel Hall for 258 acres in Fairmount, Election district 6, map #9.
1783 tax- Charles Hall 172 acres HALLS KINDNESS
1783 tax- Esther Hall 86 acres HALLS KINDNESS.
12 April 1809 Charles Hall gave to sons Samuel Hall & John Hall.

FRIENDS KINDNESS

Patented on 1 June 1696 to Richard Waters for 116 acres in Fairmount, Election district 6, map #9.
Rent Rolls 1666-1723 Richard Waters
1720 Richard Waters will, this land not mentioned.
1783 tax- Richard Waters 116 acres
8 Nov.1786 Richard Waters Sr sold to William Waters Sr. devised Richard by his father William Waters(division of lands)
15 Feb.1787 Richard Waters Sr,wife Eleanor Waters, sold to James Waters plantation where Richard lives- no name or acres.
20 Dec.1788 Richard Waters, wife Eleanor Waters sold to Isaiah Tilghman 149 1/2 acres of FLATLAND,LONDONS GIFT,FRIENDS KINDNESS.
20 Dec.1788 Richard Waters,wife Eleanor Waters sold to Thomas Lister 149 1/2 acres of FLATLAND & FRIENDS KINDNESS.
19 March 1790 John Beauchamp sold to Thomas Beauchamp 50 acres of FLATLANDS,FRIENDS KINDNESS.
10 April 1790 Richard Waters sold to Samuel Curtis 99 1/2 acres FLATLAND,FRIENDS KINDNESS.
10 April 1790 Richard Waters sold to Thomas Beauchamp 50 acres FLATLAND & FRIENDS KINDNESS.

FRIENDSHIP

Patented on 3 July 1665 to George Wale for 100 acres in Dublin,Election district 4, map #13.
16 Oct.1671 George Wale conveyed to brother Edward Wale his lands.
8 Dec.1678 Edward Wale and wife Elizabeth Wale sold to Thomas Newbold 100 acres.
1712/13 Thomas Newbold willed to son Thomas Newbold 1/2 and to son

William Newbold 1/2.
Rent Rolls 1666-1723 Thomas Newbold 100 acres.
20 Aug.1766 William Hayward of Talbot Co. sold to Purnell Newbold of
Som.Co. 100 acres as Purnell was siezed of- release of claim.
3 Feb 1767 Purnell Newbold sold to Samuel Wilson 100 acres.
1783 tax- Samuel Wilson
19 Nov.1795 Major Samuel Wilson, wife Leah Wilson sold to Littleton
Dennis 815 acres with ACQUINTICA,CONTENT,NEWTOWN,NEGLECT etc.

FRIENDSHIP

Patented in 1794 by Nathaniel Smulling for 119 3/4 acres in East
Pr.Anne,Election district 15, map #5. A resurvey of part of ADDITION TO
ROWLEY RIDGE.
17 July 1810 Zorobable Smulling sold to Levin Miller and Nancy Miller 119
3/4 acres.
1824 John Hayman willed to daughters Leah Hayman and Molly Hayman.

FRIENDSHIP

Patented on 13 Sep.1765 by Andrew Francis Cheney for 172 acres in West
Pr.Anne,Election district 1, map #3, a resurvey of DOGWOOD RIDGE.
1783 tax- Andrew F. Cheney 172 acres.
4 Dec.1798 Francis Tubman Cheney sold to Nicholas Tull 25 acres.
14 May 1802 Richard Waters son of William Waters, and wife Mary Waters
sold 218 1/2 acres to Peter Waters with HAYWARDS PURCHASE
14 May 1802 Peter Waters sold to Richard Waters same as above.
14 May 1802 Richard Waters with wife Mary Day Waters sold to Littleton
Dennis Teackle, same.
9 Dec.1805 Nicholas Tull sold to negro Amelia 3 acres for life.

FROGG POND

Patented in 1763 by Samuel Miles for 41 acres in Westover, Election
district 13, map #11.
1793 Samuel Miles willed to son William Miles, after death to grandson
John Miles.
17 Nov.1802 John Miles sold to John Swift 28 1/2 acres.
1 March 1806 John Swift sold to William Williams 28 1/2 acres.

FRUSTRATION

Patented on 16 Nov.1694 by Francis Martin for 40 acres in Asbury,
Election district 12, map #21.
Rent Rolls 1666-1723 claimed by William Brittingham as marrying the
widow.
1741 John Sterling willed to son Joseph Sterling 40 acres.
18 Aug.1742 Mary Sterling daughter of Francis Martin deceased and relic
of John Sterling gave to son Joseph Sterling 40 acres.
22 March 1744 Joseph Sterling sold to Aaron Sterling 25 acres with CHERRY
HINTON.
31 Aug 1762 Aaron Sterling (trust lease) to Southy Whittington, after
death of Aaron, then on behalf of Littleton Sterling, HAZARD, BARNETT,
JOHNSONS LOTT, FRUSTRATION, STERLINGS GOOD LUCK.

FURNISS ADVENTURE

Patented on 3 Dec.1666 to William Furniss for 200 acres in Fairmount,
Election district 6, map #9.
1762 resurveyed to CANEDY ISLAND 219 1/2 acres.

FURNISS'S CHOICE

Patented on 12 March 1663 by William Furniss for 300 acres in Fairmount,
Election district 6, map #9.
Rent Rolls 1666-1723 possessed by James Furniss son of William Furniss.
8 January 1674 William Furniss and wife Olive Furniss sold to Henry Smith
300 acres.
1717 Miles Gray willed to son-in-law William Turpin, after death to his
son John Turpin.
11 May 1756 Solomon Gray eldest son of Thomas Gray who was the eldest son
of Miles Gray of Acoc.Co. Va. sold to Whitty Turpin (that Miles Gray
devised two tracts FURNIS'S CHOICE & POYKE to William Turpin for life and
who lately died and not possessed by Solomon Gray.)
1762 resurveyed to TURPINS PURCHASE 367 1/2 acres.

GALLOWAY

Patented in 1819, a resurvey from part of SMITHS HOPE, for 291 1/2 acres
in East Pr.Anne,Election district 15, map #4 by James Stewart.

GALLOWAY

Patented on 20 April 1680 by Samuel Long for 150 acres in Lawsons,
Election district 8, map #18. Was part of WATKINS POINT.
Rent Rolls 1666-1723 possessed by John Kirk
19 Aug.1736 Littleton Townsend and Sarah Townsend(Sarah Kirk daughter of
John Kirk,sold to John McClester 150 acres, probably a mortgage.
13 Feb 1737 Littleton Townsend and wife Sarah Townsend sold to Benjamin
Lankford 150 acres.
17 Aug.1763 Benjamin Lankford sold 150 acres to Lazarus Lankford with NEW
BRITTAIN.
15 June 1807 Benjamin Lankford sold to William Williams 29 acres.
22 June 1808 William Williams sold to Benjamin Lankford.
17 March 1810 Benjamin Lankford sold to William Williams 23 1/2 acres.
10 April 1810 Matthias Dashiell, sheriff sold to William Williams Esq.
per judgement against Benjamin Lankford 29 acres.

GARLANDS LOTT

Patented in 1767 by Stephen Garland for 18 1/2 acres in Westover,
Election district 13, map #11.
1783 tax- Stephen Garland 18 1/2 acres.

GEDDES OUTLETT

Patented in1762 by Robert Geddes for 70 acres in East Pr.Anne, Election
district 15, map #4.

172

1764 ADDITION TO GEDDES OUTLETT patented by Robert Gedddes for 20 acres.
19 Nov.1768 William Geddes son of Robert Geddes and wife Mary Geddes sold
to William Pollitt all of GEDDES OUTLETT & ADDITION.
20 Nov.1772 Thomas Pollitt sold to William Pollitt 75 acres.

GELSTON

Patented in 1747 by Isaac D. Jones, a resurvey of DORMANS CONCLUSION for
363 1/8 acres in West Pr.Anne,Election district 1, map #2.

GEORGES ADVENTURE

Patented on 16 Nov.1688 by George Betts a resurvey of BETTS PURCHASE, in
St. Peters, Election district 2, map #6, for 364 acres.
1709 George Betts willed to son-in-law John Irving and wife Frances
Irving (daughter of George Betts.)
1753 resurvey to 1000 acres by George Irving.
1 Nov.1763 Thomas Sloss of Somerset Co. and George Irving sold to William
Smith part BELLFAST 75 acres being part of GEORGES ADVENTURE and added as
a vacancy by George Irving.
1783 tax- Mary Smith 14 acres
1783 tax- Thomas Irving 286 acres
1784 Thomas Irving willed to son George Irving.
5 Feb 1789 Samuel Smith, wife Esther Smith sold to Henry Walston Miles 10
acres with CHANCE, BELFAST.
11 Jan 1793 George Irving and wife Ann Irving sold 60 acres to Ballard
Reed.
19 May 1801 William Waters Sr.sold to Ann Waters wife of William Gillis
Waters 110 acres.
19 May 1801 William Gillis Waters, wife Ann Waters sold to William Waters
Sr. aame as above.
18 Oct 1804 George Irving,wife Anne Irving sold to Evans Willin 50 acres.
9 Dec.1806 George Irving now of the state of Georgia sold to Andrew Adams
of Somerset Co., except parts already sold.
22 Feb.1808 Evans Willin sold to John Wilkins.
12 Dec.1810 Thomas Rutter, marshall, sold to Joshua Dorsey of Batltimore
County, per judgement against Evans Willin, yeoman, 60 acres.

GEORGES DELIGHT

This is part of DAVIS CHOICE 330 acres.

GEORGES FORTUNE

Patented in 1770, part from MILES CHANCE, by George Miles for 500 acres
in East Pr.Anne,Election district 15, map #5.
29 Nov.1781 Matthias Miles, wife Nanney Miles sold for 5 shillings to
Samuel Miles 492 acres
1782 Samuel Miles willed, to wife Mary Miles and then to son William
Miles. If he has no issue to brother Matthias Miles.
1783 tax- Matthias Miles 8 acres
1783 tax- William Miles of Samuel 100 acres.
1818/21 Matthias Miles willed to grandsons Tubman Jones and John Jones 26
acres

1833 ADDITION TO GEORGES FORTUNE, 11 1/8 acres by William Miles.

GERNSEY

Patented in 1681 for 150 acres in West Pr.Anne,Election district 1, map
#2.
1757 resurveyed to DOUBLE PURCHASE.
1783 tax- Stephen Adams, 150 acres.

GIBBONS LAST CHOICE

Patented in 1770 to John Gibbons for 9 acres in Westover, Election
district 13, map #10
1783 tax- John Givans Sr. 9 acres.

GIDEONS LUCK

Patented on 25 Aug.1715 John Caldwell for 100 acres in Dublin,Election
district 4, map #13.
20 Aug.1715 John Caldwell assigned to Gideon Tilghman 50 acres.15
Sep.1761 John Tilghman of Worc.Co. sold to John Givans of Som.Co. 34 1/3
acres for 4 shillings.
15 Sep.1761 John Tilghman son of Gideon, of Worc.Co. sold to Elisha
Tilghman 65 2/3 acres that Solomon Tilghman grandfather of John Tilghman
had.
13 March 1762 Gideon Tilghman gave to son Nehemiah Tilghman
24 June 1763 Elisha Tilghman traded part 7 1/2 acres of TILLMANS
ADVENTURE for same of GIDEONS LUCK.
19 July 1768 Nehemiah Tilghman,wife Catherine Tilghman, sold 41 1/2
acres.
20 Jan 1769 Nehemiah Tilghman and wife Catherine Tilghman sold to Robert
Jenkins King 268 acres with WILLIAMS HOPE,PLAGUE WITHOUT PROFIT.
21 April 1772 Aaron Tilghman sold to William Givans 164 1/2 acres of
GIDEONS LUCK & TILGHMANS ADVENTURE.
17 Oct.1773 Robert Jenkins King sold to Ephraim Stevens 250 acres of
WILLIAMS HOPE,GIDEONS LUCK,TILGHMANS CARE,PLAGUE WITH PROFIT.
21 Nov.1775 William Givans sold to Samuel Wilson 116 acres of TILGHMANS
ADVENTURE,GIDEONS LUCK.
15 Oct.1779 Ephraim Stevens sold to Robert Jenkins King 250 acres of
WILLIAMS HOPE,TILGHMANS CARE,PLAGUE WITHOUT PROFIT & ADDN. TO PLAGUE.
1 May 1782 William Givans sold to Samuel Wilson part of TILGHMANS
ADVENTURE, GIDEONS LUCK.
1783 tax- John Rounds 120 acres with TILGHMANS ADVENTURE
1788 Robert Jenkins King willed to son Robert King land bought of the
Tilghmans(not named)
13 Aug.1792 William Gibbons,wife Mary Gibbons sold to Levin Miles 200
acres of POOLS HOPE,GIDEONS LUCK,TILGHMANS CHANCE, GOOD LUCK, etc.
1795 Levin Miles willed to daughters Milcah Miles and Atlanta Miles and
to son Levin Miles, conveyed me by William Gibbons.
25 March 1800 Andrew Adams,wife Mary Adams and James Taylor, wife Sophia
Taylor and Isaac Taylor & Sarah Taylor sold to Samuel Taylor, lands of
William Taylor 84 acres of GIDEONS LUCK & PLAGUE WITHOUT PROFIT.
2 Dec.1800 Thomas Taylor sold to Samuel Taylor 84 acres of GIDEONS
LUCK,PLAGUE WITHOUT PROFIT.
8 Nov.1803 Dr. Robert Jenkins Henry sold to Eli Gibbons 399 3/4 acres

TILGHMANS CARE,BROUGHTONS PURCHASE,TILGHMANS SECURITY AND WILLIAMS HOPE.
25 Oct 1803 George Broughton and James Gibbons agree to division of
lands.
10 April 1810 Stephen Taylor sold to Samuel Taylor 84 acres of GIDEONS
LUCK & PLAGUE WITHOUT PROFIT.

GIDEONS REST
see DALES ADVENTURE

GILEAD

Patented in 1741 for 285 acres in Lawsons, Election district 8, map #18.
16 Nov.1752 Kirk Gunby sold to Southy Whittington 285 acres of
GILEAD,CHANCE, to settle dispute.
22 June 1763 Southy Whittington Sr. gave to son Southy Whittington 185
acres with CANAAN,GOSHEN,CHANCE,RECOVERY.

GILLIED

This is part of DOUBLE PURCHASE, 26 acres.
29 July 1760 Levin Wilson of Worc.Co. sold to Henry Newman 26 acres,part
of DOUBLE PURCHASE.
26 April 1802 Samuel Hillman, sailor, sold to James Bennett parcel Levin
Wilson sold to Henry Newman in 1760.
20 Oct 1804 James Bennett, wife Jane Bennett sold to John Custis Wilson
land conveyed by Samuel Hillman in 1802- no name or acreage.

GILFORD

See BELLS PURCHASE

GILLIS'S DOUBLE PURCHASE

Patented in 1748, a resurvey from HARMAN by Thomas Gillis for 303 acres
in West Pr.Anne,Election district 1, map #2.
11 June 1772 Thomas Gillis gave to son Joseph Gillis 303 acres.
15 NOv.1804 Joseph J. Gillis of Worc.Co. sold to Jacob Morris Sr. 117 1/2
acres, lot #7 per plat of division of 8 lots.

GIVANS CHANCE

Patented in 1749 by John Givans for 71 acres in Westover, Election
district 13, map #10
1783 tax- John Givans 71 acres.

GLADE SWAMP

Patented in 1767 by George Corbin for 125 acres in Dublin, Election
district 4, map #12.
16 Aug.1769 George Corbin Jr. sold 45 acres to Joseph Cottman
16 Aug.1769 George Corbin Jr. sold to John Pollitt 80 acres.
1783 tax- Joseph Cottman
1783 tax- Samuel Miles
15 March 1787 Joseph Cottman, wife Margaret Cottman, sold to Samuel Miles
41 acres.
3 Oct.1787 John Pollitt sold to Samuel Miles 8 acres.

11 Sep.1810 George Miles of Samuel Miles, of Worc.Co. sold to Isaac M. Adams.

GLANVILLE'S LOTT

Patented on 11 March 1663 by William Glanville for 500 acres in West Pr.Anne, Election district 1, map #3.
March 1693 William Glanville Jr. of Kent County sold to John King
1693 John King gave to son Capell King.
Rent Rolls 1666-1723 possessed by Peter Dent in right of Capell King's orphans.
1739 Capell King sold to Rev. James Robertson.
1739 resurvey to 440 acres by James Robertson
1783 tax- Ezekiel Gillis for James Robertons's heirs 436 acres.
1783 tax- James Wilson 4 acres.

GLASGOW

Patented in 1748 by Robert Jenkins Henry for 72 acres in Brinkleys, southeast, Election district 3, map #16.
1764 Robert Jenkins Henry willed to son Robert J. Henry.
1783 tax- Robert Jenkins Henry 72 acres.

GLASCOW SWAMP

Patented in 1729 by Alexander Adams for 300 acres in West Pr.Anne, Election district 1, map #2.
1769 Alexander Adams willed to son John Adams.
1802 resurveyed to EDINBURGH 1235 acrees.

GLASCOW

Patented on 7 Mar.1687 by David Brown for 300 acres in Dames Quarter, Election district 11, map #7.
Rent Rolls 1666-1723 Alexander Brown 150 acres. Ephraim Wilson 75 acres, Peter Dent 75 acres.
19 July 1697 David Brown willed to Thomas Wilson. Thomas Wilson died intestate and Margaret Lindow became possessed as heir at law.
1710 Peter Dent willed estate to wife Jane Dent and to daughter Rebecca Dent- land unnamed.
1 Jan 1731 James Lindow and wife Margaret Lindow his wife sold 75 acres to Ephraim Wilson.
27 April 1749 John Woolford and wife Mary Woolford, late Mary Brown coheir of Thomas Brown deceased and Margaret Brown, coheir, and Sarah Brown widow, which Thomas Brown was the heir to Alexander Brown and wife Margaret Brown otherwise called in Scotland Margaret Erskin, sold to David Wilson heir of Ephraim Wilson.
28 Dec.1762 David Wilson sold to Thomas Jones of Manokin, to farm for 20 years, KILLINGHAM,SECURITY,TILBURY,WILSONS DISCOVERY,GLASGOW.
17 April 1764 David Brown and wife Ann Brown sold to Levin Wilson his 1/4th part of above lands.
13 Dec.1768 Samuel Wilson and wife Mary Wilson sold to Denwood Wilson for 5 shillings 450 acres of TILBURY,WILSONS DISCOVERY, GLASGOW, KILLIGAN, SECURITY.

GLAZIERS HALL

see CHEESEMANS CHANCE & EDEN

GLYNEATH

Patented on 23 July 1663 from KINGSAILE by Jenkins Price 400 acres, in
Brinkleys,southeast,Election district 13, map #11.
Resurveyed for Edward Howard and included in tract THE ENTRANCE for 850
acres.
15 Aug.1766 Elias White, mortgaged to John Nairn part where Elias White
lives. All not previously conveyed before to Robert Pitts, with tr.
MORRIS HOPE.
Resurveyed in 1759 to WHITES GIFT 626 acres and later resurveyed again in
1774 to WILLIAMS GREEN.

GOLDEN LYON

Patented in March 1663 by Thomas Harwood of St. Marys County for 700
acres in Brinkleys,southeast, Election district 3, map #16.
6 Sep.1676 Thomas Harwood and wife Mary Harwood sold to Teague Riggin 700
acres.
Rent Rolls 1666-1723. Possessed by-
  Teague Riggin Jr. 200 acres
  John Riggin 100 acres
  John Andrews (married Rachel Riggin) 100 acres
  Teague Riggin Sr. 300 acres.
1692 Teague Riggin,wife Mary Riggin, gave to son Ambrose Riggin 200 acres
aka AMBROSIA
13 May 1707 Teague Riggin and wife Mary Riggin gave to John Riggin 100
acres.
26 Aug.1719 Ambrose Riggin son of Teague, and wife Mary Riggin gave to
Teague Riggin the younger 200 acres.
27 Dec.1721 Teague Riggin willed 200 acres to son Solomon Riggin.
1721 Teague Riggin gave to son Solomon Riggin 100 acres bought of brother
Ambrose, AMBROSIA with 135 acres of FATHERS & MOTHERS GIFT to son Charles
Riggin.
20 Nov.1728 Samuel Riggin and wife Elizabeth Riggin sold to John Riggin
100 acres, that was deeded to John Riggin.
15 May 1730 Samuel Riggin gave to his daughter Hannah Riggin 100 acres
(land unnamed.)
22 Aug.1733 Samuel Riggin Sr. and wife Elizabeth Riggin sold 365 acres to
Joshua Caldwell, part of tract made over to him by his father and left by
him to his son Charles Riggin.
20 March 1735 Charles Riggin and wife Amey Riggin sold to John Riggin son
of Teague Riggin deceased 50 acres of GOLDEN LYON alias FATHER & MOTHERS
GIFT.
20 Aug.1736 Solomon Riggin gave 50 acres to his brother John Riggin.
16 June 1741 Charles Dickerson gave to John Riggin and Solomon Riggin
sons of Teague Riggin deceased all rights I have (trade for RIGGINS
MINES.)
21 Jan 1742 Solomon Riggin son of Teague Riggin sold 200 acres to Charles
Riggin, the land Ambrose Riggin son of Teague and Mary Riggin sold to
Teague Riggin the younger.
11 May 1743 Solomon Riggin,Henry Wauchop and Charles Bannister agree to

177

division of lands.
20 July 1745 Charles Bannister,shipright, and wife Elizabeth Bannister,
sold to John Riggin son of Elizabeth Bannister, tract SAFETY that was
part of AMBROSIA, part of GOLDEN LYON that was conveyed to John Riggin
from Solomon Riggin 50 acres.
8 Jan 1746 Charles Riggin and wife Amey Riggin sold to Charles Bannister
150 acres for 5 shillings part called AMBROSIA that was conveyed by
Solomon Riggin to Charles Bannister.
31 Jan 1746 Charles Bannister and wife Elizabeth Bannister sold 150 acres
to David Matthews.
26 March 1742 Joshua Caldwell and wife Elizabeth Caldwell sold 300 acres
to Robert Jenkins Henry, adjacent HILLARDS DISCOVERY, where Mary Riggin
lives.
29 May 1759 Charles Riggin and wife Amey Riggin sold to Robert Jenkins
Henry 335 acres that Charles had from his father Teague Riggin and
purchased by Charles Riggin from his brother Solomon Riggin, now on
resurvey only 328 acres.
29 May 1759 Robert Jenkins Henry,wife Gertrude Henry sold 50 acres to
John Riggin son of Teague Riggin.
1764 Robert Jenkins Henry gave to daughter Mary King Henry 278 acres
purchased of Charles Riggin.
1773 John Riggin gave 100 acres to son Obediah Riggin.
1783 tax- David Matthews 150 acres & 235 acres.
1783 tax- Obed Riggin 100 acres.
17 Jun 1785 William Handy and wife Mary King Handy of Worc.Co. (Mary was
the daughter of Robert Jenkins Henry son of Robert J. Henry) sold to John
Done of Worc.Co. that Robert Jenkins Henry purchased of Charles Riggin
320 acres.
17 Jun 1785 John Done of Worc.Co. returned same as above.
28 Oct.1786 David Matthews Sr. sold 100 acres to Nathan Cahoon.
24 Mar.1788 Nathan Cahoon,wife Elizabeth Cahoon sold 200 acres to George
Howard of GOLDEN LYON & COW QUARTER except 20 acres conveyed to John
Riggin.
4 Oct.1790 George Howard, wife Priscilla Howard sold to Elijah Beauchamp
90 acres of GOLDEN LYON AND LYONS WHELP.
9 Oct.1794 Elijah Beauchamp mortgaged 200 acres to Jesse Powell.
28 March 1796 Elijah Beauchamp and wife Martha Beauchamp sold to Jesse
Powell 200 acres except 50 acres conveyed to John Riggin, and 90 acres of
marsh LYONS WHELPS (LYONS WHELPS not patented so is part of original
tract GOLDEN LYON)
1796 David Matthews willed to son Edward Matthews, where I live, if no
issue to son Israel Matthews or Joshua Matthews
1 July 1799 Jesse Powell,wife Catherine Powell gave to daughter Leah
Underhill of Northampton Co.Va. GOLDEN LYON 150 acres,90 acres of marsh,
LYONS WHELP and 3 acres from Obed Riggin to George Howard on 15 Nov.1788
after death of said Jesse.
17 Dec.1799 Israel Matthews of Baltimore Co. sold to William Williams
that David Matthews willed to son Edward Matthews who had no issue, so
descended to son Israel Matthews.
9 Jan 1800 William Williams sold to Benjamin Matthews
14 April 1800 Obed Riggin sold to Robert Riggin 153 acres of GOLDEN
LYON,RIGGINS MEADOW & LYONS WHELP
16 Apr.1804 Benajmin Holland Matthews, wife Mary Matthews sold to Levi
Matthews lands in Morumsco purchased from William Williams, no name.
16 Apr.1804 Levi Matthews mortgaged to John Riggin, Robert Riggin and

Robert Milbourn lands from Benjamin H. Matthews, no name.
1804 Benjamin Holland Matthews willed land to Levi Matthews purchased
from William Williams.
25 June 1809 Jesse Powell, wife Catherine Powell sold 78 acres to George
Riggin.
27 May 1809 Samuel Handy Jr. sold all his rights to Jesse Powell.
27 May 1809 Jesse Powell mortgaged to Edward Henry of Worc.Co. 300 acres.

GOLDEN QUARTER

Patented on 25 April 1667 by William Stevens and assigned to John
Goldsmith for 150 acres in East Pr.Anne,Election district 15, map #4.
Resurvey in 1667 to include another 150 acres, total of 300 acres.
Rent Rolls 1666-1723 Possessed 150 acres by the widow of John Goldsmith.
6 April 1731 John Goldsmith son of John Jr. sold to John Owens 150 acres,
that descended to John Goldsmith Jr. from John Sr. who died intestate.
1740 150 acres resurveyed to COME BY CHANCE
14 Jan 1755 John Owens Sr, gave to son John Owens 50 acres part of two
tracts, both called GOLDEN QUARTER.
19 Mar.1756 John Owens,wife Mary Owens sold to Michael Dorman 25 3/4
acres of the two tracts.
13 Apr.1756 John Owens Sr. and John Owens Jr. sold to Isaac Holland 150
acres, except pt. sold to Michael Dorman.
19 Apr.1757 Thomas Sloss,wife Mary Sloss sold 23 acres to John Done.
18 Aug.1757 John Owens Sr,Michael Owens and Samuel Owens,wife Elizabeth
Owens, sold to John Done part of 2 tracts GOLDEN QUARTER 41 1/4 acres and
15 1/4 acres.
16 March 1757 Isaac Holland reconveyed title of 25 3/4 acres to Michael
Owens.
25 Feb.1759 Michael Dorman sold to John Done per indenture of 1756 part
of two tracts 251 1/4 acres.
27 May 1759 John Owens sold his rights to John Done.
1771 Michael Dorman willed to son Chase Dorman
1783 tax- Dolly Hall 53 acres
1783 tax- Elizabeth Dorman
1783 tax- Chase Dorman 25 1/4 acres.
1797 Chase Dorman willed dwelling plantation to son Hezekiah Dorman.
19 April 1803 Hezekiah Dorman son of Chase Dorman and wife Amelia sold to
Zadock Long.
8 May 1804 Zadock Long sold to John Done land conveyed by Hezekiah
Dorman, adjacent DONES NEST EGG 1 3/4 acres- no name.

GOLDEN QUARTER

Patented on 1 July 1667 for 150 acres by Thomas Ball in Tangier, Election
district 9, map #7.
Rent Rolls 1666-1723 Possessed by Ephraim Pollock who purchased from
Col.James Allerton of Virginia in whom the right was issued.
2 Aug.1734 Charles Pollock gave to Joy Hobbs 106 acres for 5 shillings,
patented GOLDEN QUARTER and LONG DELAY, now called HOBBS HIS CHOICE.
1735/7 Joy Hobbs gave to son Absalom Hobbs part of HOBBS HIS CHOICE.
22 Jan 1732 Robert Jones sold for 5 shillings to George Jones 120 acres
of GOLDEN QUARTER & LONG DELAY.
16 Oct.1739 Charles Polk,wife Patience Polk sold to John Laws 212 acres
of GOLDEN QUARTER & LONG DELAY.

2 Sep.1742 Absalom Hobbs sold to David Wallace for 5 shillings 106 acres
of GOLDEN QUARTER & LONG DELAY now called HOBBS HIS CHOICE.
8 Sep.1774 Joseph Wallace sold to Charles Hall 106 acres as above.
1761 Matthew Wallace willed to son Joseph Wallace dwelling plantation at
Rock Creek (unnamed)
5 Feb.1782 John Laws sold to Robert Jones part 55 acres of GOLDEN QUARTER
& LONG DELAY
1783 tax- Ann Jones 100 acres
1783 tax- Robert Jones 55 acres.
22 Mar.1787 John Laws, wife Mary Laws, sold to Robert Jones 55 acres of
GOLDEN QUARTER & LONG DELAY.
11 Dec.1795 Ezekiel Hall sold to Robert Jones 106 acres of GOLDEN QUARTER
& LONG DELAY.
21 Feb.1798 Levin Bozman and wife Mary Bozman and Elizabeth Bozman Sr.
sold to James Kelly Jr. 67 acres of GOLDEN QUARTER,LONG DELAY,LAWS
THOROFAIR.
14 Jul.1798 Robert Jones sold to James Kelly Jr. 67 acres of GOLDEN
QUARTER, LONG DELAY, LAW'S MEADOW

GOLDEN QUARTER

see LUMNS IMPROVEMENT & LUMNS INCREASE-Tangier.

GOLDSMITHS DELIGHT

see ILLCHESTER
1783 tax- William Ballard 100 acres.

GOOD HOPE

Patented in 1753 by Hope Adams for 38 acres in Brinkleys, northeast,
Election district 3, map #15.
1768 Hope Adams willed to son Hope Adams
14 Sep.1767 We Phillip Adams Jr. and Hope Adams Sr. mortgaged to Fountain
Beauchamp part of MITCHELLS ADVENTURE & GOOD HOPE (exchange for 117 acres
of LEDBOURN)
8 Jan 1770 Fountain Beauchamp sold right & title to Duncan Livingston.
1 June 1773 Phillip Adams son of Hope Adams, sold to Duncan Livingston,
tailor, 3/4 acre.
2 Mar.1789 Levi Beauchamp sold to Hope Adams of Hope 10 acres of
ADVENTURE,GOOD HOPE, called the TANYARD.
5 Aug.1797 Samuel Adams son of Hope Adams sold to Thomas Williams all
lands devised by Hope Adams, no name or acreage.
7 Feb 1803 William A. Schoolfield, wife Mary Schoolfield, sold to Elijah
Broughton 6 acres of ADVENTURE & GOOD HOPE.
1807 Elijah Broughton willed lands to wife Leah Broughton, unnamed.

GOOD LUCK

Patented in 1726 by Barnaby Willis for 90 acres in Fairmount,Election
district 6, map #9.

GOOD LUCK

Patented in 1762 by Matthias Hobbs for 275 acres, a resurvey from

ABBINGTON, in Mt.Vernon, Election district 5, map #1.
14 Jan 1768 Marcellas Hobbs and wife Agnes Hobbs sold to Mary
Waggaman,widow of Henry Waggaman, deceased, 93 acres of the lower part.
1780 Mary Waggaman, willed to son Henry Waggaman land bought of Marcellas
Hobbs, unnamed.
1783 tax- Henry Waggaman 91 3/4 acres
1783 tax- Matthias Hobbs 71 1/3 acres
12 Nov.1793 George Waggaman sold to Elias Bayley 27 acres of CARNEYS
CHANCE & GOOD LUCK.
25 Dec.1798 George Waggaman sold to Matthias Hobbs 61 acres
25 Dec.1798 George Waggaman sold to Jesse Covington 22 1/2 acres.
25 Aug.1801 Henry Dickinson and wife Harriett Dickinson of Dor.cCo. sold
to Henry Waggaman, their rights to real estate of George Waggaman, 1/4
part that Harriett Dickinson is entitled, no name or acreage given.
9 Nov.1801 John Waggaman Footman and wife Mary Footman of Charles Town
South Carolina sold to Henry Waggaman of Dorc.Co. Md. that George
Waggaman had when he died intestate- he is entitled to 1/6th part.no name
or acres.
20 Aug./1803 Henry Waggaman and wife Sarah Waggaman of Dorc.Co. sold to
Elias Bayley 64 1/4 acres of CARNEYS CHANCE & GOOD LUCK
20 Aug.1803 Henry Waggaman,wife Sarah Waggaman of Dor.Co. sold to Levin
Jones, joiner, 483 acres with WAGGAMANS PURCHASE, CARNEYS CHANCE,
CUMBERLAND, ADDITION, CONVIENCE.
20 Aug.1803 Henry Waggaman sold to Jesse Covington 68 1/2 acres of
CARNEYS CHANCE & GOOD LUCK Jesse Covington gave Henry Waggaman a
mortgage for same.
8 July 1806 Levin Dashiell Jones sold to Matthias Hobbs 47 1/2 acres of
ADDITION, CUMBERLAND, GOOD LUCK, etc.
27 July 1809 Matthias Hobbs sold to George Jones of Robert Jones, 61
acres of ABBINGTON now called GOOD LUCK.

GOOD LUCK

 Patented on 18 Oct.1715 by Archibald Smith for 210 acres on Deals Island,
Election district 14, map #8.
1783 tax- Jonathan Stanford 50 acres.

GOOD LUCK

Patented in 1753 by Henry Miles in Fairmount,Election district 6, map #9
for 50 acres.
1762 resurveyed to MILES CONCLUSION 456 acres.

GOOD LUCK

Patented in 1762 by William Polk for 50 acres in East Pr.Anne,Election
district 15, map #4.
24 Mar.1775 William Polk sold to Matthias Miles 50 acres on road from
Princess Anne to Snow Hill.
1783 tax- Matthias Miles 50 acres.

GOOD LUCK

Patented in 1767 for 27 acres on Smiths Island,Election district 10, map
#22, by John Adams.

181

1783 tax- John Adams Sr. 27 acres
14 July 1789 William Adams sold to Thomas Jones 27 acres.

GOOD LUCK

Patented in 1763 by Aaron Tilghman for 5 acres in Westover,Election
district 13, map #10.
21 Dec 1784 Isaac Marshall surviving executor of Aaron Tilghman sold to
Thomas Gibbons with TILGHMANS LUCK,ADVENTURE,POOLS HOPE,GOOD LUCK, as
Aaron Tilghman devised to be sold.
6 Mar.1787 William Gibbons mortgaged to Samuel Wilson, with all his other
lands.
13 July 1788 William Gibbons mortgaged same to Samuel Wilson,
confirmation.
13 Mar.1792 Samuel Smith, John C. Wilson, Samuel Wilson executors of
Samuel Wilson deceased, released mortgage to Levin Miles.
13 Aug.1792 William Gibbons,wife Mary Gibbons sold to Levin Miles.

GOOD LUCK

Patented in 1785 to George Austin for 55 1/4 acres in St. Peters,Election
District 2, map #6.
19 May 1797 George Austin sold 4 acres to William Jones, Esq.

GOOD LUCK

Patented on 14 May 1714 by John Parsons for 40 acres in West Pr.Anne,
Election district 1, map #2.
Rent Rolls 1666-1723 John Parsons.
22 Nov.1771 Oliver Coston sold to Samuel Sloan of Eden School, etc. 169
acres of SECOND CHOICE,BEAR QUARTER,GOOD LUCK, conveyed by Thomas Gillis
to Ahab Coston father of Oliver Coston,and his wife Abigail Coston.
25 Sep.1781 Oliver Coston son of Abigail, daughter of John Parsons the
younger, sold to Thomas Pollitt for 5 shillings 40 acres with DAINTRY.

GOOD SUCESS

Patented on 2 May 1685 by James Rounds for 300 acres in Dublin, Election
district 4, map #13.
24 June 1707 Mary Edgar relic of James Rounds deceased sold 150 acres to
William Noble.
Rent Rolls 1666-1723 Poss.by William Hickman. Since alienated to William
Noble 150 acres, and 150 acres purchased by Robert Mitchell.
6 April 1721 William Noble and wife Elizabeth Noble sold to George
Lane.150 acres.
17 July 1724 George Lane and wife Temperance Lane sold to John Purnell
150 acres.
22 Dec.1724 John Purnell and wife Martha Purnell sold to John Dennis Jr.
150 acres.
1755 Robert Mitchell gave to son Joshua, plantation where I live.
17 Nov 1743 Isaac Mitchell am bound to William Conner of Annamessex on
the condition that William Mitchell son of Isaac Mitchell will in six
months after 1741 will be age 21 and will make over tract SUCESS,4 miles
above Deep Creek Ridge. If he does not Isaac shall alienate a corner of
tract AMITY where Isaac now lives on Kings Mill Br. 200 acres

20 Aug.1755 John Dennis the elder gave to son Littleton Dennis 150 acres.
31 Aug.1761 Joshua Mitchell and wife Joyce Mitchell sold to Isaac
Mitchell 150 acres where Robert Mitchell father of Joshua Mitchell and
Isaac Mitchell lived.
9 Feb 1768 Isaac Mitchell, wife Bridget Mitchell sold to William Mitchell
200 acres where he lives for life care, lately conveyed to Isaac
Mitchell, no name.
9 Sep.1773 Littleton Dennis of Worc.Co. sold 150 acres to Samuel Sloan.
purchased by John Dennis.
1762 ADDITION pat.266 acres. Isaac Mitchell
1774 DENNIS ADDITION TO GOOD SUCESS 170 1/2 acres by Samuel Sloan
1773 will Isaac Mitchell 266 acres to son James Mitchell ADDITION to GOOD
SUCESS.
1783 tax- John Mitchell 177 acres ADDITION
1783 tax- Samuel Sloan 150 acres.
8 June 1779 James Mitchell of Worc.Co. sold to John Mitchell 166 acres of
GOOD SUCESS ADDITION.
1807 Samuel Sloan willed to wife Elizabeth Sloan GOOD SUCESS & DENNIS
ADDITION.
1836 Levin Pollitt willed to niece Mary Stevens wife of John Stevens,
part (wife of Levin Pollitt was Sarah Sloan)

GOOSE MARSH

Patented on 7 Nov.1679 by Edward Dickerson for 50 acres in Brinkleys,
southeast, Election district 3, map #16.
15 May 1724 Somerset Dickerson son of Edward Dickerson sold to Mary
Hampton 50 acres. (wife of John Hampton)
1744 Mary Hampton gave to son Robert Jenkins Henry.
1764 Robert Jenkins Henry gave all lands to son Robert Jenkins Henry.
1783 tax- Robert Jenkins Henry 50 acres.

GOSHEN

see DOUBLE PURCHASE

GOSHEN

Patented 1722 to Southy Whittington for 340 acres in Lawsons, Election
district 8, map #18.
22 Jun 1763 Southy Whitttington gave to son Southy Jr.
1783 tax- William Whittington 170 acres.

GOSHEN

Patented on 20 March 1679 by Samuel Cooper and assigned to Edward Wright
for 300 acres in Dublin,Election district 4, map #12.
2 June 1688 John Carpenter,barber, and wife Ann Carpenter sold to William
Smullen 150 acres purchased from Edward Wright.
Rent Rolls 1666-1723 Possessed 150 acres by John Winn had of Randall
Smullen but not conveyed. 150 acres Ambrose Riggin.
1743 Randall Smullen gave to sons Nathaniel Smullen and William Smullen,
adjacent Joseph Riggin.
18 Nov.1761 Edward Smullen sold 90 1/2 acres to Thomas Barnes.
8 Nov.1761 Edward Smullen and Nathaniel Smullen sold 40 1/2 acres to
William Fleming.

22 Oct 1765 Thomas Barnes and wife Rebeccah Barnes, of Worc.Co.sold to
William Fleming 90 1/2 acres.
1783 tax- Leah Smullen 100 acres.
1783 tax- Nathaniel Smullen 100 acres
12 Apr.1785 William Fleming sold to John Fleming son of William 90 acres.
29 March 1805 Lowden Smullen and wife Elizabeth Smullen sold to
(brothers) John Smullen and Zorobable Smullen, part three tracts from
father Nathaniel Smullen, sold his interest- no name or acreage given.
25 June 1807 John Fleming now of Scipio Co. Caynoga N.Y. sold to Juliana
Massey Farrow and Mary Johnson Farrow of Somerset Co. daughters of
Charles Farrow 250 acres of UNITY ENLARGED, GOSHEN, HARPERS INCREASE,
HARPERS DISCOVERY.
21 March 1809 John Fleming of Cayuga Co. N.Y. sold to Juliana Massey
Farrow and Mary Johnson Farrow of Som. Co. 250 acres of UNITY ENLARGED,
GOSHEN, HARPERS INCREASE, HARPERS DISCOVERY.
11 July 1810 Levin Miller, wife Nancy Miller sold to Zorobable Smulling
102 acres of GOSHEN & UNITY ENLARGED.
21 Aug.1810 Matthias Dashiell, sheriff, sold to John Gibbons, per
judgement against Charles Farrow.

GRANDFATHERS GIFT

Patented in 1746 by Thomas Gibbons for 100 acres in Westover,Election
district 13, map #10.
1783 tax- Thomas Gibbons 100 acres.

GRAVESEND

Patented on 22 Nov.1673 by Thomas Shilletto for 300 acres on Deals
Island, Election district 14, map #8.
4 Feb 1675 Thomas Shilletto sold to Thomas Walker.
9 Nov.1675 Thomas Walker sold to Thomas Roe 300 acres
Rent Rolls 1666-1723 possessed by Francis Gordon in right of the orphans
of Thomas Roe.
1783 tax- John Jones of Dames Quarter, 150 acres.
14 Aug.1787 John Jones of Samuel Jones gave to brother Thomas Jones 199
acres of GRAVESEND & PURGATORY.

GRAYS ADVENTURE

Patented on 13 June 1721 by William Gray in East Pr.Anne,Election
district 15, map #5 for 100 acres.
Rent Rolls 1666-1723- William Gray.
22 March 1759 William Gray sold to Robert Elzey 110 acres.
1783 tax- heirs of Robert Elzey 110 acres.
1806 patent ADDITION 4 acres by William G. Waters.
1853 resurveyed to ANNIES DELIGHT,SEDGEWICK.

GRAYS IMPROVEMENT

Patented 1 Oct.1689 by Michael Gray for 150 acres in Fairmount,Election
district 6, map #9.
Rent Rolls 1666-1723 Michael Gray.
1717 Miles Gray willed to son-in-law William Turpin,lands not named.

1736 John Turpin willed to son William Turpin, alienated from Miles Gray.
19 Aug.1806 Hugh Henry and wife Harriett Henry sold to William Waters of
John Waters lands held by Spencer Martin Waters grandfather of Harriet
Henry, GRAYS IMPROVEMENT, TEAGUES DOWN, TEAGUES ADDITION & AHILL on s/s
of the Manokin River, no acreage given.
1808 William Waters willed Pocomoke lands to son William Gillis Waters,
no name.

GRAYS LOTT

Patented on 7 Dec.1701 by James Gray for 50 acres in Lawsons, Election
district 8, map #19.
Rent Rolls 1666-1723 James Gray.
1773 resurveyed to HEARTS CONTENT 257 1/4 acres.

GRAYS PURCHASE

Patented in 1713 by Thomas Gray for 100 acres in East Pr.Anne,Election
district 15, map #5.
1732 Thomas Gray willed to daughter Mary Gray 100 acres.
28 March 1738 William Stevens and wife Mary Stevens (was Mary Gray) sold
100 acres to John Phillips.
1762 John Phillips (wife Elizabeth Phillips) willed to son John, real
estate unnamed.
31 Jan 1775 I John Phillips am bound to William Miles for 100 acres.
1783 tax- Mary Miles 30 acres
1783 tax- John Phillips 100 acres.
22 March 1786 John McDaniel and wife Elizabeth McDaniel (Elizabeth
Phillips)sold to Jonathan Stanford and wife Grace Stanford (Grace
Phillips) 100 acres with PRIVILEDGE.
4 April 1786 Jonathan Stanford and wife Grace Stanford sold 100 acres to
Pierce Riggin.
11 May 1805 John Stewart, Samuel Smith, Henry Coston and Jesse King,
comissioners to divide the land of John Phillips GRAYS PURCHASE, ROWLEY
HILL, PRIVILEDGE, DUDLEY 170 acres. sold to Jesse Dukes in right of his
wife Sarah Dukes, a representative of John Phillips.
22 May 1805 Jesse Dukes, wife Sarah Dukes of Sussex Co.Del. sold to
Pierce Riggin all rights to afsd land.
25 March 1806 Pierce Riggin sold to John Morris of Worc Co. and Kirk
Gunby 3 acres, to settle dispute.

GREAT ANNAMESSEX

Patented in 1819 by Samuel S. Horsey for 837 acres, a resurvey of BEARD
NECK & COULBOURNS RIDGE, in Lawsons,Election district 8, map #18.

GREAT HOPES

Patented in 1768, a resurvey from Arracaco in Revells Neck, by Samuel
Wilson for 774 1/2 acres, Westover,Election district 13, map #10.
8 May 1761 William Thompson sold to Samuel Wilson for 5 shillings per
older contract all lands included in a resurvey in the name of William
Beauchamp and Marcy Beauchamp.
27 Aug.1730 Randall West sold to Ephraim Wilson 165 acres that Randall
Revell and Catherine Cox sold to John West father of Randall West 165
acres GREAT HOPES.

1732 Ephraim Wilson willed to grandson Ephraim Wilson bought of Randall West.
10 Nov. 1771 Elijah West son of Anthony West, late of Kent Co. Del. sold to Isaac Coulbourn of Somerset County with Samuel Wilson part of BROTHERS UNITED & GREAT HOPES both part of DOUBLE PURCHASE 774 1/2 acres.
6 May 1772 Samuel Wilson of Som. Co. and Elijah West of Kent Co. Del. sold for life to Isaac Coulbourn.
4 Nov.1784 Anne Feddeman, heir of Randal West sold to Samuel Wilson all her rights.

GREAT HOPES

Patented in 1776 by Samuel Wilson for 787 acres in East Princess Anne, Election district 15, map #4. A resurvey from FRIENDS ADVICE & CONCLUSION
23 Nov.1770 Samuel Wilson sold to William Furniss 20 acres.
1783 tax- Grace Furniss 6 1/2 acres
1783 tax- Thomas Furniss 14 1/2 acres
1783 tax- Samuel Wilson 700 acres
10 Dec.1784 Samuel Wilson sold to Jacob Ker, Levin Gale, David Wilson, Henry Jackson, William Polk, Isaac Henry and Thomas King trustees of the Washington Academy for 1 shilling, 4 acres.
1790 Samuel Wilson willed to son John Wilson and to daughter Milcah Gale Wilson a small part.
14 May 1794 Milcah Gale Chaille sold to John Custis Wilson, 8 acres.
13 Aug.1794 Milcah Gale Chaille sold to Nehemiah King, 3 acres.
22 May 1805 William Miles of Worc.Co. son of Samuel Miles sold all rights to Matthias Miles.
23 Sep.1823 Mary Miles sold to Isaiah Hayman, part.
1831 Isaiah Hayman willed to grandaughter Eliza Pollitt.

GREENFIELD

Patented on 20 Feb.1694 by Sampson Wheatley for 125 acres in Brinkleys,southwest, Election district 3, map #17.
Rent Rolls 1666-1723 Sampson Wheatley.
1773 Sampson Wheatley willed to daughter Betty Wheatley.
1783 tax- Mary Wheatley 125 acres.

GREENFIELD

Patented on 26 Aug.1665 by Robert Jones for 300 acres in Dublin, Election district 4, map #13.
1 July 1668 Robert Jones and wife Martha Jones of Northumberland Co. Va. sold to Thomas Walker 300 acres.
8 Nov.1670 Thomas Walker sold to Walter Powell with MIDDLE & EXCHANGE.
16 Sep.1679 Walter Powell sold to Elizabeth Hudson and Violetta Hudson daughters of Nicholas Hudson 200 acres of GREENFIELD, MIDDLE & EXCHANGE now called DAUGHTERS RECOVERY.
1695 Walter Powell willed to son William Powell.
Rent Rolls 1666-1723 William Powell 300 acres.
1715 William Powell willed to son John Powell 200 acres and to son William Powell 100 acres.
9 March 1733 John Powell and wife Elizabeth Powell sold to Richard Brooks 90 acres part called HICKORY RIDGE.
25 Nov.1734 William Powell son of William sold to Richard Brooks 70 acres

part called GUMNECK.
14 Sep.1739 John Powell son of William Powell sold to Alexander Maddux 200 acres.
21 Aug.1739 Richard Brooks and wife Joyce Brooks sold to Levin Powell 89 acres- 19 acres HICKORY RIDGE, 70 acres of GUMNECK.
20 May 1740 William Powell,wife Ellen Powell of Prince William Co. Va. sold 30 acres to Thomas Benston of Somerset Co. with part of EXCHANGE.
21 Feb.1757 William Benston, wife Martha Benston, eldest son of Thomas gave 30 acres to brother Thomas Benston.
17 June 1758 triparte- Brittian Powell s/o John Powell who was the son of William Powell, who was the son of Walter Powell, Isaac Bozman Schoolfield, to Alexander Maddux 180 acres, 50 acres of which were alienated to Alexander Maddux by John Powell father of Brittian Powell.
27 May 1809 Jesse Powell mortgaged to Edward Henry of Worc.Co.
31 March 1810 Thomas Benston, James Barrett, wife Elizabeth Barrett sold to Littleton Dennis devised by Grandfather Thomas Benston.
17 Apri 1811 Thomas Dashiell, sheriff sold to Thomas Mitchell Jones, per judgement against Thomas Benston
10 Sep.1810 Thomas Mitchell Jones, wife Margaret Jones sold to Littleton Dennis.

GREENFIELD

Patented in 1815 by Nathan Cahoon in Brinkleys, Election district 3, map #17 for 9 3/4 acres.
24 April 1805 Benjamin Conner, Noah Lankford, Benjamin Bedsworth, John Broughton, Richard Hall and Mary Bedsworth sold to Mordicai Jones of St. Marys County, devised by Sampson Wheatley with WHHEATLEYS DIFFICULT PURCHASE, IRISH GROVE, etc.

GREEN MEADOW

Patented in 1768 by Thomas Benston for 36 acres in Dublin,Election district 4,map #13.
1783 tax- Thomas Benston 30 acres.
20 Aug.1787 Thomas Benston to Samuel Wilson, division of lands, MIDDLE, COW PASTURE, GREEN MEADOW,HOG YARD.
19 Nov.1795 Major Samuel Wilson son of Samuel and wife Leah Wilson sold 30 acres to Littleton Dennis with other lands
31 March 1810 Thomas Benston, James Barrett, wife Catherine sold to Littleton Dennis, devised by grandfather Thomas Benston.

GREEN PARK

Patented on 13 Oct.1688 by Somerset Dickerson, in Brinkleys southeast, Election district 3, map #16. 200 acres.
Rent Rolls 1666-1723 possessed by Peter Dickerson.
1733 Peter Dickerson willed dwelling plantation to son Charles Dickerson- unamed land.
8 Jan.1768 Jesse Dickerson son of Charles Dickerson and Benjamin Benston with wife Elizabeth Benston (Elizabeth Dickerson widow of Charles Dickerson)both of Kent Co. Del. sold to Matthias Coston of Som.Co. 200 acres.
1783 tax- Nathaniel Riggin 200 acres.

GREEN PASTURE

Patented in 1722 to James Polk, for 200 acres in Tangier, Election district 11, map #7.
1726/7 James Polk willed to Henry Polk and 100 acres to Edward Roberts.
14 Jan 1752 Henry Pollock of Queen Anne Co.Md, shipright sold 100 acres to Edward Roberts.
1783 tax- William Roberts 100 acres
1794 William Roberts willed to niece Nancy Lemon wife of Robert Lemon.
16 May 1801 George James, wife Leah James sold to Edward Fowler 200 acres.

GREENWICH

Patented on 28 Feb.1677 by William Stevens and assigned to John Laws for 50 acres on Deals Island,Election district 14, map #8.
1696/7 John Laws gave 50 acres to son Thomas Laws.
Rent Rolls 1666-1723 Thomas Laws, 50 acres.
1769 SMALL ADDITION 4 acres.
1783 tax- John Laws, 50 acres
8 July 1788 John Laws Jr, wife Dolly Laws, sold 50 acres to Henry Walston.
5 Dec.1797 Jesse Dashiell, wife Sarah Dashiell sold to Isaac Noble, from Henry Walston.
9 Sep.1803 Isaac Noble and wife Peggy Noble sold to Thomas Jones.
22 Sep.1804 Henry Evans sold to Thomas Jones, GREENWICH, OUTLETT, CHANCE & VICTORY that Henry Walston willed 1/4th part to son David Evans and grandson Henry Evans, sold all his 1/4th part of the 1/3rd part
3 Jan 1807 David Gunby, wife Grace Gunby sold all rights to land on Deals Island devised by Henry Walston to grandaughter Grace Evans, now Grace Gunby, to Benjamin Jones, no name.
9 Feb.1810 Wallace Evans sold to Benjamin Jones, as devisee of Henry Walston, land on Devils Island, no name or acreage.

GROVE

see HORSEYS CONCLUSION

GUERNSEY

Patented 1 March 1681 by William Stevens and assigned to Nicholas Toadvine,for 150 acres in West Pr.Anne,Election district 1, map #2.
Rent Rolls 1666-1723 Nicholas Toadvine 150 acres.
22 March1749 Henry Toadvine sold to Alexander Adams, rector of Stepney Parish for 5 shillings patented by Nicholas Toadvine a resident of Guernsey Island in Europe, father of Henry, called GOOD LUCK.
28 July 1756 Henry Toadvine sold 100 acres to Alexander Adams.
1757 resurveyed to DOUBLE PURCHASE.
19 Jan 1793 Stephen Adams,wife Jemimah Adams sold to James Adams GUERNSEY & DOUBLE PURCHASE.

GULLETTS ASSURANCE

Patented in 1683 by William Gullett for 100 acres, in West Pr.Anne, Election district 1, map #2
Rent Rolls 1666-1723 William Gullett s/o Wm. 100 acres.
1715 William Gullett willed to son William, all lands and plantation.

GULLETTS ADVISEMENT

Patented 14 Jan 1673 by John Brown for 100 acres in Dublin,Election district 4, map #12.
13 Jan 1686 Andrew Whittington sold to David Brown 160 acres surv. by John Brown.
Rent Rolls 1666-1723 50 acres by Peter Dent. 50 acres in right of the orphans of Thomas Wilson, 50 acres Ephraim Wilson.
1710 will of Peter Dent, to daughter Rebecca Dent.
13 Sep.1740 John Woolford and wife Mary Woolford and Margaret Brown sold 100 acres to David Wilson.
20 Nov.1761 Ephraim Wilson and Jesse King and Zorobable King sold 38 acres to David Wilson for 5 shillings.
1783 tax- David Wilson 38 acres.
4 May 1786 David Wilson and wife Sarah Wilson of Worc.Co. sold to John Wilson all not previously sold, with CLOVERFIELDS & FRIENDS CHOICE.

GULLETTS HOPE

Patented in 1671 by William Gullett for 50 acres in West Pr.Anne,Election district 1, map #2.
Rent Rolls 1666-1723 William Gullett does not hold any such land or know of.
21 Jan 1716 William Gillett willed to eldest son William Gillett.
24 Jun 1738 William Gillett sold to Thomas Lord.
20 Nov.1761 Henry Lord sold to Michael Dorman
1769 Michael Dorman willed to son Jesse Dorman
1783 tax- Jesse Dorman 50 acres
13 Aug.1793 Thomas Lord son of Francis Lord sold to Solomon Dorman 50 acres.
1787 Jesse Dorman willed to brother Solomon Dorman.

GUM NECK

see GREENFIELD

GUNBYS VENTURE

Patented in 1731 by John Gunby for 75 acres a resurvey of KIRKS PURCHASE in Lawsons, Election district 8, map #18.
1745 John Gunby gave to son James Gunby.
1783 tax- James Gunby 3 1/4 acres
9 Feb.1797 James Gunby sold to John Gunby of Worc.Co. ADDITION 92 acres.
1794 ADDITION James Gunby for 92 3/4 acres
23 Feb.1797 John Gunby son of Kirk Gunby, of Worc.Co. sold to Benjamin Lankford CONCLUSION 3 1/4 acres and ADDITION TO GUNBYS VENTURE 92 acres with MEADOW, LOW SWAMP, LITTLEWORTH RISQUE.
15 June 1807 Benjamin Lankford sold to William Williams 3 acres.
22 June 1808 William Williams sold to Benjamin Lankford 3 acres and 86 acres of ADDITION TO GUNBYS VENTURE.
17 March 1810 Benjamin Lankford sold to Jesse Maddux Lankford, all rights.
17 March 1810 Benjamin Lankford sold to William Williams, ADDITION 24 acres.
10 Apr. 1810 Matthias Dashiell, sheriff, sold to William Williams, per judgement against Benjamin Lankford 74 acres of ADDITION TO GUNBYS

VENTURE.

GUNBYS CONCLUSION

Patented in 1767 by James Gunby for 3 1/4 acres in Lawsons,Election
district 8, map #18.
9 Feb.1797 James Gunby sold to John Gunby 3 1/4 acres
23 Feb.1797 John Gunby son of Kirk Gunby of Worc.Co. sold to Benjamin
Lankford 3 1/4 acres.
17 Mar. 1810 Benjamin Lankford sold to William Williams 3 1/4 acres.
10 April 1810 Matthias Dashiell, sheriff, sold to William Williams 3 1/4
acres, per judgement against Benjamin Lankford.

GUNNERS RANGE

Patented in 1728 by Matthew Wallace for 64 acres in Tangier, Election
district 9, map #7.
1783 tax- Jacob Parks 40 acres.

HABNAB

Patented on 2 Nov.1675 by George Betts for 50 acres in St.Peters,Election
district 2, map #6.
Rent Rolls 166-1723 George Betts.
1709 George Betts willed to son-in-law John Irving and his wife Frances
Irving (Frances Betts) 100 acres and then to her son John Irving.
(Frances married 2nd. Ephraim Wilson.)
1729 resurvey by John Irving to 216 acres.
1732 Ephraim Wilson willed to his wife Frances Irving Wilson.
22 March 1743 John Irving sold 216 acres to George Irving.
1783 tax- Thomas Irving, 216 acres.
1784 Thomas Irving willed to son George Irving 216 acres.
22 Nov.1808 George Irving of Green Co. Ga. sold to Littleton Dennis 650
acres of HABNAB & MARCOMBS LOTT. John King attorney to convey. This sale
was confirmed again on 17 May 1809.
20 April 1809 Littleton Dennis Sold to Ezekiel M. Gillis 113 acres of
same.
20 April 1809 Littleton Dennis sold to James Phoebus 50 acres.
20 April 1809 Littleton Dennis sold to Thomas G. Fountain balance of
HABNAB & MARCOMBS LOTT.
13 April 1810 Thomas G. Fountain sold to Littleton Robins 100 acres of
MARCOMBS LOTT & HABNAB.

HACKELA

Patented in 1668 by John Hilliard for 200 acres in Dublin, Election
district 4, map #13.
11 Feb.1677 John Hilliard sold to Henry Smith 200 acres..
1685 Henry Smith and Ann Smith sold to William Noble Sr, cooper, who made
a deed of gift to the eldest son of James Noble of Accomack Co. Va.
10 March 1719 James Noble on of James Noble late of Acco.Co.Va. gave to
son Jonathan Noble.
1721 Jonathan Noble gave to sons William Noble and Jonathan Noble, then
to daughters Rebecca Lewis wife of John Lewis and Hannah Dryden wife of
David Dryden and Elizabeth Noble.

22 Nov.1734 John Lewis and Rebecca Lewis, Elizabeth Noble,of Sussex Co.Del. conveyed their 1/3rds shares to John Peden.
28 May 1736 John Lewis and wife Rebecca Lewis of Sussex Co.Del. , David Dryden Jr. and wife Hannah Dryden, and Elizabeth Noble of Sussex Co.Del. sold to John Peden 80 acres.
28 May 1736 John Lewis and Rebecca Lewis and Elizabeth Noble of Sussex Co.Del. conveyed 120 acres to David Dryden and Hannah Dryden.
1759 ADDITION TO HAKELA patented for 123 1/4 acres to Jonathan Dryden.
1769 Jonathan Dryden gave to son David Dryden.
1783 tax- John Peden 66 acres.
1783 tax- Michael Cluff 50 acres
1783 tax- James Dryden 88 acres
3 Feb.1786 Hannah Dryden devised her maiden dower to sons Ephraim Dryden and grandson James Dryden.
18 Aug.1804 Robert H. Dryden,wife Priscilla Dryden sold to Jesse Taylor 3 1/4 acres of ADDITION TO HAKELA.
9 March 1805 Robert H. Dryden mortgaged to Michael Cluff HACKELA & CHERRY GARDEN.
10 June 1805 William Miles of Worc.Co. sold to Isaac Dryden 76 acres.
21 Oct 1805 Robert H. Dryden sold to Teague Donoho of Worc.Co. lands from father James Dryden HACKELA, ADDN. TO HACKELA, TIMBER GROVE & CHERRY GARDEN 102 1/4 acres.
6 June 1806 Ephraim Dryden,wife Rebecca Dryden sold to Jesse Taylor 45 acres of ADDITION TO HACKELA.
10 June 1806 Teague Donoho sold to Michael Cluff his rights to CHERRY GARDEN & HACKELA.
1808 Jesse Taylor willed to Litty Taylor daughter of Hope Taylor (a minor)lands bought of Ephraim Dryden.

HACHILA

Patented on 28 March 1688 to David Brown for 300 acres in West Pr.Anne,Election district 1, map #3.
1697 David Brown willed to Alexander Brown 300 acres.
Rent Rolls,1666-1723 Alexander Brown.
2 May 1749 Margaret Brown sold 400 acres adjacent JESMINE (unnamed land) to William Skirven.
12 July 1750 John Woolford and wife Mary Woolford one of the daughters of Alexander Brown and coheir of Col. David Brown and David Brown minister of the Gospel at Newport, Glasgow Scotland son of Mary Brown, otherwise called in Scotland Mary Erskin who is the aunt of Mary Woolford sold their interst in THORNTON,JESHIMON,HACHILA to Robert Nairn and James Nairn.
1748/50 John Woolford willed to son Charles Woolford, got by my wife Margaret Woolford (Margaret Brown)
24 Aug.1750 William Skirven sold to John Woolford his right to MEDDOW, THORNTON, HACHILA,JESHIMON.
1770 part resurveyed to THOMAS'S BEGINNING 275 acres.
29 Oct 1791 Thomas D. Woolford and William P.Woolford mortgaged to Denwood Wilson, THORNTON,HACHILA,JESAMIN,THOMAS BEGINNING.
26 March 1799 Denwood Wilson released mortgage to Levin Woolford, William Pitt Woolford and James Woolford sons of Thomas Woolford.
1814 William Pollitt willed to sister-in-law Nelly Pollitt, bought of Robert Elligood
1836 John Woolford willed to son John.

1836 Nelly J. Pollitt gave to son Levin J. Pollitt.

HACKLAND

Patented 18 Oct.1662 by John VanHack for 1100 acres in West Pr.Anne,
Election district 1, map #3.
Rent Rolls 1666-1723 possessed by Levin Denwood.
1725 Levin Denwood willed to daughter Betty Gale wife of George Gale.
1730 resurveyed ADDITION TO HACKLAND to 1630 acres.
1786 Resurveyed to STONEY POINT 1968 acres.

HACKWORTHS CHARITY

Patented on 16 March 1663 by Richard Acworth 600 acres, in West
Pr.Anne,Election district 1, map #3.
1675 Richard Acworth willed to son Richard Acworth
5 April 1748/9 Charles Acworth sold to David Wilson 600 acres for 4
pistols.
1748 resurvey to WILSONS CONCUSION 1319 acres.

HALF QUARTER

Patented in 1753 by Thomas Montgomery for 35 acres in Lawsons, Election
district 8, map #19.
6 June 1767 Dennis Montgomery sold to William Roach
1783 tax- William Roach 35 acres
1785 William Roach willed to son Billy Roach lands in Annamessex,
unnamed.
7 Jan 1800 John Ward son of Stephen Ward, now of Kentucky sold to John
Cullen.

HALLS ADVENTURE

Patented on 4 Feb.1679 by William Stevens for 250 acres and assigned to
Charles Hall in Fairmount,Election district 6, map #9.
Rent Rolls 166-1723 Possessed by widow Alice Hall.
12 June 1740 Richard Hall and wife Mary Hall sold 1 acre to Littleton
Waters of Calvert County, patented Charles Hall grandfather of Richard
Hall.
2 April 1750 Richard Hall and Joshua Hall leased to Thomas Jones 250
acres.
4 Dec.1755 Richard Hall and Joshua Hall Sr. son of Richard sold to
Richard Waters, no acreage given.
1783 tax- Joshua Hall 100 acres.
13 April 1793 Joshua Hall, wife Sarah Hall sold to Littleton Dawsey 30
acres, in Potato Neck.
2 June 1801 Joshua Hall sold to Littleton Dawsey 2 acres
13 Jan 1804 Joshua Hall sold to James Tilghman, Henry H. Curtis, Josiah
Coulbourn, Tubman Mitchell, Samuel Ford,John Hall and Lazarus Maddux,
part in trust for a meeting house for use of the Methodist Epis. Church
to be called MADDUXES MEETING HOUSE, part.(later called CURTIS CHAPPEL)
13 Aug.1804 Joshua Hall sold to Littleton D. Maddux 6 1/4 acres.
4 Feb 1806 Joshua Hall sold to Littleton D. Maddux 8 acres.
4 Feb 1806 Joshua Hall sold to John Hall Sr. 91 1/4 acres.
1806/17 Joshua Hall gave to wife Sarah Hall.
12 March 1807 Joshua Hall sold to Littleton Dennis Maddux 5 7/8 acres.

1822 Thomas Byrd willed to daughter Sarah Ann Byrd.

HALLS CHOICE

Patented on 6 June 1665 by Charles Hall for 300 acres in Fairmount, Election district 6, map #9.
1708 Charles Hall willed to son Richard Hall.
Rent Rolls 1666-1723 possessed by widow Alice Hall.
1717 Alice Hall willed to Richard Hall and Charles Hall.
1783 tax- Isaac Hall 100 acres
12 April 1785 Isaac Hall traded 30 acres with Joshua Hall for SCHOOLHOUSE RIDGE.
25 April 1786 Isaac Hall and wife Anna Hall, eldest son of Charles Hall who was the eldest son of Richard Hall sold 165 acres to Henry Miles.
1787 Henry Milles willed to son Henry lands purchased of Isaac Hall.
25 March 1800 William Tull sold to Charles Hall of Ezekiel Hall-establish lines.

HALLS HAMMOCK

Patented on 22 Dec.1680 by Charles Hall for 100 acres in Fairmount, Election district 6, map #9.
Rent Rolls 1666-1723 possessed by widow Alice Hall.
1777 Richard Hall willed to cousin(nephew) Ezekiel Hall Sr.
1783 tax- Isaac Hall 30 acres
1783 tax- Joshua Hall 50 acres
ADDITION TO HALLS HAMMOCK 1784 for 197 1/2 acres by Isaac Hall.
25 April 1786 Isaac Hall, wife Anna Hall, eldest son of Charles of Richard sold 50 acres to Henry Miles and 32 1/2 acres of ADDITION TO HALLS HAMMOCK.
1787 Henry Miles willed to son Henry Miles lands purchased of Isaac Hall.
15 Dec.1794 Isaac Hall of Baltimore town sold to Joshua Hall of Somerset Co. ADDITION 82 1/2 acres.
25 March 1800 Charles Hall heir of Ezekiel Hall of Charles sold to William Tull- to establish lines.
8 Sep.1801 Isaac Hall, wife Ann Hall of Baltimore sold to Samuel Hall Jr. 82 1/2 acres of ADDITION TO HALLS HAMMOCK
1807/17 Joshua Hall willed ADDITION, to wife Sarah Hall.
1933 resurveyed to TUBMAN HALLS MARSH 399 1/4 acres.

HALLS KINDNESS

see FRIENDS KINDNESS

HALLS PASTURE

Patented on 2 July 1688 by Charles Hall for 100 acres in Fairmount, Election district 6, map #9.
Rent Rolls 1666-1723 possessed by widow Alice Hall.
1777 Richard Hall son of Charles Hall willed to cousin(nephew) Ezekiel Hall Sr.
1783 tax- Charles Hall 34 acres
1783 tax- Esther Hall 16 acres.
24 May 1791 Charles Hall sold to Thomas Davis 50 acres.
25 March 1800 Charles Hall son of Ezekiel Hall of Charles sold to William Tull- to establish boundaries.
19 May 1806 Thomas Davis sold to Beauchamp Davis all his lands, unnamed.
12 April 1809 Charles Hall gave to sons Samuel Hall and John Hall.

Patented on 24 June 1679 by Samuel Collins for 50 acres in Brinkleys, southeast,Election disrict 3, map #16.
Rent Rolls 1666-1723 Samuel Collins.

HAMILTONS FORTUNE

Patented in 1753 by Hamilton Bell, a resurvey of HAZZARD, for 882 acres in East Pr.Anne, Election district 15, map #5.
21 March 1771 Hamilton Bell traded 8 1/4 acres with John King for 2 1/4 acres of CHANCE.
1783 tax- Levin Woolford 8 1/4 acres
1783 tax- Rev.Hamilton Bell Sr. 873 3/4 acres.
12 April 1810 John Hamilton Bell sold to George Wilson 956 acres as Hamilton Bell died intestate, no name.

HAMPTON

see MARYS LOTT.

HANDYS CHOICE

Patented on 4 June 1694 by Samuel Handy fo 175 acres in Fairmount, Election district 6, map #9.
1666-1723 Rent Rolls, poss. by Samuel Handy.
1734/5 Samuel Handy willed to sons Samuel and John Handy.
1751 John Handy of Dorc.Co. and wife Elizabeth Handy sold to Samuel Handy.
2 Oct.1747 George Tucker of Isle of Baradoes and wife Mary Tucker (Mary Handy) sold to Samuel Handy 514 acres with LONDONS ADVENTURE, etc.
7 Jan.1757 Samuel Handy sold 175 acres to Thomas Seon.
2 Sep.1767 Thomas Seon sold to Whitty Turpin.
1 Aug.1796 Thomas Holbrook and wife Peggy Holbrook sold to Henry Coston and Whittington King land deeded by Thomas Seon to Whitty Turpin father of Peggy-no name or acreage.
1822 Thomas Bryd willed part to daughter Ann Byrd.
1757 according to Bensons maps this land became actually part of COW QUARTER 678 acres.

HANDYS DELIGHT

Patented in 1819 by John Handy for 317 1/4 acres, a resurvey from POMFRET, in Lawsons, Election district 8, map #18.
1813 Sarah Handy willed to son William J. Handy.

HANDYS HALL

see DALES ADVENTURE

HANDYS MEADOW

Patented on 10 Aug.1684 by Samuel Handy for 50 acres in Brinkleys southeast, Election district 3, map #16.
Samuel Handy and wife Mary Handy sold to Samuel Collins
15 April 1734 Samuel Collins,wife Rebecca Collins, son of Samuel and grandson of Samuel, sold 50 acres of OYSTERSHELL to Thomas Evans 9 acres with HANDYS MEADOW.
1 Sep 1766 Nathaniel Evans sold to William Ward part from his father Thomas Evans.

25 July 1768 Ephraim Evans mortgaged 30 acres to John Collins, that was willed to Ephraim after death of widow Rose Evans.
19 March 1792 Abigail Collins sold to Jonathan Bunting and wife Ann Bunting, Thomas Bunting and wife Rose Bunting for 5 shillings OWEN GLENDORE,OYSTERSHELL BANK,HANDYS HALL,HANDYS MEADOW.
19 March 1792 Thomas Bunting,wife Rose Bunting sold to Jonathan Bunting 45 acres of OYSTER SHELL BANKS,HANDYS MEADOW,HANDYS HALL.
6 March 1793 Jonathan Bunting,wife Nancy Bunting and Thomas Evans sold to Ralph Milbourn 3 acres of OYSTERSHELL BANK & 50 acres of marsh aka HANDYS MEADOW.
31 March 1797 Ralph Milbourn sold to James Milbourn his interest in OYSTERSHELL BANKS
19 March 1800 James Milbourn and Ralph Milbourn mortgaged to William Waters Sr. with OWEN GLENDORE.
18 Feb.1805 Thomas Ward sold to James Milbourn 125 acres of OWEN GLENDORE & HANDYS MEADOW.
9 May 1806 James Milbourn sold to Ralph Milbourn 133 acres with OYSTER SHELL BANKS & OWEN GLENDORE total 161 acres.

HANDYS PURCHASE

Patented in 1757 by Samuel Handy for 263 acres, a resurvey of STRUGGLE, in Westover,Election district 13, map #11.
4 Dec.1736 Samuel Handy, shipwright, sold 50 acres to Thomas Handy.
1778 Samuel Handy willed to son Samuel Handy and son Isaac Handy.
1783 tax- Isaac Handy 260 acres
7 Jan 1789 Isaac Handy sold to John Williams 2 1/2 acres
14 Oct.1806 William Handy of Scott Co. Ky. sold to John Calbert of Somerset Co.Md. 24 1/2 acres.
20 Nov.1812 John W. Curtis sold to William Williams land from John Williams.
1815 William Williams sold to John W. Curtis
1815 William Curtis purchased 12 1/2 acres from William Williams.

HANNAHS DELIGHT & EXCHANGE

See DOUBLE PURCHASE.

HANSLAP

Patented on 28 June 1679 by Gilbert James who assigned to John Panther for 50 acres in St.Peters,Election district 2, map #6.
Rent Rolls 1666-1723 John Panther 50 acres.
1713/4 John Panther willed to Benjamin Sasser and then to his sons Thomas Sasser and Panter Sasser, 50 acres.
5 Aug.1729 Benjamin Sasser and Thomas Sasser deeded 50 acres to William Sasser.
1783 tax- William Sasser Sr. 50 acres.

HAP AT A VENTURE

Patented in 1746 to Stephen Handy for 176 acres in Dublin,Election district 4, map #13.
18 March 1755 Stephen Handy, wife Grace Handy sold to Littleton Dennis 25 acres.
22 March 1770 Littleton Dennis sold to George Waters 75 acres.

1783 tax- Matthias Miles 80 acres.
1795 George Waters willed to son Thomas Waters, conveyed me by Littleton Dennis.
9 Jan.1810 Thomas Waters, wife Elizabeth Waters sold to Thomas Mitchell Jones 250 acres of SUFFOLK, HAP AT A VENTURE, PROVIDENCE & MIDDLESEX.

HAPHAZARD

Patented on 7 Dec.1678 by John Cullen for 70 acres in Asbury,Election district 12, map #21.
Rent Rolls 1666-1723 John Cullen.
26 Oct.1708 John Sterling bought 70 acres from John Cullen and wife Arabella Cullen.
1741 John Sterling willed to son Aaron Sterling.
18 Aug.1742 Aaron Sterling sold to Jacob Cullen 6 acres, a trade for 6 acres of JOHNSONS LOTT.
31 Aug.1762 Aaron Sterling leased to Southy Whittington (with the stipulation that after the death of Aaron Sterling then to be on behalf of Littleton Sterling his son)
1783 tax- Aaron Sterling 70 acres.
1795 Aaron Sterling willed to son Aaron Jr.

HAPHAZARD

Patented in 1697 by Jeffrey Minshull for 100 acres in Brinkleys, southwest, Election district 3, map #17.
Rent Rolls 1666-1723 claimed by Helena Minshull relic of Jeffrey Minshull.
(Jeffrey Minshull died intestate and lands descended to son Jeffrey Jr. who died before age 21, so descended to John Mitchell brother of Jeffrey.)
1741 Phillip Adams and Teague Matthews (son-in-law) Samuel Adams(nephew) and brother William Adams purchased from John Mitchell 100 acres.
1745 tax- Samuel Adams
1763 Samuel Adams willed to sons Samuel Adams and Phillip Adams.
1756 William Adams willed to sons William and Dennis Adams.
1760 Teague Matthews willed to grandson Benjamin Holland Matthews son of Phillip Matthews 1/2 of marsh on Morumsco Ck. If no issue to son Benjamin Matthews.
1783 tax- William Adams 5 acres
1783 tax- Samuel Adams 12 1/2 acres
1783 tax- Sarah Adams 5 acres
1783 tax- William Adams 8 1/4 acres
1783 tax- Phillip Adams 5 acres
1783 tax- Phillip Adams of Hope 5 acres
1783 tax- Benjamin Matthews 12 acres
1783 tax- David Matthews Jr. 12 acres.

HAPHAZARD

Patented on 22 April 1695 by William Carey for 125 acres in East Pr.Anne,Election district 15, map #4.
14 March 1698 William Carey conveyed to Roger Phillips.
1698 Robert Phillips willed to Elizabeth Phillips alias Elizabeth Crouch. Afsd Robert Phillips son and heir of Elizabeth.

27 March 1740 Robert Crouch sold to William Taylor 125 acres.
2 May 1769 William Taylor sold to William Heath 4 acres.
6 Oct.1772 William Heath sold 4 acres to Thomas Pollitt.
29 Feb.1780 William Heath sold to Abraham Taylor 5 1/4 acres
29 Feb.1780 Abraham Taylor sold 5 1/4 acres to William Heath.
1783 tax- Samuel Taylor 60 1/2 acres
1783 tax- Abraham Taylor 60 1/2 acres
31 March 1795 Abraham Heath son of William Heath, and wife Martha Heath
sold to Josiah,Hobbs with HATHS CHANCE,WILSONS FIRST, HOG RIDGE, etc.
7 Jan 1802 Sarah Taylor widow of Samuel Taylor sold to Josiah W. Heath,
released her dower rights of husband Samuel Taylor who died on 25
Dec.1797.
17 Apr.1804 Josiah Wilson Heath, wife Mary Heath, sold to James Pollitt,
William Pollitt of William, John Done, & John Cottman for 5 shillings
part in trust for schoolhouse.
11 May 1805 Matthias Coston Taylor and wife Elizabeth Taylor sold to
Levin Beauchamp and wife Nancy Beauchamp 35 acres of HAPHAZZARD &
ADDITION TO HOG QUARTER, that Abraham Taylor devised to son Levin Taylor
and if no heirs to son William Taylor; both died without issue and it
descended to sisters Nancy Taylor and Elizabeth Taylor afsd.This was a
division of lands.
5 Dec.1807 Matthias Coston Taylor, wife Elizabeth Taylor sold to Benjamin
Simpson 16 acres.
9 Feb.1808 Samuel Taylor son of Samuel of Kent Co. Del. sold to Josiah
Wilson Heath, all rights.
20 Dec.1808 Thomas Bonnawell, wife Elizabeth Bonnawell sold to George
Maddux their part of HAP HAZZARD & HOG QUARTER, per deed from Levin
Beauchamp and wife Nancy Beauchamp to Elizabeth Taylor now Elizabeth
Bonnawell, being an heir of her brother William Taylor deceased.
24 Sep.1810 Elizabeth Bonnawell, and husband Thomas Bonnawell and George
Maddux sold to Benjamin Simpson 31 acres, right of Elizabeth Taylor now
wife of Thomas Bonnawell.

HAPPY ADDITION

Patented on 17 March 1686 by Roger Woolford for 200 acres in West
Pr.Anne, Election district 1, map #3.
Rent Rolls 1666-1723 possessed by Mary Woolford relic of Roger Woolford.
2 April 1729 Roger Woolford of Dorc.Co. son of Roger gave to Martha
Woolford and Mary Woolford daughters of Levin Woolford,late, lands and
marshes Roger willed to Levin (no name or acreage given.)
1730 Roger Woolford willed to son John Woolford.
21 March 1742 Henry Waggaman and wife Mary Waggaman one of the daughters
of Levin Woolford deeded to Samuel Wilson and wife Martha Wilson also
daughter of Levin Woolford 300 acres of WOOLFORD & HAPPY ADDITION & LUNNS
IMPROVENT,LUNNS INCREASE.
1783 tax- Levin Wilson 100 acres
1783 tax- Levin Woolford 100 acres.
1791 Levin Wilson willed to nephew George W. Jackson.
4 April 1808 Elizabeth Jackson and George W. Jackson sold to William
Jones 150 acres.
1836 John Woolford willed to son William G. Woolford.

HAPPY ADDITION

Patented in 1742 by Panter Laws for 54 acres in St.Peters,Election

district 2, map #6. Repatented in 1760 by Panter Laws for 126 1/2 acres.
1783 tax- William Laws 42 acres
15 March 1788 John Laws son of Panter Laws sold 50 acres to Henry
Jackson.
1 May 1792 John Laws sold to Thomas Laws, PANTHERS DENN & HAPPY ADDN,
part.
1 May 1792 John Laws sold to John Laws HAPPY ADDITION & PANTHERS DEN.
6 March 1804 Thomas Laws of Panter Laws sold to James J. Dashiell Gillis,
balance, no acreage given.

HARD FORTUNE

Patented in 1725 by William Miles for 4 acres in East Pr.Anne,Election
district 5, map #5.

HARD FORTUNE

Patented in 1734 by Thomas Summers for 50 acres in Lawsons, Election
district 8, map #19.

HARD FORTUNE

Patented in 1767 by Obed Dougherty for 12 acres in Lawsons, Election
district 8, map #19.
24 Aug.1800 Dickerson Dougherty sold to John E. Dougherty 3 acres.
2 May 1801 John Dougherty son of Obed Dougherty and wife Mary
Dougherty,sold to Thomas Lord 35 acres of USK, MEADOW & HARD FORTUNE.
23 Arpil 1808 John Dougherty of Obed Daugherty sold to Dickerson
Dougherty 5 acres with USK.

HARD LABOUR

Patented in 1812 by Planner Puzey for 60 acres in East Pr. Anne,Election
district 15, map #4.
22 Feb 1831 Marshalls Sale at suit of Bank of Somerset against Planner
Puzey, 43 acres.

HARDY

Patented in 1793 by Thomas Rencher for 4 3/4 acres in Mt.Vernon, Election
district 5, map #1.

HARTFORD BROAD OAKE

Patented on 26 Oct.1666 by Robert Catlin for 400 acres in Westover,
Election district 13, map #11, a resurvey on CATTLYNS LOTT.
Rent Rolls 1666-1723 possesed by William Catlin heir to Robert Catlin.
30 Aug.1731 William Catlin confirmed to John Williams his holding of
HARTFORD BROAK OAKE bequeathed by Robert Catlin to his daughter Sarah
Catlin late wife of John Williams. 150 acres
20 Aug.1746 Isaac Beauchamp quitclaimed to John Williams all right to
CONTENTION- a trade for HARTFORD BROAD OAKE, no acreage given.
8 Jun 1765 William Catlin gave to William Catlin Jr., part.
21 Aug.1766 William Catlin sold to Isaac Beauchamp, part of two tracts 41
1/5 acres with CATLIN VENTURE.
21 Nov.1766 William Catlin Sr. sold to Jesse Lister 100 1/2 acres out of
CATLINS LOTT,CATLINS VENTURE, HARTFORD BROAD OAKE.
11 March 1767 William Catlin sold to Joshua Catlin 42 acres for 5
shillings.

10 March 1767 William Catlin Jr. sold to Jacob Williams 14 1/4 acres of land from father William-unnamed.
16 March 1768 William Catlin Jr. sold to John Turpin 40 acres, part of CATLINS VENTURE,HARTFORD BROAD OAKE.
21 March 1768 William Catlin gave to son William Catlin land in Annamessex, unnamed.
6 April 1768 William Catlin Jr. mortgaged to John Williams.
21 Aug.1771 John Williams released mortgage to William Catlin.
14 Oct.1772 Joshua Catlin sold to William Catlin part with BRANFIELD 49 3/4 acres that William Catlin father of Joshua deeded him.
21 July 1789 James Williams son of Jacob Williams, wife Grace Williams sold to Thomas Jones, that Robert Catlin bequeathed to his daughter Sarah Williams late wife of John Williams.
14 Oct 1800 Samuel Smith and Mary Jones widow of Thomas Jones (agreed to sell dower rights) sold to Isaac Beauchamp as Thomas Jones willed to be sold that he purchased of James Williams on 21 July 1789- no name.
14 Oct.1800 Isaac Beauchamp sold to Mary Jones, widow of Thomas Jones, same as above.
23 Aug.1802 William A. Schoolfield and wife Mary Schoolfield sold to Isaac Beauchamp 150 acres (William Schoolfield married Mary Jones)
2 Oct 1807 William Turpin son of John Turpin sold 10 acres to Tubman Mitchell father purchased from William Catlin, no name.
6 April 1808 William Turpin of John Turpin, wife Elizabeth Turpin sold to Isaac Miles.
12 Feb.1808 Tubman Mitchell, wife Sarah Mitchell sold to Isaac Miles 10 acres purchase of Wiliam Turpin of John Turpin, unamed.
25 Jan 1810 Isaac Miles, wife Rose Anna Miles, sold 10 acres to Tubman Mitchell, purchased of Tubman, no name.

HARMON

Patented on 8 Feb.1682 by John Parker for 350 acres and sold to John Booth in West Pr.Anne,Election distict 1, map #2.
1698 John Booth willed 350 acres to son Peter Booth.
6 March 1735 Marcellas Hobbs, cooper, and wife Agnes Hobbs,sole daughter and heiress of Peter Booth Jr.,deceased sold to Benjamin Bayley.
18 May 1737 Benjamin Bayley and wife Sarah Bayley sold to John Thomson 150 acres.
20 Nov.1741 John Thomson sold to Thomas Gibbs 150 acres.
1748 part resurveyed to GILLIS DOUBLE PURCHASE.
1 March 1768 Coorge Bayley and wife Frances Bayley sold to Wilson Heath 175 acres.
10 April 1768 Wilson Heath and wife Rachel Heath sold to George Bayley of Sussex Co. Del. 175 acres.
1 April 1768 George Bayley of Sussex Co.Del. sold to John Taylor of Somerset Co. 100 acres
21 Feb 1769 John Taylor, late of Som.Co. but now of Sussex Co.Del. sold to Walter Taylor of Som.Co. 100 acres.
7 Dec.1770 George Bayley sold to Walter Taylor 25 acres.
7 Dec.1770 George Bayley of Sussex Co.Del. sold to Mills Bayley 75 acres.
8 Dec.1783 Walter Taylor mortgaged to Solomon Gibbons of Worc.Co. 125 acres.
1783 tax- Walter Taylor 25 acres
1783 tax- George Bayley 75 acres.
8 April 1796 Walter Taylor of Kent Co. Del. sold to Jacob Morris of Som.

Co. his interest.

HARMSNOT

Patented on 8 March 1762 by Stephen Ward for 50 acres in East Pr.Anne, Election district 15, map #5.
13 Nov.1801 John Ward, son of Stephen Ward, and wife Leah Ward sold to William Smullen- all.

HARMSWORTH

Patented on 3 April 1c682 by William Stevens who assigned to Roger Woolford, 300 acres in Dublin, Election district 4, map #12.
1701 Roger Woolford willed to son James Woolford land in Perryhawkin.
Rent Rolls 1666-1723 Mrs. Mary Woolford.
10 Aug.1684 James Woolford and wife Grace Woolford sold to Edmund Smullen and William Smullen.
2 July 1726 Isaac Coston and wife Rose Coston and Mary Smullen agree to division of 300 acres.
1730 I Isaac Coston give to son Ahab Coston all part of land which was divided between Mary Smullen and me.
17 Nov.1731 Isaac Coston,planter and wife Rose Coston gave to son Ahab Coston upper half, 150 acres.
25 Nov.1741 Randall Smullen Sr. and Randall Smullen Jr. sold to Joseph Riggin 137 acres.
14 March 1741 Randall Smullen Sr. and wife Sarah Smullen Jr. and wife Mary Smullen sold to Ahab Coston 137 acres.
9 March 1742 Thomas Woolford of Dorc. Co. and wife Sarah Woolford sold to Joseph Riggin 137 acres.
9 March 1742 Thomas Woolford of Dorc.Co. and wife Sarah Woolford sold 137 acres to Ahab Coston.
26 Feb.1744 John Woolford and wife Mary Woolford quitclaimed to Ahab Coston 150 acres that Roger Woolford father of John, eldest son of Roger willed to John Woolford.
26 Feb.1744 John Woolford and wife Mary Woolford sold to Joseph Riggin 115 acres
1 March 1750 Ahab Coston sold to Stephen Ward 150 acres.
25 March 1775 Joseph Riggin and wife Elizabeth Riggin sold 150 acres to Stephen Ward.
1774 ADDITION TO HARMSWORTH, 317 acres by Stephen Ward.
1783 tax- Stephen Ward 317 acres.
29 March 1805 Lowden Smullen, wife Elizabeth Smullen, sold to John Dorman of Worc.Co. 65 acres. (Elizabeth Smullen was daughter of Stephen Ward)
23 Apr.1806 Robert Leatherbury, sheriff, sold to Josiah W. Heath, per suit of Stephen Ward against John Ward, no acreage given.
23 April 1806 Josiah W. Heath sold to Ballard Reed, part.
9 Jan 1807 John Ward sold to John Dorman of Worc.Co. 85 1/4 acres.
10 April 1810 Ballard Reed, John Ward and wife Nelly Ward, sold to Josiah W. Heath 41 1/2 acres.
18 Mary 1829 Estate of Eleanor Ward widow of John Ward deceased sold to James Ward.

HARPERS DISCOVERY

Patented on 21 March 1680 by William Stevens and assigned to William Harper for 200 acres in Dublin,Election district 4, map #12.

9 Aug. 1687 William Harper and wife Elizabeth Harper sold to William and Elizabeth Denson.
9 Aug.1687 William Harper, wife Elizabeth Harper sold 100 acres to William Warwick, now called WARWICKS CHOICE.
Rent Rolls 1666-1723 100 acres William Denson, 100 acres William Warwick.
5 Aug.1719 William Denson and wife Elizabeth Denson sold to John Fleming 100 acres.
William Warwick and wife Sarah Warwick sold to John Fleming 23 1/2 acres
1783 tax- William Warwick 100 acres.
18 March 1806 John Fleming sold to Charles Jones 23 1/2 acres.
19 March 1806 William Warwick sold to William Fleming 15 acres.
24 June 1807 John F. Fleming now of Scipio Cayuga N.Y. sold to Juliana Massey Farrow and Mary Johnson Farrow daughters of Charles Farrow 250 acres of UNITY ENLARGED, GOSHEN, HARPERS INCREASE, part HARPERS DISCOVERY. This same deed also recorded on 2 July 1808.
12 April 1808 Charles Jones Esq. sold to Isaac Harris 23 acres.
21 March 1809 John Fleming of Cayuga Co. N.Y. sold to Juliana Massey Farrow and Mary Johnson Farrow.
21 Aug.1810 Matthias Dashiell, sheriff sold to John Riggin, per judgement against Charles Farrow.
18 Oct.1810 Isaac Harris of John Harris, wife Sally Harris sold to Joseph Cooley Oliver 23 1/2 acres.
1817 Samuel Harper gave to daughter Catherine Q. Harper 5 acres.

HARPERS ENCREASE

Patented on 1 Oct.1683 by William Harper for 100 acres in Dublin, Election district 4, map #12.
9 Aug.1687 William Harper, wife Elizabeth Harper sold to William Denson and wife Elizabeth Denson.
9 Aug.1687 William Harper, wife Elizabeth Harper, sold to William Warwick 50 acres now called WARWICKS DISCOVERY
Rent Rolls 1666-1723 possessed 50 acres William Denson, 50 acres William Warwick.
5 Aug.1719 William Denson and wife Elizabeth Denson sold 50 acres to John Fleming.
25 June 1807 John F. Fleming now of Scipio Cayuga Co. N.Y. sold to Juliana Massey Farrow and Mary Johnson Farrow daughters of Charles Farrow 250 acres of UNITY ENLARGED, GOSHEN, HARPERS ENCREASE, HARPERS DISCOVERY. This deed was recorded again on 21 March 1809.
21 March 1810 Matthias Dashiell,sheriff, sold to John Riggin, per judgement against Charles Farrow 250 acres of above lands.

HARRINGTON

Patented 16 March 1680 by William Stevens who assigned to Thomas Holbrook for 200 acres in Mt.Vernon, Election district 5, map #1.
Rent Rolls Thomas Holbrook 200 acres.
1717 Thomas Holbrook gave plantation to son Thomas.
1793 resurveyed to BENGAL & CONCLUSION 988 acres.

HARRIS ADVENTURE
See BEAR POINT

HARRIS CHANCE

Patented in 1764 by Spencer Harris for 150 acres in Dublin,Election
district 4, map #12
1783 tax- Spencer Harris 150 acres.
1794/5 Spencer Harris willed to son Isaac Harris.
5 Jan 1813 Isaac Harris sold to James Boston
1 Dec.1814 James Boston sold part to Isaac Harris.

HARRIS CHOICE

Patented in 1792 top Spencer Harris for 208 1/4 acres in Dublin,Election
district 4, map #12.
1794 Spencer Harris willed to son Isaac Harris, HARRIS'S CHANCE now
resurveyed and vacancy added and called HARRIS CHOICE.

HARRISLAND

see MARSHALLS INHERITANCE

HARRISONS ADVENTURE

Patented on 12 June 1679 by John Harrison 600 acres, in Dublin, Election
district 4, map #12.
Rent Rolls 1666-1723 possessed by John Harrison.
1701 John Harris willed to son Caleb Harris 50 acres, to son John Harris
200 acres, to son Jeremiah Harris 15 acres, to son Robert Harris 200
acres, to son James Harris 50 acres.
1701 John Harris willed to son James Harris 150 acres.
21 March 1722 John Harris Jr. and wife Rebecca Harris, sold 200 acres to
James Harris.
3 Jan 1737 Richard Knight (son-in-law of John Harris) gave to son James
Knight and Joshua Knight 350 acres bought of Jeremiah Harris and Robert
Harris.
10 Nov 1741 Jeremiah Harris and wife (unnamed) gave to brother Caleb
Harris all lands from father John Harris (unnamed and no acreage given.)
3 July 1744 James Knight sold to Capt. Thomas Williams 175 acres at
division line between James and his brother Joshua Knight.
18 June 1746 James Knight and Thomas Williams sold 175 acres to James
Gray for 12 shillings of 350 acres.
20 March 1748/9 James Gray sold to Allen Gray 175 acres.
22 Nov.1749 John Williams and Thomas Williams sold to William Fleming 150
acres.
17 March 1752 Allen Gray and wife Mary Gray sold to James Knight.
22 Nov.1758 Joshua Knight and wife Margaret Knight sold to James Knight
175 acres.
1765 James Knight and wife Parthana Knight sold to William Fleming 30
acres.
21 Nov.1766 James Knight mortgaged 350 acres to John Harris.
8 Sep.1768 James Knight sold 350 acres to John Harris.
23 Jan 1770 James Knight and wife Elizabeth Knight sold to John Harris
265 acres (already mortgaged to him.)
1783 tax- John Harris 312 acres

1783 tax- John Riggin 238 acres.
1777 Capt. Benton Harris willed to John Riggin my sister's son.400
acres.(Hannah Harris married Teague Riggin)
1788 will of John Harris, to son Steven Harris lands bought of James
Knight (unnamed)
3 Oct.1792 John Riggin sold to Spencer Harris 2 1/2 acres of HARRISONS
VENTURE & BEAR POINT.
1794 will of Spencer Harris, to son Littleton Harris.
(many of these deeds were hard to distinguish between HARRISONS
ADVENTURE, HARRISONS VENTURE and HARRISONS ADVENTURE patented in 1749.)
25 Oct.1808 Stephen Harris mortgaged to Thomas W. Handy 312 acres.
18 April 1810 Robert Riggin, wife Peggy Riggin sold to Littleton Harris
lands of father John Riggin 340 acres with BARE POINT.
5 Jan 1813 Isaac Harris sold to James Boston
1 Dec.1814 James Boston sold to Isaac Harris, same.
1824 Isaac Harris son of John Harris possessed. he died in 1839 and his
lands were sold HARRISONS ADVENTURE,HARRISONS VENTURE,WARWICKS DISCOVERY,
WHITTINGTONS NEGLECT in excess of 700 acres.
1859 Jehu Parsons willed to son William Sydney Parsons 800 acres of
HARRISONS ADVENTURE.

HARRISONS ADVENTURE

Patented in 1749 by Benton Harris for 263 acres in Dublin, Election
district 4, map #12, a resurvey out of BEARE POINT.
1725 Laid out for John Harris being taken out of tract of Stephen Coston
Jr. BARE POINT. that Stephen Coston willed to daughter Elizabeth Coston
150 acres which part was sold to John Harris. Signed Elizabeth Townsend,
John Tull and Isaac Coston. 150 acres.
7 Nov.1762 Benton Harris of Worc.Co. sold to John Tull of Somerset County
26 acres out of 263 acres patented Benton Harris.
21 Nov. 1791 Neil Ritchie, wife Sarah Ritchie, sold to Nehemiah King land
conveyed by John Harris and wife Rebecca Harris and 25 acres conveyed by
Benton Harris to John Tull.
5 Feb. 1793 Nehemiah King sold to Henry Coston 343 1/2 acres that Neil
Ritchie conveyed to King(unnamed)
1807 Henry Coston willed lands to son Henry K. Coston -unnamed.

HARRISONS VENTURE

Patented in 1688 by John Harris for 200 acres in Dublin, Election
district, map #12.
1701 will John Harris to wife Judith Harris 50 acres to go to son Caleb
Harris at her death, and to son James Harris 150 acres.
17 June 1752 James Harris sold to Abraham Harris 115 acres of MIDDLETON,
FLEMINGS LOSS, HARRISONS VENTURE.
17 June 1752 Abraham Harris sold to James Harris 120 acres of MIDDLETON,
FLEMINGS LOSS.
1756 resurveyed to FLEMINGS LOSS.
16 Dec.1776 Abraham Harris,wife Director Harris of Sussex Co.Del.sold to
William Fleming 50 acres.
1783 tax- William Fleming 50 acres
1783 tax- Spencer Harris 150 acres.
27 Aug.1788 John Sheldon Alexander,wife Leah Alexander of Worc.Co. sold
to John Harris Jr. 50 acres with MIDDLETOWN,FLEMINGS LOSS.

6 April 1796 John Harris sold to William Fleming 50 acres.
1796 John Fleming willed lands to sons William Fleming and Joshua
Fleming, unnamed.

HASFORTS PURCHASE

Patented on 8 Nov.1675 by George Hasfort in Brinkleys, southwest,
Election district 3, map #17, for 200 acres.
Land escheated to his Lordship for want of heirs.
13 June 1682 Richard Brittain sold to Henry Potter 200 acres.
1745 resurveyed to BOSTONS PURCHASE.

HARTHBERRY

Patented on 29 May 1683 by Capt. Henry Smith for 150 acres in East
Pr.Anne,Election district 15, map #5.
Rent Rolls 1666-1723 possessed by William Polk, vide William Smith's
account.
1696 Thomas Smith willed to son William Smith 100 acres and balance to
son John Smith.
1715 John Smith son of William, grandson of Henry Smith, of Sussex
Co.Del. sold his land.
1724 ADDITION patented for 74 acres by William Smith.
1733 William Smith, wife Magdalen Smith, willed to son William Smith and
heirs HARTHBERRY & ADDITON, except part that is bequeathed to cousin
Thomas Smith Jr.
8 Feb.1743 Thomas Smith son of Robert Smith, deceased, sold to Thomas
Walton part from his uncle William Smith.
4 Apr.1767 William Smith and wife Nelly Smith, sold to William Miles 150
acres wiith 74 acres of ADDITION.
18 Aug.1768 William Miles of Manokin, and Thomas Carpenter sold to Nelly
Smith widow of William Smith, Margaret Smith and Mary Smith daughters of
William and Nelly Smith, with ADDITION.
17 Dec.1782 William Walton sold to Thomas Maddux land on Smiths Branch 18
3/4 acres unnamed.
1783 tax- John Laws, 100 acres and 74 acres of ADDITION.
28 Jan 1783 Thomas Maddux, attorney for John Laws and Eleanor Laws his
wife sold to Margaret Handy and Mary Smith daughters of Eleanor 4 1/2
acres.
1775 Maps show this was resurvyed to LAWS PURCHASE 215 acres.
19 Feb.1788 George Robertson sold to George Waggaman 13 1/2 acres with
ROWLEY RIDGE, as Thomas Maddux had) that descended to his son John
Robertson Maddux and descended to Ann Hall and Nicholas Tull.
4 June 1788 John Laws and wife Nelly Laws, Mary Smith and William Handy
and wife Margaret Handy sold 20 acres to George Waggaman.
27 Aug.1788 Nicholas Tull of Baltimore Co.Md. heir of Thomas Maddux sold
to George Waggaman, his interest.
13 Aug.1788 Ann Hall heir of Thomas Maddux sold her interest to George
Waggaman.
14 Sep.1804 John Byrd and wife Margaret Byrd and Mary Smith sold to
Zadock Long tract conveyed by Thomas Maddux to John Laws and wife Eleanor
Laws and Margaret Handy and Mary Smith 4 3/4 acres in 1783- no name.
27 May 1805 Col. William Jones, wife Eleanor Jones sold to Isaac Gibbons
35 acres of HARTHBERRY & WAGGAMANS LOTT.
24 Apr.1805 Isaac Gibbons sold to Polly Collins all interest.

HARTS CONTENT

see SUFFOLK

HATHS PURCHASE

Patented in 1743 by Abraham Hath, was part of CARLISLE, for 175 acres in
West Pr.Anne,Election district 1, map #2.

HATHS CHANCE

Patented in 1749 by William Hath for 100 acres in East Princess Anne,
Election district 15, map #4.
1768 ADDITION patented for 145 3/4 acres
1782 SECOND ADDITION patented for 184 1/2 acres William Heath
1783 tax- William Heath
1783 tax- George Brown Sr. 50 acres.
1783 tax- George Brown Jr. 50 acres
1783 will of William Heath, to son Abraham Heath, lands on west side of
the road from Princess Anne Town to George Pollitt.
31 March 1795 Abraham Heath,wife Martha Heath sold to Josiah Hobbs.

HAWFREE POINT

Patented on 2 July 1683 by William Stevens for 100 acres in
Fairmount,Election district 6, map #9.
30 Aug.1686 William Stevens and wife Elizabeth Stevens sold to Thomas
Highway 100 acres.
Rent Rolls 1666-1723 Thomas Highway, 100 acres.
14 May 1745 Whittington King and wife Eleanor King sold to William Turpin
100 acres.
1771 William Turpin willed to son Denwood Turpin.
1783 tax- Denwood Turpin 100 acres.
1783 Denwood Turpin willed to sons William Turpin, John Turpin and Thomas
Denwood Turpin,lands (no name)
24 Aug.1793 John Turpin, wife Ally Turpin of Northampton Co. Va. sold to
William Turpin of Somerset Co. all rights to where Denwood Turpin lived.

HAYMANS ADDITION

Patented 1728 by James Hayman for 100 acres in East Princess Anne,
Election district 15, map #4.
1724 John Hayman willed to son James Hayman.
1783 tax- John M. Hayman 60 acres
1783 tax- Betty Hayman 23 acres.
17 Feb.1797 Sarah Hayman sold to Hezekiah Hayman as Revel Hayman willed
lands to be sold by wife Sarah Hayman.
16 Sep.1806 John Pollitt constable of Wicomico 100, sold to Joshua Morris
15 acres per judgement against John Hayman and Hezekiah Hayman.
1819 John Morris willed to daughter Priscilla Morris 15 acres.

HAYMANS DISAPPOINTMENT

Patented in 1786 by John Pollitt for 9 1/4 acres in East Pr.Anne,
Election district 15, map #4.
1839 John Pollitt willed to son Henry Pollitt.

HAYMANS EXCHANGE

see WHITE CHAPPELL

HAYMANS PURCHASE

Patented in 1753 by James Hayman and John Hayman in East Princess Anne,
Election district 15, map #4, for 117 acres.
A second patent by the same name for 25 acres was entered by Isaac
Hayman, and was a separate piece of land.
29 Oct.1765 James Hayman sold to Robert Geddes 58 1/2 acres.
1777 Isaac Hayman willed to son Isaac Hayman.
19 Nov.1769 William Geddes and wife Mary Geddes sold 50 1/2 acres to
William Pollitt.
4 Feb.1783 John Hayman son of John and John Harris Hayman son of James
Hayman sold 68 1/2 acres to William Pollitt, land that James Hayman
conveyed to Robert Geddes.
1783 tax- William Pollitt 113 acres
1783 tax- Isaac Hayman 122 acres of PURCHASE & ADDITION.
19 Feb.1795 Isaac Hayman sold 1 acre to Stephen Baine.
15 Jan 1797 Stephen Baine,wife Ann Baine sold to Jacob Morris, 1 acre.

HAYWARDS LOTT

Patented on 2 Nov.1734 by Thomas Hayward. a resurvey from WILLIAMS HOPE
and BLAKES HOPE, for 740 acres in Dublin,Election district 4, map #13.
1765 Thomas Hayward gave to son Thomas Hayward Jr. 740 acres.
1783 tax- Thomas Hayward 740 acres.
1792 Thomas Hayward gave to son John Hayward, and then to his son Thomas
Hayward.
24 Nov.1807 Thomas Hayward mortgaged to John Cottman.
1809 Thomas Hayward willed to his mother Elizabeth Hayward land devised
me by my grandfather Thomas Hayward.
1810 Elizabeth Morris willed to son John Elzey Hayward, devised me by son
Thomas Hayward, 740 acres.

HAYWARDS PURCHASE

Patented in 1758 by William Hayward for 549 1/2 acres in West Princess
Anne, Election district 1, map #3.
20 Nov.1767 William Hayward of Talbot Co. Md. sold to Levin Ballard of
Somerset Co. 549 1/2 acres.
14 Oct.1768 Levin Ballard sold to William Geddes 372 acres of NELSONS
CHOICE,HAYWARDS PURCHASE, DORMANS ADDITION.
7 Oct.1769 William Geddes and wife Mary Geddes sold to William Winder 456
1/2 acres of NELSONS CHOICE & HAYWARDS PURCHASE.
19 Sep.1776 Levin Ballard sold to Levin Woolford and John McGrath, all
except part sold to William Geddes.
21 Nov. 1776 Levin Woolford and John McGrath sold 5 acres to Andrew
Francis Cheney.
13 March 1779 Levin Woolford and John McGrath sold to Samuel Wilkins,
balance.
1783 tax- Samuel Wilkins 356 1/2 acres.
1783 tax- Andrew Francis Cheney 5 acres.
1783 tax- Dr.John Winder 121 1/2 acres.
12 Feb.1788 John Wilkins and wife Sally Wilkins sold 30 acres to the
trustees of the poor.

29 June 1790 John Wilkins sold to Samuel McClemmy 1 1/2acres and 20 perches.
10 May 1791 John Wilkins, mortgaged to Levin Gale,Henry Jackson and John Stewart.
13 May 1792 John Wilkins and wife Sarah Wilkins sold to William Lawler 2 acres(unnamed)
1792 William Winder willed to son John Winder land bought of William Geddes.
27 Feb.1793 John Wilkins, wife Sally Wilkins sold to James Ewing 309 acres.
9 Aug.1796 Nehemiah King sold to Samuel Wilson, conveyed in 1792, with DORMANS CONCLUSION.
29 Sep.1796 Whitty Sasser, wife Sarah Sasser (Sarah McCLemmy)sold to Parker Selby 1 1/2 acres and 20 perches.
14 Nov.1797 Parker Selby,wife Loviniah Selby, sold to John Campbell 1 1/2 acres.
28 July 1801 Isaac Ewing, merchant of Pr.Anne, sold to Littleton Dennis Teackle 13 1/4 acres.
14 May 1802 Richard Waters son of William Waters and wife Mary Waters sold to Peter Waters 218 1/2 acres.
14 May 1802 Peter Waters sold to Richard Waters son of William 71 1/2 acres.
14 May 1802 Richard Waters, and wife Mary Day Waters sold to Littleton Dennis Teackle.
20 March 1804 Isaac Ewing sold to Leah Adams 50 acres with 100 acres of TURKEY RIDGE.
7 April 1808 Littleton Dennis Teackle sold to John Teackle of Georgetown DC land purchased of Richard Waters of William Waters.

HAZZARD

Patented on 2 Nov.1664 by William Thomas for 400 acres in Mt.Vernon, Election district 5, map #1.
Rent Rolls 1666-1723 poss. by Capt.Charles Ballard 400 acres.
1723/24 Charles Ballard willed to son Charles, plantation at Wicomico River, unnamed.
1783 tax- Charles Ballard 200 acres.
1790 Charles Ballard willed lands to sons Arnold Ballard and Charles Ballard, unnamed and MIDDLE ISLAND to son Benjamin Ballard.
1793 Benjamin Ballard willed to Levin Ballard son of brother Arnold Ballard land between Charles Ballard and Arnold Ballard 60 or 70 acres, unnamed.
17 June 1804 Levin Ballard sold to John Ballard land on south side of the Wicomico River devised by Benjamin Ballard- as representative of his father Arnold Ballard, BALLARDS ISLANDS at mouth of Wicomico River, unnamed.
2 May 1806 John Ballard son of Arnold Ballard sold to Charles Simpkins of Dorc.Co. Md. MIDDLE ISLAND, part of three islands called THE HAZARD patented to Thomas Jones and devised by Charles Ballard to Benjamin Ballard deceased. Benjamin Ballard devised to Levin Ballard and it was conveyed by Levin Ballard to afsd. John Ballard - no acres.
3 May 1806 Charles Simpkins of Dorc. Co.gave mortgage to John Ballard of Arnold Ballard, same as above.
14 May 1806 Samuel Timmons sold to John Ballard of Arnold Ballard, all except WIND MILL ISLAND sold to Solomon Linton- mortgage.

13 May 1807 Samuel Ballard sold to Charles Simpkins, release of mortgage.
21 March 1808 William Ballard sold to Robert Bloodsworth of Dorc.Co. all
- came Martha Ballard, mother of William Ballard and released her rights.
5 May 1809 Solomon Linton of Matthews Co.Va. sold to Matthias Wingate,
WINDMILL ISLAND at mouth of Wicomico River, part of HAZZARD, held by
Capt. Charles Ballard.

HAZZARD

Patented on 28 Sep.1721 by John King for 160 acres in East Pr.Anne,
Election district 15, map #5.
20 March 1750 Whittington King son of John sold to Rev. Hamilton Bell 160
acres.
1783 tax Thomas Pollitt(with LIBERTY 38 acres.)

HAZZARD

Patented in 1725 by Henry Miles for 32 acres in Fairmount, Election
district 6, map #9.
1756 Henry Miles willed to grandson William Miles son of Samuel Miles and
Rebecca Miles.
23 Aug.1770 William Miles son of Samuel Miles, and wife Sarah Miles sold
to Henry Miles 32 acres with NEGLECT.
1783 tax- Henry Miles 32 acres.

HAZZARD

Patented in 1752 by Smith Horsey for 16 1/2 acres in Brinkleys,northwest
Election district 3, map #14.
1783 tax- heirs of Smith Horsey 6 acres.
1782 Smith Horsey willed dwelling plantation to son John Horsey, unnamed
land.

HEARTS CONTENT

Patented in 1677 by Robert Coulbourn for 50 acres in Lawsons, Election
district 8, map #19.
1698 Robert Coulbourn of Acco.Co.Va. gave to daughter Frances Coulbourn
50 acres in Maryland at PRAYERS NECK.
Rent Rolls 1666-1723 belongs to the orphan of Robert Coulbourn in
Virginia.
1689 will of William Coulbourn, to son Robert Coulbourn.
1739 Robert Coulbourn of Accomack Co.Va. son of Robert sold to Patrick
McClemmy 50 acres.
1753 part resurveyed to CHANCE 35 acres
1763 part resurveyed to PATRICKS LOTT 165 3/4 acres.
1773 resurveyed and repatented ADDITION TO HEARTS CONTENT by Isaac
Coulbourn for 257 1/4 acres, included GRAYS LOTT.
1783 Isaac Coulbourn willed to daughters Mary Coulbourn and Sarah
Coulbourn.
28 Feb.1797 William Williams sold to Stephen Ward 8 acres
26 Jan 1797 William Williams sold to Dickerson Dougherty, 15 acres.
31 Oct.1797 William Williams,wife Polly Williams sold to John Handy 240
acres(Polly Williams heir at law of Isaac Coulbourn)
1828 Thomas Handy willed to mother Sarah Handy lands left by her father.

1830 Sarah Handy willed to son William J. Handy.

HEARTS EASE

Patented in 1762 by Stephen Ward for 19 1/2 acres in Asbury, Election district 12, map #21.
1783 tax- Stephen Ward 19 acres.
7 Jan.1800 John Ward son of Stephen Ward, now of Kentucky sold to John Cullen.

HEARTS EASE

Patented in 1663 by Robert Hart, for 200 acres in Lawsons, Election district 8, map 18.
17 June 1679 Robert Hart, wife Jane Hart, sold to William Coulbourn son of William Coulbourn 200 acres.
Rent Rolls 1666-1723 belongs to orphans of Robert Coulbourn in Manokin.
1698 Robert Coulbourn of Acco.Co.Va.willed to unborn child. If a son, if not to be divided between daughter Rebecca Coulbourn and unborn daughter.
28 July 1729 William Coulbourn of Acco.Co.Va. wife Temperance Coulbourn sold 200 acres to Henry Miles.
1728 resurveyed to 400 acres by Henry Miles.
1761 Henry Miles willed to son William Miles.
24 Oct.1765 William Miles mortgaged to Matthias Gale of London 400 acres.
1770/85 Stacey Miles willed to Henry Miles son of William Miles 1/3rd.
1783 tax- William Miles 125 acres
1783 tax- Henry Miles 250 acres.
24 March 1795 Henry Miles sold to William Coulbourn 400 acres.
24 March 1795 William Coulbourn,wife Ann Coulbourn, sold to Henry Miles 400 acres.
25 Jan.1800 John Miles,wife Mary Miles sold to William Roach 280 acres of land of Henry Miles (unnamed)
3 Sep.1802 William Miles, wife Betsy Miles, sold 200 acres to Hambleton Johnson
13 Sep.1802 William Miles and wife Betsy Miles sold to son William Miles, 1/2 of land where he lives, no name.
23 Sep.1802 Hambleton Johnson sold to William Miles 200 acres.
22 March 1806 William Miles sold 100 acres to son William.
1852 William Miles willed to son John Henry Miles.

HEATH QUARTER

Patented on 28 May 1683 by Abraham Heath for 100 acres in East Pr.Anne, Election district 15, map #5.
1691 Abraham Heath, wife Ursulla Heath, willed to sons William Heath, Thomas Heath, Jacob Heath and Abraham Heath.
1733/5 William Heath willed to unborn child.
1759 Robert Harris willed to son Zachariah Harris 100 acres.
2 Feb 1764 Zachariah Harris of Worc.Co.and Levin Ballard and Stephen Mitchell with George Hayward agreed to divisions of lands. 100 acres.
1764 resurveyed to MITCHELLS PURCHASE 157 acres.

HEATHS EXPERIMENT

Patented in 1809 by Josiah W. Heath for 739 2/4 acres, from CHANCE & pt. of HARMSWORTH, in Dublin, Election district 4, map #12.

HEATHS GIFT

Patented in 1786 by William Heath for 13 acres, in East Pr.Anne,Election district 15, map #4.
31 March 1795 Abraham Heath son of William Heath,and wife Martha Heath sold to Josiah Hobbs with HATHS CHANCE,DONES NEST EGG,HAPHAZARD,WILSONS FIRST, HOG RANGE.
5 Aug.1800 John Heath sold to Samuel Heath 13 acres.
13 May 1803 Rebecca Hobbs sold to Samuel Heath 13 acres.
13 Aug.1804 The comissioneers to divide the real estate of William Heath sold to Rebecca Hobbs 13 acres.

HENDERSONS CHANCE

Patented on 10 Sep.1688 by John Henderson for 70 acres in Fairmount, Election district 6, map #9.
26 Aug.1727 Barnaby Willis and Collebrah Willis his wife sold to William Turpin, 32 acres taken out of BARNABYS LOTT & WILLIS CHOICE.(no WILLIS CHOICE on Bensons maps but this land is adjacent.)
1789 resurveyed to SUDLERS CONCLUSION 419 3/4 acres.

HENRYS ADDITION

Patented on 31 July 1713 by John Henry for 50 acres in Brinkleys, northeast, Election district 3, map #15.
Rent Rolls 1666-1723 John Henry.
1715/7 John Henry willed 50 acres to son Robert Jenkins Henry.
1744 Mary Hampton willed to son Robert Jenkins Henry
1764 Robert Jenkins Henry willed to son Robert Jenkins Henry land from mother Mary Hampton..
1783 Robert Jenkins Henry 50 acres.

HENRYS ENJOYMENT

Patented 19 Nov.1685 by Henry Hayman, in Mt.Vernon, Election district 5, map #1, for 50 acres.
Rent Rolls 1666-1723 Know not said land vide Phillip Covingtons account.
1732 Phillip Covington, wife Eleanor Covington gave to sons Nehemiah Covington,Phillip Covinton, and Levin Covington.

HENRYS VINEYARD

Patented in 1731 by Henry Newman for 50 acres in West Pr.Anne, Election district 1, map #3.
1750 resurveyed to NEWMANS CONCLUSION.

HEPWORTHS PASTURE

Patented in 1689 by John Hepworth for 48 acres in Lawsons, Election district 8, map #18.
1749 resurved to UPPER ANDUE for 400 acres.

HEREAFTER

Patented on 1 Oct.1679 by Thomas Roe and assigned to John Spence and

James Spence for 200 acres in Mt.Vernon, Election district 5, map #1.
Rent Rolls 1666-1723 possessed 100 acres by John Spence, 100 acres by
James Spence. (they were sons of David Spence.)
22 June 1750 George Gale, brother and exec. of Levin Gale deceased,and
Leah Gale only heir of Levin Gale sold to Henry Lowes.
1761 Henry Lowes willed to son Tubman Lowes, land bought of the heirs of
Levin Gale and 1/3rd to son Henry Lowes.
9 March 1773 Henry Lowes mortgaged to James Dickinson and William Hayward
of Talbot Co. 200 acres.
1783 tax- Henry Lowes.

HICKORY RIDGE

this is part of GREENFIELD.

HICKORY RIDGE

Patented in 1740 by William Adams Jr. in Brinkleys, northeast, Election
district 3, map #15, for 55 acres.
1788 resurvyed to ADAMS SCHEME.

HIGH MEADOW

Patented on 2 Dec.1672 by Edward Surman for 250 acres in East Pr.Anne,
Election district 15, map #4.
Rent Rolls 1666-1723 poss. by Richard Chambers 250 acres.
1726/8 Richard Chambers willed land (unnamed) to daughter Mary Brereton
and her husband Thomas Brereton.
Note-Thomas Brerton died intestate in Baltimore Co.Md. and left two sons
who died without issue and four daughters, Mary Brereton who married
Alexander Hall, Sarah Brereton who married Valentine Douglas, Winifred
Brereton who married Robert Cubbins, Judith Brereton who married Benjamin
Lagoe,
Mary Hall and Alexander Hall also died intestate and had two sons and 1
daughter, Chambers Hall, Jesse Hall and Rhoda Hall wife of George
Venrant?
4 Sep.1772 Judah Lagoe of Baltimore Md. widow, and dau. of Thomas
Brereton sold to Jonathan Pollitt except part called the SAVANAH that
Jonathan Pollitt bought of Asa Hall and part COACKMORE.
21 July 1773 William Douglas of Queen Anne Co.Md. sold to Jonathan
Pollitt his rights.
1774 Chambers Hall of Mill Ck.100, New Castle Co. Del.yeoman sold to
Revel Hayman part.
1774 Charles Hayman willed to daughter Catherine Hayman.
10 Oct.1774 Came Judith Legoe, witnessed that her sister Winifred
Brereton married John Leaton and they left children Wealthy Leaton and
Mary Thrift wife of James Thrift (Hartford Co.)
10 Oct.1774 James Thrift and wife Mary Thrift of Hartford Co. sold rights
to Jonathan Pollitt.
10 Oct.1774 Weathly Leaton of Hartford Co. sold rights to Jonathan
Pollitt.
13 Oct.1774 Judah Legoe of Hartford Co. sold rights to Jonathan Pollitt.
2 Mar.1780 Charles Hall of Newcastle Co.Del. sold to Revel Hayman,
rights.
1783 tax- John Pollitt Jr. 150 acres
1783 tax- Revel Hayman 62 1/2 acrs.

11 Nov.1793 Revel Hayman sold 9 acres to Jacob Morris.
1796 Revel Hayman willed lands to son William Brown Hayman, unnamed.
4 March 1797 Sarah Hayman devisee of Revel Hayman sold to John Pollitt
son of Jonathan Pollitt.
1838 John Pollitt willed to son Henry Pollitt 211 1/2 acres.

HIGNOTTS CHOICE

Patented 8 Feb.1667 by Robert Hignott for 300 acres in Brinkleys,
northeast, Election district 3, map #15.
April 1675 Robert Hignott sold to James Sullivan of Acco.Co. Va. if John
Crews son of John attains lawful age then James Sullivan to give him 150
acres.
9 Dec.1684 Robert Hignott sold to Dennis Sullivan of Southampton Co. Va.
all.
15 Jan 1685 Dennis Sullivan of Northampton Co. Va. sold to Edmund Howard
of Somerset Co.- all
12 Dec 1687 Edmund Howard, wife Margaret Howard sold to John Emmitt 300
acres.
Rent Rolls 1666-1723 possessed 150 acres by Edward Dykes, 150 acres Major
John Cornish.
1707 Major John Cornish gave to Col. Francis Jenkins and to Mrs. Mary
Jenkins and heirs real estate(unnamed)
1734/48 tax- Edward Dykes.
10 Feb.1755 Robert Jenkins Henry, wife Gertrude Henry, sold to William
Adams, tract WHITBY being part taken out of HIGNOTTS CHOICE, no acres
given.
1761 Sarah Dykes wife of Daniel Dykes had this land.
1764 Robert Jenkins Henry gave part to son Robert Henry.
1783 tax- James Dykes 150 acres.
1791 James Dykes(James Dakes) gave to son Daniel Dykes.
12 Feb 1799 Stephen Dakes sold to Daniel Dakes 82 3/4 acres of BUCK LODGE
& HIGNOTTS CHOICE.
29 Jan.1808 Daniel Dakes sold 2 acres to William A. Schoolfield.
6 April 1810 William A. Schoolfield, wife Mary Schoolfield, sold to Isaac
Miles.

HILLARDS ADVENTURE

Patented on 2 April 1667 by John Hillard for 100 acres in Brinkleys,
southeast, Election district 3, map #16.
Rent Roll 1661-1723 assigned John Ellis, possessed by William Matthews.
16 Aug.1746 John Ellis and wife Elizabeth Ellis sold to Teague Riggin of
Morumsco 30 acres.
1747 part 30 acres resurveyed to RIGGINS AMENDMENT 245 acres.
1747 balance resurveyed to LONG MEADOW 646 acres.

HILLARDS DISCOVERY

Patented on 1 April 1667 by John Hillard and assigned to Henry Hudson for
150 acres in Brinkleys southeast, Election district 3, map #16.
1 Sep.1676 Henry Hudson,wife Lydia Hudson sold to Henry Smith
7 June 1680 Henry Smith, wife Ann Smith sold to Teague Riggin 150 acres.
Rent Rolls 1666-1723 Possessed by Teague Riggin Sr.
22 Aug.1733 Samuel Riggin Sr. and wife Elizabeth Riggin sold to Joshua

Caldwell 50 acres part of tract made over to him by his father and left
by him to his son Charles Riggin.
1738 John Riggin willed to sons John and Teague Riggin, equally.
16 Dec.1762 John Riggin son of John of Morumsco, sold to Teague Riggin
son of John Riggin.(partition of land.)
12 April 1806 William Wilson, wife Leah Wilson sold to John Riggin lands
of Teague Riggin 65 acres unnamed.

HILLS FOLLY

Patented on 18 Aug.1672 by John Hill for 150 acres in Asbury, Election
district 12, map #21.
Rent Rolls 1666-1723 possessed by Thomas Stockwell in right of his wife,
heir of John Hill.
26 Oct.1721 William Williams and wife Alice Williams gave to sister
Hannah Stockwell,150 acres.
7 June 1764 Hannah Bird sold to Solomon Bird 47 acres.
1 Aug.1769 Solomon Bird and wife Jemima Bird sold to Levin Evans 47
acres.
13 Sep.1773 Levin Evans sold 47 acres to Samuel Lawson.
1783 tax- Thomas Byrd 102 1/2 acres
1783 tax- Samuel Lawson Jr. 47 acres.

HIS OWN BEFORE

Patented in 1786 by Samuel Wilson for 15 acres in Dublin,Election
district 4, map #13.
1783 tax- Samuel Wilson
17 Nov.1795 Major Samuel Wilson son of Samuel, wife Leah Wilson, sold to
Littleton Dennis 15 acres.

HOBBS ADVENTURE

Patented in 1728 by Thomas Hobbs for 100 acres in West Pr.Anne,Election
district 1, map #2.
1760 Stephen Hobbs willed to brother Benjamin Hobbs.
18 March 1761 Benjamin Hobbs sold to John Magraw 100 acres.
20 June 1766 Levin McGrath son of John McGrath sold to John McGrath lands
from his father.(unnamed)
21 Feb 1792 David McGrath sold to Elias Bailey 44 1/2 acres with
PRIVILEDGE(Sarah McGrath came, widow of John McGrath and released her
dower rights)
21 April 1792 David McGrath gave to son Levin McGrath with REFUGE,
PRIVILEDGE, SWINE YARD.
9 April 1793 David McGrath sold to Sarah McGrath widow of John McGrath 55
acres.
22 Feb 1800 George Robertson,sherriff sold to Levin Gale Jr. the property
of David McGrath 76 acres of HOBBS ADVENTURE, PRIVILEDGE, SWINE YARD.
15 March 1803 George Robertson sheriff, confirmed deed to Henry George
Gale and Betty Ann Wilson Gale children of Levin Gale Jr., deceased.

HOBBS CONCLUSION

Patented in 1768 by Matthias Hobbs for 463 1/4 acres in Mt.Vernon, Election district 5, map #1.
1783 tax- Matthias Hobbs
8 March 1772 Matthias Hobbs sold to Thomas Holbrook 252 acres.
1793 part resurveyed to BENGAL 988 acres.
5 Jan 1799 Benjamin Hobbs,wife Rebecca Hobbs sold to Nehemiah Covington 16 acres.
12 March 1799 Nehemiah Covington and Benjamin Hobbs sold to Elias Bailey 1 1/4 acre.
8 June 1808 Benjamin Hobbs sold to George Jones 200 acres.
17 Jan.1809 Daniel Ballard, sheriff, sold to Samuel Smith 252 acres, lands of Tubman Lowes.
13 Feb.1810 George Jones sold to Benjamin Hobbs 200 acres.

HOBBS HIS CHOICE

see GOLDEN QUARTER & LONG DELAY in Dames Quarter

HOCKLEY

Patented on 20 Nov.1678 by Thomas Manlove, for 50 acres in East Pr.Anne,Election district 15, map #5.
10 Feb.1682 Thomas Manlove,wife Jane Manlove sold to Michael Harrison.
Rent Rolls 1666-1723 possessed by Richard Plunkett.
1724/8 Richard Plunkett willed to Matthew Benston son of George Benston and Rebecca Benston 50 acres after death of wife Winifritt Plunkett.
12 Dec 1775 Matthias Benston, wife Nelly Benston, sold to William Miles 50 acres.
1783 tax- Mary Miles 50 acres.

HOG PEN SWAMP

Patented in 1745 by Henry Miles in Lawsons,Election district 8,map 18, for 50 acres
24 Oct.1765 William Miles mortgaged to Matthias Gale of London, merchant, 50 acres.

HOGG HUMMOCK

Patented on 14 April 1681 by William Stevens who assigned to Robert Dukes, for 100 acres in Lawsons,Election district 8, map #18.
Rent Rolls 1666-1723 possessed by Robert Dukes son of Robert, 100 acres.
1783 tax- Sarah Long, 100 acres.
9 Feb.1809 William Coulbourn of Robert Coulbourn, sold to Thomas Merrill Tull, with BEARD NECK & COME BY CHANCE 168 acres.

HOGGLAND QUARTER

Patented in 1744 by William Juett for 12 acres in Lawsons, Election district 8, map #19.
1783 tax- Nathaniel Juett 12 acres.

HOGG NECK

on SMITHS ISLAND- see PITCHCROFT
1766 William Mister sold to Job Wilson 25 acres.

HOG QUARTER

Patented on 25 April 1689 by William Alexander for 100 acres in East
Pr.Anne,Election district 15, map #4.
Rent Rolls 1666-1723 William Alexander Sr.
1735 William Alexander willed to son Moses Alexander where William
Alexander Sr. lived.
1749 ADDITION TO HOG QUARTER 446 acres-John Alexander.
2 May 1749 Moses Alexander sold 100 acres to John Alexander.
1751 resurvey SECOND ADDITION TO HOG QUARTER 776 acres by William Jones..
6 Aug.1751 John Alexander and wife Mary Alexander, blacksmith, sold to
William Jones 446 acres of ADDITION.
1 Nov.1763 John Jones son of Capt. William Jones deseased sold to William
Taylor 151 acres SECOND ADDITION.
21 Aug.1765 William Taylor and wife Elizabeth Taylor sold to Abraham
Taylor SECOND ADDN. TO HOG QUARTER conveyed by John Jones 51 acres.
21 Aug.1765 John Jones son of William Jones sold to John Taylor 50 acres
of FIRST ADDITION TO HOG QUARTER.
6 April 1768 John Taylor, wife Sophia Taylor, sold to Thomas Jones 50
acres of ADDITION.
23 Aug.1771 William Taylor sold to brother Abraham Taylor 100 acres
SECOND ADDITION TO HOG QUARTER
29 Sep.1772 William Taylor,wife Priscilla Taylor sold to Abraham Taylor
100 acres.
7 Feb.1775 Abraham Taylor sold 150 acres to William Miles of SECOND
ADDITION.
Feb.1780 Abraham Taylor,wife Mary Taylor sold to William Miles 100 acres.
1781/2 William Miles willed to grandaughter Peggy Pollitt of Thomas
Pollitt, 100 acres purchased of Abraham Taylor (unnamed land)
1783 tax- Mary Pollitt 100 acres
1783 tax- John Jones, SECOND ADDN. 170 acres.
15 April 1788 John Sheldon Alexander,wife Leah Alexander of Worc.Co. sold
to Michael Dorman of Som. CO., ADDITION TO HOG QUARTER, description, no
acres given.
1790 John Jones willed to son Thomas Jones SECOND ADDN.
31 Jan 1795 John Dorman sold 100 ares to William Donoho
13 Nov.1801 Eleanor Jones sold to Thomas Jones farm left by John Jones
and wife Eleanor Jones- agreement, land unnamed.
18 May 1802 Peggy Pollitt sold to Littleton Dennis Teackle 100 acres
devised by her grandfather William Miles.
1803 Thomas Jones willed to sons John Jones and Tubman Jones, and Thomas
Hamilton Jones SECOND ADDITION TO HOG QUARTER.
18 Aug.1802 Peggy Pollitt sold to Littelton Dennis Teackle 100 acres
devised by grandfather William Miles.
25 May 1803 Thomas Jones sold to Matthias Miles 220 acres of SECOND
ADDITION TO HOG QUARTER.
26 May 1803 Matthias Miles sold to Betsy Jones for 5 shillings SECOND
ADDN. TO HOG QUARTER 220 acres.
23 April 1805 Matthias Coston Taylor, wife Elizabeth Taylor sold to Levin
Beauchamp and wife Nancy Beauchamp 35 acres as Abraham Taylor died and it
descended to daughters Nancy Beauchamp and Elizabeth Taylor afsd.

11 May 1805 Matthias Coston Taylor and wife Elizabeth Taylor sold to
Levin Beauchamp and wife Nancy Beauchamp 50 acres of HOG QUARTER &
HAPHAZZARD, all interest.
15 Sep.1807 Littleton Dennis Teackle sold to Benjamin Simpson 50 acres of
SECOND ADDN. TO HOG QUARTER.
5 Dec.1807 Matthias Coston Taylor sold to Benjamin Simpson, balance.
15 Sep.1807 Littleton Dennis Teackle sold to Randal Hayman 50 acres of
SECOND ADDITION TO HOG QUARTER.
1825 Randal Hayman willed to son Randal Revel Hayman HOG QUARTER & SECOND
ADDITION.
20 Dec.1808 Thomas Bonnawell, wife Elizabeth Bonnawell, sold to George
Maddux 15 acres per deed from Levin Beauchamp and wife Nancy Beauchamp to
Elizabeth Taylor, now Elizabeth Bonnawell.
7 Jan 1810 Thomas Curtis, trustee to sell the real estate of Thomas
Jones, sold to Matthias Miles, SECOND ADDITON TO HOG QUARTER.
24 Sep.1810 Elizabeth Bonnawell,and husband Thomas Bonnawell, & George
Maddux, sold to Benjamin Simpson 16 acres.

HOG QUARTER

Patented in 1737 for 50 acres in Dublin, Election district 4, map #13.
1783 tax- John Perkins 18 /2 acres.

HOG QUARTER

Patented in 1760 by Fenton Catlin for 30 acres in Brinkleys, northeast,
Election district 3,map #15.
31 Jan.1764 Fenton Catlin sold to Brittain Powell 150 acres with WOOD
HALL.
6 Aug.1764 Fenton Catlin and wife Margaret Catlin sold to Brittain Powell
4 acres.
6 Aug.1764 Fenton Catlin sold 10 acres to William Holland
9 May 1765 Fenton Catlin, wife Margaret Catlin sold to Alexander Maddux
13 acres.
16 Dec.1766 William Holland sold 10 acres to David Long.
14 Jan.1772 Alexander Maddux sold to Phillip Adams son of Thomas Adams 13
acres.
18 March 1772 Fenton Catlin sold to David Long, with WOOD HALL.
1783 tax- David Long 30 acres
1783 tax- Phillip Adams 13 acres.
23 Oct.1806 Solomon Long son of David Long, wife Eleanor Long, William
Powell and Samuel Powell sold to Eli Gibbons 142 acres WOOD HALL, HOG
QUARTER to divide lands of David Long.
5 March 1807 Eli Gibbons,wife Amelia Gibbons and Edward Beauchamp and
wife Anna Beauchamp sold to James Smith with HOG QUARTER & WOOD HALL.
1812 Phillip Adams willed to son Stephen Adams land bought of Alexander
Maddux(unnamed)

HOG QUARTER

Patented in 1762 by Jesse Ward for 16 1/2 acres in Dublin,Election
district 4, map #12.
18 March 1772 Jesse Ward of Worc.Co. sold to Joseph Ward of Somerset Co.
16 1/2 acres.
15 Apr. 1796 David Long Ward sold to William Powell for 5 shillings.

11 Feb 1806 William Powell sold to Stephen Adams of Phillip Adams 3 3/4 acres 24 sq. perches of HOG QUARTER & OAK HALL.

HOG QUARTER

Patented in 1763 by Isaac Denston for 32 1/2 acres in East Pr.Anne, Election district 15, map #4.
1771 Isaac Denston willed to son Abraham Denston 32 1/2 acres.
1795 Abraham Denston willed to brother Isaac Adams Denston, until son Isaac Denston comes of age, lands in Somerset Co.
9 Apr.1804 Isaac Adams Denston, wife Sophia Denston sold to John Puckam 32 1/2 acres.
16 Jan.1808 John Puckam sold to Elzey Maddux 32 1/4 acres.

HOG QUARTER

Patented in 1769 for 13 acres in East Pr.Anne,Election district 15, map #4.
8 Dec.1783 Walter Taylor mortgaged to Solomon Gibbons 13 acres with HARMAN.
8 April 1796 Walter Taylor of Kent Co.Del. sold to Jacob Morris 13 acres.

HOG QUARTER

Patented in 1780 by John Harris for 14 1/2 acres in Dublin, Election district 4, map #12.
1783 tax- John Harris
1788/93 John Harris willed to son John 14 acres.

HOG RANGE

Patented in 1763 to David Dryden for 30 acres in Dublin, Election district 4, map #13.
1783 tax- Littleton Dryden 30 acres.
28 March 1796 Littleton Dryden sold to Littleton Dennis 55 acres of POWELLS CHANCE & HOG RANGE.
31 March 1810 Thomas Benston & James Barrett, wife Catherine Barrett, sold to Littleton Dennis, devised by grandfather Thomas Benston.

HOG RANGE

Patented in 1812 by Thomas Brown for 62 acres in East Pr.Anne,Election district 15, map #4.

HOG RIDGE

Patented on 1 May 1680 by David Hast and assigned to George Wilson for 100 acres in Brinkleys,northwest,Election district 3, map #14.
Rent Rolls 1666-1723 George Wilson.
1709 George Wilson willed to son George land between William Wilson and myself. unnamed.
10 Oct.1712 Elizabeth Wilson gave to son William Wilson.
10 Oct.1712 William Wilson sold to Patrick Irwin.
1712 Patrick Irwin sold to Jonathan Cooper
16 March 1730 Samuel Cooper son of Jonathan Cooper sold to William Wilson.

1731 William Wilson willed to sons George Wilson and John Wilson.
24 Feb.1763 John Wilson sold 100 acres to George Howard.
29 May 1769 George Howard and wife Priscilla Howard sold to John Long 100 acres.
1783 tax- Levin Watson 100 acres.
26 March 1787 Benjamin Conner,trustee to sell the real estate of John Long, deceased, sold 100 acres to Kellum Broughton with WILSONS PURCHASE, subject to the dower right of the widow of John Long.
24 March 1788 Levin Watson and wife Mary Watson sold to Kellum Broughton (formerly prop. of John Long.)

HOG RIDGE

Patented on 5 May 1683 by Thomas Manlove for 200 acres in East Pr.Anne, Election district 15, map #4.
Rent Rolls 1666-1723 possessed by Mrs. Mary King.
5 Sep.1729 Robert King and wife Priscilla King sold to William Heath 100 acres.
1733/5 William Heath willed to son William Heath and to son Jonathan Heath dwelling plantation and to unborn child, lands. This land not named in the will.
13 Oct.1762 Jonathan Heath of Hampshire Co.Va. carpenter, sold to Wilson Heath of Somerset Co.Md. 75 acres.
22 Oct.1765 William Heath gave to brother Wilson Heath 77 3/4 acres,land devised by their father.
21 April 1780 Mark Davis of Sussex Co.Del. sold 200 acres to Wilson Heath.
1783 tax- William Heath 25 acres.
1783 tax- Wilson Heath 153 acres.
1785 Wilson Heath willed to sons Josiah Wilson Heath and Samuel Heath.
12 Feb.1793 Thomas Watson of Sussex Co.Del. sold to Josiah Wilson Heath his share.
26 May 1794 Josiah Heath and Samuel Heath mortgaged to James Diamond 200 acres with WILSONS FIRST.
31 March 1795 Abraham Heath son of William, and wife Martha Heath sold to Josiah Hobbs.
21 May 1795 James Diamond released mortgage to Josiah Heath and Samuel Heath.
5 Aug.1800 Samuel Heath sold to John Heath 1 3/4 acres.

HOGG YARD

Patented on 16 May 1704 by Thomas Beauchamp for 95 acres in Brinkleys, northeast, Election district 3, map #15.
Rent Rolls 166-1723 Thomas Beauchamp.
18 March 1729 Edmund Beauchamp gave to son Edmund.
2 June 1733 Isaac Beauchamp son of Thomas Beauchamp gave to Edward Beauchamp 95 acres.
7 Aug.1749 Edward Beauchamp gave to son William Beauchamp 100 acres out of LEDBOURN & HOG YARD.
18 June 1771 William Beauchamp gave to son John Beauchamp 80 acres.
7 Aug.1781 Elijah Beauchamp,wife Martha Beauchamp, sold to John Beauchamp 14 acres.
1783 tax- John Beauchamp 26 acres
1783 tax- Elijah Beauchamp 25 acres

21 Feb 1787 John Beauchamp and wife Mary Beauchamp sold to Samuel Smith 160 acres of LEDOURN, HOG YARD, ENLARGEMENT.
13 Feb 1787 Elijah Beauchamp divided lands with John Beauchamp.
1 Jun 1789 Elijah Beauchamp sold to Thomas Beauchamp, his rights.
8 Jan 1790 John Beauchamp, wife Ann Beauchamp sold to Thomas Beauchamp 38 acres.
8 Jan 1790 Ann Beauchamp and Thomas Beauchamp sold to Thomas Adams, THREE BROTHERS, HOGYARD, LEDBOURN, ENLARGEMENT, except 40 acres of hers.
24 Jan 1790 Thomas Beauchamp, wife Martha Beauchamp sold to Thomas Adams 203 1/4 acres of same.
20 Sep.1796 Thomas Beauchamp Sr. and wife Sarah Beauchamp sold to William Williams 166 3/4 acres of LEDBOURN, HOGYARD, ENLARGEMENT, BEAUCHAMPS VENTURE, SMALL HOPES.
11 Jan 1798 William Williams, wife Polly Williams sold to Thomas Adams 55 acres of LEDBOURN, BEAUCHAMPS VENTURE, HOG YARD, ENLARGEMENT, etc.
11 Jan 1798 William Williams, wife Polly Williams, sold to Samuel Smith 33 1/2 acres of LEDBOURN, ENLARGEMENT, HOG YARD, BEAUCHAMPS VENTURE.
1813 Samuel Smith willed lands to sons James Smith and Samuel Smith.

HOG YARD

Patented in 1750 by Thomas Benston for 16 acres in Dublin, Election district 4, map #13.
20 Aug.1787 Thomas Benston sold to Samuel Wilson, lands MIDDLE, COWPASTURE, GREEN MEADOW, HOGYARD.
19 Nov.1795 Major Samuel Wilson son of Samuel, and wife Leah Wilson, sold to Littleton Dennis 16 acres.
31 March 1810 Thomas Benston, James Barrett, wife Catherine Barrett sold to Littleton Dennis.

HOG YARD

Patented in 1752 by Aaron Tilghman for 50 acres in Westover, Election district 13, map #11.
14 Feb 1765 Elijah Tilghman sold to Edward Waters 50 acres.
1783 tax- Edward Waters
1784 John Waters willed to daughters Elizabeth Maddux, Sarah Waters and to niece Esther Waters.
1787 upper part resurveyed to DEER PARK.

HOG YARD

Patented in 1757 to John Givans for 21 acres in Westover, Election district 13, map #10
1783 tax- John Givans Sr.
1793 John Gibbons willed lands to wife Martha Gibbons and after death to son John Gibbons.

HOG YARD

Patented in 1762 by Henry Schoolfield for 30 1/2 acres in Brinkleys, northeast, Election district 3, map #15.
1783 tax- Isaac B. Schoolfield 23 acres.
1783 tax- Henry Schoolfield 10 1/2 acres
4 Aug.1780 Henry Schoolfield the younger, wife Elizabeth Schoolfield, sold

to Henry Schoolfield Sr,23 acres..
1782 Henry Schoolfield willed to son Isaac Bozman Schoolfield
1786 Isaac Bozman Schoolfield willed to wife Rachel Schoolfield,
plantation, after death to brother Benjamin Schoolfield-unnamed land.

HOLD HOLLAND

see DISPENCE

HOLLANDS CHANCE

Patented in 1759 by Michael Holland Jr. from part of FERRY BRIDGE, for
220 1/4 acres in Lawsons, Election district 8, map #18.
17 March 1773 Michael Holland Jr. sold to Robert Holland 56 3/4 acres for
5 shillings.
1783 tax- Robert Holland 50 acres.
1783 tax- Michael Holland 166 acres.
16 Oct.1789 Robert Holland and wife Mary Holland sold to Michael Holland
the younger 40 acres.

HOLLWELL

Patented in 13 March 1679 by Thomas Sewell for 100 acres in Westover,
Election district 13, map #11.
27 Dec.1681 Thomas Sewell and wife Jane Sewell sold to Robert Catlin 30
acres called CONTENTION, of BOYCES BRANCH & HOLLWELL.
1692/3 Thomas Sewell gave to daughter Mary Sewell.
Rent Rolls, 1666-1723 possessed by Jeffrey Long in right of his wife Mary
Long.
1732 Jeffrey Long gave lands (unnamed) to sons Samuel Long and Jeffrey
Long.
8 Feb.1757 William Catlin leased for 99 years to Stacey Miles and William
Long,that Thomas Sewell sold to Robert Catlin pt. BOYCES BRANCH &
HOLLWELL it became right of William Catlin for 99 years.
1783 tax- William Long 100 acres.
6 Aug.1792 John Turpin son of Nehemiah Turpin, and wife Sarah Turpin sold
to Thomas Lister 60 1/4 acres of HOLLWELL,CURTIS LOTT,WILSONS LOTT- prop
of William Long deceased and 1/4 part became the property of Sarah Turpin
wife of John Turpin.
17 Jan 1805 Samuel Long, wife Elizabeth Long sold to Isaac Beauchamp and
George Beauchamp 57 3/4 acres he received from distribution of father
William Long, estate, no name.

HOLSTONS CHOICE

Patented on 10 May 1683 by Robert Holston and William Brittingham for 150
acres in Brinkleys Southeast, Election district 3, map #16.
Rent Rolls 1666-1723 possessed by William Brittingham by survivorship.
150 acres.
1709 William Brittingham of Acco.Co.Va. willed to son Nathaniel
Brittingham. Son Samuel Brittingham to have pasture rights.
7 Nov.1720 Nathaniel Brittingham of Acco.Co.Va.and wife Sarah
Brittingham, sold to Phillip Quinton. 150 acres.
18 Nov.1729 Phillip Quinton,carpenter, and wife Abigail Quinton sold to
Thomas Hayward, upper half 75 acres.
1730 resurveyed 160 acres,by Phillip Quinton and Thomas Hayward.

18 Aug.1731 Francis Thorogood of Va. sold to Phillip Quinton 75 acres.
18 June 1740 Nathaniel Brittingham of Acco.Co.Va. traded 5 acres to John
Dennis for 5 acres of LINE LOTT.
19 June 1740 Thomas Hayward,wife Sarah Hayward, sold to Collins Adams.
19 Oct.1750 Phillip Quinton of Worc.Co. sold to Collins Adams 160 acres.
1755 Collins Adams willed to sons Jacob Adams and Phillip Adams.
27 May 1777 I Phillip Adams of Worc.Co. son of Collins Adams am bound to
Jacob Adams of Som.Co. for 500 lbs that Collins Adams gave to son Phillip
Adams, part HOUSTONS CHOICE,SNOW HILL & COLLINS ADVENTURE.
26 Feb.1778 Jacob Adams sold to Gertrude Adams 160 acres.

HONEST INTENT

Patented in 1764 by Aaron Sterling and Isaac Moore for 36 acres in
Asbury,Election district 12, map #21.

HONEST DESIGN

See LONG RIDGE in Westover.

HOPE

Patented on 2 May 1682 by John White for 100 acres in Tangier, Election
district 11,map #7.
Rent Rolls 1666-1723 possessed by John White.
29 Aug.1721 Rowland Jones,planter, and wife Jane Jones sold to Lewis
Jones 100 acres.
1744 Lewis Jones willed lands to sons Samuel Jones and Lewis Jones.

HOPE STILL

Patented on 2 Dec.1722 by Mary Hampton and conveyed to Southy Whittington
for 220 acres in Crisfield, Election district 7, map #20.
20 Aug.1734 Southy Whittington and wife Mary Whittington sold to William
Juett.
1805 Nathaniel Juett willed land to be sold. HOPESTILL 200 acres.
29 Aug.1809 John Summers Sr., & William Juett sold to Elijah Pruitt 200
acres, per will Nathaniel Juett.

HOPEWELL

Patented on 26 June 1679 by John Caldwell for 100 acres in Lawsons,
Election district 8, map #19.
16 March 1721 John Caldwell gave to Sarah Davis 50 acres.
1721 resurveyed to 50 acres.
Rent Rolls 1666-1723 possessed by Thomas Davis.
2 Aug.1769 Samuel Cox sold to Jacob Milbourn 50 acres,with pt. UPPER
UNDUE.
20 May 1772 Samuel Cox sold to Jacob Milbourn pt. 5 acres and 3 1/2 acres
that Milbourn bought of Cox before.
Rent Rolls 1774- possessed by Jacob Milbourn.
11 May 1805 Jacob Milbourn sold to Benjamin Lankford 1/4 acre.

HOPEWELL

Patented on 15 Nov.1683 by William Furniss and assigned to William Berry for 300 acres in Westover,Election district 13, map #10.
Rent Rolls 1666-1723 possessed by James Berry.
10 Nov.1716 James Berry and wife Jane Berry sold to John Gibbons 300 acres.
1735 John Gibbons willed to grandchildren John Gibbons,Thomas Gibbons sons of John Gibbons.
1 Sep.1752 Thomas Gibbons son of John sold his moity to John Gibbons grandson of John deceased. 150 acres.
24 March 1764 John Gibbons sold for 5 shillings to Aaron Tilghman 10 acres.
6 March 1782 William Gibbons mortgaged to Samuel Wilson all his lands.
1783 tax- Thomas Gibbons Jr. 150 acres
1783 tax- John Gibbons Sr. 140 acres
1783 tax- William Gibbons 10 1/2 acres
10 Sep.1787 Sarah Marshall adm. of Isaac Marshall sold to William Gibbons for 5 shillings, which Aaron Tilghman died seized of.
13 July 1788 William Gibbons mortgaged to Samuel Wilson and Levin Miles, all lands.
1789 tax- Thomas Gibbons 150 acres.
1789 tax- John Gibbons III, 150 acres.
13 Aug.1792 William Gibbons, wife Mary Gibbons sold to Levin Miles 200 acres of POOLS HOPE,TILGHMANS ADVENTURE,TILGHMANS GOOD LUCK, HOPEWELL, DUBLIN, TILGHMANS CHANCE, GIDEONS LUCK.
11 Aug.1795 Thomas Gibbons and wife Mary Gibbons sold to Isaac Gibbons 300 acres.
1793 John Gibbons willed to daughter Martha Gibbons 1/2 manor plantation and lands to son John Gibbons- no name.
6 April 1804 Edward Stogdol Miles and Levin Miles sold to George Robertson, Peter Waters and John Bell merchants, lands from father Levin Miles- no names or acreage.
1826 John Gibbons Jr. willed to father John Gibbons HOPEWELL that I purchased of him being part grandfather John Gibbons divised to my father John Gibbons and aunt Martha Gibbons. After death of father to brother William Gibbons.

HOPEWELL

Patented on 14 May 1688 by Dennis Haggarty for 350 acres in East Pr.Anne, Election district 15, map #4.
Rent Rolls 1666-1723 person fled the county since and nothing is heard of him.
1706/7 James Hayman willed to sons Henry Hayman, James Hayman and John Hayman.
28 Oct.1736 James Hayman sold to brother Charles Hayman Jr. 100 acres.
1783 tax- John M. Hayman 56 acres
1783 tax- Betty Hayman 30 acres
1783 tax- Charles Hayman 104 acres
1783 tax- James Hayman 49 acres
1783 tax- Charles Hayman 64 acres.
26 Sep.1795 John Harris Hayman,wife Sarah Hayman sold 134 acres to Kirk Gunby.
1796 Kirk Gunby willed to wife Elizabeth Gunby lands unnamed and after death to brother Elisha Gunby.
17 Feb 1797 Sarah Hayman sold to Hezekiah Hayman, as Revel Hayman willed

to wife Sarah Hayman lands to be sold.
1 March 1800 Hezekiah Hayman sold to John Pollitt 27 1/2 acres.
2 Aug.1800 Kirk Gunby sold to Hezekiah Hayman 134 acres
13 Sep.1808 John Wilkins, sheriff sold to Peter Dashiell 142 1/4 acres
per judgement against Hezekiah Hayman.
1825 John Hayman willed part to son James Hayman and grandchildren Thomas
Handy Hayman and Elizabeth Hayman.

HOPEWELL

Patented on 15 March 1705 by William Faucett for 75 acres in Fairmount,
Election district 6, map #9.
Rent Rolls 1666-1723 William Faucett.
4 March 1714 William Faucett granted to John Tull 1/2.
11 June 1720 John Tull and Esther Tull sold to Sarah Tull relic of
Thomas Tull 37 1/2 acres.
1735 William Faucett,per will, sold to William Foxen.
11 Feb.1744 Thomas Tull son of Sarah Tull deceased, and wife Rachel Tull
sold to David Wilson 37 1/2 acres.
1750 David Wilson gave part to son Ephraim Wilson.
1756 Henry Miles willed to son Henry Miles.
16 June 1762 Joshua Tull sold to William Turpin son of William 3 acres.
20 Sep.1767 Ephraim Wilson,wife Mary Wilson sold to Henry Miles for 5
shillings 103 acres of HOPEWELL & FATHERS CARE.
20 Nov.1767 Henry Miles sold to Zorobable Hall 48 acres of MILES
CONCLUSION & HOPEWELL.
1783 tax- Henry Miles 37 1/2 acres
1783 tax- Joshua Tull 34 acres.
1783 tax- Denwood Turpin 3 acres.
1785 Zorobable Hall willed to son James Hall plantation where I live
purchased of Henry Miles 49 acres, unnamed.
20 Oct.1794 Joshua Tull son of John Tull gave to son Thomas Tull 37 1/2
acres.
1811 Thomas Tull,wife Leah Tull, willed to son William Tull land between
Annamessex and Manokin Rivers, unnamed.

HOPEWELL

Patented in 1741 by William Juett for 96 acres in Asbury, Election
district 12, map #21.
13 Nov.1769 Nathaniel Juett sold to Stephen Ward 32 acres.
1783 tax- Nathaniel Juett 36 acres.
1783 tax- Stephen Ward 33 acres
7 Jan 1800 John Ward son of Stephen Ward, now of Kentucky sold to Jacob
Cullen.
1805 Nathaniel Juett willed lands to be sold- unnamed.

HOPEWELL

Patented in 1762 by Stephen Ward for 30 1/2 acres in Asbury, Election
district 12, map #21
1783 Stephen Ward willed to son John Ward, manor plantation, unnamed.

HOPKINS DESTINY

Patented on 27 Feb.1673 by George Johnson for 50 acres in Fairmount, Election district 6, map #9.
Rent Rolls 1666-1723 Poss.by Thomas Everton refused to pay rent in right of his wife, the heir and right of a minor in England.
20 May 1682 Katherine Johnson widow of George Johnson sold to Charles Hall 50 acres.
1695 Charles Hall willed to wife Alice Hall, 50 acres.
1717 Alice Hall gave 50 acres to son-in-law John Roach and wife Alice Roach.
1726/7 John Roach willed to son William Roach 50 acres.
31 Aug.1762 William Roach of Worc.Co. sold to Ballard Bozman 50 acres for 5 shilling with PARTNERS CHOICE.
20 Nov.1770 Ballard Bozman sold to Revel Horsey 50 acres.
1783 tax- Revel Horsey 50 acres.
1805 Revel Horsey willed to Henry King son of Nehemiah King 1/2 of this land.

HORSE HAMMOCK

Patented on 24 May 1700 by James Curtis for 100 acres in Fairmount, Election district 6, map #9.
Rent Rolls 1666-1723 possessed by James Curtis.
1720 James Curtis willed to son Charles Curtis and daughter Esther Curtis.
11 Oct.1734 Charles Curtis and wife Mary Curtis sold to Solomon Long 100 acres.
21 Oct.1746 Solomon Long and wife Margaret Long sold 100 acres to James Polk.
10 July 1750 James Polk and wife Betty Polk sold to William Turpin.
1783 tax- John Turpin 100 acres.
2 Jan 1807 Solomon Long, wife Nelly sold to William Parks.

HORSEYS ADDITION

Patented in 1764 by Smith Horsey for 13 1/2 acres in Lawsons, Election district 8, map #18.

HORSEYS CHANCE

Patented in 1759 by Stephen Horsey for 223 acres in Brinkleys, northwest, Election district 3, map #14.
8 Sep.1776 Stephen Horsey of Worc.Co. sold for 10 shillings to Smith Horsey of Som.Co. 223 acres.
1784 tax- heirs of Smith Horsey 223 acres.
1781 Smith Horsey willed to wife Mary Horsey 1/3rd and lands to son John Horsey, if no heir to son Smith Horsey.

HORSEYS CHANCE

Patented 1666 by Stephen Horsey for 300 acres in West Pr. Anne, Election district 1, map #2.
22 Jan 1666 Stephen Horsey sold to Alexander Mitchell
16 Dec.1734 John Mitchell sold to Peter Sirman Sr. 100 acres all moity given John Mitchell by his father John, who left it to sons Richard

Mitchell and John Mitchell, with CANTERBURY.
2 Oct.1734 Richard Mitchell and wife Mary Mitchell sold to Alexander
Adams rector of Stepney Parish 84 acres out of HORSEYS CHANCE & 16 acres
of CANTERBURY.
15 Jan.1735 resurveyed to include CANTERBURY 201 acres by Alexander Adams
and Peter Sirman.
15 Oct.1748 Peter Sirman and wife Mary Sirman sold to Thomas Gillis 187
acres, with TROUBLE CRAMBURN,CANTERBURY.
1770 Thomas Gillis willed to dau-in-law Sarah Gillis widow of son Levin
Gillis, deceased, 3 tracts CANTERBURY,CRAMBOURN & HORSEYS CHOICE 200
acres.
21 March 1750 Alexander Adams, gave to son John Adams his rights 101
acres.
1783 tax- Thomas Fountain 78 acres.
28 Sep.1790 Joseph Gillis son of Thomas Gillis, and wife Elizabeth Gillis
sold to Thomas Fountain 87 acres.
25 March 1807 Thomas Hamilton Jr. mortgaged to Benjamin F.A.C. Dashiell,
part devised by William Adams Jr.
9 Nov.1808 Thomas G. Fountain sold to Robert J. King, CRAMBURN, HORSEYS
CHANCE, WALLEYS CHANCE, EDINBURGH 165 1/4 acres.
1810 Robert J. King sold to Levin King Jr.

HORSEYS CONCLUSION

Patented in 1745 by Outerbridge Horsey for 542 acres in Brinkleys,
northwest, Election district 8, map #18.
26 Aug.1758 Stephen Horsey son of Samuel sold for 5 shillings to
Outerbridge Horsey 542 acres.
1774 There was a resurvey by Outerbridge Horsey for 507 acres, not on
Bensons Maps, assumed to be this property called THE GROVE.
1783 tax- Outerbridge Horsey
1785 Outerbridge Horsey willed to son William Horsey and then to grandson
William son of William Horsey.
11 March 1797 Outerbridge Horsey son of William Horsey grandson of
Outerbridge Horsey sold to William Hitch.
12 March 1792 William Hitch sold to Outerbridge Horsey.
13 March 1802 Outerbridge Horsey of Deleware sold to Benjamin Conner of
Md. 50 acres.
25 Oct.1802 Outerbridge Horsey of Delaware sold to John Horsey of Smith
Horsey of Somerset Co. 50 acres.
22 Oct.1803 Outerbridge Horsey, attorney of GeorgeTown Del. sold to Dr.
Thomas Robertson Jr. 154 1/2 acres.
11 Nov.1803 Noah Holland sold Thomas Robertson Jr. 51 1/2 acres and it
was returned the same day- probably a mortgage.
12 March 1807 Thomas Robertson Jr. sold to Noah Holland 51 1/2 acres.
12 March 1807 Noah Holland, wife Betsy Holland sold to William W.
Schoolfield 51 1/2 acres.
7 Aug.1807 Dr. Thomas Roertson Jr. and wife Mary Robertson sold 28 acres
to Isaac Dixon called THE GROVE.
4 Jan 1808 William W. Schoolfield, wife Catherine Schoolfield sold to
William Miles 50 1/4 acres.
26 March 1808 John Miles constable, sold to William Miles 51 1/2 acres
per judgement against William W. Schoolfield.
1 Dec.1808 Thomas Robertson Jr, physician sold to Rizdon Bozman 103
acres.

9 June 1809 Thomas Robertson, wife Hariett Robertson sold to William
Williams 13 acres 2 rods, 19 perches THE GROVE.
13 Sep.1809 Thomas Robertson, wife Hariett Robertson sold to Benjamin
Lankford 70 1/4 acres THE GROVE.
26 Aug.1809 Rizdon Bozman sold to Jesse Johnson 1 acre.
13 Sep.1809 Thomas Robertson Jr. sold to Joseph Lankford 20 acres THE
GROVE.
1810 Rizdon Bozman willed to brother William Bozman 102 acres.

HORSEYS DOWN

Patented on 29 April 1680 by William Stevens and assigned to Stephen
Horsey for 150 acres in Lawsons Election district 8, map #18.
12 Aug.1673 Stephen Horsey son of Stephen sold to Thomas Cottingham.
Rent Rolls 1666-1723 68 acres Anthony Bell by sale from Horsey & 82 acres
Stephen Horsey.
1721 Stephen Horsey willed to son John Horsey.
1741 Anthony Bell willed land, not mentioned by name to sons Thomas Bell,
Josephas Bell, Isaac Bell and daughter Rachel Bell. Wife Abigail.
4 April 1745 Thomas Bell son of Anthony Bell, and wife Elizabeth Bell
sold to Josephus Bell 68 acres.
1753 Charles Cottingham gave to children Charles Cottingham, Thomas
Cottingham, John Cottingham, Rachel Cottingham land bought from Stephen
Horsey by my father Thomas Cottingham.
12 Nov.1762 Daniel Bell of Dorc.Co. Md. son of Thomas Bell sold to Joseph
Bell 176 acres of MOREWORTH & HORSEY DOWN.
1783 tax- John Horsey, 260 acres with HORSEYS LOTT & WATKINS POINT.

HORSEYS FANCY

Patented on 15 May 1698 for 150 acres by Stephen Horsey in Lawsons,
Election district 8, map #18.
Rent Rolls 1666-1723 Stephen Horsey.

HORSEYS LOT

Patented in 1751 by Outerbridge Horsey for 51 acres in Brinkleys,
northwest, Election district 3, map #14.
1783 tax- Outerbridge Horsey 51 acres.
1785 Outerbridge Horsey willed to grandson William Horsey.
11 March 1797 Outerbridge Horsey son of William Horsey,grandson of
Outerbridge Horsey sold to William Hitch.
12 March 1792 William Hitch sold to Outerbridge Horsey.
15 April 1807 Lazarus Horsey sold to Thomas Robertson, his claim.

HORSEYS LOTT

Patented in 1768 by John Horsey for 39 acres in Lawsons,Election district
8, map #18.
1783 tax- John Horsey

HORSEYS PREVENTION

Patented in 1757 by Outerbridge Horsey for 280 1/4 acres in Brinkleys,
northwest,Election district 3, map #14.

226

9 June 1759 Isaac Dixon (division of lands) to Outerbridge Horsey of
DIXONS CHOICE,DIXONS BULL,HORSEYS PREVENTION.
17843 tax- Outerbridge Horsey 280 1/2 acres
1785 Outerbridge Horsey willed to son Isaac Horsey.
17 May 1784 Samuel Bedsworth sold 8 acres to Thomas Williams.
25 April 1807 Lazarus Horsey sold to Thomas Robertson, all his claim to
HORSEYS PREVENTION, HORSEYS LOTT, DIXONS KINDNESS, DIXONS CHOICE
ENLARGED, DAM QUARTER and 102 1/4 acre of vacant land called THE GROVE,
DIXONS BULL & DIXONS ADDITION.

HORSEYS VENTURE

Patented in 1749 by Smith Horsey for 47 acres in Brinkleys, northwest,
Election district 3, map #14.
1783 tax- heirs of Smith Horsey
1802 ADDITION patented to John Horsey for 46 3/4 acres.

HOUSTONS ADVENTURE

Patented in 1805 by Levi Houston for 176 3/4 acres in Brinkleys,
southeast,Election district 3, map #16.
19 April 1817 Daniel Boston bought of Robert Swan 100 acres.
24 Dec.1830 Ann Boston and Susan Boston bought of Daniel Boston.
1862 Ann Boston gave to nephew Solomon C. Boston all estate.
1869/72 Susan Boston deeded to nephew Solomon C. Boston her 1/2 share.

HUDSONS FOLLY

Patented on 2 Nov.1668 by Henry Hudson and assigned to Nicholas Hudson
for 200 acres in Brinkleys,southeast, Election district 13, map #16.
11 March 1673 Nicholas Hudson and wife Elizabeth Hudson sold 200 acres to
William Giles and George Phoebus.
4 Nov.1675 William Giles and wife Doris Giles, and George Phoebus sold to
Henry Smith.
1706 Jacob Adams purchased 200 acres
17 March 1739 Jacob Adams gave to son Samuel Adams.
1739 resurveyed to ADAMS FOLLY 345 acres by Samuel Adams.

HUDSONS FORTUNE

Patented on 7 Nov.1665 for 100 acres by Henry Hudson in Brinkleys,
southeast,Election district 3, map #16.
1739 resurveyed to ADAMS FOLLY 345 acres.

HUNGARY NECK

see TROUBLE & DENTRY

HUNTING QUARTER

Patented 17 March 1680 by Cornelius Anderson for 100 acres in West
Pr.Anne,Election district 1, map #2.
5 Nov.1687 Cornelius Anderson sold to William Alexander, Rent Rolls
1666-1723 William Alexander or his son.
1732/5 William Alexander willed to son Samuel Alexander land where he
lives 150 acres and to son Moses Alexander 200 acres where I live.

2 May 1749 Moses Alexander, Blacksmith gave to son Samuel Alexander 100 acres.
21 March 1751 Samuel Alexander son of Moses Alexander, wheelwright sold 100 acres to John Dorman.
1783 tax- John Dorman 26 acres.
1821 John Dorman willed estate to son James Dorman(unnamed)

HUNTSMAN FOLLY

Patented in 1757 by William Smith for 414 acres in Westover,Election district 13, map #11.
1770 ADDITION pat. 56 1/2 acres to William Miles.
14 Dec.1778 Samuel Smith, wife Esther Smith sold to Levin Miles 208 acres.
14 Dec.1778 Samuel Smith sold to Stacey Miles 114 acres.
17 Oct.1780 Stacey miles gave to son William Miles 129 acres, two parts.
24 Sep.1782 Levin Miles sold to Isaiah Tilghman, Samuel Curtis,Isaac Handy,Samuel Smith,Thomas Handy,Thomas Miles, John Beauchamp,John Milbourn, and William Tilghman, 1 acre for the Methodist Church.
1783 tax, Levin Miles 188 acres
1783 tax- William Miles 135 acres
1783 tax- Samuel Smith 55 acres.
1785 Stacey Miles willed to son William Miles 337 acres.
3 Sep 1785 William Miles son of Stacey Miles,and wife Nancy Miles sold to Levin Miles 120 acres with ADDITION 56 1/2 acres.
21 Feb.1782 Samuel Smith and wife Esther Smith sold to Samuel Wilson 9 3/4 acres
9 Sep.1788 Samuel Smith sold to Levin Miles 1/4 acre
19 May 1789 Levin Miles, released bond of, to Samuel Smith and Samuel Wilson
9 Aug.1791 Levin Miles and William Tilghman settled dispute and partition of HUNTSMANS FOLLY & SAPLIN RIDGE.
13 Mar.1792 Samuel Smith, John C. Wilson and Samuel Wilson execs. of Samuel Wilson deceased released mortgate to Levin Miles.
5 Nov.1798 Joseph Tilghman,wife Nancy Tilghman sold to George Broughton 122 1/2 acres of HUNTSMANS FOLLY, SMITHS LOTT & EXCHANGE.
24 Feb.1801 George Broughton, wife Alee Broughton sold to William Beauchamp 57 1/4 acres of HUNTSMANS FOLLY, SMYTHS LOTT & EXCHANGE.
24 Feb. 1801 William Beauchamp sold to George Broughton lands Beauchamp holds by deed from Joseph Tilghman and George Broughton 81 1/2 acres- no names.
24 Fe .1801 George Broughton, wife Alee Broughton sold to John Miles 81 1/4 acres of HUNTSMANS FOLLY, SMYTHS LOTT, EXCHANGE.
24 Feb.1801 John Miles sold to George Broughton, same as above, 126 acres.
13 Aug.1809 John Hayman, wife Nancy Hayman of Ohio sold to James Handy son of Isaac Hancy of Som. Co. devised Nancy Hayman by her father William Tilghman, deceased.

IGNOBLE QUARTER

Patented on 1 Nov.1666 by George Andrews for 100 acres in St.Peters, Election district 2, map #6.
13 Aug.1672 George Andrews sold to William Hathely.
9 June 1678 William Hathely, wife Catherine Hathely sold to John Panter

100 acres called WOOLFE HARBOR.
Rent Rolls 1666-1723 poss. by John Panter, AKA WOOLFES HARBOR.
(also see NOBLE QUARTER.)
1713 John Panter willed to Benjamin Sasser 100 acres and at his decease
to his sons Thomas Sasser and Panter Sasser, balance to John Hall Jr.
5 Aug.1729 Benjamin Sasser deeded to William Sasser 100 acres devised by
John Panter in St. Peters district.
25 March 1775 John Laws son of Panter Laws, and wife Sarah
Laws sold 45 acres to Gowan Wright.
1783 tax- William Sasser 50 acres WOOLFES HARBOR
1783 tax- Gowan Wright 43 1/2 acres WOOLFES HARBOR
1793 William Sasser willed lands to son Benjamin Sasser, unnamed.
1805 Gowan Wright willed lands to daughters Mary Wright, Sarah Wright,
Ann Wright, unnamed.

ILLCHESTER

Patented on 25 May 1683 by Henry Smith for 700 acres in East Pr.Anne,
Election district 15, map #5.
1715 John Smith of Sussex Co.Del.sole surviving male heir and grandson of
Henry Smith sold to James Strawbridge.
Rent Rolls 1666-1723 possessed by-
 John King 150 acres
 Margaret Goldsmith 100 acres
 William Knox 150 acres
 James Strawbridge 500 acres.
1721 resurveyed 100 acres, to tract CONVENIENCY.
4 July 1719 John Goldsmith and wife Catherine Goldsmith, sold to John
Gray Jr. 100 acres part called GOLDSMITHS DELIGHT.
1732 William Knox and Jemima Knox of Kent Co.Del.and John Knox of Dorc.
Co. Md. sons of John Knox sold to James Strawbridge 150 acres.
13 Feb.1735/6 Robert Knox and wife Margaret Knox sold to James
Strawbridge 150 acres that Henry Smith conveyed to William Owens and
William Owens and wife Ann Owens conveyed to William Knox, and it
descended to Robert Knox and his son.
23 Oct.1741 James Strawbridge gave to son-in-law Jacob Williams and wife
Mary Williams 150 acres.
1743 Resurveyed to WIDOWS CHANGE 1059 acres.
20 Aug.1746 Jacob Williams and wife Mary Williams sold to Jane
Strawbridge 150 acres.
16 Nov.1748 Jane Strawbrdige sold to Thomas Dixon 150 acres.
27 July 1752 Thomas Dixon sold to William Polk 150 acres.
26 Nov.1754 James Gray and William Gray sold to Jarvis Ballard 100 acres.
1762 ADDITION 156 acres by William Polk
1766 William Strawbridge gave ADDITION TO ILLCHESTER to daughter Jane
Strawbridge, 156 acres, who died intestate by 1796 and land was sold.
1783 tax- James Polk 150 acres
1783 tax- James Polk ADDITION 156 acres.
12 March 1799 William Ballard son of James Ballard sold to Levin Ballard
100 acres.
29 March 1800 William Ballard of Jarvis sold to Lambert Hyland 100 acres
of GOLDSMITHS DELIGHT.
30 March 1800 Priscilla Walston widow of Jarvis Ballard sold to Lambert
Hyland, her dower rights.
1802 William Polk willed to son John Polk ADDITION.

IMPROVEMENT

Patented in 1775 by Denwood Wilson for 47 acres in West Pr.Anne, Election disrict 1, map #3.
1798 Denwood Wilson willed lands to sons Samuel Wilson and William Witherspoon Wilson.
1849 resurveyed to EDGE HILL.

INCLOSURE

Patented in 1740 by Thomas Maddux, a resurvey from MADDUX INCLOSURE for 590 acres in Fairmount,Election district 6, map #9.
1783 tax- John Maddux, 590 acres

INCREASE

Patented on 13 Sep.1723 by Robert Weir for 350 acres in Lawsons, Election district 8, map #18.
Rent Rolls, 1666-1723 poss. by Robert Weir.

INDIAN BONES

Patented in 1723, by Jesse King,a resurvey of KINGS GLAD, for 100 acres in Dublin and East Princess Anne, Election districts 12 & 13, maps #4 & #5.
21 June 1749 Jesse King and wife Mary King sold 7 1/2 acres to Thomas Bannister.
25 Oct.1759 Mitchell Bannister and wife Abigail Bannister, and William Bannister, brothers, sold to James Furniss Jr. son of James.
23 July 1765 Zorobable King sold 106 1/2 acres of CLOVERFIELD & INDIAN BONES & KINGS GLADE to Dorman Turpin.
22 June 1768 William Turpin sold to Zorobable King and Denwood Turpin 1/3 part, his right of dower of his now wife Betty Turpin.
22 Nov.1771 Denwood Turpin sold to William Miles 106 acres of lands purchased from Zorobable King.
7 Jan 1772 William Miles sold to Isaac Handy, that Denwood Turpin conveyed to William Miles.
17 March 1772 James Furniss sold to Isaac Handy, attorney 7 1/2 acres.
25 March 1771 Denwood Turpin and wife Elizabeth Turpin sold to Isaac Handy 100 acres of CLOVERFIELDS & KINGS GLADE, INDIAN BONES.
25 May 1773 Jesse King sold to Zorobable King for 5 shilings 73 3/4 acres.
1783 tax- William Polk for heirs of Isaac Handy 7 1/2 acres
1794 Zorobable King willed lands to son Levin King, unnamed.
8 Jan 1805 Richard Henry Handy, wife Elizabeth Handy sold to Littleton Dennis Teackle, as heir of Isaac Handy.
29 Oct.1807 Littleton Dennis Teackle sold to John Teackle of Georgetown DC. land bought of Richard Henry Handy, unnamed.
12 May 1810 John Teackle of Georgetown DC sold to John Pershouse of Philadelphia Pa. part.

INDIAN RIDGE

Patented in 1758 by William Gray for 45 acres in Dublin, Election district 4, map #12.

3 Nov.1761 William Gray son of Allen Gray sold to John Tull
1770 resurveyed to BALTIMORE 482 acres.
1780 John Tull willed to daughter Sarah Tull a small piece of land bought
of William Gray 42 1/4 acres (unnamed.)

INDUSTRY

Patented in 1746 by William Adams and Aaron Sterling in Brinkleys,
southwest,Election district 3, map #17.
12 Nov.1750 William Adams sold 75 acres to Thomas Adams.
1767 Thomas Adams willed to son David Adams 212 acres formerly INDUSTRY &
other tracts, now called PRIVILEDGE.
6 Oct.1767 Thomas Adams Sr. sold for 5 shillings to son David Adams 75
acres.
1783 tax- William Adams 75 acres
1842 Patrick Causey willed 100 acres to daughter Emeline Causey.

INDUSTRY

Patented in 1748 by Aaron Sterling for 5 acres in Asbury, Election
district 12, map #21.
1783 tax- Aaron Sterling 5 acres.

INLARGEMENT

Patented on 20 Nov.1680 by Thomas Davis for 100 acres in Lawsons,
Election district 8, map #18.
1689 resurveyed to TROUBLESOME.

INTENT

Patented in 1752 by Henry Wright, a resurvey includes LOTT, for 317 acres
in St.Peters,Election district 2, map #6.
18 June 1754 Henry Wright and wife Mary Wright sold to brother Thomas
Wright 155 acres.
3 May 1759 Thomas Wright, now of Ann Arundel Co.Md. sold to Thomas Aikman
and John Webb 155 acres with CONTENTION & INTENT.
25 May 1761 Thomas Aikman and John Webb agree to partition.
14 Dec.1762 Thomas Wright of Ann Arundel Co. sold to Thomas Aikman, part.
2 May 1775 John Wright son of Henry Wright, sold to Gowan Wright 242
acres with CONTENTION & INTENT.
1783 tax- Gowan Wright 167 acres
1783 tax- Robert Cavanaugh 95 acres
3 Jan.1792 John Webb sold to Gowan Wright 40 acres.
2 Sep.1802 John Webb, wife Hetty Webb sold to Thomas Noble.
1805 Gowan Wright willed lands to Mary Wright,Sarah Wright and Ann Wright
(unnamed lands)

INTENTION

Patented in 1819 to Richard Hall for 123 1/8 acres in Brinkleys,
northwest,Election district 3, map #14.
1838 Richard Hall willed to son Henry W. Hall.

IRELAND

Patented in 1769 by Thomas Hayward a resurvey of ADDITION & PROFIT, for 353 acres in Dublin,Election district 4, map #12.
1783 tax- Thomas Hayward 350 acres.
1792 Thomas Hayward willed to son Thomas Hayward.
1836 Levin Pollitt willed to John Corbin part and part to Robert Corbin son of John.

IRISH GROVE

Patented on 10 Nov.1665 by Morris Lister for 150 acres in Brinkleys, southwest,Election district 3, map #17.
10 Aug.1669 Morris Lister sold to Daniel Donoho 150 acres with 45 acres of a small island of marsh.
10 July 1697 Daniel Donoho and wife Alice Donoho sold to Sampson Wheatley.
22 Aug.1701 Sampson Wheatley sold to Phillip Conner part.
Rent Rolls 1666-1723 possessed by-
 Phillip Conner 22 1/2 acres
 Sampson Wheatley 100 acres
 Alexander Maddux 22 1/2 acres
15 May 1724 Phillip Conner and wife Catherine Conner sold to John Outten 22 1/2 acres.
1783 tax- Mary Wheatley 100 acres.
24 June 1786 Caleb Jones and wife Betty Jones daughter of Sampson Wheatley, sold to Kellum Lankford, Elijah Coulbourn and Thomas Jones of Annamessex, IRISH GROVE, WHEATLEYS SECOND ADDITION, NEW BOSTON, etc. no acreage given.
24 April 1805 Benjamin Conner,wife Grace Conner, Noah Lankford, wife Ann Lankford, Benjamin Bedsworth, John Broughton, wife Mary Broughton, Richard Hall, wife Sarah Purnell Hall, and Mary Bedsworth sold to Mordicai Jones of St. Marys County, MERCHANTS TREASURE,GREENFIELD, WHEATLEYS SECOND ADDITION, PRIVILEDGE, LITTLEWORTH, BOSTON, DAMM SWAMP, ADAMS CHANCE, devised by Sampson Wheatley to daughter Betty Jones and conveyed by Caleb Jones, wife Betty Jones to Kellum Lankford, Elijah Coulbourn and Thomas Jones, now deceased.

IRISH GROVE

Patented on 6 Nov.1665 by Daniel Quillan for 150 acres in Brinkleys,southeast, Election district 3, map #16.
March 1673 Daniel Quillan and Lydia Quillan his wife sold to Edward Dickinson 150 acres.
26 Oct.1675 Edward Dickinson and wife Elizabeth Dickinson sold to Thomas Owens 150 acres.
Rent Rolls 1666-1723 possessed by Peter Carsley.
20 March 1744 Robert Carsley and wife Mary Carsley sold to William Carsley 89 acres.
16 Mar.1752 William Carsley and wife Elizabeth Carsley traded 50 acres with Samuel Adams for SHOEMAKERS MEADOW.
6 Feb.1764 Partition of lands- William Carlsey son of Peter Carsley, Samuel Carlsey son of Peter and William Carsley the younger son of Peter Carsley as eldest son. That Peter Carsley the elder in 1716 willed to William (father of afsd.William Carsley)Richard Carsley,Samuel Carsley,Robert Carsley and Peter Carsley. Richard died young and Peter

died, leaving William and Richard surviving brothers.
2 Dec.1767 William Carsley Jr. and wife Elizabeth Carsley sold to William
Carsley Sr. 45 acres.
According to Bensons maps this entire tract was resurveyed to KAERSLEYS
INDUSTRY in 1701 - 300 acres.
1783 tax- Peter Carsley 129 acres.

INVEY

Patented in 1748 by Thomas Seon for 104 acres in Fairmount, Election
district 6, map #9.
28 March 1757 Thomas Seon and wife Jane Seon sold to James Willis 9 1/2
acres that Barnaby Willis father of James gave to Thomas Seon.
7 Jan 1772 Jabez Willis eldest son of William Willis sold to James Willis
all BARNABYS LOTT and ENVY.
6 March 1772 James Willis sold to Thomas Seon 2 acres.
1780 Thomas Seon willed to nephew Joseph Handy land bought of James
Willis (unnamed)
26 Sep.1781 James Willis sold to Thomas Sudler 90 acres between Whitty
Turpin and Thomas Sudler(unnamed.)
1783 tax- James Willis 7 acres
1783 tax- Thomas Seon Sudler 96 1/2 acres.
1798 resurveyed to SUDLERS CONCLUSION 419 acres.

ISAACS FORTUNE

Patented in 1771 by Isaac White for 449 acres, a resurvey to include
ADDITION TO BROTHERS LOVE & CORK. in Brinkleys,southeast,Election
district 3, map #6.
1780 Isaac White willed to eldest daughter Abigail White and to daughter
Nancy White.
1783 tax- Ann White 149 acres.
13 Aug.1790 Elijah Matthews sold to Stephen Collins 156 acres of BROTHERS
LOVE, CORK,MEADOW,ADVENTURE,ISAACS FORTUNE.
3 March 1797 Josiah Lankford,wife Abigail Lankford sold to Thomas
Williams Jr.
23 Feb 1798 Thomas Williams sold to Isaac Riggin 150 acres
4 Dec.1806 Isaac Riggin, wife Nancy Riggin sold to Isaac McCready 3
acres.
1834 Isaac Riggin willed to son Stephen Riggin 150 acres.
1841 Stephen Riggin willed to son Joshua James Riggin 164 acres.

JAMES CONTENT
Patented in 1752 by James Spicer, a resurvey that includes WHITE OAK
SWAMP, for 226 acres in St.Peters, Election district 2, map #6.
12 March 1764 James Spicer sold 84 acres to William McDorman
12 Feb.1756 William McDorman and wife Mary McDorman sold 84 acres to
Samuel Sockwell.
31 Dec.1771 Samuel Sockwell and wife Elizabeth Sockwell sold to Henry
Walston Miles 84 acres.
1783 tax- Henry Walston Miles 84 acres
1783 tax- James Spicer 42 acres.

18 Oct.1806 Henry W. Miles, wife Mary Miles sold to Lewis McDorman
18 Feb.1806 Lewis McDorman, wife Sarah McDorman sold to Henry W. Miles
(signed Lewis Dorman)

JAMES DELIGHT

this is part of DAVIDS DESTINY in Dames Quarter.
1798 tax- Francis White 100 acres
18 March 1789 Francis White sold to Marmaduke Mister, all.
2 Aug.1796 Francis White gave to son William White DAVIDS DESTINY now
called JAMES DELIGHT

JAMES VICTORY OVER HIS ADVERSARY

Patented in 1841 for 63 1/2 acres by John Jones in Tangier, Election
district 9, map #7.

JAMES MEADOW(or POLKS MEADOW)

Patented on 1 June 1705 by James Polk for 200 acres in Dames Quarter,
Election district 11, map #7.
1726/7 James Polk willed plantation to son David Polk, not named.
1783 tax- William Roberts -POLKS MEADOW, 200 acres.
1794 William Roberts willed to neice Nancy Lemon wife of Robert Lemon.
23 July 1799 Charles Jones, wife Esther Jones sold to Archibald McDorman
100 acres of POLKS MEADOW.

JAMESTOWN

Patented in 1722, a resurvey from PRICES VINEYARD,by James Ward for 300
acres in Asbury, Election district 12,map 21.
1783 tax Thomas Ward 100 acres
1783 tax Henry Sterling 25 acres
7 Jan 1800 John Ward son of Stephen Ward, now of Kentucky sold to Jacob
Cullen.

JAMES WILDERNESS

Patented in 1775 by James Wilson for 39 1/2 acres in West Pr.Anne,
Election district 1, map #3.
1783 tax James Wilson 39 1/2 acres.

JENKINS MISTAKE

Patented in 1734, a resurvey of COX'S MISTAKE, for 163 acres in Mt.
Vernon, Election district 5, map #1.
1783 tax- William Jones 163 acres.
2 Oct.1793 Elias Bayley sold 47 acres to James Bennett
1795 resurveyed to RECTIFIED MISTAKE 479 1/4 acres.

JERICHO

Patented on 2 June 1688 by Ambrose London for 100 acres in
Fairmount,Election district 6, map #9.
Rent Rolls 1666-1723 possessed by Samuel Handy
26 May 1722 Thomas Handy appointed brother Ebenezer Handy attorney to
divide land left by father Samuel Handy, equally between brother Samuel

Handy and himself.
1734/5 Samuel Handy willed to sons Samuel Handy and John Handy.
2 Oct.1747 George Tucker of Isle of Barbados, and wife Mary Tucker (Mary
Handy daughter of Thomas handy) sold to Samuel Handy 514 acres of HANDYS
CHOICE,STEPHENS MEADOW,STAKE RIDGE,BLACK RIDGE and 100 acres of JERICHO.
1751 John Handy of Dorc.Co.Md., wife Elizabeth Handy, deeded to Samuel
Handy.
7 Jan 1757 Samuel Handy sold 100 acres to Thomas Seon.
2 Sep.1767 Thomas Seon sold to Whitty Turpin.
1757 maps show this was resurveyed to COW QUARTER
23 Dec.1772 William Hastings sold 42 acres to Joshua Hastings.
1783 tax- Whitty Turpin
1 Aug.1796 Thomas Holbrook and wife Peggy Holbrook sold to Henry Coston
and Whittington King, land conveyed by Thomas Seon to Whitty Turpin
father of Peggy. no name or acreage.
22 May 1804 Whittington King,wife Nancy King, Henry Coston and wife Ann
Coston sold to William King land conveyed by Thomas Holbrook, unnamed.

JERSEY

Patented on 14 May 1689 by Nicholas Toadvine for 100 acres in West
Pr.Anne, Election district 1, map #2.
28 July 1756 Henry Toadvine sold to Alexander Adams,rector of Stepney
parish 100 acres.
1767 resurveyed to DOUBLE PURCHASE.

JESHIMON

Patented on 6 Dec.1662 by David Brown for 50 acres in West Pr.Anne,
Election district 1, map #3.
1697 David Brown willed to nephew Alexander Brown.
Rent Rolls 1666-1723 Alexander Brown
1748/9 John Woolford gave to son Charles Woolford, JESHIMON got by my
wife Mary Woolford(Mary Brown) and Margaret Brown daughters of Alexander
Brown.
12 July 1750 John Woolford, wife Mary Woolford, daughter of Alexander
Brown and coheir of Col.David Brown, sold to Robert Nairn and James
Nairn, their interest.
24 Aug.1750 William Skirvin sold to John Woolford his rights.
1770 resurvey to THOMAS'S BEGINNING
1783 tax- John Marcomb -with HACKLEY 165 acres.
29 Oct.1791 Thomas D. Woolford and William P. Woolford, mortgage to
Denwood Wilson THORNTON,HACKILA,JESHIMON,THOMAS BEGINNING.
26 March 1799 Denwood Wilson released mortgage to William Pitt
Woolford,and James Woolford son of Thomas Woolford.
1836 John Woolford willed to son John Woolford.

JESHIMON

Patented on 10 Sep.1682 to Francis Roberts for 150 acres in Dames
Quarter, Election district 11, map #7, possessed by Ann Roberts the relic
of Francis Roberts.
1783 tax- Bartlett Roberts 50 acres.
1783 tax- William Roberts 48 acres.
1783 tax- John Windsor for Frank Roberts heirs.

1820 resurvey to NEGLECT 406 acres.

JOANS HOLE

Patented on 3 June 1689 by John Kirk for 230 acres in Lawsons,Election
district 8, map #18.
19 Aug.1736 Littleton Townsend and wife Sarah Townsend (Sarah Kirk
daughter of John Kirk) sold to Joseph McClester 1/3rd part of 230 acres.

JOHNS DESIRE

Patented in 1749 for 82 acres by John Adams, in West Pr.Anne, Election
district 1, map #2, a resurvey from TONYS VINEYARD.
17 Dec.1804 Thomas Hamilton and Charles Nutter and wife Louise Nutter his
wife (late Louise Adams) agree to divide the real estate of William Adams
Jr.
25 March 1807 Thomas Hamilton mortgaged to Benjamin F.A.C. Dashiell,
devised by William Adams.
18 Dec.1810 Charles Nutter sold to Daniel Whitney.

JOHNS HILL

Patented in 1768 for 12 acres by Thomas Pollitt in West Pr.Anne, Election
district 1, map #2.
1783 tax- Thomas Pollitt 12 acres
1788 Thomas Pollitt willed to son Levin Pollitt.
9 June 1796 Levin Pollitt, wife Eleanor Pollitt sold to Stephen Wright 12
acres.
1 Dec 1804 Stephen Wright sold to Belitha Wright lands bought of Levin
Pollitt in 1799.

JOHNSONS FIRST CHOICE

Patented on 2 June 1667 by William Stevens and assigned to George
Johnson, for 200 acres in Westover,Election district 13, map #11.
28 Nov.1680 George Johnson bequeathed to wife Katherine Johnson lands
during life time.
Rent Rolls 1666-1723 belongs to orphans in England. Under guardianship
assigned to Capt.Thomas Dixon attorney.
1769 resurveyed to FIRST CHOICE

JOHNSONS LOTT

Patented on 12 Feb.1663 by John Johnson for 200 acres in Asbury, Election
district 12, map #2
9 March 1686 John Johnson, wife Elizabeth Johnson sold to John Roach 63
acres.1
Rent Rolls 1666-1723, possessed by John Cullen by gift from John Johnson.
18 Aug.1742 Jacob Cullen son of John Cullen,deceased, sold 6 acres from
Aaron Sterling.
31 Aug.1762 Aaron Sterling leased, trust, to Southy Whittington 6 acres,
after death of afsd Aaron then on behalf of son Littleton Sterling.
1783 tax- Jonathan Roach 63 acres.

18 May 1791 Jonathan Roach mortgaged to William Williams 166 acres to William Williams of LONGTOWN & JOHNSONS LOTT.
1765 part resurveyed to CULLENS LOTT 149 1/4 acres.
1795 Aaron Sterling willed to son Aaron Sterling Jr.
21 Jan 1801 Jonathan Roach sold to John Thomas 166 acres, all his land in Som.Co. at Johnsons Creek, no name given.
10 March 1810 John Thomas and wife Mary Thomas sold to Isaac Lawson, 12 acres 3 rods, 12 perches.

JOHNSONS RIDGE

This is probably part of FLATLAND in Fairmount.
1710 Thomas Everton willed to Richard Waters and heirs 850 acres on Annamessex River-no name.
1752 Elizabeth Waters willed to son Richard 91 acres left me by Thomas Everton two tracts FLATLANDS,JOHNSONS RIDGE, and to daughter Sarah Waters balance of two tracts afsd.
12 Feb. 1787 Richard Waters and wife Eleanor Waters sold to Tubman Lowe Waters for 5 shillings plantation where Sarah Waters now lives. no name or acreage.
1788/9 Sarah Waters willed to James Waters JOHNSONS RIDGE.

JOHNSTOWN

Patented on 5 Sep.1663 by George Johnson for 300 acres in Westover, Election district 13, map #11.
Rent Rolls 1666-1723 belongs to grandchild of George Johnson in England.
29 May 1723 Ann Johnson,spinster only daughter of George Johnson sold to Robert King.
1729 Robert King sold to Edward Beauchamp 5 acres.
1726 resurvey to CONCLUSION 1500 acres by Robert King.
1 Oct.1744 William Beauchamp and wife Comfort Beauchamp sold to Robert King 5 acres that Robert King the elder sold to Edmund Beauchamp who died intestate. JOHNSTON
1 Apr.1745 Robert King sold to William Beauchamp son of Edward Beauchamp, 5 acres.
1 April 1745 William Beauchamp and wife Comfort Beauchamp sold to William Jones 90 acres of PUZZLE being 50 acres of DISCOVERY, part of JOHNSTON & CONTENTION.

JONATHANS ADDITION

Patented in 1742 by Jonathan Summers for 20 acres in Lawsons, Election district 8, map #19.
9 Aug.1769 Jonathan Summers sold to George Croswell 20 acres
1783 tax- George Croswell 20 acres.
7 July 1798 George Croswell sold to John Horsey of Smith Horsey 20 1/4 acres.
10 Aug.1799 John C. Horsey sold 20 acres to Hance Croswell.

JONES ADDITION

Patented in 1764 for 100 acres by George Jones in Tangier, Election district 9, map #7.
1783 tax- Robert Jones

1804 Robert Jones willed to son John Jones.

JONES ADVENTURE

Patented in Dec.1682 by Samuel Jones for 50 acres in Dames Quarter,
Election district 11, map #7.
Rent Rolls 1666-1723 Samuel Jones.
1769 ADDITION patented by George Phoebus 5 acres.
22 Aug.1771 Samuel Jones sold to George Phoebus 50 acres.
1783 tax- John Jones 50 acres
1783 tax- George Phoebus Jr. 50 acres-resurvey
1783 tax- George Phoebus 5 acres.

JONE'S CAUTION

Patented on 29 May 1689 by Walter Lane for 200 acres in Asbury, Election
district 12, map #21.
Rent Rolls 1666-1723 Walter Lane.
1708 William Scott willed to sons Abraham Scott and Benjamin Scott.

JONES CHANCE

Patented in 1744 for 533 acres by Lewis Jones in Dames Quarter, Election
district 9, map #7.
1783 tax- Lewis Jones 266 acres
1783 tax- John Jones 266 1/2 acres.
24 May 1800 John Jones, wife Margaret Jones sold to John Kelly 533 acres.

JONES CHOICE

Patented in 1663 for 500 acres by William Jones and resurveyed on 20
Feb.1699 by William Jones for 700 acres in West Pr.Anne,Election district
1, map #3.
Rent Rolls 1666-1723 possessed, 350 acres John Jones,175 acres William
Turpin, 175 acres Robert Jones.
5 Dec.1735 Thomas Dashiell exchanged with John Jones of Stepney Parish
son of Robert Jones, BATCHELORS CHOICE,LUMS PURCHASE OR LONG EXPECTED,
pat. by Samuel Worthington and wife Alice Worthington 300 acres for land
devised to John Jones by his father Robert Jones, 300 acres.
15 June 1751 Thomas Dashiell sold to Levin Dashiell of Stepney parish 1
moity purchased of John Jones 175 acres.
1783 tax- Arnold Ballard 15 acres
1783 tax- Levin Dashiell 175 acres
1783 tax- William Jones of Thomas Jones 150 acres.
1783 tax- John Jones of Little Monie 350 acres
21 March 1809 Robert Jones of John Jones, sold to John Dashiell 113 1/2
acres- mortgage.

JONES ENLARGEMENT

Patented in 1726 for 50 acres in St.Peters, Election district 2, map #6.
1749 ADDITION patented for 52 acres.
6 March 1790 John Jones Sr. sold to William Jones Sr. 50 acres.
27 March 1792 John Jones Sr. sold to William Jones 50 a cres and ADDITION
52 acres.

8 Sep.1807 William B. Jones sold to Liittleton Dennis Teackle, JONES
ENGLAREMENT & ADDITION.
29 Oct.1807 Littleton Dennis Teackle sold to John Teackle of Georgetown
D.C. purchased of William B. Jones.

JONES ISLAND

Patented on 19 March 1669 by Leonard Jones for 100 acres on Smiths
Island, Election district 10, map #23.
12 Oct 1674 Leonard Jones, wife Jane Jones sold to Henry Smith.
3 March 1682 Henry Smith,wife Anne Smith sold all to John Cowan.
Rent Rolls 1666-1723 possessed by George Hopkins in right of Robert
Hopkins Sr. Robert Hopkins died in 1701 and George is the son of Robert
but is probably the one who died in North Carolina 1749/51.
20 Nov.1746 George Hopkins and wife Elizabeth Hopkins sold to Peter
Parsley of Northumberland Co.Va., JONES ISLAND where George Hopkins now
lives for, 99 years.
1747 William Dixon gave to son Ambrose Dixon 100 acres of marsh on JONES
ISLAND.
1773 John Riggin gave to son Obediah Riggin 25 acres of marsh on JONES
ISLAND.
1780/2 Isaac White gave to daughter Nancy White, JONES ISLAND MARSH.
1783 tax- Mary Horsey
1783 tax- Thomas Robertson
1783 tax- George Croswell
1783 tax- John Milbourn
1783 tax- Levi Thomas

JONES'S MEADOW

Patented on 1 July 1696 by Samuel Jones for 300 acres in Tangier,
Election district 9, map #7.
Rent Rolls 1666-1723 Samuel Jones.
1730 John Kelly willed to son James Kelly and John Kelly and daughters
Nancy Kelly, Leah Kelly,Betsy Kelly, JONES MEADOW at head of Dames
Quarter Creek and island.
1744 resurveyed to JONES CHANCE

JONES PRIVILDEGE

Patented in 1749 for 80 acres George Jones in Tangier, Election district
9, map #7.
1783 tax- Robert Jones 80 acres.
1804 Robert Jones willed to son John Jones 80 acres
1846 John Jones son of Robert Jones willed to son Robert V. Jones 80
acres.

JONES PURCHASE

Patented in 1743 for 127 acres by Daniel Jones in Mt.Vernon, Election
district 5, map #1.
1783 tax- Phillip Jones 107 acres.

JONES PURCHASE

Surveyed in 1837 by Benjamin Jones from part of DAVIDS DESTINY & ELLIOTTS

CHOICE, for 84 3/4 acres in Dames Quarter,Election district 11, map #7.

JONES VINEYARD

see TONYS VINEYARD- Stephen Horsey, 300 acres.

JOSEPHS FOLLY

Patented in 1747 by Joseph Tilghman for 66 acres in Westover,Election District 13, map #11.
1763 Joseph Tilghman willed to son Joseph Tilghman.
1783 tax- Joseph Tilghman
5 Nov.1798 Joseph Tilghman, wife Nancy Tilghman sold to William Beauchamp 50 acres.
5 Nov.1798 Joseph Tilghman,wife Nancy Tilghman sold to George Broughton 15 1/4 acres.
24 Feb.1801 George Broughton,wife Alee Broughton sold to John Miles 81 1/4 acres with HUNTSMANS FOLLY, etc.
24 Apr.1801 John Miles sold same to George Broughton 126 acres.
24 Feb.1801 William Beauchamp, wife Minty Beauchamp sold to John Miles 25 3/4 acres.
13 March 1802 William Beauchamp, wife Minty Beauchamp sold to George Broughton 81 1/1 acres- no name.
29 July 1802 George Broughton sold to Thomas Swift 24 1/4 acres.
10 April 1804 Thomas Swift sold to John Swift 24 1/2 acres.
1 March 1806 John Swift sold to William Williams 24 1/4 acres.

JOSEPHS SECURITY

Patented in 1790 for 57 acres by Joseph Ward. This land is not on maps but in Lawsons District 8, adjacent CORK & WHITE OAK SWAMP.
16 Oct.1806 Joseph Ward sold to William Roach 12 acres of JOSEPHS SECURITY and 25 acres. of WHITE OAK.
3 Jan 1807 William Roach sold to John Dougherty 137 acres of JOSEPHS SECURITY & WHITE OAK.

KEARSLEYS INDUSTRY

Patented on 17 Dec.1701 by Peter Kearsley, a resurvey from IRISH GROVE for 300 acres in Brinkleys, southeast, Election district 3, map #16
8 Feb.1737 William Kearsley and Robert Kearsley and Samuel Kearsley, a division of lands.
20 March 1744 Robert Kearsley and wife Mary Kearsley sold to William Kearsley 30 acres with 88 acres of IRISH GROVE, that Peter Kearsley willed to son Robert Kearsley.
1745 debt books, William Kearsley
1755 debt Books Samuel Kearsley
6 Feb.1764 triparte agreement-partition of lands William Kearsley, and Samuel Kearsley sons of Peter that Peter Kearsley the elder in 1716 willed to sons Richard Kearsley, William Kearsley,Samuel Kearsley and Peter Kearsley. Richard and Peter died.

2 Dec 1767 William Kearsley Jr. and wife Elizabeth Kearsley sold to
William Kearsley Sr. 45 acres.
21 June 1769 William Kearsley gave to Isaac Adams and Mary Adams his
wife, daughter of William Kearsley,for support and maintenace of William
and wife, given him by his brother Robert Kearsley and his cousin William
Kearsley and since became the right of William by purchase except 50
acres sold to Samuel Adams. Total 147 acres.
1783 tax- Isaac Adams 147 acres
1783 tax- Peter Kearsley 121 acres

KARSLEYS IN EARNEST

Patented in 1752 by Robert Kearsley for 27 1/2 acres in Brinkleys
northwest, Election district 3, map #14.
1745 debt books- Robert Kearsley
29 June 1765 William Carsley Jr. and Mary Carsley widow of Robert Carsley
sold to William Smith 27 1/2 acres.
1782 William Smith willed lands to wife Mary Smith, after death to
grandaughter Sarah Smith.
1783 tax- Mary Smith widow of William Smith 27 1/2 acres
8 Jan 1803 Benjamin Lankford sold to Robert Lankford 27 1/2 acres.
15 Apr 1806 Robert Lankford, wife Sarah Lankford sold to Jesse Jackson
15 Apr.1806 Jesse Jackson sold to Dr. Thomas Robertson Jr.

KATHERINES GIFT
see DOUBLE PURCHASE

KEARSLEYS JOKE

see CURSLEYS YOAK

KEEP POOR HALL

Patented on 13 Nov.1694 by James Rowley for 100 acres in St.Peters,
Election district 2, map #6.
Rent Rolls 1666-1725 James Rowley
12 Nov.1739 Robert Austin son of Joseph Austin sold 100 acres to Thomas
Martin.
1783 tax- John Martin 100 acres.

KELLUMS ADDITION

This is probably part of CHANCE, 1767 pat. John Kellum for 14 acres.
9 Apr.1798 Benjamin Lankford sold 14 acres of KELLUMS ADDITION to Robert
Burcher Holland (adj.KIRKS PURCHASE & CHANCE)

KELSO

Patented in 1812 by Thomas Holbrook 20 1/2 acres in Mt. Vernon, Election
district 5, not on maps.
13 Aug.1808 Daniel Ballard, sheriff sold to Zadock Long per judgement
against Thomas Holbrook, CONCLUSION, LAST VACANCY, FLOWERFIELD & 20 1/2
acres of KELSO.

KENDALL

Patented 21 July 1683 by Bonnard Ward for 100 acres in East Pr.Anne, Election district 15, map #5.
Rent Rolls 1666-1723 Bonnard Ward is dead and no heirs in the county; no one possesses. Repatented by Thomas Horseman
5 April 1683 Thomas Horseman, wife Jane Horseman conveyed to Archibald Smith 60 acres.
2 March 1722 Archibald Smith sold to Owen Conely 60 acres
18 June 1727 Owen Conely and wife Elizabeth Conely of Dorcester County sold to George Benston 60 acres, KENDALL aka PUNCHIN HALL.
19 Nov.1728 George Benston and wife Rebecca Benston sold 60 acres to Rev. William Stewart.
1804 resurveyed 81 1/2 acre to LONELY GLADE.

(The)KEY

Patented in 1795 for 8 acres by William Jones in East Pr.Anne, Election district 15, map #5.
1753 resurvey to ANNIES DELIGHT, SEDGWICK 319 acres.
13 Sep.1806 William Jones, wife Eleanor Jones sold to William Gillis Waters 11 acres.

KILLGLAN

Patented on 29 April 1699 by Ephraim Wilson for 1000 acres in Dames Quarter,Election district 11, map #7.
28 Dec.1762 David Wilson leased to Thomas Jones of Manokin for 20 years.
17 April 1764 Thomas Jones released to David Wilson
17 April 1764 David Wilson and wife Ann Wilson sold 1/2 part to Levin Wilson
13 Dec.1768 Samuel Wilson and wife Mary Wilson sold to Denwood Wilson for 5 shillings 450 acres of TILBURY,WILSONS
DISCOVERY,GLASGOW,SECURITY,KILLGLAN.
1783 tax- Levin Wilson 350 acres
1783 tax- Denwood Wilson 250 acres
1881 resurvey to KILLGLASS ADDITION 1863 1/4 acres by Levin P. Bowland, G.Paul Jones.

KILLMAYNHAM

Patented on 18 Oct 1665 by Christopher Nutter for 150 acres in East Princess Anne, Election district 15, map #5.
12 Oct.1686 Christopher Nutter and wife Mary Nutter sold to John Dorman, all.
1670 John Dorman sold to Matthew Dorman
10 Oct.1673 Matthew Dorman and Phillipa Dorman his wife sold to John Dorman 150 acres.
13 Jan 1673 John Doman sold to Robert Millnor 150 acres.
Rent Rolls 1666-1723 John Gray
1730/2 John Gray gave to son William Gray
1743 William Gray gave to son William Gray 150 acres.
6 July 1756 William Gray son of Allen Gray sold to William Polk and Benjamin Polk 150 acres.(mortgage)
1780 William Gray sold to Charles Vaughn 150 acres.

242

27 Dec.1782 Charles Vaughn and wife Sarah Vaughn sold to Samuel Wilson
150 acres.
13 Jan 1786 Samuel Wilson gave to Elizabeth Wilson eldest daughter of
David Wilson brother of Samuel.
17 Jan 1786 Elizabeth Wilson gave to her father David Wilson
9 Apr.1794 William Jones sold 10 1/4 acres to Benjamin Polk Sr.
10 Jan 1787 David Wilson, and Elizabeth Wilson daughter of David sold to
William Jones of Manokin land conveyed by Charles Vaughn to Samuel
Wilson.
7 Nov 1798 Whittington Polk son of Benjamin Polk sold to Thomas King 10
1/4 acres with SMITHS HOPE, WILLIAMS ADVENTURE, SMALL ADDITION & ADDITION
TO SMITHS HOPE.
7 Nov.1798 Thomas King sold to Whittington Polk, same as above.
13 Sep.1806 William Jones, wife Eleanor Jones sold to William Gillis
Waters 171 acres.

KIMBALLS PURCHASE

see TANTON DEANNE

KINGS CHANCE

Patented on 16 Feb.1673 by John King for 100 acres in Dublin,Election
district 4, map #12.
1 Nov.1678 John King and wife Eleanor King sold to Duncan Olandman Sr.
1710 Duncan Olandman willed 100 acres to son William Olandman.
William Olandman died without issue and it fell to the daughters of
Duncan Olandman Jr. His second daughter Eleanor Olandman married Duncan
King.
4 Dec.1733 Duncan King and wife Eleanor King sold to William Bowland 1/3
part with DUBLIN,PREMINE,and CHANCE.
13 Jan 1734 Alexander Chain and wife Ann Chain sold to Robert King 1/3rd
part.(Ann Chain is eldest daughter of Duncan Olandman Jr.)
4 April 1745 William Bowland son of William deceased and his mother
Eleanor Bowland sold to Robert King 40 acres of DUBLIN,PEMINE,KINGS
CHANCE.
6 Sep.1748 William Bowland son of William sold to Robert King 10 acres of
swamp not contained in other deeds.
15 Aug.1755 William Bowland confirmed sold to Nehemiah King son of Robert
King.
1 Dec.1766 Nehemiah King willed to son Nehemiah land on Kings branch,
unnamed.
1783 tax- Nehemiah King

KINGS CHASE

Patented on 4 June 1683 by William Stevens and assigned to John King for
100 acres in Dublin, Election district 4, map #12.
1696 John King willed to son Upshur King 100 acres.
Rent Rolls 1666-1723 Upshur King
1738 Planner King son of Upshur King gave to brother Zorobable King 100
acres.
1783 tax- Nehemiah King 75 acres.
1810 George Wilson Jackson possessed part.

KINGS GLAD

Patented in 1750 by Zorobable King for 478 acres in Dublin,Election

district 4, map #12.

6 July 1757 Zorobable King sold 57 acres to John Porter
23 July 1765 Zorobable King sold to Dorman Turpin 106 1/4 acres of
CLOVERFIELD,INDIAN BONES,KINGS GLAD.
3 July 1765 Zorobable King sold 54 acres to John Porter
22 June 1768 William Turpin Jr. sold to Zorobable King and Denwood Turpin
1/3rd part of his right of dower of his now wife Betty Turpin.
7 Jan 1772 William Miles sold to Isaac Handy land that Denwood Turpin
conveyed and land purchased of Samuel Prior and Zorobable King 106 1/2
acres-no name.
25 March 1772 Denwood Turpin and wife Elizabeth Turpin sold to Isaac
Handy 100 acres with CLOVERFIELDS.
1783 tax- Zorobable King 324 acres
1783 tax- William Polk for Handys heirs 11 /12 acres
1783 tax- John Porter 54 acres
1794 Zorobable King willed lands to son Levin King, unnamed.

KINGSLAND

see DOUBLE PURCHASE, by Randall Revell

KINGS LOTT

Patented on 10 Feb.1666 by John King for 300 acres in Brinkleys,
northeast, Election disrict 3, map #15.
29 July 1675 John King and wife Elizabeth King of Morumsco sold 300 acres
to Phillip Adams
Rent Rolls 1666-1723 Possessed by Thomas Adams 300 acres.
1735 Thomas Adams son of Phillip Adams gave part to son Isaac Adams.
1744 resurveyed to ADAMS FIRST CHOICE 208 acres.
1753 Moses Owens who married the widow of Thomas Adams settled the bounds
of this lot.
31 Jan 1752 Phillip Adams the younger son of Abraham Adams deceased sold
to Isaac Adams 14 acres.
11 Nov.1755 Phillip Adams son of Abraham, and wife Sarah Adams sold to
Isaac Adams 90 acres.
14 Sep.1762 Mitchell King and wife Marian King of Worc.Co. Md. sold to
John Parker 22 acres.
24 March 1774 Ephraim Adams sold to Stephen Coulbourn 125 acres.
1783 tax- Ephraim Adams 204 acres
1783 tax- Sarah Adams
1783 tax- Stephen Coulbourn 125 acres
21 July 1788 Ephraim Adams sold 47 acres to Isaac Kellum

KINGS NECK

Patented on 20 Nov.1665 by Jenkins Price for 300 acres in Brinkleys,
southeast,Election district 3, map #16.
26 March 1667 Jenkins Price and wife Matthew Price sold to Malcomb Thomas
300 acres.
14 June 1687 Hugh Mannix sold to Joseph Staton 200 acres.
9 Nov.1682 Joseph Staton of Pocomoke and wife Jane Staton sold to Samuel
Collins 200 acres.
5 Jan 1687 Hugh Mannix sold to Samuel Collins 100 acres.
Rent Rolls 1666-1723 Samuel Collins 300 acres.

1707 Samuel Collins willed to son Samuel.
1700 resurveyed to COLLINS ADDITION 233 acres.

KINGS PURCHASE AND PARTNERS CHOICE UNITED

Patented in 1746 for 797 1/2 acres, in Dublin, Election district 4, map
#12, by Robert King.
1783 tax- Nehemiah King 797 1/2 acres

KINGSALE

Patented on 12 Oct.1677 by Josias Seward for 150 acres in Brinkleys,
southeast, Election district 3, map #16.
Rent Rolls 1666-1723 poss. by Matthew Parker
1759 resurvey to WHITES GIFT

KIRKMINSTER

Patented on 15 March 1694 by Thomas Davis for 225 acres in Lawsons,
Election district 8, map #18.
Rent Rolls 1666-1723 possessed by Thomas Davis
1749 resurveyed to UPPER ANDUE

KIRKS CHANCE

Patented in 1745 by Kirk Gunby for 32 acres in Lawsons, Election district
8, map #18.
1775 Kirk Gunby willed to son John Gunby
1783 tax- John Gunby Sr.
1783 tax- Sarah Gunby 1/3rds.
1788 John Gunby willed to son Kirk Gunby.
1796 Kirk Gunby willed to wife Elizabeth Gunby 1/3rds, after death lands
to brother Elisha Gunby, no name.

KIRKS PURCHASE

Patented on 29 May 1669 by John Kirk for 200 acres in Lawsons, Election
district 8, map #18.
Rent Rolls 1666-1723 John Kirk
12 Feb.1697 John Kirk gave to John Gunby son of Francis Gunby (Adria Kirk
daughter of John married John Gunby)
19 March 1755 James Gunby sold to brother Kirk Gunby, part
18 March 1761 Kirk Gunby sold to James Gunby, part.
19 Jan 1775 Kirk Gunby gave to son John Gunby
1783 tax- James Gunby 200 acres
27 Feb.1797 John Gunby son of Kirk Gunby, of Worc.Co. sold 200 acres to
Benjamin Lankford
9 Feb.1797 James Gunby sold to son John Gunby of Worc.Co. 200 acres.
15 June 1807 Benjamin Lankford sold to William Williams 200 acres.
22 June 1808 William Williams sold to Benjamin Lankford.
17 March 1810 Benjamin Lankford Sr. sold to William Williams 123 1/4
acres.
10 April 1810 Matthias Dashiell, sheriff, sold to William Williams per
judgement against Benjamin Lankford 123 1/4 acres.
1820 Benjamin Lankford gave to son Benjamin Lankford.

KNAVERY DISCOVERED

Patented in 1752 for 145 acres by William Miles in East Pr.Anne,Election district 15, map #4.
1783 tax- Matthias Miles 145 acres.

KNAVERY PREVENTED

Patented in 1760 by Sampson Wheatley for 37 1/2 acres. This land is not on the maps, probabley in Brinkleys, map #17.

KNIGHTS PURCHASE

Patented in 1730 by James Knight, a resurvey of CHANCE, for 199 acres, in Dublin,Election district 4, map #12.
1759 repatented by Stephen Tull for 119 acres
1760 resurveyed to TULLS ADDITION 212 1/4 acres.

KNIGHTS SUCESS

see NIGHTS SUCESS-Dublin district

LABANON

Patented in 1799 for 2 5/8 acres by Isaac Newman in West Pr.Anne,Election district 1, map #3.

LABOUR

Patented in 1762 by Richard Puckam for 192 acres in East Pr.Anne, Election district 15, map #4.
28 Feb.1769 Richard Puckam and wife Ann Puckam sold part to William Miles (mortgage)
21 June 1769 Richard Puckam and wife Ann Puckam sold to Levi Lankford 75 acres
19 March 1772 Richard Puckam and wife Ann Puckam sold to Levi Lankford 117 acres.
18 Aug.1773 Levi Lankford sold to Benjamin Puzey 75 acres
16 March 1774 Levi Lankford mortgaged to William Miles 117 acres.
1783 tax- Levin Lankford 117 acres
1783 tax- Benjamin Puzey 75 acres
24 March 1786 Matthias Miles released mortgaged that William Miles father of Matthias had, to Levi Lankford 117 acres.
20 April 1801 Levi Lankford sold to Benjamin Puzey 2 acres
7 June 1803 Levi Lankford deeded 54 acres to Tubman Lankford
7 June 1803 Levi Lankford,wife Leah Lankford sold to Tubman Lankford 54 acres LABOUR & 54 acre of RAINBOW.
26 Jan 1805 Levi Lankford sold to William How Lankford balance of LABOUR 138 acres.
1808 Benjamin Puzey willed all lands to son Planner Puzey (unnamed)
6 April 1809 Tubman Lankford, wife Amelia Lankford sold to Planner Puzey 43 1/8 acres LABOUR & RAINBOW.
22 Feb.1831 Marshalls sale,per garnishee of Bank of Somerset, 75 acres, against Planner Puzey.
1847 ADDITION TO LABOUR patented by Nathaniel C. Miller 12 3/4 acres.

LABOUR IN VANE

Patented by John Pollock on 11 March 1750 for 170 acres in East Pr.Anne, Election district 15, map #4.
19 Oct.1756 John Pollock now of Carolina and wife Ella Pollock sold to John Done of Somerset Co. COMEBY CHANCE, a resurvey to 170 acres LABOUR IN VANE, but now said to contain only 155 3/4 acres(except part Pollock sold to Thomas Sloss.)
1768 resurvey to DONES NEST EGG 355 3/4 acres

LADRITHS DISAPPOINTMENT

Patented in 1815 for 8 1/4 acres by Daniel Whitney in West Pr.Anne, Election district 1, map #2.

LANKFORDS CHOICE

Patented in 1808 a resurvey from LONGS CHANCE by William Lankford, for 295 1/4 acres in Brinkleys,northwest, Election district 3, map #14.
1851 Stephen Ward gave to wife Margaret Ward 17 acres bought of George F. Ward and Mary Ann Ward.
1854 Harriet Handy wife of James Handy willed to son Sidney W. Handy 17 acres.
(the Northwest corner of this land is still called LONGS CHANCE,unpatented 18 acres.)

LANKFORDS CONTENT

Patented in 1749 by John Lankford for 50 acres in Brinkleys, northwest, Election district 3, map #14.
1763 ENLARGEMENT patented for 97 acres by John Lankford .
21 April 1755 Joseph Lankford deeded to Puzey Lankford 69 acres
7 April 1755 Joseph Lankford, wife Alice Lankford sold to Joseph Lankford. 80 acres.
26 July 1766 John Lankford, wife Jane sold 97 acres to John Long Jr. LANKFORDS CONTENT ENLARGED.
23 May 1775 Mary Long sold 97 acres to Thomas Dixon of ENLARGED.
1783 tax- Puzey Lankford 81 1/2 acres
1783 tax- Joseph Ballard- ENLARGED 85 acres
1783 tax- Thomas Dixon 12 acres
9 Jan 1784 Ezekiel Lankford sold to Samuel Bedsworth 77 acres
8 Dec.1783 Joseph Lankford sold his rights to Thomas Dixon and Joseph Barrett.
8 Dec.1783 Thomas Dixon sold to Joseph Barrett 85 acres of ENLARGED.
21 July 1784 Samuel Bedsworth and wife Mary Bedsworth sold 89 acres to William Bedsworth.
15 March 1785 Ezekiel Lankford,wife Catherine Lankford, sold to Robert Hall and wife Elizabeth Hall 95 acres with TROUBLESOME.
15 March 1785 William Bedsworth sold to Robert Hall 61 1/4 acres
17 June 1790 William Bedsworth sold 58 acres to Benjamin Conner
15 Nov.1791 William Bedsworth sold to Benjamin Conner 64 acres.
15 Jan 1794 Thomas Dixon sold 11 3/4 acres to Joseph Barrett, ENLARGED.
11 April 1810 Benjamin Conner sold to Samuel Trehearn son of Obed Trehearn 64 acres.

LANKFORDS SECOND PURCHASE

see BOSTONS PURCHASE

LAST CHANCE

Patented in 1770 by John Benston for 125 acres in East Pr.Anne, Election
district 15, map #5.
1771 John Benston willed lands to be sold.
31 Jan 1792 Matthias Miles sold to Jesse King, for benefit of the
daughters of John Benston.
1 Jan 1792 Jesse King sold to Eli Furniss
22 May 1798 Jesse King sold to Eli Furniss with WOOLOVER.
Resurveyed in 1799 by Eli Furniss for 125 acres.
9 Dec.1800 Eli Furniss wife Matilda Furniss, sold to Levin Boston Jr. 50
acres.
14 Nov.1804 Levin Boston sold to Littleton Dennis Teackle, except 50
acres conveyed to Levi Ward.
12 Nov. 1805 Levi Ward sold 50 acres to Mary Broughton.
29 Oct.1807 Littleton Dennis Teackle sold to John Teackle of Georgetown
DC.

LAST CHOICE

Patented on 6 Sep.1667 by Ambrose London for 10 acres in Fairmount,
Election district 6, map #9.
9 Aug.1676 Ambrose London, wife Mary London sold to Mary Riggin alias
Mary London, wife of Teague Riggin.
Rent Rolls 1666-1723 possessed by Samuel Handy that Ambrose London sold
to Thomas Newbold who sold to Samuel Handy.
1687 Teague Riggin, wife Mary sold to Miles Gray.

LAST CHOICE

Patented in 1749 for 18 acres by Teague Riggin in Dublin, Election
district 4, map #12.
1783 tax- Teague Riggin- Dividing ck. 100
6 Jan 1807 Wrixam L. Porter and wife Priscilla Porter (daughter of Teague
Riggin) sold her share to John Riggin.

LAST CHOICE

Patented in 1757 for 37 1/2 acres by John Johnson in Lawsons, Election
district 8, map #18.

LAST CHOICE

Patented in 1760 by William Pollitt for 61 acres in East Pr.Anne,
Election district 15, map #4.
20 Nov.1772 Thomas Pollitt sold to William Pollitt with GEDDES OUTLETT,
ADDITION, FAIRMEADOW,HAYMANS PURCHASE.
1783 tax- Mary Pollitt 26 1/4 acres
1783 tax- William Pollitt 30 acres
7 Feb.1809 William Pollitt Jr. sold to George Pollitt of George 23 1/2
acres of LAST CHOICE & LITTLE PLANTATION.

LAST CHOICE

Patented in 1768 by Jonathan Pollitt for 83 1/2 acres in East Pr.Anne, Election district 15, map #4.
23 March 1770 Jonathan Pollitt sold to Matthias Miles 83 1/2 acres.
1800 Matthias Miles willed 40 acres to daughters Susan P. Miles,Emily Miles, Mary E. Miles, Harriet L. Miles and Julia P. Miles.

LAST CHOICE

Patented in 1789 for 11 1/2 acres by Samuel Smith in Brinkleys, northeast, Election district 3, map #15.

LAST CHOICE

Patented in 1795 for 8 1/2 acres by Littleton Dennis in Dublin, Election district 4, map #13.

LAST CONCLUSION

Patented in 1770 by Matthias Miles for 152 acres in East Pr.Anne Election district 15, map #4.
1783 tax- Matthias Miles 152 acres
25 May 1803 Thomas Jones of John Jones, and wife Betsy Jones sold to Littleton Dennis Teackle 152 acres.

LAST PEACE

Patented in 1815 for 34 acres by Matthias Miles in East Pr.Anne, Election district 15, map #5.

LAST PEACE

Patented in 1771 for 50 acres in Dublin, Election district 4, map #13.

LAST PURCHASE

Patented in 1724 by Thomas Walker for 618 acres in Mt.Vernon, Election district 5, map #1.
26 July 1735 Thomas Walker son of Thomas,deceased sold to Levin Gale part of two tracts ADDITION & LAST PURCHASE except lot in Whitehaven Town, no acreage given.
18 March 1763 Mary Richardson coheir of Thomas Walker sold to Thomas Holbrook her rights to part not devised by the will of Thomas Walker.
19 March 1768 Levin Gale sold to Thomas Holbrook 10 acres for 5 shillings between Whitehaven Town and Lower Ferry of Wicomico.
16 March 1771 Jacob Sarley of New York sold to Jane Lucas(as Thomas Walker willed to Jacob Sarley) 548 acres.
9 June 1778 Sarah Richardson coheir of Thomas Walker sold to Thomas Holbrook, no acres given.
1783 tax- Levin Gale 60 acres
1783 tax- Thomas Holbrook
1783 tax-Thomas Waters 300 acres
22 July 1786 Robert Dashiell and Jane Dashiell his wife, one of the daughters and coheir of Jane Lucas late, and Matilda Bounds sold to

Thomas Waters their parts that Jane Lucas had originally granted to
Thomas Waters. Jane Lucas gave to three daughters Jane Dashiell, Matilda
Bounds and Margaret Waters wife of William Waters. 322 1/2 acres
18 Aug.1791 Thomas Waters and wife Margaret Waters sold to Francis Tubman
Cheney for 5 shillings 1/3 part that descended to Margaret Waters.
19 Aug.1791 Francis Tubman Cheney sold to Thomas Waters the 1/3rd part.
1792 resurveyed to CHANCE 559 1/4 acres.

LAST VACANCY

Patented in 1750 to Thomas Holbrook for 60 acres in Mt.Vernon, Election
district 5, map #1.
11 March 1762 Daniel Jones sold to Thomas Holbrook with
PRIVILEDGE,FLOWERFIELDS, part.
1783 tax- Thomas Holbrook
2 Feb.1788 Thomas Holbrook sold to son Henry Holbrook 207 1/2 acres of
LAST VANCANCY & FLOWERFIELDS.
1789 Henry Holbrook willed to son Thomas Holbrook.
7 Jan 1794 John Holbrook sold to Thomas Holbrook that Henry Holbrook
willed 207 acres to John to pay debts. Priscilla Holbrook consented to
sell her dower rights- no name of land.
21 Aug.1804 Thomas Holbrook, wife Peggy Holbrook sold to Levin Jones Sr.
140 acres of FLOWERFIELDS, LAST VACANCY & BENGAL.
13 Aug.1808 Daniel Ballard, sheriff, sold to Zadock Long 81 1/2 acres of
FLOWERFIELDS, LAST VACANCY & CONCLUSION per judgement against Thomas
Holbrook.

LATE DISCOVERY

Patented on 22 Nov.1679 by John Robins for 600 acres in Brinkleys,
southeast,Election district 3, map #16.
31 Jan 1687 John Robins and wife Catherine Robins sold to Hugh Marnix 400
acres, who deeded 370 acres to Samuel Collins.
23 Jan 1683 John Robins,wife Katherine Robins sold to Samuel Collins 200
acres called SNOW HILL.
16 July 1686 John Robins, wife Katherine Robins sold to Hugh Mannix 400
acres.
Rent Rolls 1666-1723 Samuel Collins
1707 Samuel Collins willed to sons Samuel and John Collins.
1709 John Collins willed to brother Samuel Collins.
20 Mar.1733/4 Samuel Collins and wife Rebecca Collins sold to John Evans
151 1/2 acres.
20 March 1733 Samuel Collins and wife Rebecca Collins sold to John
Milbourn 50 acres.
25 Dec.1735 John Evans,carpenter, sold to Isaac Dickerson 151 1/2 acres.
20 June 1744 John Evans and wife Elizabeth Evans sold to Isaac Dickerson
151 1/2 acres.
2 July 1750 Samuel Collins and wife Ann Collins sold to Collins Adams 22
acres.
2 July 1750 Collins Adams and wife Tabitha Adams sold to Isaac Dickerson
22 acres of part called SNOW HILL of 200 acres.
9 June 1758 John Milbourn sold to Isaac Dickerson
1771 Isaac Dickerson willed to wife Catherine Dickerson dwelling
plantation, unnamed, after death to son James Dickerson
27 Mary 1777 I Phillip Adams son of Collins Adams am bound to Jacob Adams
for land that Collins gave to son Phillip Adams.

26 Feb 1778 Jacob Adams sold 200 acres to Gertrude Adams.
1783 tax- Catherine Dickerson 200 acres.
1 Aug.1806 James Dickerson, wife Rebecca Dickerson, sold to Esme Merrill
15 acres.

LATE PURCHASE

this is part of LONGS LOTT & LEDBOURN

LATE TO REPENT

see PITCHCROFT

LAWS ADDITION

Patented in 1769 a resurvey from part of NORTH FORELAND, by John Laws for
36 acres on Deal Island,Election district 14, map #8.
1783 tax- John Laws 36 acres
13 June 1789 John Laws Jr.wife Dolly Laws sold to William Evans 116 acres
of NORTH FORELAND & LAWS ADDITION.
10 May 1792 John Laws, wife Dolly Laws mortgaged to William Adams
1789 resurveyed to LAWS PREPOSSESSION 558 acres.

LAWS DEFENSE

Patented in 1715 on Deals Island, by Thomas Laws, Election district 14,
map #8 for 90 acres.
1783 tax- John Laws 90 acres
1789 resurveyed to LAWS PREPOSSESSION

LAWS MEADOW & LAWS THOROUGHFARE

see GOLDEN QUARTER & LONG DELAY in Tangier, 25 acres by John Laws in
1738.

LAWS PREPOSSESSION

Patented in 1789 for 558 acres by William Adams from NORTHFORELAND,
ADDITION, LAWS DEFENCE, LAWS ADDITION, on Deals Island,Election district
14, map #8.
10 May 1792 John Lawc, wife Dolly Laws, mortgaged to William Adams.
19 April 1810 John Adams sold 11 1/2 acres to Jesse Webster.

LAWS PURCHASE

Patented in 1775 for 215 acres by John Laws, from HARTHBURRY, and
ADDITION in East Pr.Anne,Election district 15, map #5.
1783 tax- John Laws
31 March 1792 John Laws sold to Margaret Byrd and Mary Smith for 5
shillings after death of their mother Nelly Laws 215 1/2 acres.
31 March 1792 John Byrd and wife Margaret Byrd and Mary Smith sold to
John Laws for his lifetime.
8 Mary 1794 John Laws sold to Polly Smith for money received from William
Heath for Polly Smith.
11 March 1799 John Byrd, wife Margaret Byrd and Mary Smith
sold to Peggy Pollitt HARTLEBURY ADDITION or LAWS PURCHASE

1 Dec.1801 Peggy Pollitt sold to Isaac Gibbons lands conveyed Peggy
Pollitt by by John Byrd and Mary Smith, no name.
14 Sep.1804 John Byrd, wife Margaret Byrd and Mary Smith sold to Zadock
Long 216 1/2 acres, except part conveyed to Peggy Pollitt.
24 April 1806 Isaac Gibbons sold all to Polly Collins of LAWS PURCHASE &
ADDITION.

LAYTONS CHANCE

Patented in 1754 for 130 1/2 acres by Samuel Jones in Dames Quarter,
Election district 11, map #7
1783 tax- John Jones 130 acres
10 May 1796 John Jones sold to Henry Walston 130 1/2 acres.

LAYTONS CONVENIENCE

Patented on 1 March 1679 by Henry Layton for 140 acres in Tangier,
Election district 9, map #7.
Rent Rolls 1666-1723 possessed by George Hutchins who married Margaret
Layton, the widow.
1783 tax- Lewis Jones 70 acres.

LAZARUS LOTT

Patented in 1740 by Lazarus Maddux, a resurvey from MATTOX ADVENTURE, for
641 acres in Fairmount,Election district 6, map #9.
1757 resurveyed to END OF STRIFE 609 acres.
17 March 1810 Benjamin Lankford Sr. sold to William Williams 5 acres.
10 April 1810 Matthias Dashiell, sheriff, sold to William Williams, per
judgement against Benjamin Lankford 5 acres.

LAZARUS LOTT

Patented in 1758 in by Lazarus Maddux for 5 acres in Lawsons Election
district 8, map #18

LEAST

Patented in 1790 for 3 1/2 acres by John Williams in East Pr.Anne,
Election district 15, map #5.
17 Oct.1794 Sarah Porter and William Porter sold to William Davis Allen
for 5 shillings WIDOWS CHANGE, CONVEINECY, ADDITION, LITTLE LESS & LEAST.
They became possessed at the death of Jane Strawbridge daughter of Dr.
William Strawbridge in right of her grandmother Mary Williams half sister
to Dr. William Strawbridge.

LEBANON

Patented in 1799 by Isaac Newman for 2 5/8 acres in West Pr.Anne,
Election district 1, map #3.
7 April 1807 Isaac Newman, wife Mary Newman sold to Jesse Wainright 2 5/8
acres.

LEDBOURN

Patented on 8 March 1679 by William Stevens for 350 acres in Brinkleys,

northeast,Election district 3, map #15.
Rent Rolls 16661-723 possessed by -
  Dockett Beauchamp 100 acres
  John Heath 150 acres
  Edward Beauchamp 100 acres
17 Dec.1681 Levin Boston bought of brother Richard Boston land purchased from Handy Beauchamp.
1727 resurvey to 926 acres by Edward Beauchamp
1733 will of Edward Hull, to son-in-law Beauchamp Davis WELL WISH being part of LEDBOURN and 100 acres adjacent to Edward Beauchamp.
1738 Edward Beauchamp and wife Naomy Beauchamp gave 160 acres to Thomas Beauchamp it being OLD RIGHTS that John Hath conveyed to Beauchamp.
7 June 1738 Edward Beauchamp and wife Naomy Beauchamp sold 45 acres to George Marshall for 5 shillings.
7 June 1738 Edward Beauchamp gave 150 acres to John Beauchamp.
6 May 1744 George Marshall and wife Mary Marshall of Morumsco sold to John White Jr.16 acres, called THE EXCHANGE.
22 March 1744 Edward Beauchamp and wife Naomy Beauchamp sold 100 acres to Marcy Beauchamp for 20 shillings.
18 July 1746 John White Jr. and wife Mary White sold to Cornelius Riggin 16 acres with LONG LOTT, now called THE EXCHANGE.
9 Feb 1748 George Marshall and Samuel Long and wife Sarah Long(daughter and coheir of Randal Long)and Thomas Cottingham and wife Mary Cottingham(d/o Randal Long) sold to Robert King the younger of Worc. Co. 45 acres, a total of 85 acres taken out of LONG LOTT & LEDBOURN called LATE PURCHASE.
7 Aug.1749 Edward Beauchamp gave to son William Beauchamp 100 acres out of HOGYARD and LEDBOURN.
14 Sep.1750 Cornelius Riggin,Samuel Long and wife Sarah Long, Thomas Cottingham and wife Mary Cottingham, sold to Thomas King the eldest son of Robert King, of Worc.Co. As Robert King had contracted for lands but money not paid or lands conveyed before his death the said Robert King being willing on behalf of the said Thomas King his grandson, to advance purchase money. ADDITION TO LATE PURCHASE taken out of LONG LOTT & LEDBOURN adjacent, formerly the right of George Marshall deceased.
1752 Edward Beauchamp, wife Naomy Beauchamp, willed part to Beauchamp Davis.
28 March 1759 Richard Boston and wife Mary Boston purchased 19 3/4 acres from Handy Beauchamp.
15 Dec.1769 Handy Beauchamp sold to William Boston 10 acres with BEAUCHAMPS VENTER.
1 Nov.1761 Marcy Beauchamp and wife Grace Beauchamp sold 49 acres to Handy Beauchamp, out of resurvey.
21 July 1762 Handy Beauchamp sold to Richard Boston 19 3/4 acres being part of 49 acres.
14 Sep.1767 Fountain Beauchamp sold to Phillip Adams and Hope Adams 117 acres left him by his brother Thomas Beauchamp (trade for MITCHELLS ADVENTURE & GOOD HOPE)
1 April 1769 Fountain Beauchamp and wife Rhoda Beauchamp sold to Phillip Adams son of Hope Adams 117 acres and part known as BEAUCHAMPS VENTURE 44 acres willed to Fountain by his father Edward in 1750.
18 June 1771 William Beauchamp gave to son John Beauchamp 5 acres.
8 Dec.1772 Beauchamp Davis Sr. sold to Beauchamp Davis Jr 176 acres.
1777 Beauchamp Davis willed to son Beauchamp Davis.
7 Aug.1781 Elijah Beauchamp and wife Martha Beauchamp sold to John

Beauchamp 14 acres.
17 Dec.1781 Richard Boston,wife Mary Boston sold to brother Levin Boston
10 acres, conveyed to William Boston who died intestate and Richard was
the eldest brother.
1783 tax- Richard Boston 19 acres
1783 tax- Levin Boston
1783 tax- Thomas King 41 acres
1783 tax- Phillip Adams of Hope Adams 117 acres
1783 tax- Joshua Beauchamp 175 acres
1783 tax- Elijah Beauchamp 70 acres
1783 tax- Beauchamp Davis 45 acres
21 Feb.1787 John Beauchamp and Mary Beauchamp sold to Samuel Smith 160
acres of LEDBOURN,HOGYARD,ENLARGEMENT with 52 acres of ADAMS CONCLUSION.
13 Feb.1787 Elijah Beauchamp sold to John Beauchamp (division of lands)
13 Feb.1787 John Beauchamp sold to Elijah Beauchamp (division of lands.)
21 March 1787 Planner Beauchamp sold 1 1/4 acres to Samuel Smith.
5 Feb.1789 Beauchamp Davis,Planner Beauchamp wife Martha Beauchamp,
William Adams of William, Levin Beauchamp,Thomas Beauchamp sold 2 1/2
acres to Samuel Smith
19 May 1789 Elijah Beauchamp,wife Martha Beauchamp sold to John Beauchamp
100 acres of THREE BROTHERS & LEDBOURN.
1 June 1789 Elijah Beauchamp sold to Thomas Beauchamp, description,no
acreage given.
8 Jan 1790 John Beauchamp,wife Anne Beauchamp sold to Thomas Beauchamp 38
acres.
8 Jan 1790 John Beauchamp,wife Anne Beauchamp, sold Phillip Adams 100
acres.
8 Jan 1790 Ann Beauchamp and Thomas Beauchamp sold to Thomas Adams THREE
BROTHERS,HOGYARD,ENLARGEMENT except 40 acres of hers, no acreage given.
24 Jan 1790 Thomas Beauchamp,wife Martha Beauchamp sold to Thomas Adams
203 1/4 acres.
13 Oct 1792 Risdon Beauchamp of Kent Co.Del. sold to Phillip Adams 12
acres
20 Sep 1796 Thomas Beauchamp,wife Sarah Beauchamp sold to William
Williams 166 3/4 acres of LEDBOURN, HOGYARD, ENLARGEMENT, BEAUCHAMP
VENTURE, SMALL HOPES.
17 April 1797 Joshua Beauchamp,wife Mary Beauchamp sold to Samuel Smith
60 acres of BEAUCHAMPS VENTURE,LEDBOURN formerly belonging to Handy
Beauchamp and 1/3rd part held by Joshua in right of his wife.
1 Jan 1798 William Williams, wife Polly Williams, sold to Thomas Adams,
part.
11 Jan 1798 William Williams, wife Polly Williams, sold to Samuel Smith
33 1/2 acres of LEDBURN, HOG YARD, ENLARGEMENT, BEAUCHAMPS VENTURE.
1809 Richard Boston willed lands to nephew Elijah Boston.
1812 Phillip Adams willed to son Henry Adams.
29 Jan.1820 Elijah Boston sold to Thomas Adams of Phillip Adams, part.
1813 Samuel Smith willed lands to sons James Smith and Samuel Smith.
1831 Thomas Adams willed to four children, Morris Henry Adams, Mary Pitt
Adams, Leah Jane Adams and Emeline Rounds land purchased of Elijah
Boston.

LIBERTY

Patented in 1744 to Robert Harris for 50 acres in East Pr.Anne, Election
district 15, map #5.

1755/9 Robert Harris willed to son Zachariah Harris.
6 acres of LIBERTY nearby on maps, no date.
2 Feb.1764 Zachariah Harris of Worc.Co. sold to Levin Ballard of Som.Co.
50 acres and Stephen Mitchell-triparte with HEATHS QUARTER & LITTLEWORTH.
22 Feb.1764 same as above but to John Mitchell.
1770 became part of GEORGES FORTUNE 500 acres.

LIBERTY

Patented in 1747 for 163 acres by Henry Waggaman in Mt.Vernon,Election
district 5, map #1.
1751 resurveyed to WAGGAMANS PURCHASE 947 1/2 acres

LIBERTY

Patented in 1767 for 55 acres by Levin Dorman in East Pr.Anne,Election
district 15, map #4.
23 Nov.1769 Stephen Mitchell sold to George Miles for 5 shillings 21 1/4
acres.
25 Aug.1775 Levin Dorman sold to Matthias Miles for 5 shillings.
12 Dec 1780 Mathias Miles sold 34 acres to Thomas Pollitt
29 Nov.1781 Stephen Mitchell and wife Priscilla Mitchell sold to Samuel
Miles 21 3/4 acres.
1782 Samuel Miles willed to wife Mary Miles until death, then to son
William Miles (Minor) if he dies to brother Matthias Miles.
5 Dec 1793 Matthias Miles sold to William Pollitt 20 3/4 acres.
1783 tax- Robert Pollitt-with HAZARD 38 acres
1783 tax- William Pollitt 20 3/4 acres
5 Feb 1793 Matthias Miles sold 20 3/4 acres to William Pollitt.
1795 William Miles willed to sons John Miles and William Miles land that
may be devised me by my father Samuel Miles, unnamed.

LIMBRICK

Patented on 10 March 1680 by William Stevens and assigned to Daniel
Quillan for 150 acres in Brinkleys,southeast and is part of SONS CHOICE.
Not on maps by the name LIMBRICK.
Rent Rolls 1666-1723 possessed by Hugh Porter and widow Lydia Quillan,
and Edmond Dickenson.
10 July 1694 Thomas Quillan and wife Sarah Quillan deeded to Thomas
Lister. Thomas Lister and wife Margaret Lister made over to Peter
Dickenson. Peter Dickinson and Sarah Dickinson sold to Edmond Dickenson
Sr.
9 June 1703 Peter Dickenson and wife Sarah Dickenson conveyed to Edmond
Dickerson Sr.
19 Aug.1729 Edmond Dickenson Sr. gave to Edmond Dickenson Jr. 85 acres.
19 April 1721 ADDITION TO LIMRICK 25 acres Edmond Dickerson
1744 will of Mary Hampton, to son Robert Jenkins Henry.
1764 Robert Jenkins Henry gave to son Robert J. Henry 1/3 of LIMBRICK
being part of SONS CHOICE.
1783 tax- Robert Jenkins Henry 133 1/2 acres
1783 tax- Cornelius Dickerson 40 acres.
1815 Cornelius Dickerson willed lands to sons Henry Dickerson and Parker
Dickerson. unnamed.

LINSEN GREEN

Patented on 25 July 1679 and assigned to Josias Seward for 100 acres in Brinkleys southwest,Election district 3, map #17.
Rent Rolls 1666-1723 possessed by Samuel Tomlinson who married Abigail Seward daughter of Josias Seward.
11 Apr.1757 Seward Tomlinson sold 50 acres to Caleb Milbourn
20 Aug.1770 Seward Tomlinson heir of Josias alias Josias Seward sold 50 acres to Littleton Dennis.
1783 tax- Jonathan Milbourn

LITTLE

Patented in 1790 for 47 acres by John Williams in Dublin, Election district 4, map #12.

LITTLE BOLTON

Patented in 1663 by Alexander Draper for 250 acres in Lawsons Election district 8, map #19.
8 April 1676 Alexander Draper and wife Katherine Draper sold 250 acres to Miles Gray.
Resurveyed on 26 Oct.1688 for 850 acres by Thomas Jones and includes WOOD STREET.
Rent Rolls 1666-1723 Possessed by Robert Catherwood in right of the orphans of Thomas Jones.(Robert Catherwood married the widow of Thomas Jones, Martha Davis.)
1700 will of Thomas Jones, to eldest son Thomas.
14 Oct 1749 triparte-Thomas Jones sold to Richard Waters. John Williams to be able to sue against Richard Waters for this land 850 acres.
13 Nov.1751 Samuel Ward and John Ward son of Samuel quitclaimed all interest to John Williams of Jones Creek.
13 Nov.1751 John Williams and wife Esther Williams sold to Samuel Ward 40 acres.
1775 resurvey to include WOOD STREET 825 1/2 acres, by Benjamin Williams and Betty Williams..
1783 tax- Stephen Ward of John Ward 75 acres
1783 tax- John Williams 850 acres
1791 John Ward willed to son John Ward, lands formerly belonging to Stephen Ward, no name mentioned.
2 Feb.1795 Ann Frazier sold to Benjamin Williams and Betty Williams and they returned on the same date-division of lands.
15 April 1796 William Ward of Wolford Co. Ky. sold to John Ward of Somerset Co. his interest in land possessed by Stephen Ward, no name or acreage.
26 Dec.1807 Benjamin Williams and Betty Williams sold to the trustees for a meeting house 1 acre.
6 Sep.1832 Hance Croswell sold to John Walker
5 Oct.1885 William Roach sold to Zachariah Walker

LITTLE DERRY

Patented on 3 Aug.1684 by John Rousells for 200 acres in Dublin, Election district 4, map #13.
Rent Rolls 1666-1723 John Rousells

10 Sep.1687 John Rousells and wife Mary Rousells sold to Thomas Tull 200 acres.
1694 Edward Stockwell sold to the Justices of Somerset Co. for a new court house until 1742.
1740 resurvey 176 acres by John Hamilton.
1775 ADDITION patented for 343 1/2 acres that includes CHANCE & CYPRESS SWAMP.by John Hamilton and Archibald Bell
1783 tax- Rev. Hamilton Bell 160 acres

LITTLE PLANTATION

Patented in 1792 for 14 acres by Evans Willin in St.Peters, Election district 2, map #6.
22 Feb.1808 Evans Willin sold to John Wilkins.

LITTLE PLANTATION

Patented in 1769 by William Heath for 7 1/2 acres in East Princess Anne, Election district 15, map #4.
6 Oct.1772 William Heath sold to Thomas Pollitt 7 1/2 acres
1783 tax- Thomas Pollitt 7 1/2 acres..
1795 Thomas Pollitt willed balance of plantation to son William Pollitt (unnamed)
7 Feb.1809 William Pollitt sold to George Pollitt of George 23 1/2 acres of LITTLE PLANTATION & LAST CHOICE.

LITTLE PROFIT

Patented in 1759, a resurvey from CHESTNUT RIDGE by John Perkins for 102 acres in Dublin,Election district 4, map #13.
1783 tax- John Perkins 102 acres
22 Feb 1785 John Perkins traded 12 acres to Jonathan Cluff for 12 acres of NEGLECT.
1797 Jonathan Cluff willed to son Robert Cluff 233 acres of unnamed land.

LITTLE SWAMP

Patented in 1747 to Joseph Ward for 29 1/2 acres in Dublin, Election district 4, map #12.
22 May 1770 Joseph Ward,wife Elizabeth Ward sold 7 1/2 acres to William Warwick.
1783 tax- Elizabeth Ward
1783 tax- William Warwick
17 April 1787 Joseph Ward, wife Elizabeth Ward, and Elizabeth Ward sold to John Perkins 121 acres of PAXON HILL, WARWICKS DISCOVERY, LITTLE SWAMP, WINDSOR SWAMP, CROOKED RIDGE, WORTHLITTLE, COME BY CHANCE.
1 May 1787 Elizabeth Ward sold to David Long and Solomon Long her 1/3rds as widow of Joseph Ward 95 acres-no name or acreage.-mortgage.
15 May 1787 Joseph Ward sold to John Fleming parts WINDSOR SWAMP,WARWICKS DISCOVERY, LITTLE SWAMP 95 1/2 acres that was not sold to John Perkins or laid off for his mother.
17 June 1789 John Fleming, John Perkins sold to David Long Ward 84 3/4 acres of WINDSOR SWAMP, WARWICKS DISCOVERY & LITTLE SWAMP.
9 Feb.1796 David Long Ward, William Warwick and Mills Dryden sold to William Fleming 218 1/4 acres of WARWICKS DISCOVERY, WINDSOR SWAMP,WORTH

NOTHING & LITTLE SWAMP.
5 Apr.1796 William Warwick, David Long Ward and Mills Dryden sold to
William Fleming 221 1/2 acres of same.
1798 William Fleming willed lands to son William Fleming -unnamed.

LITTLE USKE

Patented on 4 July 1681 by Nathaniel Dougherty in Lawsons, Election
district 8, map #19.
29 Oct.1723 Nathaniel Dougherty of Baltimore Md. gave to brother John
Dougherty USK & MEADOW on Annamessex River.
Rent Rolls 1666-1723 possessed by the sons of Cornelius Ward in right of
the child of Nathaniel Dougherty.
1752 John Dougherty willed to son Obed Dougherty.
1783 tax- Nathaniel Daugherty 44 acres
1783 tax- James Gunby 82 acres.
2 May 1802 John Dougherty son of Obed Dougherty, and wife Mary Dougherty
sold to Thomas Lord 35 acres of USK, MEADOW & HARD FORTUNE.
7 May 1803 John Dougherty of Obed Dougherty sold to Dickerson Dougherty
50 acres MEADOW & LITTLE USK.
12 May 1804 William Roach, Thomas Tyler, Elisha Gunby, Samuel Smith,
Littleton Byrd sold to Jesse Dougherty eldest son of Nathaniel Dougherty
deceased, as comissioners to divide the real estate of Nathaniel
Dougherty, LITTLE USK & MEADOW, no acres given.
23 Jan 1808 John Dougherty of Obed Dougherty sold to Dickerson Dougherty
5 acres of USK & HARD FORTUNE

LITTLEWORTH

see NEWTOWN- 1791 pat. for 1 acre by Thomas Maddux

LITTLEWORTH

Patented on 15 Sep.1676 by William Stevens and assigned to Thomas
Cottingham, in Brinkleys,southwest,Election district 3, map #17, for 50
acres.
Rent Rolls 1666-1723 possessed by the widow Furbey Rugg in her son's
right (Mary Cottingham daughter of Thomas Cottingham married Furbey Rugg)
1702 Furbey Rugg willed to daughter Mary Rugg all lands when her mother
dies.
1748 tax- Mary Rugg 50 acres(she married David Adams)
15 Dec.1772 Thomas Adams son and heir of Mary Rugg sold to George Hayward
of Worcester Co. and Josiah Polk with PLANNERS ADVENTURE(mortgaged his
part.
16 Apr.1774 Thomas Adams gave to son David Adams, recovered from George
Hayward deceased by act of the assembly.
1762 resurveyed to ADAMS CHANCE with PLANNERS ADVENTURE.

LITTLEWORTH

Patented on 3 Aug.1681 by Edward Williams and assigned to John Panter for
50 acres in St.Peters,Election district 2, map #6.
Rent Rolls 1661723 possessed by John Panter
1713/4 John Panter willed to William Laws son of Robert Laws 50 acres.
23 Nov.1769 Robert Laws son of William Laws, and wife Mary

Laws sold to Billy Laws son of Panter Laws deceased for 5 shillings.
1 Dec.1778 Robert Laws of Sussex Co. Del. sold 50 acres to Billy Laws.
1783 tax- William Laws 50 acres.
26 May 1807 William Laws sold to Henry Walston Miles 50 acres.

LITTLEWORTH

Patented on 1 April 1689 by George Phoebus for 200 acres in St.Peters, Election district 2,map #6.
Rent Rolls 1666-1723 George Phoebus
1749 ADDITION TO LITTLEWORTH 540 acres
1764 resurvey 239 1/4 acres
18 Aug.1752 Samuel Phoebus and wife Martha Phoebus sold to Joseph Reed, tailor 100 acres of ADDITION.
26 July 1763 Samuel Phoebus sold to Thomas Aikman 8 acres
29 Apr.1765 Joseph Reed sold to George Miles 100 acres of ADDITION TO LITTLEWORTH.
7 May 1768 George Miles for 5 shillings sold to Sarah Jones 100 acres for 12 years of ADDITION.
30 Aug.1775 Joseph Reed sold to Thomas Aikman 13 acres of ADDITION
30 Aug.1775 Joseph Reed sold to George Miles 17 acres of ADDITION.
1780 George Miles willed to Sarah Jones and her daughter Ruth Jones 99 acres on Morumsco,(no name)and if no issue to Matthias Miles son of Matthias.
4 Sep.1781 Job Robaman and wife Mary Robaman and Job Robaman all of Dorcester Co. sold to John Cavanaugh, as George Phoebus Sr. willed to son George and as George Phoebus the grandfather died and left to Mary Robaman wife of Job Robaman, their interest.
23 Apr.1782 Samuel Phoebus sold to John Cavanaugh part.
1783 tax- Thomas Aikman 21 1/2 acres ADDITION
1783 tax- John Cavanaugh 18 acres ADDITION
1783 tax- John Cavanaugh 55 acres
1783 tax- George Miles 100 acres & 14 acres ADDITION
1783 tax- John Phoebus 27 and 15 acres
1783 tax- Samuel Phoebus 34 1/2 acres & 120 acres ADDITION
1783 tax- Joseph Reed 69 1/2 acres
1783 Samuel Phoebus willed to wife Martha Phoebus, LITTLEWORTH & ADDITION
24 May 1786 John Phoebus,wife Jamima Phoebus sold to William Jones son of William Jones 62 1/2 acres of NICHOLSONS ADVENTURE & LITTLEWORTH.
1788 Martha Phoebus willed to Thomas Jones son of Samuel Jones, except land in dispute with Thomas Aikman, I give to Thomas Aikman.
23 Jan 1795 John Phoebus sold to John Phoebus Jr. 200 acres that includes LITTLEWORTH.
23 Jan 1795 John Phoebus Sr. sold to William Phoebus land devised by Martha Phoebus widow of Samuel Phoebus 200 acres, unnamed.
18 July 1800 Thomas Jones of Samuel Jones sold to Evans Willin 300 acres of LITTLEWORTH, ADDITION & NICHOLSONS ADVENTURE.
13 Aug.1800 Owen McGrath Sr. sold to Evans Willin lands of Martha Phoebus 300 acres of LITTLEWORTH & ADDITION TO LITTLEWORTH.
22 Feb 1808 Evans Willin sold to John Wilkins ADDITION TO LITTLEWORTH.
12 Dec.1810 Thomas Rutter, marshall, sold to Joshua Dorsey of Baltimore County, per judgement against Evans Willin, ADDITION TO LITTLEWORTH 300 acres.
1837 Ballard Reed (married Nancy Cavanaugh) willed 200 acres to grandaughters Ann Ballard and Ann Maria Montgomery daughter of Robert

Montgomery ADDITION TO LITTLEWORTH.

LITTLEWORTH

Patented on 5 Dec.1701 by Benjamin Summers for 100 acres in Crisfield, Election district 7, map #20.
1709 Benjamin Summers willed to sons William Summers, Thomas Summers and John Summers.
4 May 1723 William Summers,sailor, and Martha Summers his wife appoints William Coulbourn attorney to make over to Southy Whittington land according to our grandfather Benjamin Summers.
29 June 1725 Joseph Summers the only surviving son of William Summers deceased, son of Benjamin Summers sold his 1/3rd part of LITTLEWORTH to Southy Whittington, that his father William left to sons Benjamin Summers, William Summers and Joseph Summers. Benjamin Summers and William died intestate without issue so it fell to Joseph Summers afsd.

LITTLEWORTH

Patented in 1727 for 50 acres by Stephen Ward in Lawsons, Election district 8, map #19. ADDITION patented in 1746 for 8 acres and all resurveyed in 1751 to 72 acres by John Ward.
28 March 1772 John Ward sold to Matthias Ward 17 1/2 acres.
1782 Stephen Ward willed part to son Matthias Ward
1783 tax- Matthias Ward 57 acres.
1783 tax- John Ward 40 acres.
5 June 1784 Matthias Ward sold for 10 shillings to Stephen Ward 17 1/2 acres
14 Nov.1785 Stephen Ward sold to Jacob Ward 3 acres
18 July 1788 Stephen Ward sold to Levi Miles his rights to CORK & LITTLEWORTH.
17 Feb.1797 Ezekiel Ward sold to Littleton Johnson 27 1/2 acres of CORK, CHESTNUT RIDGE, LITTLEWORTH, WHITE OAK.
19 Apr.1797 John Ward and Elijah Ward sold to George Davey, 1 acre
18 Apr.1797 Matthias Ward and Stephen Ward of Matthias sold to George Davey 25 acres.
25 May 1797 George Davey sold to William Roach 25 acres.
14 Jan 1804 George Davey sold to David Follen 25 acres of CHESTNUT RIDGE & LITTLEWORTH.
12 May 1804 John Ward Jr. leased to William Johnson son of Littleton Johnson 75 acres of CHESTNUT RIDGE, WHITE OAK SWAMP & LITTLEWORTH & CORK.
29 Sep 1804 Levin Miles sold to George Davey 1 1/2 acres in Little Annamessex, LITTLEWORTH.
31 Dec 1807 John Ward of John sold to John Taws of William Taws, all rights.
5 March 1808 David Follen, wife Esther Follen sold to William Riggin 25 acres.
4 June 1808 John Miles sold to William Roach, per judgement against Levin Miles CORK & LITTLEWORTH.
16 July 1808 John Miles, constable, sold to George Davey 12 acres, lands of Levin Miles.
9 June 1810 William Roach sold to James Montgomery, all rights.

LITTLEWORTH

Patented in 1728 by William Turpin for 6 acres in Fairmount, Election
district 6, map #9.
10 April 1754 William Turpin sold to Barnaby Willis 6 acres.
28 March 1757 Barnaby Willis, wife Colley Willis sold to Thomas Seon 6
acres.
1783 tax- Thomas S. Sudler 6 acres.

LITTLEWORTH

Patented in 1729 by Robert Harris for 50 acres in East Priness Anne,
Election district 15, map #5.
1755/9 Robert Harris willed to son Zachariah Harris 50 acres.
2 Feb 1764 Zachariah Harris of Worc.Co. sold to Levin Ballard and Stephen
Mitchell (mortgage) with HEATHS QUARTER & LIBERTY
22 Nov.1764 Zachariah Harris, same as above, but to John Mitchell 50
acres.
29 Nov.1781 Stephen Mitchell and wife Priscilla Mitchell sold 7 acres to
Samuel Miles with LIBERTY.
1783 tax- Stephen Mitchell 42 1/2 acres
1783 tax- Mary Miles 7 acres.
12 March 1805 Thomas Mitchell and wife Mary Mitchell of Worc.Co. sold to
William Mitchell 180 1/2 acres of LITTLEWORTH, CUT CLOSE & MITCHELLS
PURCHASE.
18 May 1805 William Mitchell, wife Sally Mitchell sold 18 1/2 acres to
Kirk Gunby of LITTLEWORTH, CUT CLOSE & MITCHELLS PURCHASE. except 7 acres
belonging to William Miles of Samuel Miles.

LITTLEWORTH

Patented in 1745 by Cornelius Ward for 25 acres in Dublin, Election
district 4, map #12.
1770 resurvey to WARDS VENTURE 67 acres.
1783 tax- Jesse Ward 25 acres
7 Feb.1792 Jesse Ward and wife Esther Ward of Worc.Co. sold to John
Layfield 25 acres with COME BY CHANCE,WARDS VENTURE & LITTLEWORTH.
1799 John Layfield willed to son John Layfield land bought of Jesse Ward,
unnamed.

LITTLEWORTH

Patented in 1751 for 53 acres to Thomas White in Brinkleys, southwest,
Election district 3, map #17.
1766 Thomas White willed to wife Sarah 53 acres
7 June 1789 Sarah White sold to Nathan Cahoon
1783 tax- Nathan Cahoon 53 acres.

LITTLEWORTH

Patented in 1757 for 40 acres by James Gunby in Lawsons, Election
district 8, map #18
1783 tax- James Gunby 40 acres
27 Feb.1797 John Gunby son of Kirk Gunby of Worc.Co. sold to Benjamin
Lankford 40 acres.

9 Feb.1797 James Gunby sold to John Gunby of Worc.Co. 40 acres.
9 Apr.1798 Benjamin Lankford sold to Henry Handy 110 3/4 acres of LOW
SWAMP & LITTLEWORTH.
1813 Henry Handy willed to wife Hannah Handy land bought of Benjamin
Lankford.

LITTLEWORTH

Patented in 1759 for 3 acres by Thomas Ward in Asbury, Election district
12, map #21.

LITTLEWORTH

Patented in 1764 for 3 acres by Abraham Outten in Brinkleys, southwest,
Election district 3, map #17.
31 March 1769 Abraham Outten and wife Elizabeth Outten sold to Sampson
Wheatley 3 acres.
1773 Sampson Wheatley willed to daughter Betty Wheatley
24 June 1786 Caleb Jones and wife Betty Jones, daughter of Sampson
Wheatley, sold to Kellum Lankford,Elijah Coulbourn,Thomas Jones of
Annamessex, LITTLEWORTH, NEW BOSTON, DAMN SWAMP & ADAMS CHANCE.
24 April 1805 Benjamin Conner,wife Grace Conner, Noah Lankford, wife Ann
Lankford, Benjamin Bedsworth, John Broughton and wife Mary Broughton,
Richard Hall, wife Sarah Purnell Hall, and Mary Bedsworth sold to
Mordicai Jones of St. Marys County MERCHANTS TREASURE, GREEN FIELD,
WHEATLEYS DIFFICULT PURCHASE, PRIVILEDGE, LITTLEWORTH, BOSTON, etc.
devised by Sampson Wheatley to daughter Betty Jones and conveyed by Caleb
Jones and wife Betty Jones to Kellum Lankford, Elijah Coulbourn and
Thomas Jones now deceased.

LITTLEWORTH

Patented in 1813 for 82 3/4 acres by John Puzey in East Pr.Anne, Election
district 15, map #4.

LOCUST HAMMOCK and FRONT OF LOCUST HAMMOCK

Patented in 1682 by John Polkley for 50 acres in Tangier, Election
district 8, map #7.
11 Oct 1697 FRONT OF LOCUST HAMMOCK patented by same for 75 acres.
1702 John Polkley willed to William Kent, dwelling plantation LOCUST
HAMMOCK. If no issue to Lewis Jones and in turn to Eliza Moore in the
event of said Jones without issue.
Rent Rolls 1666-1723 possessed by Francis Craden in right of the relic
and the orphans of John Polkley.
2 Dec 1719 William Kent of Pennsylvania and wife Catherine Kent conveyed
to Ephraim Polk.
24 Aug.1764 Charles Polk of Worc Co.,son of Ephraim Polk deceased sold to
Levin Woolford and William Waller 125 acres.

262

1783 tax- Levin Woolford 37 1/2 acres (Front)
1783 tax- Levin Woolford 25 acres
1783 tax- Ann Waller 37 acres (FRONT)
1783 tax- Ann Waller 25 acres
1801 Levin Woolford willed lands to sons John Woolford,(land in Dames
Quarter) Arthur Woolford and wife Prissy Woolford.
2 Oct 1803 Priscilla Woolford sold all rights to Arthur Woolford, left by
the will of Levin Woolford, unnamed.
23 Feb.1808 John Woolford and William Waller sold to Thomas Roe 50 acres
LOCUST HAMMOCK & 75 acres of FRONT OF LOCUST HAMMOCK.
1836 John Woolford willed to son John Woolford land formerly belonging to
Uncle Charles Woolford, unnamed.

LOCUST RIDGE

Patented on 3 April 1666 by William Furniss for 50 acres, alias HUMMOCK,
in Fairmount,Election district 6, map #9.
Rent Rolls 1666-1723 John Marvell
1783 tax- Abraham Taylor
1791 will of Abraham Taylor, to son William Taylor.
17 May 1810 Louther Taylor, of Kent Co. Del. attorney of Bartholomew
Taylor and Abraham Taylor of Bracken Co. Ky, sold to Clement Johnson 93
acres.
1852 Solomon Evans willed to grandson Abraham Evans.

LONDONS ADVENTURE

Patented on 5 Sep.1667 by Ambrose London who conveyed to Samuel Handy,for
25 acres in Fairmount,Election district 9, map #6.
11 March 1678 Ambrose London and wife Mary London sold to Joseph Mason 25
acres 1 rod, 16 perches.
1734 Samuel Handy willed to sons Samuel Handy and John Handy.
2 Oct.1747 George Tucker of the Isle of Barbadoes and wife Mary Tucker
(Mary Handy daughter of Thomas) sold to Samuel Handy several parcels,
JERICHO,HANDYS CHOICE,LONDONS ADVENTURE, STEPHENS MEADOW,STAKE RIDGE AND
BLACK RIDGE.
1751 John Handy,wife Elizabeth Handy of Dorc.Co. deeded to Samuel Handy.
7 Jan 1757 Samuel Handy sold to Thomas Seon 25 acres.
2 Sep.1767 Thomas Seon sold to Whitty Turpin
23 Aug.1770 Whitty Turpin sold to Isaac Handy(released bond on tracts.)
1783 tax- Whitty Turpin
1 Aug.1796 Thomas Holbrook and wife Peggy Holbrook sold to Henry Coston
and Whittington King land conv. by Thomas Seon to Whitty Turpin father of
Peggy on 2 Sep.1767.

LONDONS ADVISEMENT

Patented on 3 June 1667 by William Furniss for 50 acres in Fairmount,
Election district 6, map #9.
William Furniss assigned to George Johnson.
23 Nov.1680 George Johnson gave to wife Katherine Johnson, to be sold.
Rent Rolls 1666-1723 belongs to the heirs of George Johnson.
1733 Benjamin King willed lands to be sold.
1753 Robert King willed to Richard Waters son of William Waters deceased
by his wife Abigail Waters and to William Walston and Thomas Walston

balance adjacent formerly belonging to Benjamin King.
1757 per Bensons maps, resurveyed to COW QUARTER
1776 William Walston willed to sons Charles Walston and Levin Walston
28 March 1789 Charles Walston and Levin Walston sold to Samuel Smith 22
acres of WINTER HARBOUR,LONDONS ADVISEMENT and all lands contiguous
4 Feb.1794 Thomas Walston of Kent Co.Del. grandson and heir of Thomas
Walston sold all rights to Samuel Smith.
20 Sep.1803 Samuel Smith sold his interest to William Walston of Obed
Walston.
19 Oct.1805 William Walston sold to Revel Roach 32 1/2 acres of WINTER
HARBOR AND LONDONS ADVISEMENT.
13 Oct.1809 William Coulbourn of Robert Coulbourn, constable, sold to
George Beauchamp 50 acres, property of Revel Roach purchased of William
Walston, unnamed.

LONDONS GIFT

Patented on 3 Jan 1667 by William Furniss for 50 acres and assigned to
George Johnson in Fairmount,Election district 6, map #9.
23 Nov.1680 George Johnson willed to wife Katherine Johnson. After death
to young child, unnamed.
Rent Rolls 1666-1723 belongs to the heirs of George Johnson
1783 tax- Richard Waters
8 Nov.1786 Richard Waters Sr willed to William Waters Sr., land devised
Richard by his father William Waters.
15 Feb.1787 Richard Waters Sr. and wife Eleanor Waters sold to James
Waters land where he now lives-no name.
20 Dec.1788 Richard Waters, wife Eleanor Waters sold to Isaiah Tilghman
149 1/2 acres of FLATTLAND,FRIENDS KINDNESS & LONDONS GIFT.
1790 Isaiah Tilghman willed to son William Tilghman.

LONELY GLADE

Patented in 1804 a resurvey from KENDALL by William Stewart for 81 1/2
acres in East Pr.Anne, Election district 15, map #5.
18 Oct.1831 Sheriff's sale at suit of Levin Miller against Henry J.
Riggin 179 acre of PANTHERS DENN, ALLENS VALE AND LONELY GLADE.

LONG ACRE

Patented on 9 Oct.1673 by Alexander Draper for 100 acres in Lawsons,
Election district 8, map #19.
Rent Rolls 1666-1723 possessed by Cornelius Ward
1701 resurvey by Cornelius Ward 525 acres.
1722 Cornelius Ward willed his land be divided between his children- no
name or acreage.
18 Nov 1742 Cornelius Ward sold to John White and Archibald White 25
acres.
14 Jan 1767 agreement of division of lands, Cornelius Ward son of Joseph
Ward, James Ward son of Thomas Ward, Cornelius Ward son of Cornelius and
John Ward son of Samuel Ward (heirs of deceased grandfather Cornelius
Ward.)
14 Jan 1767 Cornelius Ward Sr. and son Cornelius Ward Jr. and James Ward
Sr. sold to Joseph Ward son of Samuel Ward 275 acres.
June 1769 I Archibald White give to William White for the care of me and

my wife and to Samuel White,Archibald White Jr. and Martha White 12 1/2 acres.
19 Aug.1772 Jesse Ward sold to John Ward 50 acres.
1783 tax- John Ward Sr. 50 acres
1783 tax- Cornelius Ward 20 acres
1783 tax- James Ward 20 acres
1783 tax- William Ward 250 acres
1783 tax- Ann White 12 acres
1791 John Ward willed to son John 50 acres. After his death to grand son Elijah Ward son of John Ward.
1780/2 Isaac White willed LONG ACRE MARSH per deed in possession of William White, to be sold.
29 Sep.1804 Samuel Ward Sr. sold to John Dyes 25 acres.

LONG DELAY

Patented in 1729 for 90 acres by Lazarus Windsor on Deals Island, Election district 14, map #8.

LONG DELAY

Patented on 20 March 1706 by Ephraim Pollock for 274 acres in Tangier, Election district 9, map #7.
Rent Rolls 1666-1723 William Pollock to whom it was assigned.
16 Oct.1739 Charles Polk and wife Patience Polk sold to John Laws 212 acres out of GOLDEN QUARTER & LONG DELAY.
20 Aug.1734 Charles Pollock gave to Joy Hobbs 106 acres of LONG DELAY,& GOLDEN QUAARTER now called HOBBS CHOICE.
1735/6 Joy Hobbs gave to son Absalom Hobbs, now called HOBBS HIS CHOICE.
22 Jan 1732 Robert Jones sold for 5 shillings to George Jones parcel taken out of GOLDEN QUARTER & LONG DELAY 120 acres.
2 Sep.1742 Absalom Hobbs sold to Matthew Wallace 106 acres out of GOLDEN QUARTER & LONG DELAY, for 5 shillings.
1761 Matthew Wallace willed to son Joseph Wallace land,unnamed.
8 Sep.1774 Joseph Wallace sold to Charles Hall 106 acres of GOLDEN QUARTER & LONG DELAY.
13 Jan 1779 Robert Jones traded John Jones, part LONG DELAY 6 1/2 acres for 7 1/2 acres LUMS ENCREASE.
5 Feb.1782 John Laws Sr. sold to Robert Jones 55 acres of GOLDEN QUARTER & LONG DELAY.
1783 tax- Dolly Hall 53 acres
1783 tax- Ann Jones
1783 tax- Robert Jones
1783 tax- Richard Wallace 30 acres
13 Feb 1787 John Laws Sr. and wife Mary Laws sold 21 acres to George Jones.
22 March 1787 John Laws,wife Mary Laws sold to Robert Jones 55 acres of GOLDEN QUARTER & LONG DELAY.
19 Nov.1791 John Laws Sr. sold 33 acres to Thomas Jones
11 Dec.1795 Ezekiel Hall sold to Robert Jones 106 acres of GOLDEN QUARTER & LONG DELAY.
21 Feb.1798 Levin Bozman and wife Mary Bozman and Elizabeth Bozman Sr. sold to James Kelly Jr. 67 acres of GOLDEN QUARTER, LONG DELAY & LAWS THOROUGHFARE.
14 June 1798 Robert Jones sold to James Kelly Jr. 11 /4 acres of LONG

DELAY & LAWS MEADOW.

LONG GUILE

Patented in 1745 by William Heath for 50 acres in East Pr.Anne,Election district 15, map #4.

LONG HEDGE

Patented on 25 Feb.1679 by John Carter for 250 acres in Lawsons, Election district 8, map #18.
Rent Rolls 1666-1723 John Carter Jr.
1 Nov.1722 John Carter and Elizabeth Carter of Dorc.Co.Md. sold part to Sarah Davis-no acreage given.
1752 resurveyed to UPPER ANDUE 746 acres.

LONG LOOKED FOR

Patented in 1726 for 48 acres by Francis Wilson in St.Peters, Election district 2,map #6
1753 resurveyed to GEORGES ADVENTURE 1000 acres.

LONG LOOKED FOR

see DAVIS CHOICE

LONG LOTT

Patented on 19 March 1694 by James Langrell for 50 acres in St.Peters, Election district 2, map #6.
Rent Rolls 1666-1723 possessed by James Langrell.
3 Aug.1720 George Langrell of Dorc.Co.,planter, sold to Thomas Wright 50 acres
1783 tax- John Wright
1785 resurveyed to RIGHTS CONCLUSION 284 1/4 acres.

LONG LOTT

Patented in 1798 for 7 3/4 acres in Dublin,Election district 4, map #12, by Levin D. Miles, Matthias Miles, John Miles, Nelly Miles and James Miles.

LONG MEADOW

Patented in 1747, a resurvey included HILLARDS ADVENTURE,by Robert Jenkins Henry for 646 acres in Brinkleys, southeast, Election district 3,map #16.
1764/6 Robert Jenkins Henry willed to son Robert 646 acres
1783 tax- Robert Jenkins Henry 646 acres.
28 Jan.1801 Robert Jenkins Henry of Baltimore sold to George Riggin 600 acres.
20 July 1801 George Riggin,wife Elizabeth Riggin sold 218 acres to Gilbert Milbourn.
20 July 1801 George Riggin,wife Elizabeth Riggin sold to William Cox 159 acres.
1816 William Cox willed to son William Cox.
1838 Gilbert Milbourn had only daughters, land not assigned to anyone.

LONG MEADOW

Patented in 1786 for 30 acres by Henry W. Miles in Tangier, Election district 9, map #7.

LONG MEADOW

Patented on 25 May 1709 by John Tunstall for 248 acres in Dames Quarter, Election district 11, map #7.
9 Sep.1760 Edward Roberts, Samuel Jones and Lewis Jones sold to Thomas Hayward and William Hayward interest 150 acres in LONG MEADOW.

LONG MEADOW

Patented in 1746 for 78 acres by Henry Waggaman in St.Peters, Election district 2, map #6.
1783 tax- William Waggaman
1 Nov.1794 William Waggaman sold to George Waggaman, LONG MEADOW,ADVENTURE & ADVENTURES AMENDMENT.
1 Nov.1794 George Waggaman sold to John Bedsworth 78 acres but is really 75 acres with ADVENTURE.

LONG RIDGE

Patented on 22 April 1695 by Joseph Stanford for 125 acres in East Pr.Anne,Election district 15, map #4.
Rent Rolls 1666-1723 Joseph Stanford is dead and no one possesses.
20 Aug1760 Joseph Stanford,wife Sarah Stanford sold to Jonathan Pollitt 125 acres.
1783 tax- Jonathan Pollitt 125 acres
1806 Jonathan Pollitt willed to wife Mary Pollitt.

LONG RIDGE

Patented on 30 May 1689 by Robert Catlin for 135 acres in Westover, Election district 13, map #11.
2 June 1713 William Catlin heir of Robert Catlin, wife Jane Catlin sold to Timothy Sullivan 135 acres.
Timothy Sullivan and wife ELinor Sullivan sold to James Daugherty.
1716 James Daugherty willed to daughter Rose Daugherty 75 acres and to daughter Catherine Daugherty (she died young)
22 Aug.1733 William Puzey and wife Rose Puzey sold to Daniel Hull 135 acres
1735 Daniel Hull willed wife Hannah Hull to sell 60 acres.
15 Dec.1735 Hannah Hull widow of Daniel Hull sold to Dennis Adams 60 acres now called THE HONEST DESIGN.
13 Dec.1746 Marcy Beauchamp sold to Hannah Hull and Daniel Hull her son 60 acres of HONEST DESIGN being part LONG RIDGE.
30 March 1753 Dennis Adams and wife Rachel Adams sold 60 acres to William Boston.
1773 Dennis Adams willed to wife Rachel Adams.
1778 Jacob Adams willed to son John Adams
1777 William Boston willed to sons Richard Boston and Levin Boston.
1783 tax- Richard Boston 40 acres
1783 tax- Levin Boston

1783 tax- Sabrah Adams
23 Dec 1797 Sabra Adams sold to Henry Curtis devised Sabra by her father
Dennis Adams 125 acres.
17 Feb.1810 Levin Boston sold to William Williams 40 acres of BEAUCHAMPS
VENTURE & LONG RIDGE.
29 June 1820 Elijah Boston sold to Thomas Adams son of Phillip Adams.

LONG SINCE EXPECTED

see DAVIS CHOICE

LONG TOWN

Patented on 8 Jan 1676 for 150 acres by William Stevens and assigned to
Thomas Shollites for 150 acres in Asbury,Election district 12, map #21.
Rent Rolls 1666-1723 Thomas Shollites is deceased without heirs. Held by
Thomas Davis
1715 Thomas Davis willed 150 acres to son Thomas.
1726 John Roach willed to son John 150 acres
11 Nov.1758 John Roach sold 40 acres to Jacob Ward.
22 Aug.1763 John Roach,wife Rebecca Roach sold to John Sterling 17 3/4
acres.
12 Dec.1767 John Roach sold 59 acres to Isaac Summers,shoemaker.
1783 tax- Jonathan Roach 40 acres
1783 tax- Mary Sterling 17 1/2 acres
1783 tax- Isaac Summers 80 acres
18 Mary 1791 Jonathan Roach mortgaged to William Williams 166 acres of
LONGTOWN & JOHNSONS LOTT.
7 Jan 1800 John Ward son of Stephen Ward, now of Kentucky sold to Jacob
Cullen.
21 Jan 1801 Jonathan Roach sold to John Thomas 166 acres at Johnsons
Creek.-no names of tracts.
6 Nov.1801 John Cullen,wife Betsy Cullen, sold to Stephen Sterling (free
negro) 10 acres.

LONG VILE

Patented on 28 Sep.1681 for 50 acres by James Johnson in East Pr. Anne,
Election district 15, map #4.
Rent Rolls 16661-1723 -James Johnson long since dead.

LONGS CHANCE

Patented in 1741 by Samuel Long for 25 acres in Lawsons, Election
district 8, map #18.
1756 Samuel Long willed to son Randal Long
1783 tax- Sarah Long 25 acres.

LONGS CHANCE

Patented in 1740 by Daniel Long for 100 acres in Dublin, Election
district 4, map #2.
25 Feb.1755 Daniel Long sold to Elisha Long 100 acres.
6 July 1757 Elisha Long,wife Mary Long sold 100 acres to John Porter.
1763 resurveyed to PORTERS PURCHASE 319 acres.

LONGS CHANCE

Patented in 1753, a resurvey from BOSTONS ADVENTURE, by Jeffrey Long and Coulbourn Long for 1130 acres in Brinkleys,northwest,Election district 3, map #14.
28 June 1756 Coulbourn Long,wife Esther Long sold to Jeffrey Long 1130 acres.
29 June 1756 Jeffrey Long,wife Sarah Long sold to Benjamin Lankford 260 acres.
29 June 1756 Jeffrey long sold to Coulbourn Long tract now called COULBOURN LONGS CHANCE being part of LONGS CHANCE 131 1/2 acres.
29 Dec.1759 Benjamin Lankford sold to David Lankford 241 1/2 acres with tract NEWPORT.
18 March 1778 John Fleming and wife Sarah Fleming and Mary Scott sold to John Perkins and wife Rachel Perkins 160 acres, a moity of LONGS CHANCE.
18 March 1778 John Perkins and wife Rachel Perkins (Rachel Long daughter of Jeffrey Long) sold to John Fleming and wife Sarah Fleming (prob. a division of land.)
10 Apr.1780 John Fleming and wife Sarah Fleming (Sarah Long) sold to John Perkins and wife Rachel Perkins 160 acres patented Jeffrey Long.
1783 tax- John Broughton 110 acres
1783 tax- John Perkins 320 acres
1783 tax- Coulbourn Long 131 1/2 acres
1783 tax- heirs of David Lankford 277 1/2 acres
19 April 1782 John Broughton,wife Mary Broughton sold to John Perkins 160 acres, their rights.
24 Oct.1787 Samuel Long,wife Margaret Long, sold to Orpha Turpin 131 1/2 acres COULBOURN LONGS CHANCE
22 Aug.1794 Stephen Marshall and wife Rachel Marshall sold to Thomas Mills 137 3/4 acres of MITCHELLS LOTT,MARSHALLS INHERITANCE,LONGS CHANCE.
25 May 1795 Orpha Turpin sold 131 1/2 acres to William Turpin
6 Jan 1798 I Rachel Perkins am bound to William Perkins to make over 166 acres.
7 Jan.1802 William Perkins, Joseph Broughton, Esther Long Perkins, Elzey Maddux and wife Elizabeth Maddux sold 479 acres to Nathan Cahoon, formerly held by John Perkins and Rachel Perkins, deceased.
9 May 1806 Nathan Cahoon, wife Betty Cahoon sold to Henry Cahoon 244 1/2 acres.
1808 part resurveyed to LANKFORDS CHOICE 295 1/4 acres.
9 Feb.1807 William Lankford of David Lankford sold to John Ward 4 acres.
3 Oct.1808 William Wiliams, Thomas Williams, John Williams, Thomas Furniss comissioners to sell the real estate of William Turpin of Nehemiah Turpin who died intestate sold LONGS CHANCE, BOSTONS ADVENTURE & CONVENIENCE to Sewell Turpin of Worc.Co.Md.
1851 Stephen Ward willed to wife Margaret Ward 4 acres.

LONGS CHANCE

This piece of land is within the bounds of LANKFORDS CHOICE
that was resurveyed in 1751 from LONGS CHANCE by Samuel Long for 25 acres
12 Nov.1767 Benjamin Lankford gave to son-in-law George Howard for 5 shillings.18 acres conveyed by Jeffrey Long to Benjamin Lankford.
28 Feb. 1794 George Howard,wife Priscilla Howard sold to Severn Howard 18 acres.
1783 tax- George Howard 18 acres.
1844 Severn Howard willed lands to son William Howard, unnamed.

LONGS DELIGHT

Patented in 1748 by Samuel Long for 60 acres in Lawsons, Election
district 8, map #18.
1756 Samuel Long willed to son Jeffrey Long
1783 tax- Jeffrey Long 60 acres.

LONGS LOTT

Patented on 26 April 1680 by William Stevens for 100 acres and assigned
to Samuel Long in Westover,Election district 13, map #1.Resurveyed in
1667 to 200 acres.
Rent Rolls 1666-1723 John Long son of Samuel Long
1713 Randal Long and Sarah Long sold to Adrain Marshall
6 May 1744 George Marshall and wife Mary Marshall of Morumsco sold to
John White Jr. 60 acres, 44 acres of LONG LOTT & 16 acres of LEDBOURN
adj. called THE EXCHANGE.
9 Feb.1748 George Marshall, Samuel Long and wife Sarah Long, Thomas
Cottingham and wife Mary Cottingham (heirs of Randal Long)sold to Robert
King tract LOTS PURCHASE, 85 acres made up of LONG LOTT & LEDBOURN.
20 Sep.1780 Coulbourn Long sold to Samuel Long of Acco.Co.Va. 140 acres
1783 tax- Thomas King 100 acres.
19 Dec.1791 Thomas King traded 10 acres with Levin Boston for 14 acres of
CONCLUSION.
19 Dec.1791 I Thomas King agree to sell to Samuel Smith 1 acre, in
Morumsco.
2 Aug.1806 Levin Boston Sr. sold to William Williams CONCLUSION & LONGS
LOTT 102 acres and LONGS LOTT now called THE EXCHANGE 10 acres.

LONGS PREVENTION

Patented on 3 May 1689 by Samuel Long for 69 acres in Brinkleys,
northwest, Election district 3, map #14.
Rent Rolls 1666-1723 possessed by John Long.
13 Sep.1716 agreement of division- by John Long, Jeffrey Long, David Long
and Daniel Long, equal parts of 442 acres of LONGS PURCHASE,BOSTONS
ADVENTURE,LONGS PREVENTION.
30 June 1739 William Hutchison and wife Ann Hutchison sold to Solomon
Long BOSTONS ADVENTUE and 10 acres out of LONGS PREVENTION & LONGS
PURCHASE.
28 Oct.1747 David Long and wife Abigail Long sold to Jeffrey Long 110
acres of BOSTONS ADVENTURE,LONGS PURCHASE, LONGS PREVENTION.
1740 Samuel Long willed land to sons William Long and Coulbourn Long.
22 Aug.1748 William Long and wife Neomy Long of Worc.Co. sold to
Coulbourn Long his moity 16 acres.
5 Sep.1750 John Long, Jeffrey Long, David Long, wife Abigail Long, David
Long the younger, Coulbourn Long 100 acres (division of lands.)
15 Sep.1753 David Long Jr,shipwright,sold to Jeffrey Long 110 acres of
BOSTONS ADVENTURE,LONGS PURCHASE,LONGS PREVENTION
15 Oct.1767 Littleton Long sold to Nehemiah Turpin land from father David
Long 110 1/2 acres of BOSTONS ADVENTURE,LONGS PURCHASE & LONGS PREVENTION
1753 resurveyed to LONGS CHANCE 1130 acres.

LONGS PRIVILEDGE

Patented in 1762 for 7 acres by Jeffrey Long in Brinkleys, northwest, Election district 3, map #14.

LONGS PURCHASE

Patented on 2 May 1689 by Samuel Long for 123 acres in Brinkleys, northwest,Election district 3, map #14.
Rent Rolls 1666-1723 John Long heir.
13 Sep.1716 agreement as to division, by John Long,Jeffrey Long,David Long and Daniel Long.
20 June 1739 William Hutchison and wife Ann Hutchison sold to Solomon Long 10 acres.
28 Oct.1747 David Long and wife Abigail Long sold to Jeffrey Long 100 acres LONGS PURCHASE,LONGS PREVENTION,BOSTONS ADVENTURE.
22 Aug.1748 William Long and wife Neomi Long sold to Coulbourn Long 40 acres.
4 Sep.1750 John Long,Jeffrey Long,David Long,David Long the younger and Coulbourn Long(division of lands.)
15 Sep.1753 David Long Jr.,shipwright sold to Jeffrey Long part.
15 Oct.1767 Littleton Long sold to Nehemiah Turpin part.
1753 resurveyed to include LONGS CHANCE.

LOOT

Patented in 1730 for 50 acres in Dublin, Election district 4, map #12.

LOSS AND GAIN

Patented in 1726 by Edmund Beauchamp for 100 acres in Westover, Election district 13, map #11.
8 Sep.1745 I William Beauchamp eldest son of Edmund, of Kent Co. Del. blacksmith, sell to brother Edmund Beauchamp of Som.Co.planter 100 acres.
20 Aug.1746 Edmund Beauchamp and wife Elizabeth Beauchamp sold to William Jones,carpenter, aka FORKED NECK
14 Aug.1752 Edmund Beauchamp sold to William Walston 44 1/4 acres.
2 Dec 1752 William Walston,wife Ann Walston, sold to Nathaniel Dougherty 44 1/2 acres.
8 May 1752 William Jones,wife Sarah Jones, sold to Samuel Handy, aka HOGYARD
19 July 1754 Nathaniel Dougherty sold to William Turpin 44 1/2 acres
1767 William Turpin willed to son Joshua Turpin tract bought of Nathaniel Dougherty, unnamed.
7 June 1761 William Walston sold to Nathaniel Dougherty FIRST CHOICE, LOSS & GAIN, 8 acres.
12 Feb 1763 Nathaniel Dougherty and wife Rebecca Dougherty sold 40 1/4 acres to William Turpin,LOSS & GAIN,& FIRST CHOICE and 8 acres conveyed by William Walston.
1783 tax- Joshua Turpin 52 acres
1815 Joshua Turpin willed real estate to brother William Turpin, unnamed.

LOSS & GAIN

Patented in in 1804 for 5 acres by Matthias Miles in East Pr.Anne, Election district 15, map #5.
1818 Matthias Miles willed to son Levin C. Miles.

Patented in Nov.1664 by William Thomas of Virginia for 1000 acres in Mt.Vernon,Election district 5, map #1.
16 Dec.1673 William Thomas deeded to Francis Roberts.
18 Dec.1673 Francis Roberts sold to Edward Gibbs 892 acres 9 March 1683 Edward Gibbs returned to Francis Roberts 892 acres.
9 March 1683 Francis Roberts sold to William Harris now to be called SIDNEY BROWNS LOTT.
9 June 1674 Francis Roberts sold to William Wright 108 acres of part now called LOTTS WIFE.
17 Nov.1683 Francis Roberts sold to William Harris 892 acres of LOTT at Oystershell Point.
1685 William Right sold to Levin Denwood LOTTS WIFE.
1693 became GRAVE ENDS TOWN, part now RIVERLEIGH
Rent Rolls 1666-1723 892 acres possessed by William Harris son of William and 108 acres to Thomas Dashiell
26 Aug.1700 Levin Denwood and wife Priscilla Denwood deeded to Thomas Dashiell 108 acres called LOTTS WIFE.
1 Au.1718 William Harris deeded to Richard Harris.
10 Dec 1729 William Harris and wife Frances Harris sold to Sidney Brown of Pennsylvania 97 acres.
19 Dec.1729 Sidney Brown sold to Edward Fowler
11 Oct 1737 resurvey by Thomas Dashiell part of LOTTS WIFE, 85 acres to FATHERS CARE and added vacant land 166 acres adjacent.
8 May 1739 George Harris son of Robert Harris, and wife Esther Harris sold 200 acres to John Leatherbury.
29 Jan 1742 William Harris and wife Frances Harris sold to John Fowler 140 acres LOTTS SON, part of LOTT
1783 tax- Edward Fowler-LOTTS DAUGHTER 257 acres
1783 tax- Robert Leatherbury 200 acres
1783 tax- Robert Layfield
1783 tax- Tempy Harris 166 acres
1783 tax- Mary Harris 83 acres
1783 tax- John Harris 200 acres
16 Feb 1783 Clement Holliday, commissioneer to sell confiscated property sold to Robert Layfield 80 1/4 acres.
1 May 1783 Caleb Harris of Sussex Co.Del.sold to Thomas Holbrook his interest.
24 May 1799 Richard Ingersol sold to Robert Fowler,part.
2 Oct 1800 John Leatherbury of Robert Leatherbury, wife Sarah Leatherbury sold to Richard Ingersol 360 or 370 acres of COVINGTONS FOLLY, MY OWN BEFORE, SECURITY, LOTT.
7 April 1804 Richard Ingersol, wife Elizabeth Ingersol sold to William Roberts 350 acres of LOTT, SECURITY & COVINGTONS FOLLY.
24 July 1804 Robert Fowler, wife Sarah Fowler sold to John Kirwin 3 acres and 1 1/13th acres.
14 July 1805 Richard Ingersol sold to Thomas Rencher, part from father Samuel Ingersol.
16 Feb.1806 Edward Fowler and wife Eleanor Fowler sold to George Jones 84 acres.
15 Feb.1806 Edward Fowler, wife Eleanor Fowler sold to John Harris 23 1/2 acres.
12 Nov.1834 John Kirwin Jr. s/o John sold to William A.D. Bounds 31 1/3

acres.

LOTT

Patented in 1715 by David Polk for 200 acres in St.Peters, Election
district 2, map #6.
1752 resurveyed to INTENT 317 acres.

LOTT

Patented on 25 May 1724 by John Roach for 36 acres in Asbury, Election
district 12,, map #21.
1726/7 John Roach willed to son John 36 acres.
12 Dec 1767 John Roach sold to Isaac Summers, shoemaker 21 acres with
LONG TOWN.
1783 tax- Jonathan Roach 12 acres.
21 Jan.1801 Jonathan Roach sold all his land 166 acres to John Thomas.

LOTT

Patented in 1756 for 10 acres by Thomas Toadvine in East Princess Anne
Election district 15, map #4.
22 Dec.1779 Stephen Toadvine sold to Walter Taylor 10 acres
1783 tax- Walter Taylor
8 Dec.1783 Walter Taylor sold 10 acres to Solomon Gibbons of
Worc.Co.(mortgage)
8 Apr.1796 Walter Taylor of Kent Co.Del. sold to Jacob Morris part with
HARMAN,HOGQUARTER & PRIVILEDGE.

LOTT

Patented in 1760 for 3 acres by Kellum Lankford in Brinkleys, northwest,
Election district 3, map #14.
8 Dec.1767 Kellum Lankford sold to Thomas Williams 3 acres and LOT
ENLARGED total of 8 1/2 acres
1761 LOTT ENLARGED 5 1/2 acres, by Kellum Lankford..
1767 resurveyed to WILLIAMS GREEN 644 3/4 acres.

LOTT

Patented in 1766 for 5 acres by Stephen Ward in Asbury, Election district
12, map #21.
7 Jan 1800 John Ward son of Stephen Ward, now of Kentucky sold to Jacob
Cullen.

LOTT

Patented in 1790 by Matthias Miles for 56 acres in East Princess
Anne,Election district 15,map #5.
12 July 1803 Matthias Miles and wife Nancy Miles sold to John B. Slemons
56 acres.

LOTTS PURCHASED

see LONGS LOTT & LEDBOURN

LOTTS WIFE,LOTTS SON, LOTTS DAUGHTER

see LOTT of 1664.

LOW NECK

see WATERS RIVER

LOWER WOOD

Patented on 28 Aug.1677 William Green and assigned to Richard Peake for 170 acres in Mt.Vernon,Election district 5, map #1.
Rent Rolls 1666-1723 possessed by Phillip Covington
1751 resurveyed to COVINGTONS CONCLUSION 348 acres.

LOW LAND

Patented in 1749 a resurvey of CLOVERFIELDS by Thomas Bannister for 100 acres in East Pr.Anne,Election disrict 15, map #5.
1751 Thomas Bannister willed to son Ezekiel Bannister LOW GROUND.

LOWLANDS

Patented in 1758 for 34 1/2 acres by William Gray in Dublin, Election District 4, map #12.
17 June 1761 William Gray son of Allen Gray, and wife Mary Gray sold 10 1/2 acres to Isaac Coston, near Dividing Creek.
1772 Isaac Coston willed lands to sons Henry Coston, Eli Coston and Isaac Coston, this land not named.
17 Oct.1794 Henry Coston sold to John Williams of Worc.Co. land devised by father Isaac Coston to son Isaac Coston that was confiscated by my mother Laura Coston- no name.
1794 resurveyed to WINDSOR 482 1/4 acres by Henry Coston.

LOWLAND

Patented in 1762 for 45 acres and 31 acres by John Gibbons and Thomas Gibbons in Westover, Election district 13, map #10
1783 tax- Thomas Gibbons 31 1/2 acres
1783 tax- John Gibbons Sr.45 acres.

LOW SWAMP

Patented in 1754 for 100 acres by James Gunby in Lawsons ,Election district 8, map #18.
1783 tax- James Gunby 100 acres
9 Feb.1797 James Gunby sold to John Gunby of Worc.Co. 70 acres.
27 Feb.1797 John Gunby son of Kirk Gunby of Worc.Co. sold to Benjamin Lankford 70 acres.
9 Apr.1798 Benjamin Lankford sold to Henry Handy 110 3/4 acres of LOW SWAMP & LITTLEWORTH.
1813 Henry Handy willed to wife Hannah Handy land bought of Benjamin Lankford.

LOW SWAMP

Patented in 1762 for 9 acres by John Duett in Lawsons, Election district

8, map #18. Resurveyed in 1763 for 10 acres.

LOW SWAMP

Patented in 1763 by John Duett for 10 acres in Lawsons, Election district
8, map #18.
12 Aug.1801 Thomas Robertson Jr. executor of Robert B. Holland sold to
John Horsey of Smith Horsey 2 acres out of the 10 acres.
12 Aug.1801 Smith Horsey sold to Thomas Robertson Jr. 9 acres.
16 April 1806 Smith Horsey sold to John Horsey of Smith Horsey 10 acres
purchased of Thomas Robertson exec. of Robert B. Holland.

LUNS AMENDMENT

Patented in 1740 for 251 acres by Lewis Jones in Tangier, Election
district 9, map #7.
1792 resurveyed to CHANCE 227 1/4 acres

LUMNS ENCREASE

Patented in 1668 by Edward Lumn for 150 acres in Tangier, Election
district 9, map #7.
1 Apr.1669 Edward Lumn sold 100 acres to Gideon Tilghman of GOLDEN
QUARTER(this probably includes LUMNS ENCREASE.
2 Apr.1669 Edward Lumn sold 300 acres to William Hopkins at Dames
Quarter.
1675 Edward Lumn of Ann Arundel Co. Md. and wife Mary Lumn appointed
friend John Panter of Little Money Creek his attorney to sell GOLDEN
QUARTER in Dames Quarter.
5 Nov.1675 Edward Lumn and wife Mary Lumn sold to Levin Howard 150 acres.
21 March 1742 Henry Waggaman and wife Mary Waggaman one of the daughters
of Levin Woolford deceased son of Roger Woolford sold to Samuel Wilson
and wife Martha Wilson(d/o Levin Woolford) deeded 300 acres of
WOOLFORD,HAPPY ADDITION,LUMNS IMPROVEMENT,LUMNS ENCREASE on an island
called GOLDEN QUARTER.
1783 tax- Robert Jones 7 1/2 acres.
1751 resurveyed to PROSPECT 449a cres.

LUMNS IMPROVEMENT

Patented on 3 June 1667 by Edward Lumn for 250 acres in Tangier, Election
district 9, map #7.
6 Nov.1675 Edward Lumn and wife Mary Lumn sold to Roger Woolford 250
acres.
Rent Rolls-1666-1723 possessed by the widow Mrs. Mary Woolford 150
acres, and 200 acres George Hutchins
1726/7 George Hutchins willed estate to son William Hutchins and daughter
Mary Hutchins(land not named.)
21 March 1742 Henry Waggaman and wife Mary Waggaman(d/o Levin Woolford
deceased.) sold to Samuel Wilson and wife Martha Wilson(d/o Levin
Woolford) 300 acres, WOOLFORD,HAPPY ADDITION,LUMNS IMPROVEMENT,LUMNS
ENCREASE on an island called GOLDEN QUARTER
1744 Lewis Jones willed 90 acres to sons Lewis Jones,Samuel Jones.
1 Jan 1773 Martha Wilson widow of Samuel Wilson deceased and Levin Wilson
with Sarah Wilson gave to George Wilson- land on the north side of

Manokin River, unnamed.
13 Jan 1779 John Jones traded 7 1/2 acres with Robert Jones for part of
LONG DELAY
1751 resurveyed to PROSPECT, 449 acres.

LYONS WHELP

see GOLDEN LYON Pat.1788 by Obed Riggin 36 3/4 acres.

MADDUX ADVENTURE

Patented on 20 Aug.1679 by John White and assigned to Lazarus Maddux, in
Fairmount, Election district 6, map #9, for 150 acres.
Rent Rolls 1666-1723 Possessed by Lazarus Maddux son of Alexander Maddux
1740 resurveyed to LAZARUS LOTT, 641 acres.

MADDUX HIS HOPE

Patented on 14 Jan 1666 by Lazarus Maddux for 100 acres in Fairmount,
Election district 6, map #9.
Resurveyed by William Roach 150 acres.
1757 resurveyed to END OF STRIFE 609 acres
1783 tax- John Moore 100 acres.

MADDUX ENCLOSURE

Patented on 24 May 1680 by Lazarus Maddux for 100 acres in Fairmount,
Election district 6, map #9.
Rent Rolls 1666-1723 Lazarus Maddux
1695 resurveyed to 250 acres Lazarus Maddux
1740 resurveyed to INCLOSURE 590 acres.

MAIDSTONE

Patented on 28 April 1680 by Elizabeth Davis for 70 acres in Westover,
Election district 13, map #11.
Rent Rolls 1666-1723 possessed by Ephraim Wilson 70 acres.

MAKEPEACE

Patented on 9 Nov.1663 by John Roach for 150 acres in Lawsons, Election
district 8, map #19.
1709 John Roach Sr. willed 150 acres to son John Roach.
1726/7 John Roach Jr. willed to son Charles Roach 150 acres.
22 June 1757 William Roach (division of lands) to Thomas Cullen that John
Roach devised MAKEPEACE & EXCHANGE to sons John Roach and Michael Roach.
1783 tax- Daniel Cullen 122 acres
1783 tax- William Roach 100 acres
1783 tax- Rachel Roach 50 acres.

MANLOVES DISCOVERY

Patented on 20 June 1668 by Thomas Manlove for 250 acres in East Pr.Anne,
Election district 15, map #5.
Rent Rolls 1666-1723 Samuel Worthington

1717 Samuel Worthington willed to wife Alice Worthington.
1739/40 Alice Ellis widow of Samuel Worthington and Merrick Ellis
(daughter of Arnold Elzey,) willed to nephew Robert Elzey and if no heirs
to neice Sarah Elzey daughter of brother John Elzey.
1783 tax- heirs of Robert Elzey 250 acres.
19 May 1801 William Waters Sr sold to Ann Waters wife of William Gillis
Waters 250 acres
19 May 1801 William Gillis Waters, wife Ann Waters sold to William Waters
Sr. 250 acres.

MANLOVES LOTT

Patented on 25 Nov.1678 by William Manlove and assigned to Cornelius
Morris in Brinkleys, northeast, Election district 3, map #15, for 300
acres.
10 Feb.1680 Cornelius Morris and wife Ann Morris sold to Josias Seward
300 acres.
Josias Seward died intestate and his daughter Abigail Seward married
Samuel Tomlinson Jr.
22 Feb.1688 Josias Seward and wife Margaret Seward sold to Archibald
White, part. Rent Rolls 1666-1723 Samuel Tomlinson
1745 Abigail Tomlinson gave part to son Hampton Tomlinson.
1748 Sayward Tomlinson sold to John Williams of Pocomoke.
25 Aug.1748 John Williams and Esther Williams and Sayward Tomlinson and
wife Margaret Tomlinson sold to Robert Jenkins Henry 138 acres.
1764 Robert Jenkins Henry gave to son Robert J.Henry 138 1/2 19 June 1764
Archibald White gave to son William White, TULLY BRISK sold by Josias
Seward to Archibald White father of Archibald out of MANLOVES LOTT 45 1/2
acres.
3 Nov.1772 Elizabeth Tomlinson daughter of Hampton Tomlinson sold 50
acres to John J. Jordan for 5 shillings.
1775 ADDITION patented for 59 acres.
16 Dec.1777 William White sold to Jesse Hall, 9 acres, ADDITION TO
MANLOVES LOTT.
1783 tax Robert J. Henry 158 acres
23 June 1792 Samuel Tomlinson sold to John Jordan his interest.
22 Aug.1796 John Jordan,wife Rebecca Jordan sold to David Tyler of
Worc.Co.Md. 50 acres.
7 Feb 1806 Jesse Hall sold to Elijah Hall 9 acres of ADDITION TO MANLOVE
LOTT.

MANLOVES VENTURE

Patented on 19 Nov.1692 to Richard Acworth and assigned to John Manlove
for 100 acres in East Princess Anne,Election district 15, map #5.
10 Dec.1674 John Manlove and wife Elizabeth Manlove sold to Richard
Chambers 100 acres.
Rent Rolls 1666-1723 Richard Chambers
1743 Richard Chambers willed to cousin Richard Brereton and cousin Samuel
Collins.
1746 Henry Brereton of Baltimore Co. Md. and Thomas Brereton of same
place sold to Woncey McClemmy all rights 100 acres, that Richard Brereton
brother of Henry Brereton and Thomas Brereton willed to them.
7 Apr.1748 Samuel Collins and wife Elizabeth Collins of Worc.Co. sold to
Woncey McClemmy.

7 Nov.1749 creditors join to sell lands of Woncey McClemmy to Hamilton
Bell, 100 acres.

MANNINGS RESOLUTION

Patented on 16 Oct.1662 by Thomas Manning for 800 acres in
Mt.Vernon,Election district 5,map #1.
16 Jan 1684 John Manning and wife Sarah Manning sold to Cornelius
Johnson.
16 Dec.1684 Nathaniel Manning son of Thomas Manning sold to Cornelius
Johnson.
20 Jan 1679 Cornelius Johnson sold to Thomas Covington 150 acres now
called COVINGTONS PURCHASE.
1687 Cornelius Johnson willed to William Jones Jr. and Daniel Jones.
Rent Rolls 1666-1723 Samuel Covington 150 acres, Daniel Jones 400 acres,
William Jones 250 acres.
1690 William Jones of Money died and land divided by William and Daniel
Jones.
1749 Thomas Covington gave 150 acres to sons John Covington and Jacob
Covington.
14 Dec.1756 James Covington sold 20 acres to Daniel Jones.
1756 Daniel Jones willed to son Phillip Jones 20 acres.
6 May 1766 James Covington sold to Daniel Jones, his interest.
1783 tax- Daniel Jones 397 acres
1783 tax- Elizabeth Parker 133 acres.
20 June 1799 Phillip Jones,wife Peggy Jones, sold to Nancy Hill, 1 acre.
8 Jan 1802 John Leatherbury, wife Sally Leatherbury sold to Levin Jones
Sr. 220 7/8 acres of COVINGTONS COONCLUSION, SWEETWOOD & MANNINGS
RESOLUTION.
8 Jan 1802 Levin Jones sold to John Leatherbury of Robert Leatherbury,
400 acres of COVINGTONS CONCLUSION,SWEETWOOD, MANNINGS RESOLUTION.
7 Sep.1803 Thomas Holbrook sold to Levin Jones and John Leatherbury part
to settle boundary dispute.
26 April 1810 Levin Jones,wife Nancy Jones sold to Benjamin Smith 2 1/4
acres.
24 Dec.1814 Thomas Holbrook sold to Elizabeth Jones, 150 acres.
27 Apr.1830 Sheriff's sale, suit of Esther H. Cottman against Alexander
Jones and George Jones 560 acres.
1851 Elizabeth Jones widow of Alexander Jones, willed to son Daniel Jones
150 acres, deeded me by Thomas Holbrook.

MARCOMBS LOTT

Patented on 7 March 1663 by John Marcomb & Ann Marcomb for 400 acres in
St.Peters,Election district 2, map #6.
Rent Rolls 1666-1723 possessed by George Betts
3 July 1667 granted to Ann Marcomb widow and now wife of Peter Douty.
11 June 1672 Peter Douty and wife Ann Douty sold to George Andra 400
acres.
24 Feb.1674 George Andra and wife Thomason Andra sold to George Betts 400
acres.
1703 resurveyed by George Betts.
1709 George Betts gave to son-in-law John Irving and his wife Frances
Irving, his eldest daughter.
1783 tax- Thomas Irving 400 acres

1784 Thomas Irving willed to son Thomas Irving, 400 acres.
20 Nov.1808 George Irving of Green Co. Ga., wife Ann Irving sold to
Littleton Dennis 650 acres of HABNAB & MARCOMBS LOTT. Sale reconfirmed 17
May 1809.
20 April 1809 Littleton Dennis sold to Ezekiel Gillis 113 acres of HAB
NAB & MARCOMBS LOTT.
20 April 1809 Littleton Dennis sold to Thomas G. Fountain balance of
HABNAB & MARCOMBS LOTT.
13 April 1810 Thomas G. Fountain sold to Littleton Robins 100 acres of
MARCOMBS LOTT & HABNAB.

MARGRATES PURCHASE

Patented in 1761 by Margaret Hales for 15, acres in East Pr.Anne,
Election distict 15, map #4.
1783 tax- Margaret Hales 15 acres.
3 July 1792 Mary Taylor of Worc.Co. and Esther Sollas of Sussex Co.Del.
sold to Matthias Miles, 15 acres where Margaret Hailes formerly lived.
1804 ADDITION 23 acres patented Matthias Miles.

MARISH GROUND

Patented on 10 Nov.1695 by Richard Davis in Fairmount for 200 acres,
Election district 6, map #9.
Rent Rolls 1666-1723 66 2/3 acres by John Davis son of Richard Davis and
133 1/3 acres by William Davis son of Richard.
1710 William Davis granted to William Bannister father of Thomas
Bannister.
18 July 1729 Thomas Bannister sold to Henry Miles 50 acres.
16 March 1742 William Beauchamp and wife Comfort Beauchamp sold to Thomas
Bannister and wife Sarah Bannister part of FOUNTAINS ADDITION taken out
of MARISH GROUND sold to Nicholas Fountain. 110 acres
23 Aug.1770 Betty Allen sold to John Williams for 5 shillings 33 1/2
acres.
24 Aug.1770 William Miles sold to Stoughton Maddux 50 acres.
14 May 1771 Thomas Pollitt and wife Betty Pollitt sold to William
Fountain 200 acres for 5 shillings NEWFOUNDLAND,FISHING ISLAND, MARISH
GROUND.
1783 tax- William Fountain
13 Aug.1786 William Fountain and wife Sarah Turpin Fountain sold to John
Williams 1/2 of MARISH GROUND
14 Feb.1789 William Fountain and wife Sarah Fountain sold to John
Williams 1 moity.
1791 William Fountain willed to son William Fountain a piece of marsh
adj. FISHING ISLAND 40 acres unnamed.
4 May 1807 John W. Curtis, wife Margaret Curtis and William Fountain sold
to John C. Wilson 40 1/4 acres.

MARLBOROUGH

Patented on 22 Dec.1681 to Samuel Jones and assigned to Thomas Walter for
150 acres in Election district 2, map #6.
Rent Rolls 1666-1723 possessed by Thomas Shaw who purchased from the
heirs of Thomas Walter.
1783 tax- Thomas Sloss 130 acres

1783 tax- Gowan Wright 20 acres.
1805 Gowan Wright willed lands to daughters Mary Wright, Sarah Wright and
Ann Wright, unnamed.

MARSH PASTURE

Patented in 1730 for 10 3/4 acres by Thomas Holbrook, in Mt.Vernon,
Election district 5, map #1.
1783 tax- William Dockery 10 1/2 acres
1791 Thomas Holbrook willed to son Samuel Holbrook.

MARSHALLS INHERITANCE

Patented on 30 Nov.1740 to Thomas Marshall for 438 acres in Brinkleys,
northwest,Election district 3, map #14.
7 Oct.1746 Thomas Marshall sold 129 acres to Jeffrey Long
1774 Thomas Marshall gave to Stephen Marshall of Acco.Co.Va. 309 acres.
1783 tax- Stephen Marshall
20 Mach 1787 Stephen Marshall sold to William Lankford of David Lankford
4 acres
6 Aug.1794 Stephen Marshall sold 254 acres to Thomas Marshall of
MITCHELLS LOTT,MARSHALLS INHERITANCE.
22 Aug.1794 Stephen Marshall,wife Rachel Marshall sold to Thomas Miles
137 3/4 acres of MITCHELLS LOTT, MARSHALLS INHERITANCE, LONGS CHANCE.
17 May 1798 Thomas Marshall son of Stephen Marshall sold to John Harris
275 acres of MITCHELLS LOTT & MARSHALLS INHERITANCE.
1851 Stephen Ward willed to wife Margaret Handy Ward HARRISLAND
consisting of MARSHALLS INHERITANCE bought of George F. Ward and Theodore
G.Dashiell and Matilda Dashiell 200 acres.
1854 Harriet Handy wife of James Handy gave to son Sidney Handy 200 acres
called HARRISLAND

MARSHEY HOPE

Patented in 1802 for 144 1/2 acres by Samuel Trehearn in Brinkleys,
southwest, Election district 3, map #17.

MARTINS HOPE

Patented in Aug.1679 by William Green and assigned to Francis Martin for
100 acres in Asbury,Election district 12, map #21.
Rent Rolls 1666-1723 Held by William Brittingham in Virginia who married
the widow of Francis Martin.
19 June 1765 John Sterling Sr. sold 4 1/2 acres to Solomon Bird for 5
shillings(trade of lands for PARKERS PEACE.)
1772 resurveyed part to OAK HAMMOCK,pt.to STERLINGS GOOD LUCK, part to
HONEST INTENT.

MARVELLS CHANCE

Patented on 2 April 1705 by John Marvell for 27 acres in Tangier,Election
district 9, map #7.surveyed for Francis Roberts.
Rent Rolls 1666-1723 Francis Roberts
Rent Rolls 1744 John Waller

MARYS ADVENTURE

Patented on 29 Sep.1705 by Mary McGraugh for 40 acres in West Pr.Anne, Election district 1, map #3.
Rent Rolls 1666-1723 Mary McGraugh widow of Owen McGraugh
14 Apr.1725 William McGraugh, grandson of Mary McGraugh, planter and wife Elizabeth McGraugh sold to Henry Newman 40 acres.

MARYS LOTT

This is part of REHOBETH. 400 acres. Today this property is called HAMPTON.
1711 John Henry and Mary Henry sold 400 acres to Robert Mills.
1712 Robert Mills sold back to John Henry.
1715 John Henry willed 400 acres to son Robert Jenkins Henry
1744 Mary Hampton willed to son Robert Jenkins Henry
1764 Robert Jenkins Henry willed to son Robert Jenkins Henry called MARYS LOTT, part of REHOBETH.
1783 tax- Robert Jenkins Henry 400 acres.

MASONS ADVENTURE

Patented on 6 March 1687 by William Mason for 100 acres in St.Peters, Election district 2, map #6.
This is also known as WHITTYS LOTT or TROUBLE
Rent Rolls 1666-1723- Thomas Shaw on accounts of Richard Whitty.

MATES ENJOYMENT

Patented on 22 Oct.1685 by John Culhoone and John Eames for 100 acres in Brinkleys,southwest, Election district 3, map #17.
Rent Rolls 1666-1723 Jesse Ayres
1739 Randal Long willed to grandson Randal Prior
28 Nov.1741 I Sarah Long give to children Thomas Long and Ann Prior 100 acres.
1772 Ann Prior widow of Thomas willed to son Randal Prior.
1783 tax- Thomas Cottingham for orphans of Randal Prior, 100 acres.

MATTHEWS ADVENTURE

Patented in 1696 by William Matthews for 135 acres in Brinkleys, southeast, Election district 3, map #16.
Rent Rolls 1666-1723 William Matthews.
1696 William Matthews willed to sons Teague Matthews, John Matthews, Samuel Matthews.
June 1706 William Matthews sold to Somerset Dickerson
15 May 1724 Somerset Dickerson and wife Hannah Dickerson sold to Alexander McCready 135 acres.
1782 Solomon McCready willed to son Alexander McCready.
1783 tax- Joseph Bell 25 acres.
1783 Solomon McCready 35 acres
1783 tax- Andrew McCready 25 acres.
13 Feb.1808 Stephen McCready, wife Mary McCready & Hannah Milbourn his mother, sold to Stephen Collins 63 1/2 acres.

MATTHEWS FOLLY

see ADAMS FOLLY

MATTHEWS GREEN

Patented in 1749 for 48 acres by Samuel Matthews in Brinkleys, southeast,
Election district 3, map #16.
1783 tax- Samuel Matthews 35 acres

MATTHEWS RIDGE

Patented in 1728 for 60 acres by Joseph Tilghman in Westover, Election
district 13, map #11.
1783 tax- William Tilghman 60 acres
1785 ADDITION patented by William Tilghman 693 3/4 acres
1806 William Tilghman gave ADDITION to daughter
Nancy Tilghman and son William Tilghman.
13 May 1809 John Hayman, wife Nancy Hayman of Ohio sold to James Handy of
Isaac Hancy of Som. Co.Md. devised Nancy Hayman by her father William
Tilghman, ADDITION.

MATTHIAS CHANCE

Patented in 1768 by Matthias Miles for 70 acres in East Pr.Anne, Election
district 15, map #4.
1783 tax- Matthias Miles 70 acres.
resurveyed to CONSOLIDATION 820 3/4 acres in 1791.
25 May 1803 Thomas Jones of John Jones, and wife Betsy Jones sold to
Littleton Dennis Teackle 70 acres.
25 May 1803 Matthias Miles sold to Thomas Jones of John Jones 70 acres.

McCREADYS FIRST CHOICE

Patented in 1748 for 17 3/4 acres by Solomon McCready in Brinkleys,
southeast, Election district 3, map #16.
1783 tax- Solomon McCready 17 acres
1782 will Solomon McCready, to son Alexander McCready three pieces of
land, unnamed.
31 Aug.1789 Alexander McCready and wife Leah McCready of Worc.Co. sold to
Isaac McCready of Somerset Co. with RANGLE.

McDORMANS ADVENTURE

Patented by George McDorman in 1789 for 71 3/4 acres in Dames Quarter,
Election district 11, map #7.
1834 George McDorman willed to sons James McDorman,William McDorman and
Henry McDorman.
14 March 1800 George McDorman sold to William McDorman 6 1/4 acres.
1830 William White willed DORMANS VENTURE to be sold.

MEADOW

Patented on 27 March 1688 by John Brown for 55 acres in West Pr.Anne,

Election district 1, map #3
14 Aug.1688 resurveyed by David Brown for 80 acres.
1698 David Brown willed to Alexander Brown.
1701/13 Alexander Brown willed to son Thomas Brown plantation, no name
given.
3 Oct.1749 John Robertson,glover, sold to John Woolford 80 acres that
Col.David Brown had.
13 Sep.1749 John Woolford and wife Mary Woolford sold to John Robertson.
2 May 1749 Margaret Brown sold to William Skirven for 5 shillings MEADOW,
HACHALA, OWENS CHICE,BROWNS LOTT, etc.
1748/9 John Woolford willed to son Levin Woolford.
24 Aug.1750 William Skirven sold to John Woolford his rights to MEADOW,
THORNTON, HACKLAH, JESHMINE.
1783 tax- Levin Woolford 80 acres
1836 John Woolford willed to son William G. Woolford.

MEADOW

Patented in 1685 for 50 acres by Robert Catlin in Lawsons, Election
district 8, map #19.
Rent Rolls 1666-1723 claimed by William Catlin 50 acres
1731 resurveyed to 200 acres by John Gunby
1745 John Gunby willed to son James Gunby
29 Oct.1723 Nathaniel Doughterty of Baltimore Md. gave to brother John
Dougherty with LITTLE USK
1740 Dickerson Dougherty willed to son Levi Dougherty.
9 Feb.1797 James Gunby sold 100 acres to John Gunby of Worc.Co.Md.
1760 John Dougherty willed to son Obed Dougherty, with LITTLE USK and to
son James Dougherty part and marsh called LITTLE PASTURE.
27 Feb.1797 John Gunby son of Kirk Gunby of Worc.Co.sold to Benjamin
Lankford 100 acres with KIRKS PURCHASE,GUNBYS CONCLUSION, RISQUE,
LITTLEWORTH, LOW SWAMP.
2 May 1801 John Dougherty son of Obed Dougherty and wife Mary Dougherty
sold to Thomas Lord 35 acres of USK, MEADOW, HARD FORTUNE.
7 May 1803 John Dougherty of Obed Dougherty sold to Dickerson Dougherty
50 acres of MEADOW & LITTLE USK.
12 May 1804 William Roach, Thomas Tyler, Elisha Gunby, Samuel Smith,
Littleton Byrd comissioners to divide the real estate of Nathaniel
Dougherty sold to Jesse Dougherty eldest son of Nathaniel Dougherty
LITTLE USK & MEADOW, no acreage given.
15 June 1807 Benjamin Lankford Sr. sold to William Williams 100 acres.
22 June 1808 William Williams sold to Benjamin Lankford 100 acres.
17 March 1810 Benjamin Lankford Sr. sold to William Williams 100 acres.

MEADOW

Patented in 1695 by John Tull for 50 acres in Fairmount, Election
district 6, map #9.
1729 John Tull willed to son Joshua Tull lands in Manokin and Annamessex,
unnamed.
20 Oct.1794 Joshua Tull son of John Tull gave to son Thomas Tull 50 acres
with DESART,WINTER RANGE,HOPEWELL,TULLS ADDITION.
1811 Thomas Tull son of Joshua Tull, and wife Leah Tull willed plantation
to son William Tull, between Annamessex and Manokin River, no name.

MEADOW

Patented on 2 June 1721 by Richard Wallace for 50 acres in Dames Quarter, Election district 9, map #7.
13 July 1779 David Wallace gave to Richard Wallace 50 acres
29 July 1788 Richard Wallace,wife Rebecca Wallace sold to William Roberts his rights to MEADOW that descended to David Wallace heir of James Wallace deceased, and willed by Richard Wallace to sons Matthew Wallace and James Wallace father of David Wallace and conveyed by David to Richard Wallace.

MEADOW

Patented in 1727, a resurvey from ADAMS CONCLUSION for 316 acres in Brinkleys,northeast,Election district 3, map #15.

MEADOW GROUND

Patented on 21 Nov.1694 by William Matthews for 50 acres in Brinkleys, southeast,Election district 3, map #16.
Rent Rolls 1666-1723 William Matthews
10 Dec.1753 John Matthews and wife Elizabeth Matthews and Samuel Matthews Jr. sold 16 acres to Teague Matthews.
9 June 1762 John Matthews gave to son Elijah Matthews 50 acres.
1783 tax- David Matthews MEADOW 15 acres
1783 tax- Samuel Matthews 25 acres MEADOW
1784 Samuel Matthews gave to son Boaz Matthews dwelling plantation.
16 May 1788 Henry Matthews son of Boaz Matthews sold to Samuel Bedsworth and Thomas Jones
1789 Samuel Bedsworth sold to Thomas Jones land of Samuel Matthews who gave to son Boaz Matthews-no name or acres.
13 Aug.1790 Samuel Bedsworth and Thomas Jones sold to Elijah Matthews 150 acres that Samuel Matthews gave to son Boaz, no name.
13 Aug.1790 Elijah Matthews sold to Stephen Collins 50 acres.
21 July 1800 Isaac Matthews sold 119 acres to Elijah Matthews of EDWIN & MEADOW.
21 July 1800 Zachariah Matthews, Thomas Evans, wife Sophia Evans, Molly Matthews, Ruth Matthews, Eleanor Matthews sold to Isaac Matthews 119 acres of EDWIN & MEADOW.
16 Feb.1802 Elijah Matthews sold to Zachariah Matthews 119 acres of EDWIN & MEADOW.
10 Jan 1806 Zachariah Matthews sold to George Carsley 45 acres of EDWIN & MEADOW.
1844 David Walston willed to wife Betty M. Walston.

MEADOW GROUND

Patented in 1746 for 100 acres in Brinkleys, southeast, Election district 3, map #16.
1783 tax- Teague Riggin 100 acres.

MEADOW GROUND

Patented in 1760 for 22 1/2 acres by Thomas Gillis in West Pr.Anne, Election district 1, map #1.

1779 Thomas Gillis willed to grandson Thomas Gillis son of Levin Gillis
and to grandson Levin Gillis.
1783 tax- Levin Gillis 21 1/2 acres.

MEADOW GROUND

Patented in 1769 by John Scott for 18 acres. This was not found on the
maps, probably part of BEARDS NECK.
16 Apr.1806 Smith Horsey sold to John Horsey of Smith Horsey BEARDS NECK
& MEADOW GROUND 5 or 6 acres.

MEADOW GROUND

Patented in 1803 for 5 1/2 acres by William A. Schoolfield in Brinkleys,
northwest ,Election district 3, map #14.
6 April 1810 William A. Schoolfield, wife Mary Schoolfield sold to Isaac
Miles 5 1/2 acres.

MEADOW GROUND

Surveyed in 1807 for 12 3/4 acres, unpatented, by Whittington King in
East Pr.Anne,Election district 15, map #5

MEADOW LAND

Patented in 1769, a resurvey from CHANCE & vacant land by William Miles
for 120 acres in East Princess Anne,Election district 15, map #5.
1775 ADDITION TO MEADOW LAND patented for 111 acres, by Matthias Miles.
1783 tax- Matthias Miles 120 acres.

MEADLAND

Patented on 21 Nov.1697 by John Roach for 64 acres in Asbury, Election
district 12, map #21
1783 tax- Rachel Roach 12 acres
1783 tax- William Roach 22 acres
1783 tax- Jonathan Roach 32 acres
21 Jan 1801 Jonathan Roach sold to John Thomas 166 acres, all of his land
at Johnsons Creek, no name.

MENTWELL

Patented in 1766 for 248 1/4 acres by William Adams in Brinkleys,
northeast,Election district 3 map #15.
1783 tax- William Adams Jr. 100 acres
1783 tax- William Adams Sr. 140 acres

MERCHANTS TREASURE

Patneted on 9 June 1679 by Stephen Coffin who assigned to Daniel Donoho
for 150 acres in Brinkleys,southwest,Election district 3,map #17.
Rent Rolls 1666-1723 -possessed 102 acres by John Outten and 48 acres by
Phillip Conner.
10 July 1697 Daniel Donoho and wife Alice Donoho sold to Sampson
Wheatley.

8 Aug.1701 Sampson Wheatley and wife Elizabeth Wheatley sold to Phillip Conner 48 acres.
14 May 1724 Phillip Conner and wife Catherine Conner sold to John Outten 48 acres.
1735/6 John Outten Jr. gave to son John Outten
1773 Sampson Wheatley willed to daughter Betty Wheatley
1783 tax- Mary Wheatley widow of Sampson Wheatley 100 acres.
24 Apr.1805 Benjamin Conner, wife Grace Conner, Noah Lankford, wife Ann Lankford, John Broughton and wife Mary Broughton, Richard Hall, wife Sarah Purnell Hall and Mary Bedsworth sold to Mordicai Jones of St. Marys County, lands devised by Sampson Wheatley to daughter Betty Jones and conveyed by Caleb Jones to Kellum Lankford, Elijah Coulcourn and Thomas Jones now deceased.

MERRILLS FOLLY

Patented in 1754 by William Merrill for 21 acres in Lawsons, Election district 8, map #18.
1795 William Merrill of Acco.Co.Va. gave to son Maximillian Merrill,plantation where son George Merrill lives in Somerset Co.on Planners Ck. and adj. piece of swamp called MERRILLS FOLLY.
7 Nov.1804 Maximillian Merrill of Va. sold to Elisha Gunby 19 1/4 acres.

MICKLE MEADOW

Patented in 1683 by James Price for 300 acres in Asbury, Election district 12, map #21.
Rent Rolls 1666-1723 possessed by Mary Price widow of James Price.
26 Aug.1758 Cornelius Ward Sr. sold to Outerbridge Horsey 150 acres that came to Cornelius from his mother Ann Ward, daughter of James Price.
1783 tax- Outerbridge Horsey 150 acres.
1783 tax- Stephen Ward 75 acres
1783 tax- Thomas Ward 75 acres
7 Jan 1800 John Ward son of Stephen Ward, now of Kentucky, sold to John Cullen.

MIDDLE

Patented in 1665 by Robert Jones for 100 acres in Dublin, Election district 4,map #13.
14 July 1668 Robert Jones of Northumberland Co. Va.and wife Martha Jones sold to Thomas Walker
8 Nov.1670 Thomas Walker sold to Walter Powell, with GREENFIELD & EXCHANGE.
10 Sep.1670 Walter Powell sold to Elizabeth Hudson and Violetta Hudson daughters of Nicholas Hudson 200 acres of GREENFIELD, MIDDLE & EXCHANGE.
6 Feb.1686 Richard Warren and wife Violetta Warren and John Snow and wife Elizabeh Snow, Elizabeth Hafford mother of Violetta Warren and Elizabeth Snow, widow of John Hafford sold to John Lowder of Boston, New England 200 acres of EXCHANGE & MIDDLE
12 March 1687 John Lowder of Boston sold to John Starrett of Maryland,cooper, 200 acres of MIDDLE & EXCHANGE.
1715 William Powell willed to son Levin Powell
2 Oct.1740 Levin Powell sold 100 acres to Thomas Benston
21 Feb.1757 William Benston son of Thomas Benston,wife Martha Benston gave to brother Thomas Benston.

286

10 March 1767 William Benston, wife Martha Benston, sold to Samuel Wilson
110 acres of MIDDLE & EXCHANGE.
25 March 1780 Samuel Wilson sold to William Benston son of Thomas Benston
14 1/2 acres of MIDDLE & EXCHANGE
20 Aug.1787 division of lands between Samuel Wilson and Thomas Benston
1 March 1790 Thomas Benston sold to Samuel Wilson, description, no acres
given.
19 Nov.1795 Major Samuel Wilson and wife Leah Wilson sold to Littleton
Dennis 185 acres of MIDDLE, EXCHANGE, COW PASTURE, HOG YARD, GREEN
MEADOW, etc.
31 Mach 1810 Thomas Benston, James Barrett, wife Catherine Barrett sold
to Littleton Dennis, devised by grandfather Thomas Benston.

MIDDLE

Patented on 16 May 1683 by Owen McGraugh for 100 acres in West Pr.Anne,
Election district 1, map #3.
Rent Rolls 1666-1723 Owen McGraugh
1751 John McGrath willed to sons David McGrath,Levin McGrath,and John
McGrath.
28 July 1733 William McGrath of Manokin sold to John McGrath of Gr.Money
100 acres patented by Owen McGrath grandfather of William McGrath and
father of said John McGrath.
14 Feb.1764 David McGrath sold his interst to John White.
3 Oct.1766 John White sold mortgage on 100 acres to William Smith
25 June 1768 David McGrath sold to John McGrath 38 acres David had by
fathers will with vacancy added.
29 March 1769 Isaac Coulbourn,sheriff, sold to Mary Waggaman widow, as
Edward Lloyd of Talbot Co. had a judgement against, John White,David
McGrath and William Smith, sold to settle 271 acres of OWENS IMPROVEMENT,
MIDDLE, OWENS DELIGHT, REFUGE, DAVIDS CHANCE.
16 Nov.1774 David McGrath sold to John McGrath for 5 shillings all.
1780 Mary Waggaman gave to son Henry Waggaman lands conveyed me by Isaac
Coulbourn, sheriff.
1783 tax- John McGrath 52 acres
7 Feb.1792 John McGrath of Levin McGrath, Sarah McGrath widow of Levin
and Sarah McGrath widow of John McGrath, sold to Dr. Arnold Elzey 82 3/4
acres of OWENS DELIGHT,OWENS IMPROVEMENT, MIDDLE.
29 April 1792 Henry Waggaman, wife Sarah Waggaman of Dorc.Co. son of
Henry and Mary Waggaman, sold to George Waggaman of Som.Co. afsd lands.
20 Aug.1803 Henry Waggaman, wife Sarah Waggaman of Dorc.Co. sold to
Littleton Dennis Teackle 906 1/4 acres.
17 Dec.1804 Littleton Dennis Teackle sold to John Dennis 450 acres of
OWENS IMPROVENT,OWENS DELIGHT, MIDDLE & WAGGAMANS PURCHASE.
30 May 1804 Arnold Elzey, wife Henrietta Elzey of the city of Washington
DC sold to Levin Jones of Robert Jones 82 3/4a. of OWENS DELIGHT, MIDDLE,
OWENS IMPROVEMENT for which Levin Jones gave him a mortgage.
16 JUne 1807 Arnold Elzey released mortgage to Levin Jones of Robert
Jones.
23 April 1808 Levin Jones sold to Robert J. King.
23 Oct.1809 David McGrath son of John McGrath sold to Robert J. King 200
acres of OWENS DELIGHT, OWENS IMPROVEMENT & MIDDLE.
MIDDLE

Patented in 1769 by Thomas Holbrook for 32 acres in Mt.Vernon, Election

district 5, map #1.
17 Feb.1779 Thomas Holbrook sold to Samuel Ingersol with COVINGTONS
MEADOW 11 acres.
16 Feb.1779 Thomas Holbrook sold 20 1/4 acres to Thomas Roberts.
1783 tax- Samuel C. Ingersol 11 3/4 acres.
17 March 1790 John Roberts and Rachel Roberts sold to William James of
Worc.Co. prop of Samuel Ingersol in Somerset and Worcester Counties.
24 Apr.1790 Mary Ingersol sold to William James lands held by father
Samuel Ingersol. unnamed.
23 June 1795 Richard Ingersol sold to William Roberts 30 acres on the
south side of his plantaion, unnamed.
16 May 1797 Richard Ingersol sold to William Roberts 54 1/4 acres of
FATHERS CARE & MIDDLE.
1 Oct.1800 Richard Ingersol son of Samuel Ingersol, and wife Elizabeth
Ingersol sold to David Walston with FATHERS CARE & ADDITION.
27 April 1804 William Roberts, wife Sarah Roberts sold to Richard
Ingersol 279 acres of COVINGTONS MEADOW, COMFORTS ADVENTURE, MIDDLE &
FATHERS CARE.
19 Dec.1804 Richard Ingersol and wife Elizabeth Ingersol sold to Fairfax
Smith 50 acres of MIDDLE & FATHERS CARE.
1806 Thomas Rencher willed to son Thomas Rencher.
10 Nov.1807 Fairfax Smith, wife Rebecca Smith sold to Thomas Rencher 7
1/4 acres of FATHERS CARE & MIDDLE.
20 Jan 1807 Fairfax Smith, wife Rebecca Smith sold to John Kirwin 44
acres of MIDDLE & FATHERS CARE.
13 March 1808 Richard Ingersol sold to Jacob Cannon 4 1/2 acres of
FATHERS CARE & MIDDLE.

MIDDLE

Patented in 1793 for 5 3/4 acres by Thomas Rencher in Mt.Vernon, Election
district 5, map #1.

MIDDLE OF THE NECK

Patented in 1764 for 168 acres by Stephen Ward in Lawsons, Election
district 8, map #19.
1783 tax- Stephen Ward 30 acres
7 Jan 1800 John Ward son of Stephen Ward, now of Kentucky sold to John
Cullen.
6 Nov.1801 John Cullen, wife Betsy Cullen, sold to Jacob Miles (free
negro) 20 acres with BENSTONS LOTT.
15 Feb.1802 John Cullen sold to Hance Croswell 23 acres of BENSTONS LOTT,
BOTTOM OF THE SPOUNT, MIDDLE OF THE NECK & ADDITION.
23 April 1808 Hance Croswell sold to William Ward 23 acres of same as
above.

MIDDLE PASTURE

Patented in 1763 for 452 1/2 acres by Isaiah Tilghman in Dublin, Election
district 4, map #12.
1783 tax- Isaiah Tilghman 452 acres.
1790 Isaiah Tilghman willed 452 acres to son James Tilghman.

MIDDLE PLANTATION

Patented on 12 May 1663 by William Harper for 175 acres in Dublin,

Election district 4, map #12.
1702 William Harper (married Elizabeth Harper widow of Francis Harper)
willed to grandsons William Harper,Francis Harper and Edward Harper Jr.
Rent Rolls 1666-1723 possessed by the widow Harper
and Edward Harper in right of his children.
1721 Teague Riggin gave to son Charles Riggin 175 acres
3 Nov.1740 John Fleming traded 175 acres of MINSHALLS ADVENTURE for
MIDDLE PASTURE.
1743 Teague Riggin willed to wife Mary Riggin and then to son Teague
Riggin.
19 March 1746 Bond of George Benston and wife Mary Benston one of the
executors of Teague Riggin husband of Mary Riggin, for Teague Riggin son
of Teague.
1783 tax- Teague Riggin 160 acres.
6 Jan 1807 Wrixam L. Porter, wife Priscilla Porter sold to John Riggin
her share of MIDDLE PLANTATION, RIGGINS CHANCE, LAST CHOICE, FLEMINGS
CONCLUSION, UNCLES KINDNESS, as Teague Riggin died intestate leaving
three children, Priscilla Porter w/o Wrixam Porter, Ann Riggin wife of
Henry Coston and John Riggin.

MIDDLE PLANTATION

see DOUBLE PURCHASE

MIDDLE RIDGE

Patented on 9 July 1677 by William Stevens for 200 acres, and assigned to
John Kirk, in Lawsons, Election district 8, map #18.
Rent Rolls 1666-1723 possessed by John Gunby.
1741 resurveyd to 248 acres by Kirk Gunby.
24 July 1741 John Gunby gave to son Kirk Gunby 200 acres.
20 Aug.1746 Southy Whittington and Kirk Gunby settle dispute of
boundaries of MIDDLE RIDGE & GALLOWay.
1780 Kirk Gunby willed land to son John Gunby.
1783 tax- John Gunby
1791 John Gunby son of Kirk Gunby willed to son Kirk.
1796 Kirk Gunby gave to wife Elizabeth Gunby, lands, then to go to
brother Elisha Gunby.
10 Nov.1804 Elisha Gunby sold to Benjamin Lankford 8 1/2 acres of CHANCE
& MIDDLE RIDGE.
1848 Elisha Gunby willed lands to son Elisha James Gunby and Dr. Hiram H.
Gunby, unnamed.

MIDDLESEX

Patented on 28 April 1680 by William Morris of Kent Co.Del. for 450
acres, in Dublin,Election district 4, map #13.
14 Nov.1688 William Morris sold to Griffin Thomas 100 acres
16 March 1720 William Morris son of Samuel Morris of Kent Co.Del. sold to
Criffin Thomac 100 aorcc.
16 Mar 1720 William Morris sold to Richard Aldridge 100 acres possessed
by Griffin Thomas being heir at law of Richard Aldridge, 100 acres.
1719/20 William Morris son of Samuel Morris,late son of William Morris
Sr. of Kent Co.Del. sold 180 acres to Joseph Lankford.
18 Nov.1725 Joseph Lankford,wife Alice Lankford sold to Robert Mitchell
250 acres.
20 Aug.1726 Griffin Thomas and Marthew Thomas his wife sold 200 acres to
William Handy.

1753 Robert Mitchell gave to son Isaac Mitchell 250 acres bought of Joseph Lankford and Mary Smith.
25 Sep.1770 Isaac Mitchell sold 200 acres to John Handy son of William Handy.
25 Sep.1770 John Handy son of William Handy sold 250 acres to Isaac Mitchell.
1773 Isaac Mitchell willed 250 acres to son Joshua Mitchell.
14 June 1774 John Handy sold 100 acres to John Mitchell
18 April 1775 John Handy sold 12 acres to John Mitchell
28 May 1776 John Handy sold 87 1/2 acres to John Mitchell.
1783 tax- John Handy 100 acres
1783 tax- Henry Handy 100 acres
1783 tax- Jane Mitchell 250 acres
12 March 1785 John Mitchell,wife Sally Mitchell sold to John Handy 83 3/4 acres
12 March 1785 John Handy,wife Priscilla Handy, sold to Samuel Sloan 83 3/4 acres.
4 June 1785 George Waters,wife Betty Waters sold to John Handy 7 1/2 acres
7 June 1785 John Handy sold to Samuel Sloan 7 1/2 acres
7 June 1785 Samuel Sloan,wife Elizabeth Sloan sold to John Mitchell 1 1/4 acres.
2 Aug 1787 John Mitchell sold to Joshua Mitchell for 5 shillings 250 acres with WILLIAMS HOPE and a small piece between Isaac Mitchell father of John Mitchell and Joshua Mitchell that was left by Isaac Mitchell to son Joshua Mitchell.
17 Nov.1791 Joshua Mitchell sold to Isaac Mitchell Adams for 5 shillings 3 1/4 acres.
22 May 1798 John Mitchell mortgaged 100 acres to Henry Coston.
10 June 1800 William Handy son of John Handy of Worc.Co. sold to Teague Donoho MIDDLESEX & part of SUFFOLK.
20 July 1803 William Handy son John Handy, of Worc. Co. sold to Teague Donaho 200 acres.
22 May 1805 Teague Donoho of Worc.Co.sold to John Dennis and William Whittington 40 acres.
24 June 1806 William Whittington of Worc.Co. sold to Levin Pollitt of John Pollitt 40 acres.
9 June 1806 John Dennis sold to Levin Pollitt of John Pollitt. no acreage mentioned.
28 July 1806 Teague Donoho, wife Betsy Donoho of Worc.Co. sold 40 acres to Levin Pollitt of John Pollitt.
26 Nov.1806 Joshua Mitchell, wife Nancy Mitchell sold to Joseph Richards of Worc.Co. 239 1/2 acres of MIDDLESEX & COLEMANS ADVENTURE.
20 Jan 1807 Joseph Richards gave mortgage to Joshua Mitchell for same.
6 Oct.1807 Henry Coston, wife Ann Coston released mortgage to John Mitchell.
1807 Rev.Samuel Sloan gave to daughter Sarah Pollitt wife of Levin Pollitt, 90 acres bought of John Handy son of William Handy.
1807 Henry Coston willed lands to son Henry K. Coston -unnamed.
9 Jan 1810 Thomas Waters son of George Waters, wife Elizabeth Waters sold to Thomas Mitchell Jones.
1815 Burton Cannon gave to son Caleb N. Cannon 150 acres bought of Joseph Richards.
18 July 1817 William Melvin sold 72 acres to James Boston
18 July 1817 James Boston sold 72 acres to Samuel Taylor

1836 Levin Pollitt gave part to Ann B. Porter daughter of George Porter.

MIDDLESEX PLANTATION

see DOUBLE PURCHASE

MIDDLE STRAND

Patented in 1744 by John Williams for 85 acres in Westover, Election district 13, map #11.
1760 John Williams willed to son Josiah Williams 85 acres
2 April 1768 Josiah Williams and mother Elizabeth Williams sold to Thomas Tull 85 acres.
22 March 1769 Thomas Tull, wife Esther Tull sold 85 acres to Thomas Davis
1783 tax- Thomas Davis 85 acres.
19 May 1806 Thomas Davis sold all his lands to Beauchamp Davis, no names.
18 May 1807 Thomas M. Jones, wife Margaret Jones sold to Thomas Beauchamp 1/3rd part DISCOVERY & MIDDLE STRAND devised by Thomas Davis to sons Robert and Thomas Davis who died intestate leaving brother James Davis and sisters Hetty Furniss and Margaret Jones.
18 May 1807 James Davis, wife Mary Davis, sold 1/3rds to Thomas Beauchamp.
9 June 1807 James Furniss and wife Hetty Furniss sold 1/3rd part to Thomas Beauchamp.
13 Jan 1810 Isaac Miles, wife Rose Miles, sold to Thomas Beauchamp 6 1/2 acres.

MIDDLE TOWN

Patented on 12 May 1683 by John Harris for 175 acres in Dublin, Election district 4, map #12.
Rent Rolls 1666-1723 possessed by John Harris.
1701 John Harris willed to wife Judith Harris and then to son Caleb Harris.
21 March 1723 Caleb Harris and Rosannah Harris (Rose) his wife sold 50 acres to Edward Harper.
20 March 1749/50 Edward Harper and wife Esther Harper sold 50 acres to Abraham Harris.
17 June 1752 James Harris sold to Abraham Harris 115 acres
17 June 1752 Abraham Harris sold 120 acres to James Harris
18 Aug.1763 James Harris sold to Abraham Harris 50 acres.
16 Dec.1776 Abraham Harris,wife Director Harris of Sussex Co.Del. sold to William Fleming 90 acres.
1783 tax- William Fleming 136 acres
1783 tax- Sarah Harris 30 acres
27 Aug.1788 John Sheldon Alexander, wife Leah Alexander of Worc.Co. sold 17 acres to John Harris.
6 Apr.1796 John Harris sold 175 acres to William Fleming with FLEMINGS LOTT,FLEMINGS CONCLUSION,HARRISONS VENTURE.

MILBOURNS MISTAKE

see DALES ADVENTURE

MILBOURNS PURCHASE

Patented in 1775 by John Milbourn for 126 3/4 acres in Westover,Election

district 13, map #11.
1783 tax- John Milbourn
19 Jan 1787 John Milbourn sold 7 acres to Elijah Boston son of Levin Boston
29 Jan.1820 Elijah Boston sold to Thomas Adams.
1831 Thomas Adams willed to children Morris Henry Adams, Mary Pitt Adams,Leah Jane Adams and Emeline Rounds land purchased of Elijah Boston.

MILE END

Patented on 20 May 1680 by William Brereton for 250 acres in West Pr.Anne,Election district 1, map #2.
1690 William Brereton willed to son John Brereton.
1718 William Brereton sold to John Waltham 100 acres.
26 Oct.1728 William Brereton conveyed to Alexander Adams, he to pay John Caldwell except pt. convyed to John Waltham.
1783 tax- William Brereton 10 cres
23 Nov.1790 William Brereton gave to Salathiel Griffith to keep during lifetime all realestate, no name.
1799 Joseph Brereton gave to brother Scott Brereton.
23 Oct.1803 William Brereton gave to Scott Brereton with BRERETONS CHANCE & SMITHS ADVENTURE.

MILES ADDITION

Patented in 1750 to Samuel Miles for 474 3/8 acres in Dublin,Election district 4, map #12.
21 Feb 1787 Samuel Smith sold to Samuel Miles 15 acres in consideration of his conveying to Nehemiah King part of MILES ADDITION.
21 Feb.1787 Samuel Smith, wife Esther Smith and Samuel Miles and William Waters Sr. sold 15 acres to Nehemiah King.
21 March 1787 Nehemiah King sold to Levin King son of Robert Jenkins King 15 acres.
1785 Samuel Miles willed manor plantation to grandson Samuel Duer.
14 March 1804 Samuel M.Duer, wife Martha Duer sold to George Miles of Worc.Co. 227 1/2 acres of MILES LOTT, MILES ADDITION, WATERFORD, from grandfather Samuel Miles.
15 Feb.1805 George Miles of Worc.Co., mortgaged to Littleton Robins, MILES ADDITION, MILES LOTT, WATERFORD, BAD LUCK.
16 June 1808 George Miles of Worc.Co. sold to Littleton Robins.
28 Nov.1808 Levin King sold for 5 shillings to Mary A. King, MILES LOTT & ADDITION TO MILES ADDITION, BAD LUCK & BACHELORS HOLE.

MILES ADDITION

Patented in 1785 for 230 1/4 acres by Thomas Miles in Westover, Election district 13, map #11.

MILES CHANCE

Patented in 1763 for 397 acres by William Miles in East Pr.Anne, Election district 15, map #5.
1769 William Miles sold to George Miles for 5 shillings, 371 acres.
1770 resurveyed to GEORGES FORTUNE, 500 acres.
1783 tax- Matthias Miles 23 acres

1818/21 Matthias Miles willed to grandsons Tubman Jones and John Jones. 41 acres.

MILES CHOICE

Patented in 1721 by Henry Miles for 77 acres in Fairmount, Election district 6, map #9.
22 May 1755 Henry Miles sold 77 acres to Richard Waters.
1783 tax- Richard Waters
18 March 1789 Henry Miles son of William Miles sold to Richard Waters 77 acres
23 Dec.1789 Richard Waters,wife Eleanor Waters sold to Joshua Tull the younger 77 acres.
2 Apr.1797 Joshua Tull the younger, sold to Elisha Walston 77 acres with tr.ENVY.

MILES CONCLUSION

Patented in 1762 by Henry Miles, a resurvey from WHITE OAK, for 458 acres in Fairmount,Election district 6, map #9.
20 Nov.1767 Henry Miles sold to Zorobable Hall 48 acres.
1783 tax- Henry Miles 408 acres.
1787 Henry Miles willed part to son William Miles
1787 Zorobable Hall, to son James Hall, plantation purchased of Henry Miles 49 acres.
11 June 1804 Samuel Miles sold to Isaac Beauchamp 250 acres.

MILES DISCOVERY

Patented in 1757 for 200 acres by Samuel Miles, a resurvey of part of GIDEONS LUCK in Westover,Election district 13, map #10.
1773 part resurveyed to SECURITY 234 acres.
25 Oct.1803 George Broughton and James Gibbons agree to division of lands.

MILES LAST CHOICE

Patented in 1767 for 514 acres by Samuel Miles in Dublin, Election district 4, map #12.
1783 tax- Samuel Miles 442 acres
15 March 1787 Samuel Miles,wife Rebecca Miles sold to Joseph Cottman 48 acres.
11 Sep.1810 George Miles son of Samuel Miles, of Worc.Co. sold to Isaac M. Adams 509 acres of MILES LAST CHOICE, GLADE SWAMP, COSTONE VENTURE, as trustee for Eliza Atkinson Miles and Molly Henny Miles daughters of afsd. George Miles.

MILES LOTT

Patented on 22 July 1749 by Samuel Miles for 150 1/2 acres in Dublin, Election district 4, map #12.
22 Nov.1758 Samuel Miles and wife Rebeccah Miles,carpenter, sold to William Smith,.weaver, 45 acres.
1783 tax- Samuel Miles 81 acres
1783 tax- Samuel Smith 24 acres
1783 tax- William Miles of Samuel Miles 80 acres.

1785 Samuel Miles willed land to grandson Henry Summers, no name.
21 Feb 1787 Samuel Smith sold to Samuel Miles 15 acres.
21 Feb.1787 Samuel Smith,wife Esther Smith,Samuel Miles,William Waters,
sold to Nehemiah King 102 acres.
21 March 1787 Nehemiah King sold to Levin King son of Robert Jenkins King
33 acres.
21 Feb 1787 Samuel Smith, wife Esther Smith sold to William Waters Sr. 7
acres.
1793 Samuel Miles willed manor plantation to grandson Samuel Duer, no
name.
20 March 1802 Henry Summers sold to George Beauchamp 134 acres devised
him by his grandfather Samuel Miles
26 Nov.1803 Samuel M. Duer sold to James Smith of Samuel Smith 25 acres
of MILES LOTT & WATERFORD.
26 Jan 1804 James Smith, wife Elizabeth Smith sold to William Gillis
Waters 125 acres of MILES LOTT & WATERFORD.
17 March 1804 Samuel M. Duer, wife Martha Duer sold to George Miles of
Worc.Co. 227 1/2 acres of MILES ADDITION, MILES LOTT, WATERFORD.
14 Feb.1805 George Miles of Worc.Co. mortgaged to Littleton Robins
WATERFORD, MILES LOTT, MILES ADDITION & BAD LUCK where Samuel Miles
lived.
16 June 1808 George Miles of Worc.Co.son of Samuel Miles sold to
Littleton Robins.
28 Nov.1808 Levin King sold for 5 shillings to Mary A. King.
18 April 1809 William Waters sold to John Miles of William Miles, 40
acres.
31 Jan 1810 George Beauchamp sold to William King of William, land
purchsed of Henry Summers that was devised Henry Summers by the will of
Samuel Miles, 133 acres, no name.

MILL POINT

Patented in 1745 by Panter Laws for 18 1/2 acres in St.Peters, Election
district 2, map #6.
21 June 1782 John Laws son of Panter Laws sold to Benjamin Sasser Jr. 18
1/2 acres
1783 tax- Benjamin Sasser Jr. 18 1/2 acres.

MILL SUPPORT

Patented in 1794 for 112 1/2 acres by Matthias Miles in East Pr.Anne,
Election district 15, map #4.

MINSHALLS ADVENTURE

Patented on 18 Jan 1667 by Jeffrey Minshull for 400 acres in Dublin,
Election district 4, map #12.
30 July 1668 Jeffrey Minshull and wife Frances Minshull deeded 200 acres
to William Green.
25 Feb.1669 Jeffrey Minshull and wife Frances Minshull sold 200 acres to
Thomas Ball.
1676 Thomas Ball sold to Thomas Smith 200 acres.
21 Sep.1679 Jeffrey Minshull Jr. and Frances Minshull his mother deeded
ADVENTURE to William Stevens.
1687 William Stevens of Rehobeth willed his plantation to wife Eliza

Stevens her dower rights and to widow Sarah White, to hold land
bequeathed to Stevens White. unnamed.
1709 Thomas Layfield sold 400 acres to Phillip Adams.
1 Nov.1735 William Green of Kent Co.Del son of William Green deceased of
Dorc.Co. sold 200 acres to John Fleming, that Thomas Ball deeded to
William Green who died intestate.
3 Nov.1740 Robert Harris quitclaimed to John Fleming, a trade for CHANCE,
no acrege.
2 Nov.1740 Teague Riggin sold for 5 shillings to John Fleming, trade for
MIDDLE PLANTATION, no acreage.
1743 I John Fleming of Worc.Co. sell to William Fleming of Som.Co. 200
acres.
3 Feb.1747 Phillip Adams gave to son Hope Adams 180 acres, after his
death to grandson Phillip Adams second son of Hope Adams.
28 Feb.1756 William Adams sold 122 acres to Jacob Adams now called THE
ADVENTURE.
27 Feb.1756 Phillip Adams sold to William Adams 233 1/2 acres
14 Sep.1767 Phillip Adams Jr. and Hope Adams Sr. sold to Fountain
Beauchamp part with GOOD HOPE, a trade for 117 acres of LEDBOURN.
1768 Hope Adams willed to son Hope Adams.
1 June 1773 Phillip Adams son of Hope Adams sold 94 acres to Duncan
Livingston,tailor with part of GOOD HOPE.(as Phillip and Hope Adams did
mortgage to Fountain Beauchamp who on 8 Jan.1770 made over to Duncan
Livingston the right and title to these lands.)
30 Feb.1779 Fountain Beauchamp Jr. and wife Rhoda Beauchamp and Levin
Beauchamp sold to Fountain Beauchamp Jr. 3 acres.
30 Dec.1779 Fountain Beauchamp Sr. and Rhoda Beauchamp and Levi Beauchamp
sold to Beauchamp Davis Sr. 37 3/4 acres
18 Jan 1790 Levi Beauchamp and Rhoda Beauchamp sold 35 acres to Beauchamp
Davis.
20 Apr.1790 Isaac Beauchamp son of Fountain Beauchamp, wife Eunice
Beauchamp, and Hope Adams of Jesse Adams, Phillip Adams of Hope Adams and
Rhoda Beauchamp sold to Fountain Beauchamp, now called ADVENTURE.
1795 Fountain Beauchamp willed to son David Beauchamp 38 acres purchased
of brother Isaac Beauchamp, not named.
2 Sep.1803 Beauchamp Davis sold to Thomas Davis 72 3/4 acres.
1 June 1805 Elisha Beauchamp, wife Milly Beauchamp sold to Thomas Cullen
parcel Fountain Beauchamp devised to son David Beauchamp and it descended
by the death of David to Elisha Beauchamp afsd. 12 3/4 acres being 1/3rd
of parcel, no name.
7 June 1808 Leah Beauchamp widow of Fountain Beauchamp Jr, Elisha
Beauchamp, wife Milly Beauchamp and Mary Beauchamp sold to Robert Catlin
tract conveyed to Levin Beauchamp on 13 Dec.1779, no name.

MIRTLEY SWAMP

Patented in 1761 by William Heath for 50 acres in East Princess Anne,
Election district 15, map #4.
1783 tax- William Heath 45 acres.

MISFORTUNE

Patented in 1763 by Isaac Denston for 35 acres in East Pr.Anne Election
district 15, map #4.

1771 Isaac Denston willed to daughter Rachel Denston.
28 Sep.1779 William Townsend and wife Rachel Townsend of Worc.Co. sold 17
3/4 acres to William Denston of Som.Co.
22 Apr.1794 Ephraim Denston sold to Samuel Banks 35 acres.
24 July 1798 Samuel Banks sold to David Brown 35 acres.

MISORY

Patented in 1817 for 16 1/4 acres by Levin Miller in East Pr.Anne
Election district 15, map #5.

MISTAKE

Patented on 8 May 1702 by Matthew Jones for 400 acres in Lawsons,Election
district 8, map #19.
Rent Rolls 1666-1723 possessed by Robert Catherwood for the orphans of
Matthew Jones.
14 Oct.1749 Thomas Jones,merchant, sold 400 acres to John Williams.
11 Nov.1768 John Williams sold part to Kirk Gunby.
29 Dec.1768 John Williams sold 1/4 part to Josephus Bell.
1775 Kirk Gunby willed to son John Gunby.

MISTAKE

Patented in 1757 for 7 acres by John Dougherty in Lawsons, Election
district 8, map # 19.
12 Dec.1807 Dickerson Dougherty sold to Leah Ward of Stephen Ward 1 1/2
acres of ADDITION TO MISTAKE.

MITCHELLS CHOICE & IMPROVEMENT

Patented on 2 March 1663 by George Mitchell for 500 acres, in West
Pr.Anne, Election district 1, map #3.
1669 resurveyed 500 acres to MITCHELLS IMPOVEMENT.
George Mitchell had no living sons. George Downs married Margaret
Mitchell daughter of George Mitchell
Rent Rolls 1666-1723 possessed 250 acres by George Downs, 250 acres by
Thomas Dashiell.
5 Dec.1729 Thomas Dashiell, Elizabeth Dashiell, George Dashiell Sr. and
Priscilla Dashiell, Joseph McCLester and Isabell McClester deeded to
George Downs and Mary Downs 250 acres.(this was a division of lands)
26 Dec.1729 George Downs and Margaret Downs his wife gave to children
Robert Downs, Margaret Downs and Sarah Downs 250 acres.
25 Dec.1729 George Downs and wife Margaret Downs gave to daughters 1/4th
part Margaret Downs and Sarah Downs. If either marry, the single one to
inherit. no acres given.
24 Dec.1731 Thomas Dashiell and wife Elizabeth Dashiell gave to son
George Dashiell.
1748 George Dashiell willed to son Thomas Dashiell, where my father now
lives, if no issue to son Benjamin Dashiell.
22 March 1753 Levin Dashiell and wife Bridget Dashiell sold to Isaac
Dashiell 115 acres of MITCHELLS IMPROVEMENT, MEECHES HOPE & CHOICE, from
father Thomas Dashiell.
12 Dec.1758 Robert Downs deeded part to Levin Dashiell, part.
12 Dec 1758 tripple voucher, Robert Downs,inholder, 250 acres to William

Hayward and Levin Dashiell.
21 June 1759 Robert Downs, wife Betty Downs, sold 250 acres to Levin
Dashiell.
1783 Levin Dashiell 500 acres.

MITCHELLS CHOICE

Patented on 17 March 1694 Thomas Potter for 180 acres in
Brinkleys,southwest, Election district 3, map #17.
Rent Rolls 166-1723 Thomas Potter.
1726/7 Thomas Potter willed to son Thomas, at head of MITCHELLS CHOICE
and lands to son Elijah Potter, unnamed.
1783 tax- Henry Potter 180 acres.
17 March 1785 Henry Potter sold 160 acres to Jesse Powell.
17 Apr.1786 Jessee Powell sold to Henry Potter for 5 shillings OWENS LOTT
& MITCHELLS CHOICE.
25 April 1786 Henry Potter and wife Mary Potter and Sarah Matthews sold
46 acres to Merrill Maddux.
1828 Jesse Powell willed to grandson Jesse Powell King 160 acres.
unnamed.

MITCHELLS DISCOVERY

Patented in 1765 by Isaac Mitchell for 12 1/2 acres in Dublin, Election
district 4, map #12.
1773 Isaac Mitchell willed to sons James Mitchell and Joshua Mitchell.
2 Apr.1787 John Mitchell sold for 5 shillings to Joshua Mitchell, part
with MIDDLESEX, WILLIAMS HOPE.

MITCHELLS LOTT

Patented in 1679 by Randall Mitchell for 400 acres in Brinkleys, Election
district 3, map #14.
1698 Randall Mitchell and wife Alice Mitchell sold 150 acres to John
Moore.
1698 Randall Mitchell and wife Alice Mitchell sold 100 acres to John
White, now called MARSHALLS PURCHASE.
Rent Rolls 1666-1723 Possessed by Richard Mitchell 150 acres, 150 acres
John Moore,100 acres John White.
31 Dec.1716 John Moore willed to sons John and Thomas Moore.
7 March 1719 Randall Mitchell assigned 150 acres to the Vestry of
Coventry Parish.
18 June 1740 John White, eldest son of Stevens White, son of John White
the elder, with wife Mary White, sold to Thomas Marshall and wife Jane
Marshall 100 acres.
20 March 1744 Josephus Potter of Worc.Co. and wife Ann Potter,John Wilson
of Som. Co. and wife Elizabeth Wilson, Thomas Lankford and wife Sarah
Lankford sold to Beauchamp Davis CHANCE 150 acres part of MITCHELLS LOTT.
18 July 1745 Beauchamp Davis and wife Mary Davis sold to Thomas Moore 75
acres.(John Moore had four daughters, Ann Moore now wife of Josephus
Potter, Elizabeth Moore wife of John Wilson, Sarah Moore wife of Thomas
Lankford, Mary Moore wife of Beauchamp Davis.)part called FATHERS GIFT
SECURED.
22 Jan 1757 Beauchamp Davis and wife Mary Davis sold to Thomas Marshall
75 acres of part called CHANCE.

17 Dec.1759 Nathaniel Whitaker rector of Coventry Parish sold 150 acres
to Nathaniel Roach where Joseph Potter lives known as GLEBE LAND
belonging to Coventry Parish for 20 years.
1783 tax- Beauchamp Davis 37 1/4 acres
1783 tax- Stephen Marshall 75 acres
1783 tax- William Moore 75 acres
6 Aug.1794 Stephen Marshall sold to Thomas Marshall 254 acres of
MITCHELLS LOTT, MARSHALLS INHERITANCE.
22 Aug.1794 Stephen Marshall,wife Rachel Marshall sold to Thomas Miles
137 3/4 acres of MITCHELLS LOTT,MARSHALLS INHERITANCE & LONGS CHANCE.
17 May 1798 Thomas Marshall son of Stephen Marshall sold to John Harris
275 acres of MITCHELLS LOTT,MARSHALLS INHERITANCE
6 April 1810 William A. Schoolfield, wife Mary Schoolfield, sold to Isaac
Miles 5 1/2 acres.
1851 Stephen Ward gave to wife Margaret Ward.
1854 Harriet Handy wife of James Handy willed to son Sidney W. Handy 74
acres.

MITCHELLS PURCHASE

Patented in 1764 for 157 acres by Stephen Mitchell, a resurvey of HEATHS
QUARTER, in East Pr.Anne,Election district 15, map #5.
1783 tax- Stephen Mitchell 157 acres.
17 June 1788 Stephen Mitchell sold to Esau Boston 46 acres.
1798 Tubman Lankford occupied land owned by Esau Bostons heirs.
May 1802 court awarded to James Boston son of Esau Boston.
13 March 1804 James Boston sold to Parker Puzey 46 acres.
12 March 1805 Thomas Mitchell, wife Mary Mitchell of Worc.Co. sold to
William Mitchell 180 1/2 acres except 46 acres sold Esau Boston of
LITTLEWORTH, CUT CLOSE & MITCHELLS PURCHASE..
18 May 1805 William Mitchell, wife Sally Mitchell sold 180 1/2 acres to
Kirk Gunby, of LITTLEWORTH, CUT CLOSE & MITCHELLS PURCHASE.

MONMOUTH

Not patented but is part of WALLEYS CHANCE & WINDSOR, 100 acres in West
Pr.Anne,Election district 1, map #2.
16 June 1704 George Goddard sold 50 acres each of the above lands to
Griffith Jones.
25 Nov.1720 Griffith Jones and wife Mary Jones of Albarmarle North
Carolina sold to William Alexander Jr. of Som.Co.Md.
with WHALEYS CHANCE
11 Oct.1721 Griffith Jones of Paspetank North Carolina confirms that he
sold 50 acres to George Goddard.
18 Sep.1722 George Goddard, cooper,wife Mary Goddard sold to Alexander
Adams 40 acres of each WALLEYS CHANCE & WINDSOR.
2 May 1749 Moses Alexander son of William Alexander, blacksmith gave to
son Samuel Alexander 100 acres with HUNTING QUARTER.

MOORS BARROW

Patented in 1748, a resurvey of DEEP & SHIPWAYS CHOICE by Mary
Whittingham, for 323 acres in East Pr.Anne,Election district 15, map #4.
14 Dec 1769 Heber Whittingham and Mary Whittingham relic of Heber
deceased sold 309 acres to John Jones of William Jones

1783 tax- John Jones 309 acres.
(this was named for MOORSBOROUGH Parish of Middlewick England)
1790 John Jones willed lands to son Thomas Jones(unnamed)
6 July 1792 Elizabeth Jones daughter of John Jones sold to Thomas Jones
son of John Jones.
20 May 1800 Bridget Miles, Eleanor Jones & Henry Jones, wife Elizabeth
Jones sold to Capt. Thomas Jones all rights, that Tubman Jones died
possessed of.
1803 Thomas Jones willed to sons John Jones and Tubman Jones.
11 June 1808 Thomas Curtis, trustee to sell the real estate of Thomas
Jones sold 209 acres to Matthias Miles.

MORE AGAIN

Patented in 1796 for 16 3/4 acres by Matthias Miles in East Pr.Anne,
Election district 15, map #5.
1818/21 Matthias Miles willed to grandsons Tubman Jones and John Jones.

MORE AND CASE IT

Patented on 11 Nov.1662 by William Bozman for 1200 acres in West Pr.Anne,
Election district 1, map #3.
1664/5 William Bozman willed to sons John Bozman and George Bozman.
14 April 1722 William Bozman son of George Bozman traded 150 acres with
William Bozman son of John Bozman deceased for 120 acres of same.
Rent Rolls 1666-1723 John Bozman 600 acres, Luke Valentine 600 acres.
19 April 1722 William Bozman and wife Catherine Bozman sold to brother
George Bozman 150 acres.
1725 William Bozman Sr. and wife Sarah Bozman sold to James Robertson,
minister of Coventry Parish 420 acres.
10 Feb.1735 William Bozman sold to Joseph Gillis and his wife Eleanor
Gillis- no acreage mentioned.
20 March 1746/7 William Bozman sold 12 acres to Rev. James Robertson.
1750 Levin Bozman son of George gave to brothers Daniel Bozman and
Philomen Bozman.
6 Nov.1770 Thomas Robertson son of James Robertson, and wife Martha
Robertson sold to Rev. Hamilton Bell 420 acres with BOZMANS ADDITION
5 May 1777 Joseph Gillis and wife Eleanor Gillis gave to son William
Gillis.
12 Aug.1783 Hamilton Bell sold for 5 shillings to brother William Bell
all land purchased of Dr.Thomas Robertson on the Manokin River, unnamed.
1783 tax- Isaac Bozman 130 acres
1783 tax- William Bell 420 acres
1783 tax- William Giles 158 acres
1783 tax- Henry Jackson 221 acres
23 Nov 1787 John Denwood, high sheriff, sold to Ezekiel Gillis, for
judgement of Samuel Chase against Peter Waters and William Gillis, 342
acres with OAK HALL.
27 Nov.1787 William Gillis sold to Ezekiel Gillis 342 acres.
30 Oct.1790 George Bozman and Isaac Bozman sold to William Williams 200
acres, mortgage.
6 Sep.1794 George Bozman gave to Sally Bozman, Ann Bozman and Dolly
Bozman 200 acres.
1795 Ezekiel Gillis willed to son James J.Dashiell Gillis if daughter
Nelly Gillis has no issue. If he has no issue to son Ezekiel Gillis.

15 May 1802 Littleton Dennis trustee to sell the plantation MORE & CASE IT, of George Bozman, sold at public sale to Ezekiel McClemmy Gillis, no acreage given.
4 April 1808 Elizabeth Jackson and George W.Jackson sold to William Jones 221 acres of CASE IT.
24 Feb.1810 Ezekiel M. Gillis sold to John Cottman lands devised to James D. Gillis.
24 Oct.1810 John Cottman sold to Ezekiel M. Gillis
27 June 1810 William Jones, Esq., wife Eleanor Jones, sold to Ezekiel M. Gillis 200 3/4 acres of Goose Creek purchased of George W. Jackson, no name.
27 June 1810 Ezekiel M. Gillis, wife Sally Gillis, sold to William Jones 318 1/2 acres.
24 April 1827 Village Herald- Sherrif's sale at suit of John Woolford and Josiah Johnson against Levin Ballard Sr. John King Sr. Dr. L.W. Ballard and Samuel McBryde, 150 acres of MORE & CASE IT.
1832 Elizabeth Jones widow of Charles Jones gave to sons Charles Jones and Alfred Jones, no acreage mentioned.
1841 Eliza William Ann King daughter of John King gave to brother John Trippe King, no acreage.

MOREWORTH

Patented on 18 Sep 1676 by William Stevens and assigned to John Horsey for 200 acres in Lawsons,Election district 8, map #18.
Rent Rolls 1666-1723 Stephen Horsey 132 acres and Anthony Bell 68 acres purchased of the heirs of John Horsey.
1741 will of Anthony Bell, this land not mentioned, gave to sons Thomas Bell, Josephus Bell and Isaac Bell.
4 Apr.1745 Thomas Bell son of Anthony Bell, and wife Elizabeth Bell sold to Josephus Bell, 200 acres now called BELLS PURCHASE, includes HORSEY DOWNS
12 Nov.1762 Daniel Bell of Dorcester County son of Thomas Bell sold to Josephus Bell of Som.Co. pt. two tracts MOREWORTH, HORSEY DOWN 176 acres.
1799 Josephus Bell willed to wife Sophia Bell, all lands.

MOREWORTH

Patented in 1762 for 8 acres by William Duett in Asbury, Election district 12, map #21
1783 tax- Nathaniel Duett
7 Jan 1800 John Ward son of Stephen Ward, now of Kentucky sold to Jacob Cullen.

MORRIS ADVISEMENT

Patented on 5 Oct 1683 by William Stevens who assigned to Francis Jenkins 150 acres, in Dublin, Election district 4, map #13.
Rent Rolls 1666-1723 Edward Harper.

MORRIS'S HOPE

Patented on 8 Feb.1670 by Morris Lister for 250 acres in Brinkleys, southeast,Election district 3, map #16.
12 March 1676 Morris Lister and wife Winifred Lister of Deleware River

sold to Cornelius Morris 250 acres
1 Dec.1678 Cornelius Morris and wife Ann Morris sold to William Manlove 250 acres.
1 Feb.1686 William Manlove, wife Alice Manlove sold to Thomas Lister 250 acres with PERSIMON.
27 Feb 1734 Mark Manlove son of William Manlove sold to Robert Boyer, 250 acres.
21 June 1737 Robert Boyer of Pocomoke, wife Elizabeth Boyer gave to grandson George Clifton 40 acres with 50 acres of PERSIMON POINT.
24 Aug.1761 Michael Clifton of Cowan Co. South Carolina son of John Clifton of Som.Co.Md. sold to Elias White PERSIMON POINT 5 acres and MORRIS HOPE, total of 94 acres conveyed to George Clifton uncle of Michael Clifton afsd.
15 Aug.1766 Elias White mortgaged to John Nairn 44 acres with GLENEATH.
20 Nov.1766 Elias White sold to John Nairn part 44 acres that Elias had from his brother Stevens White with PERSIMON POINT & THE ENTRANCE.
2 June 1767 George Dickerson of Acco. Co.Va. sold to Robert Pitts 25 acres.(that Robert Boyer willed to George Dickerson and Elias White who released to Dickerson.
1 June 1767 George Dickeson of Acco.Co.Va. sold to Isaac Dickeson 100 acres, balance of MORRIS HOPE.
25 Nov.1768 Elias White of Som.Co. sold to Littleton Dennis 44 acres
26 June 1769 Elias White sold to Samuel Wilson 400 acres of dwelling plantation at Pocomoke river- mortgage, no name.
3 July 1770 Littleton Dennis of Worc.Co. sold 44 acres to David Williams with PERSIMON POINT & COXES BITT.
21 Nov.1770 Robert Pitts and wife Milcah Pitts sold to Thomas Robertson 25 acres
24 Aug.1771 Thomas Robertson sold to David Williams 25 acres of land George Dickerson recovered by arbitration of Elias White.
22 Nov.1773 Elias White, wife Sarah White sold 44 acres to David Williams.
1784 Dr. Thomas Robertson and wife Martha Robertson sold 25 acres to William Waddy.
1784 James Dickerson son of Isaac Dickerson,sold to Jesse Ward 22 1/2 acres.
16 May 1785 James Dickerson, silversmith,son of Isaac Dickerson sold to Thomas Handy 45 acres.
2 Sep 1785 William Waddy,wife Mary Sewell Waddy and Thomas Handy with wife Mary Handy sold to William Miles 212 3/4 acres of ENTRANCE, ADVENTURE, MORRIS HOPE.
3 Sep 1786 Thomas Handy,wife Mary Handy sold 35 acres to Matthias Coston.
29 Oct.1796 William Miles,wife Nancy Miles sold to Thomas Williams 212 3/4 acres of ADVENTURE, ENTRANCE, MORRIS HOPE.
19 Aug.1805 Samuel Smith, wife Esther Smith sold 25 acres to Ralph Milbourn.
21 Aug.1807 Thomas Williams sold to Asa Dix, as Thomas Williams of David Williams died intestate at Pocomoke, John Gale and wife Amelia Gale and Thomas Williams Sr. heirs at law and Thomas Williams Sr. died before division, divised his share to Thomas Williams afsd and Thomas Williams Wilkins, his grandson (minor) no name acreage. This could be other lands.
8 July 1809 Thomas Williams Wilkins sold to Lodowick Milbourn, land Thomas William of David Williams purchased of William Miles, no name or acreage.

MOTHER AND SONS ENJOYMENT

see BOSTONS ADVENTURE 150 acres.

MOTHERS CARE

Patented in 1663 as BOZMANS CHOICE by Lazarus Maddux for 300 acres in West Pr.Anne,Election district 1, map #3.
1687 part resurveyed 164 acres to CARYS CHANCE.

MOTHERS CARE

Patented in 1740, a resurvey of DAVIS CHANGE,DAVIS CONQUEST,DAVIS LOTT, for 795 acres in Westover,Election district 13, map #11.
1783 tax- John Wilson of Samuel Wilson 705 acres.
1791 Levin Wilson willed to nephew Robert Jackson son of Henry Jackson and Elizabeth Jackson.
9 May 1803 Leah Gale and George Wilson Jackson sold to John Dennis with MOUNT EPHRAIM.
28 June 1803 John Dennis, wife Elinor Dennis sold 1/4 part to George Wilson Jackson of MOUNT EPHRAIM & MOTHERS CARE.
24 March 1804 Elizabeth Jackson gave to son George W. Jackson and daughter Ann Wilson Jackson (under 21) with any tracts contiguous.

MOUNT EPHRAIM

Patented in 1726 by Ephraim Wilson for 375 acres in Westover, Election district 13, map #11.
1750 David Wilson willed to son Ephraim Wilson.
1783 tax- John Wilson of Samuel Wilson 375 acres.
1791 Levin Wilson willed to nephew Robert Jackson son of Henry Jackson and Elizabeth Jackson.
9 May 1803 Leah Gale and George Wilson Jackson sold to John Dennis with MOTHERS CARE
28 June 1803 John Dennis,wife Elinor Dennis sold 1/4th part of MOTHERS CARE & MT. EPHRAIM to George Wilson Jackson.
24 March 1804 Elizabeth Jackson gave to son George W. Jackson and daughter Ann Wilson Jackson, with any tracts contiguous.

MOUNT PLEASANT

Patented in 1784 by Ezekiel Gillis for 238 1/4 acres in St.Peters, Election district 2, map #6.
1790 John Evans willed to wife Elizabeth Evans 225 acres.
6 May 1794 William Waller and Ezekiel Gillis agreed on lines between WALLERS ADVENTURE,MT. PLEASANT & COLEBROOK.
1807 Thomas Cannon willed to son Thomas, no acreage.
1842 Gabriel Webster willed to brother Hamilton Webster 60 acres.

MOUNT PLEASANT

Patented in 1819 for 763 1/2 acres by Joseph Cottman in Mt.Vernon, Election district 5, map #1.

see ERLINDY

MUMFORD

Patented in 1741 by Thomas Lindzey for 100 acres in Brinkleys, southwest, Election district 3, map #17.
27 Feb.1756 Thomas Lindsey sold to Charles Cottingham 50 acres part of BOSTON & MUMFORD.
12 May 1761 Thomas Lindsey sold 140 acres to Nehemiah Turpin of GLAZIERS HALL,BOSTON & MUMFORD.
23 Oct 1764 Nehemiah Turpin sold to Thomas Lindzey 140 acres of same.
23 Oct.1764 Thomas Lindzey sold 95 acres to Nehemiah Turpin of CHEESEMANS CHANCE,MUMFORD,BOSTON resurveyed and lately called EDEN.
1783 tax- David Lindsey 92 acres
1783 tax- William Cottingham 15 acres & 7 acres.
24 June 1795 John Turpin and wife Sarah Turpin of Worc.Co. sold to Thomas Whittington 91 1/4 acres of CHEESEMANS CHANCE,MUMFORD, BOSTON.
10 March 1796 Thomas Whittington sold to Isaac Whittington 95 acres of BOSTON,EDEN,MUMFORD
10 Mach 1796 David Lindzey sold to Thomas Whittington 95 acres of BOSTON,EDEN,MUMFORD.
23 June 1834 Josiah Cottingham son of William Cottingham sold to Levin Conner.

MUNGARS CHOICE

Patented in 1751 by Matthias Mungar for 82 1/2 acres in West Pr.Anne, Election district 1, map #3.
20 Nov.1761 Matthias Mungar sold 82 1/2 acres to Thomas Whitney.
1783 tax- Thomas Whitney 82 acres
1796 Thomas Whitney willed to son David Whitney.
25 Aug.1807 David Whitney sold to Littleton Dennis Teackle 82 1/2 acres.

MUSKETA HUMMOCK

Patented on 23 Sep.1683 by Benjamin Summers for 200 acres in Crisfield,Election district 7, map #20
1709/15 Benjamin Summers willed 200 acres to sons William Summers, Thomas Summers and John Summers.

MUSKETT HOLE

Unpatented and surveyed in 1714 by Levin Denwood for 360 acres in St.Peters, Election district 2, map #6.

MY OWN

Patented in 1768 for 115 1/2 acres by Matthias Miles in Dublin, Election district 4, map #12.
1836 Levin Pollitt willed to William Bowland son of John Bowland.
1889 Jehu Parsons willed to wife Sarah Parsons 4 acres part of THE RIDGE, MY OWN, in Dublin district.

MY OWN BEFORE

Patented in 1752 by John Leatherbury for 61 acres in Mt.Vernon, Election
district 5, map #1.
1756 John Leatherbury willed to son Robert Leatherbury
1783 tax- Robert Leatherbury
1784 Robert Leatherbury willed to son John Leatherbury.
2 Oct.1800 John Leatherbury of Robert Leatherbury, wife Sarah Leatherbury
sold to Richard Ingersol 360 or 370 acres of COVINGTONS FOLLY, MY OWN
BEFORE, SECURITY & LOTT.
24 Dec.1800 Richard Ingersol sold to Robert Leatherbury with SECURITY &
COVINGTONS FOLLY, no acres given, description.
4 Dec.1830 Sheriff's sale, at suit of Robert Leatherbury against Major
Simpkins, Charles Simpkins, Alexander Jones and Samuel G. Holbrook, with
LOTT 86 acres.

MYRTLE SWAMP

Patented in 1764 for 100 acres by Henry Walston Miles in St.Peters,
Election district 2, map #6.
1783 tax- Henry Walston Miles 100 acres.

NAN ELLIS'S RIDGE

Patented in 1737 by Esau Boston for 40 acres in Brinkleys, southeast,
Election district 3,map #16.
1768 Esau Boston sold to William Wood and Naomi Wood.
1786 William Wood and wife Naomi Wood sold to Jacob Boston
9 Feb.1786 William Wood,wife Naomi Wood sold to Jacob Adams part 45 acres
of TULLY BRISK,SUPPORT,NAN ELLIS RIDGE or BOSTONS ADVENTURE.

NASWORTHYS CHOICE

Patented on 10 March 1663 by George Nasworthy and resurveyed by Capt.
Henry Smith. 1000 acres in West Pr.Anne,Election district 1, map #3.
Repatented again by Thomas Jones in 1672.
3 June 1679 Thomas Jones sold to William Stevens
16 Oct.1679 William Stevens sold to Henry Smith Stevens..
Possessed by John Tunstall and several others being found but 700 acres,
called SMITHS RECOVERY being all part of THOMPSONS PURCHASE.

NEARNS ADDITION

Patented on 27 Aug.1720 by Robert Nairn for 87 acres in Brinkleys,
southeast,Election district 3, map #16.
31 March 1724 Robert Nairn, merchant willed to son Robert Nairn.
1783 tax- Eleanor Nairn

NAIRNS CHANCE
see THE ENTRANCE
NEED

Patented in 1769 by Ephraim Cottingham for 35 1/2 acres in Brinkleys
southwest, Election district 3, map #17.
12 March 1774 Ephraim Cottingham sold 22 1/2 acres to David Cottingham

1783 tax- David Cottingham 22 acres
1798 tax- Ephraim Cottingham

NEGLECT

Patented in 1749 for 15 acres by Henry Miles in Fairmount, Election
district 6, map #9.
1756 Henry Miles willed to grandson William Miles son of Samuel Miles and
Rebecca Miles, part 4 acres..
23 Aug.1770 William Miles son of Samuel Miles, wife Sarah Miles sold to
Henry Miles 7 acres with NEGLECT.
1783 tax- Henry Miles 9 acres.
1787 Henry Miles willed lands, unnamed, to son Samuel Miles.

NEGLECT

Patented in 1761 for 72 acres by Jonathan Cluff in Dublin, Election
district 4, map #13.
1762 resurveyed to 193 acres, by Jonathan Cluff.
16 Aug.1769 Jonathan Cluff and wife Betty Cluff sold to Michael Cluff 50
acres.
1783 tax- Jonathan Cluff 149 1/2 acres
3 Jan 1786 Jonathan Cluff and Samuel Wilson adjusted lines between
ACQUANTICO & NEGLECT.
22 Feb.1786 John Perkins traded 12 acres of LITTLE PROFIT for 12 acres of
NEGLECT.
19 Nov 1795 Samuel Wilson son of Samuel, and wife Leah Wilson sold to
Littleton Dennis 815 acres of ACQUINTICO, POWELLS CHANCE,MIDDLE &
EXCHANGE, etc.
21 April 1807 Robert Leatherbury, sheriff, sold to Robert Cluff 83 acres.
of NEWTOWN, LITTLEWORTH, NEGLECT, CHESTNUT RIDGE, per judgement against
William Perkins.

NEGLECT

Patented in 1795,by George Gale and Samuel Wilson, a resurvey from
COVINGTONS ADVENTURE, for 102 1/4 acres in Mt.Vernon, Election district
5, map#1.
25 Oct.1800 George Gale of Cecil Co., wife Ann Gale sold his interest to
John Leatherbury and Levin Jones.
25 Oct.1800 Littleton Gale of Cecil Co. Md. sold his part to John
Leatherbury and Levin Jones.
18 May 1801 Samuel Wilson and wife Leah Wilson (Leah Gale) sold to John
Leatherbury and Levin Jones.
3 Aug.1801 John Leatherbury of Robert Leatherbury, and wife Sally
Leatherbury sold to Lucretia Jones.

NEGLECT

Patented in 1802 by Matthias Miles for 110 1/2 acres in Lawsons,Election
district 8, map #18 a resurvey with DOE PARK.

NEGLECT

Surveyed in 1820 but not patented,by George Jones, a resurvey on EDWARDS

LOTT & JESIMON, for 406 acres in Dames Quarter, Election district 1, map #7
16 May 1801 George Jones,wife Leah Jones sold to Edward Fowler part.
16 May 1801 George Jones,wife Leah Jones sold to Underwood Roberts 111 acres.
16 May 1801 George Jones and wife Leah Jones sold to John Roberts, 91 1/2 acres.

NEIGHBORS AGREEMENT

Patented in 1750 by Marcy Fountain for 87 acres in Westover, Election district 13, map #11.
12 July 1754 Marcy Fountain and wife Betty Fountain sold to William Turpin son of William 46 acres.
23 May 1775 Thomas Fountain sold 20 acres to William Fountain.
3 Sep.1775 Thomas Fountain sold part to William Fountain- no acres given.
1783 William Turpin willed to wife Betty Turpin 1/3 of lands and mills,after death to son Denwood Turpin.
1783 tax- William Fountain 50 acres
1783 tax- Denwood Turpin 45 acres
7 July 1800 Whitty Turpin Fountain and William Turpin agreed to division of lands.
1 Nov.1805 Thomas Robertson Jr. sold to Custis Jenkins of Acco.Co. Va. all rights to property of William Turpin deceased, on Morumsco creek. No name.

NEIGHBORS CONCLUSION

Patented in 1773, a resurvey from WILLIAMSTON by Thomas Williams and Planner Williams, for 624 1/2 acres in Brinkleys, northwest,Election district 3, map #14.
17 Nov.1773 Levin Williams sold to Planner Williams and Thomas Williams 438 1/2 acres.
18 Nov.1773 Planner Williams and Thomas Williams sold to Robert Jenkins King 438 1/2 acres
21 Feb.1775 Robert Jenkins King sold 400 acres to Thomas Robertson
1783 tax- Thomas Robertson 438 1/2 acres
1783 tax- Levin Wilson 180 acres
13 Apr.1796 Thomas Williams sold 100 acres to William Williams.
1816 Thomas Robertson willed to son Thomas lands in Annamessex, unnamed.

NEIGHBORS CONTENT

Patented in 1769 for 10 3/4 acres by Benjamin Lankford in Brinkleys, northwest, Election district 3, map #14.
22 Nov.1773 Benjamin Lankford sold to Thomas Dixon and Isaac Dixon 6 1/4 acres and all his title to lands on the south side of the ditch adjacent.
1794 Thomas Dixon willed to daughter Sarah Dixon Furniss wife of Thomas Furniss 3 1/4 acres, after death to William Furniss son of Thomas Furniss.

NEIGHBORS EXCHANGE

Patented in 1788 for 3 3/4 acres by Samuel Smith in Brinkleys, northeast, Election district 3, map #15.
1786 Henry Schoolfield willed to grandson Henry Schoolfield 3 1/2 acres north of Rehobeth Town landing, no name.

NEIGHBORS NEGLECT

Patented in 1760 by William Tull for 80 acres in Dublin, Election district 4, map #12.
29 Oct.1765 William Tull son of Noble Tull sold to Isaac Mitchell 80 acres
1773 Isaac Mitchell willed to son James Mitchell 80 acres.
8 June 1779 Isaac Mitchell of Worc.Co. sold to John Mitchell 2 1/2 acres.
1783 tax- John Mitchell 53 acres.
1825 NEIGHBORS NEGLECT land of Joseph Stevenson, yeoman, sold at Sheriff's sale to Robert Swan for judgement against Joseph Stevenson.

NEIGHBORS REQUEST

Patented in 1788 by Samuel Smith for 98 1/2 acres in Brinkleys, northeast,Election district 3, map #15.
5 Feb 1789 Samuel Smith sold 12 1/4 acres to Beauchamp Davis.
5 Feb.1789 Samuel Smith,wife Esther Smith, sold to Phillip Adams son of Hope Adams 18 1/4 acres.

NELSONS CHOICE

Patented on 22 March 1663 by John Nelson for 300 acres in West Pr.Anne, Election district 1, map #2.
20 Dec.1668 John Nelson and wife Katherine Nelson, alienated to Christopher Nutter.
12 June 1671 Christopher Nutter and Mary Nutter his wife conveyed to John Dorman 300 acres.
11 Aug.1673 John Dorman,cooper, gave to Matthew Dorman 300 acres.
Rent Rolls 1666-1723 Matthew Dorman 300 acres.
1692 Matthew Dorman gave part to son Matthew Dorman
1 March 1724 John Dorman and wife Christian Dorman sold to brother Matthew Dorman his share from their father Matthew Dorman.
25 Nov.1757 Nehemiah Dorman sold to Levin Ballard part that Matthew Dorman willed to him 75 acres.
7 Dec.1757 Nehemiah Dorman quitclaimed to William Hayward a small piece of land- no acres.
21 June 1758 Levin Ballard released to Nehemiah Dorman part, mortgage.
8 July 1758 triparte agreement between Nehemiah Dorman, 75 acres to William Allen and William Hayward
16 June 1762 Matthew Dorman son of Matthew sold to Levin Ballard 55 acres that Matthew Dorman grandfather willed to son John Dorman 175 acres.no name given.
20 Nov.1767 William Hayward of Talbot Co.Md. sold to Levin Ballard of Som.Co. 75 acres.
15 Oct.1768 Levin Ballard sold to William Geddes 372 acres of NELSONS CHOICE,HAYWARDS PURCHASE.
7 Oct.1769 William Geddes,wife Mary Geddes sold 372 acres to William

Winder of NELSONS CHOICE,HAYWARDS PURCHASE.
1769 Michael Dorman gave to son Chase Dorman.
27 June 1772 William Geddes of Kent Co. sold to Charles Dorman 55 acres.
1783 tax- Chase Dorman 55 acres
1783 tax- John Winder 250 1/2
1793 Chase Dorman gave to son Hezekiah Dorman
1792 William Winder willed to son John Winder land bought of William
Geddes, unnamed.
29 April 1803 Hezekiah Dorman son of Chase Dorman, and wife Amelia Dorman
sold to Zadock Long.
9 Nov.1808 Thomas Chase Dorman sold to Samuel Chase Dorman 60 acres
divised by Charles Dorman father of Both, to son Jesse Dorman now
deceased- no name of land.

NEW BOSTON

Patented in 1741 by Sampson Wheatley for 50 acres in Brinkleys,
southwest, Election district 3, map #17.
1773 Sampson Wheatley willed to daughter Betty Wheatley.
24 June 1786 Caleb Jones and wife Betty Jones daughter of Sampson
Wheatley sold to Kellum Lankford,Elijah Coulbourn, and Thomas Jones with
MERCHANTS TREASURE,PRIVILEDGE,WHEATLEYS SECOND ADDITION, etc.
1783 tax- Mary Wheatley 28 3/4 acres.
17 Feb.187 Caleb Jones of Parish of St. Marys in Co. York, New Brunswick
and wife Betty Jones sold to Mordicai Jones of St. Mary Co. USA 28 3/4
acres.
23 Aug.1807 Mordicai Jones and wife Mary Jones of St. Marys Co.Md. sold
to Robert Bell of Som. Co. 28 3/4 acres.
11 Sep 1807 Robert Bell sold 28 3/4 acres to Samuel Tull.

NEW BRITIAN

Patented in 1741 by Benjamin Lankford for 50 acres in Lawsons, Election
district 8, map #18.
17 Aug.1763 Benjamin Lankford sold to Lazarus Lankford 50 acres.
15 June 1807 Benjamin Lankford Sr. sold to William Williams 23 acres.
22 June 1808 William Williams sold to Benjamin Lankford 23 acres.
10 April 1810 Matthias Dashiell, sheriff, sold to William William Esq.,
per judgement against Benjamin Lankford 23 acres.

NEWFOUNDLAND

Patented on 16 Nov.1699 by Francis Roberts, a resurvey of part of DAVIDS
DESTINY for 125 acres in Dames Quarter,Election district 11, map#7.
Rent Rolls 1666-1723 possessed by the widow Roberts.

NEWFOUNDLAND

Not patented by this name, probably in Fairmount District.
14 May 1771 Thomas Pollitt and wife Betty Pollitt sold to William
Fountain 20 acres for 5 shillings, with FISHING ISLAND & MARSH GROUND
13 Aug.1786 William Fountain and wife Sarah Turpin Fountain sold to John
Williams, 1 moity of NEWFOUNDLAND & FISHING ISLAND.
14 Feb 1789 William Fountain and wife Sarah Fountain sold to John
Williams, MARSH GROUND,NEWFOUNDLAND & FISHING ISLAND.

rch 1807 John W. Curtis, wife Margaret Curtis and William Fountain
sold to John C.Wilson 314 1/4 acres of NEWFOUNDLAND, FISHING ISLAND &
MARISH GROUND.

NEW INVENTION

Patented in Nov.1695 by William Fassitt for 425 acres in Fairmount,
Election district 6, map #9.
23 July 1700 William Fassitt conveyed to John Roach Jr.
14 Aug.1703 John Roach sold to Samuel Handy.
Rent Rolls 1666-1723 Samuel Handy.
1721 Samuel Handy willed to son Ebenezer Handy 1/2 of marsh bought of
John Roach containing 425 acres.
2 Dec.1735 Ebenezer Handy willed to son Robert Handy 212 1/2 acres.
18 Nov.1747 Robert Handy sold to Thomas Seon 212 1/2 acres
1783 tax- Thomas Sudler 212 acres (grandson of Thomas Seon.)
18 March 1790 Thomas Seon Sudler sold to Milcah Gale Wilson 212 1/2 acres
29 Sep.1795 Milcah Gale Chaille sold to Samuel Miles 106 1/4 acres
29 Sep.1795 Milcah Gale Chaille sold to Levin Miles 106 1/4 acres.

NEW PROVIDENCE

Patented in 1801 for 255 acres,by Samuel Sloan, a resurvey of PROVIDENCE,
in Dublin,Election district 4, map #13.
26 Aug.1806 Samuel Sloan gave to daughter Sarah Pollitt.
9 Jan 1810 Thomas Waters son of George Waters, wife Elizabeth Waters sold
to Thomas Mitchell 250 acres of SUFFOLk, HAP AT A VENTURE, MIDDLESEX.

NEW RUMNEY

Patented on 20 Aug.1669 by John Winder for 150 acres in Fairmount,
Election district 6, map #9.
10 June 1672 John Winder and wife Bridget Winder sold to Mark Conden of
St.Marys Co.Md. 150 acres.
1690 Mark Conden willed this land to be sold to Nicholas Fountain
Rent Rolls 1666-1723 Nicholas Fountain 150 acres.
1709 Nicholas Fountain willed 150 acres to son Nicholas and son Stephen
Fountain.
25 Aug.1727 Nicholas Fountain and wife Tabitha Fountain and Stephen
Fountain son of Nicholas sold to Nicholas Fountain of Acco.Co.Va. son of
Marcy Fountain late of Somerset County.
1731 resurveyed to 287 acres by Nicholas Fountain.
26 Nov.1741 Nicholas Fountain and wife Mary Fountain sold to David
McDonald 244 acres.
1783 tax- David McDonald 244 acres
1783 tax- John Waters 43 acres
10 Aug.1790 William Fountain and Thomas Fountain with wife Sarah Fountain
sold to Josiah Furniss son of William Furniss.

NEW VIRGINIA

Patented in 1773 by George Miles for 70 acres in St.Peters, Election
district 2, map #6.
1783 tax- George Miles
1780/91 George Miles willed to Sarah Jones and then to her daughter Ruth

Jones.

NEW WOOD HALL

Patented on 10 Nov.1686 by Peter Dent 200 acres in Brinkleys, northeast, Election district 3, map #3.
Rent Rolls 1666-1723 Moses Fenton
23 June 1758 John Anderson of Augusta Co.Va. sold to Moses Catlin 200 acres NEW WOOD HALL patented by Peter Dent.. John Anderson son and heir of the daughter of Peter Dent.
2 Aug.1764 Fenton Catlin and wife Margaret Catlin sold 8 acres to BRITIAN POWELL.
6 Aug.1764 Fenton Catlin and wife Margaret Catlin sold 100 acres to William Holland.
9 May 1765 Fenton Catlin and wife Margaret Catlin sold to Alexander Maddux 99 acres.
16 Dec 1766 William Holland sold 100 acres to David Long
14 Jan 1772 Alexander Maddux sold to Phillip Adams son of Thomas Adams 94 1/4 acres
1774 tax- Phillip Adams 94 acres
1783 tax- Phillip Adams 94 1/4 acres
1783 tax- David Long 105 acres
23 Aug. 1805 Solomon Long sold to William Powell and Samuel Powell lands that descended from father David Long, 142 acres and 80 acres of marsh, no name.
1812 Phillip Adams willed to son Stephen Adams lands I now live on bought of Alexander Maddux,unnamed.

NEWBERRY

Patented on 26 Nov.1676 by William Stevens and assigned to Richard Kimball, for 150 acres in Mt.Vernon,Election district 5, map #1.
1702 Richard Kimball willed to Thomas Serman of Wicomico.
Rent Rolls 1666-1723 Possessed by widow of Thomas Serman 150 acres.
(Richard Kimball married Jane Jamison in 1674 and Thomas Surman married Margaret Jamison- they are brothers-in-law.)
1704 Thomas Serman willed to son Thomas Serman, land of Richard Kimball. unnamed.

NEWMANS CHANCE & CONCLUSION

Patented in 1743 by Henry Newman for 100 acres in West Pr.Anne, Election district 1, maps #2 & #3.
1755 ADDITION pat for 192 3/4 acres by Henry Newman.
1750 patent NEWMANS CONCLUSION 280 acres by Henry Newman
1768 resurv. to NEWMANS LAST CONCLUSION 667 acres by Henry Newman.
1783 tax- Joseph McVey 10 acres LAST CONCLUSION
1783 tax- Sarah Newman 100 acres CONCLUSION
1783 tax- Alice Newman 219 acres LAST CONCLUSION
1783 tax- Thomas Newman 488 acres LAST CONCLUSION
25 May 1782 Henry Newman attorney of Isaac Newman of Fayette Pa. sold to William Newman of Som.Co. 333 acres of NEWMANS LAST CONCLUSION and pt. 6 acres of ADDITION formerly prop. of Levi Ballard
29 Jan 1793 William Newman and Mary McVey sold to Arnold Elzey 12 1/2 acres.

24 Feb.1793 Thomas Newman Sr. and William Newman sold 50 acres to Joseph Whitney NEWMANS LAST CONCLUSION.
15 Apr.1794 Arnold Elzey conv. to Denwood Wilson, to settle dispute, NEWMANS LAST CONCLUSION
7 Oct.1794 Thomas Newman,William Newman and Isaac Newman sons of Isaac Newman sold 40 acres to Joseph Whitney.
24 Nov.1795 William Newman and wife Nelly Newman sold to Arnold Elzey 137 1/2 acres of ADDITION & NEWMANS LAST CONCLUSION
21 March 1796 Isaac Newman sold to Joseph Whitney 1 3/4acres 21 perches LAST CONCLUSION.
25 Sep.1798 Isaac Newman, wife Polly Newman, sold to George Waggaman 50 acres of NEWMANS CONCLUSION.
13 Nov.1798 Isaac Newman of Thomas Newman sold to William Newman 65 acres of NEWMANS LAST CONCLUSION.
1 Jan 1799 Isaac Newman sold to Joseph Whitney 1 acres and 12 perches of NEWMANS LAST CONCLUSION.
12 March 1800 Henry Waggaman of Dorcester Co. sold to Matthew Mongar 50 acres NEWMANS CONCLUSION
9 May 1801 Isaac Newman, wife Polly Newman sold to Littleton Dennis Teackle 12 acres.
3 Aug.1804 Arnold Elzey,wife Henrietta Elzey of Washington DC sold to Levin Jones of Robert NEWMANS LAST CONCLUSION 12 1/2 acres and ADDITION 137 acres. On the same day Levin Jones gave him a mortgage.
9 Oct.1804 Elizabeth Newman sold to Isaac Newman all rights of dower from husband Thomas Newman.
7 April 1807 Isaac Newman, wife Mary sold to Jesse Wainright 181 3/4 acres NEWMANS LAST CONCLUSION.
16 JUne 1807 Arnold Elzey released mortgage to Levin Jones of Robert Jones.
7 April 1807 Littleton Dennis Teackle sold to John Teackle of Georgetown D.C.land purchased of Isaac Newman.
23 April 1808 Levin Jones of Robert Jones, sold to Robert J. King, ADDITION, NEWMANS LAST CONCLUSION 150 acres.
17 Oct.1808 Joseph Whitney and wife Ann Whitney, sold to Robert Jenkins King 50 acres and 1 acres 11 perches and 1 3/4 acres.
2 Aug.1809 Matthew Mungar sold to Matthew Mungar Jr. 50 acres NEWMANS CONCLUSION.
13 Jan 1810 Robert Jenkins King sold to Jesse Heath Winright NEWMANS LAST CONCLUSION 1 acre 12 perches, NEWMANS CONCLUSION 1 3/4 acres 21 perches.
12 Sep.1814 Robert H. King sold 18 1/2 acres to Thomas Curtis of NEWMANS LAST CONCLUSION.
1841 Joseph Whitney willed dwelling plantation to daughters Priscilla Whitney and Harriett Whitney, unnamed.

NEWPORT PAGNELL

Patented on 20 Feb.1679 by John King and assigned to John Panter for 50 acres in St.Peters,Election district 2, map #6.
Rent Rolls 1666-1723 John Panter
1713 John Panter willed to Benjamin Sasser Jr. 50 acres
5 Aug.1729 Benjamin Sasser and Thomas Sasser deeded to William Sasser. 50 acres.
(note NEWPORT PAGNELL is a town in Bucks Co.England)

NEWPORT

Patented in 1753 for 36 acres by Benjamin Lankford in Brinkleys,
northwest, Election district 3, map #4
29 Dec.1768 Benjamin Lankford sold to David Lankford 36 acres.
20 March 1787 William Lankford sold 12 acres to Stephen Marshall.

NEWTOWN

Patented on 2 Oct.1665 by Jenkins Price for 450 acres in Dublin, Election
district 4, map #13.
1667 Jenkins Price and wife Matthew Price sold 225 acres to John Kinney.
12 June 1671 John Kinney and wife Mary Kinney and Edward Waller and wife
Elizabeth Waller sold to Alexander Murray 450 acres, of Pungateague in
Acco.Co.Va.
1674 resurveyed for 480 acres by William Hobbs.
12 Aug.1672 Alexander Murray of Pungateague Va. and wife Sarah sold to
John Kibble 225 acres.
1695 John Kibble sold 450 acres to Alexander Maddux.
Rent Rolls 1666-1723 225 acres by Alexander Maddux, 225 acres John
Perkins.
11 June 1745 Alexander Maddux son of Lazarus Maddux, and wife Rachel
Maddux sold 25 acres to John Perkins.
18 June 1750 Alexander Maddux sold to Thomas Maddux 50 acres now called
DOUBLE PURCHASE, part of NEWTOWN.
11 July 1750 Alexander Maddux son of Lazarus Maddux sold to John Perkins
part, sold to Alexander Maddux grandfather of afsd Alexander who
bequeathed to son Lazarus, 225 acres
16 Nov.1754 Alexander Maddux sold to Edward Cluff 27 acres.
1755 John Perkins gave to son John Perkins, plantation except 30 acres.
To son William Perkins tract bought of Alexander Maddux adj. and 30 acres
afsd.-no named.
10 July 1758 triparte agreement, Alexander Maddux son of Lazarus Maddux
who was the son of Alexander, to Michael Perkins and Michael Cluff 225
acres.
6 June 1759 Michael Cluff sold to Benjamin Henderson Blades 119 acres.
22 June 1759 Michael Cluff and wife Sarah Cluff to John Perkins son of
John Perkins 25 acres.
22 June 1759 Michael Cluff sold to William Perkins 15 acres
22 June 1759 Michael Cluff sold to Thomas Newbold Maddux son of Lazarus
Maddux 50 acres.
1 Sep.1759 Alexander Maddux sold to Thomas Newbold Maddux 10 acres.
1 Sep.1759 Michael Cluff sold to Alexander Maddux 30 acres.
11 Sep.1759 Alexander Maddux sold 20 acres to Thomas Newbold.
29 Sep.1760 Thomas Newbold and wife Marianne Newbold sold 20 acres to
John Newbold.
18 March 1761 Court appointed John Broughton guardian of John Perkins son
of John Perkins- tract NEWTOWN.
14 March 1765 Sophiah Maddux and Ann Maddux daughters of Alexander Maddux
of Worc.Co. sold 19 acres to Thomas Newbold Maddux.
18 Sep.1766 Thomas Newbold Maddux sold 13 acres to William White.
6 June 1767 Littleton Dennis of Worc.Co. sold 20 acres sold to Samuel
Wilson.
20 Nov.1767 20 Nov.1767 John Perkins sold 25 acres to Samuel Wilson.
30 July 1767 John Newbold son of Thomas Newbold,and wife Leah Newbold now

of Carteret North Carolina, sold 20 acres to Samuel Wilson.
21 March 1770 Thomas Newbold Maddux sold to William White and Benjamin
Henderson Blades 13 acres and another part of same 21 acres.
21 March 1770 Thomas Maddux sold 1 acre to Jesse Blades.
19 Nov.1776 William Perkins late of North Carolina sold to John Perkins
of Som.Co. 45 acres.
22 Dec.1778 John Perkins sold to John Broughton Sr. 4 1/2 acres
1778 Benjamin Henderson Blades willed to wife Comfort Blades 150 1/2
acres.
26 Aug.1778 Jesse Blades sold to Aaron Tilghman 1 acres bou/o Thomas
Maddux and 21 acres that Elizabeth Maddux mother of Jesse Blades wife
recovered of Benjamin Blades 22 acres.
15 Oct.1779 Benston Blades sold to brother Jehu Blades of Worc.Co. 4
parcels 119 acres 2 rods 33 sq.perches, 13 acres,15 acres and 6 acres.
25 March 1780 John Blades sold to Samuel Wilson 153 acres.
25 March 1780 Samuel Wilson sold to John Blades, same as above.
1783 tax- John Broughton 41 acres
1783 tax- Michael Cluff 21 acres
1783 tax- Thomas Maddux 60 acres
1783 tax- John Perkins 240 acres
1783 tax- Benston Blades 110 acres.
6 March 1784 Aaron Tilghman sold 1 acre to Thomas Maddux.
6 March 1784 Thomas Maddux sold to John Broughton Jr. 1 acre
6 March 1784 Thomas Maddux Sr. and wife Jemima Maddux, mortgaged to
Robert J. King.
20 Feb.1786 John Perkins gave 2 1/2 acres to Samuel Wilson to adjust
boundaries
8 Apr.1790 Samuel Wilson sold 5 acres to Thomas Newbold Maddux to raise
the water in his well.
1790 Samuel Wilson willed to son Samuel Wilson
15 Oct.1795 Samuel Wilson son of Samuel,and wife Leah Wilson sold to Eli
Gibbons 126 acres
19 Nov.1795 Major Samuel Wilson,wife Leah Wilson sold 25 acres to
Littleton Dennis.
1795 Thomas Newbold Maddux willed to son Elzey Maddux plantation where I
live except 1 acres, to son John Maddux called LITTLEWORTH bought of
Samuel Wilson.
29 March 1799 Richard Hamilton and Martha Eldridge of Chatham Co.
Barnstable Mass. sold to Elzey Maddux of Somerset County 1 acre of
LITTLEWORTH, that John Maddux died intestate and it became the right of
brother Elzey Maddux and representatives of his sister Polly Furniss and
Leah Hamilton and Martha Eldridge.
27 July 1801 Josiah Broughton,wife Esther Broughton sold to William
Perkins 795 acres, no name.
27 July 1802 William Perkins sold to Josiah Broughton 30 1/4 acres.
27 July 1801 William Perkins sold to Josiah Broughton 100 acres, no name.
27 July 1801 William Perkins sold to John Fleming 185 acres lands where
he now lives, no name.
10 July 1802 William Perkins sold to Josiah Broughton 30 acres during
natural life of wife Peggy Perkins.
10 July 1802 William Perkins sold to Josiah Broughton 581/2 acres.
22 March 1804 William Perkins sold to Nancy Perkins 90 acres where he now
lives adjacent Elzey Maddux and Eli Gibbons, no name.
22 March 1804 John Fleming released mortgage of 185 acres to William
Perkins, no name.

22 March 1804 William Perkins, wife Peggy Perkins sold to Josiah Broughton 203 acres, no name.
25 May 1805 Eli Gibbons, wife Amelia Gibbons sold 126 acres to Henry Cluff.
6 June 1806 Jesse Taylor, wife Diletta Taylor, sold to Littleton Dennis ACQUINTICA & NEWTOWN, no acres given.
21 April 1807 Robert Leatherbury, sheriff, sold to Robert Cluff, per judgement against William Perkins.
25 July 1807 William Furniss of George Furniss, William Taylor and wife Priscilla Taylor, Thomas Furniss of George Furniss sold to Elzey Maddux their interest, divised to John Maddux by his father Thomas Maddux who died intestate and it descended to above.
12 April 1808 John Miles, constable, sold to Amelia Gibbons, now Amelia Bell, per judgement against William Perkins, 5 acres.
6 April 1809 Henry Cluff sold to Elizabeth Morris Hayward 126 acres.
17 May 1810 Elizabeth Morris Hayward of Worc. Co. sold to Levin Pollitt of Som.Co. 126 acres NEWTOWN & 29 acres AQINTICA.

NIBLETS LOTT

Patented in 1734 by Burrell Nibletts for 28 acres in Westover, Election district 13, map #11.
13 June 1744 Burrell Nibletts of Worc.Co. sold 28 acres to Marcy Beauchamp.
1749 resurveyed to THREE BROTHERS 722 acres.

NICHOLSONS ADVENTURE

Patented on 23 Oct.1666 by James Nicholson for 150 acres in St.Peters, Election district 2, map #6.
Rent Rolls 1666-1723 possessed by George Phoebus
4 Sep.1781 Job Robaman and wife Mary Robaman and Job Robaman all of Dorc.Co. sold to John Cavanaugh, as George Phoebus willed to grandson George and as George Phoebus the grandfaer died and left to Mary wife of Job Robaman, all lands-no name or acreage.
1783 tax- John Phoebus 97 acres
1783 tax- Samuel Phoebus 41 acres
1783 tax- John Cavanaugh with LITTLEWORTH 55 acres.
25 March 1783 Samuel Phoebus sold to John McGrath 41 acres with LITTLEWORTH
26 Mach 1783 John McGrath sold to Samuel Phoebus, same as above.
1783 Samuel Phoebus willed to wife Martha Phoebus.
24 May 1786 John Phoebus,wife Jamima Phoebus sold to William Jones son of William 62 1/2 acres of NICHOLSONS ADVENTURE & LITTLEWORTH
7 Dec.1785 John Phoebus and William Gillis defined boundaries on 150 acres.
4 June 1787 John Phoebus,wife Ann Phoebus sold to Ezekiel Gillis-description,no acreage given.
1788 Martha Phoebus willed to Thomas Jones of Samuel Jones, dwelling plantation.
23 Jan 1795 John Phoebus Sr. sold to John Phoebus Jr. for 5 shilings 200 acres of NICHOLSONS ADVENTURE,BROTHERS AGREEMENT,LITTLEWORTH.
28 Apr.1795 John Phoebus sold for 5 shillings to Lewis Phoebus 16 3/4 acres.
16 June 1800 Thomas Jones of Samuel Jones sold to Evans Willin with

314

LITTLEWORTH 300 acres.
22 Feb.1808 Evans Willin sold to John Wilkins.
12 Dec.1810 Thomas Rutter, marshall, sold to Joshua Dorsey of Baltimore
Co. per judgement agains Evans Willin 40 acres.

NIGHTS SUCESS

Patented in 1749, a resurvey from TURKEY COCK HILL by James Knight for
206 acres in Dublin,Election district 4, map #12.
16 March 1757 James Knight,wife Parthena Knight sold 93 acres to William
Matthews.
16 March 1757 James Knight sold 100 acres to William Benston.
23 Jan 1770 James Knight,wife Elizabeth Knight sold to John Harris 13
acres.
11 Aug.1772 William Benston sold to William Miles Sr.100 acres.
20 Dec.1772 James Knight sold to William Miles for 5 shillings balance of
KNIGHTS SUCESS, exept pt. conv. to William Benston & William Matthews and
John Harris.
1781 William Miles willed to grandson William Miles son of Samuel Miles
lands conveyed me by William Benston and James Knight, unnamed lands.
1783 tax- John Harris 13 acres
1783 tax- William Matthews 95 acres
1783 tax- Mary Miles 25 1/2 acres
1783 William Matthews willed lands to wife Prissa Matthews.
20 April 1790 Denwood Matthews son of William Matthews sold to Matthias
Miles 93 acres where Priscilla Matthews now lives.
16 June 1794 Denwood Matthews sold to Levi Matthews 100 acres
16 Feb.1796 Denwood Matthews,wife Tabitha Matthews sold to Levi Matthews
100 acres.
1818/21 Matthias Miles willed to grandson Robert Miles of Matthias Miles
93 acres bought of Denwood Matthews.
19 Sep.1889 Jehu Parsons willed to wife Sarah Parsons real estate
purchased of Robert Bratten trustee to sell the real estate of Mrs.
Adaline W. Miles deceased 37 3/4 acres of KNIGHTS SUCESS and lot 3 of
same and another part purchased of John F. Miles containing 3 acres
adjacent.

NO NAME

Patented on 14 Aug.1688 by David Brown for 350 acres in West Pr.Anne,
Election district 1, map #3
Rent Rolls 1666-1723 Alexander Brown the heir.
1697 David Brown willed to Alexander Brown all lands, unnamed.
This land is also called THORNS ADDITION.
1 March 1738 Thomas Brown eldest son of Alexander Brown, Mary Brown and
Margaret Brown two daughters of Alexander Brown gave to brother David
Brown, THORNS ADDITION,SOUTH BRERETON and sundry other tracts.
27 April 1749 John Woolford and wife Mary Woolford late Mary Brown coheir
of Thomas Brown, Margaret Brown, Sarah Brown widow sold to David Wilson
heir of Ephraim Wilson 350 acres pat.by David Brown in 1695.
2 May 1749 Margaret Brown sold to William Skirvin 250 acres 1/2 part of
THORNTON,MEDDOW,HACKALA,OWENS CHOICE,BROWNS LOTT and patent for 350 acres
by David Brown, except part conveyed to David Wilson.

NONE SUCH

Patented on 15 Nov.1694 by Anthony Bell for 50 acres in Lawsons, Election
district 8, map #18.
1765 resurveyed to EXPENSE 340 1/4 acres.

NORFOLK

Patented on 11 June 1679 by William Harper for 500 acres in
Dublin,Election disrict 4, map #12.
1702 William Harper willed to wife Elizabeth Harper and then to grandson
John Harper 500 acres.
Rent Rolls 1666-1723 possessed by widow of Harper
1734 John Harper gave to son William Harper, plantation where brother
Francis Harper lives-unnamed.
28 Sep.1745 William Harper sold to Matthias Coston,joyner, 250 acres.
12 March 1750 Matthias Coston and wife Elizabeth Coston sold to Stephen
Coston 250 acres.
19 Apr.1750 Stephen Coston sold to Thomas Hayward 250 acres, mortgage
2 April 1751 Thomas Hayward released mortgage to Stephen Coston
3 Apr.1751 Stephen Coston, wife Rhoda Coston sold to Samuel Adams 250
acres.
26 Oct.1756 John Harper sold to Samuel Adams 10 1/2 acres
1758 Samuel Adams willed to sons Samuel and Phillip Adams 250 acres.
7 Feb 1763 John Harper and wife Catherine Harper sold to Samuel Adams 230
1/2 acres
1763 Samuel Adams willed to son Samuel lands bought of John Harper and
Stephen Coston.
13 Aug.1782 Phillip Collins Adams sold to Samuel Adams 209 acres out of
ADAMS PURCHASE & NORFOLK.
1783 tax- Phillip C. Adams 200 acres
1783 tax- Samuel Adams 50 acres
15 Nov.1785 Samuel Adams Harper,wife Sarah Harper of Worc.Co. son of John
Harper who was the eldest son of John who was the son of William Harper
sold to Philip Collins Adams 250 acres.
15 Nov.1785 Samuel Adams Harper,wife Sarah Harper, of Worc.Co. sold to
Joshua Boston 101 acres.
19 Feb.1787 Samuel Adams Harper,wife Elizabeth Harper of Worc.Co. sold to
Samuel Adams of Som.Co. 140 acres.
8 March 1791 Joshua Boston,wife Mary Boston sold 101 acres to Zorobable
King and William Turpin.
26 May 1792 Joshua Boston,wife Nancy Boston and Zorobable King and
William Turpin sold to Samuel Adams 30 acres.
1793 ADDITION TO NORFOLK 21 acres, pat. Phillip C. Adams.
29 Nov.1794 Phillip Collins Adams sold to George Miles son of Samuel
Miles 250 acres of NORFOLK, ADAMS PURCHASE.
13 April 1799 George Miles sold to Phillip Collins Adams 250 acres of
NORFOLK & ADAMS PURCHASE.
15 Aug.1803 Phillip Collins Adams, wife Priscilla Adams sold to Jonathan
Mills 105 1/2 acres of ADAMS PURCHASE & NORFOLK.
12 June 1804 Jonathan Mills sold to William Williams, merchant 105 1/2
acre purchased in 1803 from Phillip Collins Adams, unnamed.
14 March 1804 Joshua Boston sold to son Levin Boston 74 acres out of
ADAMS PURCHASE, BECKLES & NORFOLK.
13 March 1803 Joshua Boston, John Morrison and Levin King sold to James

Boston of Joshua Boston 100 acres of NORFOLK & ADAMS PURCHASE.
2 May 1804 Samuel Adams sold to Burton Cannon and Isaac Mitchell Adams,
NORFOLK, ADAMS DELIGHT & ADAMS PURCHASE, no acreage given.
2 July 1805 Phillip C.Adams sold to Collins Adams 200 acres of NORFOLK,
ADDN. TO NORFOLK, ADAMS DELIGHT.
11 Feb 1806 James Boston sold to Isaac Mitchell Adams 10 1/4 acres of
NORFOLK & ADAMS PURCHASE.
11 Feb 1806 Jonathan Mills and wife Leah Mills, William Williams and
Alexander McAllen of Worc. Co. sold to James Boston 30 acres of NORFOLK &
ADAMS PURCHASE.
12 April 1810 Matthias Dashiell, sheriff, sold to William Williams 75 1/2
acres per judgement against Mary Bedsworth.
26 July 1831 Sheriff's sale- suit of George Dashiell against Isaac M.
Adams.
1836 Levin Pollitt willed to William T. Hargis son of Thomas Hargis.
1838 Jonathan Mills willed to wife Leah Mills.

NORMANDY

Patented in Nov.1670 by Nicholas Fountain for 50 acres in Westover,
Election district 13, map #11.
Rent Rolls 1666-1723 Nicholas Fountain
1708 Nicholas Fountain willed to sons Nicholas and Stephen Fountain.
29 July 1727 Stephen Fountain sold to Nicholas Fountain son of Marcy
Fountain 50 acres.
7 June 1732 I Nicholas Fountain give to Nicholas Fountain Jr. one moity
of OLD RIGHTS 126 1/2 acres adjacent NORMANDY-unnamed.
14 June 1735 Nicholas Fountain and wife Tabitha Fountain sold to William
Turpin son of William westmost moity of FOUNTAINS LOTT,NORMANDY and his
right to CONVENIENCY.
1758 resurvyed to include FOUNTAINS LOTT 261 acres.
1783 tax- William Fountain 261 acres
1783 tax- Denwood Turpin 25 acres
1791 William Fountain willed to son Henry Fountain.
(1976 Marylander and Hearld newspaper-this land has the longest history
of ownership by a family in Som.Co. 205 acres owned by William Fountain.)

NORTH BORDER

Patented in 1749 for 100 acres by John Williams in Westover, Election
district 13, map #11
1783 tax- John Williams 100 acres.
12 July 1791 John Williams sold to Levin Ballard 100 acres and returned
by Levin Ballard to him on the same date probably a mortgage.
1815 William Williams sold to William Curtis 100 acres.
20 Nov.1812 John W. Curtis sold to William Williams.

NORTH FORELAND

Patented on 28 Apr.1675 by Thomas Walker and assigned to Thomas Roe for
300 acres on Deals Island,Election district 14, map #8.
2 June 1677 Thomas Roe and wife Ann Roe sold to John Laws.
Rent Rolls 1666-1723 possessed by John Laws in right of his brother
George Laws.
1696 John Laws willed to son Thomas Laws.

24 May 1755 Thomas Laws gave 100 acres to Thomas Laws Jr.
1783 tax- John Laws 300 acres
1785 resurveyed to LAWS PREPOSSESSION 558 acres
12 June 1789 John Laws Jr.wife Dolly Laws sold to William Evans 116 acres
of NORTHFORELAND, LAWS ADDITION.
12 Dec 1797 William Evans sold to Isaac Noble 12 acres.
4 March 1799 I Stephen Adams make over to John Adams of Stephen Adams
that descended to me from brother William Adams, deceased, all rights.
5 Aug.1800 Charles Nutter, wife Louisa Nutter sold to John Adams of
Stephen Adams, all rights.
1 Sep.1801 John Whittingham Adams sold to John Adams of Stephen Adams,
part, all rights, no acres given.
8 Oct.1805 John Adams of Stephen Adams sold to Thomas Jones 1/4th acre to
settle dispute.
11 April 1810 Lambert Hyland & Henry James Carroll trustees to sell the
real estate of William Adams, sold 480 acres to John Adams of Stephen
Adams.
19 June 1810 John Adams sold to Jesse Webster now called LAWS
PREPOSSESSION 11 1/2 acres.

NORWICH

Patented on 10 Apr.1681 by Thomas Shank for 100 acres in East Pr.Anne,
Election district 15, map #4.
Rent Rolls 1666-1723 Thomas Shank dead without heirs, land escheatable.
23 Mar.1752 George Wilson sold to William Pollitt 100 acres.
1785 resurveyed to POLLITTS SCURITY 343 1/4 acres

NOTHING

Surveyed in 1792 for 4 3/4 acres by Matthias Miles in East Pr.Anne,
Election district 15,map #5.

NOVA FRANCIA

Patented on 25 Aug.1679 by John White and assigned to Nicholas Fountain
for 100 acres in Westover,Election district 13, map #11.
1708 Nicholas Fountain willed to son Marcy Fountain, at his death to son
William Fountain.
Rent Rolls 1666-1723 Nicholas Fountain
13 Nov.1729 William Fountain of Dorc. Co. and wife Sarah Fountain sold
100 acres to Nicholas Fountain son of Marcy Fountain.
14 March 1755 Marcy Fountain sold to Ephraim Wilson lands from father
Nicholas Fountain-unnamed.
1755 resurveyed to CONVIENCY 344 acres.

NUTTERS DELIGHT

Patented on 23 Sep.1665 by Christoper Nutter in West Pr.Anne Election
district 1, map #3, for 150 acres.
3 July 1667 Christoper Nutter and wife Mary Nutter sold 150 acres to
Richard Acworth.
7 Nov.1685 Richard Acworth and wife Sarah Acworth sold to Levin Denwood
150 acres.
Rent Rolls 1666-1723 Arthur Denwood.

16 Sep.1740 Thomas Denwood and George Denwood divided the lands of grandfather Levin Denwood.
16 Sep.1741 George Denwood sold to David Wilson 420 1/2 acres of NUTTERS DELIGHT,BROWNSTONE,WEATHERLYS CHANCE,FIRST CHOICE,DENWOODS INCLUSION.

NUTTERS PURCHASE

Patented on 6 March 1666 by Christopher Nutter for 300 acres, in West Pr.Anne, Election district 1, map #3.
Rent Rolls 1666-1723 Charles Ballard
12 Nov.1672 Christopher Nutter and wife Mary Nutter sold to Charles Ballard.
1725 Charles Ballard willed to son Henry Ballard land on Manokin River, unnamed.
17 Aug.1723 Charles Ballard Jr. gave to members of the Presbyterian Congregation of Manokin 1/4 acre.
9 Oct.1745 Robert Ballard sold 300 acres to William Hayward.
4 Jan 1757 Mary Ballard widow of Henry Ballard sold to William Hayward for 5 shillings land as you go to Princess Anne Town and houses, no name or acreage.
31 May 1763 William Hayward traded 8 1/2 acres with James Laws for part of DOGWOOD RIDGE.
20 March 1764 James Laws and wife Jane Laws sold to William Hayward 8 1/2 acres DOGWOOD RIDGE-part of trade.
29 March 1764 William Hayward, wife Margaret Hayward sold 8 1/2 acres to Andrew Francis Cheney with DOGWOOD RIDGE
21 Nov.1767 Levin Ballard sold 7 1/2 acres to Andrew Francis Cheney.
1758 resurveyed to HAYWARDS PURCHASE 549 1/2 acres.
1783 tax- Andrew Francis Cheney 79 acres.
1980-this land is within the bounds of Princess Anne Town.

OAK HALL

Patented in 1761 by Thomas Benson for 30 1/2 acres in Dublin, Election district 4, map #13.
31 March 1810 Thomas Benston & James Barrett, wife Catherine Barrett sold to Littleton Dennis devised by grandfather Thomas Benston.

OAK HALL

Patented in 1762 for 100 acres by Isaac Bozman Schoolfield in Dublin, Election district 4, map #13.
1783 tax- Isaac B.Schoolfield 90 acres.
7 Feb.1784 Isaac Bozman Schoolfield,wife Rachel Schoolfield sold 100 acres to Phillip Adams.
1805 Stephen Adams son of Phillip Adams sold to William Powell.
11 Feb 1806 William Powell sold to Stephen Adams of Phillip Adams 3 3/4 acres of HOG QUARTER & OAK HALL.
1812 Philip Adams willed to grandson John Adams of James Adams, OAK HALL bought of Isaac Bozman Schoolfield.
1823 John Adams of James Adams sold to Samuel Smith land devised by Phillip Adams.
10 Aug.1830 Constable's sale at suit of Samuel A. Cahoon against John Adams of James Adams with THREE BROTHERS.

7 June 1831 Sheriff's sale at suit of Isaac W. Copes against Beauchamp D.
Adams 100 acres.

OAK HALL

Patented in 1792 for 5 1/2 acres in West Pr.Anne,Election district 1, map
#3.

OAK HAMMOCK

Patented in 1762 for 100 acres, by William Miles, a resurvey of part of
MARTINS HOPE,in Asbury,Election district 12, map #21
1783 tax- Aaron Sterling 100 acres.
1854 John S. Tyler willed to son Alexander Tyler.

OUTLETT

Patented in 1758 for 50 acres William Miles in East Pr.Anne, Election
district 15, map #5.
1770/1 James Hayman willed 50 acres to Hezekiah Hayman of HAYMANS
OUTLETT.

OUTLETT

Patented on 22 Sep.1701 by John White for 100 acres in Dames Quarter,
Election district 11, map #7.
Rent Rolls 1666-1723 John White.
1783 tax- Francis White 200 acres
2 Aug.1796 Francis White gave to son William White.
17 Jan 1799 William White of Francis White, wife Nancy White sold to
Thomas White Sr. 22 1/2 acres.
24 April 1800 William White and wife Nancy White sold to Stephen White 50
acres.
31 Jan 1804 William White of Francis White, sold to Stephen White 3
acres.
1830 William White willed 30 acres to daughter Eleanor Ann White.

OUTLETT
see DAVIDS DESTINY, Dames Quarter

OUTLETT

Patented in 1740 for 50 acres in Brinkleys, northwest, Election district
3, map #14

OUTLETT

Patented in 1764 by William Coulbourn for 15 acres in Lawsons, Election
district 8, map #18.
1775 Isaac Coulbourn willed to newphew William Coulbourn of brother
Wiliam, conveyed me by brother William Coulbourn.
1783 tax - William Coulbourn 15 acres.

OUTLETT

Patented in 1774 for 24 acres by William Polk in Mt.Vernon, Election
district 5, map #1.
1819 resurveyed to MT PLEASANT 763 1/2 acres.

OUTLETT

Patented in 1784 for 24 acres by Henry Walston on Deal Island, Election district #14, map #8.
1796 Henry Walston willed lands in Muddy Hole to son David Walston, no name.
9 Sep.1803 Isaac Noble and wife Peggy Noble sold to Thomas Jones, as Henry Walston bequeathed to son David Walston and daughter Peggy Noble 1/3rd part.
22 Sep.1804 Henry Evans sold to Thomas Jones his 1/4th part of the 1/3rd part of GREENWICH, OUTLETT, CHANCE & VICTORY that Henry Walston willed to son David Walston and grandson Henry Evans.

OUTLETT

Patented in 1792 for 12 acres by William McDorman in Dames Quarter, Election district 11, map #7.
1799 ADDITION TO OUTLETT 8 acres by William McDorman
11 Aug.1800 William McDorman Sr. gave to son Lewis McDorman 12 acres.

OUTTENS ADDITION

Patented on 28 May 1685 by John Outten for 150 acres in Brinkleys, southwest,Election district 3, map #17.
Rent Rolls 1666-1723 John Outten.
1783 tax- Isaac Outten 125 acres
1783 tax- Purnell Outten 25 acres.
1795 Purnell Outten willed lands to wife Mary Outten and then to son Purnell Outten, unnamed.
17 Jan 1799 Isaac Outten, wife Margaret Outten of Acco.Co.Va. sold to John Conner 569 acres of several tracts, unnamed.
6 April 1810 John Conner sold to Henry James Carroll.
27 July 1810 Mordicai Jones of St. Marys Co. sold to Thomas Jones of Som.Co. part.

OUTTENS VENTURE

Patented in 1758 for 45 acres by Abraham Outten in Brinkleys, southwest, Election district 3, map #17. AKA OUTTENS ADVENTURE.
26 May 1806 John Conner, wife Mary Conner sold to Mordicai Jones of St. Marys County.
6 April 1810 John Conner sold to Henry James Carroll.

OWEN GLINDORE

Patented on 1 March 1663 by Garman Gillett for 300 acres in Brinkleys, southeast,Election district 3, map #16.
Rent Rolls 1666-1723 Garman Gillett in his life, is included in a survey for John Waughop of 800 acres called PINEY POINT.
1707 Samuel Collins gave to son Samuel 300 acres.
15 Apr.1734 Samuel Collins son of Samuel,and wife Rebecca Collins sold to Thomas Evans 300 acres that Owen Guyther sold to Samuel Collins grandfather of afsd Samuel and 9 acres of OYSTER SHELL.
16 Aug.1751 Thomas Evans,shipwright, and wife Rose Evans sold to Jabez Pitts 15 acres.

1757 Thomas Evans willed to wife Rose Evans 90 acres.
14 Apr.1762 Rose Evans widow of Thomas Evans and William Evans eldest son
of Thomas gave to William Evans son of Thomas and Rose 90 acres.
22 Dec.1764 Jabez Pitts gave 15 acres to son Robert Pitts.
1 Sep.1766 Nathaniel Evans son of Thomas Evans sold to William Ward 188
acres.
25 July 1768 Ephraim Evans son of Thomas Evans sold to John Collins 95
acres.
21 Nov.1770 Robert Pitts and wife Milcah Pitts sold 15 acres to Thomas
Robertson.
1784 Dr. Thomas Robertson and wife Martha Robertson sold to William Waddy
15, acres
1783 tax- Ephraim Evans 100 acres
1783 tax- Jesse Ward 50 acres
1783 tax- William Ward 158 acres
27 Aug.1787 William Ward sold 50 acres to Daniel Boston.
13 Aug.1790 William Waters son of John Waters sold to James Milbourn and
Ralph Milbourn tracts conveyed by William Waddy to Waters now called
ENTRACT OF MORRIS HOPE.
19 March 1792 Thomas Bunting and wife Rose Bunting, Jonathan Bunting and
wife Ann Bunting sold 105 acres to Ralph Milbourn.
19 March 1792 Abigail Collins sold to Jonathan Bunting, wife Ann Bunting,
and Thomas Bunting, wife Rose Bunting for 5 shillings that Ephraim Evans
mortgaged to John Collins.
19 March 1792 Thomas Bunting, wife Rose Bunting sold to Jonathan Bunting
for 5 shillings 45 acres of afsd mortgage.
31 March 1797 Ralph Milbourn sold all his interest to James Milbourn.
19 March 1800 James Milbourn and Ralph Milbourn mortgaged to William
Waters Sr. with OYSTER SHELL BANK, CROOKED ISLAND & HANDYS MEADOW.
18 Feb 1805 Thomas Ward sold to James Milbourn 125 acres of OWEN GLENDORE
& HANDYS MEADOW.
9 May 1806 James Milbourn sold to Ralph Milbourn 161 acres of OWEN
GLENDORE, OYSTERSHELL BANK & HANDYS MEADOW.
13 Jan.1855 Samuel Charles Henry son of Daniel Henry sold to his brother
Daniel Henry his share.

OWENS CHOICE

Patented on 9 March 1663 by Owen Magraugh for 300 acres in West Pr.Anne,
Election district 1, map #3.
1691 Owen Magraugh willed to son Owen 200 acres
Rent Rolls 1666-1723 possessed by widow Mary Magraugh.
18 March 1733 William Magraw,grandson and heir of Owen Magraw, and wife
Elizabeth Magraw sold 17 acres to Henry Newman.
13 Feb 1734 William McGrath son of Owen McGrath who was the son of Owen
McGrath, and wife Elizabeth McGrath sold to David Brown, balance of land.
2 May 1749 Margaret Brown, heir of Thomas Brown sold to William Skirven
OWENS CHOICE except small part devised to Henry Newman.
12 July 1750 John Woolford and wife Mary Woolford (Mary Brown) sold their
rights to William Skirvin
18 June 1762 William Skirvin and wife Mary Skirvin sold 14 acres to Henry
Newman
7 Sep.1774 William Miles sold to Samuel Phoebus and Martha Phoebus for 5
shilings 150 acres purchased of Esther McGrath.
22 March 1775 Samuel Phoebus and wife Martha Phoebus sold to Denwood

322

Wilson for 5 shillings OWENS CHOICE in right of wife Martha Phoebus.
1783 tax- Mary Skirvin 172 1/2 acres.
7 Dec.1785 Denwood Wilson and wife Margaret Wilson sold to James Wilson
all tracts which descended to Margaret Wilson as only child of William
Skirvin-no names.
12 Dec.1786 James Wilson sold to Denwood Wilson all tracts William
Skirvin died seized of, no name or acres.
1798 Denwood Wilson willed to sons William Witherspoon Wilson, and George
Wilson land of Mr.William Skirvin.
1849 resurveyed to EDGE HILL 520 acres.

OWENS DELIGHT

Patented on 8 Sep.1675 by Owen McGraugh for 100 acres in West Pr.Anne,
Election district 1, map #3.
1691/2 Owen McGraugh gave to son John McGraugh 100 acres.
28 July 1733 William McGraw of Manokin,son of William sold to John McGraw
of Gr.Money 100 acres.
1751 John McGrath willed to sons David McGrath,Levin McGrath and John
McGrath.
14 Feb.1764 David McGrath son of John McGrath,sold to John White his
part.
3 Oct.1766 John White sold to William Smith 100 acres.
29 March 1769 Isaac Coulbourn, sheriff sold to Mary Waggaman widow 271
acres of OWENS IMPROVEMENT,MIDDLE, OWENS
DELIGHT, REFUGE, DAVIDS CHANCE, as Edward Lloyd had a judgement.
16 Nov.1774 David McGrath sold to John McGrath for 5 shillings, all his
share.
1780 Mary Waggaman willed to son Henry Waggaman lands purchased of Isaac
Coulbourn sheriff, unnamed.
1783 tax- John McGrath 100 acres.
16 June 1790 John McGrath sold for 10 shillings to Denwood Wilson- no
acreage given.
1791 John McGrath willed to sons David Gahergan McGrath and nephew John
McGrath Jr.
7 Feb.1792 John McGrath of Levin McGrath, Sarah McGrath widow of Levin
McGrath and Sarah McGrath widow of John McGrath sold to Arnold Elzey 82
3/4 acres of OWENS DELIGHT, OWENS IMPROVEMENT, MIDDLE.
29 Apr.1792 Henry Waggaman,wife Sarah Waggaman of Dorc.Co. sold to George
Waggaman of Somerset County.
20 Aug.1803 Henry Waggaman of Dorc.Co. sold to Littleton Dennis Teackle.
30 May 1804 Arnold Elzey,wife Henrietta of City of Washington DC sold to
Levin Jones of Robert Jones 82 3/4 acres of OWENS DELIGHT, OWENS
IMPROVMENT, MIDDLE, with other lands.
13 May 1804 Levin Jones of Robert Jones mortgaged to Arnold Elzey of
Washington D.C. 233 acres of above.
11 Dec.1804 Littleton Dennis Teackle sold to John Dennis 450 acres of
OWENS IMPROVEMENT, OWENS DELIGHT, MIDDLE, WAGGAMANS PURCHASE.
16 June 1807 Arnold Elzey, wife Henrietta Elzey of Washington DC released
mortgage to Levin Jones of Robert Jones.
23 April 1808 Levin Jones of Robert Jones sold 82 1/2 acres of OWENS
DELIGHT, OWENS IMPROVEMENT & MIDDLE to Robert J. King.
12 April 1809 Sarah McGrath and son David G. McGrath sold to Robert J.
King 50 acres, unnamed.
23 Oct.1809 David McGrath Jr. son of John McGrath sold to Robert J. King

200 acres of MIDDLE, OWENS DELIGHT & OWENS IMPROVEMENT.

OWENS IMPROVEMENT

Patented on 24 Apr.1667 by Owen McGraugh for 150 acres in West Pr.Anne, Election district 1, map #3.
1691 Owen McGraugh gave to son William McGraugh 150 acres.
Rent Rolls possessed by Mary widow of Owen McGraugh.
28 July 1733 William MaGraw son of William,of Manokin sold to John McGraw of Gr.Money 150 acres.
1751 John McGrath willed to sons David McGrath, John McGrath and Levin McGrath.
14 Feb.1764 David McGrath sold his part to John White, mortgage.
3 Oct.1766 John White sold the mortgage 150 acres to William Smith.
29 March 1769 Isaac Coulbourn,sheriff sold to Mary Waggaman widow, to settle judgement of Edward Lloyd of Talbot County.
16 Nov 1774 David McGrath sold to John McGrath for 5 shillings, his interest.
1780 Mary Waggaman willed to son Henry Waggaman land from Isaac Coulbourn,sheriff(unnamed land)
1783 tax- John McGrath.
1791 John McGrath willed to son David Gahergan McGrath and nephew John McGrath Jr.
7 Feb 1792 John McGrath son of Levin McGrath and Sarah McGrath widow of Levin McGrath and Sarah McGrath widow of John McGrath sold to Dr. Arnold Elzey 82 3/4 acres of OWENS DELIGHT,OWENS IMPROVEMENT & MIDDLE.
29 Apr.1792 Henry Waggaman, wife Sarah Waggaman of Dorc.Co. sold part to George Waggaman of Somerset County.
20 Aug.1803 Henry Waggaman of Dorc. Co. sold to Littleton Dennis Teackle.
20 May 1804 Arnold Elzey,wife Henreitta Elzey, of Washington DC sold to Levin Jones of Robert Jones 82 3/4 acres of OWENS DELIGHT, OWENS IMPROVEMENT, MIDDLE, with other lands.
13 May 1804 Levin Jones of Robert Jones, mortgage to Arnold Elzey of Washington DC, 233 acres of same.
11 Dec 1804 Littleton Dennis Teackle, sold to John Dennis 450 acres of OWENS IMPROVEMENT, OWENS DELIGHT, MIDDLE, WAGGAMANS PURCHASE.
1 Dec 1804 John Dennis sold to Elias Bailey OWENS IMPROVEMENT, & part of DAVIDS CHANCE.
16 June 1807 Arnold Elzey, wife Henrietta Elzey of Washington DC released mortgage to Levin Jones of Robert Jones.
23 April 1808 Levin Jones sold to Robert J. King.
12 April 1809 Sarah McGrath widow of John McGrath & son David G.McGrath sold to Robert J. King.
23 Oct.1809 David McGrath son of John McGrath sold to Robert J. King.

OWENS LOTT

Patented on 18 Sep.1701 by Moses Owens for 100 acres in Brinkleys,southwest,Election district 3, map #17
Rent Rolls 1666-1723 Moses Owens.
1722 Aaron Owens and wife Elizabeth Owens sold to Patrick (unreadable name)
1726 Thomas Potter willed to son Thomas Potter (MOSES LOTT)
1778 Thomas Potter, Sarah Matthews and Henry Potter (her son) sold to Nathan Cahoon.

1783 tax- Henry Potter 100 acres.
17 April 1786 Jesse Powell sold for 5 shillings to Henry Potter, with
MITCHELLS CHOICE, no acres.
25 Apr.1786 Henry Potter and wife Mary Potter and Sarah Potter sold 46
acres to Nathan Cahoon.

OXFORD

Patented on 2 May 1682 by John White for 100 acres in Dames Quarter,
Election district 11, map #7.
Rent Rolls 1666-1723 John White.
1761 John White willed to son John White 100 acres.
8 March 1774 John White gave to son John White.
1783 tax- John White Jr. 100 acres.
6 Oct.1790 John White Jr. sold 64 acres to Joshua Dennis Jr.
16 July 1793 John White sold to Francis White 303 acres of DAM
QUARTER,OXFORD,FRIENDS CONTENTMENT, lease during the life of John White.
1830 William White willed land bought of Francis White on Rock Creek to
be sold.
22 Jan 1799 Francis White Jr. sold to Peter White 64 acres.
27 April 1807 Abraham Furniss, wife Polly Furniss and Joshua Furniss,
wife Sarah of Elizabeth Co. Va. sold to Francis White of Somerset Co. Md.
64 acres.

OXHEAD

Patented in 1663 by James Price for 300 acres, in East Pr.Anne Election
district 15, map #5.
8 Aug.1676 James Price sold to John King of Manokin 300 acres.
Rent Rolls 1666-1723 possessed by Peter Dent
1696 John King willed to wife Elizabeth King 300 acres during life (he
married Elizabeth Ballard, she married third Peter Dent)then to son
Charles King.
7 Sep.1734 David Wilson guardian of Planner King inspect plantation
OXHEAD.
1738 Planner King gave to brother Jesse King.
1782 resurvey to 245 acres by Jesse King
1783 tax- Mary King for heirs of Jesse King 230 acres.
1810 Jesse King willed to brother William King.
1816 William King of Jesse King sold to Thomas Leeds Jr.

OYSTER SHELL BANKS

this is part of HANDYS MEADOW.

OYSTER SHELL LANDING

this is part of TWO BROTHERS on Smiths Island

PADENS PUZZLE

Patented in 1792 a resurvey by John Peden from CHERRY GARDEN for 56 3/4
acres in Dublin,Election district 4, map #13.
1796 John Peden willed lands to son John, unnamed.
10 June 1805 John Peden sold to Isaac Dryden 5 1/2 acres with part
HACKELA.

PAINTERS DEN

Patented on 12 May 1707 by Archibald Smith for 100 acres in East Pr.Anne, Election district 15, map #5.
Rent Rolls 1666-1723 Archibald Smith
20 March 1723 Archibald Smith of Sussex Co.Del.sold to Owen Conely of Dorc. Co.Md. 100 acres.
18 July 1727 Owen Conely and wife Elizabeth Conely of Dorc.Co. sold to George Benston 100 acres.
19 Nov 1728 George Benston and wife Rebecca Benston sold 100 acres to Rev. William Stewart
1763 resurvey to include BUCKRIDGE 217 1/2 acres by William Stewart.
1783 tax- William Stewart 217 acres.

PANTHERS DEN

Patented on 11 Nov.1666 by John Panter for 200 acres in West Pr.Anne, Election district 1, map #3.
Rent Rolls 1666-1723 John Panter
1713/4 John Panter willed to wife Dorothy Panter,after death to Catherine Laws and her children (dwelling plantation)
1728 resurvey 340 acres by Robert Laws
1756 resurvey 288 1/2 acres by Panter Laws
1783 tax- William Laws 96 acres
1783 tax- Benjamin Sasser 192 1/2 acres
1 May 1792 John Laws sold to Thomas Laws all rights except that already sold.
1 May 1792 Thomas Laws sold to John Laws, same as above.
8 May 1802 Thomas Laws of Panter Laws, wife Eleanor Laws sold to Robert Robertson 288 acres.
18 Aug.1808 James Robertson son of James, sold to John Leatherbury. As Robert Robertson deceased had lands on Money Creek purchased of Thomas Laws and Robert willed to Ann H. Robertson wife of Robert Robertson and then to children of James Robertson and George Robertson brothers of Robert. He sold all interest, no name of land given.

PARKERS FORTUNE

Patented in 1750 by John Parker for 26 acres in East Pr.Anne Election district 15, map #5.
22 June 1770 John Parker sold to William Miles 22 acres
1783 tax- John Parker
25 Nov.1791 John Parker,wife Elizabeth Parker,sold to John Parker and George Parker 176 acres of PARKERS FORTUNE & DAVIS CHOICE.
12 March 1800 John Parker sold to George Parker, DAVIS CHOICE & PARKERS FORTUNE
12 Mar.1800 George Parker sold to John Parker, same as above

PARKERS PEACE

Patented on 29 May 1689 by Francis Martin for 130 acres in Asbury, Election district 12, map #21.
Rent Rolls 1666-1723 the relic of Francis Martin married William Brittingham in Va. claims the land in right of Martin's orphans.
16 Aug.1721 Francis Martin heir to Francis, and wife Catherine Martin

sold 60 acres to Samuel Moore son of Thomas Moore.
18 Aug.1742 Mary Sterling daughter of Francis Martin and widow of John Sterling gave 130 acres to son Samuel Moore.
3 Oct.1763 Samuel Moore of Dorc.Co. Md.and wife Mary Moore and Thomas Moore of Som.Co. and wife Susanna Moore sold 130 acres to Solomon Bird.
19 June 1765 John Sterling Sr. sold 68 acres to Solomon Bird.
19 June 1765 Solomon Bird sold 43 acres to John Sterling.
1783 tax- Solomon Bird 45 acres.
22 Aug.1786 Solomon Bird sold 87 acres to Butler Tyler

PARKS SAFEGUARD

Patented in 1844 by Charles Parks for 112 1/2 acres in Dames Quarter, not found on maps.
1850 Charles Parks lives in Dames Quarter
1852 Charles Parks, willed to son Jacob 112 1/2 acres.

PARTNERS AGREEMENT

Patented on 17 Dec.1701 by Furbey Rugg and Charles Cottingham for 200 acres in Brinkleys,southwest,Election district 3,map #17.
Rent Rolls 1666-1723 possessed by widow of Furbey Rugg and Charles Cottingham.
23 Aug.1723 Charles Cottingham and wife Ann Cottingham and Mary Rugg sold 200 acres to David Adams.
1761 David Adams willed to son David Adams.
28 Feb.1763 David Adams sold to Sampson Wheatley.
17 June 1763 Sampson Wheatley and wife Mary Wheatley sold to Thomas Adams 200 acres.
6 Oct.1767 Thomas Adams Sr. sold to son David Adams 200 acres.
1782 Thomas Adams gave to grandson Thomas Adams
1783 tax- Peggy Adams 200 acres.
1770 resurveyed to ADAMS TROUBLE 182 acres.

PARTNERS CHOICE
AND KINGS PURCHASE UNITED

8 July 1682 Randall Revell assigned to Arnold Elzey 150 acres called PARTNERS CHOICE in Dublin Election district 3, map #12.
20 Sep.1688 Arnold Elzey and wife Mary Elzey sold to Robert Horsey.
Rent Rolls 1666-1723 - Robert Horsey 150 acres.
11 June 1727 Robert Horsey, cooper, sold to Robert King 150 acres.
UNITED patented in 1746 - see KINGS PURCHASE, Robert King

PARTNERS DESIRE

Patented on 10 Oct.1679 by Richard Waters,John Waters and Charles Hall, for 375 acres in Fairmount,Election district 6, map #9.
1708 John Waters willed to son John Waters and William Waters plantation on Gr.Annamessex River,unnamed.
Rent Rolls 1666-1723 John Roach Jr. 144 acres, 231 acres by John Waters.
1726 John Roach willed to son William Roach 144 acres.
31 Aug.1762 William Roach of Worc.Co. sold to Ballard Bozman of Som.Co.(part conv. by Charles Hall and wife and John Waters to John Roach)140 acres.

25 May 1763 Richard Waters traded with John Waters of Calvert Co. Md. ENVY for tract PARTNERSHIP 70 acres (Richard Waters afsd, grandson of Richard Waters.)
20 Nov.1770 Ballard Bozman sold to Revel Horsey 140 acres.
1783 tax- Revel Horsey of Manokin 140 acres.
1783 tax- Littleton Waters 125 acres.
1805 Revel Horsey willed to Henry King son of Nehemiah King.

PARTNERSHIP

Patented in 1763 by Arthur Williams and Solomon Bird for 70 1/2 acres in Asbury,Election district 12, map #21.

PARTNERSHIP

Patented in 1822 for 23 acres by John White in Dames Quarter, Election district 11, map #7.

PASTURAGE

Patented in 1746 by Robert Harris for 50 acres in East Pr.Anne,Election district 15, map #5.
1755/9 Robert Harris willed to son John Harris 50 acres.
1788/93 John Harris willed to son John Harris 50 acres.
1848 ADDITION patented for 261 acres, includes CHANCE & ADDITION TO CHANCE.

PASTURAGE

Patented in 1762 by William Hayward for 387 acres in Dames Quarter, Election district 11, map #7.
1783 tax- William Hayward
2 Apr.1793 George Hayward of Talbot Co.Md. sold to Thomas White of Somerset Co. 120 acres.
2 April 1793 George Hayward of Talbot Co. sold to George McDorman 100 acres.
2 Apr.1793 George Hayward sold 130 acres to Lewis McDorman
2 Apr.1793 George Hayward sold to William McDorman 37 acres.
1799 Thomas White willed to son Gowan White tract bought of George Hayward and William White, no name.
3 Dec.1799 George McDorman sold to William White of Thomas White 15 acres.
11 Aug.1800 William McDorman gave 6 1/4 acres to son Lewis McDorman
12 Aug.1800 Louis McDorman gave to George McDorman 6 1/4 acres.
14 March 1800 Gowan White son of Thomas White, wife Biddy White sold to William White 88 acres.
1834 George McDorman willed to son George McDorman.

PATRICKS FOLLY

Patented on 2 Feb.1721 by John Gray for 118 acres in East Pr.Anne, Election district 15, map #5.
1730 John Gray willed to daughter Margaret Gray
1772 Margaret Smith willed to grandson Edward Smith dwelling plantation, unnamed.

1783 tax- Edward Smith 118 acres.
25 Oct.1803 Stoughton Smith sold to John Puzey Jr. of Worc.Co. 33 acres.
This was also recorded on 15 Nov.1804.
29 March 1831 Constables sale against Peter Puzey 60 acres.

PATRICKS LOTT

Patented in 1763 by Patrick McKemmy for 165 3/4 acres out of HEARTS
CONTENT, in Lawsons,Election district 8, map #17.
26 June 1769 Patrick McKemmey sold to Isaac Coulbourn 165 3/4 acres.
1775 Isaac Coulbourn willed to wife Comfort Coulbourn plantation where
Patrick McKenney lives, if she has a son, to him and if not to daughter
Sarah Coulbourn (unnamed)

PAXEN HILL

Patented on 14 June 1682 by William Winslow for 100 acres in Dublin,
Election district 4, map #12.
14 June 1682 William Winslow willed to son William Winslow.
Rent Rolls 1666-1723 William Winslow the heir declaims it.
17 Nov.1760 Joseph Ward gave to son Joseph Ward 100 acres.
1775 Joseph Ward Sr. gave part to sons Joseph Ward and Saul Ward.
1783 tax- Elizabeth Ward
12 Apr.1785 Saul Ward sold to Joseph Ward 44 1/2 acres
21 Feb.1786 Joseph ward sold to Matthias Miles 44 1/2 acres.
22 March 1786 Joseph Morris,wife Elizabeth Morris sold 9 acres to John
Layfield.
17 Apr.1787 Joseph Ward,wife Elizabeth Ward,and Elizabeth Ward sold to
John Perkins 121 acres of PAXON HILL,WARWICKS
DISCOVERY,WORTHLITTLE,WINDSOR SWAMP,COME BY CHANCE,CROOKED RIDGE.
1 May 1787 Elizabeth Ward sold to David Long and Solomon Long 95 acres,
her 1/3rds.
28 March 1789 John Perkins,wife Rachel Perkins sold to Mary Broughton 216
acres of PAXON HILL,WARDS VENTURE,COME BY CHANCE,CROOKED RIDGE, etc.
13 Oct.1795 Mary Broughton sold to John Layfield 8 acres of above land.
20 Oct.1807 Mary Broughton gave to son Edward Broughton.
28 March 1808 Thomas Layfield, wife Henny Layfield sold to Isaac Mitchell
Adams.
29 March 1808 Isaac Mitchell Adams sold to Josiah W. Heath.

PEMINE

Patented in 1681 by Duncan Olandman for 50 acres in Dublin,Election
district 4, map #12.
Rent Rolls 1666-1723 possessed by Duncan Olandman
1710 Duncan Olandman gave 50 acres to son William Olandman.
13 Jan.1734 Alexander Chain and wife Ann Chain eldest daughter of Duncan
Olandman, sold to Robert King 33 1/3 acres.
4 Dec.1733 Duncan King and wife Eleanor King sold to William Bowland
1/3rd part.
29 March 1738 Jane Olandman sold to Robert King 58 1/3 acres of three
tracts CHANCE,DUBLIN & PEMINE that descended to the daughters of Duncan
Olandman Jr.Ann Olandman now wife of Alexander Chain, Eleanor Olandman

329

wife of Duncan King and Jane Olandman the youngest being age
21 last February.
4 Apr.1745 William Bowland son of William deceased and his mother Eleanor
Bowland sold to Robert King 40 acres part of KINGS CHANCE, PEMINE,
DUBLIN.
15 Aug.1755 William Bowland son of William and Eleanor Bowland widow,
sold to Nehemiah King son of Robert King -confirmation of last sale.
1 Dec.1766 Nehemiah King willed to son Nehemiah(under 21) land on Kings
Branch-unnamed.

PENNISULA

see PITCHCROFT

PENNY WISE

Patented on 24 July 1679 by Thomas Bloyd for 50 acres in St.Peters,
Election district 2, map #6.
Rent Rolls 1666-1723 possessed by Bloyce Wright heir of Thomas Bloyd.
5 June 1688 resurveyed for 45 acres by William Wright.
1775 ADDITION 63 1/2 acres by Thomas Sloss
1783 tax- Thomas Sloss 50 acres and 30 acres.
1787 resurveyed to BLOOMSBURY 820 1/4 acres.

PERSIMON POINT

Patented on 28 Nov.1678 by Walter Lane and assigned to William Manlove
for 50 acres in Brinkleys,southeast,Election district 3, map #16.
1 Feb 1686 William Manlove and wife Alce Manlove sold to Thomas Lister 50
acres.
Rent Rolls 1666-1723 know not who owns this land.
1731 William Wilson willed to wife Elizabeth Wilson
21 June 1737 Robert Boyer of Pocomoke with wife Elizabeth Boyer gave to
grandson George Clifton according to Sampson Allison alienation, 50
acres, with MORRIS HOPE.
24 Aug.1761 Michael Clifton son of John Clifton, nephew of George
Clifton, of Cowan Co. South Caroline,sold to Elias White of Somerset
Co.,50 acres.
20 Nov.1766 Elias White sold to John Nairn 27 acres.
3 July 1770 Littleton Dennis of Worc.Co. sold to David Williams 50 acres
with MORRIS HOPE, COXES BITT.
22 Nov.1773 Elias White and wife Sarah White sold to David Williams 23
acres.

PERTH

This is part of WILLIAMS HOPE in Dublin District.
1722 Walter Taylor and wife Esther Taylor sold to James Robertson 260
acres PERTH purchased of Robert Smith of Sussex Co.Del. out of Williams
Hope.
1 Aug.1723 James Robertson sold 260 acres to Stephen Handy.
1725 Stephen Handy willed to nephew Stephen Handy son of William Handy,
and to wife Sarah Handy PERTH bought of James Robertson.

PETERS HILL

Patented in 1753 by Thomas Sloss for 35 acres in West Pr.Anne,Election
district 1, map #2.

22 Aug.1772 Thomas Sloss sold 45 acres to Jesse Dorman.
1783 tax- Jesse Dorman 35 acres
20 Nov.1788 Thomas Sloss sold to Solomon Dorman for 5 shillings 35 acres-confirmation of last sale.
1787 Jesse Dorman willed to brother Solomon Dorman
1812 ADDITION patented Solomon Dorman for 4 3/4 acres.
1847 resurveyed to GELSTON 363 2/8 acres.

PETERS LOTT

Patented in 1791 for 5 acres by Samuel Smith in Dublin, Election district 4,map #12.
18 April 1810 Samuel Smith sold all to Littleton Harris.

PHILLIPS CONCLUSION

Patented in 1771 by John Phillips for 439 acres in East Pr.Anne,Election district 15, map #5.
1783 tax- John Phillips 389 1/2 acres
21 Feb.1786 Joseph Ward sold to Matthias Miles 72 acres with PAXON HILL,WORTH LITTLE, CROOKED RIDGE.
22 March 1786 Joseph Ward,wife Elizabeth Ward sold to John Layfield 29 acres.
20 June 1787 Matthias Miles sold to John Perkins for 5 shillings 4 1/2 acres and 8 1/2 acres, two parcels.
17 July 1787 John McDaniel,wife Elizabeth McDaniel and Phillip Riggin sold to Matthias Miles 389 1/2 acres except tract DUDLEY 50 acres that PHILLIPS CONCLUSION was resurveyed from.
28 March 1789 John Perkins,wife Rachel Perkins sold 216 acres to Mary Broughton of PAXON HILL,CROOKED RIDGE,PHILLIPS CONCLUSION,WORTH LITTLE, etc.
17 March 1792 Jonathan Stanford,wife Grace Stanford sold to Pierce Riggin 77 3/4 acres
18 Oct.1793 I William Sullivan,wife Bridget Sullivan of Sussex Co. Del. appoint John Fleming son of William Fleming attorney to sell.
28 Nov.1793 John Fleming sold to John Smullen all rights
13 Oct.1795 Mary Broughton sold to John Layfield 8 acres of WARWICKS DISCOVERY, PAXON HILL, PHILLIPS CONCLUSION, etc.
31 Jan 1775 I John Philips am bound to Mathias Miles to make over 150 acres of PHILLIPS CONCLUSION
31 Jan 1775 I John Phillips am bound to William Miles to make over balance of PHILLIPS CONCLUSION.
17 March 1801 Matthias Miles sold to John Layfield 29 acres.
17 Nov.1801 John Riggin of Worc.Co. sold to Pierce Riggin all rights.
20 Oct.1807 Mary Broughton gave to son Edward Broughton.
1832 resurveyed to ADDITION TO ROWLEY RIDGE 492 7/8 acres.

PIG PEN RIDGE

Patented in 1761 for 8 acres by John Harris in Dublin, Election district 4, map #12.
1783 tax- John Riggin 8 acres.

PIMORE

Patented on 20 Jan.1665 by Mark Manlove 300 acres in Brinkleys,
southeast,Election district 3, map #16.
1666 Mark Manlove willed unnamed lands, 400 acres to wife Eliza Manlove
and to sons Mark Manlove, William Manlove and Christopher Manlove.
20 Nov.1685 Christopher Manlove son of Mark Manlove sold 130 acres to
John Walton.
15 Feb.1693 John Walton sold to William Jones 200 acres.
Rent Rolls 1666-1723 possessed by -
  Pierce Bray 70 acres
  Orphans of Thomas Jones 200 acres
  John Walton an inhabitant of Pennsylvania 30 acres.
11 Dec 1741 John Walton of Sussex Co. Del son of John sold to James Nairn
30 acres.
18 Feb.1742 John Hall and wife Ann Hall bonded to James Nairn part of
PIMORE & TERSO a small peice of land between plantations, no acreage
given.
22 Feb.1765 John Walton of Sussex Co.Del. grandson of John Walton, sold
to James Nairn of Somerset Co. his interest in PIMORE & BROTHERS LOVE.
8 May 1795 James Nairn of Worc.Co. sold to Levi Wood Hall his interest in
PIMORE & TERSO for 10 shillings
15 Aug.1795 Levi Wood Hall and John Hall sold to James Harper 164 acres
and 12 acres of marsh and 3rd part unnamed, adjacent PIMORE.
23 Nov.1805 John Harper, William Harper, Robert Harper, Averilla Harper
all of Lincoln Co. Ga. sold to Isaac Riggin 164 acres PIMORE & TERSOE and
10 acres of marsh and 15 acres purchased by James Harper from Thomas
White except widows dower of late William Hall named Martha Hall her
1/3rds.
1834 Isaac Riggin gave to son John T.W. Riggin tract purchased of the
heirs of James Harper, 164 acres of PIMORE & TARSO.

PINEY GROVE

Patented in 1774 by Levin Gale for 21 1/4 acres in West Pr.Anne,Election
district 1, map #3.
1783 tax- Levin Gale 21 1/4 acres

PINEY HALL

Patented in 1792 for 10 3/4 acres James Wilson in West Pr.Anne, Election
district 1, map #3.

PINEY ISLAND

Patented on 28 Nov.1717 by Robert King for 10 acres on Deals
Island,Election district 14, map #8.
1753 Robert King willed to son Nehemiah King land in Manokin-unnamed.
1766 Nehemiah King willed to son Nehemiah King
1783 tax- Nehemiah King 10 acres
1816 Joshua Donoho willed to sons Fillmuroh Donoho, Joshua Donoho and
William Donoho
1849 Joshua Thomas willed to son Aaron Thomas.

PITCHCROFT

Patented on 7 June 1679 by William Stevens who assigned to Henry Smith

1000 acres on Smith Island, Election district 10, map #24.
17 June 1672 George Smith and wife Martha Smith sold to Edward Price
SMITH ISLAND now called PENNSISULA on the northwest side of said Island
150 acres and 1/2 part now called LATE TO REPENT 75 acres.- Land not
patented under these other names.
20 April 1685 Henry Smith and wife Ann Smith sold to John Evans of
Acco.Co.Va. 200 acres of PITCHCROFT at Dogwood Ridge.
Rent Rolls 1666-1723 possessed by -
  John Evans in Virginia 200 acres
  John Taylor 200 acres
  to be sold for payment of Smith's debts 600 acres.
1720 John Evans of Acco.Co.Va. gave to son John 200 acres and to son Mark
Evans 200 acres and son Richard Evans the old plantation where Arthur
Parks lives on SMITHS ISLAND.
2 May 1720 Matilda Wise of Acco.Co.Va. widow and executrix of John Wise
deceased and William Pritchett of same sold to John Caldwell. 500
acres.(whereas the property of Capt.Henry Smith was sold to satisfy a
claim in 1707 to John Wise who willed on 27 March 1717 his wife Matilda
Wise to sell his part of SMITHS ISLAND & MARSHES in Somerset Co.Md.)
5 Apr.1725 John Caldwell attorney for John Smith and his wife Sarah Smith
now deceased sold to John Evans 100 acres on SMITHS ISLAND now called
WHAT YOU PLEASE.
13 Sep.1729 John Evans son of John,wife Arabella Evans sold to William
Mister.
14 June 1736 Thomas Summers and wife Sarah Summers sold to William Mister
75 acres that John Smith grandson of Henry Smith conveyed to Arthur Parks
and Thomas Summers a total of 150 acres.
1743 Arthur Parks Sr. willed to youngest son Job Parks manor and tr. HOG
NECK on SMITH ISLAND being part of tract DOGWOOD RIDGE CREEK 75 acres.
20 Aug.1746 Mark Evans of Acco.Co.Va. and wife Susannah Evans sold 248
acres to Job Evans, on SMITH ISLAND.
28 Jan 1747 Stephen Horsey Jr. and Smith Horsey 150 acres part 4 tracts
SMITHS ISLAND, YORKSHIRE ISLAND, PRICES CONCLUSION & PERSIMMON HAMMOCK
17 June 1762 Abraham Mister, wife Alice Mister of Dorc.Co. sold 100 acres
to William Mister of Acco.Co.Va.
3 Nov.1766 Smith Horsey sold to Samuel Lawson and George Croswell 150
acres.
10 Jan 1766 William Mister sold to Job Wilson 25 acres of HOGG NECK that
William Mister devised to three sons William Mister,Abraham Mister and
Marmaduke Mister.
July 1774 I Henry Smith of Sussex Co.Del do impower Smith Horsey to
execute a deed to Littleton Tyler for 50 acres.
1783 tax- Richard Bratcher 50 acres
1783 tax- Thomas Evans 100 acres
1783 tax- Richard Evans 200 acres
1783 tax- Elijah Linton 25 acres
1783 tax- Marmaduke Mister 100 acres
1783 tax- Thomas Tyler 200 acres
1783 tax- John Parks 130 acres
21 June 1786 John Evans sold 200 acres to Esme Bayley
21 June 1786 Esme Bayley sold to John Evans 200 acres
8 July 1785 Hance Lawson, wife Ann Lawson and George Croswell, wife Mary
Croswell sold to Nathan Linton
25 Aug.1788 John Evans sold to Jesse Evans son of John 100 acres
21 Aug.1789 John Evans gave to son Jesse Evans 100 acres

14 Mar.1796 Job Parks Jr. sold to John Parks Jr. 25 acres of PITCHCROFT &
HOG NECK on Smiths Island.
28 July 1798 Butler Tyler sold to Thomas Tyler 200 acres.
28 July 1798 Thomas Tyler sold to Butler Tyler 200 acres.
28 July 1798 Butler Tyler sold to David Tyler 200 acres.
25 July 1799 Thomas Evans sold to Solomon Evans 1/4th part surveyed for
Spencer Martin Waters of Dorc.Co. land on island between Cajor Streights
and Smiths Isalnd thorofare called SMITHS ISLAND or TANGIER ISLANDS.
1 May 1794 George Gale of Dorc.Co. sold to Nathan Evans, Thomas Evans and
Ezekiel Simkins, lower part where they live surveyed for Spencer Martin
Waters of Dorc.Co. on Smiths Island.
7 July 1801 William Mister of Virginia sold to Sarah Mister of Maryland,
two parcels on SMITHS ISLAND devised William by his father Marmaduke
Mister, 125 acres, unnamed.
11 Aug.1801 Sarah Mister sold to Elijah Evans 14 acres of HOG NECK (part
of PITCHCROFT)
4 Sep.1802 Francis Evans sold 100 acres to Thomas Williams Jr.
4 Sep.1802 Thomas Williams Jr sold to Francis Evans 100 acres.
4 Sep.1802 Richard Evans,wife Fanny Evans sold to Elijah Evans 100 acres.
18 Aug.1804 Zachariah Crockett, wife Polly Crockett, Richard Evans, wife
Rachel Evans, Thomas Evans, wife Fannie Evans, William Linton, wife
Hannah Linton sold to Josiah Evans 100 acres at the north end.

PLAGUE WITHOUT PROFIT

Patented in 1751 by Gideon Tilghman for 144 acres in Dublin, Election
district 4, map #13.
19 March 1755 Gideon Tilghman sold to Thomas Hayward 1/2 acre of TILLMANS
LUCK and PLAGUE WITHOUT PROFIT.
13 March 1762 Gideon Tilghman gave to son Nehemiah Tilghman 100 acres
10 July 1765 Thomas Hayward gave to son Thomas Jr. 1/2 acre bought of
Gideon Tilghman, unnamed.
19 Apr.1766 Gideon Tilghman gave to son Nehemiah Tilghman 100 acres of
WILLIAMS HOPE,TILGHMANS CARE,PLAGUE WITHOUT PROFIT
26 Apr.1766 Gideon Tilghman gave to son Gideon Jr. 92 acres of same.
19 July 1768 Nehemiah Tilghman,wife Catherine Tilghman sold 43 acres to
William Taylor.
14 Feb 1768 Gideon Tilghman and wife Tabitha Tilghman sold to Robert
Jenkins King 84 1/4 acres of WILLIAMS HOPE,TILGHMANS CARE, PLAGUE WITHOUT
PROFIT.
20 Jan 1769 Nehemiah Tilghman son of Gideon Tilghman, wife Catherine
Tilghman sold to Robert Jenkins King 268 acres of WILLIAMS HOPE,GIDEONS
LUCK & PLAGUE
17 Oct 1773 Robert Jenkins King sold to Ephraim Stevens 250 acres of
WILLIAMS HOPE GIDIONS LUCK, SECOND ADDITION TO PLAGUE WITHOUT PROFIT,
etc.
1786 SECOND ADDITION patented by Robert Jenkins King for 297 1/4 acres.
25 Oct 1779 Ephraim Stevens sold to Robert Jenkins King 250 acres as of
above.
Resurvyed to 290 acres.
1783 tax- William Taylor 43 acres
1783 tax- Robert Jenkins King
1788/9 Robert Jenkins King willed to son Robert King part of resurvey and
land purchase of the Tilghmans.
25 March 1800 Andrew Adams and wife Mary Adams and James Taylor,wife

Sophia Taylor, Isaac Taylor and Sarah Taylor sold to Samuel Taylor their
rights to the lands of William Taylor
84 acres of GIDEONS LUCK & PLAGUE WITHOUT PROFIT.
2 Dec.1800 Thomas Taylor sold to Samuel Taylor 84 acres of PLAGUE WITHOUT
PROFIT and GIDEONS LUCK.
19 Aug.1806 Thomas Hayward sold to Henry King 1/2 of PLAGUE WITHOUT
PROFIT & TILGHMANS LUCK.
10 April 1810 Stephen Taylor sold to Samuel Taylor 84 acres of GIDEONS
LUCK & PLAGUE.

PLAIN HARBOUR

Patented on 18 Dec.1701 by Isaac Horsey and Nathaniel Horsey for 500
acres in Asbury,Election district 12, map #21.
1721 Nathaniel Horsey willed to four sons 250 acres at Cedar Island.
Rent Rolls 1666-1723 250 acres Isaac Horsey, 250 acres Nathaniel Horsey.
1752 Isaac Horsey willed to Sarah Bozman 250 acres.
28 Jan.1748 Isaac Horsey sold to Outerbridge Horsey, pat. Isaac Horsey
and Nathaniel Horsey grandfather of Outerbridge, which said Isaac Horsey
has survived Nathaniel Horsey- all.

PLANNERS ADVENTURE

Patented on 6 April 1664 by William Planner for 100 acres in Brinkleys,
southwest,Election district 3,map #17.
Rent Rolls 1666-1723 possessed by widow of Furbey Rugg.
1666 William Planner and wife Rebecca Planner sold to Thomas Cottingham
100 acres.(Mary Cottingham daughter of Thomas married Furbey Rugg)
1702 Furbey Rugg willed to daughter Mary Rugg after her mother died.
1733 debt books- Mary Rugg widow of Furbey Rugg
1735 debt books- Possessed by David Adams who married first Mary Rugg
daughter of Furbey Rugg and Mary Cottingham Rugg.
1762 Thomas Adams son of David Adams resurveyed 39 acres to ADAMS CHANCE.
15 Dec.1772 Thomas Adams son and heir of Mary Rugg mortgaged his share to
George Hayward of Worc.Co. and Josiah Polk.
16 Apr.1774 Thomas Adams gave to son David Adams.

PLANNERS BLOSSOM

Patented in 168 by Planner Williams, a resurvey from SECURITY for 577
acres, in Brinkleys northwest,Election district 3, map #14.
1783 tax- Planner Williams
1788 Planner Williams willed to Thomas Robertson and George Robertson.
1837 John Planner Gale willed to son John Gale 837 acres of CEDAR GROVE &
PLANNERS BLOSSOM.

PLANNERS PURCHASE

This is part of CHEAP PRICE possessed by William Planner.

PLEASANT MEADOW

Surveyed in 1784 for 106 acres by Jesse King in Dublin, Election district
4, map #12.

PLEASURE

Patented in 1762 by William Miles for 49 1/2 acres in Lawsons,Election district 8, map #18.
24 Oct.1765 William Miles sold to Matthias Gale 49 1/2 acres with HEARTS EASE,DIXONS LOTT,CHANCE,FORTUNE,PLEASURE.
1783 Isaac Coulbourn, willed to daughter Mary Coulbourn 49 1/2 acres purchased by Matthias Gale.

PLUNDER

Patented in 1736 by William Smith for 58 1/2 acres in Brinkleys, northwest, Election district 3, map #14.
1783 tax- Puzey Lankford
2 Oct.1785 Benjamin Lankford son of Lazarus Lankford, and Sarah Archibel Lankford his wife released to Joseph Lankford son of Puzey Lankford title in land that William Smith by his bond gave to Puzey Lankford.
2 Oct.1784 Benjamin Lankford and wife Sarah Archibel Lankford sold to Samuel Bedsworth 33 1/3 acres that William Smith willed part to Sarah Smith now wife of Benjamin Lankford-unnamed.
22 Aug.1789 Samuel Bedsworth sold to Thomas Jones, tract sold by Benjamin Lankford son of Lazarus Lankford, and wife Sarah Lankford sold to Samuel Bedsworth
8 Jan 1803 Benjamin Lankford sold to Robert Lankford 58 1/2 acres.
15 April 1806 Robert Lankford, wife Sarah Lankford sold to Jesse Jackson all land purchased from Benjamin Lankford in 1803, 168 1/2 acres, unnamed.
15 April 1806 Jesse Jackson sold to Dr. Thomas Robertson Jr.

POINT JONES

Patented in 1800 for 4 1/2 acres by John Jones, in Tangier, Election district 9, map #7.

POINT NEXT TO WORST

Patented on 18 Aug.1701 by John Collins for 25 acres in Asbury,Election district 12, map #21
Rent Rolls 1666-1723 possessed by John Collins.

POYK

Patented on 9 July 1679 by Henry Smith for 70 acres in Fairmount,Election district 6, map #9.
1709 Nicholas Fountain gave to son Nicholas 10 acres bought of Capt.Henry Smith.
Rent Rolls 1666-1723 possesed by Nicholas Fountain 10 acres and 60 acres by Michael Gray.
1717 Miles Gray willed to son-in-law William Turpin and then to son John Gray.
11 May 1756 Solomon Gray eldest son of Thomas Gray who was the eldest son of John Gray who was the eldest son of Miles Gray of Acco.Co.Va., sold to Whitty Turpin with FURNACES CHOICE, that Miles Gray devised to William Turpin for life, who lately died and now possessed by Solomon Gray.
1783 tax- Whitty Turpin 50 acres
1783 tax- Denwood Turpin 10 acres.

POLKS FOLLY

Patented on 7 March 1687 by Robert Polk for 100 acres in Dames Quarter,
Election district 11, map #7.
Rent Rolls 1666-1723 possessed by widow Magdalen Polk.
1702 Robert Polk willed to son David Polk.
1726/7 William Polk of Dorc.Co.willed to daughter Jane Polk.
16 Aug.1748 Joseph Pollock of Dorc.Co. sold to John Shores and William
Shores of Somerset Co. 100 acres.
1783 tax- George Austin
8 April 1800 George Austin, wife Mary Austin sold to Archibald McDorman
per conveyance of 1 Nov 1782 of James Hitch who died before conveyance
and son Thomas Hitch had the rights 100 acres.

POLKS LOTT

Patented on 7 March 1687 for 50 acres by Robert Polk in Dames Quarter,
Election district 11, map #7.
Rent Rolls 1666-1723 possessed by Magdalen Pollock widow of Robert
Pollock

POLKS MEADOW
see JAMES MEADOW   1707 James Polk 200 acres.

POLLITTS ADVENTURE
POLLITTS ENLARGEMENT

Patented in 1790 for 245 acres a resurvey on part of BECKLES, in Dublin,
Election district 4, map #12.
1797 resurveyed to POLLITTS ENLARGEMENT 332 1/2 acres Levin Pollitt.
1836 Levin Pollitt gave to Levin P.Bowland son of John Bowland
ENLARGEMENT.

POLLITTS CHANCE

Patented in 1728 by Thomas Pollitt for 100 acres in East Pr.Anne,Election
district 15, map #4.
1 July 1727 John Finch sold to John Tunstall merchant POLLITTS CHANCE
being part of DEEP conveyed to Thomas Pollitt 100 acres.
24 Aug.1733 John Pollitt of Dorc.Co. sold to John Finch 100 acres

POLLITTS DELAY

Patented in 1790 for 52 acres by William Pollitt in East Pr.Anne,
Election district 15, map #4.

POLLITTS INTENT

Patented in 1811 by John Pollitt for 20 1/2 acres in East Pr. Anne,
Election District 15, not on maps.
1838 John Pollitt willed to son Henry with HIGH MEADOW & HAYMANS
DISAPPOINTMENT.

POLLITTS SECURITY

Patented in 1786, a resurvey of part of NORWICH,by Thomas Pollitt for 343
1/4 acres in East Pr.Anne,Election district 15, map #4.
1795 Thomas Pollitt willed to son Tubman Pollitt.
21 Oct.1801 Tubman Pollitt son of Thomas Pollitt sold to Evans Willin 200
acres.
8 Dec.1801 Evans Willin sold to Peggy Pollitt daughter of Thomas Pollitt
200 acres.
Resurveyed in 1819 for 343 1/8 acres by Mary Riggin, John Riggin & George
Pollitt.
25 Jan 1809 William Pollitt son of Thomas Pollitt sold to John Riggin,
merchant 174 acres.
1810 John Riggin of Worc.Co. willed lands in Somerset Co. to be sold by
son London Riggin.

POLLITTS VICTORY

Patented in 1748 by Willliam Pollitt for 198 acres in East Pr.Anne,
Election district 15, map #4.
21 Oct.1766 William Pollitt sold for 5 shillings part to William Heath
that is included in Heaths land called LONG GUILE,no acreage given.
1783 tax- Thomas Pollitt 194 acres.

POMFRETT

Patented in 1663 by William Coulbourn for 1000 acres in Lawsons,Election
district 8, map #18.
13 June 1679 resurvey to 1400 acres,William Coulbourn
11 Sep.1688 William Coulbourn gave to daughter Penelope Holland wife of
Michael Holland 50 acres.
1719/21 ADDITION patented by William Coulbourn 631 1/4 acres.
1722 resurvey to 1700 acres by William Coulbourn.
7 May 1721 William Coulbourn, Solomon Coulbourn sons of William Coulbourn
of Col. William agree to divide the lands.
Rent Rolls 1666-1723 possessed by -
 Orphans of Robert Colbourn in Acco.Co.Va.
 William Coulbourn by escheat 200 acres
 John Taylor 66 acres
 Michael Holland 50 acres
 widow Ann Coulbourn 260 acres
9 Nov.1743 William Coulbourn and Solomon Coulbourn traded 750 acres of
same land.
18 Aug.1750 Samuel Handy, wife Elizabeth Handy sold to William Coulbourn
55 acres 15 rods, FATHERS INTENT which is part of POMFRETT
18 May 1750 William Coulbourn Sr. and William Coulbourn J. sold to
Michael Holland 77 acres part formerly given by William Coulbourn to his
daughter Penelope Coulbourn who married Michael Holland Sr.
10 Nov.1763 Stephen Horsey and Michael Holland sold 2 acres to the Vestry
of Somerset Parish.
27 Feb.1764 Michael Holland the elder gave part to son Michael Holland.
1765 William Coulbourn willed to wife Elizabeth Coulbourn and then to son
John Coulbourn.
7 Apr.1767 Michael Holland Jr. sold to Smith Horsey 23 acres of COLEBOURN
& POMFRETT
2 Feb 1769 Michael Holland the elder gave to son Michael Holland part not
before conveyed. All I possess.

6 Sep.1774 John Coulbourn sold 50 acres to Isaac Coulbourn
1783 Isaac Coulbourn willed to wife and unborn son or to daughter Sarah
Coulbourn, after death to nephew William Coulbourn.
10 May 1783 Benjamin Coulbourn sold to Aaron Coulbourn 172 acres given
him by the will of Solomon Coulbourn on 3 Aug.1744.
1783 tax- heirs of Isaac Coulbourn 600 acres
1783 tax- Sarah Coulbourn 200 acres
1783 tax- Benjamin Coulbourn 180 acres
1783 tax- William Henderson 83 acres
1783 tax- Michael Holland 45 acres
1783 tax- Michael Holland 27 acres.
23 May 1787 John Coulbourn,wife Ruth Coulbourn sold 150 acres to Benjamin
Schoolfield.
22 June 1787 Michael Holland eldest son of Michael who was the eldest son
of Penelope Holland deceased sold to Robert Burcher Holland that Penelope
had from her father William Coulbourn.
21 Oct.1789 John Coulbourn sold 90 acres to Thomas Williams
29 Dec.1790 Thomas Williams released mortgage of 90 acres to John
Coulbourn.
29 Dec.1790 John Coulbourn,wife Ruth Coulbourn sold to brother William
Coulbourn 44 3/4 acres.
10 Nov.1792 Michael Holland sold to John Horsey 21 1/2 acres of FERRY
BRIDGE & POMFRETT.
25 Jan.1796 John Coulbourn sold to William Williams 60 acres.
11 Nov.1796 Benjamin Schoolfield gave to William Williams Schoolfield son
of Benjamin Schoolfield.
13 Apr.1796 Robert Burcher Holland,wife Peggy Holland sold to Jesse
Holland 50 acres.
13 Apr.1796 Jesse Holland sold to William Williams,merchant 50 acres.
29 June 1796 John Coulbourn sold 60 acres to William Williams.
4 Apil 1797 Jesse Holland son of Michael Holland sold to William
Williams, his rights to POMFRET & FERRY BRIDGE.
17 July 1802 John Coulbourn sold to Joshua Hall 1 acre 93 sq.perches.
8 Jan 1805 William Williams Schoolfield son of Benjamin Schoolfield now
of Baltimore Md. sold to William Williams of Som. Co. 160 acres.
11 Sep.1807 Robert Coulbourn, wife Jane Coulbourn sold to Thomas Ward 68
1/2 acres.
17 Oct.1808 Robert Coulbourn of Robert, sold 190 acres to William
Williams
14 Jan 1809 Thomas Ward, wife Ann Ward sold to William Miles of Henry 68
1/2 acres.
14 Jan 1809 Thomas Ward, wife Ann Ward, sold to William Miles of Henry
Miles 68 1/2 acres.
14 Jan 1809 William Miles of Henry sold to William Williams 68 1/2 acres.
14 Jan 1809 William Williams, wife Mary Williams sold to Thomas Ward 150
acres.
5 May 1810 John Williams sold to William Wilkins 2 acres.

POOLS HOPE

Patented on 15 April 1667 by Thomas Pool for 300 acres in Westover,
Election district 13, map #11.
30 March 1669 Thomas Pool and wife Elizabeth Pool sold to James Davis 200
acres.
30 March 1669 James Davis and wife Margaret Davis, sold 100 acres to

William Thompson of Va., of DAVIS CHANCE now called THOMPSONS ADVENTURE out of POOLS HOPE.
1670/1 William Thompson sold to Henry Smith.
Nov.1674 Henry Smith sold to Gideon Tilghman 100 acres now called THOMPSONS ADVENTRUE.
30 May 1678 James Davis sold 100 acres to Gideon Tilghman called DAVIS CHANCE
6 Oct.1674 Henry Smith sold 100 acres to William Furniss bought of Thomas Pool called SMITHS CHANCE
Rent Rolls 1666-1723 100 acres James Furniss, 200 acres Gideon Tilghman.
11 Dec.1740 Gideon Tilghman son of Gideon sold to Benjamin Tilghman 100 acres.
15 Dec 1744 Benjamin Tilghman sold 100 acres to Robert King of DAVIS CHANGE
12 May 1753 Robert King released mortgage to Benjamin Tilghman of 100 acres
10 May 1753 Benjamin Tilghman and wife Mary Tilghman sold to Aaron Tilghman 100 acres of DAVIS CHANGE
22 March 1764 Elijah Tilghman gave to brother Aaron Tilghman Jr. TILLMANS ADVENTURE with vacancy added and pt. POOLS HOPE.
17 Sep 1765 Elijah Tilghman eldest son of Aaron Tilghman deceased sold 100 acres to Josiah Tilghman
26 Apr.1766 Gideon Tilghman sold to Josiah Tilghman 100 acres
1783 tax- Joseph Tilghman 50 acres
1783 tax- William Givans Sr. 60 acres
1783 tax- Grace Furniss 100 acres
21 Feb.1784 Isaac Marshall surviving executor of Aaron Tilghman sold to Thomas Gibbons-no acres given.
2 Aug.1786 William Gibbons and wife Mary Gibbons sold to Samuel Wilson 38 1/4 acres
6 March 1782 William Gibbons mortgaged all his lands to Samuel Wilson
21 June 1787 Joseph Tilghman,wife Nancy Tilghman sold 76 1/2 acres to John Beauchamp.
1 Jan 1789 Ephraim Furniss and Thomas Furniss sons of William Furniss sold 100 acres to Samuel Wilson.
18 March 1789 John Beauchamp,wife Anne Beauchamp and Joseph Tilghman sold 76 1/2 acres to Isaiah Tilghman
17 Aug.1789 Samuel Wilson sold to Isaiah Tilghman-to establish lines.
1790 Isaiah Tilghman willed to son William Tilghman
13 Aug.1792 William Gibbons and wife Mary Gibbons sold to Levin Miles 200 acres
18 Aug.1795 Milcah Gale Chaille sold to William Tilghman 129 acres of POOLS HOPE,FAIR SPRING,CEDAR HILL.
23 Oct.1804 Eli Gibbons and wife Amelia Gibbons sold to William Tilghman of Isaiah. Whereas Isaiah Tilghman deceased devised to daughter Amelia Tilghman now Amelia Gibbons.
1806 William Tilghman willed to daughter Nancy Tilghman land purchased of Milcah Gale Chaille 106 3/4 acres
3 Jun 1806 Nancy Tilghman daughter of William Tilghman sold to Stephen Tilghman, he to support his sister Sally Tilghman during life, 169 3/4 acres.
1817 Stephen Tilghman willed to brother William Tilghman 169 3/4 acres, unnamed land.

POOR DEPENDENCE

Patented in 1784 by Littleton Timmons and Jabez Webster for 18 acres on
Deal Island, Election district 14, map #8
14 June 1796 Littleton Timmons sold to Jabez Webster 18 acres.

POOR SWAMP

Patented in 1748 by John White for 100 acres in Lawsons, Election
district 8, map #18.
1748/9 John White willed part to daughter Alice White and daughter
Rachel White.
15 Oct.1765 John Juett and wife Alice Juett sold to William Juett 108
acres of three tracts BUCK RIDGE,POOR SWAMP,SCOTLAND, from John White
father of Alice Juett.
18 Mar.1788 George Disharoon and wife Alice Disharoon of Worc.Co. sold to
William Juett for 5 sh. her son by John Juett.
13 Dec.1789 William Juett,wife Alice Juett daughter of John White sold to
William Kellam lands from her father in Chappel Swamp.
11 Jan 1790 Elijah Coulbourn Sr.,wife Rachel Coulbourn daughter of John
White and Rachel White, and John Tull son of James Tull sold to Benjamin
Conner.
11 Jan 1790 Benjamin Conner sold to Elijah Coulbourn, same as above.
8 Mar.1791 Nathan Cahoon exec. of William Kellam sold to Robert Burcher
Holland-no acres given in Chappel Swamp.
1800 Robert Burcher Holland willed land to be sold to pay debts, 20 acres
unnamed in Chappel Swamp

PORTERS PURCHASE

Patented in 1763 by John Porter, that includes BENJAMINS ADVICE & LONGS
CHANCE, for 319 acres in Dublin,Election district 4, map #12.
1783 tax- John Porter 319 acres.

POSSESSION

Patented in 1792 for 4 1/4 acres by Nathan Cahoon in Brinkleys,
southwest, Election district 3, map #17.

POUND PASTURE

Patented in 17654 by Kellum Lankford for 17 acres in Brinkleys,
southwest, Election district 17,map #3.
1783 tax- Kellum Lankford 17 acres
1796 Kellum Lankford willed to son Noah Lankford.
5 April 1803 Noah Lankford son of Kellum Lankford sold to William
Williams all lands in Morumsco, no name.

POWELLS ADDITION

Patented on 2 April 1683 for 50 acres and assigned to Walter Powell in
Dublin,Election district 4, map #14.
1695 Walter Powell willed to son William Powell.
1715 William Powell willed to son John Powell.
14 Sep.1739 John Powell sold 50 acres to Alexander Maddux.

17 June 1758 triparte agreement Brittain Powell son of John who was son of William Powell of Walter Powell, and Isaac Bozman Schoolfield to Alexander Maddux 50 acres.
1763 Alexander Maddux willed to son Alexander 50 acres.
1774 Alexander Maddux sold 50 acres to Jesse Powell.
1783 tax- Jesse Powell
1809 Jesse Powell willed to George Washington Powell.
27 May 1809 Jesse Powell mortgaged to Edward Henry of Worcester Co.

POWELLS CHANCE

Patented in 1733 by John Powell for 165 1/2 acres in Dublin,Election district 4, map #13.
1757 Brittain Powell son of John Powell sold to David Dryden 165 1/2 acres.
22 Feb 1760 David Dryden the younger and wife Mary Dryden sold to Jonathan Dryden 55 acres.
1769 Jonathan Dryden son of David Dryden willed to son Thomas Dryden 50 acres.
1775 David Dryden willed 115 1/2 acres to son William Dryden.
1783 tax- Littleton Dryden 115 1/2 acres
1783 tax- Thomas Dryden 50 acres.
16 June 1790 William Dryden son of David Dryden sold to Littleton Dryden 110 acres.
19 Nov.1795 Major Samuel Wilson, wife Leah Wilson sold to Littleton Dennis 815 acres of POWELLS CHANCE, NEGLECT, MIDDLE, EXCHANGE, COWPASTURE, CONTENT,etc.
28 March 1796 Littleton Dryden sold to Littleton Dennis 55 acres of POWELLS CHANCE,HOG RANGE.

PREVENT

Patented in 1792 for 32 acres in East Pr.Anne, Election district 15, map #5.

PREVENTION

Patented in 1768 for 50 acres by Josiah Polk in East Pr.Anne, Election district 15, map #4.

PREVENTION

Patented in 1769 by Spencer Harris for 12 1/2 acres in Dublin,Election district 4, map #12.
1783 tax- Spencer Harris 12 acres
1794/5 Spencer Harris gave to son Isaac Harris, from John Riggin.

PRICES CONCLUSION

Patented on 15 Nov.1694 by Edward Price, alias SMITHS ISLAND, for 500 acres in Crisfield,Election district 7, map#2.
Rent Rolls 1666-1723 100 acres Samuel Horsey, 400 acres Thomas Ward.
26 Jan 1738 Cornelius Ward sold 50 acres to John Riggin.
1738 John Riggin willed to sons John and Teague Riggin.
18 Nov.1742 Cornelius Ward sold to John White and Archibald White 25

acres.

28 Jan 1747 Stephen Horsey sold to Smith Horsey 150 acres his right to four tracts SMITHS ISLAND,YORKSHIRE ISLAND, PRICES CONCLUSION,PERSIMMON HAMMOCK.

15 Oct 1768 Cornelius Ward Sr.and Cornelius Ward Jr. sold 37 1/2 acres to James Ward son of Cornelius.

16 Nov.1768 James Ward the elder sold to James Gunby and Littleton Dennis 100 acres.

19 March 1772 Teague Riggin son of John Riggin sold to Jacob Milbourn 25 acres of marsh near James Island conveyed to father by Cornelius Ward.

1783 tax- Cornelius Ward 75 acres

1783 tax- James Ward 75 acres

1783 tax- Jeremiah Riggin 25 acres.

PRICES HOPE

Patented in 13 Feb.1663 by Edward Price for 200 acres in Asbury, Election district 12, map #21.

1677 Edward Price and wife Jane Price sold to Edward Furlong.

1676 resurveyed to LONG TOWN 150 acres.

PRICES VINEYARD

Patented on 16 Feb 1663 by Edward Price for 200 acres and resurveyed in 1676 by James Price, in Asbury,Election district 12, map #21.

11 March 1689 James Price willed to daughter Margaret Price, daughter Ann Price and cousin James Price.

Rent Rolls 1666-1723 possessed by Mary Price widow of James Price 200 acres.

Rent Rolls 2nd entry- possessed by Thomas Ward in right of an heiress.(he married Margaret Price.)

18 Nov.1736 Cornelius Ward son of Cornelius deceased and wife Alice Ward sold to Jacob Ward son of Thomas Ward their 1/2 interest that James Price willed to daughters Margaret and Ann. Cornelius Ward heir to Ann Price wife of Cornelius Ward Sr.

21 Dec 1736 I James Ward son of Thomas Ward am bound to Jacob Ward, Thomas Ward and and Margaret Ward his wife- division of lands of Thomas and Margaret with sons James and Jacob Ward.

1783 tax- Stephen Ward 100 acres

1783 tax- Thomas Ward 50 acres.

1722 maps show a resurvey to JAMESTOWN.

7 Jan 1800 John Ward son of Stephen Ward, now of Kentucky sold to John Cullen.

3 July 1802 John Cullen and wife Betsy Cullen sold 10 acres to Nathan Bratcher.

PRINCESS ANNE TOWN

see BECKFORD

PRIVILEDGE

Patented in 1732 for 62 acres by Sampson Wheatley in Brinkleys, Election district 3, map #17.

17 June 1763 Sampson Wheatley and wife Mary Wheatley sold to Thomas Adams 212 1/2 acres of PARTNERS AGREEMENT and 10 1/2 acres of PRIVILEDGE

1767 Thomas Adams willed to son David Adams 212 Acres of PRIVILEDGE

formerly called INDUSTRY, and other tracts.
1773 Sampson Wheatley willed to daughter Betty Wheatley
1783 tax- Peggy Adams
1783 tax- Mary Wheatley 40 1/2 acres.
24 June 1785 Caleb Jones and wife Betty Jones daughter of Sampson
Wheatley sold to Kellum Lankford, Elijah Coulbourn and Thomas Jones of
Annamessex, MERCHANTS TREASURE, ADAMS CHANCE, LITTLEWORTH, DAM SWAMP,
PRIVILEDGE, IRISH GROVE & WHEATLEYS DIFFICULT PURCHASE.
24 Apr.1805 Benjamin Conner, Noah Lankford, Benjamin Bedsworth, John
Broughton and wife Mary Broughton, Richard Hall and Mary Bedsworth sold
to Mordicai Jones of St. Marys County WHEATLEYS DIFFICULT PURCHASE, IRISH
GROVE, GREENFIELD, WHEATLEYS SECOND ADDN, etc. divised by Sampson
Wheatley to daughter Betty Jones who conveyed to Kellum Lankford, Elijah
Coulbourn, and Thomas Jones.

PRIVILEDGE

Patented in 1734 by Levin Gale for 7 acres in Mt. Vernon, Election
District 5, map #1.
1783 tax- Levin Gale 7 acres
23 Nov.1787 Levin Gale sold to James Elzey Jr.
25 March 1794 James Elzey sold to Nehemiah King and William Jones of
Thomas Jones of Manokin.
8 Aug 1794 Nehemiah King and William Jones sold to James Elzey -probably
a settlement of land boundaries.
19 Aug.1794 James Elzey and wife Sarah Elzey sold to William Jones of
Thomas Jones.
PRIVILEDGE

Patented in 1740 for 14 acres by George Gale in Mt.Vernon, Election
district 5, map #1.
1783 tax- Levin Gale 14 3/4 acres.

PRIVILEDGE

Patented in 1744 by Thomas Holbrook for 106 1/2 acres in Mt.Vernon,
Election district 3, map #1.
11 March 1762 Daniel Jones sold to Thomas Holbrook PRIVILEDGE surveyed
for Thomas Holbrook taken out of COXES CHOICE, LAST VACANCY & pt.
FLOWERFIELDS.
1793 resurveyed to BENGAL 988 acres
1795 Thomas Holbrook willed resurvey of lands, to sons Thomas Holbrook
and Samuel Holbrook.

PRIVILEDGE

Patented in 1748 for 53 acres by Isaac Williams in Brinkleys, northwest
Election district 3, map #14.
8 Feb 1762 Isaac Williams of Dorc.Co.Md. sold 53 acres to Thomas Marshall
of Somerset County.
20 April 1774 Thomas Marshall gave to son Stephen Marshall of Acco.Co.Va.
53 acres with TURKEY TRAP, MARSHALLS INHERITANCE, MITCHELLS LOTT.
1783 tax- Stephen Marshall 50 acres.
22 Aug.1794 Stephen Marshall, wife Rachel Marshall sold to Thomas Miles,
50 acres.

344

PRIVILEDGE

Patented in 1750 for 50 acres by John Phillips in East Princess Anne,
Election district 15, map #5. and 30 acres adjacent patented in 1758.
1783 tax- John Phillips 50 acres
1762 John Phillips willed to daughters Elizabeth Phillips and Grace
Phillips- no lands mentioned in well.
31 Jan 1775 I John Phillips am bound to William Miles for 30 acres and
50 acres with ROWLEY HILL, and other land.
22 March 1786 John McDaniel and wife Elizabeth McDaniel sold to Jonathan
Stanford and wife Grace Stanford 30 acres and 5 1/2 acres.
3 Jan 1789 Jonathan Stanford and wife Grace Stanford of Worc.Co. sold to
John Handy 5 1/2 acres.
17 March 1792 Jonathan Stanford and wife Grace Stanford sold 30 acres to
Phillip Riggin
21 May 1794 Phillip Riggin and wife Mary Riggin sold to Esau Boston.
5 Jan 1796 Elizabeth McDaniel coheir of John Phillips sold 35 acres to
Caleb Bevanc McDaniel.
1798 Tubman Lankford occupied the land owned by the heirs of Esau Boston.
1802 Commissioners awarded to James Boston son of Esau Boston, he to pay
others their share.
1804 James Boston sold to Joshua Morris and Kirk Gunby.
22 May 1805 Commisioners to divide the RE of John Phillips sold to Jesse
Dukes of Sussex Co.Del. and wife Sarah Dukes, in right of Sarah Dukes
PRIVILEDGE 30 & 50 acres, ROWLEY HILL, GRAYS PURCHASE, DUDLEY
22 May 1805 Jesse Dukes and wife Sarah Dukes of Sussex Co.Del. sold to
Pierce Riggin of Som. Co. all rights to afsd land.

PRIVILEDGE

Patented in 1774 for 2 3/4 acres by Aaron Sterling in Lawsons, Election
district 8, map #19.
1795 Aaron Sterling gave to son Aaron 2 3/4 acres purchased from Richard
Barnes.

PRIVILEDGE

Patented in 1783 for 21 acres by Nathan Cahoon in Brinkleys, southwest,
Election district 3, map #17.

PRIVILEDGE

Patented in 1787 by David McGrath for 30 acres in West Pr.Anne, Election
district 1, map #3.
1783 tax- John McGrath
1788/91 John McGrath willed to nephew David McGrath
21 Feb.1792 David McGrath sold 20 acres to Elias Bailey(came Sarah
McGrath widow of John McGrath and released her Dower rights).
9 April 1793 David McGrath sold to Sarah McGrath widow of John McGrath 5
acres.
21 Apr.1797 David McGrath gave to son Levin McGrath with REFUGE, HOBBS
ADVENTURE & SWINE YARD.
22 Feb.1800 George Robertson, sheriff, court sale to Levin Gale Jr.,
property of David McGrath 75 acres of HOBBS ADVENTURE with PRIVILEDGE &
SWINE YARD.

15 March 1803 George Robertson,sheriff, confirmed sale to Henry Gale and Betsy Ann Wilson Gale children of Levin Gale Jr. deceased.

PROFFET

Patented in 1728 by Thomas Hayward for 250 acres in Dublin, Election district 4, map #12.
10 July 1765 Thomas Hayward sold to Thomas Hayward Jr. 250 acres
1769 resurveyed to IRELAND 353 acres
1792 Thomas Hayward willed resurvey of tracts PROFIT & ADDITON to son Thomas Hayward.

PROMISE LAND

Patented on 2 June 1688 by Thomas Walston for 100 acres in Fairmount, Election district #9.
Rent Rolls 1666-1723 possessed by Hugh McNeale
1716/7 Hugh McNeale willed to wife Alice McNeale and daughter Katherine McNeale, real estate, unnamed.
1757 resurveyed to COW QUARTER

PROPERTY RESTORED

see POLLITTS CHANCE & DEEP.

PROSPECT

Patented in 1751 a resurvey of LUMNES IMPROVEMENT by Martha Wilson for 499 acres in Tangier, Election district 9, map #7.
1783 tax- heirs of Nehemiah Bozman
20 Dec.1766 Bond- I Martha Wilson make over to Nehemiah Bozman.
31 Dec 1797 Joseph Bozman assigned rights to John Jones.
2 Jan 1798 Benjamin Dashiell sold to James Bennett 52 1/21 acres.
4 April 1808 John Jones sold all rights to Elizabeth Jackson.
22 Apr.1827 Sheriff's sale of suit of William Hearn against John Jones of Dames Quarter, 237 acres - Village Herald Newspaper.
1824 John Jones willed to sons James Jones and Samuel Jones, where Lewis Jones lived.
3 May 1831 Sheriff's sale, suit of State of Md. against John Jones of Dames Quarter 273 acres.

PROVIDENCE

Patented on 3 Aug.1684 for 200 acres by John Rousells in Dublin,Election district 4, map #13.
Rent Rolls 1666-1723 John Rousells.
20 Sep.1687 John Rousells, wife Mary Rousells sold to Richard Tull 200 acres.
1708/19 Francis Jenkins willed to wife Mary Jenkins 200 acres.
1715 John Henry,wife Mary Henry, willed to son Robert Jenkins Henry 200 acres
1744 Mary Hampton gave to son Robert Jenkins Henry.
1763 Resurveyed by Robert Jenkins Henry 379 acres.
1764 Robert Jenkins Henry gave to daughter Ann Henry 400 acres at Dividing Creek.

19 Oct.1772 Benjamin Scott and wife Mary Scott sold to Edward Rounds of Worc.Co. PROVIDENCE on dividing Creek devised by the will of John Scott deceased called SMITHS FOLLY- his interest in, no acreage given.
17 June 1786 Henry Stevenson and wife Ann Stevenson sold to Samuel Sloan a resurvey by Robert Jenkins Henry 343 2/4 acres of PROVIDENCE.
1801 resurvey 255 acres to NEW PROVIDENCE.

PROVIDENCE

Patented in 1732 by Edward Harper, a resurvey of CHANCE, in Dublin, Election district 4, map #12, for 36 acres.
8 Nov.1747 Edward Harper sold 36 acres to Stephen Tull.
1760 resurveyed to TULLS ADDITION 212 1/4 acres.

PROVIDENCE

Patented in 1753 for 215 1/2 acres by John Bedsworth in Brinkleys, northwest Election district 3,map #14.
1783 tax- Samuel Bedsworth 215 acres
21 March 1787 Samuel Bedsworth sold to Thomas Jones 215 1/2 acres.
17 April 1800 Lambert Hyland trustee conveyed to Thomas Jones as Jones in Dec.1797 obtained a decree against Samuel Bedsworth.
22 April 1800 Thomas Jones sold to William Williams.

PRYERS ADVENTURE

Patented in 1746 by Samuel Prior for 24 acres in Brinkleys, northwest,Election district 3,map #14.
27 Jan 1748 Ann Prior widow of Thomas Prior, Samuel Prior eldest son of Thomas Prior and John Scott sold to Outerbridge Horsey 24 acres with DIXONS KINDNESS (This was a trade for BEARD NECK.)
11 March 1797 Outerbridge Horsey son of William Horsey and grandson of Outerbridge Horsey sold to William Hitch COULBOURN, HORSEYS CONCLUSION, HORSEYS LOTT and moity of marsh between, unnamed.
12 March 1797 William Hitch returned to Outerbridge Horsey, same as above.

PURGATORY

Patented on 28 Oct.1701 by Thomas Roe for 160 acres on Deals Island,Election district 14, map #8, and found to be only 130 acres.
Rent Rolls 1666-1723 Thomas Roe 75 acres and Francis Gradon.
1783 tax- John Jones 19 acres
1783 tax- Nicholas Roe 37 1/2 acres
14 Aug.1787 John Jones of Samuel Jones gave to brother Thomas Jones 199 acres of GRAVESEND,PURGATORY on Deals Island.
4 April 1805 Nicholas Rowe sold to Thomas Rowe 36 acres.

PUZZLE

see DISCOVERY,CONTENTION,JOHNSTON- 90 acres

PUZZLE

see CHESTNUT RIDGE,CORK,WHITE OAK SWAMP, aka TROUBLESOME 175 acres.

347

PUZZLE

Patented on 3 June 1689 by John Kirk for 170 acres in Lawsons,Election district 8, map #18.
Rent Rolls 1666-1723 John Kirk
1719/20 John Kirk willed lands to wife Bridget Kirk and daughter Sarah Kirk.
19 Aug.1736 Littleton Townsend and wife Sarah Townsend,(Sarah Kirk daughter of John Kirk) mortgaged to Joseph McClester and John Dennis Jr.170 acres.
3 May 1746 Littleton Townsend and wife Sarah Townsend of Worc.Co. sold to Southy Whittington 170 acres.
1755 ADDITION patented for 6 acres
14 Apr.1763 Southy Whittington gave to son William Whittington 170 acres.
1783 tax- William Whittington 170 acres

PUZZLE

Patented in 1762 by Elijah Coulbourn for 10 3/4 acres in Lawsons,Election district 8, map #18
1783 tax- Elijah Coulbourn 10 1/2a.
11 Jan 1790 Elijah Coulbourn Sr. and wife Rachel Coulbourn and John Tull son of James Tull, to Benjamin Conner with POOR SWAMP,ACCIDENT,COME BY CHANCE,SCOTLAND.
11 Jan 1790 Benjamin Conner sold to Elijah Coulbourn, same as above-prob. establishment of boundaries.

PUZZLE CAP

Patented in 1795 for 30 1/2 acres by John Hayman in East Pr.Anne, Election district 15,map #4.
8 March 1806 John Hayman, wife Henrietta Hayman of Worc.Co. sold to Joshua Morris 30 acres.
1819 Joshua Morris willed to daughter Priscilla Morris.

RACOONS POINT

This is probably part of DOUBLE PURCHASE, not found on maps.
23 Feb 1683 Randall Revell and wife Katherine gave to son Randall and his wife Sarah Revell 500 acres of RACOON POINT of 3000 acres.
1718 Randall Revell Jr. willed to son William Revell RACOON POINT.

RAINBOW

see LABOUR

RAINSBURY

Patented on 10 Nov.1679 by Thomas Walker for 200 acres in St.Peters, Election district 2, map #6.
Rent Rolls 1666-1723 possessed by Thomas Shaw who purchased from Walker's heir.
1716/7 Thomas Shaw willed estate to wife Mary Shaw and grandson William Robinson. He also gave to preacher Thomas Hudson but no land mentioned in will.
18 June 1729 William Stoughton on behalf of William Robinson sold to Thomas Wright 50 acres of BLOYCES HOPE,CHANCE & RAINSBURY.

26 Feb.1782 John Wright sold to Gowan Wright lands that William Stoughton deeded in 1729 to Thomas Wright grandfather of John Wright-unnamed.
1783 tax- Thomas Sloss 170 acres
1783 tax- Gowan Wright 30 acres.
1787 part resurveyed to BLOOMSBURY 820 1/4 acres.

RANE WATER

Patented by George Howard in 1768 by George Hayward for 6 1/2 acres in Brinkleys, northwest,Election district 3, map #14.
1783 tax- George Hayward 6 1/2 acres.

RANGLE

Patented in 1770 by Solomon McCready for 18 1/2 acres in Brinkleys, southeast,Election district 3,map #16.
1783 tax- Solomon McCready
31 Aug.1789 Alexander McCready,wife Leah McCready of Worc.Co. sold to Isaac McCready of Somerset Co. 16 1/2 acres.

RECOVERY

Patented on 3 Nov.1676 by William Stevens for 200 acres and assigned to John Kirk, in Lawsons,Election district 8, map #18.
1719 John Kirk willed to wife Bridget Kirk and daughter Sarah Kirk, lands, no named.
19 Aug.1736 Littleton Townsend and wife Sarah Townsend(Sarah Kirk dau/o John Kirk) sold 200 acres to Joseph McClester and John Dennis Jr.-mortgage.
3 May 1746 Littleton Townsend and wife Sarah Townsend of Worc.Co. sold 200 acres to Southy Whittington.
1752 resurveyed to 273 1/2 acres by Southy Whittington
22 June 1763 Southy Whittington gave 18 1/2 acres to son Southy Whittington Jr.
14 Apr 1763 Southy Whittington gave 125 acres to son William Whittington.
1770 Southy Whittington gave to son Isaac Whittington 130 acres.
1783 tax- William Whittington 125 acres
1783 tax- Isaac Whittington 28 acres
1783 tax- Thomas S. Sudler 48 acres
9 Aug.1809 Thomas S. Sudler sold to Edward M. Waters, to establish dividing lines, part..

RECOVERY or DISCOVERY

Patented in 1757 for 14 acres by Thomas Pollitt in West Pr.Anne Election district 1, map #2.

RECTIFIED MISTAKE

Patented in 1797, a resurvey from JENKINS & COXES MISTAKE by William Jones for 479 1/2 acres in Mt.Vernon,Election district 5, map #1.
5 Sep. 1798 William Jones gave to son Levin Jones.
27 April 1830 Sheriff's sale, suit of Esther H. Cottman against Alexander Jones, George Jones and Robert Leatherbury 138 acres.
17 Oct.1808 Levin Jones, wife Elizabeth Jones sold 80 acres of RECTIFIED

MISTAKE & FLOWERFIELDS.

REFUGE

Patented on 12 July 1722 by Richard Carey for 50 acres in West Pr.Anne,
Election district 1, map #3.
Rent Rolls 1666-1723 Richard Carey
1722 /3 Richard Carey willed 50 acres to John McGrath.
1751 John McGrath willed to sons David McGrath, Levin McGrath and John
McGrath.
14 Feb 1764 David McGrath son of John McGrath sold to John White, his
interest.
3 Oct.1766 John White mortgaged to William Smith 50 acres with OWENS
IMPROVEMENT,OWENS DELIGHT,REFUGE,MIDDLE,etc.
10 Nov.1768 William Carey of Sussex Co.Del.,Solomon Carey of Worc.Co. and
Levin Carey of Worc.Co. sold 50 acres to John McGrath.
2 Aug.1768 Levin McGrath son of John McGrath sold brother John McGrath.
29 March 1769 Isaac Coulbourn,sheriff sold to Mary Waggaman widow. As
Edward Lloyd had judgement against John White, David McGrath and William
Smith 271 acres of OWENS IMPROVEMENT, MIDDLE, OWENS DELIGHT,REFUGE,DAVID
CHANCE.
12 Nov.1774 Thomas Carey Jr. of Sussex Co.Del.carpenter, sold all to Mary
Waggaman
1783 tax- John MGrath 50 acres.
1788 John McGrath willed to nephew David McGrath
21 Apr.1792 David McGrath gave to son Levin McGrath 50 acres.
29 Apr.1792 Henry Waggaman,wife Sarah Waggaman of Dorc.Co. son of Henry
Waggaman and Mary Waggaman sold to George Waggaman of Somerset County.

REHOBETH AND REHOBETH TOWN

Patented on 16 July 1665 by William Stevens for 1000 acres in Brinkleys,
northeast,Election district 3, map #15.
1665 Town patented for 2 acres by Vestry of Coventry Parish.
1687 William Stevens willed, to Stevens White son of Sarah White widow,
plantation where she lives and property on which testator lives 600
acres, to child of John White and heirs 200 acres, to cousin William
White 500 acres, unnamed. To Edward Howard and his son William Stevens
Howard, lands, to Benjamin Keyser 300 acres, part REHOBETH TOWN.
1691 Benjamin Keyser of Pocomoke willed to Lawrence Crawford 300 acres
left by Col. William Stevens.
Rent Rolls 1666-1723 600 acres Stevens White, 400 acres Col.Francis
Jenkins.(married 1st Lucy Weeden)
400 acres resurveyed-see MARYS LOT
4 Feb 1664 William Stevens and wife Elizabeth Stevens sold to James
Weeden 400 acres.
18 June 1735 Robert Jenkins Henry gave to Rev. James Robertson and
vestrymen of Coventry Parish 2 acres in REHOBETH TOWN where church now
stands and adjacent land.
1751 Stephen Ward willed to wife Margaret Ward 230 acres.
1754 Harriet Handy willed 230 acres to son Henry J. Handy.
17 June 1760 Stevens White and wife Elizabeth White sold to Littleton
Dennis part of REHOBETH & CALDICOTT(sworn at Norfolk Va,)
1760 Stevens White willed 500 acres to brother Elias White.
7 Sep.1776 Thomas Bruff and wife Betty Bruff sold to William Stevens

White(as Stevens White father of William Stevens White had CALDICUT &
REHOBETH. Betty White was the wife of Stevens White and since married
Thomas Bruff and is entitled to her dower part.
4 Aug.1780 Henry Schoolfield sold to Henry Schoolfield the younger, part
(page torn)
1782 Henry Schoolfield left part to son John Schoolfield.
1783 tax- Robert Jenkins Henry 10 acres in Rehobeth Town
1783 tax- George Schoolfield 100 acres
1783 tax- John Schoolfield 100 acres
1783 tax- Isaac B.Schoolfield 97 acres
1783 tax- Susannah Dennis 26 acres
1783 tax- William S. White 550
10 Apr.1786 Martha Henry leased 100 sq.ft. to Daniel Sturgis, blacksmith,
until Robert Jenkins King son of Martha Henry be age 14.
12 Jan 1788 George Schoolfield sold to Henry Schoolfield 1/4 acre at
Rehobeth Landing
1 June 1789 Henry Schoolfield sold 3 3/4 acres to William Davis.
13 Aug.1790 Thomas Adams sold 30 acres to William Davis, at Rehobeth.
27 Apr.1791 William Davis sold to John Turpin as conveyed by Henry
Schoolfield with 30 acres of wood land bought of Thomas Adams.
11 May 1791 William Stevens White sold to Littleton Dennis of Worc.Co. 16
1/4 acres of REHOBETH & CALDICOTT
23 Sep.1793 Henry Schoolfield leased 30 sq.ft. in Rehobeth Town to
William Porter.
21 Feb.1794 William Stevens White sold all his rights to Littleton Dennis
29 June 1796 William Porter,wife Sarah Porter sold to James Jordan lot in
Rehobeth Town, leased from Henry Schoolfield for 99 years.
11 Oct.1797 I George Schoolfield son of Henry Schoolfield am bound to
Joshua Silverthorn of Acco.Co.Va. or part of REHOBETH per will of Henry
Schoolfield.
23 Feb.1798 Joshua Silverthorn sold 3 acres to Henry Schoolfield.
1798 Benjamin Schoolfield willed to wife Polly Schoolfield plantation on
the Pocomoke River, no name.
13 May 1799 Joshua Silverthorn, wife Leah Silverthorn sold to Henry
Schoolfield 15 acres.
1797 George Schoolfield willed to Joshua Silverthorn, part.
28 Jan 1801 Robert Jenkins Henry of Baltimore sold to George Beauchamp,
warehouse lot.
28 Jan 1801 Robert Jenkins Henry of Baltimore sold to John Jordan of
Som.Co. 3/8 acre.
28 Jan 1801 Robert Jenkins Henry of Baltimore sold to Lazarus Adams, lot
in Rehobeth Town, 3/8 acre.
7 Feb.1803 Lazarus Adams sold to Michael Murray lot in Rehobeth Town.
4 Apr.1803 John G. Schoolfield sold to Risdon Bozman two lots at Rehobeth
Landing 3/4 acre.
8 Nov.1803 Michael Murray sold to Josias Cox lot in Rehobeth Town
2 Oct.1804 John G. Schoolfield sold to Josias Cox 1/2 lot in Rehobeth
Town.
5 Apr.1806 Risdon Bozman sold to Thomas Robertson house and lot at
Rehobeth, in right of wife Elizabeth Bozman.
18 Feb.1809 John Rogers and wife Polly Rogers of Acco. Co.Va. sold to
William A. Schoolfield REHOBETH formerly of Benjamin Schoolfield who
devised to Polly Rogers.
9 Jan 1809 John Schoolfield Sr. sold to Lazarus Adams, as Isaac Bozman
Schoolfield willed plantation to brother Benjamin Schoolfield 23 acres

who devised to brother George Schoolfield who devised to brother John
Schoolfield, no name.
3 Sep.1816 Heirs of Joshua Silverthorn sold to Elijah Boston 132 acres.
17 Oct.1818 Elijah Boston sold 12 acres to Henry Moore.
29 Jan 1824 Anne Boston widow of Elijah Boston, of Baltimore gave to
Obediah Riggin.
1826 Samuel Tull willed to son Henry Tull house and lot in Rehobeth Town.

RELPHS PURCHASE

see ROBINSONS LOTT

REMANANT

Patented in 1746 by William Jones for 13 acres in Westover, Election
district 13, map #11.
12 Apr.1753 William Jones,carpenter,wife Sarah Jones sold to Isaac
Beauchamp 13 acres.
1783 tax- Jean Beauchamp 13 acres.

RENCHERS SECURITY

Patented in 1714 by Thomas Rencher for 100 acres in Mt.Vernon, Election
district 5, map #1.
1743 ADDITION patented for 66 acres
25 June 1753 Thomas Rencher sold to William Rencher 37 acres.
21 Oct.1769 William Rencher Sr. and wife Martha Rencher sold to Thomas
Rencher Jr. 37 acres.
1783 tax- Thomas Rencher

REVENGE

Patented in 1760 by William Cottingham for 30 acres in Brinkleys,
southwest,Election district 3, map 17.
1783 tax- William Cottingham 30 acres.
23 March 1811 Josiah Cottingham son of William Cottingham sold part to
Thomas Cottingham
4 Oct.1813 Josiah Cottingham sold 1 acre to Samuel Tull
29 Aug.1832 Josiah Cottingham sold pt. to Nathan Horsey
23 June 1834 Josiah Cottingham sold balance to Levin Conner

RICH RIDGE

This is part of REHOBETH, not patented as RICH RIDGE
1687 William Stevens gave to Benjamin Keizer part of REHOBETH
called RICH RIDGE
1691 Benjamin Keizer sold to Lawrence Crawford
1727 Thomas Smith of Dorc.Co. willed to son-in-law John Brown of Somerset
Co. Md. 50 acres.

RICH SWAMP

Patented in 1754 for 50 acres by John Johnson in Lawsons, Election
district 8, map #18.
1783 tax- John Johnson Jr. 50 acres

1792/5 John Johnson willed to son John and to grandson Josiah Johnson.

RIDGE

Patented in 1724 for 60 acres by James Strawbridge in Dublin, Election district 4, map #12.
1 March 1757 James Strawbridge, wife Jean Strawbridge, sold to George Gillett formerly belonging to George Waggaman and Henry Waggaman, purchased of Littleton Teackle 60 acres.
4 Aug.1772 George Gillett sold to Saul Ward,60 acres
12 Apr.1785 Saul Ward sold to Matthias Miles 60 acres
1783 tax- Matthias Miles
1800 John Dennis willed to daughters Betsy Henry,Susan Upshur and Henrietta Dennis
1829 Henrietta Dennis willed to brother John Dennis.
1889 Jehu Parsons willed to wife Sarah Parsons, 4 acres of THE RIDGE & MY OWN had from William T. Mariner.

RIGGINS AMENDMENT

Patented in 1747, a resurvey by Teague Riggin from HILLIARDS DISCOVERY & HILLIARDS ADVENTURE, for 285 acres in Brinkleys, southeast,Election district 3, map #16.
1783 tax- Teague Riggin 210 acres.
1783 tax- Jemimah Riggin 75 acres.
23 May 1795 Teague Riggin sold 356 3/4 acres to George Riggin
1794 resurveyed to AYR 357 3/4 acres.
21 Feb 1804 George Riggin sold 50 acres to John Riggin Sr.
6 April 1809 John Riggin sold to Robert Riggin

RIGGINS CHANCE

Patented in 1743, a resurvey by Teague Riggin of part of MINSHALLS ADVENTURE,for 45 acres in Dublin, Election district 4, map #12.
6 Jan 1807 Wrixam L. Porter and wife Priscilla Porter sold her share to John Riggin.
1810 ADDITION TO RIGGINS CHOICE surveyed for 1 1/4 acres by John Riggin.

RIGGINS MEADOW

Patented in 1762 by John Riggin for 50 acres in Brinkleys, southeast, Election district 3, map #16.
1783 tax- Obed Riggin 50 acres.
14 April 1800 Obed Riggin sold 153 acres to Robert Riggin of GOLDEN LYON & RIGGINS MEADOW.

RIGGINS MINE

Patented on 7 June 1683 by William Stevens who assigned to Teague Riggin, for 100 acres in Brinkleys, southeast, Election district 3, map #16.
Rent Rolls 1666-1723 Ambrose Riggin
16 June 1741 John Riggin,Solomon Riggin sons of Teague Riggin deceased traded to Charles Dickerson for part of GOLDEN LYON, no acreage given.
8 Jan.1768 Jesse Dickerson son of Charles Dickerson and Benjamin Benston,

wife Elizabeth Benston both of Kent Co.Del. sold 100 acres to Matthias
Coston with GREEN PARK,DICKERSONS HOPE.
1774 ADDITION resurveyed by Matthias Coston 412 3/4 acres.
1783 tax- Levin Riggin 100 acres.
15 Aug.1805 Samuel Smith, wife Esther Smith sold to Ralph Milbourn 35
acres of ADDITION TO RIGGINS MINE
19 Aug.1805 Samuel Smith, wife Esther Smith sold to Stephen Collins 10
1/4 acres of ADDN. TO RIGGINS MINE.
15 Oct.1805 Samuel Smith, wife Esther Smith sold to Levi Houston of
Worc.Co. ADDITION TO RIGGINS MINE 90 acres.

RIGHTS CONCLUSION

Patented in 1785 by John Wright, a resurvey from LONG LOTT,WORST IS
PAST,FRIENDS ADVICE and 25 acres of vacancy in St.Peters,Election
district 2, map #6, for 264 1/4 acres
27 March 1787 John Wright and wife Attlanta Wright of Worc.Co. sold to
Levin Dashiell 264 1/4 acres.
1792 Levin Dashiell willed to son John Dashiell land purchased of John
Wright.
1817 John Dashiell willed to son Robert K. W. Dashiell
17 Dec.1800 William Waller, wife Bridget Waller sold to John Dashiell 75
acres of FRIENDS ADVICE & RIGHTS CONCLSUION tracts that William Wright
has rights to.

ROAD

Patented in 1789 for 6 acres by William Heath in East Pr.Anne, Election
district 15, map #4.
12 June 1804 Rebecca Hobbs sold to Whittington Polk, all.
13 Aug.1804 Samuel Smith, Josiah W. Heath, Matthias Miles, Evans Willin,
Thomas Pollitt comissioners to sell lands of William Heath sold to
Rebecca Hobbs 6 1/4 acres. She to pay his other heirs, Abraham Heath,
John Heath, Rebecca Hobbs, Nelly Morris, Leah Beauchamp, Polly Anderson,
Betsy Pollitt, Priscilla Morris and Esther Fooks. Lands to be divided,
with DONES NEST EGG, HEATHS GIFT.

ROACHS FOLLY

Patented in 1734 by Samuel Roach for 74 acres in Lawsons, Election
district 8, map #19.
1736 Samuel Roach willed to cousin Michael Roach 74 acres.
11 June 1785 William Wheatley sold to Jesse Cullin 14 3/4 acres of CABIN
SWAMP & ROACHS FOLLY
21 March 1787 William Wheatley Sr. sold his rights to Benjamin
Schoolfield ROACHS FOLLY & CABIN SWAMP.
10 Oct.1787 Daniel Cullen sold to William Wheatley and Michael Wheatley 7
acres of ROACHS FOLLY & CABIN SWAMP.
27 Feb.1808 John Riggin sold to Littleton Johnson 25 acres of ROACHS
FOLLY & CABIN SWAMP.

ROACHS PRIVILEDGE

Patented in 1695 by John Roach for 57 acres in Asbury, Election district
12, map #21.

Rent Rolls 1666-1723 John Roach Sr.

ROBERTS ADVENTURE

Patented in 1761 by Francis Roberts for 10 acres in Dames Quarter,
Election district 11, map #7.

ROBERTS LOTT

Patented on 27 Aug.1679 by Francis Roberts and assigned to Charles
Williams for 100 acres in Tangier,Election disrict 9, map #7.
Rent Rolls 1666-1723 possessed by Charles Williams 100 acres.
1783 tax- Elizabeth Williams 100 acres
1829 Zorobable Williams willed to brother Elijah Williams.

ROBERTS RECOVERY

Patented on 10 Sep.1682 by Francis Roberts for 100 acres in Dames
Quarter,Election district 11, map #7.
Rent Rolls 1666-1723 possessed by widow Ann Roberts relic of Francis
Roberts.
1783 tax- William Roberts 59 acres
1794 William Roberts willed to niece Nancy Lemon wife of Robert Lemon.
16 May 1801 George Jones and wife Leah Jones sold to Edward Fowler,
NEGLECT,RECOVERY, VENTERS PRIVILDEGE, GREEN PASTURE total 510 acres.

ROBERTSONS ADDITION

Patented in 1754 by John Robertson for 37 acres in St. Peters Election
district 2, map #6.
11 Apr.1760 George Robertson son of John Robertson deceased, sold to
Nehemiah Bozman, 27 acres
18 Apr.1760 George Robertson,wife Elinor Robertson sold 10 acres to
Arnold Elzey
15 Nov.1779 Dr. Arnold Elzey once of Somerset Co. now of Baltimore Town
sold to Henry Jackson and John Jones of Goose Creek with BOZMANS
ADVENTURE.
1783 tax- John Jones of Goose Creek
1783 tax- Henry Jackson
28 Feb.1791 John Jones of Goose Creek and Henry Jackson settled division
lines.
6 March 1791 John Jones Sr. sold to William Jones Sr.part.
27 March 1792 John Jones Sr. sold to William Jones Sr.no acres mentioned
(sold with other lands)
1794 Henry Jackson, willed to son George Wilson Jackson land bought of
Arnold Elzey, unnamed.
8 Sep.1807 William B. Jones sold to Littleton Dennis Teackle 300 acres
per deed of 27 March 1792.
29 Oct.1807 Littleton Dennis Teackle sold to John Teackle of Georgetown
DC.
4 April 1808 Elizabeth Jackson and George W. Jackson sold to William
Jones 27 acre plus 110 acres of BOZMANS ADVENTURE & ROBERTSONS ADDITION.

ROBINSONS LOTT

355

Patented in 1665 for 300 acres by William Robinson, and resurveyed on 28 June 1676 for 325 acres in Mt.Vernon, Election district 5, map #1.
13 June 1681 William Robinson, wife Elizabeth Robinson sold to Thomas Relfe 80 acres called RELFS PURCHASE.
1696 William Robinson willed lands to two sons equally (unnamed)
21 Apr.1733 William Robinson son of William sold to John Robinson plantation left by father at Wic.Creek.
22 June 1750 George Gale brother and exec. of the will of Levin Gale and Leah Gale, only heir of Levin sold to Henry Lowes part of ROBINSONS LOTT conveyed to Betty by John Robinson and wife Elizabeth Robinson. in 1727 Betty Gale willed to Levin Gale one moity.
1755 William Robinson gave lower part to son Ezekiel Robinson 147 acres
17 May 1766 Thomas Holbrook and wife Sarah Holbrook sold to James Polk all rights to ROBINSONS LOTT & COW PASTURE.
15 Apr.1766 William Robertson and Walter Lane Robertson sold all inteest to Thomas Holbrook with COW PASTURE.
5 Aug.1766 John Robinson son of John and wife Priscilla Robinson sold 65 acres to William Polk.
13 June1767 John Robinson sold to William Polk, all.
8 Sep.1767 Rachel Robinson relic of William Robinson sold to William Polk her 1/3ra dower of ROBINSONS LOTT & COW PASTURE.
21 Feb 1769 John Robinson and wife Priscilla Robinson sold to William Polk, all his interest.
25 Sep.1770 James Polk sold to William Polk all rights.
9 March 1773 Henry Lowes, mtg. to James Dickinson and William Hayward of Talbot Co.Md. 15 acres.
1783 tax- William Polk 285 1/2 acres
1783 tax- Henry Lowes 30 acres
1795 resurvey to WILLIAMS LOTT 460 acres.

ROODY

Patented on 4 June 1688 by John Panter for 200 acres in St.Peters, Election district 2, map #6. AKA RONDIE
Rent Rolls 1666-1723 John Panter.
1713 John Panter willed to Benjamin Sasser 200 acres
5 Aug.1729 Benjamin Sasser and Thomas Sasser deeded to William Sasser 200 acres.
1783 tax- William Sasser Sr. 200 acres
1793 William Sasser willed to son Benjamin Sasser, lands (unnamed.)

ROWLANDS RIDGE
see ELLIOTTS CHOICE

ROWLEY HILL

Patented on 28 May 1693 by William Stevens and sold to Abraham Heath in 1684, for 100 acres in East Pr.Anne,Election district 15, map #5.
10 June 1723 Anthony Moore who moved to Carolina sold 100 acres to James Strawbridge that Abraham Heath willed to son William and that William Heath and wife Mary Heath sold to Anthony Moore.
1735 James Strawbridge,wife Jean Strawbridge sold to John Phillips 100 acres
1762 John Phillips willed land (unnamed) to son John.
31 Jan 1775 I John Phillips am bound to William Miles for 100 acres.
1783 tax- John Phillips 100 acres

22 March 1786 Jonathan Stanford and wife Grace Stanford (Grace Phillips) sold to John McDaniel and wife Elizabeth McDaniel for 5 shillings.
5 Jan 1796 Elizabeth McDaniel, cohier of John Phillips sold to David McDaniel 57 1/2 acres of ROWLEY HILL & DUDLEY.
22 May 1805 The comissioners to divide the RE of John Phillips sold to one of the representatives of John Phillips, Jesse Dukes and wife Sarah Dukes 170 acres of DUDLEY, ROWLEY HILL, GRAYS PURCHASE & PRIVILEDGE.
22 May 1805 Jesse Dukes and wife Sarah Dukes of Sussex Co.Del. sold his rights to same, to Pierce Riggin of Som.Co.
1832 resurveyed to ROWLEY RIDGE

ROWLEY RIDGE

Patented on 16 March 1680 by Richard Chambers for 100 acres in East Pr.Anne,Election district 15,map #1 and map #5..
Rent Rolls 1666-1723 Richard Chambers 100 acres
1726 Richard Chambers gave to daughter Olive Chambers 100 acres.
1743 Richard Chambers gave to cousin William Douglas
7 Jan 1752 William Douglas of Kent Co.Md. sold to John Maddux, 100 acres
13 Nov.1773 John Maddux gave 100 acres to son Thomas Maddux
1776 John Maddux patented 68 1/4 acres.
19 Oct.1787 Nicholas Tull of Baltimore Co. sold to George Robertson property of Thomas Maddux deceased- his interest in.
19 Feb.1788 George Robertson sold to George Waggaman 100 acres
14 Feb.1797 George Waggaman sold to Elizabeth Jackson 33 1/4 acres of WAGGAMANS LOTT,ROWLEY RIDGE,ADDITION.
27 Dec.1803 Col. William Jones son of William and wife Elinor Jones sold to John Bloodsworth 13 1/4 acres.
1832 ADDITION pat. 492 7/8 acres includes ROWLEY HILL & PHILLIPS CONCLUSION.

ROXBUROUGH

Patented on 2 April 1695 by Roger Phillips for 210 acres in East Pr.Anne,Election district 15, map #4.
1698 Roger Phillips willed to son Thomas Phillips and daughter Dorothy Phillips.
Rent Rolls 1666-1723 Possessed by Thomas Phillips for his sister who hath the right 105 acres and Richard Phillips for his sisters right.
27 Aug.1739 William Polk gave to son David Polk 210 acres purchased from Alexander Vance.
5 March 1776 David Polk gave to son Gillis Polk.
1783 tax- Gillis Polk 210 acres.
1791 resurvey to CONSOLIDATION 820 3/4 acres.

ROYAL EXCHANGE

Patented in 1769 by Joseph Venables for 12 acres in East Pr.Anne,Election district 15, map #5.
19 March 1772 Joseph Venables and wife Nelly Venables sold to William Polk 12 1/2 acres
1783 tax- James Polk 12 1/2 acres.

RUCK PREVENTED

Patented in 1732 from COXES BILL by William Cox for 145 acres in

Brinkleys, southeast,Election district 3, map #16.
1 Nov.1785 Jesse Ward sold to William Cox 145 acres.
1742 resurveyed to CALF PASTURE 247 acres.

RUMBLING POINT

Patented on 20 Nov.1694 by Phillip Conner for 100 acres in Brinkleys,
southwest,Election district 3, map #17.
1702 Phillip Conner willed to sons John Conner and William Conner.
Rent Rolls 1666-1723 possessed by the widow Conner
17 June 1724 John Conner and wife Elizabeth Conner sold 90 acres to
Randal Long and Charles Cottingham.
1783 tax- William Cottingham 75 acre.
1783 tax- Thomas Cottingham 15 acres
1783 tax- Isabelle Conway 10 acres.

RUSCOMMON

Patented on 3 May 1689 by Phillip Conner for 100 acres in Brinkleys,
southwest,Election district 3, map #17.
26 Sep.1694 Phillip Conner Sr. bequeathed to son Phillip 100 acres.
Rent Rolls 1666-1723 possessed by widow Conner.
30 July 1764 Bell Maddux and wife Margaret Maddux sold 23 acres to Sarah
Potter widow of Thomas Potter.
20 March 1783 Zorobable Maddux, wife Esther Maddux formerly of Som.Co.
and Margaret Maddux sold rights to Merrill Maddux of Worc.Co. 150 acres.
1784 Samuel Matthews willed return to wife Sarah Matthews her dower
land.(married Sarah Potter)
7 March 1791 Henry Potter of Pittsylvania Co.Va.sold to Nathan Cahoon 73
acres of RUSCOMMON & FATHERS CARE.
15 Apr.1791 Merrill Maddux sold to Nathan Cahoon 206 1/2 acres of
RUSCOMMON,CONVIENCY,MITCHELLS CHOICE.

RYANS PURCHASE

see TONYS VINEYARD

RYESK

Patented in 1758 by James Gunby for 82 acres in Lawsons Election district
8, map #18
9 Feb.1797 James Gunby sold to John Gunby of Worc.Co. 82 acres.
27 Feb.1797 John Gunby son of Kirk Gunby of Worc.Co. sold 82 acres to
Benjamin Lankford.
1820 Benjamin Lankford willed to sons Lazarus Lankford,Henry Lankford and
Benjamin Lankford.
15 June 1807 Benjamin Lankford Sr. sold to William Williams 80 acres.
22 June 1808 William Williams sold to Benjamin Lankford 80 acres.
17 March 1810 Benjamin Lankford sold to William Williams 82 acres.

SAFETY

part of GOLDEN LYON, the part called AMBROSIA

ST.GILES

Patented on 12 June 1683 by George Betts for 200 acres in St.Peters, Election district 2, map #6.
1709 George Betts willed to son-in-law John Irving and his wife Frances Irving (Frances Betts).
1753 resurveyed to GEORGES ADVENTURE 1000 acres.

St.PETERS NECK

Patented on 2 May 1663 by Peter Elzey for 400 acres in St.Peters,Election district 2, map #6.
Rent Rolls 1666-1723 resurvey lines for 750 acres -Peter Elzey
1715 Peter Elzey willed to daughters Frances Elzey and Elizabeth Elzey.
18 Jan.1721 William Wallace sold to William Stoughton
1733 resurvey for 720 acres.
2 Nov.1763 Thomas Sloss of Som.Co. and George Irving sold to William Smith with GEORGES CHANCE & BELL FAST, that was conveyed to William Stoughton.
1783 tax- Robert Cavanaugh 88 acres
1783 tax- Lambert Hyland 517 acres
1783 tax- Mary Smith 140 acres
2 Aug.1785 Patrick Glascow and wife Mary Glascow sold to Lambert Hyland(as Mary Glascow formerly Mary Rigby and Elizabeth Rigby married Lambert Hyland and Sarah Rigby married John Jones, were daughters of John Rigby deceased, became entitled to 1/3rds ST PETERS NECK. Sarah Done died without issue and Mary Glascow became entitled.-sold their rights.
5 Feb.1789 Samuel Smith and wife Esther Smith sold to Henry Walston Miles 68 1/2 acres
5 Feb.1789 Samuel Smith sold to Gowan Wright 33 1/2 acres for the use and benefit of Rebecca Smith widow of Thomas Smith and her daughter Margaret Smith.

St.THOMAS ISLAND

Patented in 1803, a resurvey on SARA by Thomas Jones, for 152 3/4 acres on Smiths Island,Election district 10 map #22.
1923 resurvey to SPORTSMANS DELIGHT 2270 acres.

SALEM

Patented in 1750 for 490 acres by John Waters in Fairmount, Election district 6, map #9.
1783 tax- John Waters 490 acres
31 March 1787 Francis Hutchings Waters sold to John Gale that my father John Waters willed in 1784, plantation in Annamessex after death of his wife Elizabeth Waters, now dead. no name or acreage of land.
1789 resurveyed by Francis Hutchings Waters 648 1/4 acres.
16 May 1800 Francis Hutchings Waters sold to Littleton Dawsey 32 acres.

SALISBURY

Patented on 3 April 1667 by John Rhodes for 200 acres in Fairmount,Election district 6, map #9.
1668 John Rhodes, sold to Thomas Tull and Richard Tull.
(Richard Tull married a Martha Rhodes and left county)
Rent Rolls 1666-1723 possessed by Nathaniel Roach in right of James

Curtis the purchaser.
1720 James Curtis willed to daughter Elizabeth Roach. (married Nathaniel
Roach)
28 March 1750 Nathaniel Roach and wife Hannah Roach sold 75 acres to
Thomas Seon
6 Aug.1752 Nathaniel Roach sold to John Waters Jr. balance 125 acres.
16 Sep.1752 John Waters the younger, sold 35 acres to Thomas Seon, part
called STRUGGLE.
21 March 1757 Nathaniel Roach sold to Thomas Seon(as Nathaniel mortgaged
to John Waters part that was returned)
19 Aug.1758 John Waters and wife Elizabeth Waters sold to Thomas Seon
(prob.release of Mortgage.)
17 Dec.1769 Nathaniel Roach sold part to Nathaniel Whitaker rector of
Coventry Parish.
13 Aug.1761 Nathaniel Whitaker sold to Thomas Seon his interest in
BARNABYS LOTT & SALISBURY.
22 Nov.1770 Thomas Seon sold 3 acres to Sewell Handy
1783 tax- Stephen Garland 50 acres
1783 tax- Thomas Seon Sudler 197 14 acres.
3 Apr.1783 Nathaniel Roach sold 200 acres to Thomas Sudler
6 Nov.1683 Nathaniel Roach and wife Hannah Roach sold to Thomas Seon
Sudler (heretofore conveyed by Roach to Thomas Seon grandfather to Thomas
Seon Sudler) 200 acres.

SALSBERYS LOTT

Patented in 1752 by Stephen Garland for 50 acres in Westover, Election
district 13, map #11.
2 Jan.1766 Stephen Garland sold to Thomas Dashiell,sheriff 50 acres for a
certain prisoner languishing in jail.
10 March 1767 Thomas Dashiell, sheriff sold to John White 50 acres.
10 March 1767 John White sold 50 acres to Stephen Garland.
12 Sep.1763 Stephen Garland mortgaged to John Logan in city of
London,merchant his interest.

SAMPIRE

Patented on 15 May 1704 by James Curtis for 80 acres in Fairmount,
Election district 6, map #9.
Rent Rolls 1666-1723 James Curtis
20 Aug.1740 Charles Curtis son of James and wife Mary Curtis sold to
Solomon Long 130 acres with COW QUARTER.
1756 Solomon Long gave to son David Long 130 acres with COW QUARTER.
1772 Solomon Long willed to son David Long 130 acres.
23 March 1775 William Long sold 80 acres to Brittian Powell.
23 March 1775 David Long and wife Elizabeth Long sold to William Long 80
acres.
1776 Sewell Handy son of Thomas and Jane Handy (Jane Long) willed to son
Thomas Handy and part to son Sewell Handy.
19 March 1778 James Hammond sold to Solomon long and Zadock Long (as
William Long willed his estate to James Hammond and John Long and John
Howard, no names of land or acreage).
1780 Solomon Long sold to John Howard
1783 tax- John Howard 97 1/4 acres of NORTH SAMPIRE.
24 Aug.1786 John Howard sold to Samuel Long 1/2 part devised him and

James Hammond and Solomon Long by William Long deceased, SOUTH SAMPIRE, no acreage given.
17 March 1790 John White sold to John Howard SOUTH SAMPIRE and 1/2 mill thereon.
17 March 1790 John Howard sold to John White 1 moity of land and mill on SOUTH SAMPIER
25 May 1792 John White, wife Rebecca White and John Howard sold to Solomon Long his rights to SOUTH SAMPIER.
23 March 1795 William Done sold to William Lawson SOUTH SAMPIER, (this was returned the same date.)
14 Aug.1800 Sewell Handy son of Thomas Handy sold to Thomas Beauchamp, real estate of Thomas Handy, no name or acreage.
1 Nov.1803 William Done sold to William Denston of Lancaster Co. Va. his rights to SOUTH SAMPIER.
4 Nov.1803 William Denston of Lancaster Co. Va. sold to William Parks, SOUTH SAMPIER.
17 Jan.1805 Mary Handy sold right of dower to Thomas Beauchamp that land Thomas purchased of Sewell Handy, being his distributed share of his father Capt Thomas Handy estate, no name or acreage.
2 Jan 1807 Solomon Long, wife Nelly Long sold to William Parks 80 acres of ADVENTURE, HORSE HAMMOCK, SAMPIER & COW QUARTER.
1815 Thomas Beauchamp son of Thomas Beauchamp willed to son Isaac Beauchamp SAMPIER bought of Sewell Handy.

SAMUELS ADVENTURE

Patented on 7 Jan 1665 by Col.Samuel Smith in Virginia for 1000 acres in West Pr.Anne,Election district 1, map #2.
Rent Rolls 1666-1723 367 acres Ann Brereton, 133 acres not found, 50 acres Peter Presley, possessed by Jonathan Raymond.
1675 resurvey 300 acres to BRERETONS CHANCE
1680 resurvey 250 acres to MILE END
1721 resurvey 510 acres to END OF STRIFE
11 March 1802 Scott Brerton sold to William Brereton 27 1/2 acres of BRERETONS CHANCE & SMITHS ADVENTURE.
4 May 1802 William Brereton,wife Ann Brereton sold to Scott Brereton 60 1/4 acres of same.
23 Oct.1803 William Brereton sold to Scott Brereton the balance.

SAMUELS LOT

Patented in 1771 by Samuel Miles for 9 acres in East Pr.Anne,Election district 15,map #5.
29 May 1782 Samuel Miles,wife Mary Miles sold to Matthias Miles 9 acres.

SAMUELS PART

Patented in 1728 by Samuel Fountain for 64 acres in Westover,Election district 13, map #11.
11 Apr.1749 Samuel Fountain of Dorc.Co.merchant,sold to Robert Jenkins Henry 64 acres.

SAPLIN RIDGE

Patented in 1749 for 19 acres by Joseph Tilghman and resurveyed in 1763

and 84 acres added, in Westover Election district 13, map #11, by Joseph Tilghman.
1763 Joseph Tilghman willed to son William Tilghman 19 acres and 84 acres ADDITION
1783 tax- William Tilghman
9 Aug.1791 Levin Miles and William Tilghman settled dispute of boundaries of HUNTSMANS FOLLY & SAPLIN RIDGE.
1785 resurveyed to TILGHMANS PRIVILEDGE, 113 acres.

SARA

Patented in 1723 for 50 acres by Alexander Adams on Smiths Island, Election district 10, map #22.
14 July 1789 William Adams Jr. sold 50 acres to Thomas Jones, land on island on south side of Holland Streights.
1803 resurveyed to St.Thomas Island 152 /34 acres.

SARAHS JOY

see DOUBLE PURCHASE

SASSAFRAS NECK

Patented in 1681 by John Covington for 150 acres in Mt.Vernon,Election district 5, map #1. AKA SUFFOLK NECK.
Rent Rolls 1666-1723 Phillip Covington 150 acres
1683/4 John Covington willed to son John Covington 150 acres and if no heirs to son Phillip Covington
1713 resurveyed by Phillip Covington for 206 acres.
6 July 1757 Phillip Covington, Daniel Jones (married Elizabeth Covington)Nehemiah Covington of Dorc.Co. sold to Thomas Jones.
1783 tax- Arnold Ballard 67 acres(married Elizabeth Jones widow of Thomas Jones)
1783 tax- John Jones for heirs of Thomas Jones 137 acres.
22 Oct.1792 George Jones son of Thomas Jones sold to Thomas Rencher.
1806 Thomas Rencher Sr. willed to son John Rencher, where Richard Ingersoll now lives.

SATISFACTION

Patented on 25 April 1714 by George Dashiell for 116 acres in Mt. Vernon, Election district 5, map #1.
Rent Rolls 1666-1723 George Dashiell
1748 George Dashiell willed 116 acres to son Benjamin Dashiell.
20 Nov.1759 Joseph Dashiell son of George Dashiell, and wife Martha Dashiell sold to Thomas Simms 116 acres.
1783 tax- Smith Simms son of Thomas Simms 116 acres
1828/33 Smith Simms willed to son Smith Simms.

SAUCERS ADDITION

Patented on 5 June 1688 for 50 acres by Benjamin Sasser in St.Peters, Election district 2, map #6.
Rent Rolls 1666-1723 Benjamin Sasser.
1712 Benjamin Sasser willed to son William Sasser 50 acres.

SAUCERS FOLLY

Surveyed on 5 July 1679 by Benjamin Sasser for 100 acres in St.Peters, Election district 2,map #6.
Rent Rolls 1666-1723 Benjamin Sasser.
1712 Benjamin Sasser willed to son William Sasser and heirs 100 acres.
1783 tax- William Sasser Sr. 100 acres

SAUCERS LOT

Surveyed on 1 Oct.1681 by Benjamin Saucer for 50 acres in St.Peters but not located on Benson's maps.
Rent Rolls 1666-1723 Benjamin Saucer
5 Nov.1685 Benjamin Saucer and wife Ann sold to John Rickins 50 acres.
1783 tax- William Saucer 50 acres.

SCHOOLFIELDS CHANCE

Patented in 1757 by Henry Schoolfield for 51 acres in Brinkleys, northeast, district 3, map #15.
1777 Henry Schoolfield Jr. willed to son Henry.
1783 tax- Henry Schoolfield 50 acres
17 July 1784 Henry Schoolfield Jr,wife Elizabeth Schoolfield sold 7 acres to Brittain Powell.
12 Jan 1788 Leah Schoolfield gave her interest to son Henry Schoolfield
12 Jan 1788 Henry Schoolfield,wife Elizabeth Schoolfield sold to Pierce Chapman ADDITION TO CHANCE SCHOOLFIELDS CHANCE, BEAUCHAMPS VENTURE, CHANCE, 69 1/2 acres
1 March 1790 Henry Schoolfield,wife Elizabeth Schoolfield sold to Brittain Powell 14 1/2 acres.
27 June 1795 Brittain Powell,wife Sarah Powell sold to Rebecca Chapman 11 7/8 acres.
1795 Pierce Chapman willed to son John Chapman, if he dies before of age, to wife Rebecca Chapman estate- no name.
1796 Brittain Powell willed to son Samuel Powell 80 acres adjacent land of John Bruff, and Rebecca Chapman- not named.
15 June 1810 Samuel Powell sold to William Williams, unnamed 80 acres devised by father Brittain Powell.

SCHOOLHOUSE RIDGE

Patented in 1753 by Richard Waters for 98 acres in Fairmount, Election disrict 6, map #9.
4 Dec.1756 Richard Waters sold to Joshua Hall for 5 shillings 98 acres.
1783 tax- Isaac Hall 50 acres
12 Apr.1785 Joshua Hall traded Isaac Hall 98 acres for HALLS CHOICE.
1786 resurveyed to 100 acres.
25 Apr.1786 Isaac Hall son of Charles Hall, wife Anna Hall, sold to Henry Miles, no acreage mentioned,description.
1787 Henry Miles willed to son Henry lands bought of Isaac Hall.
20 July 1789 Ann Hall and James Hall adjusted division lines with Henry Miles.
Resurveyed in 1803 by Henry Miles for 100 acres.

SCOTLAND

Patented on 12 July 1677 by William Stevens and assigned to William Scott
for 300 acres in Lawsons,Election district 8, map #18.
1708 William Scott willed dwelling plantatin to son William (no name) and
lands to sons George Scott, David Scott and John Scott.
Rent Rolls 1666-1723 William Scott.
1722 ADDITION patented for 65 acres by William Scott
19 March 1728 Capt.John Scott son of William Scott,sold to William
Merrill of Acco.Co.Va. one moiety.
19 March 1728 William Merrill of Acco.Co.Va. sold to Jacob Merrill the
moiety in exchange of 50 acres of ARRACOCO.
21 Apr.1729 George Scott son of William Scott sold part to John White.
17 May 1733 Edward Hearn and wife Deborah Hearn and Joshua Atkinson and
wife Elizabeth Atkinson sold to John White, their interest; that Wiliam
Scott willed to son George Scott who sold to John White. Deborah Hearn
and Elizabeth Atkinson were coheirs and daughters of William Scott eldest
son of William.
6 June 1737 articles of agreement-Joshua Atkinson sold to Southy
Whittington 150 acres, as William Scott deceased father of Elizabeth
Scott now wife of Joshua Atkinson was seized of SCOTLAND, 50 acres SCOTTS
FOLLY, CANAAN(Joshua Atkinson and Samuel Atkinson bound to agreement.)
13 Oct.1765 John Juett sold to William Juett 108 acres to BUCK RIDGE,POOR
SWAMP, SCOTLAND willed by John White to his daughter Alice White now wife
of John Juett.
12 Nov.1767 James Ward Sr, wife Rachel Ward, sold to Samuel Kellum 17
acres purchased by Thomas Ward his father from Robert Dukes on 17
Aug.1708.
11 Nov.1768 Samuel Kellum sold to Elijah Coulbourn 17 acres with COME BY
CHANCE.
1783 tax- James Hearn 185 acres
1783 tax- William Merrill 117 acres.
18 March 1788 George Disharoon,wife Alice Disheroon, of Worc.Co. sold to
William Juett for 5 shillings (her son by John Juett and left to Alice
Disharoon by her father John White in 1749) no name or acreage.
11 Jan 1790 Elijah Coulbourn and wife Rachel Coulbourn and John Tull son
of James Tull sold to Benjamin Connner.
11 Jan 1790 Benjamin Conner sold to Elijah Coulbourn,same.
1795 William Merrill of Acco.Co.Va. willed to son Maximillian Merrill,
plantation where son George Merrill now lives in Somerset Co. on Planners
Ck. SCOTTLAND.
7 Nov.1804 George Merrill of Acco.Co.Va. sold to Southy Whittington, no
acreage mentioned.

SCOTTS FOLLY

Patented on 15 March 1683 by William Scott for 50 acres, in Lawsons
Election district 8, map #18.
1712 William Scott willed to son William, plantation, after his wife
dies.
6 June 1737 Joshua Atkinson,wife Elizabeth Atkinson (Elizabeth Scott d/o
William Scott) SCOTTS FOLLY now called CANAAN.50 acres.

SEWARDS PURCHASE

Patented on 1 Nov.1677 by Josias Seward for 400 acres in
Brinkleys,northeast,Election district 3, map #15.
29 March 1678 Josias Seward and wife Margaret Seward sold to Cornelius
Morris all.
1688 Cornelius Morris,wife Anne Morris, sold to Isaac Boston and Esau
Boston.
Rent Rolls 1666-1723 possessed by Adrain Marshall (married Elizabeth
Boston widow of Isaac Boston) 200 acres and 200 acres by Esau Boston.
1688 Esau Boston resurveyed 200 acres called BOSTONS PURCHASE with
vacancy land adjacent.
13 Jan 1756 Isaac Boston sold 19 2/3 acres to Samuel Adams
6 July 1756 Isaac Boston, mortgaged to Thomas Marshall 181 acres that
came him from his father Isaac Boston
1774 Thomas Marshall deeded to son Isaac Marshall 19 acres.
10 July 1757 resurvey part to BOSTONS CHANCE, total 260 1/2 acres.
7 July 1757 Rachel Boston widow of Isaac Boston, sold to Thomas Marshall
her 1/3rds.
20 Apr.1774 Thomas Marshall gave to son Isaac Marshall 19 2/3rds acres.
(see BOSTONS PURCHASE)

SECOND CHOICE

Patented on 14 Feb.1666 by Henry Hayman for 200 acres in Mt.Vernon,
Election district 5, map #1.
25 Nov.1687 Henry Hayman, cooper, wife Martha Hayman and Eleanor Hayman
relic of Henry Hayman sold to John Covington
Rent Rolls 1666-1723 possessed by Phillip Covington heir of John
Covington
17 Oct.1693 John Covington willed 200 acres to wife Mary Covington and
then to son Nehemiah Covington and then to son Phillip Covington.
1732/3 Phillip Covington son of John willed to wife Mary Covington, then
to son John Covington.
4 Sep.1750 Nehemiah Covington and Elinor Covington sold to Henry
Waggaman.

SECOND CHOICE

Patented in 1675 by John Parsons for 300 acres in West Pr. Anne and East
Pr.Anne,district 15, maps #2 & #4.
Rent Rolls 1666-1723 John Parsons.
15 Oct.1748 Ahab Coston and wife Abigail Coston (Abigail Parsons dauchter
of John Parsons) sold 20 acres to Thomas Gillis.
15 Oct.1748 Thomas Gillis sold to Ahab Coston part 20 acres- trade of
lands.
15 Feb.1760 Thomas Gillis sold to Levin Gillis 20 acres.
31 March 1763 triparte-Matthias Coston,wife Abigail Costen,sold to Jesse
Lister and Coulbourn Long (except part conveyed by Abigail and Ahab
Coston her then husband to Thomas Gillis.
20 Sep.1763 Matthias Coston and wife Abigail Coston sold to Thomas
Pollitt(dispute of lands) SECOND CHOICE & DAINTY.
10 Apr.1764 Matthias Coston and wife Abigail Coston leased for 7 years to
John Davis.
24 Apr.1771 Oliver Coston and wife Sophia Coston sold to Rev. Samuel
Sloan and Eden School part.
13 Apr.1771 Oliver Coston sold to brother Ahab Coston 110 acres.

22 Nov.1771 Oliver Coston sold to Samuel Sloan of Eden School. part.
Probably confirmation of above deed.
18 July 1773 Ahab Coston,wife Betty Mary Coston sold to Gillis Polk.
13 Oct.1788 Oliver Coston son of Abigail Coston sold 300 acres to Andrew
Adams.
1791 resurveyed to CONSOLIDATION 820 3/4 acres.

SECOND CHOICE

Patented in 1744, a resurvey from FIRST CHOICE,by William Dixon for 215
acres in Brinkleys,northwest,Election district 3, map #14.
19 May 1750 William Dixon sold 215 acres to son Thomas Dixon Jr.
1783 tax- Thomas Dixon 215 acres
1799 William Cottingham, willed to wife Mary Cottingham (Mary Dixon) and
to son Charles Cottingham and dwelling plantation to son Josiah
Cottingham.
17 Jan 1799 Thomas Dixon sold to William Cottingham 107 1/2 acres.
3 Feb 1805 Josiah Cottingham son of William Cottingham sold to James
Rounds Mills, tract from father, no name.
23 Feb 1805 James Rounds Mills sold to Josiah Cottingham, probably a
mortgage.

SECOND PURCHASE

Patented in 20 Nov.1676 by Francis Roberts for 250 acres in Mt.Vernon,
Election district 5, map #1.
5 Feb.1678 Francis Roberts sold to Edward Gibbs.
1681 Edward Gibbs mortgaged to Benjamin Lawrence.
10 Jan 1718 Henry Gibbs son of Edward, received payment of mortgage.
Henry conveyed to Benjamin Lawrence, John Bell and Lucy Bell his wife
heirs of Benjamin Lawrence deceased.
1783 tax- Ann Elzey
1794 resurveyed by Ann Elzey 238 1/4 acres.
25 March 1794 James Elzey sold to Nehemiah King and William Jones of
Thomas Jones of Manokin for 5 shillings.
18 Aug.1794 Nehemiah King and William Jones sold to James Elzey,same as
above.
19 Aug.1794 James Elzey,wife Sarah Elzey sold to William Jones of Thomas
Jones.

SECURITY

Patented in 1726 for 300 acres by Ephraim Wilson in Dames Quarter,
Election district 11,map #7.
28 Dec.1762 David Wilson leased to Thomas Jones for 20 years.
17 Apr.1764 Thomas Jones releases above
17 Apr.1764 David Wilson and wife Ann Wilson sold to Levin Wilson his
1/4th part.
13 Dec.1768 Samuel Wilson and wife Mary Wilson sold to Denwood Wilson 450
acres for 5 shillings,SECURITY,KILLGAN, TILBURY, WILSONS DISCOVERY,
GLASGOW.
1783 tax- Levin Wilson 75 acres
1783 tax- Denwood Wilson 75 acres

SECURITY

Patented in 1727 by William Planner for 150 acres in Brinkleys,

northwest, Election district 3, map #14.
1733 William Planner willed to Elizabeth Owens part, after death to
Thomas Williams.
1768 Resurveyed to PLANNERS BLOSSOM 577 acres.

SECURITY

Patented in 1731 for 172 acres by Samuel Miles in Fairmount, Election
district 6, map #9.
1756 Henry Miles willed to son Henry Miles.
1762 resurveyed to MILES CONCLUSION

SECURITY

Patented in 1739, by William Dixon,a resurvey from DICKESONS CHOICE for
405 acres in Brinkleys, northwest, Election district 3,map #14.
1783 tax- William Dixon Sr. 202 1/2 acres
1783 tax- Ambrose Dixon 202 1/2 acres

SECURITY

Patented in 1741 for 243 acres by George Wilson in Brinkleys, southwest,
Election district 3, map #17.
1768 George Wilson willed to son William and after death to grandson
George Wilson of William Wilson.
1783 tax- William Wilson of George Wilson 100 acres
1783 tax- Rhoda Wilson 200 acres.
1784 William Wilson willed to son George.

SECURITY

Patented in 1745 by John Cahoon for 100 acres in Brinkleys, southwest,
Election district 3, map #17.
8 Oct.1765 Henry Cahoon son of John Cahoon sold to Abraham Outten 100
acres.
7 Sep.1776 Isaac Outten sold to Nathan Cahoon, with CHEESEMANS CHANCE, no
acres mentioned.
1783 tax- Nathan Cahoon 100 acres
1783 tax- Isaac Outten 100 acres
17 Jan 1799 Isaac Outten, wife Margaret Outten of Acco.Co.Va. sold to
John Conner 569 acres of several tracts, unnamed.
11 Nov.1805 John Conner sold to William Coulbourn and William Lankford,
land bought of Isaac Outten, no name.

SECURITY

Patented in 1740 by Daniel Maddux for 310 acres for Fairmount, Election
district 6, map #9.

SECURITY

Patented in 1772 by Henry Lowes for 152 1/2 acres in Mt.Vernon, Election
district 5, map #1.
1783 tax- Henry Lowes 153 acres.

SECURITY

Patented in 1773 by Samuel Miles, a resurvey on MILES DISCOVERY, for 234 acres in Westover Election district 13, map #10.
1826 John Gibbons Jr. willed 17 acres to be sold of SECURITY.

SECURITY

Patented in 1794 by Robert Leatherbury for 9 acres in Mt.Vernon, Election district 5, map #1.
2 Oct 1800 John Leatherbury, wife Sarah Leatherbury sold to Richard Ingersol, with LOTT & MY OWN BEFORE, etc.
24 Dec 1800 Richard Ingersol, sold to Robert Leatherbury with COVINGTONS FOLLY & MY OWN BEFORE.
1 Aug.1800 Robert Leatherbury, wife Elizabeth Leatherbury sold to John Leatherbury 9 acres in Hungary Neck .
7 April 1804 Richard Ingersol, wife Elizabeth Ingersol sold to William Roberts 350 acres of COVINGTONS FOLLY, SECURITY & THE LOTT.

SELAHAMMALETOTH

Patented in 1793 by James Wilson, a resurvey from SUPPORT & JAMES WILDERNESS, for 95 3/4 acres for West Pr.Anne,Election district 1, map #3.

SELF POSSESSION

Patented in 1744 by Robert King for 204 acres on Deals Island, Election district 14, map #8.
30 Nov.1747 Robert King sold to Thomas Laws 29 acres.
1783 tax- John Laws 29 acres
24 Feb.1794 Nehemiah King sold 152 acres to David Wilson.

SEVEN BROTHERS

Patented in 1772 by Samuel Chase and Esther Gale for 784 acres on Smiths Island, Election district 10, map #23.
27 Apr.1792 Samuel Chase, wife Hannah Killy Chase of Baltimore Town sold to Richard Evans, part.
1805 resurveyed to KING RICHARDS GARDEN 714 acres.

SHIPWAYS CHOICE

Patented on 25 Apr.1680 by John Shipway for 250 acres in East Pr.Anne, Election disrict 15, map #4.
1687 John Shipway willed to John Heath at majority, if no issue to sister Mary Heath.
Rent Rolls 1666-1723 possessed by Henry Dorman(married Mary Heath.)
15 Apr.1728 Henry Dorman Jr. son of Henry and Mary Dorman sold part to Matthew Dorman.
1740 resurvey DEEP to SHIPWAYS CHOICE 36 acres.
1748/9 Heber Whittingham per will, lately sold SHIPWAYS CHOICE now called MOORSBOROUGH, with DEEP 197 acres.
3 March 1731 /2 Henry Dorman gave to son Henry 250 acres of DEEP & SHIPWAYS CHOICE.

17 June 1732 Henry Dorman Jr. and wife Catherine Dorman sold to John
Finch part of two tracts that is not included in part belonging to
Abraham Heath cont. 150 acres and 100 acres sold by John Shipway to
Thomas Pollitt.
24 Aug.1733 John Pollitt of Dorc.Co.sold to John Finch 100 acres,
POLLITTS CHOICE which is part of DEEP & SHIPWAYS CHOICE.
13 May 1749 Peter Spence Hack release to Heber Whittingham (mortgage) 1/2
of DEEP & SHIPWAYS CHOICE divised Peter Hack by his grandfather John
Tunstall.
7 March 1769 I Heber Whittingham son of Heber assign rights to John Jones
of William Jones. no acres given.

SHELL TOWN

see DALES ADVENTURE

SHOEMAKERS MEADOW

Patented on 6 May 1685 by John Rowell for 109 acres in Brinkleys,
southeast,Election district 3,map #16.
Rent Rolls 1666-1723 John Rowell deceased.know not the rights.
1739 resurveyed by Jacob Adams 109 acres.
19 March 1739 Jacob Adams gave to son Samuel Adams, after death to
Catherine Adams wife of Jacob Adams.
1740 resurveyed by Samuel Adams to 99 acres.
1745 Jacob Adams deeded to son Samuel.
6 March 1758 Samuel Adams sold 58 2/3 acres and 19 2/3 acres of BOSTONS
PURCHASE & balance of SHOEMAKERS MEADOW.
16 March 1752 William Kersley and wife Elizabeth Kersley sold 50 acres to
Jacob Adams, trade for IRISH GROVE 50 acres.
21 June 1769 William Kersley gave to Isaac Adams and Mary Adams his wife
daughter of William Kersley 147 acres of KERSLEYS INDUSTRY, DISCOVERY,
SHOEMAKERS MEADOW-50 acres.
1774 Thomas Marshall,wife Grace Adams Marshall, gave to son Isaac
Marshall 39 acres.
1783 tax- Samuel Adams 20 acres
1763 tax- Isaac Marshall 39 acres.

SKIPPERS PLANTATION

Patented on 20 Sep.1663 by Matthew Armstrong for 600 acres in Westover,
Election district 13, map #11.
resurveyed 1667 to ARMSTRONGS PURCHASE & ARMSTRONGS LOTT.

SLIPE

Patented in 1791 for 7 1/2 acres by George Miles in St.Peters, Election
district 2, map #6.

SMALL ADDITION

see SMITHS HOPE 6 1/4 acres

SMALL ADDITION

Patented in 1769 for 4 1/2 acres by James Windsor on Deals Island,
Election district 14, map #8.

1780 James Windsor willed to wife Elizabeth Windsor and sons James
Windsor and Isaac Windsor and Henry Windsor COME BY CHANCE & SMALL
ADDITION on Devils Island.

SMALL ADDITION

Patented in 1775 for 3 3/4 acres by Denwood Wilson in West Pr.Anne,
Election district 1, map #3.

SMALL HOPES

Patented on 28 Dec.1668 by William Thorns for 100 acres in Westover,
Election district 13, map #11.
1665 William Thorns willed to wife Winifred Thorns, estate.
Rent Rolls 1666-1723 Posseessed by Gideon Tilghman 100 acres.
1720 Gideon Tilghman gave to sons Solomon Tilghman and Moses Tilghman 50
acres each.(Solomon died before division)
9 March 1730 Moses Tilghman sold to Aaron Tilghman 100 acres.
21 Aug.1735 Gideon Tilghman of Coventry Parish gave to brother Aaron
Tilghman(with THOMPSONS ADVENTURE)
1747 resurveyed PART TO TILGHMANS ADVENTURE 180 acres.

SMALL HOPES

Patented in 1788 by Samuel Smith for 1 1/2 acres in Brinkleys, northeast,
Election district 3, map #15.
5 Feb.1789 Samuel Smith sold 1 1/2 acres to Thomas Beauchamp.
20 Sep.1796 Thomas Beauchamp,wife Sarah Beauchamp sold to William
Williams.
11 Jan 1798 William Williams, wife Polly Williams sold to Thomas Adams
part.
11 Jan 1798 William Williams, wife Polly Williams, sold to David Potter
78 1/4 acres of BEAUCHAMPS VENTURE & SMALL HOPES
11 Jan 1798 David Potter sold to Phillip Adams 78 1/4 acres of BEAUCHAMPS
VENTURE & SMALL HOPES.
14 Sep.1804 David Potter, wife Mary Potter sold to Phillip Adams 78 1/4
acres of BEAUCHAMPS VENTURE & SMALL HOPES.

SMALL LOT

Patented on 9 Oct.1747 by William Jones for 8 acres in Westover, Election
district 13, map #11.
8 May 1752 William Jones,wife Sarah Jones, sold to Samuel Handy 8 acres.

SMALL LOT

Patented in 1802 for 8 1/4 acres by William White in Dames Quarter,
Election district 11, map #7.

SMITHFIELD

Patented on 8 July 1682 by Randal Revell and assigned to James Ingram for
100 acres in East Pr.Anne,Election district 15, map #4.
12 June 1688 James Ingram of Wicomico and wife Mary Ingram sold 100 acres
to Roger Phillips.

Rent Rolls 1666-1723 Roger Phillips.
1698 Roger Phillips willed to daughter Phoebe Phillips.
1743 Thomas Pollitt willed to wife Sarah Pollitt.

SMITHFIELD

see SMITHS RESOLVE

SMITHS HOPE

Patented on 25 May 1683 by Capt.Henry Smith for 100 acres in East
Pr.Anne,Election district 15, map #5.
20 Jan 1687 Capt.Henry Smith, wife Ann Smith, sold to Henry Phillips who
died intestate and it descended to son Charles Phillips.
Rent Rolls 1666-1723 Henry Phillips.
16 Aug.1727 William Owens and wife Sarah Owens sold to William Polk 100
acres bought of Charles Phillips.
1750 resurvey ADDITION 220 acres.
2 Apr.1754 James Polk sold to William Heath ADDITION 220 acres.
1770 SMALL ADDITION surveyed for 6 1/2 acres.
1783 William Heath willed to son Abraham Heath lands on west side of road
from Princess Anne Town tothe lands of George Pollitt, and to son John
Heath part. of afsd. no name.
21 June 1770 James Polk gave to son Benjamin Polk 220 acres.
1783 tax- James Polk 236 acres
1783 tax- Benjamin Polk 100 acres & ADDITION 194 acres & SMALL ADDITION 6
1/4 acres.
29 Apr.1794 Benjamin Polk Sr. sold 10 1/4 acres to William Jones
7 Nov.1798 Whittington Polk son of Benjamin Polk sold to Thomas King 100
acres and ADDITION TO SMITHS HOPE 95 acres.

SMITH ISLAND

see PITCHCROFT, TWO BROTHERS & BLUFF HAMMOCKS.

SMITHS ADVENTURE

see SAMUELS ADVENTURE

SMITHS LOTT

Patented in 1740 by Henry Smith for 45 acres in Brinkleys, northwest,
Election district 3, map #14.
1746/7 Henry Smith willed to son Henry Smith
1757 resurveyed to HORSEYS PREVENTION 280 1/4 acres.

SMITHS POLICY

Patented on 9 March 1723 by Isaac Stitt for 75 acres in East Pr.Anne,
Election district 15, map #5.
1774 Archibald Stitt sold 75 acres to William Knox son of Robert Knox of
North Carolina.
29 Nov.1774 William Knox of Pitt Co. North Carolina sold 75 acres to John
Pollitt.
1783 tax- John Pollitt 75 acres.

SMITHS RECOVERY

Patented on 2 Dec.1679 by Henry Smith from part of THOMPSONS PURCHASE &
NASWORTHYS CHOICE for 700 acres in West Pr.Anne, Election district 1, map
#3.
17 Aug.1720 John Caldwell kinsman and attorney for John Smith heir at law
of Capt. Henry Smith deceased conveyed to John Everton 99 acres.
24 Dec 1726 John Everton sold to the debtors for the Public School 99
acres now called EVERTONS CHOICE.
Rent Rolls 1666-1723 Phillip Fitzgerald in right of the orphans of
Edward Wheeler 150 acres.
 John Tunstall 300 acres
 Thomas Everton 100 acres
 John Pollock 150 acres.
2 Sep.1727 William Wheeler son of Edward Wheeler sold to John Tunstall
120 acres now called WHEELERS DESIRE.
1750 David Wilson gave to son David Wilson, purchased of Kendal Hack in
Indian Town where John Tunstall formerly lived.
1751 triparte-Tunstall Hack of Northumberland Co.Va. and grandson of John
Tunstall of Som.Co. deceased sold to Ephraim King and Thomas Jones of
Manokin for 5 shillings part that John Tunstall devised to his grandson
310 acres and by which tract WHEELERS DESIRE was purchased by William
Wheeler adj. 120 acres.
1 Nov.1751 Charles Hall of Kent Co. Md. sold to William Raisen,150 acres
sold by John Polk and wife to Alexander Hall called BILLENDUE being part
of SMITHS RECOVERY.
11 June 1752 William Raisen of Kent Co. Md. sold to Ephraim Wilson
17 Jan 1786 David Wilson son of David,wife Sarah Wilson gave to James
Wilson son of David. If no heirs to Ephraim Wilson son of David Wilson.
1764 resurveyed to WILSONS PURCHASE 609 acres.
9 Nov.1802 James Wilson sold to John B. Slemons, SMITHS RECOVERY all not
included in resurvey by Daniel Wilson.
9 Nov.1802 John King, wife Harriett Hamilton King sold to Rev. John B.
Slemons, land divised by grandfather Isaac Holland and conveyed to Isaac
Holland by visitors of Eden School 100 7/8 acres.
9 Nov.1802 Whittington King sold to John B.Slemons 1/2 acre.
9 Nov.1802 John B. Slemons sold to Whittington King 1/2 acre.

SMITHS RESOLVE

Patented on 29 May 1683 by Capt.Henry Smith for 350 acres in East
Pr.Anne, Election district 15, map #5.
1697 Thomas Smith willed to son Roger Smith.
13 June 1688 Capt. Henry Smith, wife Ann Smith sold to Samuel Johnson and
Joan Wallace 250 acres.
2 Sep.1719 Robert Smith son of Thomas Smith, and wife Mary Smith sold 100
acres to John Gray Jr. sold by Henry Smith to Thomas Smith part called
SMITHFIELD.
Rent Rolls 1666-1723, 250 acres William Pollock, 100 acres William Smith.
26 Nov.1754 James Gray and William Gray sold to Jarvis Ballard part of
SMITHSFIELD,that is part of SMITHS RESOLVE 100 acres.
22 Apr.1760 Jarvis Ballard sold to Thomas Jones 17 acres
1783 tax- William Ballard 100 acres
1783 tax- Jesse Walston 100 acres.
1795 resurveyed to CONCLUSION 380 acres.

12 March 1799 William Ballard of Jarvis Ballard sold 100 acres to Levin Ballard.
29 March 1800 William Ballard of Jarvis Ballard, sold to Lambert Hyland 100 acres of SMITHFIELD.
30 March 1803 Priscilla Walston widow of Jarvis Ballard sold to Lambert Hyland her dower rghts.
27 Dec.1803 Col. William Jones son of William Jones, wife Eleanor Jones sold to John Bloodsworth 17 acres.

SMYTHS LOT

Patented in 1762 for 60 acres in Westover,Election district 13, map #11 by William Smith.
21 Feb.1782 Samuel Smith,wife Esther Smith sold 60 acres to Joseph Tilghman.
1783 tax- Samuel Smith 60 acres.
10 Jan 1786 Mary Smith widow of William Smith sold to Samuel Smith her dower right for 5 shillings, land between Manokin and Pocomoke Rivers, no name.
5 Nov.1798 Joseph Tilghman, wife Nancy Tilghman sold to George Broughton.
24 Feb.1801 George Broughton, wife Alee Broughton, sold to John Miles 81 1/4 acres of HUNTSMANS FOLLY, JOSEPHS FOLLY, SMYTHS LOTT & EXCHANGE.
24 Feb 1801 John Miles sold to George Broughton 126 acres of same.
24 Feb 1801 George Broughton, wife Alee Broughton sold to William Beauchamp 57 1/4 acre of HUNTSMANS FOLLY, SMYTHS LOTT, & EXCHANGE.
24 Feb.1801 William Beauchamp sold to George Broughton lands William Beauchamp holds by deed from Joseph Tilghman and George Broughton 81 1/2 acres.

SNOW HILL

see LATE DISCOVERY

SNOW WATER

Patented in 1768 by Benjamin Lankford for 18 1/2 acres in Brinkleys, northwest, Election district 3, map #14.
1783 tax- Benjamin Lankford 18 1/2 acres
1784/88 Benjamin Lankford willed to son Kellum Lankford 9 acres, and to daughter Priscilla Howard (wife of George Howard)
28 Feb.1794 George Howard,wife Priscilla Howard sold to Severn Howard, 9 acres.
1832 Mary Ann Lankford (widow of Noah Lankford) willed to daughter Mary Ann Holland.

SOMERSET

Patented on 8 Aug.1723 by John Jones and Thomas Dashiell for 50 acres in St.Peters,Election district 2, map #6.
1755 Thomas Dashiell willed tract where Money Church stands to said church.

SOMERSETSHIRE

Patented in 1764 by Stephen Garland in Westover,Election district 13 map#11.
2 Jan 1766 Stephen Garland sold to Thomas Dashiell,sheriff, 13 1/2 acres for bail of prisoner in jail.

10 March 1767 Thomas Dashiell, sheriff, sold to John White.
10 March 1767 John White sold 13 1/2 acres to Stephen Garland
1783 tax- Stephen Garland.

SOMETHING WORTH

Patented in 1724 by Jonathan Shaw for 44 acres in Westover, Election
district 13, map #10.
16 Jan 1759 Teague Riggin of Worc. Co.,tailor, and wife Mary Riggin only
child of Jonathan Shaw deceased sold 44 acres to William Furniss son of
James Furniss for 5 shillings.
1765 James Furniss willed to son George Furniss.
16 Aug.1769 William Furniss Jr.son of William, and wife Sarah Furniss
sold to brother George Furniss.
21 Aug.1772 George Furniss Jr. sold 44 acres to Isaiah Tilghman.
1783 tax- Isaiah Tilghman 44 acres
1790 Isaiah Tilghman willed to son James Tilghman 44 acres.

SOMETHING WORTH

Patented in 1701 by John Panter for 675 acres in St.Peters,Election
district 2, map #6.
1702 John Panter willed to cousin Catherine Laws and her children.
1713 /4 John Panter willed to William Sasser 150 acres and part to
William Laws son of Robert Laws.
24 Nov.1769 Robert Laws son of William Laws,and wife Mary Laws sold to
Whitty McClemmy and Robert Elzey for 5 shillings.
24 Nov.1769 Robert Laws and wife Mary Laws sold to Billy Laws son of
Panter Laws 50 acres.
1 Dec.1778 Robert Laws of Sussex Co.Del. sold 50 acres to Billy Laws.
1783 tax- William Sasser Jr. 150 acres
1783 tax- Benjamin Sasser 134 acres
1783 tax- heirs of Robert Elzey 68 acres
1783 tax- William Laws 50 acres
1783 tax- John Laws 66 1/2 acres
1783 tax- Whitty McClemmy 68 1/2 acres

SONS CHOICE

Patented in 1665 for 300 acres in Brinkleys, southeast, Election district
3, map #16.
1764 Robert Jenkins Henry willed to son Robert J. Henry 1/3rd part of
LIMBRICK being part of SONS CHOICE.

SONS CHOICE

see BROTHERS LOVE

SONNES CHOICE

Patented in 1776 for by Mark Manlove for 300 acres in Brinkleys,
southeast, Election district 3, map #16.
1666 Mark Manlove willed to wife Eliza Manlove and to sons Mark Manlove,
William Manlove and Christopher Manlove, lands unnamed.
18 Sep 1678 Mark Manlove sold to David Lindzey 133 1/3 acres
27 Feb.1679 William Manlove and wife Alice Manlove sold to Mark Manlove

133 1/3 acres now called BROTHERS LOVE.
22 Feb.1688 Josias Seward and wife Margaret Seward sold to William
Traille 25 acres.

SOUTH BETHERTON

Patented on 15 Sep.1665 by William Thorn for 300 acres in West
Pr.Anne,Election district 1, map #3.
1665 William Thorn willed to John Richards at age 21, 300 acres
1697 David Brown willed to John Brown.
Rent Rolls 1666-1723 John Brown, given by the widow of Thomas Brown who
had the right.
1 March 1738 Thomas Brown eldest son of Alexander Brown and Mary Brown
and Margaret Brown two daughters of Alexander Brown gave to brother David
Brown, that David willed to John Brown and his male heirs.
part resurveyed to BROWNS LOTT 132 acres
part resurveyd to NO NAME by David Brown.

SOUTH FORELAND

Patented on 28 Apr.1675 by Thomas Walker and assigned to Thomas Roe, for
50 acres on Deals Island,Election district 14, map #8.
5 March 1678 Thomas Roe, wife Ann Roe sold to Henry Leaton.
6 April 1684 Henry Leaton and wife Margaret Leaton sold to John Windsor.
Rent Rolls 1666-1723 Graves Jarrett
1783 tax- Nehemiah King 37 1/2 acres.

SOUTH LOTT

Patented in 1727 for 200 acres by Thomas Williams in Brinkleys,
northwest, Election district 3, map #14.
2 Dec.1767 Thomas Williams gave to grandson Thomas Williams Jr. 200
acres.
1767 resurveyed to WILLIAMS GREEN 644 3/4 acres

SPITTLE

Patented on 4 Nov.1706 by Abraham Heath for 22 acres in East Pr.Anne,
Election district 15, map #4.
Rent Rolls 1666-1723 Abraham Heath
7 June 1740 Dorman Heath gave to wife Perthenia Heath and to daughters
Rachel Heath and Sarah Heath DEEP & SPITTLE.
4 Dec.1783 Wilson Heath and Jesse Heath sold to Josiah Hobbs of Sussex
Co.Del. 22 acres.
1783 tax- Wilson Heath 22 acres
7 Apr.1795 Josiah Hobbs and wife Rebecca Hobbs sold to Ezekiel Haynie 22
acres.
1 June 1808 Thomas Curtis trustee to sell the RE of Thomas Jones sold 20
acres to Matthias Miles.

SPORTING FIELD

Patented in 1749 for 50 acres by John Adams in East Pr.Anne Election
district 15, map #4.
1 Aug.1792 William Adams Jr.,wife Louise Adams sold 50 acres to Thomas
Pollitt Jr.

STAKE RIDGE

Patented on 6 Sep.1667 by Ambrose London for 10 acres in Fairmount, Election district 6, map #9.
19 March 1685 Ambrose London sold to Michael Williams.
1699 Michael Williams willed to son Nathaniel Williams.
2 Sep.1723 Nathaniel Williams sold to Samuel Handy 10 acres
Rent Rolls 1666-1723 Samuel Handy.
7 Apr.1724 Samuel Handy sold to Thomas Handy
2 Oct.1747 George Tucker of Isle of Barbadoes and wife Mary Tucker (Mary Handy d/o Thomas Handy) sold 10 acres to Samuel Handy.
24 Sep.1751 John Handy of Dorc. Co. and wife Elizabeth Handy sold to brother Samuel Handy
7 Jan 1757 Samuel Handy sold 10 acres to Thomas Seon.
2 Sep.1767 Thomas Seon sold to Whitty Turpin
1 Aug.1796 Thomas Holbrook,wife Peggy Holbrook daughter of Whitty Turpin, sold to Henry Coston and Whittington King land conveyed by Thomas Seon to Whitty Turpin. unnamed

STANSTEADS ABBY

Patented on 4 Dec.1677 by William Stevens and assigned to Richard Barns and John Sterling for 50 acres in Asbury,
Election district 12, map #21.
Rent Rolls 1666-1723- 25 acres by Richard Barns and 25 acres by John Sterling son of John.
1710 Richard Barnes,wife Avis Barnes, left land to son Richard Barnes at age 20.
2 Jan 1718 John Sterling with Richard Barnes bought of James Ward and wife Mary Ward, Morris Dougan and wife Sarah Dougan of Dorc.Co. and from a son of Richard Barns.
1783 tax- Mary Sterling 50 acres.

STARLINGS CHANCE

Patented on 4 Apr.1748 by John Sterling for 38 acres in Asbury,Election district 12, map #21.
1783 tax- Mary Sterling

STERLINGS CHOICE

Patented on 17 July 1670 by John White and assigned to John Sterling for 50 acres in Asbury,Election district 12, map #21
Rent Rolls 1666-1723 John Sterling son of John.
1783 tax- Aaron Sterling
1795 Aaron Sterling son of John Sterling willed to son Aaron Sterling Jr.

STERLINGS FANCY

Patented in 1758 for 9 acres by John Sterling in Asbury, Election district 12, map #21.
1783 tax- Mary Sterling 9 acres

STERLINGS GOOD LUCK

Patented on 9 Sep.1761 by Aaron Sterling for 58 3/4 acres in
Asbury,Election district 12, map#21.
31 Aug.1762 Aaron Sterling -lease trust, to Southy Whittington, after
death of Aaron, then on behalf of Littleton Sterling.
1783 tax- Aaron Sterling 50 acres.

STERLINGS TRIUMPH

Patented in 1809 for 15 acres by Aaron Sterling in Lawsons, Election
district 8, map #19.

STEVENS MEADOW

Patented on 20 Sep.1701 by William Stevens for 188 acres in Fairmount,
Election district 6, map #7.
1699 Michael Williams willed to son Nathaniel Williams.
2 Sep.1723 Nathaniel Williams sold to Samuel Handy 188 acres.
Rent Rolls 1666-1733 Samuel Handy
7 Apr.1724 Samuel Handy sold to Thomas Handy 1/2.
2 Oct.1747 George Tucker of Isle of Barbadoes and wife Mary Tucker sold
to Samuel Handy 188 acres.
24 Sep.1751 John Handy of Dorc.Co. wife Elizabeth Handy sold to Samuel
Handy
7 Jan 1757 Samuel Handy sold 188 acres to Thomas Seon
2 Sep.1767 Thomas Seon sold to Whitty Turpin.
1 Aug.1796 Thomas Holbrook and wife Peggy Holbrook, daughter of Whitty
Turpin, sold to Whittington King and Henry Coston.
22 May 1804 Whittington King, wife Nancy King, and Henry Coston, wife
Anna Coston sold to William King land conveyed by Thomas Holbrook,
unnamed.

STONEY POINT

Patented in 1730 by Levin Denwood for 1963 acres, a resurvey from
ADDITION TO HACKLAND in West Pr.Anne, Election district 1, map #3.
Rent Rolls 1666-1723 possessed by Betty Gale wife of George Gale and
daughter of Levin Denwood.
12 Apr.1796 Littleton Gale of Cecil Co. Md. sold to Levin Gale 125 acres,
alloted Robert Gale by division of the Real Estate of Levin Gale and
descended to Littleton Gale by the death of Robert Gale.
23 Sep.1796 George Gale of Cecil Co.Md. and Samuel Wilson, wife Leah
Wilson sold to Levin Gale 1/2 of land conveyed by Denwood Wilson and by
the death of Robert Gale.
10 Feb.1797 Levin Gale of Somerset Co. and Littleton Gale of Cecil Co.
sold 58 acres to William Whitney.
1801 Levin Gale willed to son Henry George Gale
(this is probalby the plantation of TUSCULUM)

STONIDGE

Patented on 4 Apr.1680 by Nicholas Smith for 50 acres in West Pr.Anne,
Election district 1, map #3.
Rent Rolls- is part of a later survey by special warrent for Levin
Denwood in 1681
1709 resurveyed by Levin Denwood for 300 acres..
1783 tax- Levin Gale 300 acres.

STREIGHTS

Patented on 4 Sep.1663 by George Johnson for 600 acres in Westover,
Election district 3, map #11.
Rent Rolls 1666-1723 belongs to heirs of George Johnson in
England.Possessed by John Heath 300 acres and Thomas Beauchamp 300 acres.
1681 George Johnson willed to wife Frances Johnson.
9 May 1723 Ann Johnson daughter of George Johnson of parish of
St.Pauls,Covent Garden, of Middlesex county England sold to Robert King
600 acres.
1726 resurvey to CONCLUSION by Robert King 1500 acres.

STRIFE

Patented in 1751 for 1 1/4 acre by William Heath in East Pr.Anne Election
district 15, map #4.
1783 tax- William Heath

STRIFE

Patented in 1767 by Henry Walston Miles for 38 3/4 acres in St.Peters,
Election district 2, map #6.
1783 tax- Henry Walston Miles 38 3/4 acres.

STRUGGLE

Patented in 1747 for 200 acres by William Jones in Westover, Election
district 13, map #11.
1757 resurveyed to HANDYS PURCHASE 263 acres.
1778 Samuel Handy willed to sons Samuel and Isaac Handy
1781 Samuel Handy willed to wife Mary Handy and then to Levin Colbert son
of Isaac Colbert.
1806 William Handy of Scott Co.Ky sold 24 1/2 acres to John Colbert.
23 Jan 1805 William Moore, Neal Colbert,wife Alice Colbert and Elizabeth
Williams sold to John Colbert 30 1/2 acres.
Lands formerly held by Nancy Colbert who married William Moore, no name.

STRUGGLE

see SALISBURY

SUCESS

Patented in 1752 by Arnold Ballard for 121 acres in St.Peters,Election
district 2,map #6.
1783 tax- Arnold Ballard 121 acres
9 Aug.1785 Arnold Ballard sold 61 acres to son William Ballard.
27 Oct 1795 William Ballard,wife Jane Ballard sold to Thomas Ballard 61
acres
27 Oct.1795 Thomas Ballard sold 10 acres to Ballard Reed
1806 Arnold Ballard willed to son Thomas Ballard.

SUCESS

Patented on 26 Feb.1663 by Thomas Bloyd for 300 acres in St.Peters,
Election district 2, map #6.
Rent Rolls 1666-1723 possessed by Bloyce Wright heir of Thomas Bloyd.
1757 resurveyd to BLOOMSBURY 820 3/4 acres.

SUDLERS CONCLUSION

Patented in 1789, a resurvey of BARNABYS LOTT, for 419 3/4 acres by
Thomas Seon Sudler in Fairmount, Election district 6, map #9.
1978-possessed by Mr.and Mrs. Joseph Eberly- the house build c.1800-
Marylander and Hearld newspaper.

SUFFOLK

Patented on 11 June 1679 by William Morris for 1000 acres in Dublin,
Election district 4, map #13.
20 March 1677 William Stevens, wife Elizabeth Stevens sold to Thomas
Jarvis of Elizabeth City Va. who assigned the rights to William Morris of
Elizabeth City Va.
23 Feb.1682 William Morris and wife Rebecca Morris sold to John Tripshaw
75 acres now called HARTS CONTENT.
23 Feb 1682 William Morris and wife Rebecca Morris sold to Richard
Aldridge 75 acres now called FREE CHOICE.
4 Feb 1688 William Morris, wife Elizabeth Morris sold to John Tripshaw 75
acres.
16 March 1719 William Morris of Kent Co. Del. sold 200 acres to William
Mills.
Rent Rolls 1666-1723 Possessed by -
 Robert Hitch 446 acres
 held by Archibald Smith in right of the orphans of John Tripshaw, 75
 acres
 John Tull who hath sold to Williams Mills vide Samuel Morris account
 200 acres.
1721 Samuel Handy gave to son William Handy
1733 William Handy willed to son Samuel Handy 444 acres
1748/9 William Mills willed to grandsons Stephen Mills and William Mills
plantation where I live next to Samuel Handy
20 Aug.1750 William Mills willed to son William Mills
11 Sep.1764 William Mills sold to Stephen Mills 137 1/2 acres.
1 Apr.1768 Samuel Handy son of William Handy,and wife Mary Handy of
Worc.Co. sold to George Hayward. 448 acres.
22 March 1775 John Handy sold 13 acres to George Watson
18 Apr.1775 John Handy sold 23 acres to John Mitchell
23 Aug.1776 John Handy sold 44 acres to George Waters.
1783 tax- Stephen Mills 275 acres
1783 tax- John Mitchell 20 1/2 acres
1783 tax- George Waters 446 1/2 acres
4 March 1785 John Handy sold 39 acres to George Waters.
4 March 1785 George Waters,wife Betty Waters sold to John Handy 13 acres
and 20 acres of same.
1795 George Waters gave part to son Thomas Waters and part to son John
Watters.
10 June 1800 William Handy son of John Handy, of Worc.Co. sold his
interest to Teague Donoho.
18 April 1807 John Waters, wife Elizabeth Waters sold to Whittington Polk
330 acres.
9 Jan 1810 Thomas Waters son of George Waters, wife Elizabeth Waters sold
to Thomas Mitchell Jones, part.
1829 Harriet Dryden gave to Robert W. Swan 140 acres belonging to father
Thomas M. Jones.

1836 Levin Pollitt willed to Ann B. Porter daughter of George Porter, part.
1848 Samuel S.Bonnewell gave to wife Ann Bonnewell 139 1/2 acres.

SUFFOLK NECK
see SASAFRAS NECK

SUIEKIERKE

Patented on 1 June 1683 by William Stevens for 50 acres in St.Peters, Election district 2, map #6.
Maps indicate it is out of GEORGES ADVENTURE.
Rent Rolls 1666-1723 possessed by John Irving who married Frances Betts.
1753 resurveyed to GEORGES ADVENTURE 364 acres.

SUMMERS ADDITION

Patented in 1785 for 19 3/4 acres by Thomas Summers in Lawsons, Election district 8, map #19.

SUNKEN GROUND

Patented on 16 Nov.1694 by George Hey for 100 acres in Brinkleys, southwest, Election district 3, map #17.
Rent Rolls 1666-1723 George Hey
1708 George Hey of Annamessex, willed to wife Sarah Hey 100 acres of dwelling plantation, she to convey to John Dukes 100 acres.
1716 John Dukes willed to wife Ann Dukes 100 acres.
1 March 1719 Ann Dukes relic of John Dukes sold to Thomas Potter
1783 tax- Thomas W. Potter 100 acres.
7 April 1810 Elijah Potter, wife Dolly Potter, sold to Isaac Adams 2 acres.

SUPPORT

Patented on 8 Aug.1775 by Levin Boston for 36 acres in Brinkleys, southeast, Election district 3, map #16.
16 Dec.1777 Levin Boston sold 3 acres to William White and 26 acres to Jesse Hall.
10 Oct.1779 Jesse Hall sold to Thomas Wilson 17 acres.
1783 tax- Thomas Wilson 3 acres
9 Feb.1786 William Wood,wife Naomi Wood sold to Jacob Adams 45 acres of TULLY BRISK,SUPPORT,NAN ELLIS RIDGE or BOSTONS ADVENTURE.
5 Sep.1785 Thomas Wilson sold to William Wood 17 acres.
7 Sep.1806 Jesse Hall sold to Elijah Hall 26 1/4 acres.

SUPPORT

Patented in 1733 for 30 acres by Robert Geddes in East Pr.Anne, Election district 15, map #5.

SUPPORT

Patented in 1744 by Col.Robert King for 37 acres on Deal Island,Election district 14, map #8.
24 Feb.1795 Nehemiah King sold 37 acres to David Wallace.

27 Dec 1797 Esme Merrill, wife Gertrude Merrill sold to Thomas White 7 acres of SUPPORT on road from Rehobeth to Oystershell town.
5 May 1806 Esme Merrill, wife Gertrude Merrill sold to Stephen Collins 5 acres of ADDITION TO SUPPORT.

SUPPORT

Patented in 1747 by Thomas Gillis for 138 acres in West Pr.Anne,Election district 1, map #2.
15 Feb 1760 Thomas Gillis sold to Levin Gillis 138 acres
1783 tax- Levin Gillis

SUPPORT

Patented in 1774 by Matthias Miles for 57 acres in East Pr.Anne,Election district 15, map #5.
1778 William Badley willed to son James Dean Badley 57 acres.
1802 resurveyed to WINTER HARBOUR 183 acres

SUPPORT

Patented in 1774 by James Elzey for 42 acres in West Pr.Anne,Election district 1, map #3.
2 June 1783 Nathaniel Ramsey,commissioner to sell British confiscated property sold 42 1/2 acres to William Polk.
4 Feb.1792 William Polk sold to Samuel Williams 42 1/2 who repatented it for 42 1/2 acres.acres.
1793 resurveyed to SELAHAMMALEKOTH 95 3/4 acres.

SWEETWOOD

Patented on 12 Feb.1663 by Sarah Jordan for 300 acres in Mt.Vernon, Election district 5, map #1.
13 June 1665 Sarah Ballard now wife of Charles Ballard, relic of John Elzey and widow of Thomas Jordan repatented.
11 June 1672 Charles Ballard of G. and wife Sarah Ballard sold to Cornelius Johnson 300 acres.
1687 Cornelius Johnson willed to William Jones and Daniel Jones.
1752 repatented by Nehemiah Covington 300 acres.
4 Jan 1754 Nehemiah Covington and Philip Covington sold 100 acres to Daniel Jones.
1758 Daniel Jones gave to son Phillip Jones 100 acres bought of Nehemiah Covington and 20 acres bought of James Covington.
20 June 1759 Nehemiah Covington and wife Betty Covington of Dorc.Co. and Daniel Jones and wife Elizabeth Jones of Som.Co. sold to Phillip Covington all interest in SWEETWOOD.
9 July 1766 Mary Covington admx. of Phillip Covington deceased sold 300 acres to Levin Gale(highest bidder).
1783 tax- Levin Gale 200 acres.
25 Oct.1800 Littleton Gale of Cecil Co. Md. sold to Levin Jones and John Leatherbury of Som.Co. COVINGTONS CONCLUSION, COVINGTONS ADVENTURE & SWEETWOOD part of the real estate of Levin Gale, total 650 acres.
18 May 1801 Samuel Wilson and wife Leah Wilson (late Leah Gale) sold to Levin Jones and John Leatherbury, their claim.
8 June 1802 John Leatherbury,wife Sally Leatherbury sold to Levin Jones

220 7/8 acres of COVINGTONS CONCLUSION, SWEETWOOD, MANNINGS RESOLUTION
8 Jan 1802 Levin Jones sold to John Leatherbury of Robert Leatherbury 400
acres of same as above.
3 Aug.1807 John Leatherbury and wife Sally Leatherbury sold to Lucretia
Jones.

SWINE YARD

Patented in 1755 by David McGrath for 21 acres in West Pr.Anne, Election
district 1, map #2.
20 June 1766 Levin McGrath sold to John McGrath.
1788 John McGrath willed to nephew David McGrath
21 Apr.1792 David McGrath gave to son Levin McGrath
9 Apr.1793 David McGrath sold to Sarah McGrath widow of John McGrath,
21 acres.
24 Feb 1800 Sheriff's sale, property of Levin McGrath, to Levin Gale,
HOBBS ADVENTURE, PRIVILEDGE & SWINE YARD 75 acres
15 March 1803 George Robertson, sheriff confirmed deed to Henry George
Gale and Betsy Ann Wilson Gale children of Levin Gale Jr. deceased.

TAMROONS RIDGE

Patented on 28 June 1679 by Gilbert James and assigned to Phillip Ascue
for 250 acres in East Pr.Anne,Election District 15, map #4.
Rent Rolls 1666-1723 Phillip Ascue son of Phillip.
27 Aug.1739 William Polk gave to son David Polk 125 acres bought of Bryan
Snee
1743 Thomas Pollitt willed to wife Sarah Pollitt.
20 Aug.1760 Joseph Stanford,wife Sarah Stanford sold 50 acres conveyed to
Joseph Stanford by Thomas Pollitt, sold to Jonathan Pollitt.
1770 ADDITION patented for 217 1/2 acres
5 March 1776 David Polk gave to son Gillis Polk
4 Apr.1780 George Pollitt sold to Jonathan Pollitt 21 1/2 acres, the
right of survey between LONG RIDGE & TAMAROONS RIDGE.
1783 tax George Pollitt 172/12 acres, ADDITION
1783 tax- Jonathan Pollitt 50 acres, ADDITION 21 1/2 acres.
1791 resurvey to CONSOLIDATION 820 3/4 acres
1806 Jonathan Pollitt willed to wife Mary Pollitt 50 acres and ADDITION
21 1/2 acres.

TAN YARD

see ADVENTURE & GOOD HOPE 10 acres

TAUNTON DEANNE

Patented on 27 June 1669 by Capt.William Thorn 300 acres in Mt.Vernon,
Election district 5, map #1.
29 Sep.1668 William Thorn and wife Winifred Thorn sold to Francis Roberts
300 acres.
20 June 1670 Francis Roberts and wife Rosanna Roberts sold to Benjamin
Cottman.
5 June 1677 Benjamin Cottman, wife Mary Cottman sold 50 acres to Richard
Kimball, called KIMBALLS PURCHASE.
Rent Rolls 1666-1723 Possessed by Benjamin Nesham who married the widow
of Benjamin Cottman who was vested in the right and holds for the orphans

of Benjamin Cottman.
7 March 1720 Benjamin Cottman sold to Thomas Serman 70 acres.
2 4 March 1721 Thomas Serman and wife Elizabeth Serman sold to Benjamin
Cottman Sr. 2 parcels now called WELCOME HOME AGAIN & CHANCE within the
bounds of TAUNTON DEANNE.
20 Aug.1733 Benjamin Cottman gave to son William Cottman 150 acres
31 Oct.1734 Benjamin Cottman gave to son Benjamin Cottman Jr. now of
Pennnsylvania, lower part.
7 Feb.1743 Benjamin Cottman the younger of Philadelphia Co.Pa. sold 186
acres to Joseph Cottman of Somerset Co.
15 Sep.1750 William Cottman gave to son Benjamin Cottman 150 acres.
1783 tax- Joseph Cottman 186 acres
1783 tax- Benjamin Cottman

TAYLORS CHOICE

Patented on 9 March 1663 by Walter Taylor for 600 acres in West Pr.Anne,
Election district 1, map #3.
1665 resurveyed to SOUTH BETHERTON

TAYLORS GOOD LUCK

Patented in 1762 by Walter Taylor for 50 acres in East Pr.Anne,Election
district 15, map #4.
1783 tax- Stephen Taylor 25 acres
1783 tax- George Bayley 25 acres
3 Feb.1784 Walter Taylor sold to Mills Bayley 24 acres.
1 Sep.1790 Walter Taylor of Kent Co.Del. sold 23 3/4 acres to Henry
Banks.

TAYLORS PRIVILEDGE

Patented in 1768, a resurvey by Walter Taylor, includes CHADWICKS
ADVENTURE, for 163 1/2 acres in West Pr.Anne, Election district 1, map
#2.
1783 tax- Stephen Taylor 98 3/4 acres
1783 tax- Walter Taylor 131 acres
8 Dec.1783 Walter Taylor mortgaged to Solomon Gibbons of Worc.Co. 13 1/2
acres with HARMON, HOGQUARTER, LOTT,
1 Sep.1790 Walter Taylor of Kent Co.Del. sold to Henry Banks of Som.Co.
102 1/4 acres.
8 Apr.1796 Walter Taylor of Kent Co.Del.sold to Jacob Morris 13 1/2
acres.

TERSOE

Patented in 1665 for 300 acres by Mark Manlove in Brinkleys, southeast,
Election district 3, map #16.
3 March 1724 Robert Nairn, gave to son Robert 1/2 of NAIRNS SECURITY 300
acres and 50 acres of GEORGES MARSH and part of TERSO and NAIRNS ADDITION
10 acres
18 Dec.1742 John Hall and wife Ann Hall sold to James Nairn part of
PIMORE & TERSO, a small piece between their plantations.
1783 tax- Robert Marshall 150 acres
8 May 1795 James Nairn of Worc.Co. sold for 10 shillings his interest in
to Levi Wood Hall

15 May 1795 Levi Wood Hall and John Hall sold to James Harper 164 acres and 12 acres of marsh of PIMORE & TERSOE.
1814 Robert Marshall willed to Robert Nearn Marshall
1834 Isaac Riggin willed to son John T.W. Riggin 164 acres PIMORE & TERSO.

TEAGUES ADDITION

Surveyed in 1730 by John Teague for 78 acres. This land not patented but could be in Fairmount Election District 6, not on maps.
20 Feb.1756 John Teague of Worc.Co. sold to Spencer Waters AHILL & LOWES HAMMOCK at Manokin River.
19 Aug.1806 Hugh Henry and wife Harriett Henry sold to William Waters of John Waters land held by Spencer Martin Waters grandfather to Harriett, GRAYS IMPROVEMENT, TEAGUED DOWN, TEAGUES ADDN. & AHILL on the south side of the Manokin River, no acreage given.
1808 William Waters willed Pocomoke lands 1100 acres to son William Gillis Waters.

TEAGUES DOWNE

Patented on 6 Sep.1667 by Ambrose London for 16 acres in Fairmount, Election district 6, map #9.
9 Aug.1676 Ambrose London, wife Mary London sold to Mary Riggian alias Mary London, wife of Teague Riggin.
July 1687 Teague Riggin, wife Mary Riggin sold to Miles Gray 16 acres with LAST CHOICE.
Rent Rolls 1666-1723 Belongs to Samuel Handy who purchased from Thomas Newbold purchaser from Ambrose London.
1721 Samuel Handy gave lands to sons Samuel Handy and Thomas Handy.
19 Aug.1806 Hugh Henry and wife Harriett Henry sold to William Waters of John Waters, land held by Spencer Martin Waters grandfather of Harriett Henry, GRAYS IMPROVEMENT, TEAGUES DOWN, TEAGUES ADDITION & AHILL, no acreage mentioned.
1808 William Waters willed Pocomoke lands 1100 acres to son William Gillis Waters.

THIRD CHOICE

Patented in 1727 for 64 acres by Isaac Williams in Brinkleys, northwest, Election district 3, map #14.
2 Apr.1751 Isaac Williams son of Thomas Williams,and wife Ann Williams traded with Thomas Williams 20 acres for land in Dorc.Co. Md.
2 Dec 1767 Thomas Williams gave to grandson Thomas Williams Jr. 20 acres.
2 Dec 1767 Thomas Williams gave to grandson Planner Williams 1000 acres in Annamessex where brother Isaac Williams lived.
1773 resurv. to NEIGHBORS CONCLUSION 624 1/4 acres.

THOMAS'S BEGINNING

Patented in 1770, a resurvey from HACHILA & JEMIMON, for 275 acres by Charles Woolford, in West Pr.Anne, Election district 1, map #3.
29 Oct.1791 Thomas D. Woolford and William P. Woolford mortgaged to Denwood Wilson, THORNTON, HACHILA & JESHAMIN
4 Nov.1794 William Pitt Woolford son of Charles Woolford, sold to Tubman Woolford devised by Charles Woolford to son John Woolford now deceased.
9 Dec.1797 Thomas Denwood Woolford sold to Levin Woolford for 5 shillings, no acres given.

26 March 1799 Denwood Wilson, Levin Woolford and William Pitt Woolford
sold to James Woolford son of Thomas Woolford, THORNTON, HACHILA, JESEMAN
& THOMAS'S BEGINNING, release of mortgage.
1801 Levin Woolford willed to sons John Woolford, Arthur Woolford land
purchased of Thomas D. Woolford, unnamed.
1836 John Woolford willed to son John Woolford.

THOMAS'S CHANCE

Patented in 1750 by Thomas Gibbons for 91 acres in Westover, Election
district 13, map #10.
1783 tax- Thomas Gibbons 91 acres
1795 Thomas Gibbons Sr. gave lands,unnamed, to sons William Gibbons and
Robert Gibbons.
13 March 1810 Isaac Gibbons sold to James Tilghman 17 1/4 acres.
2 May 1837 Theodore Thomas Gibbons sold to Nathan Adams.

THOMPSONS ADVENTURE

see POOLS HOPE
5 Aug.1677 Henry Smith assigned to Gideon Tilghman 100 acres of POOLS
HOPE,purchased of William Thompson called DAVIS'S CHANGE, now called
THOMPSONS ADVENTURE.
21 Aug.1735 Gideon Tilghman gave to brother Aaron Tilghman
1 Aug.1735 Gideon Tilghman gave to brother Joseph 70 acres.
1763 Joseph Tilghman willed to son Joseph Tilghman 50 acres.

THOMPSONS PURCHASE

Patented on 30 Dec.1668 for 500 acres by William Stevens and assigned to
William Thompson in West Pr.Anne,Election district 1,map #3.
28 Nov.1673 William Thompson sold to Henry Smith 500 acres.
Rent Rolls 1666-1723 this tract is included in a later survey made for
Capt.Henry Smith, this and NASWORTHYS CHOICE was but 700 acres and now
called SMITHS RECOVERY.

THORNS ADDITION

Patented on 10 Oct.1695 by David Brown for 350 acres- see tract NO NAME,
West Pr.Anne.

THORNS INTENTION

Patented on 8 May 1671 by David Brown for 50 acres in West Pr.Anne,
Election district 1, map #3.
1697 David Brown gave lands to nephew Alexander Brown
Rent Rolls 1666-1723 Alexander Brown.
17 March 1738 Thomas Brown eldest son of Alexander Brown deceased, and
wife Mary Brown, and Margaret Brown two daughters of Alexander Brown,
gave to brother David Brown 50 acres
27 Apr.1749 John Woolford and wife Mary Woolford, (Mary Brown coheir of
Thomas Brown) Margaret Brown cohier which Thomas Brown was hier to
Alexander Brown, and Margaret Brown his wife otherwise called in Scotland
Margaret Erskin, and Sarah Brown widow, sold to David Wilson heir of
Ephraim Wilson 50 acres.

THORNTON

Patented on 2 Nov.1662 by William Thorn for 600 acres in West Pr.Anne,
Election district 1, map #3.
12 Feb.1665 William Thorn willed to wife Winifred Thorn.
2 Dec 1672 David Brown and wife Winifred Brown (late widow of
Capt.William Thorn) sold to William Scott 600 acres.
20 March 1672 William Scott sold to David Brown and Winifred Brown his
wife.
1697 David Brown willed to Alexander Brown 600 acres, or to Ephraim
Wilson if Alexander does not cultivate.
1748/9 John Woolford, willed to son Charles Woolford, got by my wife Mary
Woolford, and Margaret Brown.
2 May 1749 Margaret Brown sold 300 acres to William Skirvin.
12 July 1750 John Woolford and wife Mary Woolford, David Brown minister
of Gospel at Newport Glasgow Scotland son of Mary Brown sold their
interest to Robert Nairn and James Nairn.
24 Aug.1750 William Skirvin sold to John Woolford his rights
29 Oct.1791 Thomas D. Woolford and William Pitt Woolford mortgaged to
Denwood Wilson
4 Nov.1794 William Pitts Woolford sold to Tubman Woolford devised by
Charles Woolford to son John Woolford,deceased.
26 March 1799 Denwood Wilson released mortgage to Levin Woolford, William
Pitts Woolford and James Woolford son of Thomas Woolford.
13 July 1802 William Pitts Woolford sold to John Woolford land entitled
to by the death of nephew James Woolford, one moity 75 1/2 acres on
Manokin River, no name.
13 Nov.1802 John Wilkins, sheriff, sold to John Woolford, per judgement
against Tubman Woolford who became entitled at death of nephew James
Woolford 75 1/2 acres.
1836 John Woolford willed to son John Woolford.

THREE BROTHERS

Patented in 1749 by Marcy Beauchamp, survey includes NIBLETTS LOTT, for
722 acres in Westover,Election district 13, map #11.
17 June 1751 Marcy Beauchamp,carpernter, and wife Grace Beauchamp sold
200 acres to William Beauchamp
10 Nov.1761 Marcy Beauchamp and wife Grace Beauchamp sold 265 acres to
Stephen Garland,merchant.
16 Nov.1761 Marcy Beauchamp sold 200 acres to Samuel Curtis.
12 Sep.1763 Stephen Garland mortaged to John Logan of the City of
London,merchant.
2 Jan 1766 Stephen Garland conveyed to Thomas Dashiell,sheriff 265 acres
on behalf of a certain prisoner languishing in jail.
10 March 1767 Thomas Dashiell sheriff, sold to John White 265 acres
10 March 1767 John White sold to Stephen Garland 265 acres.
18 June 1771 William Beauchamp gave to son John Beauchamp 29 acres.
1783 tax- Samuel Curtis 200 acres.
1783 tax- Elijah Beauchamp 205 acres
1783 tax- Stephen Garland 237 1/2 acres
27 Aug.1787 Elijah Beauchamp sold to James Adams son of Phillip Adams 19
acres
19 Mary 1789 Elijah Beauchamp leased for 13 years, 50 acres to Edward
Beauchamp.

19 May 1789 Elijah Beauchamp,wife Martha Beauchamp sold to John Beauchamp 100 acres of THREE BROTHERS & LEDBOURN
1 June 1789 Elijah Beauchamp sold part to Thomas Beauchamp, no acreage given.
8 Jan 1790 Ann Beauchamp and Thomas Beauchamp sold to Thomas Adams THREE BROTHERS,HOGYARD,LEDBOURN,ENLARGEMENT,except 40 acres of hers.
24 Jan 1790 Thomas Beauchamp,wife Martha Beauchamp sold to Thomas Adams 203 1/4 acres of LEDBOURN,HOGYARD,THREE BROTHERS, ENLARGEMENT
8 Jan 1790 John Beauchamp,wife Anne Beauchamp sold to Philip Adams 100 acres of LEDBOURN,THREE BROTHERS.
13 Oct.1792 Risdon Beauchamp of Kent Co.Del.sold to Phillip Adams 12 acres of THREE BROTHERS & LEDBOURN.
15 Feb.1798 Samuel Curtis sold to Henry H. Curtis for 5 shillings 200 acres with CURTIS LOTT, 100 acres
1812 Phillip Adams gave to grandson John Adams son of James Adams.
10 Aug.1830 Constable's sale at suit of Samuel Cahoon against John Adams of James Adams, THREE BROTHERS & OAK HALL.
7 Sep.1830 Constable's sale at suit of Thomas Robertson against John Adams of James Adams, 20 acres.

TICK RIDGE

Patented in 1762 for 25 acres by Solomon Long in Dublin, Election district 4,map #12.
1775 ADDITION TO TICK RIDGE patented for 98 1/4 acres by John Porter.
17 March 1773 David Long sold part to John Porter 23 acres.
1783 tax- John Porter 23 acres.
21 June 1791 John Porter sold to Matthias Miles 37 acres for 5 shillings of ADDITION.

TILBURY

Patented in 1683 by Robert Sterling as surveyed by Roger Shirley in Dames Quarter, Election district 11, map #7 for 100 acres.
Rent Rolls 1666-1723 Ephraim Wilson
28 Dec.1762 David Wilson leased to Thomas Jones for 20 years.
17 Apr.1764 Thomas Jones releases back to David Wilson
17 Apr.1764 David Wilson and wife Ann Wilson sold his 1/4th part to Levin Wilson
13 Dec.1768 Samuel Wilson and wife Mary Wilson sold to Denwood Wilson 450 acres for 5 shillings of TILBURY,WILSONS DISCOVERY, GLASGOW, KILLGLAS, SECURITY.
1881 resurveyed to ADDTION TO KILLGLASS 1863 1/4 acres.

TILGHMANS ADVENTURE

Patented on 12 Sep.1682 by Gideon Tilghman for 50 acres in Brinkleys, southeast,Election district 3, map #16.
Rent Rolls 1666-1723 declaimed by Gideon Tilghman pending a cut by an older survey
1707 Samuel Collins died in possession.

TILGHMANS ADVENTURE

Patented in 1668 by Gideon Tilghman, fpr 100 acres and resurveyed in 1747 by Gideon Tilghman from SMALL HOPE and GIDEONS LUCK,in Westover,Election

district 13, map #13, 180 acres..
Rent Rolls 1666-1723 Gideon Tilghman
2 March 1749 Aaron Tilghman gave to son Elijah Tilghman 100 acres of OLD
PLANTATION where Moses Tilghman lived.
24 June 1763 Elisha Tilghman exchanged 7 1/2 acres with John Gibbons
25 Nov.1763 Elisha Tilghman sold his rights to Aaron Tilghman.
22 March 1764 Elijah Tilghman son of Aaron gave to his brother Aaron
Tilghman.
21 Apr.1772 Aaron Tilghman sold 164 1/2 aces of GIDEONS LUCK AND
TILGHMANS ADVENTURE to William Gibbons.
1774 Resurveyed by Aaron Tilghman for 266 1/4 acres.
1783 tax- John Gibbons Sr. 7 1/2 acres
1783 tax- William Gibbons 47 acres
1783 tax- John Rounds 120 acres
1783 tax- Isaiah Tilghman 100 acres
1 May 1782 William Gibbons sold to Samuel Wilson
21 Dec.1784 Isaac Marshall surviving exec. of Aaron Tilghman sold to
Thomas Gibbons part devised by Aaron to be sold.
13 Feb. 1787 William Gibbons and wife Mary Gibbons sold to Levin Miles 5
acres.
6 March 1787 William Gibbons mortgaged to Samuel Wilson with all his
other lands.
13 July 1788 William Gibbons mortgaged to Samuel Wilson and Levin Miles.
3 Jan 1792 John C. Wilson,Samuel Wilson and Samuel Smith executors of
Samuel Wilson sold 125 acres to Thomas King.
13 Aug.1792 William Gibbons and wife Mary Gibbons mortgaged to Levin
Miles.
25 Oct.1802 James Gibbons of Somerset Co. and George Broughton divided
land that was held by John Gibbons deceased.
29 March 1820 Jabez Tilghman sold to James Boston, part.

TILGHMANS CARE

Patented on 11 Aug.1720 by Gideon Tilghman in Dublin,Election district 4,
map #13.for 138 acres.
26 Nov.1746 Gideon Tilghman and wife Esther Tilghman sold 76 acrs to
Thomas Maddux
26 Apr.1766 Gideon Tilghman sold 7 1/2 acres to John Broughton.
19 Apr.1766 Gideon Tilghman gave to son Nehemiah Tilghman 100 acres out
of WILLIAMS HOPE,TILGHMANS CARE,PLAGUE WITHOUT PROFIT.
26 Apr.1766 Gideon Tilghman gave to son Gideon Jr. 99 acres of the same
as above.
14 Feb 1769 Gideon Tilghman and wife Tabitha Tilghman sold part to Robert
Jenkins King.
20 Jan 1769 Nehemiah Tilghman and wife Kathryn Tilghman sold to Robert
Jenkins King 268 acres of WILLIAMS HOPE,TILGHMANS CARE,PLAGUE WITHOUT
PROFIT,BROUGHTONS PURCHase.
1783 tax- John Broughton 76 acres
1783 tax- Robert Jenkins King 350 1/2 acres
1783 tax- Thomas Maddux 23 acres
1785 John Broughton willed to sons George Broughton and Josiah Broughton,
lands.
1789 Robert Jenkins King willed to son Robert lands bought of the
Tilghmans.
17 Oct.1773 Robert Jenkins King sold to Ephraim Stevens

15 Oct.1779 Ephraim Stevens sold back to Robert Jenkins King.
1795 Thomas Maddux willed to son Elzey Maddux plantation where I live, no name.
5 Nov.1798 George Broughton son of John Broughton, wife Alice Broughton sold to Elzey Maddux 63 3/4 acres of WILLIAMS HOPE & TILGHMANS CARE.
8 Nov.1803 Dr.Robert Jenkins King sold to Eli Gibbons 399 3/4 acres of BROUGHTONS PURCHASE,TILGHMANS LUCK,WILLIAMS HOPE.

TILGHMANS CHANCE

Patented in 1759 by Aaron Tilghman for 50 acres in Westover, Election district 13, map #11.
25 May1773 Elijah Tilghman of Dorc.Co. sold 50 acres to Samuel Wilson of Somerset Co.
2 Aug.1796 Samuel Wilson sold 38 1/4 acres to William Gibbons
16 March 1787 William Gibbons mortgaged to Samuel Wilson
13 July 1788 William Gibbons mortgaged to Samuel Wilson and William Miles.
3 Jan 1792 John C. Wilson,Samuel Wilson and Samuel Smith sold to Thomas King 125 acres that Samuel Wilson purchased of William Gibbons, no name
13 Aug.1792 William Gibbons and wife Mary Gibbons sold to Levin Miles.
7 Aug.1802 Henry James Carroll, wife Eliza Barnes Carroll sold to James Gibbons 125 acres ROUNDS on Back Creek conveyed by John C. Wilson, Samuel Wilson, Samuel Smyth executor of Samuel Wilson, to Thomas King.

TILGHMANS ENLARGEMENT

Patented in 1763 for 150 acres by Isaiah Tilghman in Dublin, Election district 4, map #12.
1783 tax- Isaiah Tilghman 150 acres
1790 Isaiah Tilghman willed to daughter Amelia Tilghman
1784 resurveyd to FOUL MEADOW 183 /34 acres, unpatented.

TILGHMANS FORTUNE

Patented in 1762 for 90 acres by Isaiah Tilghman in Dublin, Election district 12, map #12.
1783 tax- Isaiah Tilghman
1790 Isaiah Tilghman willed to son James Tilghman 90 acres.

TILGHMANS LOTT

see TILGHMANS PURCHASE Pat 1724 John Tilghman, 50 acres.

TILGHMANS LUCK

Patented in 1762 by Aaron Tilghman for 30 acres in Westover, Election district 13, map #11.
1783 tax- William Gibbons 30 acres.
1783 ADDITION patented by Levin Miles for 13 acres.
13 Feb.1787 William Gibbons and wife Mary sold to Levin Miles 20 acres.
6 March 1787 William Gibbons mortgaged to Samuel Wilson
13 Aug.1788 William Gibbons mortgaged to Samuel Wilson and Levin Miles.
21 Dec 1784 Isaac Marshall executor of Aaron Tilghman sold to Thomas Gibbons.

13 Aug.1792 William Gibbons and wife Mary Gibbons sold to Levin Miles
with his other lands.
19 Aug.1806 Thomas Hayward sold to Henry King part PLAGUE WITHOUT PROFIT
& TILGHMANS LUCK.

TILGHMANS PRIVILEDGE

Patented in 1785 by William Tilghman for 113 3/4 acres in Westover,
Election district 13, map #11.
1806 William Tilghman willed to daughter Nancy Tilghman and son William
Tilghman.
13 May 1809 John Hayman, wife Nancy Hayman of Ohio sold to James Handy of
Isaac Handy, of Som. Co.Md. devised Nancy Hayman by her father William
Tilghman.

TILGHMANS PURCHASE

Patented in 1723 by John Tilghman in Westover Election district 13, map
#11 for 30 acres AKA TILGHMANS LOTT.
1733 John Tilghman willed to sons John Tilghman and Moses Tilghman.
Repatented in 1734 by Moses Tilghman
3 Nov.1735 Moses Tilghman,wife Barbara Tilghman sold to Barnaby Niblett
30 acres between back Creek and Morumsco at HANDYS RIDGE-unnamed.
13 Oct.1752 John Tilghman sold to Edward Waters land at Back Creek of
Manokin.
1752 resurveyed to BEAUCHAMPS PRIVILEDGE.

TILGHMANS REST
see DALES ADVENTURE
TILGHMANS SECURITY

Patented in 1715 for 100 acres by Nehemiah Tilghman, a resurvey from
GIDEONS LUCK in Dublin,Election district 4, map #13.
1 Aug.1771 Nehemiah Tilghman and wife Catherine Tilghman of Worc.Co. sold
Robert Jenkins King 4 acres.
1783 tax- Robert Jenkins King 4 acres
8 Nov.1803 Robert Jenkins King sold to Eli Gibbons with other land total
399 3/4 acres..
13 March 1790 Joseph Tilghman of Worc.Co. sold 18 acres to Samuel Taylor
of Somerset Co.
1813 ADDITION patented for 32 acres by Samuel Taylor.

TIMBER GROVE

Patented on 9 June 1683 by William Noble for 150 acres in Dublin,Election
district 4, map #13.
Rent Rolls 1666-1723 William Noble
10 Dec.1687 Isaac Noble, wife Mary Noble sold to Robert Kimball 100
acres.
1721 Jonathan Noble willed to sons William Noble and Jonathan Noble.(they
both died in minority)
22 Nov.1734 John Lewis and Rebecca Lewis(Rebecca Noble daughter of
Jonathan Noble) and Elizabeth Noble deeded 1/3rd part to David Dryden and
Hannah Dryden (Hannah Noble), that William Noble conveyed to his son
James Noble who died intestate so it descended to his son James Noble Jr.

who conveyed to Jonathan Noble.
2 Nov.1735 James Noble Jr.son of William Noble, and wife Alice Noble sold
to Edward Cluff 75 acres.
1760 Edward Cluff willed to sons Michael Cluff and Jonathan Cluff.
1783 tax- James Dryden 30 acres
1783 tax- Jonathan Cluff 37 acres.
1786 Hannah Dryden devised her dower right to sons Ephraim Dryden and
grandson James Dryden(unnamed land)
5 Oct 1791 Jonathan Cluff sold 37 acres to Michael Cluff son of Michael.
15 March 1793 Michael Cluff son of Michael sold 37 acres to Robert Cluff.
21 Oct.1805 Robert H. Dryden son of James Dryden sold to Teague Donoho of
Worc.Co. 102 1/4 acres of HACKLEY, TIMBER GROVE, CHERRY GARDEN.

TIMBER GROVE

Patented in 1726 by Phillip Covington for 150 acres in Mt.Vernon,
Election district 5, mmap #1.
1732 Phillip Covington willed to sons Nehemiah Covington,Phillip
Covington,Levin Covington and John Covington.
3 June 1748 Nehemiah Covington conveyed to Henry Waggaman
23 June 1748 Eleanor Covington and Nehemiah Covington sold 150 acres to
Henry Waggaman
21 Feb.1756 Daniel Jones and Nehemiah Covington sold to Henry Waggaman.
18 June 1756 Daniel Jones,wife Elizabeth Jones and Nehemiah
Covington,wife Betty Covington and Phillip Covington,wife Mary Covington
sold to Henry Waggaman.

TIMBER TRACT

Patented in 1748 by Robert King for 809 acres in Dublin, Election
district 4,map #13.
1754 resurveyed for 834 acres by Robert King
1750 Robert King willed to grandson Robert Jenkins King.
Feb.1755 Robert King Esq. for 10 shillings gave pt. to Littleton
Dennis-no acreage given.
14 Dec.1762 There was a bond from Col.Robert King in his life to Edward
Waters for conveyence of part and King willed tract to Edward Waters
since money paid to Nehemiah King due on said lands.
1764 resurvey 626 acres called WATERS ADDITION to TIMBER TRACT.TO DEER
PARK.
3 May 1775 Robert Jenkins King sold 21 /12 acre to John Broughton Sr.
1783 tax- John Broughton 21 acres.
1783 tax- Robert Jenkins King 500 1/2 acres
1783 tax- Edward Waters.
1788 Robert Jenkins King willed to son Levin King part that bounds Josiah
Broughton and to daughter Mary King balance of TIMBER TRACT.

TINSON

Patented on 9 June by William Bozman Jr. for 300 acres in West Pr.Anne,
Election District 1, map #2.
9 July 1677 William Bozman Jr. sold to Isaac Noble.
Rent Rolls 1666-1723 Possessed by Isaac Noble son of Isaac 300 acres.

1 Oct 1719 Isaac Noble Jr,cooper and wife Susannah Noble sold 200 acres
to John Leatherbury.
17 July 1730 William Bozman son of John Bozman sold to John Leatherbury
150 acres.
15 Sep.1750 William Cottman gave to son Benjamin Cottman with TAUNTON
DEAN
25 Nov.1762 Isaac Noble sold to John Leatherbury 150 acres, with YOUNG
TINSON
1756 John Leatherbury willed to son Charles Leatherbury, lands purchased
of Isaac Noble Sr. and Isaac Noble Jr. unnamed.
26 Sep.1763 John Noble and wife Priscilla Noble and Alice Noble and Isaac
Noble of North Carolina eldest son of Isaac of Somerset Co. sold to John
Adams 154 acres of TINSON alias YOUNG TINSON
2 Apr.1771 Charles Leatherbury and wife Priscilla Leatherbury sold 150
acres to Benjamin Cottman
1783 tax- Benjamin Cottman.
25 March 1807 Thomas Hamilton mortgaged to Benjamin F.A. C. Dashiell.

TONYS VINEYARD

Patented on 15 Oct.1665 by Stephen Horsey for 300 acres in West Pr.Anne,
Election district 1, map #2.
16 Aug.1666 Stephen Horsey leased for 20 years to Anthony Johnson(negro)
June 1670 Stephen Horsey leased for 99 years to Mary Johnson relic of
Anthony, then to her sons John Johnson and Richard Johnson(negros.)
1715 William Ryan willed to Benjamin Mitchell son of John Mitchell and
wife Mary Mitchell, dwelling plantation.
1746 resurvey   84 acres
28 Aug.1747 Stephen Horsey sold to Alexander Adams. Stephen Horsey and
Hannah Horsey conveyed to John Ryan 112 acres but lately by warrent found
to be but 84 acres and an older tract TINSON now possessed by Isaac Noble
and John Leatherbury cuts off a great part of TONYS VINEYARD. 7 acres.
3 July 1742 Benjamin Mitchell son of John Mitchell, and wife Mary
Mitchell devisee of William Ryan sold to Alexander Adams 112 acres for 5
shillings of RYANS PURCHASE it being part of TONYS VINEYARD, that John
Ryan willed to Benjamin Mitchell.
1746 repatented by Alexander Adams 84 acres.
1754 Stephen Horsey willed to sons Revel Horsey, Stephen Horsey and
grandson John Horsey.
21 March 1750 Alexander Adams, gave to son John Adams 84 acres with part
of HORSEYS CHANCE.
17 Dec.1804 Thomas Hamilton and Charles Nutter, wife Louisa Nutter, late
Louisa Adams agree to divide the RE of William Adams Jr.
25 March 1807 Thomas Hamilton mortgaged to Benjamin F.A.C. Dashiell.
1810 Dr. Charles Nutter sold part to Daniel Whitney.

TOSSITER

Patented on 18 March 1680 by William Stevens who assigned to William
Bradshaw for 150 acres in Dublin,Election district 4, map #3.
20 Dec 1685 William Bradshaw, wife Anne Bradshaw sold to William Noble
150 acres.
Rent Rolls 1666-1723 William Noble.
25 May 1734 James Noble and wife Alice Noble sold to Samuel Dorman 150

acres that William Bradshaw alienated to William Noble willed to son
James Noble afsd.
1760 resurveyed to DORMANS DISCOVERY 128 acres.

TOTTONAIS

Patented on 21 March 1680 by William Turpin for 250 acres in Westover,
Election disrict 13, map #11.
Rent Rolls 1666-1723 John Turpin
1736 John Turpin willed to son William Turpin 1/2 and 1/2 to wife Hannah
Turpin during widowhood, then to son William Turpin and heirs.
1783 tax- John Turpin 149 acres.
6 April 1810 William Turpin of John Turpin, wife Elizabeth Turpin sold to
John Custis Wilson 147 acres.

TRAHEARNS LOTT

Patented in 1749 by James Trehearn for 55 acres in Brinkleys, northwest,
Election district 3,map #14.
1769 James Trehearn willed lands to son Samuel Trehearn unnamed.
1783 tax- Samuel Trehearn 55 acres.

TREHEARNS TROUBLE

Patented in 1771 for 4 acres by Samuel Trehearn in Brinkleys, northwest,
Election district 3, map #14.
7 Aug.1807 James Trehearn of Worc.Co. sold to Nathaniel Bell of Somerset
Co. 2 1/2 acres.

TRIBLE PURCHASE

see DOUBLE PURCHASE, part of CATHERINES CONTENT

TROUBLE

Patented on 20 Aug.1679 by John White who assigned to Henry Miles, for 50
acres in Fairmount,Election district 6, map #9.
1695 Henry Miles willed to daughter Alice Miles 50 acres
Rent Rolls 1666-1723 possessed by Alice Miles.
9 June 1746 Samuel Miles sold to Stacey Miles 50 acres.
7 June 1755 Stacey Miles sold to Thomas Seon 50 acres
1783 tax- Thomas Seon Sudler 50 acres.(gr.son of Thomas Seon)
1789 resurveyed to SUDLERS CONCLUSION 419 3/4 acres.

TROUBLE

Patented on 13 Oct.1677 by Thomas Strawbridge who conveyed to William
Alexander Jr. for 250 acres in West Pr.Anne, Election district 1, map #2.
Rent Rolls 1666-1723 William Alexander Jr.
1732 William Alexander willed to son Liston Alexander
1737 Liston Alexander willed to William Alexander son of Moses Alexander
part, to sister Agnes Alexander and heirs balance.
24 June 1736 Moses Alexander,clocksmith,son of William Alexander sold for
5 shilings all interest in land of William Alexander HUNGARY NECK being
part of TROUBLE & DENTRY.

2 Nov.1738 Moses Alexander sold to Agnes Alexander 20 acres.
1743 Thomas Pollitt willed to son Thomas Pollitt, TROUBLE & DAINTRY.
27 March 1749 John Laws and wife Agnes Laws sold to Thomas Pollitt 20
acres deeded by Moses Alexander to Agnes Alexander now wife of John Laws.
9 Apr.1745 Moses Alexander and his son John Alexander, blacksmith of
Wicomico 100 sold to Alexander Adams rector of Step. Parish 230 acres(as
William Alexander had several children and all his sons died childless
except his 2nd son Moses Alexander afsd.)
15 Oct.1748 Peter Serman and wife Mary Serman sold to Thomas Gillis 50
acres conveyed by George Goddard 50 acres with CRAMBURN,HORSEYS CHANCE,
CANTERBURY.
1768 Alexander Adams gave to grandson Alexander son of Alexander Adams.
1783 tax- Josiah Adams
1783 tax- Thomas Pollitt 20 acres
1788 Thomas Pollitt willed to son Thomas Pollitt.
1790 Joseph Gillis son of Thomas Gillis,wife Elizabeth Gillis sold 50
acres to Thomas Fountain with CRAMBURN, HORSEYS CHANCE,CANTERBURY.
15 Feb 1798 John Woolford and wife Ann Woolford sold to Levin Pollitt 78
acres as Joseph Gillis had and died intestate and Ann Woolford coheir of
him. no name.

TROUBLE

Surveyed in 1787 for 48 acres by Ezekiel Gillis, was part of MASONS
ADVENTURE, unpatented in St.Peters,Election district 2, map #6.

TROUBLESOME

Patented in 1749 by Thomas Tull for 24 acres in Brinkleys, southwest,
Election district 3,map #17.
24 March 1760 Thomas Tull sold to William Tull 24 acres
29 June 1765 William Tull of Annamessex sold to Thomas Tull that was
conveyed to Thomas Tull by deceased father of William and Thomas.
1766 part resurveyed to CHANCE
1759 part resurveyed to WILLIAMS LOTT
27 Jan 1806 Thomas Tull Sr. sold to William Merrill Tull 170 acres of
BOSTON, TROUBLESOME & CHANCE.
9 Feb.1809 Thomas Merrill Tull, wife Polly Tull sold to Joshua Tull 203
1/2 acres of BOSTON,GOSHEN, TROUBLESOME & WILLIAMS LOTT.

TROUBLESOME

Patented in 1689 by Thomas Davis for 260 acres in Lawsons, Election
district 8, map #18.
2 Apr.1720 Thomas Davis granted to John Davis.

TROUBLESOME

see VULCANS VINEYARD 9 acres
see CANES CHOICE 100 acres
see CHESTNUT RIDGE,WHITE OAK SWAMP,CORK, PUZZLE 65 acres.

TROUBLESOME

Patented on 15 Nov.1694 by Francis Martin for 130 acres in Asbury,
Election district 12, map #21.

Rent Rolls 1666-1723 possessed by William Brittingham in Virginia by marrying the widow.

TULLS ADDITION

Patented as ADDITION in 1728 by John Tull for 100 acres in Fairmount, Election district 6, map #9.
1783 tax- Joshua Tull
1787 resurvey to 95 acres by Joshua Tull
20 Oct.1794 Joshua Tull son of John Tull gave to Thomas Tull 95 acres.

TULLS ADDITION

Patented in 1760 by Stephen Tull, a resurvey of part of CHANCE, for 212 1/2 acres in Dublin,Election district 4, map #12.
1783 tax- Samuel Tull 212 acres.

TULLS ADVENTURE

Patented in 1761 by Jonathan Tull for 13 acres in Dublin, Election district 4, map #12.
1783 tax- Jonathan Tull Sr. 13 acres

TULLY BRISK ADDITION

Patented in 1749 by Archibald White for 76 acres in Brinkleys, southeast, Election district 3, map #16.
19 June 1764 Archibald White gave to son William White part of TULLY BRISK, sold by Josias Seward to Archibald White father of afsd, out of MANLOVES LOTT 45 1/2 acre and part of ADDN. TO TULLY BRISK 50 acres and WHITES DESIRE 11 acres.
26 Oct.1765 Archibald White sold to Robert Taylor 13 3/4 acres.
28 Oct.1765 Robert Taylor sold to Stephen Garland part of TULLY BRISK and 13 3/4 acres of ADDITION purchased of Archibald White.
14 March 1772 Robert Taylor sold to Jesse Hall 60 acres.
9 Nov.1774 Wiliam Allen executor of will of Thomas Dashiell of Worc.Col sold to Robert Taylor- a release of mortgage.
16 May 1774 Robert Taylor and wife Rebecca Taylor sold to Jesse Hall 60 acres TULLY BRISK & ADDITION.
10 Oct 1779 Jesse Hall sold to Thomas Wilson 17 acres of ADDITION & SUPPORT
1783 tax- Jesse Hall 13 acres & ADDITION 42 acres
1783 tax- Thomas Wilson 14 acres
1783 tax- William White 50 acres
1783 tax- William White 45 1/4 acres TULLY BRISK.
5 Sep.1785 Thomas Wilson sold 17 acres of ADDITION & SUPPORT to William Wood.
9 Feb.1786 William Wood,wife Nancy Wood sold to Jacob Adams prts of TULLY BRISK,SUPPORT,NAN ELLIS RIDGE,BOSTONS ADVENTURE.
7 Oct.1806 Jesse Hall sold to Elijah Hall 66 acres of TULLY BRISK & ADDITION TO TULLY BRISK.

TURKEY COCK HILL

Patented on 29 oct 1679 by John King who assigned to John Bennett for

145 acres in Dublin,Election district 4, map #12.
2 Aug.1682 John Bennett of Manokin sold to James Conner
1749 resurveyed to KNIGHTS SUCESS 206 acres.

TURKEY PINE

Patented in 1760 by Abraham Outten for 56 acres in Brinkleys, southwest,
Election district 3,map #17.
18 Apr.1771 Isaac Outten,wife Sarah Outten sold 56 acres to David
Cottingham.
13 Sep.1801 Samuel Cottinham son of David Cottingham sold to William
Williams, BOSTON, VULCANS VINEYARD, TURKEY PINE- no acres.
22 Feb.1809 Richard Hall, wife Sally Hall and Nathan Cahoon sold to Noah
Lankford Hall part.
22 Feb.1809 Samuel Cottingham and William Williams sold to Richard Hall
20 acres.
22 Feb.1809 Richard hall, wife Sarah hall sold to William Williams 20
acres.

TURKEY RIDGE

Patented in 1687 by Matthew Dorman for 100 acres in West Pr.Anne,Election
district 1, map #2.
1692 Matthew Dorman willed to son Henry Dorman.
Rent Rolls 1666-1723 Charles Ballard
9 Oct.1756 Robert Ballard sold 100 acres to William Hayward
20 Nov.1767 William Hayward of Talbot Co. sold to Levin Ballard
19 Sep. 1776 Levin Ballard sold to Levin Woolford and John McGrath 100
acres.
13 March 1779 Levin Woolford and John McGrath sold 100 acres to Samuel
Wilkins
1783 tax- Samuel Wilkins 100 acres
27 Feb.1793 John Wilkins,wife Sally Wilkins sold to James Ewing 100
acres.
20 March 1804 Isaac Ewing sold to Leah Adams 100 acres.

TURKEY RIDGE

Patented in 1758 for 10 1/2 acres by William Gray in Dublin, Election
district 4, map #12.
1764 resurveyed to FLATLAND

TURKEY SWAMP

Patented in 1749 by Abraham Outten for 94 acres in Brinkleys, southwest,
Election district 3, map #17.
18 March 1769 Abraham Outten sold to John Cottingham
1778 John Cottingham willed to son Ephraim Cottingham, all lands.
1773 John Cottingham conveyed to Thomas Cottingham during life only.
1783 tax- Thomas Cottingham 10 acres
1783 tax- Ephraim Cottingham
8 March 1794 Ephraim Cottingham,wife Leah Cottingham sold 40 acres to
Kellum Lankford.
1 June 1801 Samuel Cottingham sold 20 acres to Robert Hall, he calls it
TURKEY POINT
28 Dec 1801 Levi Holland and wife Sally Holland sold to Samuel Tull

BOSTON & TURKEY SWAMP, all land Ephraim Cottingham died possessed.
16 Jan 1810 Kellum Lankford sold 40 acres to Nathaniel Bell.

TURKEY TRAP

Patented in 1736 by Thomas Adams for 44 1/4 acres in Brinkleys,northwest,
Election district 3, map #14.
1735 Thomas Adams willed part to son David Adams.
1756 repatented by Thomas Marshall
1761 tax- William Adams son of Thomas Adams
1774 Thomas Marshall (married Grace Adams) gave to son Stephen Marshall
of Acco.Co.Va. 44 acres
1783 tax- Stephen Marshall 44 1/4 acres
22 Aug.1794 Stephen Marshall,wife Rachel Marshall sold to Thomas Miles,
44 1/4 acres.

TURKEY TRAP

Patented in 1775 for 5 3/4 acres in Dublin,Election district 4, map #12.
1783 tax- John Harris
1788/93 John Harris willed to son John Harris.

TURNERS PURCHASE

see DAVIS CHOICE

TURPINS CHOICE

Patented in 1753 by William Turpin for 100 acres and repatented by him in
1762 for 350 acres in Dublin, Election district 4,map #12.
1753 resurvey 100 acres
23 March 1769 William Turpin Sr. and William Turpin Jr. sold to Levin
Gale part of 350 acres except 100 acres which was contained in the
original patent.
4 Apr.1769 William Turpin sold to David Prior 100 acres
23 Jan 1778 David Prior sold 100 acres to Jesse King
21 March 1778 Levin Gale sold 250 acres to Alexander Dean and Hugh Dean
1783 tax- Alexander Dean 250 acres
1783 tax- Jesse King 100 acres.
25 May 1792 Jesse King sold 100 acres to Nehemiah King for 5 shiillings.
1832 Dr. John B. Slemons willed TURPINS CHOICE be sold.

TURPINS PURCHASE

Patented in 1762 a resurvey from FURNISS CHOICE, by Whitty Turpin for
367 1/2 acres in Fairmount,Election district 6, map #9.
2 March 1801 Thomas Seon Sudler sold to Whitty Turpin Fountain part of
land between them, no name or acreage, 1st bounder of TURPINS PURCHASE
2 March 1801 Whitty Turpin Fountain sold to Thomas Seon Sudler, same as
above.

TWO BROTHERS

Patented in 1722 for 200 acres by John Hopkins on Smiths Island,Election
district 10, map #23.

1 Aug.1746 John Hopkins sold to George Hopkins Sr. for 5 shillings 100 acres called OYSTER SHELL LANDING at Cagers Island.
20 Nov.1746 George Hopkins and wife Elizabeth Hopkins sold 100 acres at Cagers Island to Peter Presley of Northumberland Co. Va.
1752 John Hopkins willed to son John, marsh at Cagers Island, no name or acreage given.
20 Oct.1746 Hance Lawson and wife Elizabeth of Dorc.Co. sold to William Haynie of Northumberland Co. Va. part of Cagers Island 52 acres-no named.
1771 Stephen Hopkins willed to sons Stephen Hopkins and Charles Hopkins tract at Cagers Island(unnamed.)
1772 resurveyed to SEVEN BROTHERS 784 acres.

UNDUE

Patented on 2 Apr.1664 by Stephen Horsey for 300 acres in Lawsons, Election district 8, map #18.
8 Feb.1686 Stephen Horsey and wife Hannah Horsey deeded to Thomas Davis 131 acres
8 Feb.1686 Stephen Horsey, wife Hannah Horsey sold to John Hepworth 108 acres.
Rent Rolls 1666-1723 Thomas Davis
1715 Thomas Davis willed to son Thomas Davis and son John Davis.
2 Apr.1720 Thomas Davis sold 131 acres to John Davis.
1754/61 Stephen Horsey willed to grandson Isaac Horsey my old plantation except 150 acres out of a patent called OLD UNDUE and 45 acres out of COW QUARTER which 195 acres my father Stephen Horsey sold to Thomas Davis.
1749 resurvey to UPPER ANDUEY 400 acres.

UNCLES KINDNESS

Patented in 1789 by William Fleming out of MINSHULLS ADVENTURE for 105 3/4 acres in Dublin,Election district 4, map #12.
19 Jan 1790 William Fleming Sr. sold 43 acres to John Harris Hayman and Samuel Curtis.
6 Jan 1807 Wrixam L. Porter, wife Priscilla Porter sold her share to John Riggin (Priscilla Porter as daughter of Teague Riggin)

UNEXPECTED

Patented on 27 Sep.1705 by Arthur Denwood for 40 acres in West Pr.Anne, Election district 1, map #3.
Rent Rolls 1666-1723 Arthur Denwood
16 Jan.1747 Levin Denwood son of John Denwood, son of Arthur Denood, of Dorc.Co. Md. sold 40 acres to David Wilson.
1749 resurvyed to WILSONS CONCUSION 1319 acres.

UNITY

Patented on 22 July 1721 by John Fleming for 20 acres in Dublin,Election district 4, map #12.
1757 UNITY ENLARGED 350 acres- William Fleming
17 Nov.1772 William Fleming sold to Nathaniel Smullen 82 acres of UNITY ENLARGED.
25 May 1773 William Fleming sold to Edmund Smullen 49 3/4 acres
1783 tax- John Fleming 349 acres

1783 tax- Leah Smullen 49 acres
1783 tax- Nathaniel Smullen 42 acres, UNITY ENLARGED.
12 Apr.1785 William Fleming sold to John Fleming son of William Fleming part.
1798 tax- John Ward
1803 Eleanor Ward sold 181 acres to James Ward.
29 Mar.1805 Louden Smullen and wife Elizabeth Smullen sold to John Smullen and Zorobable Smullen, part of three tracts father Nathaniel Smullen had, no names..
25 June 1807 John Fleming now of Scipico Co. Cayuga N.Y. sold to Juliana Massey Farrow and Mary Johnson Farrow of Som.Co. daughters of Charles Farrow, 250 acres of UNITY ENLARGED, GOSHEN, HARPERS INCREASE, HARPERS DISCOVERY.
13 April 1809 John Fleming of Cayuga Co. N.Y. sold to Severn Johnson of Worc. Co. Md. 87 acres UNITY ENLARGED.
3 APril 1809 John Fleming of Cayuga N.Y. sold to William Fleming of Som. Co.Md. 6 1/4 acres of UNITY ENLARGED.
11 July 1810 Levin Miller, wife Nancy Miller sold to Zorobable Smulling 102 acres of GOSHEN & UNITY ENLARGED.
11 July 1810 Zorobable Smulling sold to Levin Miller and Nancy Miller 54 acres.
24 Aug.1810 Matthias Dashiell, sheriff, sold to John Riggin, per judgement against Charles Farrow, with GOSHEN, HARPERS INCREASE, HARPERS DISCOVERY.

UPPER ANDUE

Patented in 1752 a resurvey of UNDUE & KIRKMINSTER & LONG HEDGE, by John Davis for 746 acres in Lawsons Election district 8, map #18.
2 Aug 1769 Samuel Cox sold to Jacob Milbourn 50 acres.
8 Nov.1769 Samuel Cox sold to Solomon Byrd 11 1/4 acres
27 Dec.1771 Samuel Cox sold to William Darcus 50 acrs
17 Jan 1772 Samuel Cox sold to John Horsey 70 acres with part of BRICKLEY HOE.
20 May 1772 Samuel Cox sold to Jacob Milbourn part of two tracts, unnamed 5 acres and 3 1/2 acres that Jacob Milbourn bought of Samuel Cox before.
1783 tax- Jacob Milbourn 108 acres
1783 tax- Solomon Byrd 127 1/2 acres.
1783 tax- Martha Cox 300 acres
1783 tax- William Darcus 50 acres.
10 Nov.1804 John D. Cox sold to Benjamin Lankford 1/2 willed by grandfather Samuel Cox, 120 acres.
15 June 1807 Benjamin Lankford Sr. sold to William Williams 35 acres.
26 Dec.1807 Thomas Cox, wife Peggy Cox sold to Jacob Tylor 35 acres.
13 Dec.1808 Benjamin Lankford Sr. sold to William Roach 120 acres with other parcels of same land and all his other possessions.
17 March 1810 Benjamin Lankford Sr. sold to William Williams 8 acres LOGN HEDGE.
10 Aug.1810 Matthias Dashiell, sheriff, sold to William Williams Esq. per judgement against Benjamin Lankford 8 acres of LONG HEDGE.
10 March 1810 Jacob Tyler, wife Betsy Tyler sold to Samuel Miles 3 acres.
10 march 1810 Peggy Cox sold to Samuel Miles 3 acres.

UPPER ANDUEY

Patented in 1749, part resurvey of HEPWORTHS PASTURE and UNDUE by John Davis for 400 acres in Lawsons,Election district 8, map #18.
1767 resurveyed to DAVIS GOOD WILL 777 acres.

VACANCY

Patented in 1748 for 19 acres by Isaac Williams in Brinkleys, northwest, Election district 3, map #14.
2 Apr.1751 Isaac Williams and wife Ann Williams traded 19 acres to Thomas Williams for land in Dorc.Co.
1773 resurveyed to NEIGHBORS CONCLUSION 624 1/4 acres.

VALE OF MISERY

Patented on 4 Apr.1696 to John Roach for 88 acres in Fairmount, Election district 6, map #9.
Rent Rolls 1666-1723 John Roach Jr.
1726 John Roach willed 88 acres to son Stephen Roach
19 March 1755 Stephen Roach and wife Deborah Roach sold to Absalom Ford.
27 March 1764 Absalom Ford sold to Charles Ford 88 acres
1778 Littleton Waters willed this tract to be purchased for son Littleton Waters.
1783 tax- John Wilson

VENTURE

Patented on 6 July 1679 by John Brown and assigned to Robert Smith for 100 acres in Brinkleys,southeast,Election district 3, map #16.
Rent Rolls 1666-1723 by Samuel Tomlinson vide Richard Chambers.
1745 Abigail Tomlinson gave to son Hampton Tomlinson.
19 June 1769 Sayward Tomlinson of Gloster Co.Va. sold to Samuel Tomlinson of Som.Co. 100 acres
20 Aug.1770 Sayward Tomlinson of Va. gave to Samuel Tomlinson son of Sayward 100 acres.
3 Nov.1772 Elizabeth Tomlinson daughter of Hampton Tomlinson sold to William Kersey.
1783 tax- William Kersey 90 acres.
23 April 1789 Littleton Carsley sold to Thomas White 6 1/2 acres.
4 June 1800 Littleton Carsley sold to Stephen Collins 100 acres.
29 March 1856 Renatus T. Hastings sold to Daniel Boston
23 Sep.1885 Solomon Boston mortgaged to the Hall brothers 38 acres inherited from father Daniel Boston.

VENTURE

Patented in 1734 by Francis Carey for 50 acres in Brinkleys, northwest, Election district 3, map #14.
20 May 1747 Francis Carey and wife Sarah Carey of Princess Anne County, North Carolina,planter sold to Thomas Marshall of Somerset County 50 acres.
1817 Thomas Connerly willed to son John Connerly.

VENTURE

Patented in 1751 for 80 acres by John Milbourn in Brinkleys, southeast, Election district 3, map #16.
1783 tax- Susay Milbourn 80 acres

VENTURE

Patented in 1775 for 27 1/4 acres by William Miles in Dublin, Election District 4, map #12.
1809 resurveyed to HEATHS EXPERIMENT 739 3/4 acres.

VENTURE

Patented in 1807 by William Pollitt for 16 1/4 acres in Eeast Pr.Anne,Election district 15, map #4.
1814 William Pollitt willed to sister-in-law Nelly Pollitt 150 acres of HACKALAH & VENTURE
1836 Nelly J. Pollitt willed to son Levin J. Pollitt 150 acres of HACKALAH & VENTURE.

VENTURE PRIVILEDGED

Patented in 1744 for 100 acres by Edward Roberts in Dames Quarter, Election district 11, map #7.
1783 tax- William Roberts 100 acres
1794 William Roberts willed to niece Nancy Lemon wife of Robert Lemon.
16 May 1801 George Jones and wife Leah Jones sold to Edward Fowler 100 acres.

VICTORY

Patented in 1763 for 14 acres in West Princess Anne,Election district 1, map #2.

VICTORY

Patented in 1784 for 12 acres by Henry Walston on Deal Island, Election district 14, map #8.
5 Dec.1797 Jesse Dashiell, wife Sarah Dashiell sold to Isaac Noble, as Henry Walston deceased willed 1/3 part to son David Walston and to said daughter Sarah Dashiell, on Devil's Island.
12 Dec.1797 Isaac Noble sold to William Evans 12 acres.
9 Aug 1803 Isaac Noble and wife Peggy Noble sold to Thomas Jones 1/3rd part that Henry Walston bequeathed to daughter Peggy Noble.
22 Sep.1804 Henry Evans sold to Thomas Jones, as Henry Walston willed 1/4th part to son David Jones and grandson Henry Evans- sold all his part of a 1/3rd.

VULCANS FORGE

Patented on 16 March 1680 by William Stevens and assigned to Richard Chambers in East Princess Anne,Election district 15, map #5, for 100 acres.
Rent Rolls 1666-1723 Richard Chambers 100 acres
1743 Richard Chambers gave to cousins Richard Brereton and Samuel Collins
1743 Richard Brereton willed to brother Henry Brereton lands left by

uncle Richard Chambers-unnamed.
6 Oct.1746 Henry Brereton of Baltimore Co.Md. and Thomas Brereton of same
sold all to Woncey McClemmy.
7 Apr.1748 Samuel Collings and wife Elizabeth Collings of Worc.Co. sold
to Woncey McClemmy
7 Nov.1749 creditors join to sell lands of Woncy McClemmy to Hamilton
Bell.
1783 Hamilton Bell willed lands to son Rev. Hamilton Bell, no name.

VULCANS VINEYARD

Patented on 10 March 1677 by Thomas Cottingham for 200 acres in
Brinkleys, southwest,Election district 3, map #14.
16 Oct.1708 Charles Cottingham and Ann Cottingham sold 14 acres to
Jonathan Cottingham
19 March 1718 Charles Cottingham and wife Ann Cottingham sold 75 acres to
Jonathan Cottingham.
Rent Rolls 1666-1723 Charles Cottingham s/o Thomas Cottingham. 200 acres.
1 Nov.1723 Jonathan Cottingham and Margaret Cottingham of Sussex Co.Del.
sold to Joseph Lankford 89 acres.
4 Sep.1742 Charles Cottingham gave to son Thomas Cottingham balance.
19 March 1746 Thomas Cottingham Jr. and wife Mary Cottingham sold 9 acres
to Joseph Lankford(part called TROUBLESOME.)
1783 tax- David Cottingham 35 acres
1783 tax- Ezekiel Lankford 86 acres
9 Jan.1784 Ezekiel Lankford sold to Samuel Bedsworth 9 acres.
21 July 1784 Samuel Bedsworth and wife Mary Bedsworth sold to William
Bedsworth 9 acres.
15 March 1785 Ezekiel Lankford,wife Catherine Lankford sold to Robert
Hall and wife Elizabeth Hall 9 acres with LANKFORDS CONTENT & TROUBLESOME
95 acres.
15 March 1785 William Bedsworth sold to Robert Hall part.
17 June 1790 William Bedsworth sold to Benjamin Conner 1 acre TROUBLESOME
out of VULCANS VINEYARD with LANKFORDS CONTENT.
13 Sep.1801 Samuel Cottingham son of David Cottingham sold to William
Williams BOSTON, VULCANS VINEYARD, TURKEY PINE.

WAGGAMANS LOTT

Patented in 1748 by Henry Waggaman a survey of part of BRIDGERS LOTT, for
384 acres in West Pr.Anne,Election district 1, map #3.
1759/61 Henry Waggaman willed to son William Elliott Waggaman.
23 June 1775 William Elliott Waggaman sold to Henry Waggaman for 5
shillings.
26 Nov.1776 William Elliott Waggaman and Henry Waggaman sold 384 acres to
George Waggaman with lot in Pr.Anne Town.
1780 George Waggaman sold to Henry Jackson, 23 acres
1783 tax- Henry Jackson 23 acres
1794 Henry Jackson willed to son George Wilson Jackson land adj. Pr.Anne
Town-unnamed.
19 Nov.1795 George Waggaman sold to Major William Jones WAGGAMANS LOTT &
ADDITION.
14 Feb 1797 George Waggaman sold to Elizabeth Jackson 33 1/4 acres of
WAGGAMANS LOTT,ROWLEY RIDGE, & ADDITION.

25 Aug.1801 Henry Dickinson and Harriett Dickinson of Dorc.Co. sold to
Henry Waggaman - that George Waggaman died intestate and Harriett
Dickinson is entitled to 1/4th part. no name, or acreage.
9 Nov.1801 John Waggaman Footman and wife Mary Footman of Charles Town,
South Carolina, sold to Henry Waggaman of Dorc.Co. Md. that George
Waggaman died intestate, sold /6th part his share, no name or acres.
2 May 1805 Col. William Jones, wife Elinor Jones sold to Isaac Gibbons 35
acres of HARTHBERRY & WAGGAMANS LOTT.
24 April 1806 Isaac Gibbons and wife Hetty Gibbons sold all interest to
Polly Collins 85 acres of WAGGAMANS LOTT, HARTHBERRY, ADDITION & LAWS
PURCHASE.
12 May 1810 John Teackle, wife Elizabeth Teackle of Georgetown DC sold to
William Williams Co.Md. 15 acres with saw mill and grist mill.
22 June 1810 William Williams sold same to Zadock Long.
12 April 1810 Daniel Ballard, sheriff, sold to William Williams, per
judgement against William Hurley, grist mill, saw mill and 15 acres of
WAGGAMANS LOTT.

WAGGAMAN PURCHASE

Patented on 20 Nov.1666, a resurvey from CARYS ADVENTURE,by Henry
Waggaman in Mt.Vernon, Election district 5 ,map #1.
for 300 acres.
1742 resurveyed to 436 acres by Henry Waggaman
1751 resurvey 947 1/2 acres that includes WASHFORD.
1759/61 Henry Waggaman willed to son John Waggaman
1783 tax- Henry Waggaman
10 Nov.1781 William Elliott Waggaman released to Henry Waggaman devised
by Major Henry Waggaman.
29 Apr.1792 Henry Waggaman,wife Sarah Waggaman of Dorc.Co. son of Henry
and Mary Waggaman sold to George Waggaman of Som.Co. 947 1/2 acres.
20 Aug.1803 Henry Waggaman, wife Sarah Waggaman sold to Littleton Dennis
Teackle,part.
20 Aug.1803 Henry Waggaman, wife Sarah Waggaman of Dorc.Co.sold to Levin
Jones.
Dec.1804 Littleton Dennis Teackle sold to John Dennis 450 acres of
WAGGAMANS PURCHASE, MIDDLE, OWENS DELIGHT & OWENS IMPROVEMENT.
15 Feb.1806 Littleton Dennis Teackle sold to Daniel Whitney 100 acres.
4 Nov 1808 John Teackle of Georgetown DC & Littleton Dennis Teackle sold
to Tubman Lowes 356 acres.
5 May 1810 Tubman Lowes, wife Anne Lowes, sold to Henry Nicols of
Baltimore Md. 200 acres.
1848 Ephraim Nutter (blackman) willed 10 acres to wife Esther Nutter.

WALLERS ADVENTURE

Patented on 1 Nov.1666 by John Waller for 300 acres in St.Peters,
Election district 2,map #6.
Rent Rolls 1666-1723 possessed by William Waller son of John Waller.
1783 tax- Ann Waller
6 May 1794 William Waller and Ezekiel Gillis agreed on boundaries of
lands.
1841 Isaac Newman gave to son Thomas William Newman and son Isaac Newman,
purchased of William Waller-no acres mentioned.

WALLEYS CHANCE

Patented on 9 June 1665 by Thomas Walley for 300 acres in West Pr.Anne, Election district 1, map #2.
1669/70 Thomas Walley willed to son John Walley 300 acres.
Aprl 1687 John Walley conveyed 300 acres to Michael Judd
9 Oct.1693 Michael Judd conveyed to Edward Day.
3 June 1695 Edward Day conveyed to George Goddard 300 acres
1705 George Goddard conveyed 20 acres to Alexander Carlysle
Aug.1709 Alexander Carlisle sold back to George Goddard 20 acres.
15 June 1704 George Goddard sold part 50 acres to Griffith Jones who resurveyed to tract MONMOUTH.
Rent Rolls 1666-1723 George Goddard
4 Nov.1720 Griffith Jones of Albarmarle,North Caorolina and wife Mary Jones conveyed to William Alexander Jr. 80 acres of WALLEYS CHANCE & MONMOUTH.
25 Oct.1721 William Alexander Jr. confirmed the purchase.
23 Feb.1725 George Goddard conveyed to John Goddard inhertiance 150 acres-unnamed.
22 Nov.1721 George Goddard alienated to Alexander Adams
Nov.1722 Rev. Alexander Adams conveyed 1/2 acre for a chappel of Stepney Parish, GODDARDS CHAPPEL.
21 Aug.1755 Day Scott son of Betty Scott who was Betty Day daughter of Edward Day sold to Alexander Adams rector of Stepney Parish 300 acres that Edward Day on 3 June 1695 with wife Mary Day deeded to George Goddard at head of Wicomico River.1769 Alexander Adams willed to grand son Alexander son of Alexander Adams.
1769 part resurveyed to ANDREWS DISAPPOINTMENT
25 March 1807 Thomas Hamilton sold to Benjamin F.A.C. Dashiell, devised by William Adams to Thomas Hamilton.
9 Nov.1808 Thomas G. Fountain sold to Robert J. King 165 1/4 acres of CRAMBURN, WALLEYS CHANCE, HORSEYS CHANCE, EDINBURGH.
1810 Robert J. King sold to Levin King Jr.

WALLERS INLET

Patented in 1744 for 64 acres by John Waller in Tangier, Election district 9, map #7.
1829 Zorobable Williams willed to brother Elijah Williams.

WALLERS POINT

Surveyed in 1794 for 7 acres in St.Peters, Election district 2, map #6.

WALSTONES HOPE

Patented in 1793 for 32 1/4 acres Obed Walston in Fairmount, Election district 6, map #9.

WALTONS IMPROVEMENT

Patented in 1750 by William Walton for 294 acres in East Pr.Anne, Election district 15, map #5.
6 Apr.1757 William Walton and wife Jane Walton sold 55 1/2 acres to Hamilton Bell

7 July 1761 William Walton exchanged 1 1/4 acres with Thomas Jones for 2 1/4 acres of WINTER QUARTER.
14 Aug.1782 William Walton sold to William Jones 51 1/4 acres
1783 tax- Rev.Hamilton Bell Sr. 55 1/2 acres
1783 tax- William Walton 150 acres
24 June 1783 William Walton,wife Rhoda Walton sold to William Handy 13 1/2 acres
26 Aug.1800 John Howard sold to William Hurley 50 acres with WINTER QUARTER.
30 Dec. 1800 William White of Francis White,and wife Nancy Ann White sold to John Bloodsworth 92 acres, 1/2 of tracts of William Walton deceased. divides lands from Rhoda Walton and Ann Walton- unnamed land.
9 March 1803 John Bloodsworth sold to Thomas Walston, several tracts of William Walston deceased, 92 acres unnamed.
17 Feb.1803 Col. William Jones son of William Jones, and wife Elinor Jones sold to John Bloodsworth 1 1/4 acres and 51 1/4 acres.
22 May 1804 William Hurley and wife Rhoda Hurley and William White of Francis White, and wife Ann White agreed to division of lands as William Walton left issue Ann White and Rhoda Hurley, 184 acres.
14 Sep.1804 John Byrd and wife Margaret Byrd, Mary Smith sold to Zadock Long 13 1/2 acres.
1826 Thomas Walston willed to son William Edward Walston.

WALTONS ADDITION

Patented on 22 Nov.1686 by John Walton for 200 acres in Brinkleys, southeast,Election district 3,map #16.
Rent Rolls 16661-1723 Land sold by John Walton who removed to Pennsylvania.
3 March 1719 John Walton and wife Hannah Walton sold to Alexander Davis-no acreage given.
1707 resurveyed to CORK 200 acres.

WANSBOROUGH

Patented on 20 Nov.1679 by Thomas Manlove for 100 acres in East Pr.Anne, Election district 15,map #4.
Rent Rolls 1666-1723 possessed by Madam Mary King
5 Sep.1729 Robert King and wife Priscilla King sold 50 acres to William Heath.
23 March 1752 George Wilson sold 50 acres to William Pollitt
1783 tax- William Heath 50 acres
1783 tax- Thomas Pollitt 50 acres.

WARDS AND HORSEYS CHANCE

Patented in 1762 for 18 acres by Thomas Ward and Outerbridge Horsey in Asbury, Election district 12, map #21
1783 tax- Outerbridge Horsey 18 acres.

WARDS CONCLUSION

Patented in 1787 by John Perkins for 209 acres in Dublin, Election district 4, map #12.
29 March 1789 John Perkins,wife Rachel Perkins sold to Mary Broughton 216

acres of PAXON HILL,WARDS VENTURE,COME BY CHANCE,WARWICKS DISCOVERY,
WARDS CONCLUSION,etc.
13 Oct.1795 Mary Broughton sold to John Layfield 8 acres of WARWICKS
DISCOVERY,WINDSOR SWAMP,WARDS CONCLUSION,etc.
20 Oct.1808 Mary Broughton gave to son Edward Broughton.
28 March 1808 Thomas Layfield, wife Henny Layfield sold to Isaac Mitchell
Adams.
29 March 1808 Isaac Mitchell Adams sold Josiah W. Heath.

WARDS FOLLY

Patented in 1769 by Stephen Ward in Lawsons,Election district 8, map
#19.
13 Nov.1769 Stephen Ward sold 4 1/2 acres to Nathaniel Juett.

WARDS FOLLY

Patented by Stephen Ward in 1748 for 52 acres by Jacob Ward in Asbury,
Election district 12, map #21.
7 Jan 1800 John Ward son of Stephen Ward, now of Kentucky sold to John
Cullen.

WARDS FOLLY

Patented in 1753 for 16 1/2 acres by James Ward in Asbury, Election
district 12, map #21.
1783 tax- Traves Sterling 16 1/2 acres.

WARDS VENTURE

Patented in 1770 by Joseph Ward, a resurvey from LITTLEWORTH, for 67
acres in Dublin,Election district 4, map #12.
28 March 1789 John Perkins,wife Rachel Perkins sold to Mary Broughton 216
acres of WARDS VENTURE,PAXON HILL,COME BY CHANCE,CROOKED RIDGE,PHILLIPS
CONCLUSION, etc.
8 April 1790 John Perkins sold to Jesse Ward of Worc.Co. 6 3/4 acres for
5 shillings.
7 Feb.1792 Jesse Ward,wife Esther Ward of Worc.Co. sold 6 3/4 acres to
John Layfield
13 Oct.1795 Mary Broughton sold 8 acres to John Layfield of PAXON HILL,
WARDS VENTURE, COME BY CHANCE, etc.
1799 John Layfield willed to son Thomas Layfield 8 acres bought of Mary
Broughton and to son John Layfield tract bought of Jesse Ward, unnamed.
20 Oct.1807 Mary Broughton gave to son Edward Broughton.
28 March 1808 Thomas Layfield, wife Henny Layfield to Isaac Mitchell
Adams.
29 March 1808 Isaac Mitchell Adams sold to Josiah W. Heath.

WARE POINT

Patented on 13 March 1663 by Garman Gillett for 100 acres in Brinkleys,
southwest,Election district 3,map #17.
6 March 1667 Garman Gillett of Acco.Co.Va. and wife Sarah Gillett sold
100 acres to Donnock Dennis.
Rent Rolls 1666-1723 possessed by John Outten in right of the child of

Phillip Conner. 50 acres possessed by widow Conner.
1731 ENLARGED pat. 168 acres by Purnell Outten, John Outten and Abraham Outten.
1733 John Outten gave to son Purnell Outten 50 acres his father John Outten alienated from Phillip Conner.
23 Sep.1755 Abraham Outten sold for 5 shillings to Purnell Outten 34 acres
23 Sep.1755 Purnell Outten sold to Abraham Outten for 5 shillings 34 acres of WARE POINT ENLARGED.
1783 tax- Isabelle Conway 50 acres ENLARGED
1783 tax- Purnell Outten 34 acres ENLARGED
1783 tax- Isaac Outten 125 acres ENLARGED
1783 tax- Neil Ritchie 87 acres.
1795 Purnell Outten willed to wife Mary Outten and son Purnell Outten,lands.
17 Jan.1799 Isaac Outten, wife Margaret Outten sold to John Conner 569 acres of several tracts, with WEBLY & WARE POINT ENLARGED.
26 May 1806 John Conner, wife Jane Conner sold to Mordicai Jones of St.Marys Co. WARE POINT, CONNERS ADDITION & OUTTENS VENTURE.
6 April 1810 John Conner sold to Henry James Carroll, WARE POINT, WARE POINT ENLARGED.

WARWICKS CHOICE
see HARPERS INCREASE & HARPERS DISCOVERY

WARWICKS DISCOVERY

Patented in 1763 by William Warwick for 360 3/4 acres in Dublin, Election district 4, map #12, a resurvey from LITTLESWAMP & ADDITION.
6 Apr.1768 William Warwick sold 80 acres to John Benston for 5 shillings.
22 May 1770 William Warwick,wife Martha Warwick sold to Joseph Ward 40 acres.
1775 Joseph Ward willed to son Joseph Ward.
31 Aug.1772 William Warwick,wife Martha Warwick sold 145 1/2 acres to William Miles Sr.
1781 William Miles willed to grandson William Miles son of Samuel Miles, lands conveyed me by William Warwick,unnamed.
1783 tax- William Warwick 121 acres
1783 tax- William Warwick Jr. 50 acres
1783 tax- Mary Miles 55 1/2 acres
1783 tax- Matthias Miles 20 acres.
20 Oct.1786 Joseph Ward sold to David Long and Solomon Long WINSOR HALL,WARWICKS DISCOVERY, bond-no acreage- as David Long and Solomon Long were suritys for Saul Ward and Elizabeth Ward.
17 Apr.1787 David Long and Solomon Long released bond to Joseph Ward.
17 Apr.1787 Joseph Ward,wife Elizabeth Ward, and Elizabeth Ward sold to John Perkins 121 acres of PAXON HILL,WARWICKS DISCOVERY,WINDSOR SWAMP, WORTH LITTLE, etc.
15 May 1787 Joseph Ward sold to John Fleming parts of afsd. land that was not conveyed to John Perkins.95 1/2 acres
28 March 1789 John Perkins sold 216 acres to Mary Broughton of PAXON HILL, WINDSOR SWAMP.WARWICKS DISCOVERY, etc.
16 June 1789 John Fleming and John Perkins sold to David Long Ward 84 3/4 acres of WINDSOR SWAMP,LITTLE SWAMP & WARWICKS DISCOVERY.
21 Oct.1790 Mary Broughton sold 1 acre to William Warwick

21 Oct.1790 William Warwick sold to Mary Broughton 1 acre.
20 March 1792 William Warwick, wife Sarah Warwick sold to Isaac Harris of John Harris 29 3/4 acres.
13 Oct.1795 Mary Broughton sold to John Layfield 8 acres.
9 Feb.1796 David Long Ward,William Warwick, Mills Dryden sold to William Fleming 218 1/2 acres of WARWICKS DISCOVERY,WINSOR SAVANAH,WORTH NOTHING, LITTLE SWAMP.
5 Apr.1796 William Warwick, David Long Ward & Mills Dryden sold to William Fleming Jr. 221 1/2 acres of same as above.
20 Oct 1807 Mary Broughton gave to son Edward Broughton.
28 March 1808 Thomas Layfield, wife Henny sold to Isaac Mitchell Adams.
29 March 1808 Isaac Mitchell Adams sold to Josiah W. Heath.

WASHFORD

Patented on 6 Feb.1672 by Henry Hayman for 150 acres in Mt.Vernon, Election district 5, map #1.
11 Nov.1674 Henry Hayman and wife Eleanor Hayman sold 150 acres to Thomas Carey.
Rent Rolls 1666-1723 75 acres John Webb-75 acres Thomas Carey.
29 Jan 1724 William Carey, wife Elizabeth Carey,
gave to Thomas Carey otherwise called Thomas Crouch 72 acres at Gr.Money Creek.
7 Oct 1740 Thomas Carey(Thomas Crouch) sold to Edward Chambers one moity of WASHFORD.
11 March 1750 Samuel Carey eldest son of John Carey deceased, of Sussex Co.Del., Stephen Hobbs grandson of Joy Hobbs deceased, Robert Austin heir of Joseph Austin sold to Henry Waggaman 75 acres, that John Carey sold to Joy Hobbs.
1751 resurveyed to WAGGAMANS PURCHASE 947 1/2 acres.

WATERFORD

Patented on 26 June 1679 by Roger O'Keen and assigned to John Mackitt for 450 acres in Brinkleys,southeast,Election district 3, map #16.
1715 Thomas Davis willed to wife Sarah Davis.
1726 Sarah Davis gave to daughter Mary Cox wife of William Cox.
13 Aug.1736 Sarah Davis,widow sold to William Cox for 5 shillings, all.
1745 William Cox willed to wife, and then to son John Cox.
1783 tax- William Cox 450 acres.

WATERFORD

Patented in 1767 for 569 acres by Isaiah Tilghman, in Dublin District, Election district 4, map #12.
18 March 1772 Isaiah Tilghman sold 65 acres to Samuel Miles.
6 Dec.1782 Edward Waters Sr.and Isaiah Tilghman agree to make a ditch on tract.
1783 tax- Isaiah Tilghman 50 acres
1783 tax- William Miles of Samuel Miles 65 acres.
1787 corrected to 550 1/4 acres.
1793 Samuel Miles willed manor plantation to grandson Samuel Duer, unnamed.
1795 WATERFORD CORRECTED 559 1/4 acres by Isaiah Tilghman
1799/1802 Isaiah Tilghman willed to son James Tilghman, CORRECTED to 159

acres.
26 Nov.1803 Samuel M. Duer sold to James Smith of Samuel Smith 125 acres
of MILES LOTT & WATERFORD.
26 Jan 1804 James Smith with wife Elizab-th Smith sold to William Gillis
Waters 125 acres of MILES LOTT & WATERFORD.
17 March 1804 Samuel M. Duer and wife Martha Duer sold pt. to George
Miles.
14 Feb.1805 George Miles of Worc.Co. Md., mtg. to Littleton Robins
WATERFORD, MILES LOTT, MILES ADDITION & BAD LUCK.
7 Feb.1809 James Tilghman sold 14 acres to John Miles.
7 Feb.1809 John Miles son of William Miles sold to James Tilghman 6 3/4
acres.

WATERS ADDTION & ENLARGEMENT

Patented in 1757 by George Waters,for 11 acres and in 1761 ENLARGEMENT
for 165 acres pat. by Edward Waters, in Dublin, Election district 4, map
#12
1783 tax- George Waters- both
1 Nov.1791 George Waters sold to William Cottman son of Joseph Cottman 11
acres and 165 acres
9 Oct.1794 George Waters sold to William Cottman son of Joseph Cottman
-same as above.
1805 William Cottman willed all property to be sold to pay debts.

WATERS ADDITION TO TIMBER TRACT

Patented in 1764 for 625 acres by Edward Waters in Dublin, Election
district 4, map #12.
1784 Edward Waters,to kinsman of William Waters son of John Waters for
Mary Ann Hannah Waters all lands.
1840 resurveyed to ADDITION TO WINTER RANGE 887 1/8 acres.

WATERS RIVER

Patented on 5 Sep.1663 by William Waters for 1280 acres in Westover,
Election district 13, map #9.
William Waters of Northampton Co. Va. sold 150 acres to Thomas Tull, now
called DEAR PURCHASE..
Rent Rolls 1666-1723 150 acres Thomas Tull Sr.-700 acres John Waters- 430
acres Richard Waters.
1720 Richard Waters willed to son William Waters 620 acres.
3 Aug.1739 Thomas Tull and wife Rachel Tull sold 150 acres to William
Waters conveyed to Thomas Tull grandfather of said Thomas Tull.
1762 ADDITION patented for 192 acres William Waters..
1783 tax- Richard Waters 525 acres
1783 tax- Rose Waters 352 1/2 acres
1783 tax- Rose Waters ADDITION 136 acres
8 Nov.1786 Richard Waters Sr. sold to William Waters Sr. land devised
Richard by father William Waters-division of lands.
15 Feb.1787 Richard Waters Sr. and wife Eleanor Waters sold to James
Waters part where Richard Waters now lives.
15 Feb.1787 Richard Waters and wife Eleanor Waters sold for 5 shillings
to Tubman Lowe Waters plantation where Sarah Waters now lives at
WATERWORK GUTT.

24 Jan 1793 William Waters son of William sold to Henrietta Elzey w/o
Dr.Arnold Elzey- as Ephraim Wilson father of Henrietta Elzey had bound
him from William Waters deceased. both died before conveyeance.
24 Jan 1793 John Custis Wilson and wife Peggy Wilson traded William
Waters of William for WILSONS LOTT, that Ephraim Wilson agreed to
exchange, that Ephraim Wilson willed to daughter Peggy Wilson who married
John Custis Wilson.
4 May 1793 Thomas Seon Sudler,wife Nelly Sudler sold for 5 shillings to
James Waters land conveyed by Richard Waters and Eleanor Waters to James
Waters- unnamed land.
4 May 1793 William Curtis wife Betsy Curtis (Betsy Waters) sold to James
Waters for 5 shillings their rights.
4 May 1793 Richard Ezekiel Waters sold to James Waters, his rights.
10 Feb.1795 John Custis Wilson sold 1/2 acres of DEAR PURCHASE to John
Irving.
19 Feb.1802 Francis Hutchins Waters sold to Thomas Seon Sudler;
settlement of boundaries of land that bounds WATERS RIVER- no acres
mentioned.
19 Feb.1802 Thomas Seon Sudler sold to Franics Hutchings Waters, same as
above.
12 June 1802 William Curtis,wife Elizabeth Curtis sold to Richard E.
Waters parcel conv. by Richard Waters and wife Eleanor Waters deceased to
Tubman Lowes Waters, at WATER WORK GUTT- no name.
12 June 1802 Daniel Ballard and wife Dolly Ballard sold to James Waters
for 5 shillings, parcel where James Waters now lives, conveyed by Richard
Waters and Eleanor Waters to James Waters at HALL CREEK GUTT. no name.
12 June 1802 Thomas Seon Sudler and wife Nelly Sudler sold to Richard E.
Waters, same as above.
12 June 1802 James Waters, wife Peggy Waters sold to Richard Ezekiel
Waters, same as above.
12 June 1802 Daniel Ballard,wife Dolly Ballard sold to Richard Ezekiel
Waters,same as above.
5 Oct.1802 William Gillis Waters, wife Ann Glasco Waters sold to James
Waters, land conveyed by Richard Waters and wife Eleanor Waters, no name
or acres.
5 Oct.1802 William Waters and wife Ann Glasco Waters sold to Richard
Ezekiel Waters same as above.
18 Jan 1803 Joseph Gillis Waters sold for 5 shillings to James Waters,
same as above.
18 Jan 1803 Joseph Gillis Waters sold to James Waters, same as above.
18 Jan 1803 Joseph Gillis Waters sold to Richard Ezekiel Waters, same as
above.
24 Jan 1803 James Waters sold to members of the Methodist Episcopal
Church and Protestant Episc. Church 1/2 a lot, no name.
1 Dec.1803 William Waters of William gave part to son William Hayward
Waters.
1 Dec.1803 Wiliam Waters gave to son Edward Marriott Waters, part.
4 June 1804 Richard Waters of William Waters, wife Mary Waters sold to
Whitty Fountain 55 3/4 acres.
9 Oct.1804 Whitty Fountain sold to William Turpin of Denwood Turpin 15
1/2 acres.
22 Feb 1805 Whitty Turpin Fountain sold to Thomas Seon Sudler 4 3/4
acres.
4 March 1806 Ann Hack Robertson sold to Richard Ezekiel Waters land
conveyed by Richard Waters and wife Eleanor Waters to Tubman Lowe Waters.

19 July 1806 Ann Hack Robertson sold to James Waters all except part sold
to Tubman Lowe Waters, no name.
2 Nov.1830 Sheriffs sale-suit of Elisha Whitlock against Edward M.
Waters.

WATERTON

Patented in 1705 by John Waters for 120 acres in Westover, Election
district 13, map #11.
1708 John Waters willed 120 acres to Richard Tull.
1710 Richard Tull willed part to son Solomon Tull
18 June 1766 Solomon Tull and wife Rachel Tull sold to William Waters Jr.
part 97 1/4 acres
1783 tax- Solomon Tull 2 1/2 acres
1783 tax- William Waters Jr. 97 1/4 acres
31 Dec.1798 Solomon Tull sold to William Waters of William for 5
shillings all interst in WATERTON,WILSONS LOTT.
1803 William Waters of William, willed to son Edward Marriott Waters,
part.
2 Nov.1830 Sheriff's sale-suit of ELisha Whitlock against Edward M.
Waters.

WATKINS POINT

Patented on 20 Feb.1664 by John Horsey for 150 acres in Lawsons,Election
district 8, map #18.
12 Aug.1721 Stephen Horsey son of John Horsey conveyed to Stephen Horsey
Jr. except part John Horsey conveyed to Anthony Bell and part John Horsey
gave to John Horsey son of Stephen Horsey and Hannah Horsey.
1721 Stephen Horsey willed to son Stephen Horsey.
7 Apr.1750 Capt.Stephen Horsey,wife Elizabeth Horsey sold 150 acres to
Josephus Bell now called BELLS & HORSEYS CONCLUSION.
1754 Stephen Horsey willed to grandson John Horsey,and 50 acres to
Jonathan Darkus.
22 Aug.1751 Josephus Bell sold 33 acres to Benjamin Lankford of BELLS &
HORSEYS CONCLUSION, part conveyed called COMPLYANCE.
18 Jan 1730 Benjamin Lankford sold to Benjamin Lankford son of Lazarus
Lankford 33 acres of above.
1781 Revel Horsey willed to son Stephen Horsey.
1783 tax- William Darcus 50 acres
1783 tax- John Horsey
1783 tax- Sarah Horsey 150 acres
1783 tax- Benjamin Lankford 94 1/2 acres
18 March 1789 Stephen Horsey sold 1 1/2 acres to Benjamin Lankford
9 Apr.1792 Stephen Horsey sold to Benjamin Lankford 65 3/4 acres
9 Apr.1792 Stephen Horsey sold 100 acres to Robert Burcher Holland.
3 Oct.1792 Stephen Horsey sold 13 1/2 acres to Henry Miles.
1 May 1794 Stephen Horsey sold all his rights to Edward Horsey and Revel
Horsey
7 Jan 1795 Edward Horsey of Worc.Co. and Stephen Horsey sold 126 1/2
acres to Aaron Sterling son of John Sterling.
13 Apr.1796 Robert Burcher Holland, wife Peggy Holland sold 33 1/4 acres
to Jesse Holland.
1798 Edward Horsey willed to brother Stephen Horsey land he conveyed me
and to his son Revel Horsey.
1800 Robert Holland willed 66 2/3 acres to be sold.

411

20 Jan 1798 Jesse Hudson sold to Jesse Holland 23 1/2 acres
26 Sep.1800 Thomas Robertson Jr. executor of Robert Burcher Holland deceased, sold to Jesse Holland, lot and wind mill on Coulbourns Creek.
1 Oct.1800 Jesse Holland sold to John Wilkins same as above.
3 Oct.1800 Margaret Holland widow of Robert Burcher Holland released her dower rights to Jesse Holland.
22 Aug.1804 John Wilkins administrator for Jesse Holland, sold 2 acres to William Williams with wind mill conveyed by Jesse Holland. Mary Ann Hall widow of Jesse Holland relinquishes her dower rights.
1 Sep 1804 Thomas Robertson executor sold to William Miles 66 2/3 acres that Robert Burcher Holland willed to be sold.
29 Sep.1804 William Miles sold to Henry Miles 33 1/2 acres.
17 March 1806 Henry Miles, wife Rachel Miles sold to John Miles 42 acres.
8 Dec.1806 Stephen Horsey sold to Thomas Purnell 700 acres.
15 June 1807 Benjamin Lankford sold to William Williams 100 acres.
22 June 1808 William Williams sold to Benjamin Lankford 100 acres.
Jan 1809 Revel Horsey of Worc.Co. sold to Aaron Sterling of John Sterling 127 1/2 acres.
17 March 1810 Benjamin Lankford Sr. sold to William Williams 101 1/4 acres.
10 April 1810 Matthias Dashiell, sheriff sold to William Williams, per judgement against Benjamin Lankford 101 acres.
1840 William Sterling willed to son William Sterling 51 acres and to daughter Betsy Horsey 31 acres and son Thomas Sterling 51 acres.
1852 William Miles willed to son John Henry Miles, part.

WEATHERLYS CHANCE

Patented on 16 Dec.1679 by James Weatherly for 150 acres in West Pr.Anne, Election district 1, map #3.
17 Nov.1686 James Weatherly, wife Ann Weatherly sold 150 acres to Levin Denwood.
Rent Rolls 1666-1723 Arthur Denwood 150 acres
16 Sep.1740 Thomas Denwood and George Denwood agree to partition of land.
16 Sep.1741 George Denwood sold to David Wilson 420 1/2 acres of WEATHERLYS CHANCE,BROWNSTONE,FIRST CHOICE,NUTTERS DELIGHT,DENWOOD INCLUSION, from grandfather Levin Denwood.
1783 tax- James Wilson 20 acres.

WEBLEY

Patented in Dec.1679 by Henry Smith and assigned to Andrew Whittington for 250 acres in East Pr.Anne,Election district 15, map #5.
12 Jan 1687 Court of Somerset drew conveyance for 10 acres from Andrew Whittington and wife.
18 June 1682 Andrew Whittington and wife Ursulla Whittington conveyed to Francis Jenkins and other Justices of Peace for Som.Co. 10 acres for UNITY COURTHOUSE.
Rent Rolls 1666-1723 possessed by John King, who married Ursula Whittington daughter of Andrew Whittington.
25 Aug.1765 John Bozier and wife Priscilla Bozier sold to John King 1/3 pt. of WEBLEY & CHANCE, right of dowery of Priscilla who was the widow of Whittington King.
1773 John King gave to son Whittington King.
1783 tax- Levin Woolford 250 acres.

17 Jan 1799 Isaac Outten and wife Margaret Outten of Acco.Co.Va. sold to
John Conner 569 acres of several tracts, no name.
3 March 1801 Whittington King,wife Ann King sold to the trustees of the
WASHINGTON ACADEMY 7 1/2 acres.
This was the original site of GEORGE WASHINGTON UNIVERSITY 1 mile south
of Pr.Anne Md.

WEBLEY

Patented on 18 Nov.1677 by Josias Leonard for 150 acres in Brinkleys,
southwest,Election district 3, map #17.
Rent Rolls 1666-1723 Josias Leonard assigned to Donnock Dennis. now
possessed by John Outten.
1709 John Outten Sr. died and lands went to sons Samuel Outten,John
Outten,Thomas Outten and Abraham Outten. This land not mentioned in the
will.
1783 tax- Isaac Outten

WEBSTERS MISCHANCE

Patented in 1783 for 7 acres on Deal Island, Election district 14, map
#8.
21 Feb 1805 Meshack Webster, wife Ann Webster sold to William Wallace 7
acres.

WELCOME POOL

see DOUBLE PURCHASE, Randall Revel patented.

WELL MENT

Patented in 1753 for 15 acres by John Webb in St.Peters, Election
district 2, map #6.
2 Jan 1792 John Webb sold to Gowan Wright 8 acres with pt. INTENT.
2 Sep.1800 John Webb and wife Hetty Webb sold to Thomas Noble with
CONTENTION,DISCOVERY.

WELL WISH

see LEDBOURN

WHARTONS FOLLY

Patented on 1 Dec 1719 by Charles Wharton for 100 acres in Dublin,
Election district 4, map #13.
Rent Rolls 1666-1723 Charles Wharton
1720 Charles Wharton willed to Mary Hipes, at decease to Mary
Broughton,Elizabeth Broughton and Rachel Broughton daughters of John
Broughton.
21 June 1732 Charles Richardson of All Hollows Parish and wife Mary
Richardson (late Mary Broughton) cohier with Elizabeth Broughton and
Rachel Broughton spinsters, sold 100 acres to William Booth
21 Nov.1733 William Booth and wife Sarah Booth sold to Nehemiah King 100
acres.

1750 Robert King of Acco.Co.Va.-codicil to will, to grandson Robert
Jenkins King, purchased of my son Nehemiah and by him this day conveyed
to me.
12 July 1754 Nehemiah King sold for 5 shillings to Robert King Esq. no
acres given.
14 Feb 1762 There was a bond from Col.Robert King in his life to Edward
Waters for conveyance of part of TIMBER TRACT and also pt. WHARTONS
FOLLY, that King willed to Edward Waters, who since paid to Nehemiah King
all money due on land.
1783 tax- Edward Waters
12 Feb 1788 Nehemiah King sold 100 acres to Robert Jenkins King.
27 Aug.1788 Robert Jenkins King sold 66 acres to William Waters son of
John Waters.
1788 Robert Jenkins King willed to daughter Mary King.
1787 part resurveyed to DEER PARK

WHAT YOU PLEASE

Patented on 21 March 1694/5 to Phillip Askew for 150 acres in East
Pr.Anne, Election district 15, map #4.
Rent Rolls 1666-1723 Phillip Askew son of Phillip Askew
2 Dec 1709 Philip Askew conveyed to James Adams who sold to Alexander
Vance, 150 acres.
20 Nov.1723 Alexander Vance sold 50 acres to Joseph Stanford.
6 Apr.1772 Joseph Stanford gave 69 acres to son David Vance Stanford.
16 Feb.1773 Henry Dorman and wife Sarah Dorman sold 60 acres to Mills
Bailey part conveyed to Joseph Stanford and Stephen Redding
22 March 1775 Mills Bailey and wife Rebeccah Bailey sold 3 acres to
Duncan Baine for 5 shillings.
1783 tax- Stephen Baine 3 acres
1783 tax- David Stanford 69 acres
1783 tax- George Bailey 57 acres
15 Jan 1798 Stephen Baine, wife Ann Baine sold 3 acres to Jacob Morris.
5 May 1804 James Bailey sold to Jacob Morris
21 Aug.1805 James Bailey sold to negro Jesse Purnell(formerly belonging
to the heirs of Stephen Disharoon, dec'd.)28 acres of WHAT YOU PLEASE,
HENRYS ENDEAVOUR, BAINES ADDITION.

WHAT YOU WILL

Patented in 1769 by Stephen Garland for 7 acres in Westover, Election
district 13, map #11.
1783 tax- Stephen Garland 7 acres.

WHEATLEYS PLEASURE

Patented in 1756 by William Wheatley for 16 1/2 acres in Lawsons,Election
district 8, map #19.
22 Jan 1763 Williiam Wheatley and wife Alice Wheatley sold 16 acres to
Daniel Cullen
8 June 1771 Daniel Cullen sold 16 acres to Outerbridge Horsey
17 Aug.1774 Outerbridge Horsey sold 16 acres to Daniel Cullen
25 June 1775 Daniel Cullen,shop carpenter, sold 16 acres to Isaac
Coulbourn
3 Feb 1792 Daniel Cullen sold to John Handy with EXCHANGE, & CABBIN SWAMP

133 3/4 acres.
31 Oct 1797 William Williams and wife Polly Williams (Polly was heir of
Isaac Coulbourn) relesed claim to John Handy.
8 Jan 1803 John Handy, wife Sarah Handy sold to John Lawson 130 3/4 acres
of CABIN SWAMP, EXCHANGE & WHEATLEYS PLEASURE

WHEATLEYS SECOND ADDITION

Patented in 1734 for 45 acres by Sampson Wheatley in Brinkleys,southwest,
Election district 3, map #17.
1773 Sampson Wheatley willed to daughter Betty Wheatley.
1783 tax- Mary Wheatley 45 acres
24 June 1786 Caleb Jones and wife Betty Jones (daughter of Sampson
Wheatley) sold to Kellum Lankford,Elijah Coulbourn and Thomas Jones of
Annamessex, WHEATLEYS DIFFICULT PURCHASE,IRISH GROVE,MERCHANTS
TREASURE,PRIVILEDGE,WHEATLEYS SECOND ADDITION,LITTLEWORTH,NEW BOSTON, DAM
SWAMP and 17 acres of ADAMS CHANCE.
24 April 1805 Benjamin Conner, Noah Lankford, Benjamin Bedsworth, John
Broughton and wife Mary Broughton, Richard Hall and Mary Bedsworth sold
to Mordicai Jones of St. Mary Co.devised by Sampson Wheatly to daughter
Betty Jones.

WHEELERS DESIRE

see SMITHS RECOVERY

WHITE CHAPPEL

Patented on 23 Oct.1676 by William Stevens who assigned to Robert Crouch
for 200 acres in West Pr.Anne,Election district 1, map #2.
Rent Rolls 1666-1723 Robert Crouch 200 acres
10 June 1719 Jacob Crouch and wife Jane Crouch sold to John Christopher
50 acres that Adrain Gordon sold to Jacob Crouch.
10 June 1719 Jacob Crouch youngest son of Jacob Crouch,and wife Jane
Crouch sold to William Hayman 100 acres now called HAYMANS EXCHANGE.
2 March 1725 William Hayman and wife Mary Hayman sold 100 acres to Thomas
Gillis (now called HAYMANS EXCHANGE.)
1732 ADDITION 52 acres
1748 Thomas Gillis leased to Mary Serman part where John Thompson
formerly lived, for her lifetime.
1757 resurvey to 502 acres. Thomas Gillis
18 June 1766 Clement Christopher sold to Thomas Gillis his rights to
WHITE CHAPPEL,WHITE CHAPPEL GREEN now included in resurvey called WHITE
CHAPPEL.
15 Dec.1767 Thomas Gillis sold 35 acres to Constant Disharoon.
11 June 1770 Thomas Gillis gave to son Joseph Gillis except part sold to
Constantine Disharoon,502 acres.
1783 tax- Joseph Gillis 167 acres
1783 tax- Constant Disharoon 50 acres.
28 May 1794 Thomas Handy Gillis sold to Eleanor Wilson 154 3/4 acres for
5 shilings.
3 June 1794 Richard Bounds sold to James Wilson Jr. and Levin Irving 154
3/4 acres.
3 June 1794 James Wilson Jr. and wife Eleanor Wilson sold to Richard
Bounds 154 3/4 acres
4 Aug.1798 George Handy, sheriff, sold to highest bidder Levin Irving,

per judgement against Thomas Handy Gillis 130 acres, no name of land.
24 Apr.1827 Village Herald newspaper- tr. of George A. Porter at suit of
Samuel Brown executor of Stephen Disharoon - sheriff's sale.
1802 part resurveyed to BRERETONS MISTAKE 177 3/4 acres.
12 Jan 1803 Richard Bounds, wife Rebecca Bounds, sold to John Whittingham
Adams part purchased of James Wilson
25 March 1807 Thomas Hamilton mortgaged to Benjamin F.A. C. Dashiell.
8 Jan.1807 John Whittingham Adams sold to Joshua Disharoon 54 acres.

WHITE CHAPPELL GREEN

Patented in 1682 by Adrain Gordon for 50 acres in West Pr.Anne, Election
district 1, map #2.
Rent Rolls 1666-1723 possessed by Robert Crouch.
1711 Robert Crouch and wife Mary Crouch willed to grandsons John Taylor
and Jacob Taylor 100 acres, formerly belonging to Adrain Gordon and sold
testator by Sampson Powers.
1732 resurveyed to WHITE CHAPPELL 502 acres.

WHITE HAVEN TOWN

Incorporated in 1702 and was part of tract THE LOTT, in Mt.Vernon.
Lot #1 taken up by Samuel Worthington
13 Nov.1731 John McClester,gentleman,sold to Patrick Stewart, surgeon,
lot #3 in the original platt.
3 Aug.1730 Thomas Covington Jr,ship carpenter, sold to Merrick Ellis lot
#2 (Thomas Covington heir at law of Isaac Covington)
Lot #4 Col. Elzey
Lot #6 Col.George Gale
13 July 1733 Thomas Dashiell Sr. sold to Alice Ellis, Spinster, lot #5.
26 July 1735 Thomas Walker son of Thomas sold to Levin Gale tracts
ADDITION & LAST PURCHASE, except lot in WHITEHAVEN Town.
30 Sep.1738 Dr. Patrick Stewart sold to Alexander Buncle 1/2 of lot #3.
1739/40 Alice Ellis willed to nephew John Elzey lots in town.
6 July 1739 Patrick Stewart sold to Matthias Gale lot taken up by John
McClester lot #3.
22 Aug 1746 Alexander Buncle of Worc Co.merchant sold to Matthias Gale
1/2 of lot #3.
21 Nov.1747 Matthias Gale sold to George Douglas of Acco.Co.Va. 1/2 of a
lot
24 Aug.1750 George Douglas of Acco.Co.Va. sold to Robert Heron of Som.Co.
1/2 where Patrick Stewart lived.
1761 Henry Lowes willed house on Chappel St. to be sold.
22 Apr.1763 Robert Heron esq. sold to John Elzey Jr. 1/2 lot.
1766 William Shephard willed to wife Alice Shephard two houses on Bracken
Street.
23 Nov.1787 Levin Gale sold to James Elzey Jr.
1733 Littleton Upshur Dennis, willed to nephews Henry Emerson Dennis and
Francis Dennis land at White Haven on Wicomico River devised from late
wife by her father George Robertson which descended to our children
George Dennis and Elizabeth Dennis.

WHITE OAK

Patented on 30 July 1683 by William Stevens for 250 acres in Fairmount,

Election district 6, map #9.
3 Aug.1686 William Stevens, wife Elizabeth Stevens sold to Henry Miles.
1695 Henry Miles willed to sons Samuel Miles and Henry Miles.
Rent Rolls 1666-1723 Samuel Miles son of Henry Miles 250 acres.
1756 Henry Miles willed to son Henry Miles
1762 resurveyed to MILES CONCLUSION 458 acres

WHITE OAK SWAMP

Patented on 1 March 1680 by Cornelius Ward for 150 acres in
Lawsons,Election district 8, map #19.
Rent Rolls 1666-1723 Cornelius Ward
1722 Cornelius Ward willed to son Samuel Ward plantation where he is
living-unnamed.
7 July 1726 Samuel Ward son of Cornelius Ward and wife Mary Ward sold to
Francis Lord 150 acres of CHESTNUT RIDGE,WHITE OAK SWAMP.
28 March 1747 Randall Lord sold to son Henry Lord 75 acres.
a part now called TROUBLESOME.
1761 Samuel Ward willed to daughter Keziah Taws.
15 Oct.1768 Cornelius Ward Sr. and Cornelius Ward Jr. sold 50 acres to
James Ward son of Cornelius Ward Sr.
1783 tax- Cornelius Ward 25 acres
1783 tax- James Ward 25 acres
1783 tax- William Ward 50 acres.
28 Aug.1790 Isaac Dougherty and Capt. John Taws and wife Keziah Taws sold
22 1/2 acres to John Ward.
28 Aug.1790 Isaac Doughtery sold to Ann Ward and Joseph Ward 2 1/2 acres
27 Aug.1795 John Lord,wife Jemima Lord, Ann Lord and Nathaniel Dougherty
and wife Betty Dougherty sold to Joshua Dougherty 30 1/2 acres of WHITE
OAK SWAMP,CORK,CHESTNUT RIDGE.
13 July 1796 Stephen Ward of John Ward, wife Leah Ward sold to Littleton
Johnson of Lame Johnson 29 1/2 acres of CORK,CHESTNUT RIDGE,WHITE OAK
SWAMP.
17 Feb.1797 Ezekiel Ward sold to Littleton Johnson 17 1/4 acres of CORK,
CHESTNUT RIDGE,LITTLEWORTH,WHITE OAK SWAMP.
17 Feb.1797 Hance Croswell sold to Ezekiel Ward 5 acres of FOLLY,WHITE
OAK SWAMP,CORK.
7 Jan 1800 John Ward son of Stephen Ward, now of Kentucky sold to John
Cullen.
9 Jan 1800 Mary Lord sold to Isaac Daugherty all rights with CORK &
CHESTNUT RIDGE.
12 May 1804 Ezekiel Ward, planter transfered to John Miles,constable of
Little Annamessex, to pay debts 150 acres with FOLLY & DUBLIN
12 May 1804 John Ward Jr. leased to William Johnson son of Littleton part
during life of John Ward.
22 Sep. 1804 Samuel Ward sold to Joseph Ward 15 acres.
22 Sep 1804 Samuel Ward Sr. sold to Samuel Ward Jr. 15 acres.
1 Feb 1806 John Miles, planter sold to Ezekiel Ward 150 acres of WHITE
OAK SWAMP, FOLLY & DUBLIN
1 Feb.1806 Ezekiel Ward sold to Thomas Ward 150 acres of WHITE OAK SWAMP,
FOLLY & DUBLIN.
8 March 1806 Keziah Taws sold to Ezekiel Taws land left by father Samuel
Ward, except part of WHITE OAK SWAMP.
25 Aug.1806 Samuel Ward sold to John Lord 40 or 50 acres of CORK, BAKERS
LOTT & WHITE OAK.

16 Oct.1806 Joseph Ward sold to William Roach 25 acres of WHITE OAK &
part of JOSEPH SECURED
3 Jan 1807 William Roach sold to John Dougherty 137 acres of WHITE OAK &
JOSEPHS SECURITY.
1 Dec.1807 Littleton Johnson sold to Mary Parremore and Stephen
Parremore.
31 Dec.1807 Mary Parremore and Stephen Parremore sold all rights to John
Ward.
31 Dec.1307 John Ward of John sold to John Taws son of William Taws, all
rights.
13 Aug.1808 John Miles, constable sold to William Ward lands of Ezekiel
Ward, 100 acres of DUBLIN, CORK, WHITE OAK SWAMP.
16 Feb.1809 Mary Parremore & Stephen Parremore sold 4 acres to Littleton
Johnson.
21 July 1810 Keziah Taws, spinster, sold to Henry Ward, blacksmith, 5 or
6 acres.
1829 John Dougherty willed lands next to Henry Ward and Joshua Dougherty
to be sold, all other lands to John Thomas Cox at age 21, unnamed lands.
1832 Village Herald newspaper-Easter Daugherty admx. of Joshua Daugherty
deceased, against William Ward of Elijah Ward, taken to settle debts.

WHITE OAK SWAMP

Patented in 1673 by Richard Carey for 100 acres in St.Peters, Election
district 2, map #6.
23 Dec.1682 Richard Carey and wife Mary Carey sold to Edward Carey.
Rent Rolls 1666 1723 - Possessed by Joy Hobbs whose father purchased of
Richard Carey.
1735 Robert Givans willed this land to be sold 100 acres.
2 Nov.1750 John Pollock and James Pollock of Worc.Co. sold 100 acres to
James Spicer.
1783 tax- James Spicer 100 acres
1752 resurveyed to JAMES CONTENT 226 acres.

WHITE OAK SWAMP

Patented in 1745 for 30 acres by Isaac Hayman and James Hayman in East
Princess Anne,Election district 15, map #4.
1770 Isaac Hayman willed to sons Joshua Hayman and Isaac Hayman.
1783 tax- Joshua Hayman 18 acres.

WHITES GIFT

Patented in 1759 by Elias White, a resurvey from GLINEATH and THE
ENTRANCE for 626 acres in Brinkleys,southeast,Election district 3, map
#16.
19 March 1768 Elias White sold to Jacob Adams GLINEATH now called WHITES
GIFT.
26 June 1769 Elias White mortgaged to Samuel Wilson 400 acres of dwelling
plantation- no name
3 July 1770 John Nairn, Jacob Adams, Samuel Wilson, Littleton Dennis of
Worc.Co. sold to David Wilson- as Elias White had tract on resurvey, 400
acres (balance not sold) to pay all debts to afsd.
1767 resurveyed to WILLIAMS GREEN 664 3/4 acres.
21 Nov 1770 Robert Pitts and wife Milcah Pitts sold to Thomas Robertson

140 acres of ENTRANCE or WHITES GIFT.
22 Nov.1773 Elias White,wife Sarah White sold 400 acres to David
Williams.
1784 Dr. Thomas Robertson and wife Martha Robertson sold to William Waddy
141 acres with ENTRANCE,ADVENTURE,MORRIS HOPE,GLENDORE.

WHITBY RECITFIED

Patented in 1750 for 245 acres by Robert Jenkins Henry in Brinkleys,
northeast,Election district 3, map #15.
1764 Robert Jenkins Henry willed to son Robert Jenkins Henry 245 acres.
10 Feb.1755 Robert Jenkins Henry sold to William Adams WHITBY being part
of HIGNETTS CHOICE at head of Morumsco.
1756 William Adams willed to son William Adams and son Phillip Adams.
1783 tax- Robert J. Henry 245 acres
28 Jan.1802 Robert Jenkins Henry of Baltimore sold to William A.
Schoolfield 245 acres.
7 Feb.1803 William A. Schoolfield,wife Mary Schoolfield sold to William
Adams 36 1/2 acres.
(is part of HIGNOTTS CHOICE resurveyed- no date on maps.)
23 April 1806 Samuel Smith sold to Isaac Gibbons 200 acres of WHITBY,
ADAMS CONCLUSION & ADAMS SCHEME.
27 July 1809 William Adams Schoolfield sold to Outerbridge Horsey of
Wilmington Del. 230 acres.
2 July 1809 William Adams Schoolfield mortgaged to Lemuel Taylor of
Baltimore md. 230 acres.

WHITNEYS DELIGHT

Patented in 1751 by Thomas Whitney for 132 acres in West Pr.Anne,Election
district 1, map #3.
1783 tax- Thomas Whitney 132 acres
2 Apr.1790 Thomas Whitney, wife Sarah Whitney sold to Denwood Wilson,wife
Peggy Wilson (division of lands, pt.WHITNEYS DELIGHT & WOLFS DEN that
bounds WILSONS CONCLUSION)

WHITTINGTONS CONCLUSION

Patented in 1813 for 163 3/4 acres, by Isaac Whittington, a resurvey from
ADDITION, in Lawsons, Election district 8, map #18.
1749 James Whittington willed to wife Sally Whittington.

WHITTINGTONS NEGLECT

Patented in 1749 by William Benston for 156 acres in Dublin, Election
district 4, map #12.
13 Feb 1759 William Benston sold to William Warwick 156 acres
probably a mortgage.
22 May 1770 William Benston, wife Leah Benston sold 7 1/2 acres to
William Warwick.
11 Aug.1772 William Benston sold to William Miles Sr. 135 acres, except
part conveyed William Warwick.
1781 William Miles willed to grandson William Miles son of Samuel Miles
ands conveyed me by William Benston-unnamed.
1783 tax- Matthias Miles 110 acres

1783 tax- Henry Miles 9 acres
1783 tax- William Warwick 7 acres
20 March 1792 William Warwick and wife Sarah Warwick sold to Isaac Harris
of John Harris 6 acres.
1839 Pr.Anne Herald-newspaper, Land of Isaac Harris son of John Harris to
be sold
1847 William Mills willed to Hester A. Johnson daughter of Henry McDonal.

WHITTYS LOT

Patented on 28 Nov.1685 by John Whitty for 50 acres in St.Peters,Election
district 2, map #6.
Rent Rolls 1666-1723 possesssed by William Turpin
19 March 1756 William Shores sold to John Shores and Henry Spear 50
acres.
1762 ADDITION 20 acres by William Shores AKA MASONS ADVENTURE.
1783 tax- George Austin 50 acres with ADDITION 20 acres.

WIDOWS CHANGE

Patented in 1743 by William Strawbridge for 1059 acres, a resurvey from
ILLCHESTER, in East Pr.Anne Election district 15, map #5.
1766 William Strawbridge died and land descended to daughter Jane
Strawbridge who died intestate by 1796 and lands sold.
1783 tax- William Strawbridge 1059 acres.
17 Oct.1794 Sarah Porter and William Porter sold to William Davis Allen
for 5 shillings,-became possessed at death of Jane Strawbridge daughter
of William Strawbridge in right of her grandmother Mary Williams half
sister to Dr.William Strawbridge with CONVIENCY,ADDITION,LITTLE LESS &
LEACH.
15 Apr.1796 John Williams of Worc.Co. sold to William Davis Allen, as
John Williams was the eldest male heir of Jane Strawbridge daughter of
William and descended to John Williams and James Williams, Sarah Porter
wife of William Porter,Mary Willis wife of Elijah Willis, Elizabeth
Williams, Nancy Williams and Amelia Williams all of James Williams
deceased and Levin Layfield,William Layfield,Priscilla Dryden wife of
William Dryden,all of Hannah Layfield deceased. Isaiah Furniss, Mary
Stevens wife of Levi Stevens, Levin Boston and James Boston all of Sarah
Boston,tracts WIDOWS CHANCE,CONVIENCY & ADDITION 1128 acres and lot in
Pr.Anne Town.
1797 resurveyed to ALLENS VALE 1297 acres.

WIDOWS HOPE

Patented in 1750 by Rosannah Baine for 13 acres in East Pr.Anne,Election
district 15, map #4.
1783 tax- Stephen Baine 10 acres
1794 resurveyed to BAINES THIRD ADDITION 212 1/4 acres.

WILDERNESS

Patented in 1757 for 21 acres by Thomas Williams in Brinkleys, northwest,
Election district 3, map #14.

WILLIAMS ADVENTURE

Patented on 22 Dec.1723 by William Owens for 64 acres in East Pr.Anne,
Election district 15, map #4.
16 Aug.1727 William Owens and wife Sarah Owens sold 64 acres to William
Polk.
21 June 1770 James Polk gave to son Benjamin Polk 64 acres.
1783 tax- Benjamin Polk 64 acres.

WILLIAMS ADVENTURE

Patented on 9 June 1696 to Michael Williams for 100 acres in Brinkleys,
northwest,Election district 3, map #14.
Rent Rolls 1666-1723 possessed by no one, belongs to heirs of Michael
Williams.
23 Apr.1729 James Dickinson and wife Elizabeth Dickinson sold to Thomas
Williiams 100 acres purchased of Michael Williams
2 Dec.1767 Thomas Williams gave to grandson Thomas Williams Jr.
1767 resurveyed to WILLIAMS GREEN 644 /34 acres.
7 Nov.1798 Whittington Polk son of Benjamin Polk sold to Thomas King 64
acres with SMITHS HOPE,SMALL ADDITION,KILMANNAN,SMITHS HOPE ADDITION
7 Nov.1798 Thomas King sold to Whittington Polk same as above.

WILLIAMS BEGINNING

Patented in 1754 for 50 acres by William Roberts in Dames Quarter,
Election district 11, map #7.
1783 tax- William Roberts 50 acres
1794 William Roberts willed to neice Nancy Lemon wife of Robert Lemon.
23 July 1799 Charles Jones,wife Esther Jones sold to Archibald McDorman
100 acres of this and JAMES MEADOW

WILLIAMS CONQUEST

Patented on 4 Sep.1663 by Michael Williams for 300 acres in Brinkleys,
northwest,Election district 3, map #14.
11 Jan 1696 Michael Williams sold part to brother Thomas Williams 10
acres and balance went to wife Patience Williams.
1720 Thomas Williams gave his part to son Isaac Williams.
1733 William Planner died and gave to Thomas Williams land after decease
of Elizabeth Owens.
2 Apr.1751 Isaac Williams and wife Ann Williams traded 20 acres with
Thomas Williams for tract in Martins 100 and HOOPERS CHANCE in Dorc.Co.
2 Dec.1767 Thomas Williams gave to grandson Planner Williams land where
brother Isaac Williams lived-unnamed.

WILLIAMS GREEN

Patented in 1774 a resurvey from WHITES GIFT,GLINEATH for 488 1/4 acres
in Brinkleys,southeast,Election district 3, map #16.
1783 tax- Martha Williams widow of David Williams 488 acres.
1780 David Williams, to wife Martha Williams, 1/4 pt. of estate and to
son Thomas Williams plantation on Pocomoke River,unnamed.
1802 Thomas Williams willed to John Wilkins, land bounder of WILLIAMS
GREEN.
26 Oct.1809 Gen. John Gale, wife Amelia Gale sold to Ralph Milbourn 1

moity 326 acres, Amelia Gale was entitled to after death of Thomas
Williams of David Williams- they held a mortgage.

WILLIAMS GREEN

Patented in 1767 for 644 3/4 acres by Thomas Williams, a resurvey from
DOUBLE PURCHASE & SOUTH LOTT, in Brinkleys northwest,Election district 3,
map #14.
1783 tax- Benjamin Schoolfield 229 1/2 acres
1783 tax- Thomas Williams 315 acres
1837 William Adams willed to son William G. Adams.

WILLIAMS HARD LOTT

Patented in 1725 for 25 acres in Dame Quarter,Election district 11, map
#7.
13 March 1792 William Roberts made over to David Polk for 5 shillings,
land no name or acresge.
10 Dec.1798 Phillip Hughs, wife Esther Hughs of Sussex Co Del. (sister
and heir of David Polk) sold to George Jones of Som.Co., no name or
acreage.
7 Jan 1799 George Jones,wife Leah Jones sold to Charles Jones, land
bounds JESHIMON & EDWARDS LOTT in Dames Quarter, purchased of Phillip
Hughs. no name.
13 Aug.1809 Charles Jones sold to Thomas White, land purchased of George
Jones in Dames Quarter 27 acres, no name.

WILLIAMS HOPE

Patented on 13 March 1663 by William Smith for 1000 acres in Dublin,
Election district 4, map #13.
1688 resurvey 1002 acres by Henry Smith
1667 William Smith willed to wife Mary Smith. She died intestate and it
descended to Hannah Atchison wife of Vincent Atchison only sister of Mary
Smith.
28 Feb.1671 Vincent Atchison and wife Hannah Atchison sold to
Capt.William Colebourn.
1672 William Colebourn and wife Margaret Colebourn sold to Henry Smith.
1717 Charles Wharton willed to son William Wharton and unborn child 1/2
of tract 100 acres each.
9 March 1722 John Caldwell attorney of John Smith of Sussex Co.Del heir
of Capt. Henry Smith sold 500 acres to Walter Taylor.
20 March 1722 Walter Taylor and wife Esther Taylor sold to James
Robertson 260 acres of PERTH out of WILLIAMS HOPE.
1 Aug.1723 James Robertson sold to Stephen Handy 260 acres of PERTH out
of WILLIAMS HOPE.
18 March 1724 Thomas Dukes and wife Elizabeth Dukes sold to Edward Cluff
60 acres of ADVENTURE out of WILLIAMS HOPE purchased by Walter Taylor who
sold to Thomas Dukes.
11 Dec.1733 Edward Cluff and wife Sarah Cluff sold 60 acres to Thomas
Hayward ADVENTURE out of WILLIAMS HOPE
11 May 1734 John Taylor son of Walter Taylor sold to Thomas Hayward 260
acres.
1734 part resurveyed to HAYWARDS LOTT 560 acres.
21 Nov.1734 Thomas Lindzey eldest son of David Lindzey sold to John

Broughton 80 acres sold by Walter Taylor to David Lindzey who willed to son Levin Lindzey 80 acres, who died a minor and it fell to Thomas Lindzey.

17 Feb.1734/5 John Broughton traded 25 acres with Thomas Hayward for 21 acres of BLAKES HOPE.

18 Nov.1735 William Wharton and wife Mary Wharton sold to John Dennis Jr. 100 acres.

20 June 1738 Mary Smith (Mary Wharton daughter of Charles Wharton) sold to John Dennis Jr. 37 1/2 acres.

21 May 1738 Mary Smith sold 62 1/2 acres to Robert Mitchell

7 Apr.1738 William Kitchen appointed Robert Jenkins Henry to be attorney to convey all property to his last wife Temperance Scarborough. Receipt acknowledge from Walter Taylor attorney of John Smith of Sussex Co. Del. 500 acres being part of WILLIAMS HOPE.

24 Nov.1739 Henry Smith of Sussex Co.Del.son of John Smith deceased sold 550 acres to Thomas Hayward of Som.Co.

24 Nov.1739 I Henry Smith of Sussex Co.Del. sell to John Broughton 180 acres.

15 Jan 1739/40 Henry Smith son of John Smith sold to Gideon Tilghman 40 acres

15 Jan 1740 Henry Smith sold to John Dennis Jr. 137 acres

1743 Robert Mitchell willed to son Isaac Mitchell.

1755 John Broughton gave 100 acres to son William Broughton and then to his wife Jemima Broughton and to his son John Broughton part.

20 Aug.1755 John Dennis gave to son Littleton Dennis 100 acres.

19 Apr.1766 Gideon Tilghman gave to son Nehemiah Tilghman 100 acres out of WILLIAMS HOPE,TILGHMANS CARE & PLAGUE WITHOUT PROFIT.

26 Apr.1766 Gideon Tilghman gave to son Gideon Jr. same as above.

14 Feb.1769 Gideon Tilghman and wife Tabitha Tilghman sold to Robert Jenkins King 84 1/2 acres of WILLIAMS HOPE,TILGHMANS CARE,PLAGUE WITHOUT PROFIT.

20 Jan 1769 Nehemiah Tilghman son of Gideon Tilghman and wife Kathryn Tilghman sold to Robert Jenkins King 268 acres of WILLIAMS HOPE,GIDEONS LUCK,PLAGUE WITHOUT PROFIT.

9 Sep.1773 Littleton Dennis sold to Samuel Sloan of Worc.Co. 100 acres purchased of William Wharton and 37 1/2 acres purchased of Mary Wharton.

1773 Isaac Mitchell gave to son Joshua Mitchell 62 /12 acres.

17 Oct.1773 Robert Jenkins King sold to Ephraim Stevens 250 acres of GIDEONS LUCK,WILLIAMS HOPE,PLAGUE WITHOUT PROFIT,SECOND ADDITION, TILGHMANS CARE.

15 Oct.1779 Ephraim Stevens sold to Robert Jenkins King 250 acres of WILLIAMS HOPE,GIDEONS LUCK,PLAGUE etc.

1783 tax- John Broughton Jr.100 acres

1783 tax- John Broughton 21 acres

1783 tax- Jane Mitchell 62 acres

1783 tax- Samuel Sloan 137 acres.

1785 John Broughton willed to sons George Broughton and Josiah Broughton.

2 Apr.1787 John Mitchell sold for 5 shillings to Joshua Mitchell 62 1/2 acres.

1788 Robert Jenkins King willed to son Robert King lands bought of the Tilghmans.

5 Nov.1798 George Broughton son of John Broughton, wife Alce Broughton sold to Elzey Maddux with TILGHMANS CARE 63 3/4 acres.

28 Feb.1803 John Broughton gave to son Isaac Broughton 185 acres of BLAKES HOPE & WILLIAMS HOPE.

7 May 1803 John Wilkins,sheriff, per judgement against John Broughton
sold to Kellum Broughton 134 acres of BLAKES HOPE & WILLIAMS HOPE.
11 Nov.1806 Pierce Riggin constable sold to Kellum Broughton 36 acres of
WILLIAMS HOPE & BLAKES HOPE per judgement against Isaac Broughton Esq.

WILLIAMS LOTT

Patented in 1769 by William Cottingham for 60 3/4 acres in Brinkleys,
southwest, Election district 3, map #17.
1783 tax- William Cottingham 60 acres
1799 William Cottingham willed to wife Mary Cottingham and son Josiah
Cottingham.
9 Jan 1807 Josiah Cottingham, wife Elizabeth Cottingham sold to Thomas
Merrill Tull 32 1/2 acres and 1 acre lot contiguous.
9 Feb.1809 Thomas Merrill Tull, wife Polly Tull, sold to Joshua Tull 203
1/2 acres of BOSTON, GOSHEN, TROUBLESOME & 32 1/2 acres of WILLIAMS LOTT.
23 July 1834 Josiah Cottingham sold to Levin Conner.

WILLIAMS LOTT

Patented in 1726 for 200 acres by John Williams in Westover,Election
district 13, map #11.
1755 resurveyed ENLARGED to 223 1/4 acres.
1760 John Williams Sr. possessed in will.
1783 tax- Solomon Tull 24 acres
1783 tax- John Williams 200 acres
12 July 1791 John Williams sold 200 acres to Levin Ballard
12 July 1791 Levin Ballard sold to John Williams 200 acres
20 Nov.1812 John W. Curtis sold to William Williams
1815 William Williams sold to William Curtis 223 1/4 acres.

WILLIAMS LOTT

Patented in 1784 by William Polk for 70 acres in Mt.Vernon, Election
district 5, map #1
1783 tax- William Polk
1795 resurvey to include ROBINSONS LOTT 460 acres.

WILLIAMS PURCHASE

see DOUBLE PURCHASE-Randall Revell

WILLIAMS PURCHASE

Patented in 1819 for 54 1/2 acres by William Williams in Lawsons,
Election district 8, map #18.

WILLIAMSTON

Patented on 4 Sep.1663 by Thomas Williams for 300 acres in Brinkleys,
northwest,Election district 3,map #14.
Rent Rolls 1666-1723 Thomas Williams
1720 Thomas Williams willed to son John Williams
3 June 1712 Thomas Williams Sr. and wife Frances Williams sold to Thomas
Williams Jr.

2 Apr.1751 Isaac Williams and wife Ann Williams sold 80 acres to Thomas Williams.
2 Dec.1767 Thomas Williams gave to Thomas Williams Jr. 500 acres of CHANCE,SOUTH LOTT,WILLIAMS ADVENTURE, WILLIAMSTON. etc.
2 Dec.1767 Thomas Williams gave to grandson Planner Williams plantation where brother Isaac Williams lived.
1773 resurveyed to NEIGHBORS CONCLUSION 624 1/4 acres.

WILLINGS ADVICE

Patented in 1801 for 6 acres by Nathaniel Bell in Brinkleys, northwest, Election district 3, map #14.

WILINGS LOTT

Patented in 1797 for 6 acres by Evans Willin in Dames Quarter, Election district 11, map #7.

WILLS LOTT

This is part of AMITY, in Westover, Election district 13, map #10.
1684 William Furniss deeded this part of AMITEE 100 acres to John Bennett and wife Sarah Bennett
1703 John Bennett and Sarah Bennett sold to William Turpin.

WILSONS ADDITION

Patented in 1775 by Denwood Wilson for 31 3/4 acres in West Pr.Anne, Election district 1, map #3.
1792 James Wilson willed to wife Catherine Wilson and then to grandson James Wilson lands adjacent WILSONS ADDITION.

WILSONS ADDITION

Patented in 1770 by James Wilson for 50 acres in West Pr.Anne,Election district 1, map #3.
1783 tax- James Wilson 50 acres
1793 resurveyed to SELAHAMMALEKOTH 95 3/4 acres.

WILSONS CONCLUSION

Patented in 1749 from part of ARCADIA by David Wilson for 1319 acres in West Pr.Anne,Election district 1, map #3.
1783 tax- Denard Wilson 1001 acres a resurvey of 1319 acres.
20 Aug.1772 triparte- James Wilson and Josiah Polk, to George Hayward (that David Wilson deceased devised to James Wilson part) 315 1/4 acres) mortgage.
12 Nov.1783 James Wilson son of David Wilson sold to Samuel McClemmy 315 1/4.
12 Nov.1793 Samuel McClemmy sold to James Wilson, same-division.

WILSONS CONCLUSION

Patented in 1803 for 158 1/2 acres by George Wilson in Brinkleys, northwest, Election district 3, map #14.

23 Feb.1805 George Wilson sold to Richard Hall, 2 acres.
22 Feb 1809 Richard Hall, wife Sally Hall & Nathan Cahoon sold part to
Noah Lankford Hall.

WILSONS DISCOVERY

Patented on 31 Mar.1707 by Ephraim Wilson for 100 acres in Dames Quarter,
Election district 11, map #7.
28 Dec.1762 David Wilson leased to Thomas Jones of Manokin for 20 years.
17 Apr.1764 Thomas Jones returned to David Wilson
17 Apr.1764 David Wilson and wife Ann Wilson sold to Levin Wilson 1/4 the
part.
13 Dec.1768 Samuel Wilson and wife Mary Wilson sold to Denwood Wilson 450
acres of TILBURY,WILSONS DISCOVERY,GLASGOW,SECUIRTY & KILLGLAN for 5
shillings.
1783 tax- Levin Wilson 75 acres.
1783 tax- Denwood Wilson 25 acres.
1881 resurveyed to ADDITION TO KILLGLASS

WILSONS FINDING

Patented on 31 July 1713 by Alexander Carlisle and assigned to Robert
Wilson for 68 acres in East Pr.Anne,Election district 15, map #4.
23 March 1752 George Wilson sold to William Pollitt 68 acres.
1783 tax- Thomas Pollitt 68 acres.

WILSONS FIRST

Patented in 1754 by Wilson Heath for 100 acres in East Pr.Anne,Election
district 15, map #4.
23 Oct.1765 Wilson Heath gave to son William Heath 2 3/4 acres.
1783 tax- William Heath 2 1/2 acres
1783 tax- Wilson Heath 97 1/2 acres
1785 Wilson Heath willed to sons Josiah Wilson Heath and Samuel Heath.
1789 ADDITION pat. Josiah W. Heath for 14 acres.
26 May 1794 Josiah Heath and Samuel Heath sold to James Diamond 100 acres
with HOG RIDGE-mortgage.
31 March 1795 Abraham Heath son of William Heath, and wife Martha Heath
sold to Josiah Hobbs.
21 May 1795 James Diamond released mortgage to Josiah Heath and Samuel
Heath, with HOG RIDGE.

WILSONS FOLLY

Patented on 25 April 1714 by William Wilson for 50 acres in West
Pr.Anne,Election district 1, map #2.
Rent Rolls 1666-1723 William Wilson
1729 part resurveyed to GLASCOW SWAMP
10 June 1747 William Wilson formerly of Somerset Co.,now of Queen Annes
Co.Md. sold to Alexander Adams 50 acres.
1783 tax- John Adams 50 acres
1802 Balance resurveyed to EDINBURGH
25 March 1807 Thomas Hamilton mortgaged to Benjamin F.A. C. Dashiell.

WILSONS LAST SURVEY

Patented in 1770 by William Wilson for 16 acres in Brinkleys, northwest, Election district 3, map #14.
1794 William Wilson willed to son George Wilson and after death to grandson William Wilson.
10 Jan 1805 George Wilson sold to nathaniel Bell 3/4 acre now called WILSONS CONCLUSION & SECURITY.

WILSONS LOTT

Patented in 1734,by David Wilson, a resurvey from BERERS LOTT, for 800 acres in Westover,Election district 13, map #11.
29 Apr.1737 David Wilson sold 20 acres to William Wharton.
20 Apr.1737 David Wilson sold 24 acres to Solomon Tull
21 July 1732 David Wilson and wife Betty Wilson sold 68 acres to Samuel Long.
1742 William Wharton and wife Mary Wharton sold 20 acres to Edward Rook.
15 Dec.1746 Edward Rook and wife Sarah Rook, mariner, sold 20 acres to John Howard.
1750 David Wilson willed to son Ephraim Wilson
25 Feb 1751 John Howard and wife Christian Howard sold to William Waters 20 acres.
1756 Samuel Long gave to wife Sarah Long 68 acres and then to son William Long.
9 Apr.1771 William Long sold 2 acres to Ephraim Wilson
9 Apr.1771 Ephraim Wilson son of David Wilson sold to William Long son of Samuel 68 acres.(confirmation of sale to Samuel Long from David Wilson)
1777 Ephraim Wilson willed to daughter Peggy Wilson
1783 tax- William Long 66 acres
1783 tax- Levin Wilson 463 acres
1783 tax- William Waters Jr. 20 acres
1783 tax- Thomas S.Sudler 30 acres
23 Dec 1789 John Wilson, wife Peggy Wilson sold to Thomas Seon Sudler 30 acres.
6 Aug.1792 John Turpin and wife Sarah Turpin sold to Thomas Lister 60 1/4 acres of HOLWELL,CURTIS LOTT, WILSONS LOTT(prop. of William Long deceased and 1/4 part became right of his daughter Sarah Long now wife of John Turpin.
24 Jan 1793 John Curtis Wilson and wife Peggy Wilson traded part of WATERS RIVER for WILSONS LOTT that Ephraim Wilson willed to daughter Peggy Wilson who married John Curtis Wilson.
13 Dec.1798 Solomon Tull sold to William Waters of William, all interest in WATERTON, BEACH & PINE, WILSONS LOTT
2 Dec 1801 William Long sold to George Beauchamp interest in the real estate of William Long deceased near branch of Annamessex where Samuel Long now lives 57 1/2 acres- no name.
2 Nov.1830 Sheriff's sale- suit by Elisha Whitlock against Edward M. Waters.

WILSONS LOTT

see DOUBLE PURCHASE-part of CATHERINES CONTENT

WILSONS PURCHASE

Patented in 1764, a resurvey by David Wilson on SMITHS RECOVERY,by James

Wilson for 609 acres in West Pr.Anne,Election district 1, map #3.
1783 tax- James Wilson 609 acres.

WILSONS PURCHASE

Patented in 1769 by William Wilson for 41 3/4 acres in Brinkleys,
northwest, Election district 3, map #14.
31 March 1772 William Wilson sold 14 3/4 acres to John Long for 5
snillings.
1783 tax- William Wilson of George Wilson 21 acres.
26 March 1787 Benjamin Conner trustee, sold to Kellum Broughton 14 acres
by decree of the court, to sell property of John Long deceased, subject
to dower right of the widow of John Long.
24 March 1788 Levin Watson and wife Mary Watson sold to Kellum Broughton,
property of John Long, no acreage given.
1797 William Wilson willed 20 acres to son Jesse Wilson.
1 June 1801 Jesse Wilson son of William Wilson sold to George Wilson all
his fathers land.
1816 George Wilson willed lands to son William Wilson, no name.

WINDERS PURCHASE

Patented on 1 April 1666 by John Winder for 200 acres in Westover,
Election district 13, map #11.
4 June 1672 John Winder and wife Bridget Winder sold 200 acres to
Nicholas Fountain
1728 resurvey by Nicholas Fountain 160 acres.
Rent Rolls 1666-1723 possessed by Marcy Fountain
5 Oct.1754 Marcy Fountain and wife Betty Fountain sold to Benjamin
Fransway and Ephraim Wilson-triparte agreement.
1755 resurveyed to CONVIENCY 344 acres

WINDSOR

Patented in 1794 by Henry Coston for 482 1/4 acres in Dublin, Election
district 4, map #12, a resurvey of FLATLAND,BEARE POINT,LOW LAND,TURKEY
RIDGE.
11 June 1799 Henry Coston sold 26 acres to William Cottman

WINDSOR

Patented on 13 June 1683 by William Stevens and assigned to George
Goddard and John Goddard, in West Pr.Anne,Election district 1, map#2, for
100 acres.
1769 Alexander Adams willed to Sarah Adams widow of son Alexander and
then to her son Alexander Adams.
23 May 1775 Alexander Adams sold to George Dashiell son of George, 1
acre.
1783 tax- John Adams Sr. 1 3/4 acres
1783 tax- William Adams 30 1/2 acres
1783 tax- Josiah Adams 184 acres.
25 March 1807 Thomas Hamilton sold to Benjamn F.A. C. Dashiell, devised
him by William Adams.

428

WINSOR CASTLE

Patented on 28 Sep.1681 by William Winslow for 200 acres in East Pr.Anne, Election district 15, map #5.
1 June 1687 William Winslow, wife Mary sold to James Barrey 200 acres.
Rent Rolls 1666-1723 possessed by Capt.John West.
1715/6 John West willed to be sold,that William Winslow and wife Mary Winslow conveyed to James Barrey and wife Jean Barrey who conveyed to Capt. John West.
6 Jan 1724 Katherine West daughter of John West sold 200 acres to Patrick Dailey (confirmed by Randal West and Anthony West.)
15 May 1738 Patrick Dailey sold to William Sullivan 100 acres.
1 Apr.1763 William Sullivan and wife Bridget Sullivan sold 100 acres to John Puzey.
1783 tax- John Puzey 100 acres
20 Feb.1806 John Puzey mortgaged to Jesse Winright, WINDSOR CASTLE & ADDITION.
5 Apr.1814 John Puzey willed 182 acres to children(with ADDITION)
29 March 1831 Constables sale- at suit of William Clayville against Peter Puzey,William Puzey,Jeptha Puzey and Joseph M. Puzey- WINDSOR CASTLE & ADDITION TO- 100 acres property of John M. Puzey
1867 Sarah Jones granted to William Puzey,Eleanor Townsend wife of William Townsend,John F. Puzey,Sarah E. Carter w/o John P. Carter, and Thomas Puzey heirs at law of William Puzey deceased- all rights to WINDSOR CASTLE and AADDITION and all interest 1/4 part being my brother William's share.

WINDSORS PREVENTION

Patented on 28 Oct.1701 by Thomas Roe for 60 acres on Deals Island, Election district 14, map #8.
Rent Rolls 1666-1723 possessed by Francis Craydon
1783 tax- John Jones 30 acres
1783 tax- David Wallace 30 acres
28 Nov.1797 David Wallace sold 14 acres to Isaac Noble and wife Peggy Noble that Henry Walston devised to Peggy Walston now wife of Isaac Noble.

WINSOR SWAMP

Patented in 1752 for 70 1/2 acres by Joseph Ward Jr.in Dublin, Election district 4, map #12.
20 Oct.1786 Joseph Ward sold to David Long and Solomon Long WINDSOR HILL & WARWICKS DISCOVERY.mortgage.
17 Apr.1787 David Long and Solomon Long released mortgge to Joseph Ward.
17 Apr.1787 Joseph Ward,wife Elizabeth Ward, and Elizabeth Ward sold to John Perkins 121 acres of PAXON HILL,WARWICKS DISCOVERY,WINSOR SWAMP,CROOKED RIDGE,LITTLEWORTH, etc.
15 May 1787 Joseph Ward sold to John Fleming 95 1/2 acres of WINSOR SWAMP,WARWICKS DISCOVERY,LITTLE SWAMP.
28 March 1789 John Perkins,wife Rachel Perkins sold to Mary Broughton 216 acres of WINSOR SWAMP,PHILLIPS CONCLUSION, WORTH LITTLE, WARDS CONCLUSION,etc.
16 June 1789 John Fleming and John Perkins sold to David Long Ward 84 3/4 acres of WINSOR SWAMP, LITTLE SWAMP, WARWICKS DISCOVERY.

29 Oc t.1793 James Ward sold to David Long Ward 118 acres of WORTH
NOTHING,WINSOR SWAMP.WINSORS SAVNAH.
22 Sep.1795 James Ward son of Joseph Ward sold to Mills Dryden 82 1/2
acres of WORTH NOTHING,WINSOR SWAMP,WINSOR SAVANAH
13 Oct.1795 Mary Broughton sold to John Layfield 8 acres of WINSOR SWAMP,
WARDS CONCLUSION, COME BY CHANCE, WORTH LITTLE,etc.
9 Feb.1796 David Long Ward, William Warwick and Mills Dryden sold to
William Fleming 218 1/2 acres of WARWICKS DISCOVERY, WINSOR
SWAMP,WORTHNOTHING, LITTLE SWAMP.
5 April 1796 William Warwick, David Long Ward and Mills Dryden sold to
William Fleming Jr. 221 1/2 acres of WARWICKS DISCOVERY,LITTLE
SWAMP,WORTH NOTHING, etc.
20 Oct.1807 Mary Broughton gave to son Edward Broughton.
28 March 1808 Thomas Layfield, wife Henny Layfield, sold to Isaac
Mitchell Adams.
29 March 1808 Isaac Mitchell Adams sold to Josiah W. Heath.

WINSORS SAVANAH

Patented in 1773 by Joseph Ward for 47 1/2 acres in Dublin, Election
district 4, map #12.
1775 Joseph Ward Sr. willed 47 1/2 acres to son James Ward.
29 Oct.1793 James Ward sold to David Long Ward 118 acres of WINSORS
SAVANAH, WORTH NOTHING,WINSORS SWAMP.
22 Sep.1795 James Ward son of Joseph sold 82 1/2 acres to Mills Dryden
WINSOR SWAMP,WINSOR SAVANAH,WORTH NOTHING.
5 Apr.1796 William Warwick,David Long Ward & Mills Dryden sold to William
Fleming, afsd.lands 221 1/2 acres.
1789/1803 William Fleming willed lands to son William Fleming, unnamed.

WINTERBOURNE

Patented on 4 Oct.1677 by John White and assigned to Isaac Noble for 100
acres in West Pr.Anne,Election district 1, map #2.
Rent Rolls 1666-1723 Isaac Noble son of Isaac Noble.
25 Nov.1752 Isaac Noble sold to John Leatherbury 164 acres of TINSON,
WINTERBURN and vacancy.
1665 resurveyed to TINSON 300 acres.

WINTERHARBOUR

Patented on 22 Dec.1688 by Capt.John King for 86 acres in Fairmount,
Election district 6, map #9.
1696 John King willed to son Benjamin King 86 acres.
Rent Rolls 1666-1723 Benjamin King.
20 Oct.1773 Ephraim King sold to William Walston and Thomas Walston for 5
shillings.
1776 William Walston willed to sons Charles Walston and Levin Walston
1783 tax- William Walston 51 3/4 acres.
28 March 1789 Charles Walston and Levin Walston sold to Samuel Smith 22
acres of WINTER HARBOUR,LONDONS ADVISEMENT and all lands contiguous.
1790 Isaiah Tilghman willed to son William Tilghman, purchased of Thomas
Walston.
4 Feb.1794 Thomas Walston of Kent Co.Del. grandson and heir of Thomas
Walston sold 10 1/2 acres to Samuel Smith

4 Feb.1794 Thomas Walston of Kent Co.Del. sold to William Tilghman 20 1/2 acres
20 Sep.1803 Samuel Smith sold his interest to William Walston of Obed Walston.
19 Oct.1805 William Walston sold to Revel Roach 32 1/2 acres of WINTER HARBOUR & LONDONS ADVISEMENT.
13 Jan 1809 William Coulbourn, of Robert Coulbourn, constable, sold to George Beauchamp 50 acres, property Revel Roach bought of William Walston, unnamed.

WINTER HARBOUR

Patented on 9 Aug.1688 by John Perkins for 150 acres in Asbury,Election district 12, map #21.
21 July 1769 John Perkins sold 150 acres to Planner Williams,Thomas Williams,Levin Williams,Isaac Williams and Thomas Dixon 30 acres each.
1783 tax- Thomas Dixon 30 acres
1783 tax- Planner Williams 100 acres.
9 April 1792 Thomas Dixon of Worc.Co. sold to Isaac Dixon of Som.Co. all lands father bought in Apes Hole with Planner Williams and others in Little Annamessex.

WINTER HARBOUR

Patented in 1802, a resurvey by Matthias Miles of SUPPORT & PRIVILEDGE, for 183 acres in East Pr.Anne Election district 15, map #5.

WINTER QUARTER

see COSTONS VENTURE

WINTER QUARTER

Patented in 1755 by Thomas Jones for 255 3/4 acres in East Pr. Anne, Election district 15, map #5.
22 Apr.1760 Thomas Jones of Money 100, sold to Jarvis Ballard 17 acres in exchange for SMITHS RESOLVE.
7 July 1761 Thomas Jones sold 2 1/2 acres for 5 shillings to William Walton in exchange for part WALTONS IMPROVEMENT
10 Aug.1782 William Jones sold to William Walton 15 3/4 acres
1783 tax- William Walton 51 3/4 acres
26 Aug.1800 John Howard sold to William Hurley 50 acres with WALTONS IMPROVEMENT
27 Dec 1803 Col. William Jones son of Thomas Jones sold to John Bloodsworth 185 1/2 acres.
1826 Thomas Walston willed to son William Edward Walston

WINTER RANGE

Patented on 2 July 1688 by Thomas Tull for 200 acres in Fairmount, Election district 6, map #9.
Rent Rolls 1666-1723 Thomas Tull
1717 Thomas Tull willed to son John Tull 50 acres and to William Cox son of wife Ann Tull 150 acres.
1729 John Tull willed to son Joshua Tull.
19 Nov.1729 Thomas Tull and wife Rachel Tull sold to John Tull 150 acres

(Thomas Tull as grandson and heir at law to Thomas Tull deceased.)
1783 tax- Thomas Tull 200 acres
20 oct.1794 Joshua Tull son of John Tull gave to son Thomas Tull 150
acres.

WINTER RANGE

Patented in 1760 by Thomas Hayward and William Hayward for 172 acres in
Dublin, Election district 4, map #12.
21 Nov.1766 Thomas Hayward of Som.Co. and William Hayward of Talbot
Co.Md. sold 172 acres to Joseph Cottman for 5 shillings.
1783 tax- Joseph Cottman 172 acres
10 Aug.1793 I Joseph Cottman give to wife Margaret Cottman and son
Lazarus Cottman the produce of tract and at decease to be divided between
then.
1793 Joseph Cottman willed to son Lazarus Cottman 172 acres.

WOLFES DEN

Patented on 12 March 1687 by Owen Magraugh for 120 acres in West Pr.Anne,
Election district 1, map #3.
1691 Owen Magraugh willed to son Richard Magraugh.
Rent Rolls 1666-1723 possessed by widow Mary Magraugh.
17 July 1738 William Magraugh grandson of Owen Magraugh and son of Owen
the younger deceased sold to Richard Magraugh son of Richard Magraugh for
10 shillings 120 acres.
14 Apr.1747 Richard Magraugh and wife Elizabeth Magraugh sold 120 acres
to Henry Ballard.
24 March 1752 Henry Ballard and wife Mary Ballard sold to Thomas Whitney
53 1/2 acres
4 Jan 1757 Mary Ballard widow of Henry Ballard sold to William Hayward
lands and houses- no name or acreage given.
2 Apr.1790 Thomas Whitney and wife Sarah Whitney and Denwood Wilson,wife
Peggy Wilson divided lands WHITNEYS DELIGHT & WOLFES DEN
7 March 1797 Thomas Ballard sold to George Waggaman for 5 shillings.

WOLF DEN

Patented in 1757 by William Furniss for 49 acres in Westover, Election
district 13, map #10.
1765 James Furniss willed to son George Furniss.
15 Aug.1769 William Furniss Jr.son of James Furniss,
and wife Sarah Furniss sold to George Furniss 49 1/2 acres.
21 Aug.1772 George Furniss Jr. schoolmaster, sold to Isaiah Tilghman 49
1/2 acres.
1783 tax- Isaiah Tilghman 49 1/2 acres
1790 Isaiah Tilghman willed to son James Tilghman.

WOLFS DEN

Patented in 1766 by Levin Ballard for 9 acres in West Pr.Anne, Election
district 1, map #3.
19 Sep.1776 Levin Ballard sold to Levin Woolford and John McGrath 9
acres.
13 March 1779 Levin Woolford and John McGrath sold 9 acres to Samuel

Wilkins.
6 March 1782 John Wilkins sold to Elias Bailey 5 3/4 acres
3 Apr.1792 John Wilkins sold to Elias Bailey 5 3/4 acres
1817 Elias Bailey willed lands to sons Benjamin Bailey & Isaiah Bailey,
no name.

WOLFSPITT RIDGE

Patented on 24 May 1688 by Richard Chambers for 115 acres in East
Pr.Anne, Election district 15, map #4.
Rent Rolls 1666-1723 Richard Chambers.
20 Aug.1735 Stephen O'Dear son of John O'Dear, of Queen Anne Co.Md. sold
115 acres to Isaac Hayman that Richard Chambers conveyed to John O'Dear
who died intestate.
1774 ADDITION pat by Joshua Hayman for 284 1/2 acres.
1770 Isaac Hayman willed to son Joshua Hayman and ADDITION to son Isaac
Hayman.
1783 tax- Isaac Hayman 70 acres
1783 tax- Joshua Hayman 288 acres
14 Dec 1785 Joshua Hayman sold 9 acres to Stephen Baine ADDITION.
18 March 1790 Joshua Hayman sold 29 acres to Isaac Hayman of ADDTION.
15 Jan 1798 Stephen Baine, wife Ann Baine sold to Jacob Morris 5 acres.
5 Apr.1797 James Pollitt,wife Betty Pollitt sold 28 1/2 acres to Jacob
Morris son of John Morris.
14 May 1803 David Hayman of Worc.Co. sold to Jacob Morris of John Morris
43 acres that fell him by the death of sister Polly Hayman.
31 March 1821 Tubman Lankford and wife Amelia Lankford sold to Randal
Hayman brother of Amelia Lankford, land of Joshua Hayman, 1/2.

WOOD BRIDGE
see DISPENCE

WOOD HALL & WOOD HALL REGAINED

Patented on 24 Aug.1679 for 200 acres by John White who assigned to John
Woodard for 200 acres in Brinkleys, northeast, Election district 3, map
#15.
7 Feb 1606 John Woodward, wife Ellinor Woodward sold to Richard Farewell.
Rent Rolls 1666-1723 Moses Fenton possessed.
1723/7 Moses Fenton willed estate to daughters Elizabeth McDonnell,Naomi
Fenton,Margaret Fenton,Sarah Fenton, Agnes Fenton.
13 May 1758 Moses Craig of Kent Co.Del,tailor and wife Sarah Craig (Sarah
Fenton) sold to Fenton Catlin of Somerset Co.her 1/4 right.
2 July 1759 Hugh Craig of Kent Co.Del. son of Hugh Craig and Agnes Craig
(Agnes Fenton) both now deceased, sold to Fenton Catlin their 1/4 part.
24 July 1753 William Dickinson of Kent Co.Del. son of Walter Dickinson
and wife Naomi Dickinson (Naomi Catlin) deceased, sold to Robert Blair
his share.
19 Nov.1762 David Dryden appointed guardian of John Blair son of Robert
Blair who had part of WOOD HALL.
31 Jan 1764 Fenton Catlin sold 79 acres to Brittain Powell.
9 May 1765 Fenton Caltin, wife Margaret Catlin, sold to Alexander Maddux
120 acres out of NEW WOOD HALL,WOOD HALL & HOG QUARTER.
22 Jan.1770 John Blair sold 40 acres to Elisha Brittingham and Brittain
Powell.
14 Jan 1772 Alexander Maddux sold 8 acres to Phillip Adams son of Thomas

Adams.
18 March 1772 Fenton Catlin sold to David Long(debt to Duncan Livingston
and Nehemiah Catlin) while Fenton Catlin was in jail, they attorneys to
convey to Nehemiah Catlin 30 acres.
1783 tax- Phillip Adams 8 acres
1783 tax- David Long 13 acres
1783 tax- Brittain Powell 198 acres
1788 resurvey WOOD HALL REGAINED 136 3/4 acres by Brittain Powell..
17 May 1796 Samuel Powell sold to William Powell 97 1/4 acres as Brittain
Powell willed them to be divided.
17 May 1796 William Powell sold to Samuel Powell 80 acres.
23 Oct.1806 Solomon Long son of David Long, wife Elinor Long and William
Powell and Samuel Powell sold to Eli Gibbons 142 acres of WOOD HALL & HOG
QUARTER- division of lands of David Long.
5 March 1807 Eli Gibbons, wife Amelia Gibbons, and Edward Beauchamp, wife
Anna Beauchamp sold to James Smith.

WOODLAND

Patented on 21 March 1680 by William Stevens and assigned to Andrew
Whittington for 150 acres in East Pr.Anne,Election district 15, map #5.
13 Jan 1686 Andrew Whittington sold to David Brown 150 acres
13 Sep.1740 John Woolford and wife Mary Woolford (Mary Brown) and
Margaret Brown sold to David Wilson 150 acres.
1749 resurveyed to CLOVERFIELDS by David Wilson

WOOD STREET

Patented on 13 Nov.1677 by John Emmett and assigned to Thomas Jones for
300 acres in Lawsons,Election district 8, map #9.
Rent Rolls 1666-1723 Robert Catherwood in right of the orphans of Thomas
Jones (widow Martha Jones married Roert Catherwood.)
1701 Thomas Jones willed to son John Jones LITTLE BOLTON.
1775 resurveyed to LITTLE BOLTON 825 1/2 acres.

WOODSTOCK

Patented in 1747 for 50 acres by Thomas Williams in Brinkleys, northwest,
Election district 3, map #14.

WOODS CONTENT

Patented in 1751 for 161 acres, by William Wood, a resurvey from ALLENS
CONTENT in Brinkleys,northeast,Election district 3, map #15.
1773 Levi Wood gave to sister .Martha Wood ALLENS CONTENT, if no issue to
Levi Wood son of Elijah Wood.
1783 tax- William Wood 161 acres
1795 William Wood willed to son Joshua Wood.

WOOLEDGE

Patented on 28 Feb.1677 by Henry Leaton for 150 acres on Deals Island,
Election district 14, map #8.
26 April 1684 Henry Leaton and wife Margaret Leaton sold to John Winsor
150 acres.

Rent Rolls 1666-1723 John Winsor 150 acres
1730 John Winsor willed to son Lazarus Winsor.
1738/48 Lazarus Winsor willed to son Isaac Winsor, 150 acres on Devils
Island.
19 Nov.1731 John Winsor, planter sold to son Lazarus Winsor 150 acres.
1783 tax- Richard Wallace
1823 resurvey to 212 acres (includes LONG DELAY.)

WOOLFES HARBOR

Patented in 1714 for 150 acres by Daniel Morrow in East Pr.Anne,Election
district 15, map #5.
17 March 1721 John King and wife Ursulla King sold to Daniel Morrow and
Alexander Morrow his son 150 acres.
25 Apr.1744 Alexander Morrow and wife Rachel Morrow sold 150 acres to
Thomas Bannister 150 acres.
25 Oct 1759 Mitchell Bannister,wife Abigail Bannister and William
Bannister both sons of Thomas Bannister sold to James Furniss Jr. son of
James Furniss 150 acres
22 March 1769 James Furniss mortgaged to John Hall.
11 Oct.1769 John Hall sold to Isaac Handy the mortgage.
17 March 1772 James Furniss sold to Isaac Handy, attorney 150 acres.
8 Jan 1805 Richard Henry Handy, wife Elizabeth Handy sold to Littleton
Dennis Teackle, as heir to Isaac Handy Esq.
19 Oct.1807 Littleton Dennis Teackle sold to John Teackle of Georgetown
DC. land bought of Richard Henry Handy, no name.

WOOLFS HARBOR

see IGNOBLE QUARTER

WOOLFORD

Patented on 11 Nov.1672 by Roger Woolford for 700 acres in West Pr.Anne,
Election district 1, map #3.
1701 Roger Woolford gave plantation to son Roger Woolford.
Rent Rolls 1666-1723 possessed by Mary Woolford relic of Roger Woolford.
1713 resurveyed to 900 acres John Woolford
1730 Roger Woolford willed to son John Woolford 900 acres
21 March 1742 Henry Waggaman and wife Mary Waggaman (one of the daughters
of Levin Woolford son of Roger Woolford) deeded to Samuel Wilson and wife
Martha Wilson(daughter of Levin Woolford) part of WOOLFORD & HAPPY
ADDITION which Roger Woolford willed to son Levin. Robert Woolford heir
at law to Roger Sr. deeded on 2 Apr.1729 to Mary Woolford and Martha
Woolford heirs of Levin Woolford.
23 Aug.1759 Martha Wilson and Levin Wilson gave to Thomas Wilson.
1 Jan 1773 Martha Wilson widow of Samuel Wilson and Levin Wilson and wife
Sarah Wilson gave to George Wilson for love.
1783 tax- Levin Woolford 900 acres
6 May 1807 Dr. Arthur Woolford, wife Elizabeth Woolford sold to Rev.
James Laird 203 acres.
25 Feb.1807 Arthur Woolford sold to John Woolford 479 1/2 acres, willed
by Levin Woolford.
1836 John Woolford willed to son William G. Woolford, MIDDLE PLACE, part
of WOOLFORD.

WOOLFORDS CHANCE

435

Patented on 22 Nov.1667 by Roger Woolford for 300 acres in St.Peters,
Election district 2, map #6.
1701 Roger Woolford willed to son Roger Woolford, plantation.
Rent Rolls 1666-1723 Mary Woolford relic of Roger Woolford.
1730 Roger Woolford of Dorc.Co. willed to son John Woolford.
18 May 1734 John Woolford sold to George Bozman 300 acres except part
taken out by William Jones son of John.
1750 Levin Bozman willed to brothers Daniel Bozman and Phillomon Bozman.
6 March 1790 John Jones Sr. sold to William Jones 36 1/2 acres.
27 March 1792 John Jones Sr. sold to William Jones Sr. 36 1/2 acres.
6 Sep.1807 William B. Jones sold to Littleton Dennis Teackle.
29 Oct.1807 Littleton Dennis Teackle sold to John Teackle of Georgetown
DC.

WOOLFORDS VENTURE

Patented on 14 Oct.1696 by Roger Woolford for 50 acres in Tangier,
Election district 9, map #7.
Rent Rolls 1666-1723 Mary Woolford relic.
1730 Roger Woolford of Dorc.Co. willed to son John Woolford 50 acres
1783 tax- Levin Woolford 50 acres
29 May 1804 Dr. John Woolford sold to Robert Jones 50 acres.

WOOLVER MARSH

Patented on 20 April 1680 by John Kirk for 150 acres in Lawsons,Election
district 8, map #18.
1719 John Kirk willed to wife Bridget Kirk and to daughter Sarah Kirk.

WOOLVER

Patented on 3 Oct.1681 by Nathaniel Dougherty and assigned to Andrew
Whittington for 100 acres in East Pr.Anne, Election district 15, map #5.
Rent Rolls 1666-1723 possessed by William Fassitt and John King 100
acres.(William Fassitt married Elizabeth Whittington and John King
married Ursulla Whittington)
1771 John Benston willed to be sold
1783 tax- Rebecca Benston
13 July 1788 Rebecca Benston sold to Richard Bounds
31 Jan.1792 Matthias Miles sold to Jesse King (as John Benston deceased,
appointed Stephen Ward now deceased and Matthias Miles to sell with LAST
CHANCE 100cres for the benefit of the daughters of John Benston.
1 Jan 1792 Jesse King sold 100 acres to Eli Furniss with LAST CHANCE
22 May 1798 Jesse King sold to Eli Furniss 100 acres-same as above.

WORKINGTON

Patented in 1794 by James Elzey, a resurvey from SECOND PURCHASE,COXES
LOTT & pt.BENGAL for 502 1/2 acres in Mt.Vernon, Election district 5, map
#1.
site of WORKINGTON PLANTATION built 1793 by Henry Jackson from Workington
England.
21 Feb 1795 Henry Jackson willed estate to wife Elizabeth Jackson. (Levin
Gale married Leah Jackson daughter of Henry Jackson)
1837 John Planner Gale willed to daughter Maria Gale and children William

Gale,Francis Gale and George Gale 976 acres.

WORKINGTON

Patented in 1813 for 44 acres by Alfred Whitney in East Pr.Anne, Election
district 15, map #4.

WORST IS PAST

Patented on 25 Oct.1666 by James Nicholson for 50 acres in St.Peters,
Election distict 2, map #6.
9 Feb.1671 James Nicholson and wife Mary Nicholson sold 50 acres to
Richard Whitty.
8 June 1680 Richard Whitty and wife Alice Whitty sold to Richard Lumn.
Rent Rolls 1666-1723 possessed by James Langrell on behalf of orphans 50
acres
1729 resurveyed to 150 acres.
1783 tax- John Wright 150 acres
1785 resurveyed to RIGHTS CONCLUSION 264 1/4 acres.

WORTHLESS

Patented on 28 Nov.1694 by William Matthews for 100 acres in Brinkleys,
southeast,Election district 3, map #16.
Rent Rolls 1666-1723 William Matthews
1726 William Matthews willed to son David Matthews.
21 June 1745 David Matthews sold 100 acres to Teague Matthews.
1760 Teague Matthews willed to grandson Benjamin Holland Matthews 100
acres
1783 tax- Benjamin Matthews 100 acres
16 July 1791 Benjamin Holland Matthews sold for 5 shillings to Stephen
Collins
16 July 1791 Stephen Collins sold to Benjamin Holland Matthews, same.

WORTH LITTLE

Patented in 1759 for 50 acres by Joseph Ward in East Pr.Anne, Election
district 15, map #5.
12 Apr.1785 Saul Ward sold to Joseph Ward 50 acres
21 Feb 1786 Joseph Ward sold to Matthias Miles part
22 March 1786 Joseph Ward and wife Elizabeth Ward sold to John Layfield
38 acres
17 Apr.1787 Joseph Ward,wife Elizabeth Ward and Elizabeth Ward sold to
John Perkins, part.
28 March 1789 John Perkins,wife Rachel Perkins sold to Mary Broughton
13 Oct.1795 Mary Broughton sold to John Layfield,part.
20 Oct.1807 Mary Broughton gave to son Edward Broughton
28 March 1808 Thomas Layfield, wife Henny sold to Isaac Mitchell Adams.
28 March 1808 Isaac Mitchell Adams sold to Josiah W. Heath.

WORTH NOTHING

Patented in 1773 for 50 acres by James Ward in East Princess Anne,
Election district 15, map #5.
1833 resurveyed to FRIENDS GOODWILL 175 acres.

WORWICKS DEPARTURE

Patented in 1808 by William Warwick for 20 acres in Dublin, Election district 4, map #12.

WRANGLE

see RANGLE

WRIGHTS FOLLY

Patented in 1765 by Thomas Aikman for 127 acres in St.Peters, Election district 2, map #6.
16 Apr.1770 Thomas Aikman sold 17 acres to Samuel Sockwell.
17 Apr.1770 Thomas Aikman sold 62 3/4 acres to Gowan Wright
31 Dec.1771 Samuel Sockwell and wife Elizabeth Sockwell sold 17 acres to Henry Walston Miles.
1783 tax- Thomas Aikman 41 acres
1783 tax- Henry Walston Miles 17 acres
1783 tax- Gowan Wright 62 3/4 acres
1805 Gowan Wright willed to daughters Mary Wright,Sarah Wright and Ann Wright lands-unnamed.

YORKSHIRE

Patented in 1764 for 28 1/2 acres by Stacey Miles in Westover, Election district 13, map #11
1770 Stacey Miles willed to son Thomas Miles.

YORKSHIRE ISLAND

Patented on 2 June 1664 for 100 acres by William Wilkinson in Crisfield, Election District 7, map #20
Rent Rolls 1666-1723 found to be 150 acres in right of Samuel Horsey, occupied by Rice Morgan.
1724/6 Samuel Horsey willed to sons Smith Horsey and Stephen Horsey bought of Cornelius Ward.
28 Jan.1748 Stephen Horsey Jr. sold to Smith Horsey his rights.
2 April 1760 Smith Horsey sold to Stephen Horsey for 5 shillings land where Stephen Horsey lives, no name or acreage.

YOUNG TINSON

Patented in 1743 by Isaac Noble from part of TONYS VINEYARD for 168 acres in West Pr.Anne,Election district 1, map #2.
25 Nov.1752 Isaac Noble sold to John Leatherbury 168 acres
1756 John Leatherbury willed to son Charles Leatherbury purchased of Isaac Noble.
21 June 1757 Charles Leatherbury,wife Priscilla Leatherbury, sold 10 acres to Benjamin Cottman
2 Apr.1771 Charles Leatherbury,wife Priscilla Leatherbury sold 4 acres to Benjamin Cottman.
17 Dec.1804 Thomas Hamilton and Charles Nutter, wife Louisa Nutter (late Louisa Adams) agree to divide the real estate of William Adams Jr.
25 March 1807 Thomas Hamilton sold to Benjamin F.A. C. Dashiell lands devised by William Adams Jr. to Thomas Hamilton 1235 1/8 acres. WALLEYS CHANCE, WINDSOR, CRAMBURN, TINSON, WILSONS FOLLY, GLASGOW SWAMP, YOUNG

TINSON, TONYS VINEYARD, JOHNS DESIRE, ADAMS DISCOVERY, HORSEYS CHANCE,
WHITE CHAPPEL, ANDREWS DISAPPOINTMENT, EDINBURGH. Mortgage.
1810 Dr. Charles Nutter, sold part to Daniel Whitney.

444

445

(continued from previous col.)

(continued from previous col.)

452

(continued from previous col.)

(continued from previous col.)

457

459

461

465

467

(continued from previous col.)

474

475

478

482

(continued from previous col.)

484

MAPS OF TRACTS OF SOMERSET COUNTY
Compiled and drawn by Harry L. Benson, Baltimore,
Maryland, 1942.

Shown are names of tracts, date of survey and acreage.

Map No.	Region within Election District [Map numbers have been changed to accommodate this reprinting and differ from Benson's original work.]
1	All of Mt. Vernon (E.D. #5).
2	Upper part of West Princess Anne (E.D. #1)
3	Lower part of West Princess Anne (E.D. #1)
5*	Upper part of East Princess Anne (E.D. #15)
4*	Lower part of East Princess Anne (E.D. #15)
6	All of St. Peters (E.D. #2)
7	All of Tangier (E.D. #9) & Dame Quarter (E.D. #11)
8	All of Deal Island (E.D. #14)
9	All of Fairmount (E.D. #6)
10	Upper part of Westover (E.D. #13)
11	Lower part of Westover (E.D. #13)
12	Upper part of Dublin (E.D. #4)
22*	Lower part of Dublin (E.D. #4)
14	Northwestern part of Brinkley (E.D. #3)
15	Northeastern part of Brinkley (E.D. #3)
16	Southeastern part of Brinkley (E.D. #3)
17	Southwestern part of Brinkley (E.D. #3)
18	Eastern part of Lawsons (E.D. #8)
19	Western part of Lawsons (E.D. #8)
20	All of Crisfield (E.D. #7)
21	All of Asbury (E.D. #12)
13*	South Marsh part of Smiths Island (E.D. 10)
23	Upper part of Smiths Island (E.D. #10)
24	Lower part of Smiths Island (E.D. #10)

* Benson's original numbers, 4 and 5 have been interchanged
and numbers, 13 and 22 have been interchanged for ease in
use.

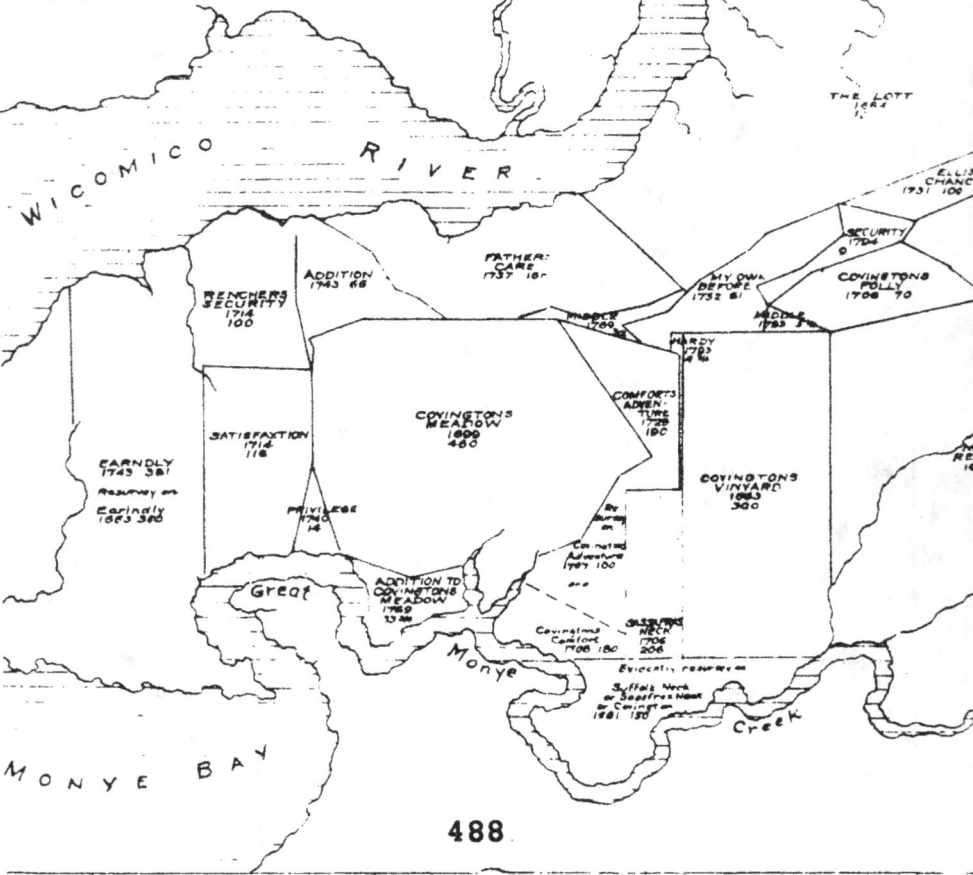

NOTE: This map shows the outlines, names and acreage of tracts of land recorded in the Land Commissioner at Annapolis, Md. The names of the resurveyed tracts are ... the courses are shown by broken lines (— — —) original tracts have been resurveyed more than ... are shown by broken lines (—·—·—·—)

Compiled and drawn by Harry L. Benson, ...
February 28, 1940

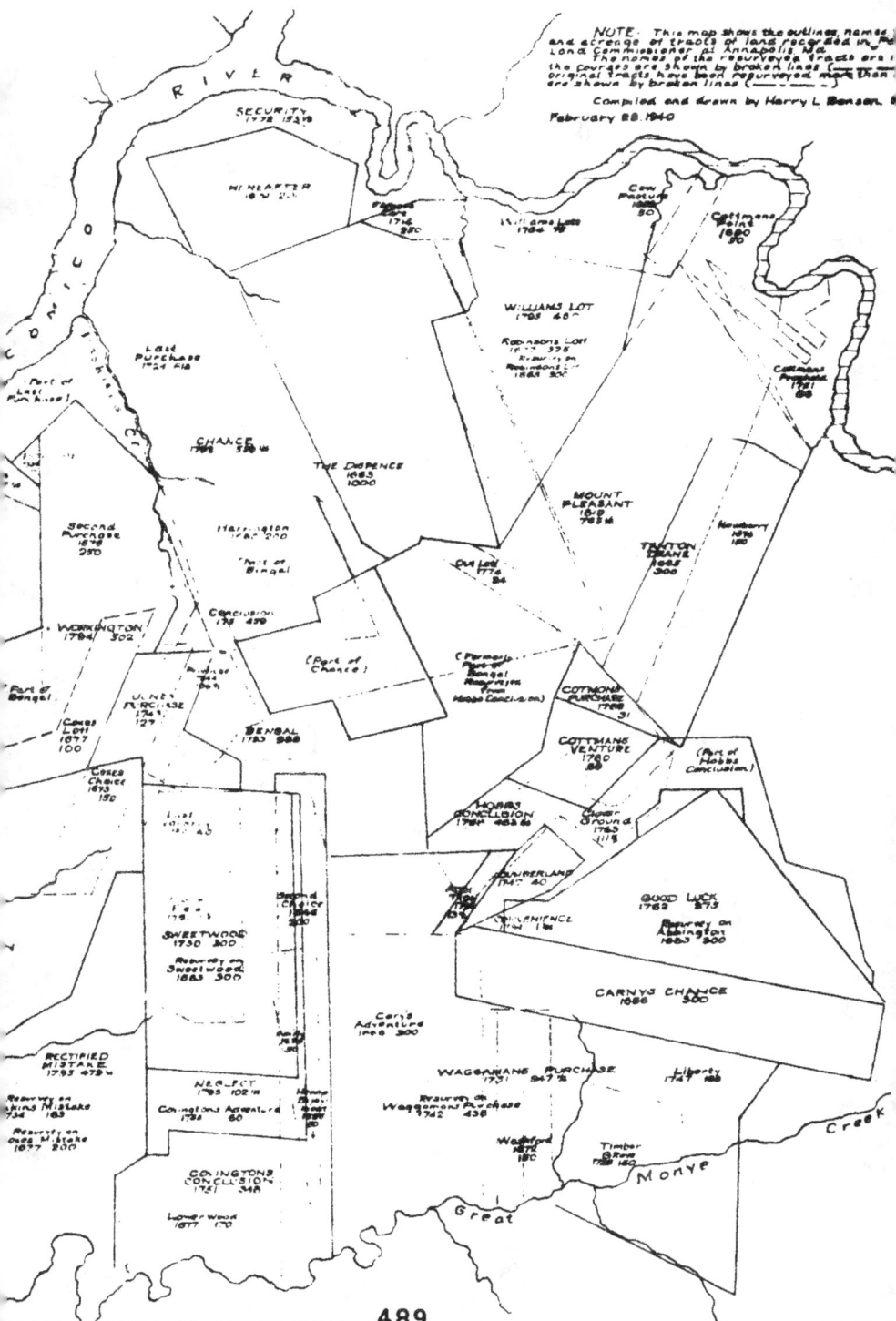

RIVER

ONIO ... RIVER

SECURITY
1778 1539

HEREAFTER
1672 251

FOUND
1714
350

WILLIAMS LOT
1784 48

COW PASTURE
50

COTTMANS POINT
1660
50

WILLIAMS LOT
1793 48

ROBINSONS LOT
1675 375
Resurvey on
Robinsons Lot
1683 350

COTTMANS PURCHASE
1761
88

LAST PURCHASE
1724 518

Part of
Last Purchase

CHANCE
1785 579

THE DEFENCE
1663
1000

MOUNT PLEASANT
1619 785

Newberry
1696
180

TALTON PLAINE
1685 300

SECOND PURCHASE
1678
250

HARRINGTON
1760 200

Part of
Bengal

OUR LOT
1774
84

WORKINGTON
1784 302

CONCLUSION
1778 470

(Part of
Chance)

(Formerly Part of
Bengal Resurveyed
from Hobbs Conclusion)

COTTMANS PURCHASE
1788
31

Part of
Bengal

U NEY
PURCHASE
1749
127

Bridge
1744
60

BENGAL
1753 988

COTTMANS VENTURE
1780
88

(Part of
Hobbs
Conclusion)

CONES LOTT
1677
100

CONES CHANCE
1693
150

Second
Chance
1724
200

HOBBS CONCLUSION
1784 483

CLEAR GROUND
1783
118

CUMBERLAND
1747 40

SWEETWOOD
1730 300

Resurvey on
Sweetwood
1883 500

GOOD LUCK
1762 373

Resurvey on
Addington
1663 300

CONVENIENCE
1704 18

CARNYS CHANCE
1688
300

RECTIFIED MISTAKE
1793 479

Resurvey on
kins Mistake
734 183

Resurvey on
Cones Mistake
1677 300

NEGLECT
1795 102

Covingtons Adventure
1794 60

Cary's Adventure
1666 300

WAGGAMANS PURCHASE
1731 547

Resurvey on
Waggamans Purchase
1742 438

LIBERTY
1747 188

COVINGTONS CONCLUSION
1751 348

Longwood
1677 170

WEXFORD
1675
180

TIMBER GROVE
1766 180

Monye

Great

Creek

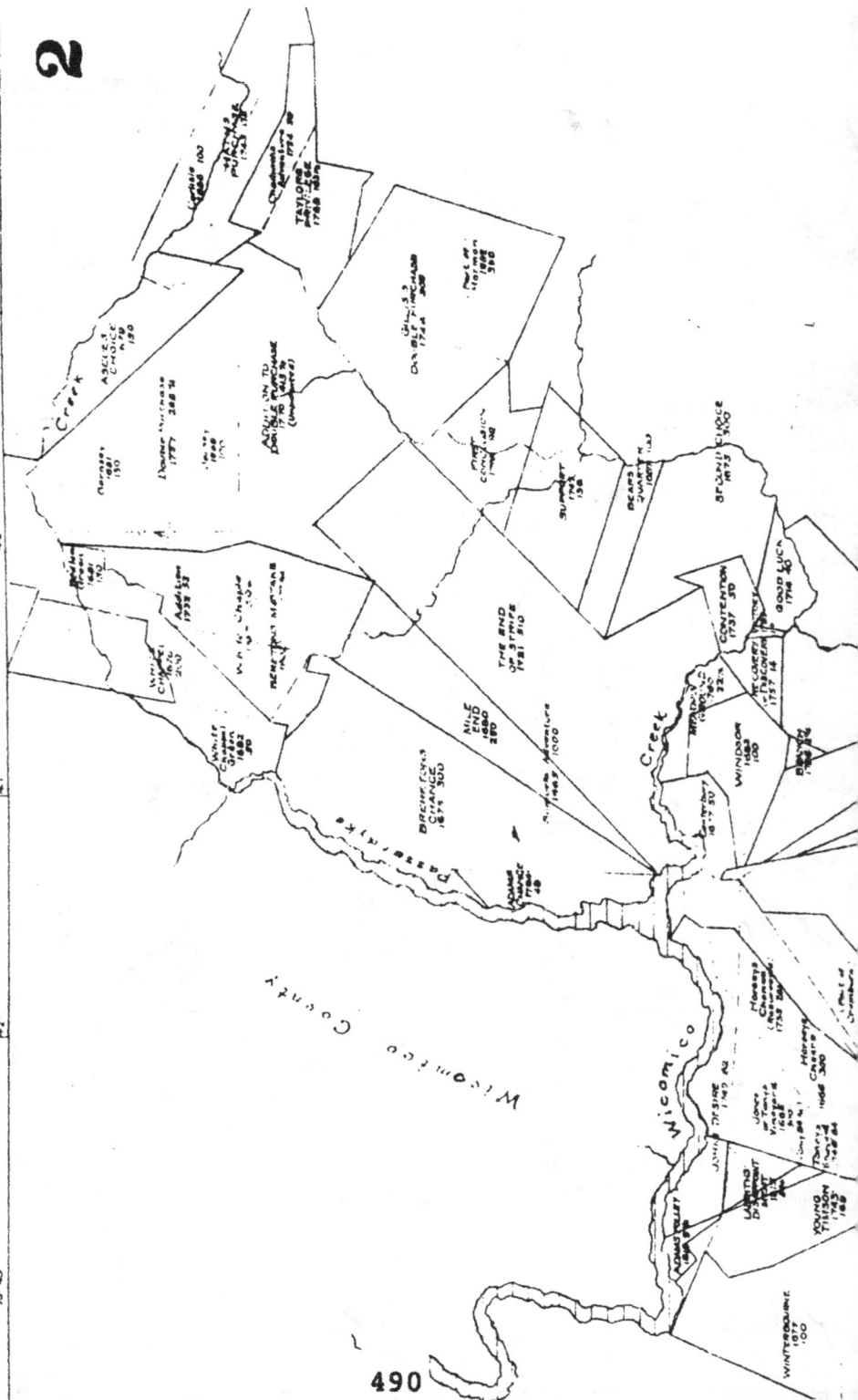

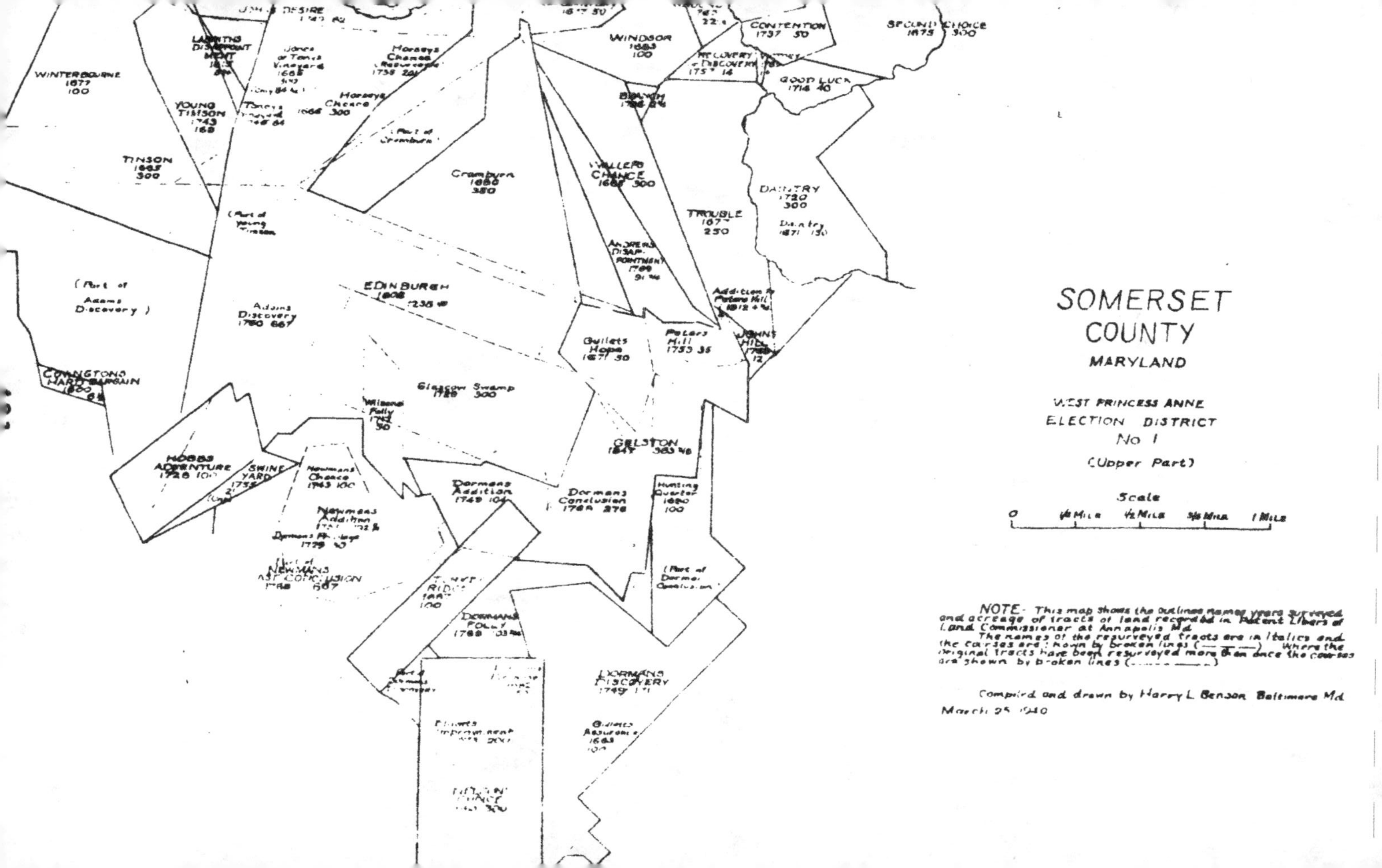
SOMERSET
COUNTY
MARYLAND
WEST PRINCESS ANNE
ELECTION DISTRICT
No 1
(Upper Part)
Scale
0 1/4 Mile 1/2 Mile 3/4 Mile 1 Mile
NOTE- This map shows the outlines names years surveyed and acreage of tracts of land recorded in Patent Libers of Land Commissioner at Annapolis Md.
The names of the resurveyed tracts are in Italics and the courses are shown by broken lines (— — —). Where the original tracts have been resurveyed more than once the courses are shown by broken lines (- - - - — —)
Compiled and drawn by Harry L Benson Baltimore Md
March 25 1940
WINTERBOURNE 1677 100
YOUNG TIMSON 1743 168
TINSON 1665 300
Horseys Chance 1666 300
Crambyrn 1680 380
(Part of Crambyrn)
(Part of Young Timson)
(Part of Adams Discovery)
Adams Discovery 1780 667
EDINBURGH 1808
Glasgow Swamp 1728 300
HOBBS ADVENTURE 1728 100
SWINE YARD
Newmans Chance 1743 100
Dormans Addition 1749 104
Dormans Conclusion
GELSTON
Hunting Quarter 1680 100
Gullets Hope 1671 50
Peters Hill 1753 35
WALLERS CHANCE 1663 300
TROUBLE 250
DAINTRY 1720 300
Daintry
WINDSOR 1683 100
CONTENTION 1737 50
SECOND CHOICE 1675 300
GOOD LUCK 1714 40
DORMANS DISCOVERY
Gullets Assurance 1663
(Part of Dormans Conclusion)
Part of NEWMANS LAST CONCLUSION 1788 667
CONNINGTONS HARD BARGAIN
Jones or Tones Vineyard 1668

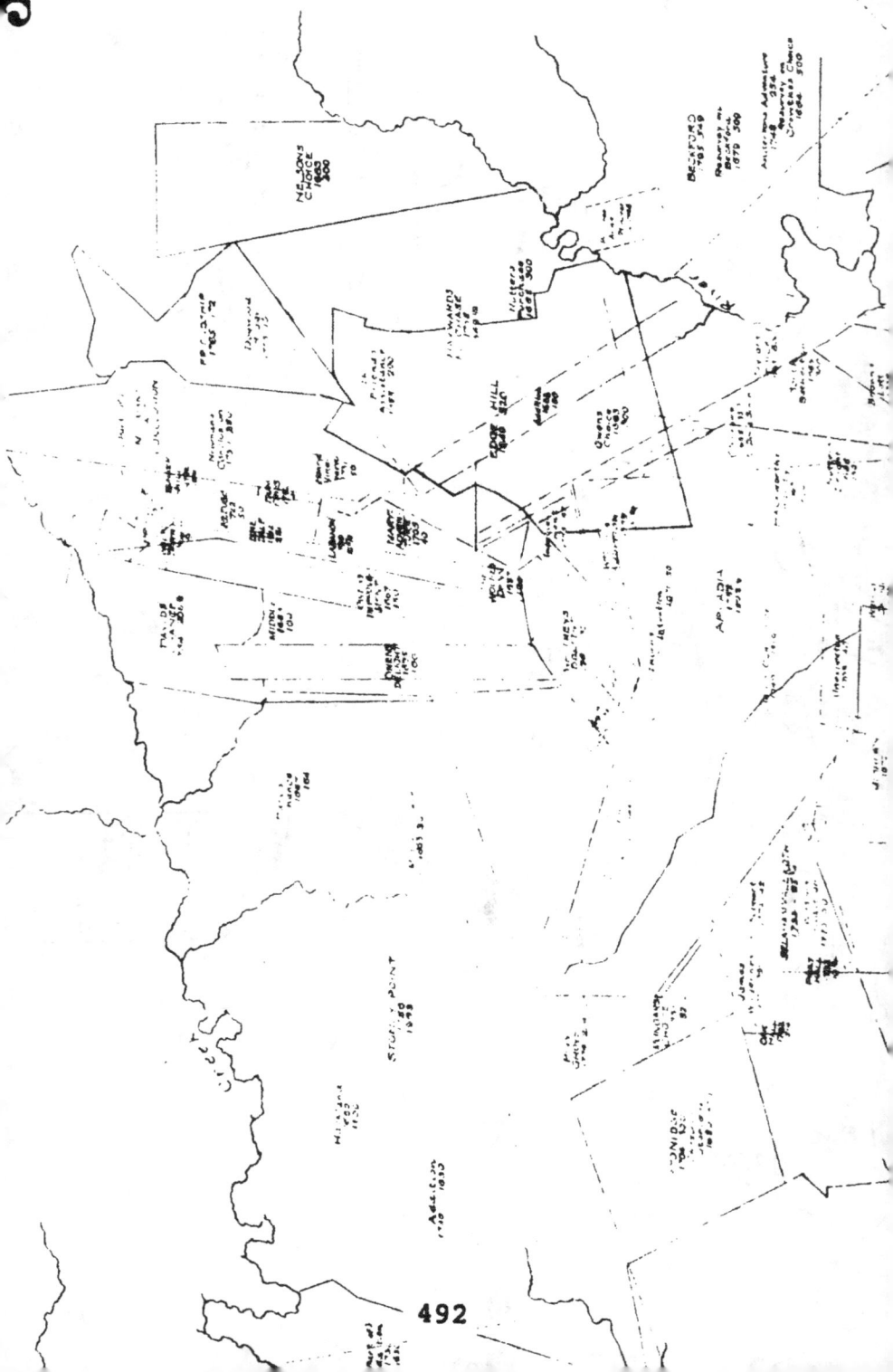

SOMERSET
COUNTY
MARYLAND

WEST OF CREEK AT ...
ELECTION DISTRICT
No I
(Lower Part)

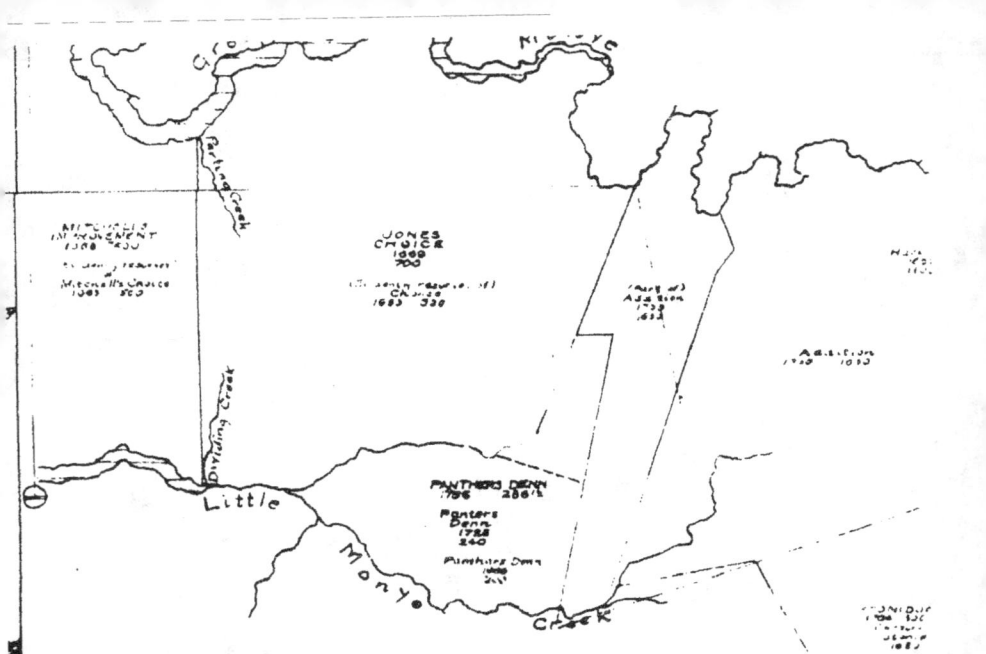

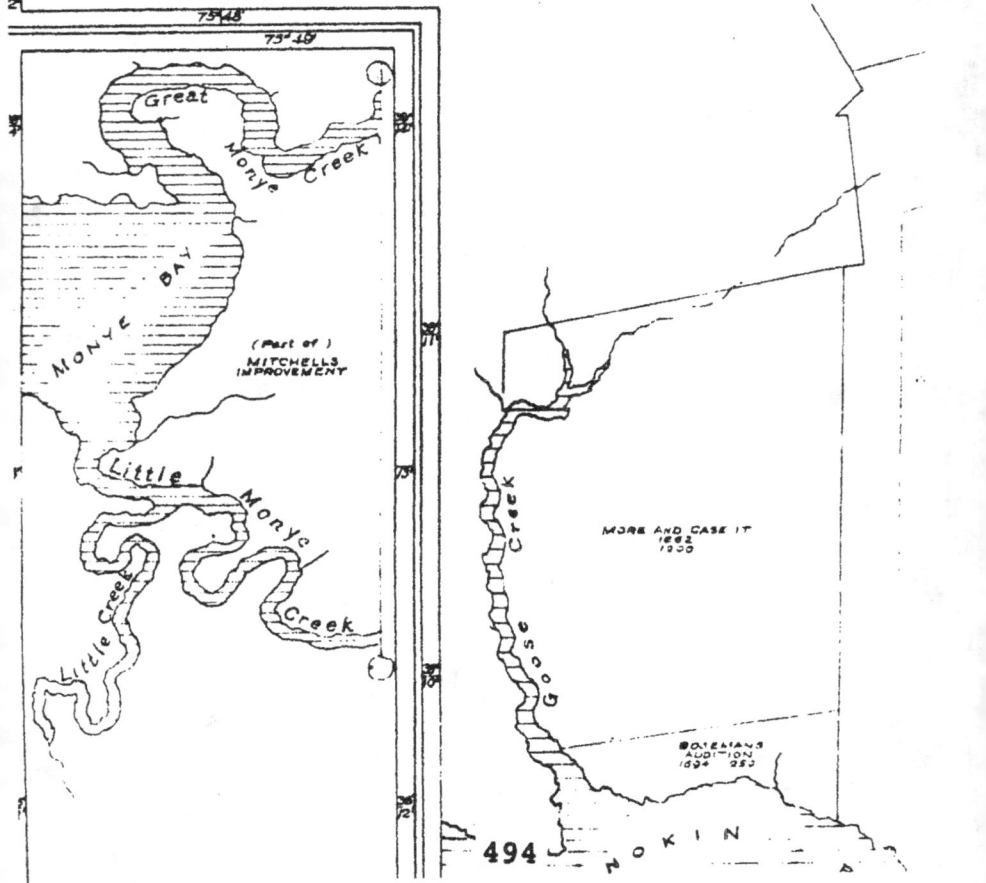

494

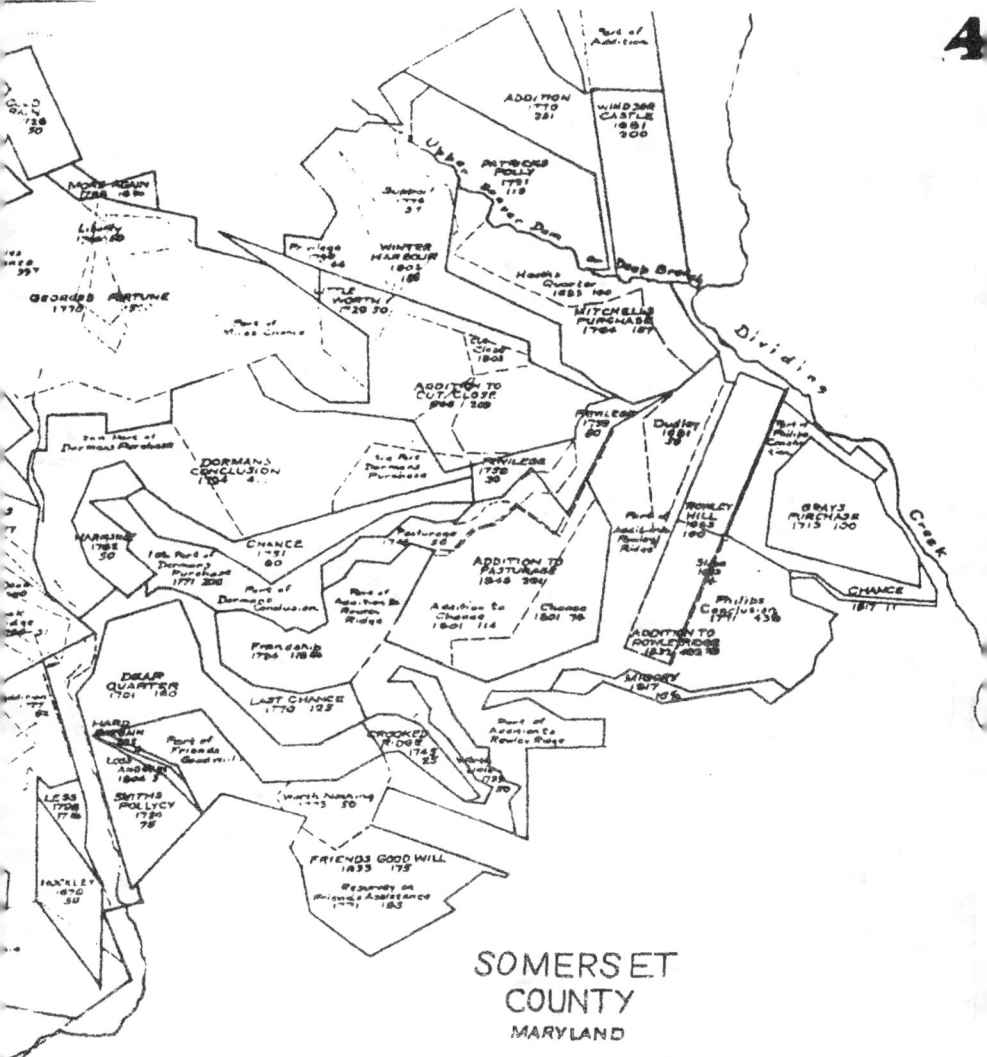

SOMERSET
COUNTY
MARYLAND

EAST PRINCESS ANNE
ELECTION DISTRICT
No. 15

(Lower Part)

Exclusive of small part below Kings Creek
shown on map of Election District No.13

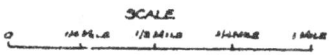

SCALE

NOTE: This map shows the outlines, names, years surveyed,
and acreage of tracts of land recorded in Patent Libers at
Land Commissioner at Annapolis Md.
The names of the resurveyed tracts are in italics and
the courses are shown by broken lines (————) where the
original tracts have been resurveyed more than once the courses
are shown by broken lines (— · — · —).

Compiled and drawn by Harry L. Benson, Baltimore Md
September 2, 1940

495

Minokin River

South   of   Shibwiry's Branch

KILLNONMAN
1663
150

DUB...
...

HANLONS
DISCOVERY
1686
250

FRIENDS
ADVICE
1753
356

Part of
Smiths
Resolves 63

ANNESBURY
SECONUER
1833 318

Good...
CHANCE
84

Gr 19
ADVENTURE
1721
110

CONCLUSION
1755
560

DERRY
1721
77

AT... ...
...
ADVENTURE
...

Primrose
Anne
28 ...

Anderson's
Adventure
748 394

The
Richmond
700

IULO...
166...

Resurvey on
Cranuba Choice
1664 500

Crown.m
756 65

SMITHS
RESOLVES
1663 350

BECKFORD
1753 549

Branch

Resurvey on
Beckford
699 5...

WINTER
QUARTER
495 235

BRIDGERS
LOTT
1263 370

Sparks's

ALI...
1...
R...
Wic...
1...

Rowley Ridge
680 100

Part of
Hartsbury

Carpenters
Ridge
68
50

Bridgers Lott
525 100

Resurvey on
Bridgers Lott
1583 350

Hartsberry
1663 150

WALTONS
IMPROVEMENT
1750 294

Resurvey
on Amag
Lott
1787
97

Upper   Fork

JAMES
FORTUNE
1773 215

Addition
724 46

Part of
Winter
Quarter

DAVIDS   CHOICE
1693 600

LOT...

HAMILTONS
FORTUNE
1739
662

HARLEYS
FORTUNE
1753 28

MEADOW
GROUND
ROOT
(Lost)

LOT...

Part of
Hamiltons Fortune

HAZARD
1721
100

Manloves
Venture
1672 100

Part of
Cloverfields

Vulcans Forge
1760 100

PHOENIX
CHOICE
1673
300

WESLEY
1670
250

...VELS
...9

CHANCE
1673
90

FRIENDS
KINDNESS
1723 100

CLOVERFIELDS
1749
1250

WOOLFES
HARBOR
1714 150

Kings

OXHEAD
1732
243

Part of
Cloverfields

Woodland
1690
150

Resurvey on
Oxhead
1683 300

...CA...
...H...
...3

or

Trading

Branch

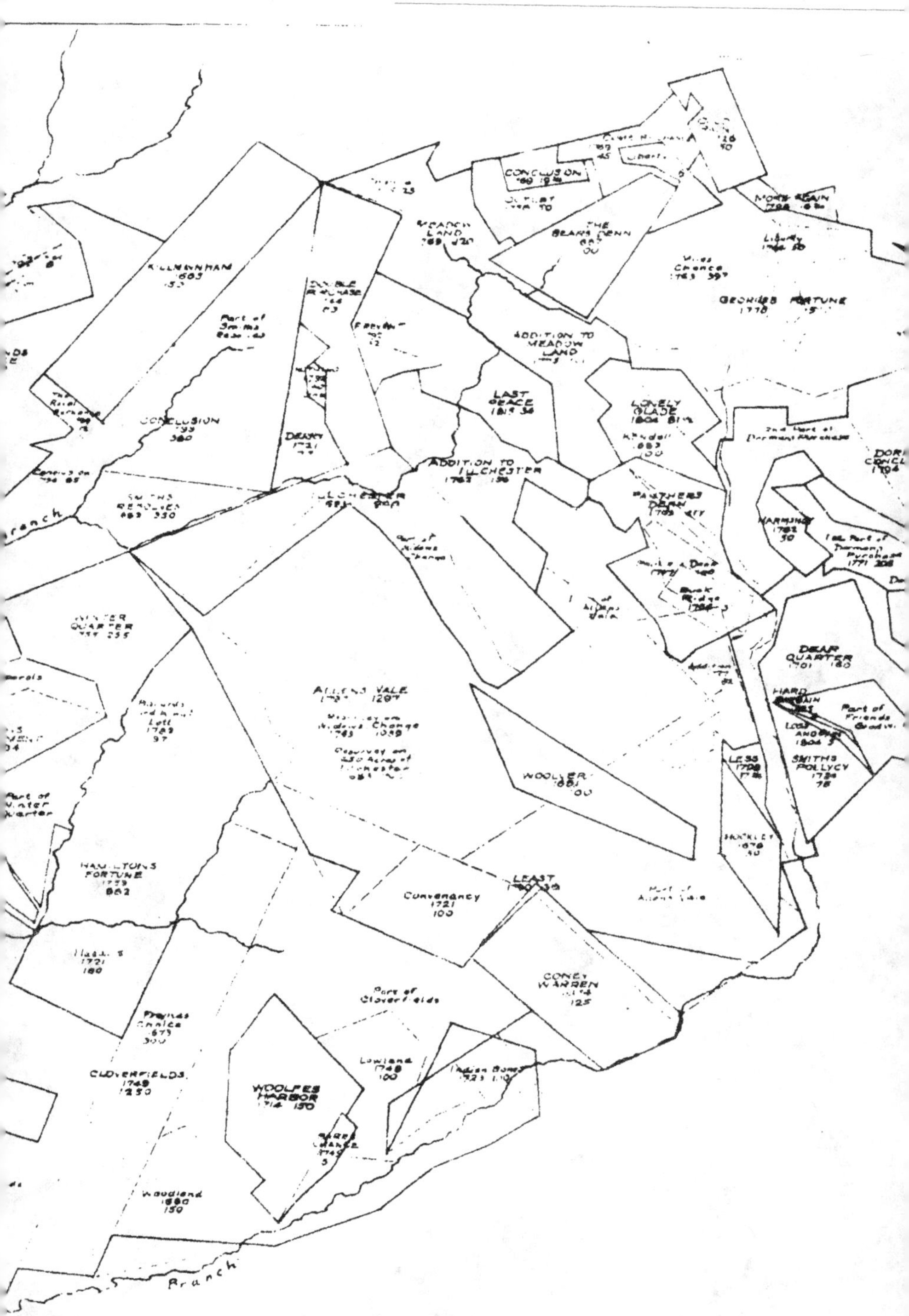
CONCLUSION
THE BEARS DENN
MEADOW LAND
Moles Chance
GEORGES FORTUNE 1770
DOUBLE PURCHASE
Part of Smiths Resolve
ADDITION TO MEADOW LAND
LAST PEACE 1815 34
LONELY GLADE
Kendall
2nd Part of Dormant Purchase
CONCLUSION 1793 380
DEARY 1721
ADDITION TO ILLCHESTER 1763 156
ILLCHESTER
SMITHS RESOLVE
PANTHERS DENN
HARMONY 1782 50
1st Part of Dormant Purchase 1771
Buck Ridge
DEAR QUARTER 1701 160
WINTER QUARTER
Part of Friends Goodwill
SMITHS POLLYCY 1736 75
ALLENS VALE
Part of Winter Quarter
HAMILTONS FORTUNE
Convenancy 1721 100
LEAST
Part of Allens Vale
CONEY WARREN 125
Part of Cloverfields
CLOVERFIELDS 1749 1230
WOOLFES HARBOR 1714 150
Lowland 1749 100
Woodland 1680 150
Branch

SOMERSET
COUNTY
MARYLAND

EAST PRINCESS ANNE
ELECTION DISTRICT
No. 15
(Upper Part)

SCALE

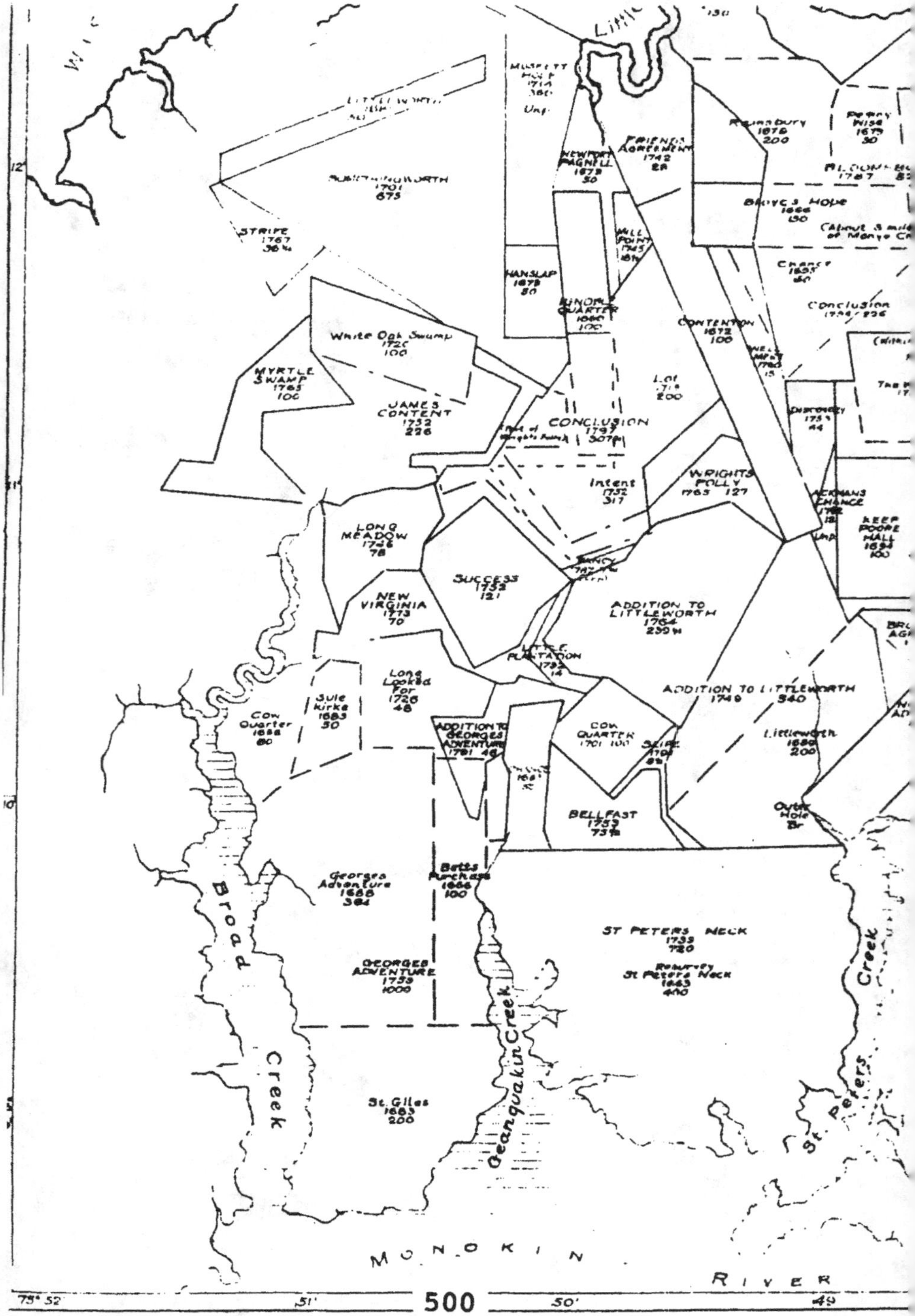
MUSKETT HOLE 1714 380
Unp.
NEWPORT PAGNELL 1673 30
FRIENDS AGREEMENT 1742 28
Penny Wise 1679 30
200
BRUCES HOPE 1666 150
SUBSTITUTE WORTH 1701 675
STRIFE 1767 36¾
HANSLAP 1679 80
Chance 1697 60
Conclusion
CONTENTION 1672 100
White Oak Swamp 1720 100
MYRTLE SWAMP 1765 100
JAMES CONTENT 1752 226
Lot 1718 200
CONCLUSION 1797 307½
Intent 1752 317
WRIGHTS FOLLY 1765 127
KEEP POORE HALL 1684 100
LONG MEADOW 1746 78
SUCCESS 1752 121
NEW VIRGINIA 1773 70
ADDITION TO LITTLEWORTH 1764 259¼
LITTLE PLANTATION 1752 14
Lone Looked For 1726 48
Sule Kirke 1683 50
Cow Quarter 1686 80
ADDITION TO GEORGES ADVENTURE 1761 46
ADDITION TO LITTLEWORTH 1749 340
COW QUARTER 1701 100
Littleworth 1680 200
BELLFAST 1753 73½
Betts Purchase 1666 100
Georges Adventure 1688 364
GEORGES ADVENTURE 1733 1000
ST PETERS NECK 1733 720
Resurvey St Peters Neck 1663 400
St. Giles 1683 200
Broad Creek
Geanquakin Creek
St. Peters Creek
MONOKIN RIVER
75° 52'
51'
50'
49'

6

FRIENDS
ADVICE
1700 45

CONCLUSION
1703 6¼
(Unsd)

HAPPY
ADDITION
1700 120¼

HAB NAB
1759
316

ADDITION TO
HAB NAB
1716 89½

PILGRIMS
1679
80

Conrad
Adams

Resurvey
Hab Nab
1679 80

SOMERSET
1723
50

PILGRIMS REST
1787 820¼

HOLE
(About .5 mile west
of Manya County)

THE SUCCESS
1685 300

WALLERS
ADVENTURE
1699
300

MARCOMBS
LOTT
1699
400

Resurvey
Marcombs Lott
1643 400

ROBERTSONS
ADDITION
1784
57

Conclusion
1766 325

(Within 8 miles of Princess Anne)

MOUNTS SURVEYIOR
1787 264½

FRIENDS
Adv.
1742
40

Lowe
LOTT
1702
50

The Worst is Best
1729 130

The Worst
is Best
1665
50

DAWSMANS
ADVENTURE
1734 280

ADDITION TO WHITTIS LOT
1703 20

ADDITION
1703
52

JONES
ENLARGEMENT
1787
50

WOOFFORDS
CHANCE
1667
300

BECKMANS
CHANCE
1786
181
Unsd

KEEP POORE
HALL
1684
100

AUSTINS
CHANCE
1787 42¾

WHITTIS LOT
or ALSONS
1703 48

GOOD
LUCK
1786 28½

MOUNT
PLEASANT
1786
238½

Addition to Alsons
WHITTIS LOT
1702

TROUBLE
1767 46
Unsd

COLEBROOKE
1662
550

Goose
Creek

SOMERSET
COUNTY
MARYLAND

(ST PETERS)
ELECTION DISTRICT
No. 2

BROTHERS
AGREEMENT
1749
79

NICHOLSONS
ADVENTURE
1686 150

Scale:

0   ¼ MILE   ½ MILE   ¾ MILE   1 MILE

ALMODINGTON
1672 1800

Resurvey
Almodinut
1665 1800

R I V E R

This map shows the outlines, names,
years surveyed and acreages of tracts of
land recorded in Patent Liber of Land
Office at Annapolis Md.
The resurveyed tracts are in Italics.

St. Peters Creek

Creek

M O N O K I N

Compiled and drawn by Harry L. Brown

Baltimore July 10 1939

R
49   48   501   47'   75° 46'

WICOMICO CO

TANGIER SOUND

GOLDEN QUARTER 1867 150

LONG DELAY 1703 274

JONES WORRY OVER HIS ADVENTURY 1841 41½ (Unm)

LUMS AMENDMENT 1740 251

LUMS ENCREASE 1688 150

Chance 1732 22

CHANCE 1792 227½ (Unm)

Lumes Improvement 1681 230

FRONT JONES 1800 4½ (Unm)

PROSPECT 1731 440

THE DOINS 1673 100

WOODLAND VENTURE 1696 20

JONES ADDITION 1784 100

JONES PRIVILEGE 1749 60

WICOMICO

Bails Creek

OXFURD 1682 100

A Friends Ch 1666 200

WILDINGS LOTT

LAYTONS CHANGE 1794 180½

LAYTONS CONVENIENCE 1867 140

COME OUR 1818 86 (Unm)

CHARLES HIS ADVENTURE 1703 140

ROBERTS LOTT 1678 100

MARVELS CHANCE 1703 27

JONES ADVEN 1682

LOCUST HUMMOCK 1682 30

FRONT OF LOCUST HUMMOCK 1687 75

MEADOW 1736 25

WALLERS INLET 1744 64

GREEN PASTUR 1722 200

LONG MEADOW 1786 60

Lowes

SOMERSET
COUNTY
MARYLAND

TANGIER
ELECTION DISTRICT
No 9
AND

DAMES QUARTER
ELECTION DISTRICT
No 11

SCALE

0   ¼ MILE   ½ MILE   ¾ MILE   1 MILE

GUNNERS RANGE 1728 64

Thoroughfare

WHITEHURST 1937 166

NOTE· This map shows the outlines names years surveyed and acreage of tracts of land recorded in Patent Libers of Land Commissioners at Annapolis Md. The names of the resurveyed tracts are in Italics and the courses are shown by broken lines (— —·—) where the original tracts have been resurveyed more than once the courses are shown by broken lines (— — — —)

Compiled and drawn by Harry L Benson Baltimore Md.
October 10, 1940

502

75°57'   56'

TUMS QUARTER 1688 150

FRIENDS CONTENT 1726 870

Resurvey on A Friends Choice 1666 300

FATHER AND SONS DESIRE 1690

Newfound Land 1680 131

DAVIDS DESTINY 1686 350

ELLIOTTS CHOICE 1686 200

EDWARDS LOTT 1750 230

Resurvey on Edwards Lott 1705 200

JONES PURCHASE 1687 64¾ (Unp)

RALLY BRAKE 1700 300

EDWARDS CHANCE 1743 166 (Unp)

RAFFELS Chance 1743 100

BOEMANS MATCH 1723 440

James (or Punplo) Meadow 1705 200

FORLORN HOPE 1685 100

FORLORN HOPE ADDITION 1712 50

DELAY 1808 80

FRIENDS ACCEPTANCE 1784 50

WILLIAMS HARD LOT 1775 25

WILLIAMS BEGINNING 1734 50

CLONMELL 1700 100

FOLKS LOTT 1687 50

THE ADVENTURE 1688 200

NEGLECT 1836 406 (Unp)

Additon 1752 10

JONES ADVENTURE 1682 30

Jedimon 1682 150

MEADOW 1781 50

FOLKS FOLLY 1687 100

PARTNERSHIP 1823 (Unp)

ADVENTURE AMENDMENT 1728 37

Francis's 1761 17 (Unp)

CHARLES HIS VENTURE 1703 140

THE OUTLETT 1701 130

SMALL LOTT 1836 64

OUTLETT 1793 14

ROBERTS RECOVERY 1683 100

KEEP OUT 1808 25

VENTURE PRIVILEGE 1744 100

PASTRIDGE 1782 567

Security 1738 300

McDORMANS VENTURE 1788 71¾

English Branch Noll's

Jones Quarter Election District 1888

GREEN PASTURE 1722 200

THE HOPE 1682 100

LONG MEADOW 1786 50

LONG MEADOW 1709 246

ADDITION TO KILLGLASS 1681 1683¾

Killglass 1698 1000

JONES CHANCE 1744 523

Jones Meadow 1686 300

WILLSONS DISCOVERY 1707 100

WHITEHURST 1927 168

Tilbury 1683 100

Gladstone 1687 300

Fishing Creek

BROAD CREEK

MANOKIN RIVER

8

SOMERSET
COUNTY
MARYLAND

DEAL ISLAND
ELECTION DISTRICT
No. 14

SCALE

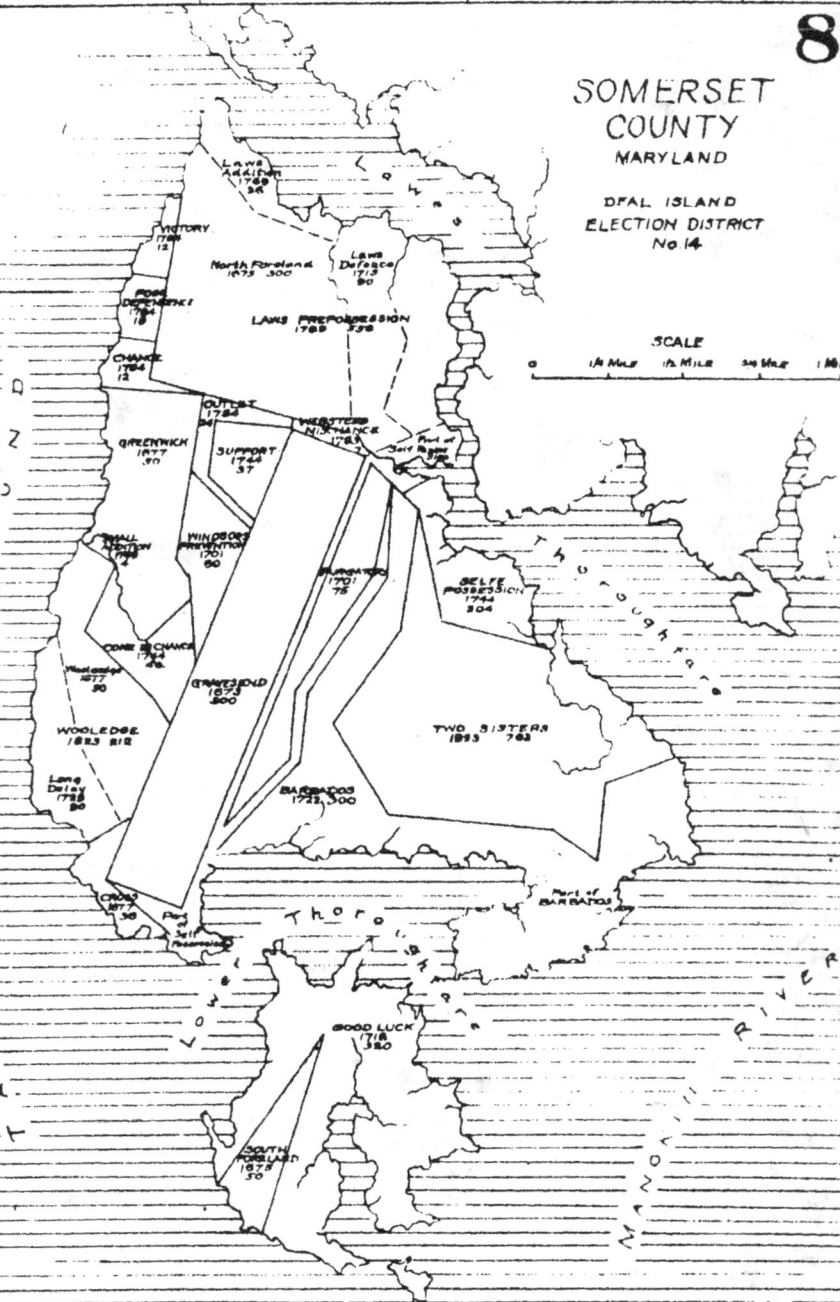

NOTE: This map shows the outlines, names, years surveyed
and acreage of tracts of land recorded in Patent Library at
Land Commissioner at Annapolis, Md.
The names of the resurveyed tracts are in italics and
the courses are shown by broken lines.

Complied and drawn by Harry L. Benson, Baltimore Md.
September 15, 1940

504

9

INCLOSURE
1750 300

CANES
CHOICE
1683
200

Mattos
Inclosure
1688
100

Prat
1673 90

Part of
Tomkins
Purchase

Barnabye
1685 200

Wandowes
Choice
1659
70

SUDLERS
CONCLUSION
1740 210

TURPINS
PURCHASE
1762 307½

Matthews
His Hope
and
100

Trouble
1657
50

Pomfrees
Choice
1685
300

SECURITY
1750 570

Maburv
Adventure
1659 160

Good
Luck
1733 50

Arovy
1749 104

Conveyency
1672
100

...burs Adventure
1670 170

CONVEYENCY
1701 60

SECURITY
1730 50

SALEM
1750 460

WATERS RIVER
1668
1280

HALLS
ADVENTURE
1673
250

SALISBURY
1667
200

Nanticoke & Halls Cr.

RIVER

ANNEMESSEX

Nanemess Bay

...DS
...NESS
250

HALLS
HANOCK
1680 100

...ddison to
...lls Hammocks
1784 197½

...MANS HALL MARSH
1833 399 ¼

Halls
Pasture
1688 100

Piney
...tale

...Bays
...Cove Addition
1782 11

NOTE. This map shows the outlines, names, years surveyed
and acreage of tracts of land recorded in Patent Libers of
Land Commissioner at Annapolis, Md.
The names of the resurveyed tracts are in Italics and
the courses are shown by broken lines. Where the
original tracts have been resurveyed more than once the courses
are shown by broken lines.

Compiled and drawn by Harry L. Benson, Baltimore Md.
November 26, 1940.

SOMERSET
COUNTY
MARYLAND

FAIRMOUNT
ELECTION DISTRICT
No. 6

SCALE
0   1/8 MILE   1/2 MILE   3/4 MILE   1 MILE

RIVER

MANOKON

DRUM C.

SOUND

Winders or Goose Creek

Mine Creek

TANGIER

BONFIRE
1709 50

COW
QUARTER
1883
50

NEW INN
1665

ADVENTURE
1663 200

HORSE
HAMMOCK
1706 100

TREASURY
BOWNE
1667

GRAVE
IMPROVEMENT
1666 130

Furnace or Tangues Creek

HAW TREE
POINT
1665
100

(Part of
Fashons
Care)

Wagners Creek

LOCUST
RIDGE
1666
50

THE
LAST
CHOICE
1667
10

(Part of Grove Improvement)

LONDONS GIFT
1667 50

New Rumney
1669 130

NEW RUMNEY
1751 267

Canaa
Island
1663
50

CANEDY ISLAND
1762 3/8 %

Fannin's
Adventure
1696
200

Winter
Harbour
1660
55

(Part of
Flattland)

LONDONS
ADVENTURE

STONE
HOUSE

HOGS
RIVER
1667

STEVENS
MEADOW
1702 150

Hazard

(Part of
Flattland)

FLATTLAND
1696 850

FRIENDS
KINDNESS
1695
110

(Part of
Fashons
Desire)

Flattland

COW QUARTER
1731 678

LONDONS
ADVENTURE
60

JEFFERS
1663
50

MOUNT
LIME
1694
130

Handys Choice
1694

(Part of Cow Quarter)

ANNEMESSEX   RI

506

MARISH GROUND 1693 200

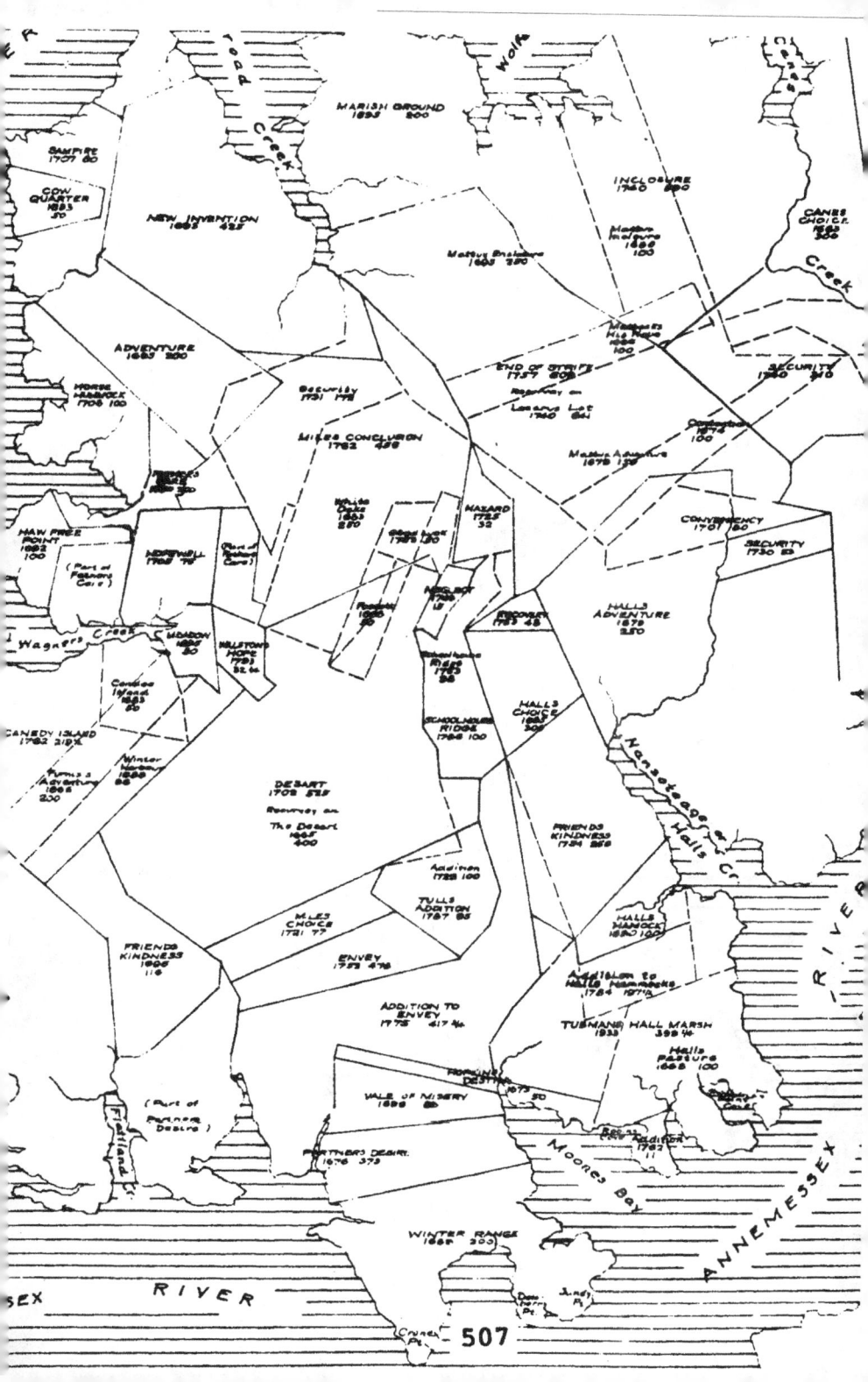

SAMPIRE 1707 60

COW QUARTER 1683 50

NEW INVENTION 1683 425

INCLOSURE 1760 290

CANES CHOICE 1686 350

Mattox Inclosure 1686 100

Mattox Enclosure 1663 250

ADVENTURE 1683 200

HORSE HAMMOCK 1708 100

Security 1731 178

Mattox's His Note 1686 100

END OF STRIFE 1757 800

Resurvey on Lanens Lot 1760 641

SECURITY 1730 240

Covington 1674 100

MILES CONCLUSION 1762 450

Mattox Adventure 1678 125

CONVENIENCY 1701 180

SECURITY 1730 80

White Oaks 1683 280

HAZARD 1725 52

MAW FREE POINT 1683 100

(Part of Pedmore Care)

HOPEWELL 1708 78

(Part of Redmore Care)

MEADOW 1685 50

HILLSTOWN HOPE 1723 52.66

NEGLECT 1735 19

Redmore 1698 50

HALLS ADVENTURE 1678 250

DISCOVER 1783 48

Richard Lemins River 1763 55

Wagner's Creek

Canoe Island 1683 50

CANEDY ISLAND 1762 218½

Tulls Adventure 1695 200

Winter Harbor 1685 86

DESART 1708 525

Resurvey on The Desart 1765 400

SCHOOLHOUSE RIDGE 1766 100

HALLS CHOICE 1682 500

FRIENDS KINDNESS 1754 250

Nanseastago & Halls Co.

HALLS HANNOCK 1690 100

Addition 1725 100

TULLS ADDITION 1767 85

MILES CHOICE 1721 77

ENVEY 1753 478

Addition to Halls Hammocks 1784 137½

FRIENDS KINDNESS 1696 116

ADDITION TO ENVEY 1775 417½

TUSMANS HALL MARSH 1933 399¼

Halls Pasture 1685 100

FORTUNES DESTINY 1673 50

VALE OF MISERY 1698 85

FARTHERS DESIRE 1676 373

BRAY NEIGHBOR 1762 11

(Part of Former Desire)

WINTER RANGE 1685 200

RIVER

SEX RIVER

Moores Bay

ANNEMESSEX

507

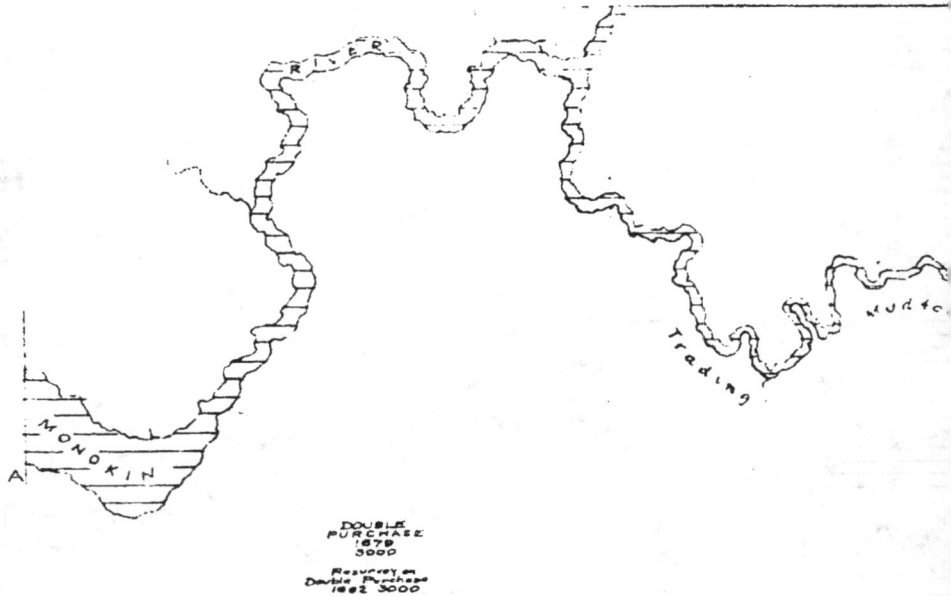

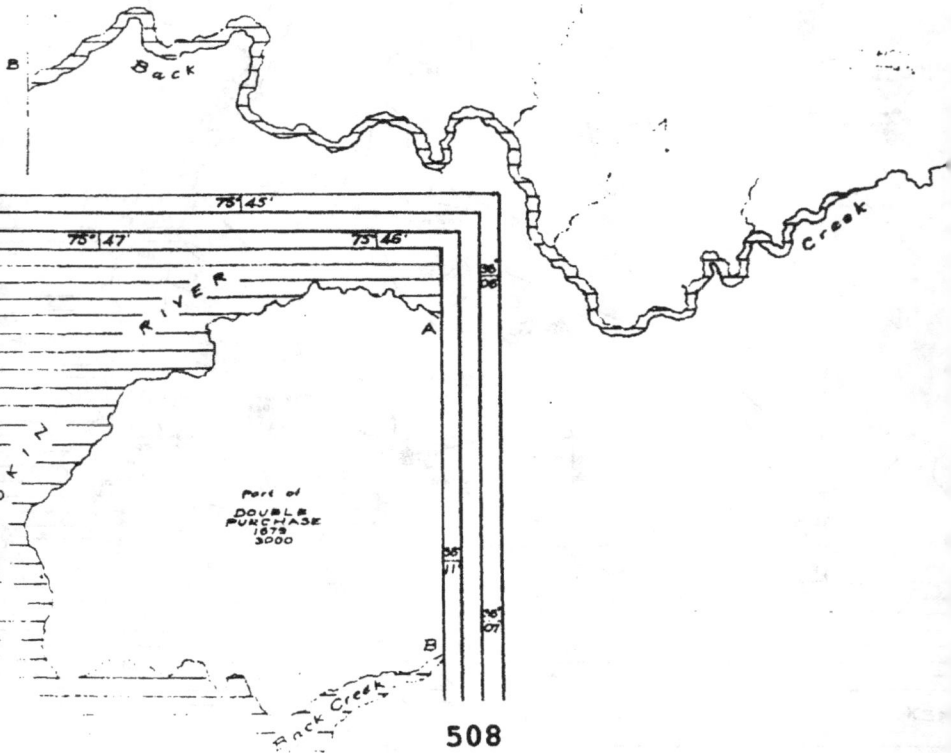

508

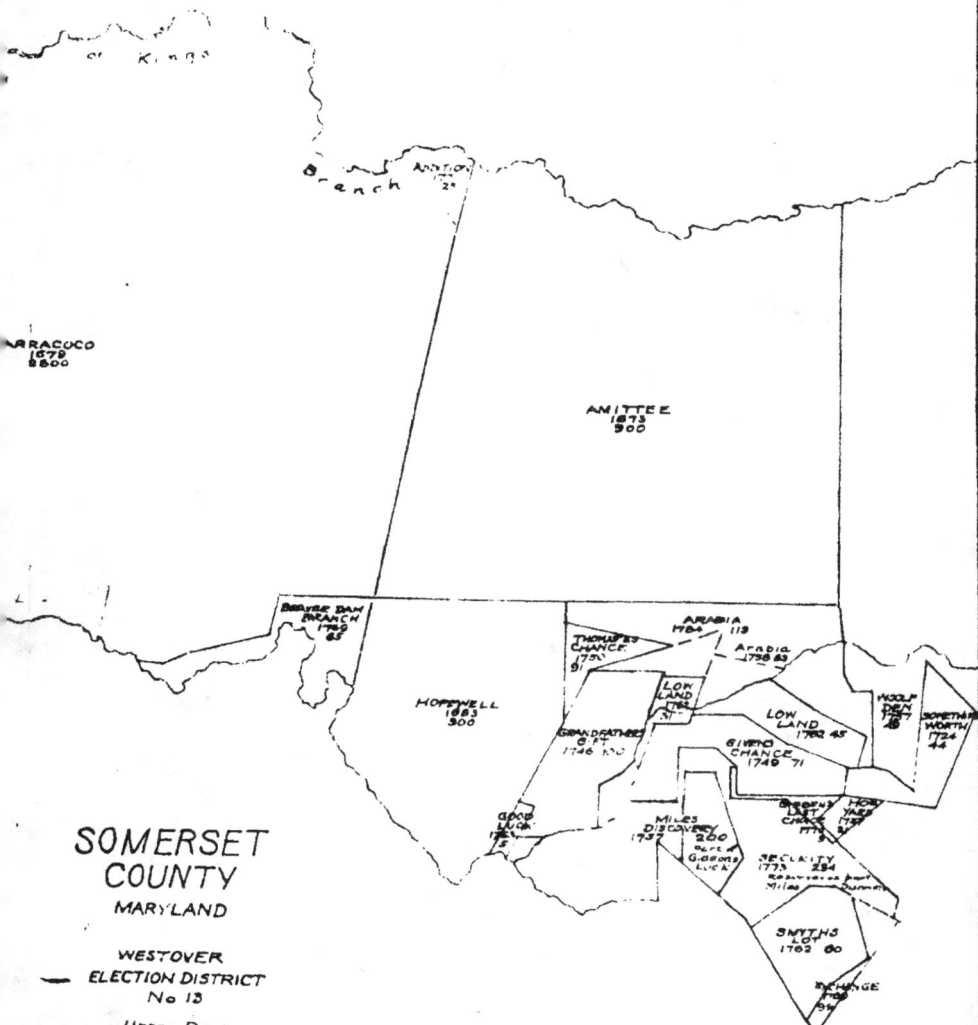

SOMERSET
COUNTY
MARYLAND

WESTOVER
ELECTION DISTRICT
No 13

Upper Part

SCALE

0   1/4 Mile   1/2 Mile   3/4 Mile   1 Mile

NOTE: This map shows the outlines names years surveyed and acreage of tracts of land recorded in Patent Libers of Land Commissioner at Annapolis, Md.
The names of the resurveyed tracts are in Italics and the courses are shown by broken lines (———). Where the original tracts have been resurveyed more than once the courses are shown by broken lines (———).

Compiled and drawn by Harry L Benson, Baltimore Md
December 26, 1940.

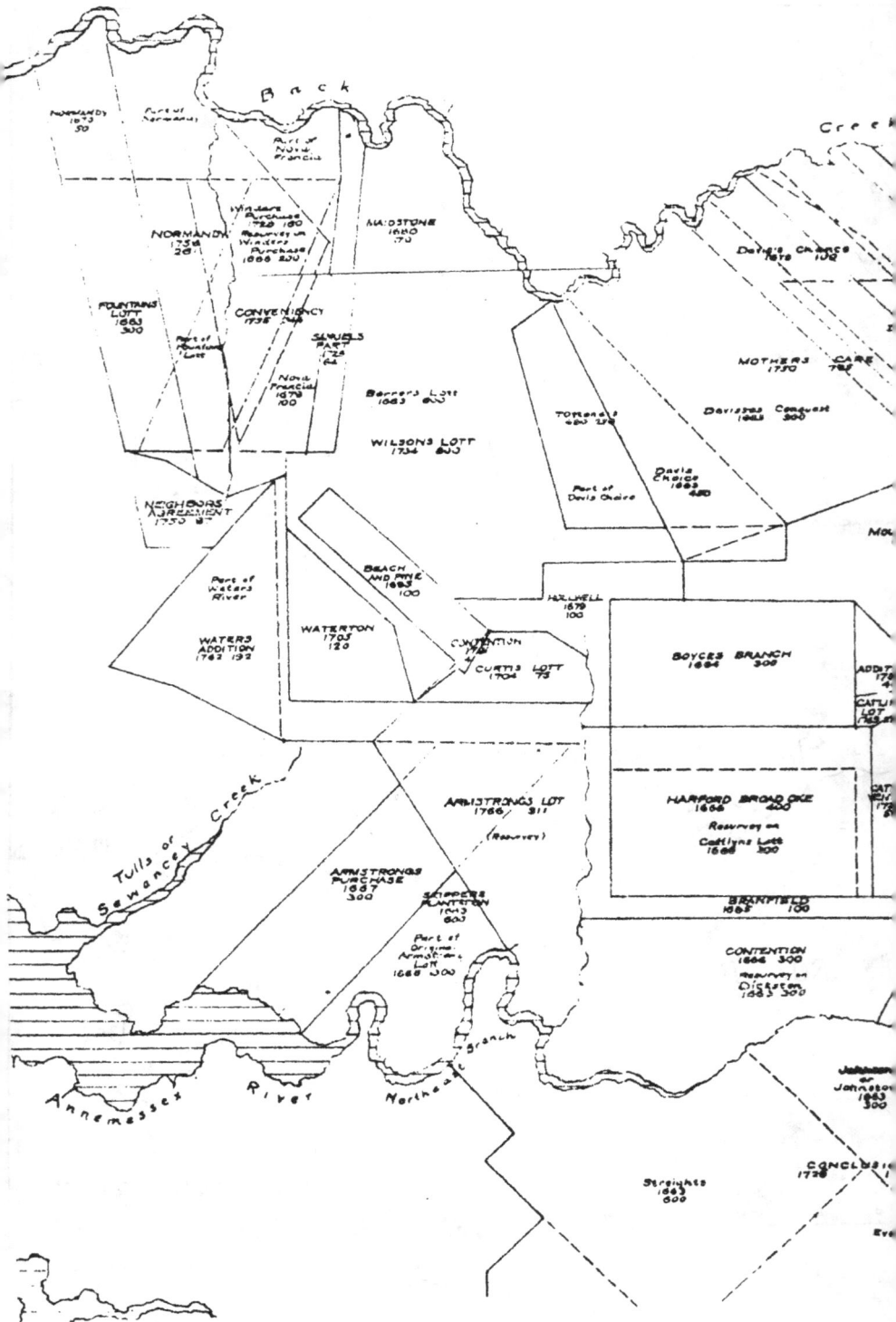

11

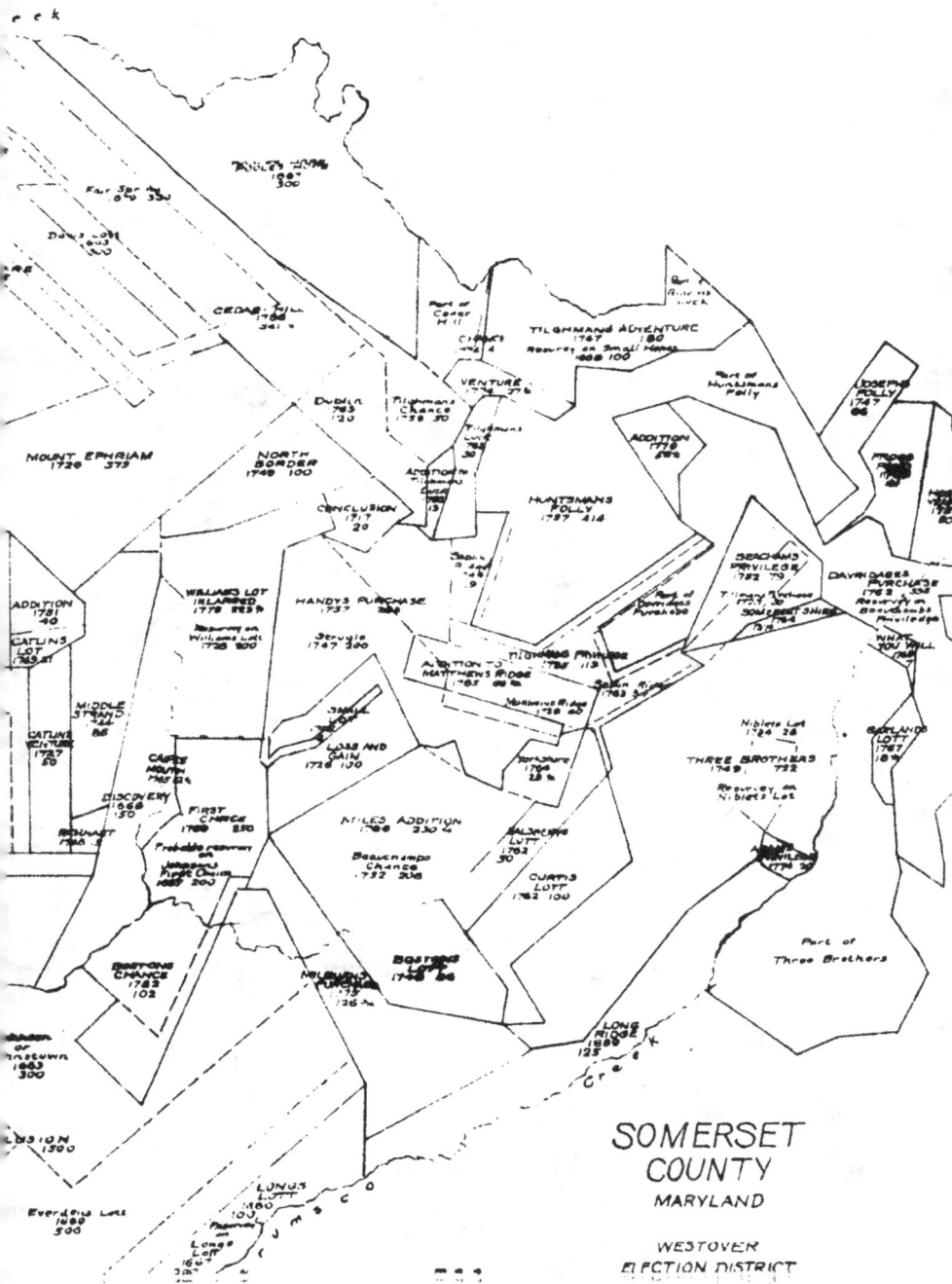

SOMERSET
COUNTY
MARYLAND

WESTOVER
ELECTION DISTRICT

Trading or Kings Creek

LIMIT

NIGHTS SUCCESS 1748 204

Reservion on Turkey Cock Hill 1876 145

MY OWN 1768

COLRANE 1682 200

Longs Chance 1740 100

ADDITION TO TICK RIDGE HDG 1773 90½

JUNIPER 1762

TICK RIDGE 1762 73

AUXRESS C 1792

Kalise Danese 1729 100

Kings Chase 1683 100

Beginnings Addison 1781 50

PORTERS PURCHASE 1763 510

THE BOARS HEAD 1762 73

PREVENTION 1763 9½ (Unp)

Part of Bullsrs Agrisemnt 1673 100

KINGS GLAD 1750 478

Part of Longs Choice

Index Ridge 1788 45 (Unp)

DUBLYN 1683 125

Kings Purchase

BALTIMORE 1790 482

Addition to Flashland 941

Flation 10

EMINIE 1681 50

KINGS CHANCE 1673 100

PARTNERS CHOICE AND KINGS PURCHASE UNITED 1746 797½

TURNING CHOICE 1762 350

PLEASANT MEADOW 1784 108 (Unp)

Flashland 1764 277

TURKEY RIDGE 1762 19½

W

Le 17 34

Partners Choice

Turning Choice 1763 100

WATERS ADDITION 1751 ½

WATERS INLARGEMENT 1761 165

TILGHMANS FORTUNE 1761 80

Bear Ridge 1791 49

Part of Baltimore

Part of Addition to Beech Ridge

COSTS VEN 17

AD BE 17

nck Creek

WATERFORD CORRECTED 1787 559½

Reservion on Waterford 1787 559

FOUL MEADOW 1784 183½ (Unp)

Part of Castons Venture

MIDDLE PASTURE 1763 452½

Tilghmans Enlargement 1763 130

Parcel Miles Last Choice

Part of Addams Purchase

MILES LAST CHOICE 1767 514

BLADE SWAMP 1762 125

Bare Hole 1700 50

Exchange 1762 80

Blue Luck 1750 162

Winter Range 1760

Part of Miles Last Choice

MILES LOT 1740 150½

MILES ADDITION 1760 474½

ADDITION TO WINTER RANGE 1840 887½

Part of Miles Last Choice

Part of 1739 350

IRELAND 1769 383

more 1754

Part of ADDITION TO BATCHELDER HOPE 1773 80

Part of Waters Addition to Timber Tract 1764 620

AGGI 1740

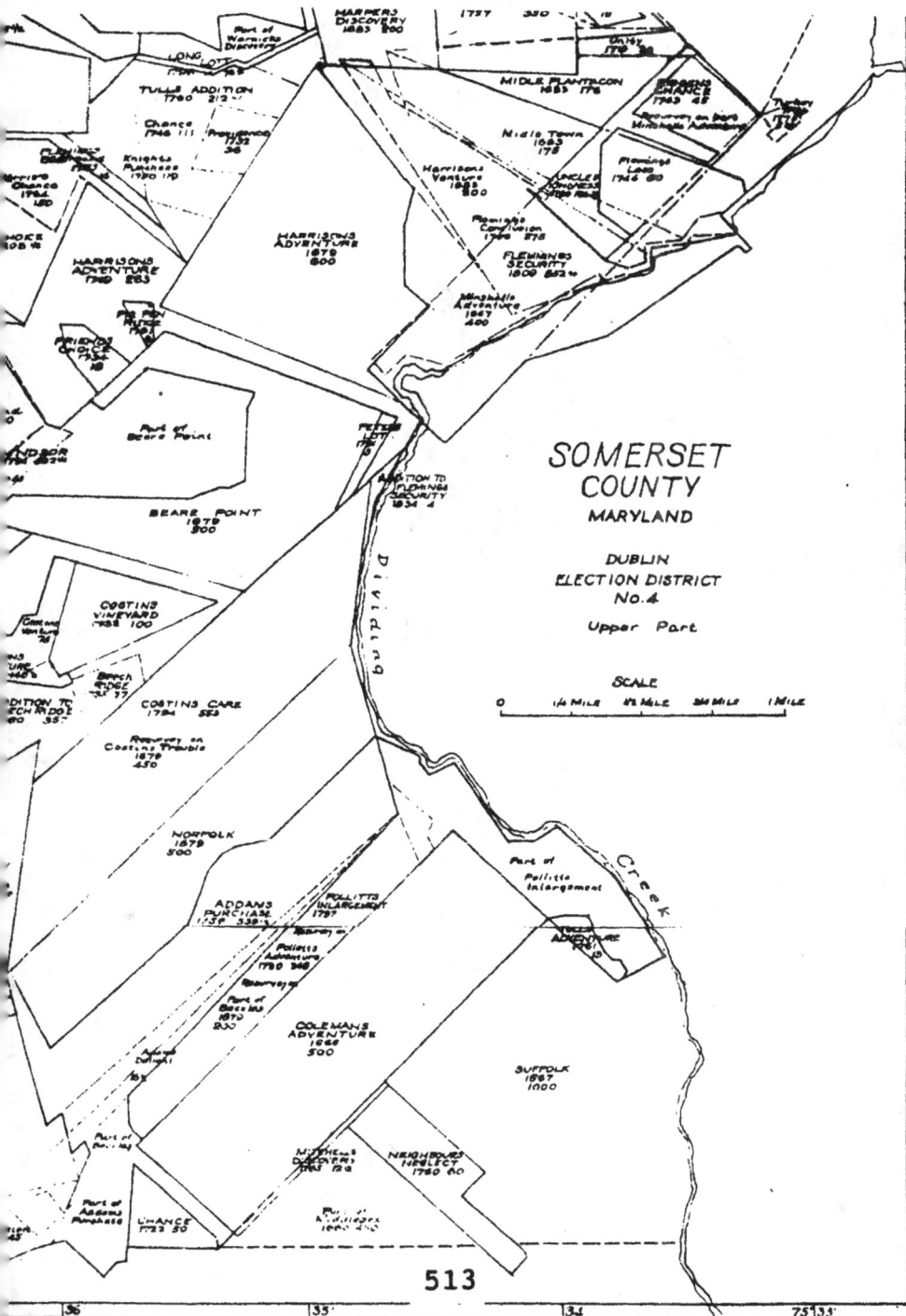

SOMERSET
COUNTY
MARYLAND

DUBLIN
ELECTION DISTRICT
No. 4

Upper Part

SCALE

0   1/4 MILE   1/2 MILE   3/4 MILE   1 MILE

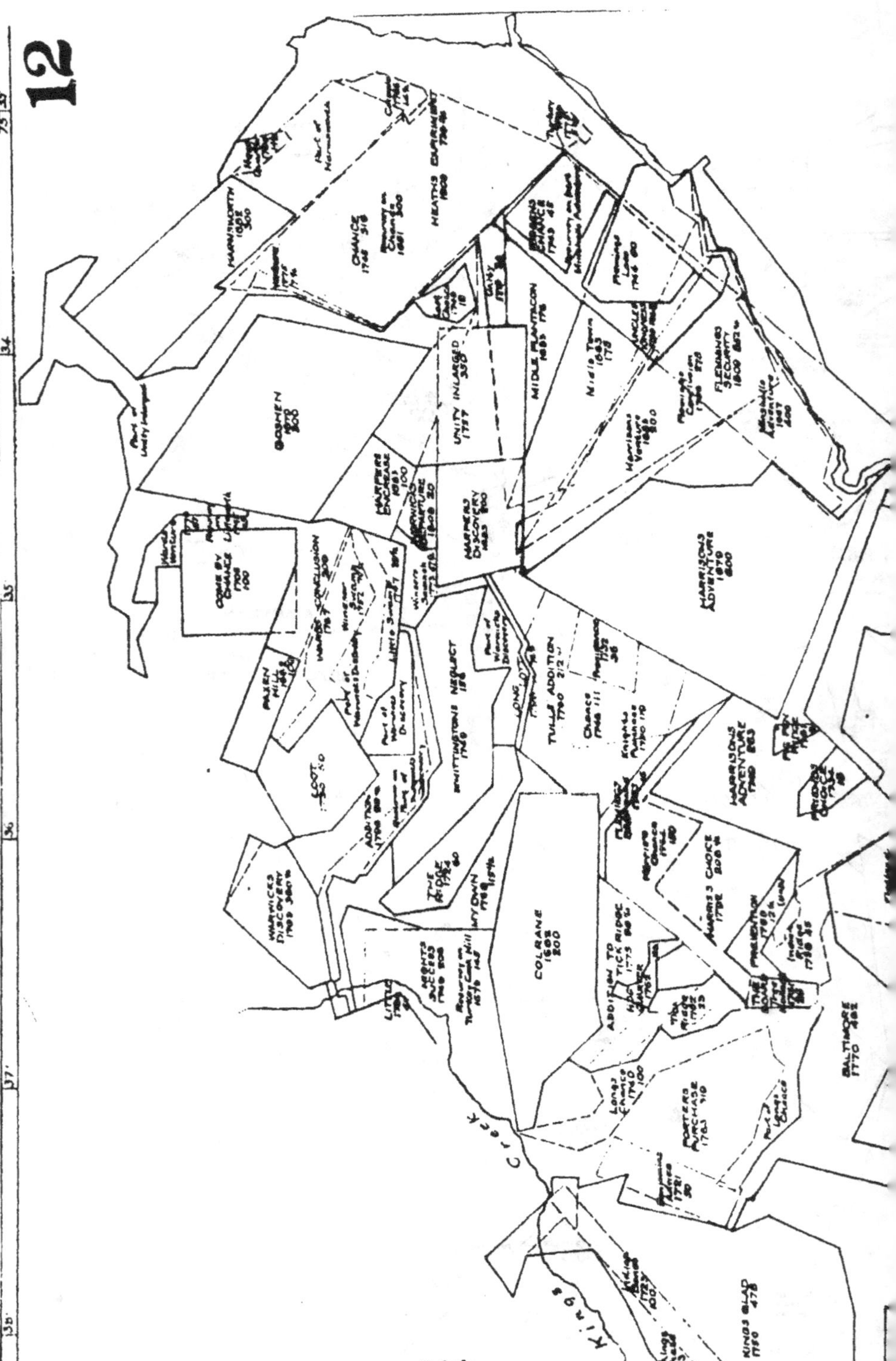
12
GOSHEN
COLRANE 1682 300
HARRISONS ADVENTURE 1670 600
HARRISONS ADVENTURE
BALTIMORE 1770 282
KINGS GLAD 1750 478
PORTERS PURCHASE
UNITY INLARGED 1757 330
HEATHS EXPERIMENT
MIDLE PLANTACON
WARWICKS DISCOVERY
WHITTINGTONS NEGLECT
TULLS ADDITION
PAXEN HILL
THE RIDGE
HARRISONS CHOICE
HARPERS DISCOVERY
HARPERS ENCREASE
CHANCE
FLEMMINGS SECURITY
Kings Creek

SOMERSET
COUNTY
MARYLAND

SMITHS ISLAND
ELECTION DISTRICT
No.10

South Marsh Part

SCALE

515

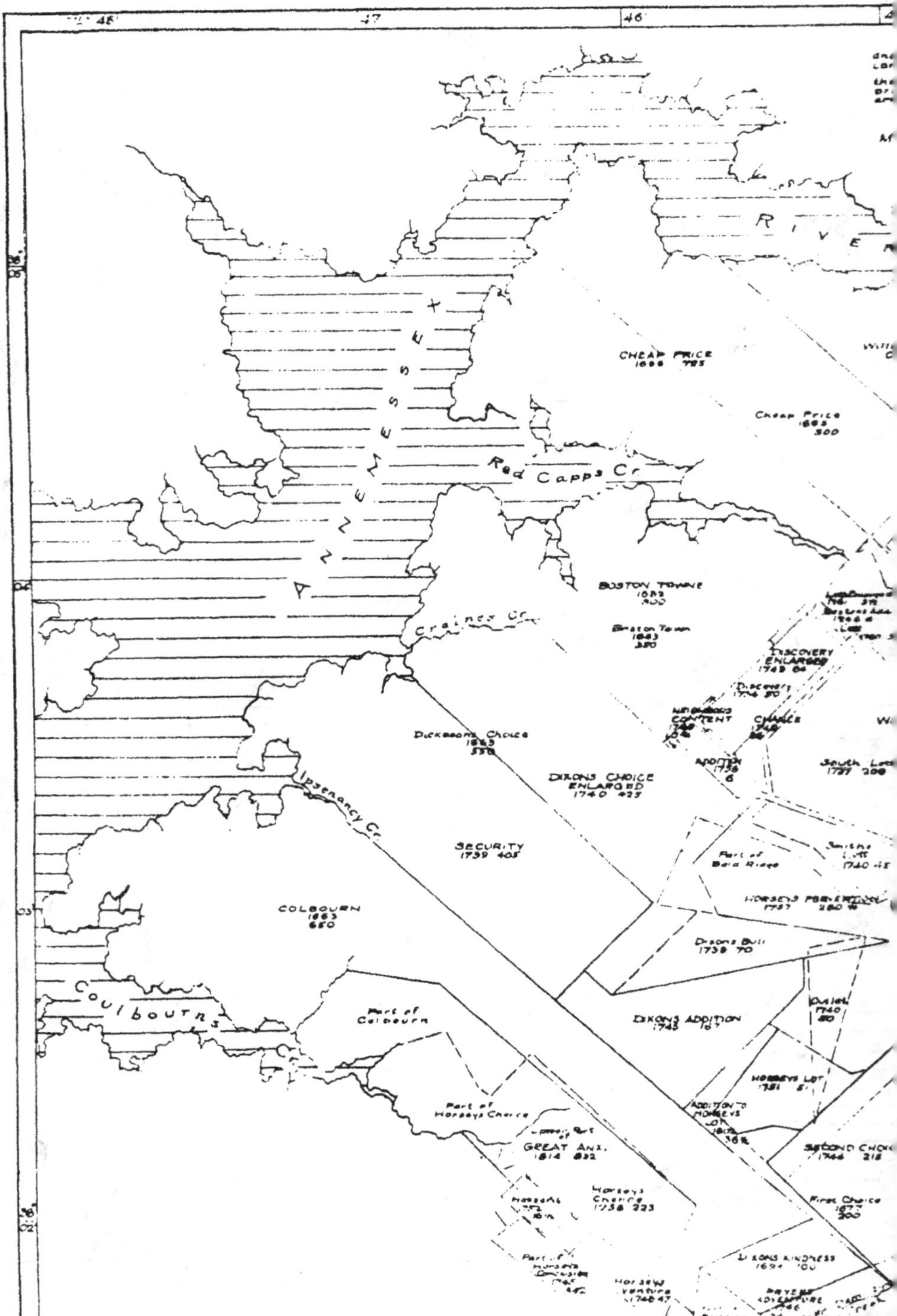
48
47
46
Red Capps Cr
R I V E R
CHEAP PRICE
1666 725
Cheap Price
1663
300
BOSTON TOWNE
1683
300
Boston Town
1663
350
DISCOVERY
ENLARGED
Dickesons Choice
1663
550
DIXONS CHOICE
ENLARGED
1740 425
SECURITY
1739 405
COLBOURN
1663
650
Part of
Bold Ridge
Dixons Bull
1739 70
Part of
Colbourn
DIXONS ADDITION
HORSEYS LOT
Part of
Horseys Choice
GREAT ANX.
1814 832
Horseys
Choice
1738 223
SECOND CHOI
First Choice
200
DIXONS KINDNESS
Coulbourns Cr

NOTE This map shows the outlines names years surveyed and acreage of tracts of land recorded in Patent Libers at Land Commissioner at Annapolis, Md. The names of the resurveyed tracts are in italics and the courses are shown by broken lines (_____) Where the original tracts have been resurveyed more than once the course are shown by broken lines (_____)

Compiled and drawn by Harry L Benson Baltimore, Md
May 3 1941

14

SOMERSET COUNTY
MARYLAND

BRINKLEYS
ELECTION DISTRICT
No.3

Northwestern Part

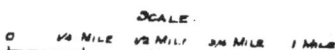

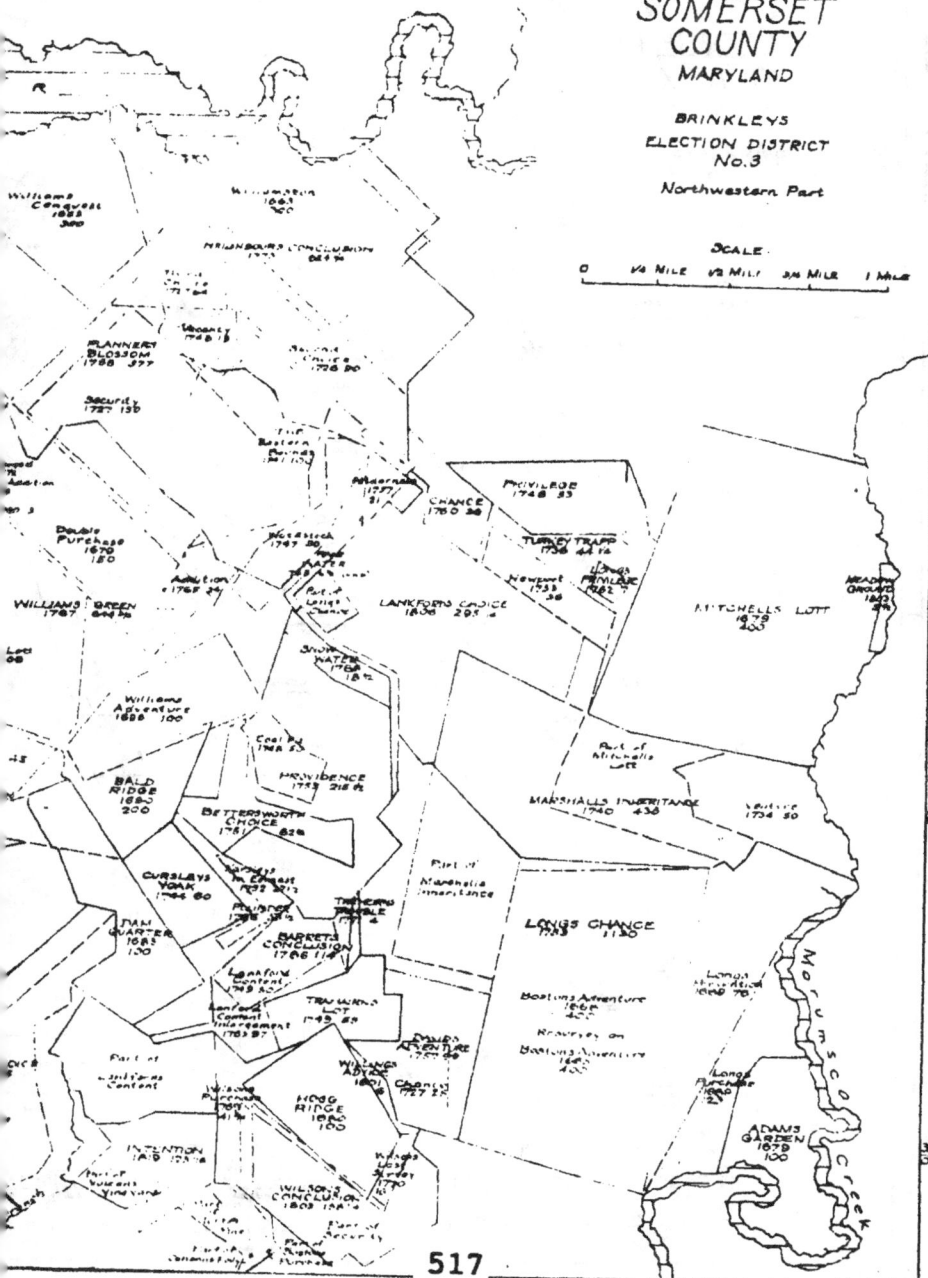

SCALE

0   ¼ MILE   ½ MILE   ¾ MILE   1 MILE

Williams Congress 1683 300

Wilmington 1663

Neighbours Conclusion 1679

FLANNERS BLOSSOM 1768 377

Security 1727 130

Double Purchase 1670 180

WILLIAMS GREEN 1767

Addition 1765 24

PRIVILEGE 1748 33

CHANCE 1760 36

TURKEY TRAPP 1736

Newport 1733

MITCHELLS LOTT 1679 100

LANKFORDS CHOICE 1808 295

Williams Adventure 1688 100

Part of Mitchells Lott

PROVIDENCE 1733

BALD RIDGE 1680 200

BETTERSWORTH CHOICE 1781 820

MARSHALLS INHERITANCE 1740 430

Venture 1734 50

CURSLEYS YOAK 1744 60

Part of Marshalls Inheritance

LONGS CHANCE 1733 1130

HAM QUARTER 1683 100

BARRETS CONCLUSION 1766

Lankford Content 1749

Bostons Adventure 1668 400

Longs Adventure 1668 70

Resurvey on Bostons Adventure 1668 400

HOGG RIDGE 1685 100

Chance 1727

Longs Purchase 1668

ADAMS GARDEN 1679 100

INTENTION

WILSONS CONCLUSION 1808

517

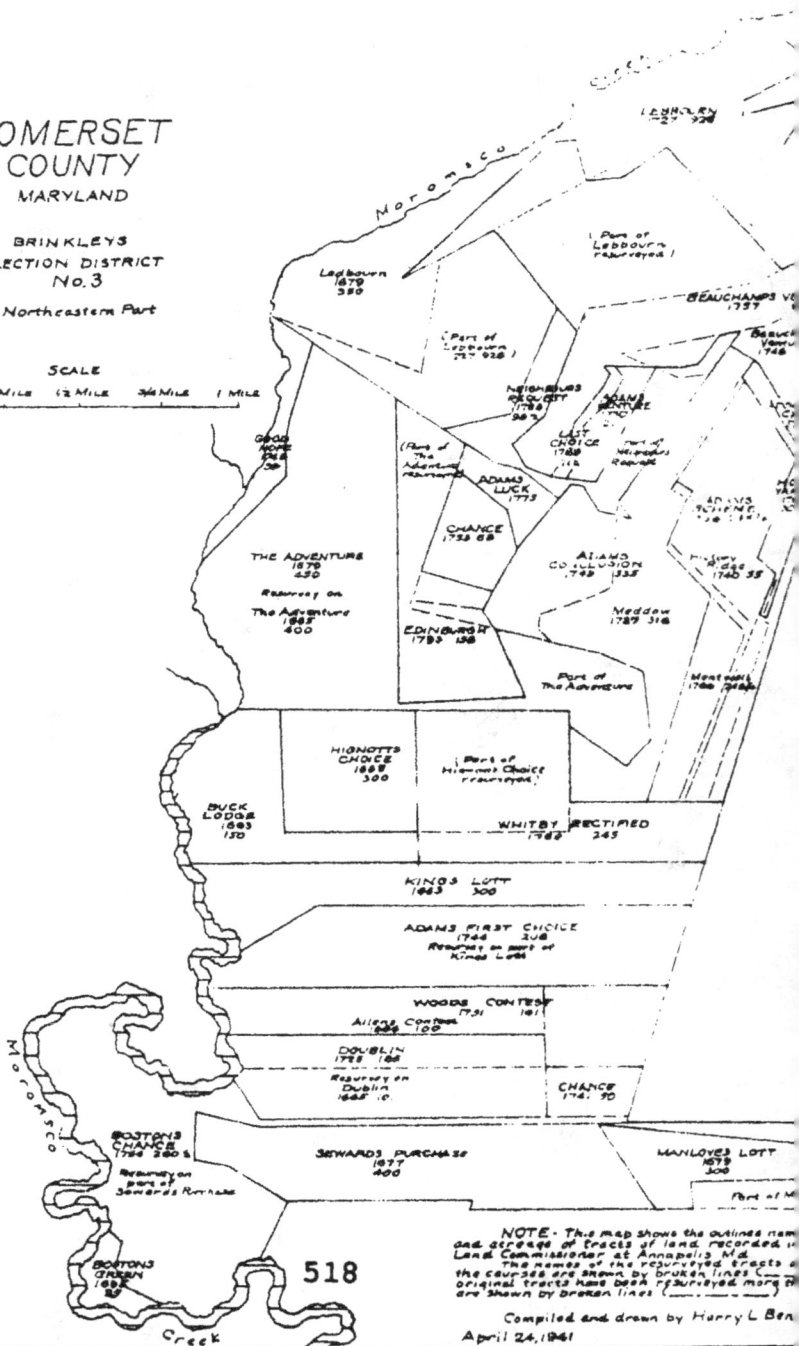

SOMERSET
COUNTY
MARYLAND

BRINKLEYS
ELECTION DISTRICT
No. 3

Northeastern Part

SCALE

0   1/4 MILE   1/2 MILE   3/4 MILE   1 MILE

NOTE - This map shows the outlines names
and acreage of tracts of land recorded in
Land Commissioner at Annapolis Md.
The names of the resurveyed tracts are
the courses are shown by broken lines (_____)
original tracts have been resurveyed more and
are shown by broken lines (_____)

Compiled and drawn by Harry L Ben

April 24, 1941

518

15

Part of Three Brothers?

HOG YARD 1704 95

INLARGEMENT 1763 109

NEW WOOD HALL 1648 200

LENBOURN 1727 928

HOG QUARTER 1700 50

Part of Lebbourn resurveyed

SMALL HOPE 1788 12

WOOD HALL REGAINED 1788 139½

BEAUCHAMPS VENTURE 1737 606

Beauchamps Venture 1748 165

CHANCE 1737 50

SCHOOLFIELDS CHANCE 1737 51

WOOD HALL 1679 203

NEIGHBOURS QUEST 1760

ADAMS REFUGE 1750

LAST CHOICE 1788 11½

Part of Neighbours Request

ADDITION TO CHANCE 1760 30

CORRECTION 1788

NEIGHBOURS EXCHANGE 1737 346

CALDICUT 1867 500

ADAMS SCHEME 1742 111½

HOG YARD 1704

ADAMS CO-ILLUSION 1748 533

MILLERY RIDGE 1740 55

Meddow 1737 318

Montpoint 1766 744½

Part of The Adventure

REHOBETH 1683 1000

...BY ...CTIMED 1788 343

...HOICE ...

CHANCE 1741 90

HENRYS ADDITION 1713 50

MANLOVES LOTT 1679 500

Part of Manloves Lot Resurveyed

Part of Manloves Lot

P O N D O T

WORCESTER COUNTY

E. This map shows the outlines names years surveyed ...s of tracts of land recorded in Patent Liber of ...denser at Annapolis Md. ...names of the resurveyed tracts are in italics and ...s are shown by broken lines (———) where the ...cts have been resurveyed more than once the courses by broken lines

...piled and drawn by Harry L Benson Baltimore Md 1941

519

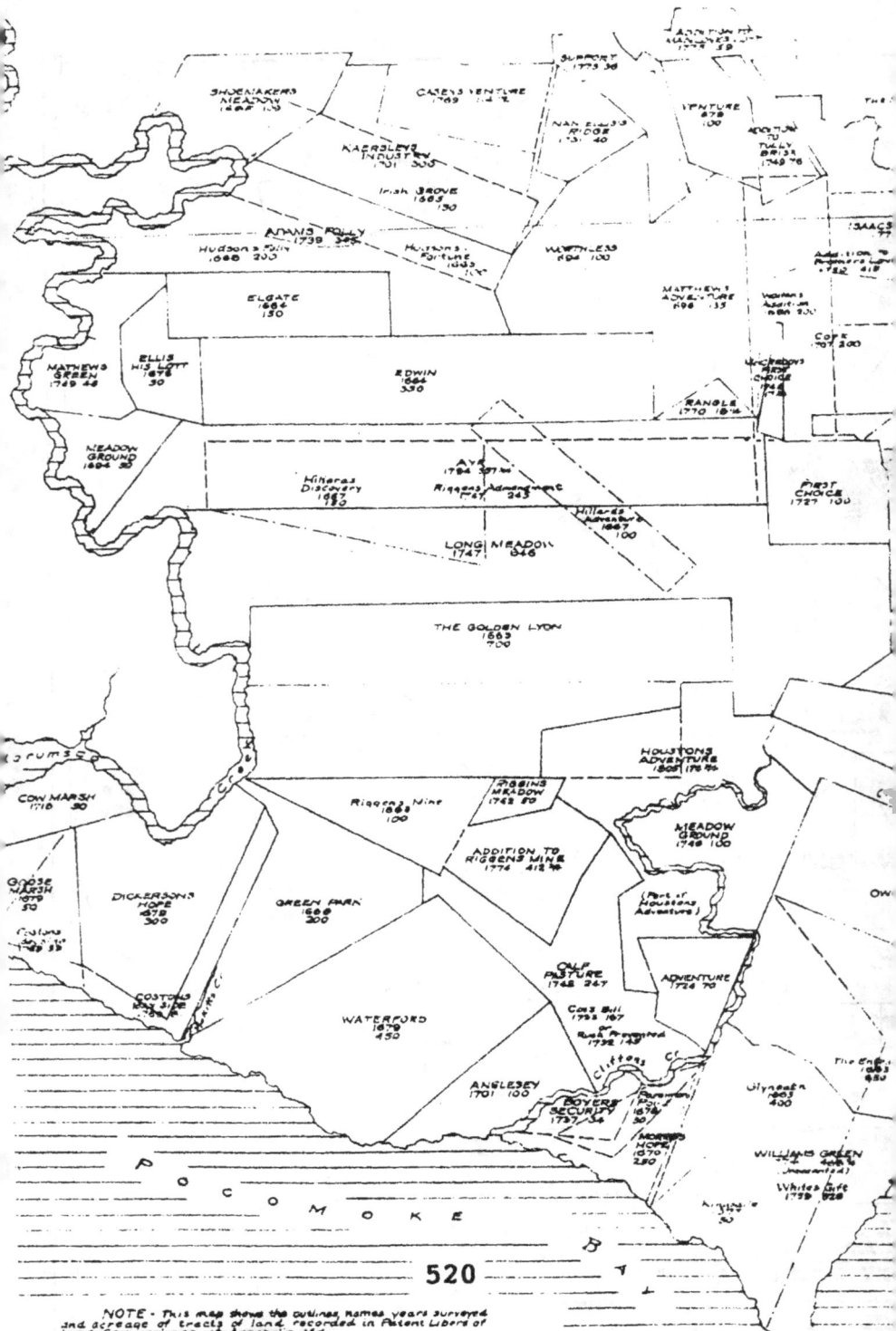

520

NOTE · This map shows the outlines, names, years surveyed and acreage of tracts of land recorded in Patent Libers of Land Commissioner at Annapolis, Md. The names of the resurveyed tracts are in italics and the ...

16

SUPPORT
1775 30

NAN EVANS'S
RIDGE
1731 40

ADDITION TO
GLASGOWS LOT
50

VENTURE
1679
100

ADDITION
TO
TULLY
BRISK
1748 76

THE SINNERS CHOICE
1665
300

GLASGOW
1748 72

CLOUDWELL
1800 40

PRIVILAGE
1731 2710

WORTHLESS
1694 100

MATTHEWS
ADVENTURE
1698 135

NOIRNS
ADDITION
1684 200

ISAACS FORTUNE
1771
449

ADDITION TO
Rigmore's Love
1782 418

PIMMORE
1663
500

BEAUCHAMPS
ENDEAVOR
181?   281

NAIRNS
ADDITION
1720 8?

COTE
1679 200

COLLINS
ADVENTURE
1718

TERSOE
1665
300

McCREEDYS
FIRST
CHOICE
1746

RANGLE
1770 1834

Hillards
Adventure
1867
100

COLLINS ADVENTURE
AMENDED
1799 84

CHANCE
1782
14

FIRST
CHOICE
1727 100

THE LATE DISCOVERY
1679
600

HALSTONS
CHOICE
1720 160

Halstons
Choice
1683
160

COLLINS
LOT?
1783 3

Collins Co

NAB
1679
30

CAHILS
LOTT
No. 11

COLLINS ADDITION
1700   223

VENTURE
1731 60

The KAYS NECK
1663
300

HOUSTONS
ADVENTURE
1805 176 44

DALES ADVENTURE
252

MEADOW
GROUND
1748 100

(Part of
Addition to
Rigmors
Mine)

OWIN GUNDORE
1663
500

Golinors Cr

TILGHMANS
ADVENTURE
1682
30

(Part of
Houstons
Adventure)

ADVENTURE
1726 70

(Gundar
Island)

CALFS
PASTURE
1748 247

HANDS
MEADOW
1681
50

Cows Bill
1792 167

Rush Preserved
1772 143

MILFORDS
MISTAKE
1722 19

BOYERS
SECURITY
1727 34

Ulyneath
1663
400

The Entrance
1663
480

MODESTY
HOPE
1670
250

WILLIAMS GREEN
4eb 34
(Unsurveyed)

(Part of
The Meadows
GROUND)

Whites Gift
1759 826

Rigmans
180

SOMERSET COUNTY
MARYLAND

BRINKLEYS
ELECTION DISTRICT
No. 3

Southeastern Part

SCALE

0   1/4 MILE   1/2 MILE   3/4 MILE   1 MILE

SOMERSET
COUNTY
MARYLAND

BRINKLEYS
ELECTION DISTRICT
No. 3

Southwestern Part

SCALE

0   .4 Mile   .3 Mile   .6 Mile   1 Mile

522

POCOMOKE   BAY

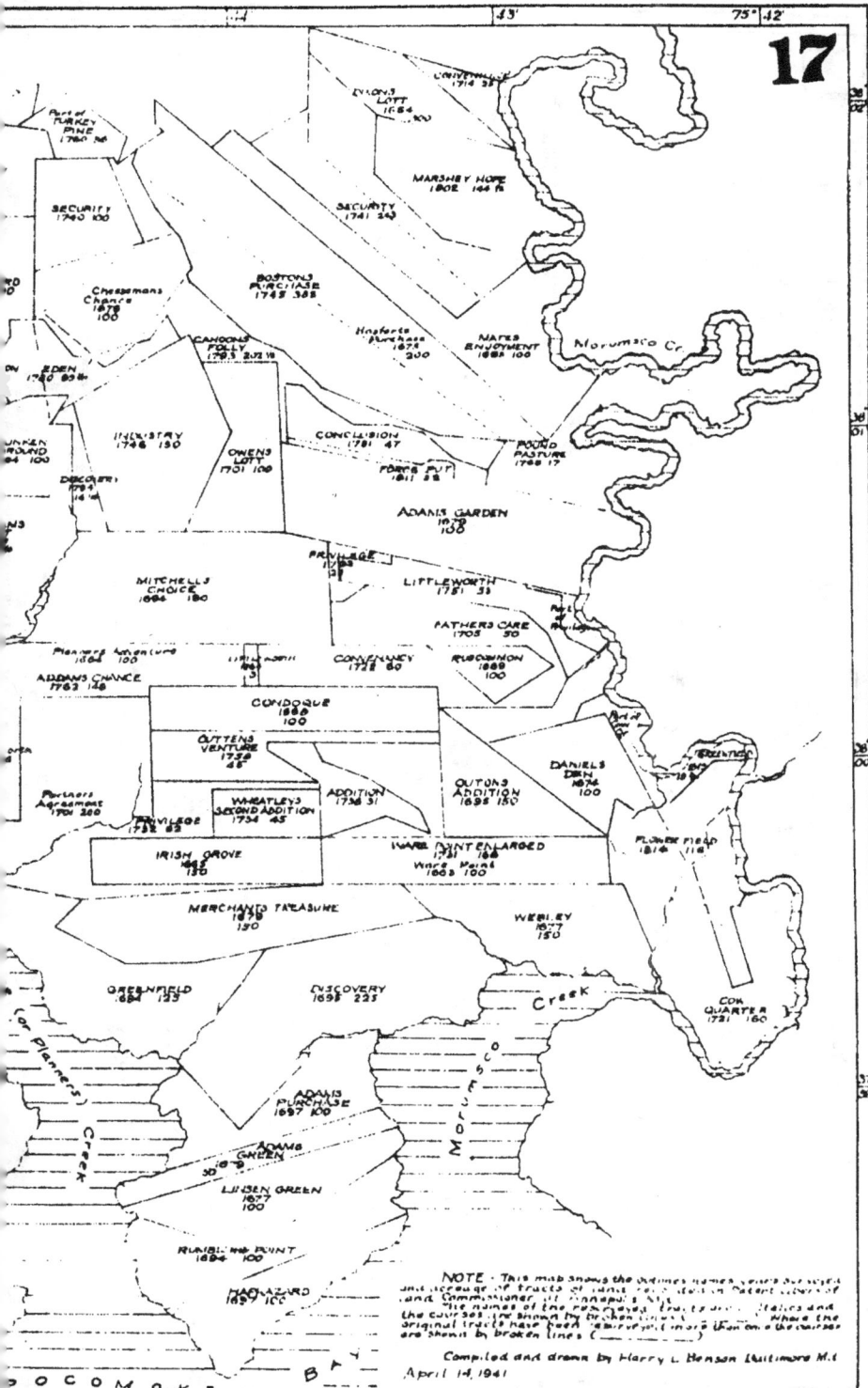

17

NOTE - This map shows the outlines, names, years surveyed and acreage of tracts of land rare listed in Patent Liber of Land Commissioner at Annapolis, M.d.
The names of the remaining tracts are shown in italics and the courses are shown by broken lines. Where the original tracts have been resurveyed (in more than one the courses are shown by broken lines.

Compiled and drawn by Harry L. Benson, Baltimore Md.

April 14, 1941

523

SOMERSET COUNTY
MARYLAND

LAWSONS
ELECTION DISTRICT
No. 8

Eastern Part

SCALE

1/4 Mile   1/2 Mile   3/4 Mile   1 Mile

NOTE: This map shows the outline names (rare) surveyed lines of each tract of land recorded in Patent Liber of Land Commissioner. Original tract names are in italics and the courses are shown by broken lines ( ). Where the original lines are broken or preserved mile given in the course are shown by broken lines ( )

Compiled and drawn by Harry L. Benson, Baltimore, Md.

MANOKIN RIVER

COLD. INE

ANNE LUTE TO POMPEY 1730 651/4

JOHNSON JR POMPRET 1652 185

TEAR LAND 1732 79 1/4

MANAKIN CHANCE 1720 4

HICKETTS CONCLUSION 1742 162

ACCIENT 1732 37

PORT (or LITTLE BRIDGE 1745 200)

PITT PERIL BRAWL

DUDLEY 1737 82

ALL LENS 1733 PURCHASE 1720 341 1/2

HAMEY LAND 1720 420

HALEY'S PLUS 1732 20

FORTUNE 1730 266

NEGLECT 1607 20

PLEASURE 1732 48 M

RICH SWAMP 1724 10

PINE SWAMP

LOVES DELIGHT 1748 80

COME BY CHANCE 1764 103

L BELLE 1752 76

RICH RIDGE 1720 100

HOWARD ENGLISH PURCHASE 1818

LATT PURCHASE 1783 110

BRAND 1678 300

JONES CHANCE 1761 25

524

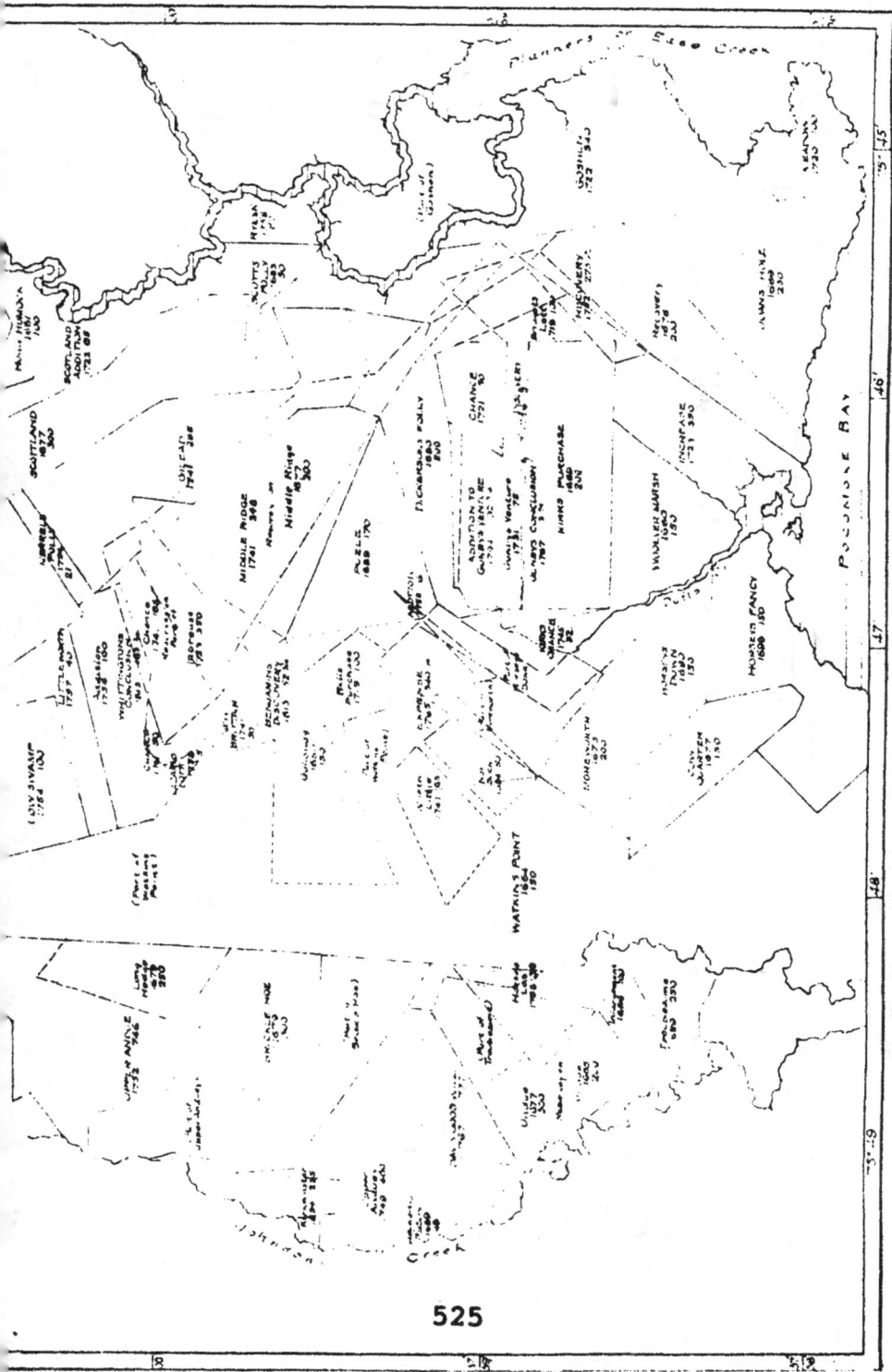

525

ANNEMESSEX RIVER

Sandy Point Creek

TANGIER SOUND

THE MISTAKE
1702 400

FLAT CAPP
1687 50

ANNEMESSEX MARSH
1731 250

(Part of Meadow)

Meadow
50

Wood Str
1972 300

LITTLE BOLTON
1773 833½

Resurvey on
Little Bolton
1688 858

ROCK HOLE CREEK

LONG ACRE
1731 583

Little Acre
1673 100

MEADOW
1731 500

LITTLE USKE
1677

Litt
Es
230

TRAINHEROPS ADVENTURE
1718 6

MISTAKE
1727 4

HARD FORTUNE
1718 12

CHESTNUT RIDGE
1677 100

COACHS FOLLY
1732 74

DAUGHERTY'S PURCHASE
1810 36½

CORK
1678 500

LITTLEWORTH
1781 75

LINCOLN
1706 8

HEART OF THE NECK
1690 180

MIDDLE OF THE NECK
1744 367

CAP
579
180

LITTLEWORTH
1727 50

WINDOW
1747

ADDITION
1773 10

FORCES ADV
1716 155

POLLY
1778 12

PORTION OF THE SPRINGS
1760 4½

HARD FORTUNE
1734 30

DOUBLIN
1743 73

HALF QUARTER
35

THE EXCHANGE
1673 200

SUMMERS ADDITION
1726 79 2/46

LEVIATHANS ADDITION
1762 50

HOGLAND QUARTER
1742 12

PRIVILEGE
1773 2 3/4

SOMERSET
COUNTY
MARYLAND

LAWSONS
ELECTION DISTRICT
No 8

Western Part
Including Eastern Part of
Crisfield Election District No.7

526

NOTE - This map shows the outlines, names and acreage of tracts of land recorded in Land Commissioner at Annapolis, Md.
The names of the resurveyed tracts are shown by broken lines (
original tracts have been resurveyed more than are shown by broken lines (

SCALE
0 ¼ MILE ½ MILE ¾ MILE 1 MILE

Compiled and drawn by Harry L Benson
October 10, 1940

19

ANNEMESSEX RIVER

Sandy Point Creek

CAMP
30

NNEMESSEX
MARSH
31 230

(Part of
Kleadun)

Meadow
50

Woods Street
1972
300

LITTLE BOLTON
1773 825 75

Resurvey on
Little Bolton
1858
858

LONG ACRE
1751 555

Long Acre
1875
130

DAUGHERTYS
PURCHASE
1815
59 95

MEADOW
1725
200

LITTLE USKE
1827
100

TAUGHERTYS
ADVENTURE
1818
5

MISTAKE
1787 7

HARD
FORTUNE
1760 12

Little Bolton
230

Patricks Lott
1783 169 3/4

Resurvey on
Harts Content
1773 367 3/4

HARTS CONTENT
1773 367 3/4

Good
Luck
1751 512

WHEATLEYS
PLEASURE
1729
16 3/4

HOPEWELL
1751 90

HOPEWELL
1772
100

CORK
1678
500

CHESTNUT
RIDGE
1877
100

ROACHS
FOLLY
1732 74

STIRLINGS
TRIUMPH
1800
15

LITTLE WORTH
1781 78 3/4

Little Worth
1766
6

WHITES
GOOD
LUCK
1880
183

MIDDLE
OF THE
NECK
1760
30

CABBIN
SWAMP
1880
100

(Part of
The Exchange)

LITTLEWORTH
1787 30

WOODS
1867

ADDITION
1773
10

FORCE
PUT
1748
165

MAKE
PEACE
1733 150

HARD FORTUNE
1734 30

POLES
1778
13

BOTTOM
OF THE
BAGG
1760 4 3/4

DOUBLIN
1762 73

HALF
QUARTER
1753
33

THE
EXCHANGE
1678
200

Resurvey on
Make
Peace
1863
150

SANDERS
ADDITION
1868 74 3/4

JONATHANS
ADDITION
1762 30

HUSBAND
QUARTER
1744 12

PRIVILEGE
1773 12 3/4

NOTE - This map shows the outlines, names, years surveyed
and acreage of tracts of land resurveyed in Patent Libers at
Land Commissioner at Annapolis, Md.
The names of the resurveyed tracts are in italics and
the courses are shown by broken lines ( ) where the
original tracts have been resurveyed more than once the courses
are shown by broken lines.

Compiled and drawn by Harry L. Benson, Baltimore Md.
October 10, 1940

1 MILE   1 MILE

20

SOMERSET
COUNTY
MARYLAND

CRISFIELD
ELECTION DISTRICT
No. 7

SOUND

PRICES
CONCLUSION
1664 800

DIXONS HOPE
1681
Resurvey in
Dixons Lott
1884 1000

RIVER

LITTLEWORTH
1784 100

(Part of
Hopewell)

RUCEBOK
1879 250
Resurvey on
Emmanuales
1683

HOPESTILL
1724 750

ANNE ARUNDEL

YORKSHIRE ISLAND
1664 100

MUSKETA
HUMMOCK
1843
150

TANGIER

LITTLE

BACK

CREEK

SOMERSET
COUNTY
MARYLAND

ASBURY
ELECTION DISTRICT
No. 12

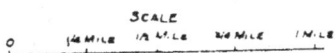

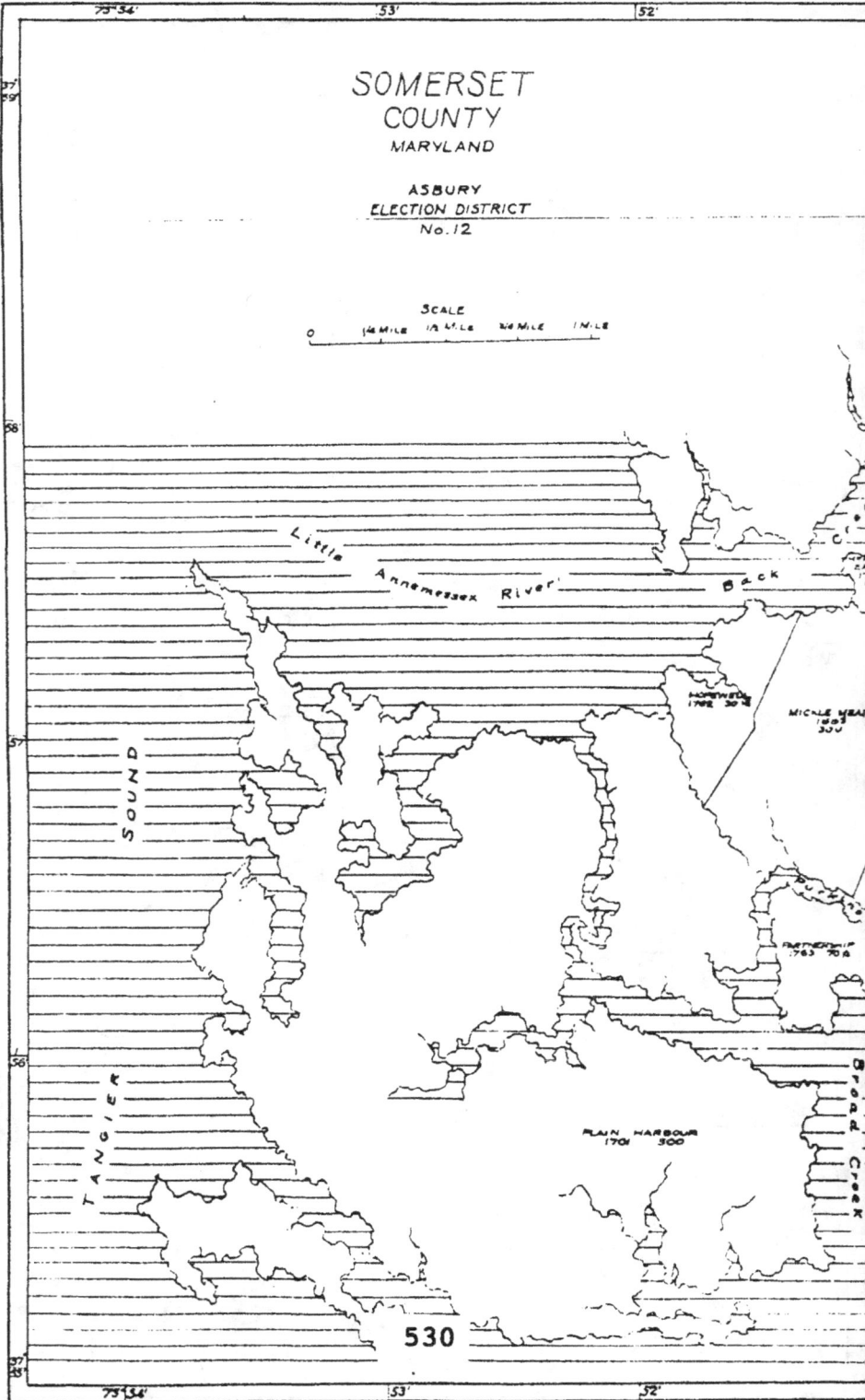

SCALE

0   ¼ MILE   ½ MILE   ¾ MILE   1 MILE

Little Annemessex River Back

SOUND

TANGIER

Broad Creek

HOPEWELL
1782   30 A

MICHLE WEAR
1683
300

PARTNERSHIP
1763   70 A

PLAIN HARBOUR
1701   300

530

NOTE: This map shows the outlines, names, years surveyed, and acreage of tracts of land recorded in Patent Libers at Land Commission, now at Annapolis, Md. The names of the resurveyed tracts are in italics and the courses are shown by broken lines (— — —). Where the original tracts have been resurveyed more than once the courses are shown by broken lines (· — · — ·).

Compiled and drawn by Harry L. Benson Baltimore Md.

September 25, 1941.

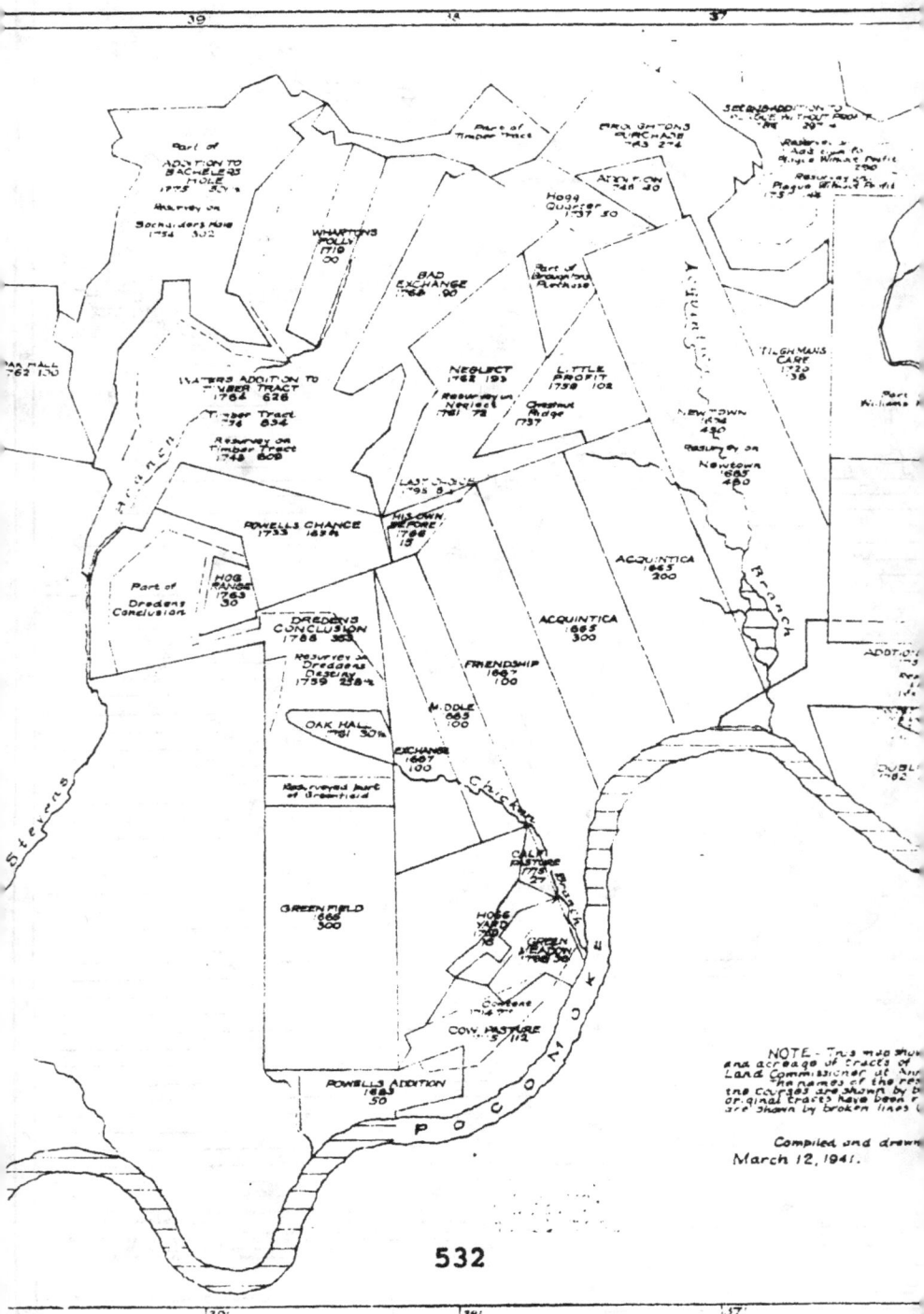

Part of
ADDITION TO
BACHELERS
HOLE
1775   305

Harvey on
Bachelders Hole
1754   302

WHARTONS
FOLLY
1719
00

Part of
Timber Tract

BROUGHTONS
PURCHASE
1743   274

SECOND ADDITION TO
EAGLE WITHOUT PROOF
1748   39

Addition to
Eagle without Profit
1750

Resurvey on
Plague without Profit
1753   48

ARY'S COW
1748   40

Hogg
Quarter
1737   50

Part of
Broughtons
Purchase

BAD
EXCHANGE
1768   00

NEGLECT
1762   193

LITTLE
PROFIT
1758   102

TILGHMANS
CARE
1720
38

Part
Williams

OAK HALL
1762   170

WATERS ADDITION TO
TIMBER TRACT
1764   626

Resurvey on
Neglect
1781   72

Chestnut
Ridge
1737

NEW TOWN
1750
480

Resurvey on
Newtown
1685
480

Timber Tract
1774   834

Resurvey on
Timber Tract
1745   809

LAST CHANCE
1795   8½

POWELLS CHANCE
1733   185½

HIS OWN
BEFORE
1786
15

ACQUINTICA
1665
200

Part of
Dredens
Conclusion

HOG
RANGE
1763
50

DREDENS
CONCLUSION
1788   315

Resurvey on
Dredens
Destiny
1759   238½

ACQUINTICA
1665
300

ADDITION

Rev
1

DUBL
1762

FRIENDSHIP
1667
100

OAK HALL
1781   30½

MIDDLE
665
100

EXCHANGE
1667
100

Resurveyed part
of Greenfield

CALFE
PASTURE
1775
27

Stevens

GREEN FIELD
665
500

HOGS
YARD
1726
10

GREEN
MEADOW
1766   36

Contene
1746

COW PASTURE
5   112

POWELLS ADDITION
1883
50

22

SOMERSET
COUNTY
MARYLAND

DUBLIN
ELECTION DISTRICT
No 4

Lower Part

SCALE

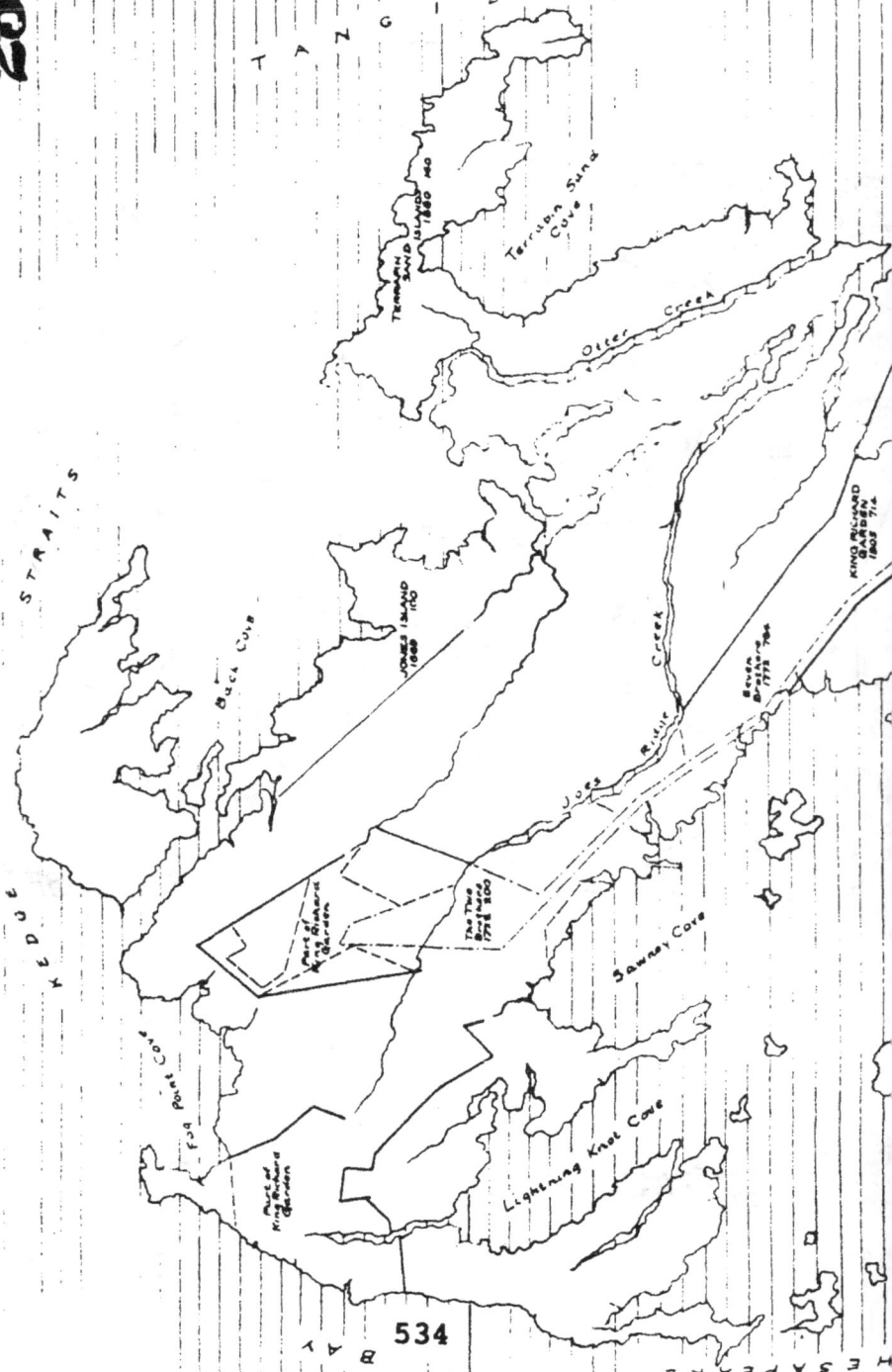

23

T A N G I E R

S T R A I T S

K E D G E

Buck Cove

Terrapin Sand Island
1460 40

Terrapin Sand Cove

Otter Creek

Jones Island
1880 1100

Joes Ridge Creek

Bruce Brothers
1773 766

King Richard Garden
1803 716

Part of King Richard Garden

Part of King Richard Garden

The Two Brothers
1776 200

Sawney Cove

Fog Point Cove

Lightning Knot Cove

534

B A Y

C H E S A P E A K E

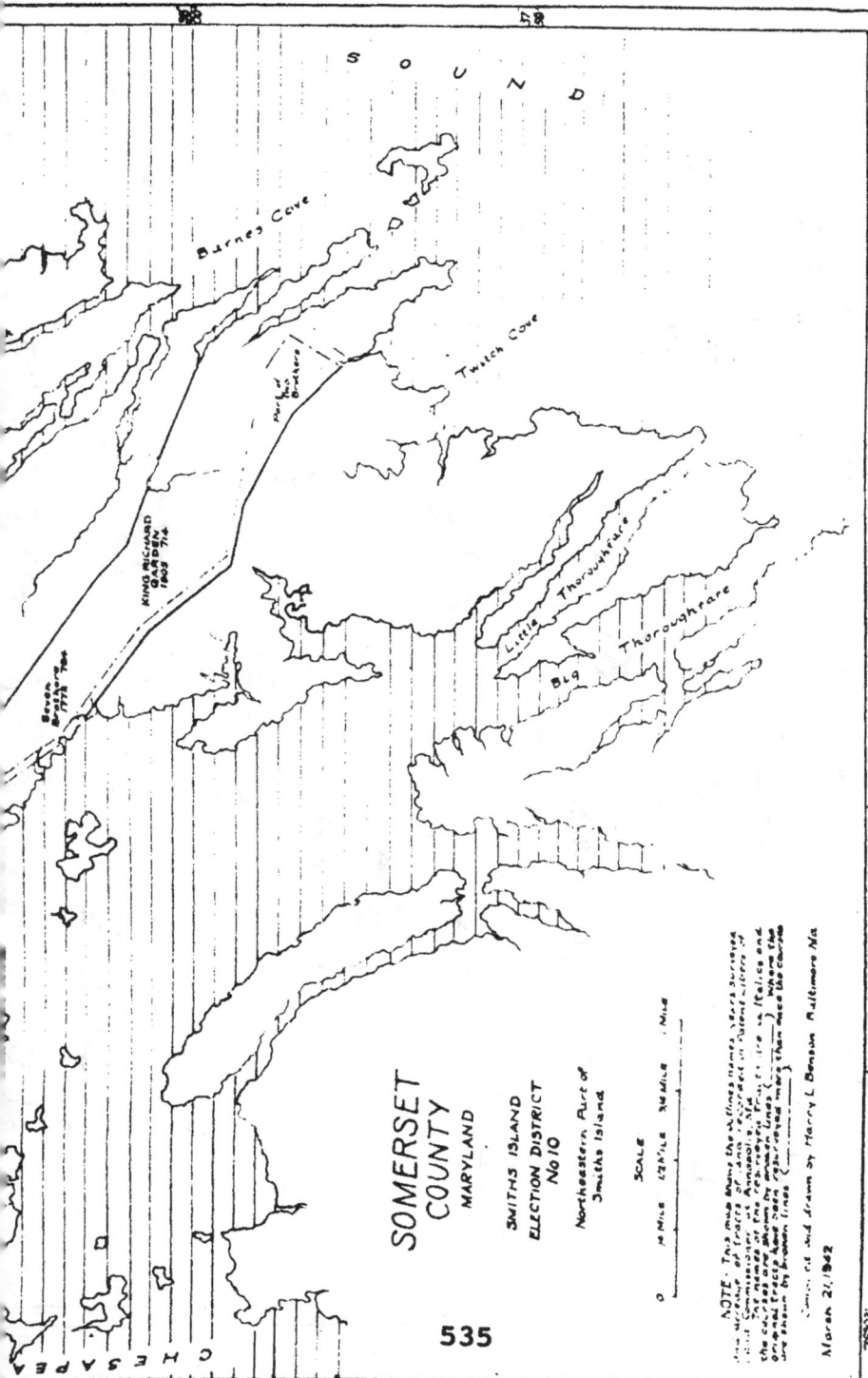

S O U N D

Barnes Cove

Twitch Cove

Parks Brothers

KING RICHARD
GARDEN
1803 714

Seven
Brothers Too

Little Thoroughfare

Big Thoroughfare

C H E S A P E A

SOMERSET
COUNTY
MARYLAND

SMITHS ISLAND
ELECTION DISTRICT
No 10

Northeastern Part of
Smiths Island

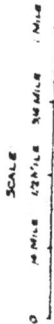

SCALE

0   1/8 Mile   1/4 Mile   3/8 Mile   1 Mile

NOTE: This map shows the outlines names, areas, surveys
and acreage of tracts of land, recorded in patent offices of
Land Commissioner for Annapolis, Md.
The acreages are shown by broken lines ( ) where
the original tracts have been reproduced more than once the course
are shown by broken lines ( )

March 21, 1942

Compiled and drawn by Harry L. Benson Baltimore Md

535

76°03'   76°02'   76°01'   76°00'   75°59'

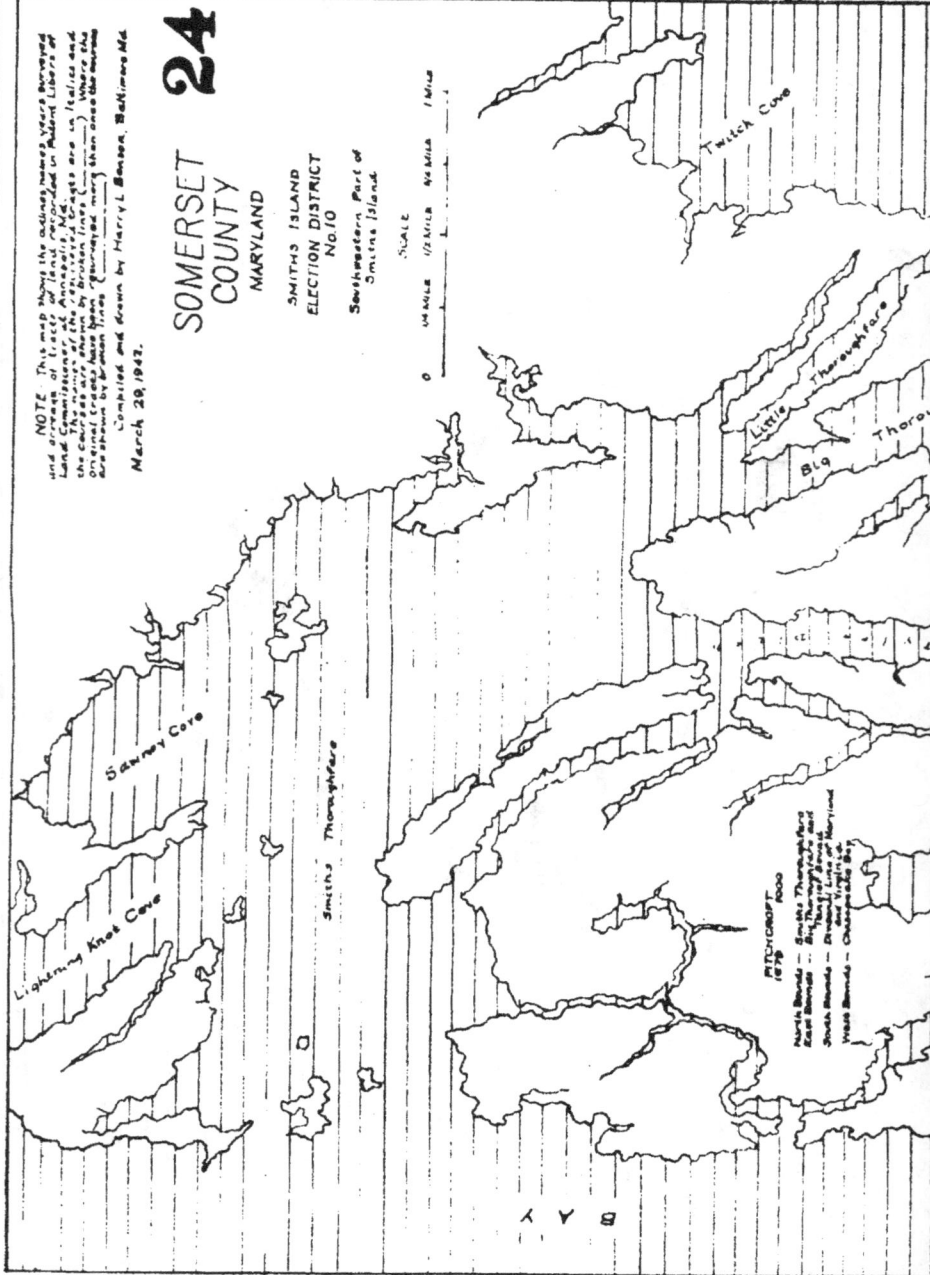

Heritage Books by Ruth T. Dryden:

Cemetery Records of Somerset County, Maryland

Cemetery Records of Worcester County, Maryland

Land Records of Somerset County, Maryland

Land Records of Wicomico County, Maryland

Land Records of Worcester County, Maryland

Maryland Mortality Schedule: 1850 and 1860

Parish of Somerset: Records of Somerset County, Maryland

Rent Rolls of Somerset County, Maryland, 1663–1723

Somerset County Will Books, 1748–1749

Somerset County Will Books, Liber EB1, 1788–1799

Somerset County Will Books, Liber WK, 1777–1788

Stepney Parish Records of Somerset County, Maryland

Worcester County, Maryland 1850 Census

*Worcester County, Maryland Administration
Bonds and Inventories, 1783–1790*

Worcester County, Maryland Wills, Liber LPS, 1834–1851

Worcester Will Books, Liber JBR, 1799–1803

Worcester Will Books, Liber JBR, 1803–1806

Worcester Will Books, Liber JW, 1790–1799

Worcester Will Books, Liber JW4, 1769–1783

Worcester Will Books, Liber MH, 1806–1813

Worcester Will Books, Liber MH, 1813–1822

Worcester Will Books, Liber MH, 1822–1833

www.ingramcontent.com/pod-product-compliance
Lightning Source LLC
Chambersburg PA
CBHW060948280326
41935CB00009B/656